Chinese Communist Politics in Action

Studies in
Chinese Government and Politics

1. CHINESE COMMUNIST POLITICS IN ACTION
Edited by A. Doak Barnett

Sponsored by the Subcommittee on
Chinese Government and Politics
of the Joint Committee
on Contemporary China of the
American Council of Learned Societies
and the Social Science Research Council

Chinese Communist Politics in Action

EDITED BY A. DOAK BARNETT

CONTRIBUTORS

ROY HOFHEINZ, JR.

ILPYONG J. KIM

MARK SELDEN

MICHEL OKSENBERG

YING-MAO KAU

RICHARD H. SOLOMON

THOMAS P. BERNSTEIN

R. J. BIRRELL

JAMES R. TOWNSEND

JOHN GARDNER

JOYCE K. KALLGREN

UNIVERSITY OF WASHINGTON PRESS

SEATTLE & LONDON

"Revolutionizing Chinese Youth: A Study of *Chung-kuo Ch'ing-nien*" by James R. Townsend appeared in slightly different form as part of his book, *The Revolutionization of Chinese Youth: A Study of* Chung-kuo Ch'ing-nien (Berkeley: Center for Chinese Studies, China Research Monograph No. 1, 1967)

Preface

The Joint Committee on Contemporary China, of the American Council of Learned Societies and the Social Science Research Council, sponsors a variety of activities designed to foster scholarship on contemporary China. Its Subcommittee on Chinese Government and Politics is organizing a series of conferences on topics relating to the political system of Communist China. General planning of this series is the responsibility of the entire Subcommittee.

The first meeting in the series, a conference on the Microsocietal Study of the Chinese Political System, was held at Wentworth-by-the-Sea, Portsmouth, New Hampshire, August 29–September 1, 1967, under the chairmanship of A. Doak Barnett. The studies included in this volume were first presented there.

In addition to the authors of papers—Thomas P. Bernstein, Robert J. Birrell, John Gardner, Roy Hofheinz, Jr., Joyce K. Kallgren, Yingmao Kau, Ilpyong J. Kim, Michel Oksenberg, Mark Selden, Richard H. Solomon, and James R. Townsend*—those attending the conference included Jeremy R. Azrael, University of Chicago; A. Doak Barnett, Columbia University; Sidney Greenblatt, Columbia University; John W. Lewis, Cornell University; John M. H. Lindbeck, Columbia University; Lucian W. Pye, Massachusetts Institute of Technology; Kay K. Ryland, Social Science Research Council; Robert A. Scalapino, University of California, Berkeley; George E. Taylor, Univer-

* Information on each author is given at the end of the book.

v

sity of Washington; A. Lynn Williams, Columbia University; and Bryce Wood, Social Science Research Council.

The editor would like to acknowledge the help that Bryce Wood of the Social Science Research Council has given at every stage in the planning and preparation of this volume, the assistance provided to the editor during 1967–68 by the Center for International Studies and Political Science Department of the Massachusetts Institute of Technology, and the efficient manuscript typing of Mrs. Roy C. Smith.

Contents

PART IV. RURAL CONTROL AND MOBILIZATION

PART V. POLICIES TOWARD YOUTH,
THE BOURGEOISIE, AND THE WORKERS

APPENDIX

ABBREVIATIONS USED IN NOTES

CB	*Current Background*
CFJP	*Chieh-fang Jih-pao* (Liberation Daily)
CKCN	*Chung-kuo Ch'ing Nien* (Chinese Youth)
CKCNP	*Chung-kuo Ch'ing Nien Pao* (Chinese Youth Journal)
ECMM	*Extracts from China Mainland Magazines*
JMJP	*Jen-min Jih-pao* (People's Daily)
JPRS	*Joint Publications Research Service*
KJJP	*Kung-jen Jih-pao* (Workers' Daily)
NFJP	*Nan-fang Jih-pao* (Southern Daily)
NCNA	New China News Agency
SCMM	*Selections from China Mainland Magazines*
SCMP	*Survey of the China Mainland Press*
TKP	*Ta Kung Pao* (Impartial Daily)
URI	Union Research Institute
URS	Union Research Service

A. DOAK BARNETT

Introduction

This volume presents eleven studies of Chinese politics, which are representative of some of the best research now being done on the political system in Communist China by a new generation of young scholars. It is a product of a conference on the Microsocietal Study of the Chinese Political System, held in the summer of 1967.

There has been an increasing recognition in recent years among political scientists in the United States of the importance of understanding the character of political institutions and behavior in contemporary China. This is not simply the result of a growing awareness of the problems which the United States faces in dealing with Communist China, although the need for scholarly research to help inform public policy is widely acknowledged. More fundamentally, it reflects a new sensitivity to the crucial importance of comparative studies in the formulation of valid generalizations about political phenomena. Accompanying this there has been a growing realization that broad, generalizing propositions about political systems and political development which do not at least take into account data on China, or are not tested in application to China, are subject to challenge for having ignored the political experience of more than a fifth of mankind.

China's historical importance can hardly be questioned; it has had a longer continuous existence as a political unit than any other extant entity. Moreover, during two millennia it has ruled—as it does today —a larger number of people than any other nation. Equally important, in contemporary terms, Communist China represents not only one of the most important examples of totalitarian rule but also one of the most significant experiments in modernization. For decades, under the impact of the West, it has been undergoing processes of political development which, while unique in some respects, also share many of the characteristics and problems of modernizing nations elsewhere.

Unfortunately, however, until recently there was a tendency among many scholars—not least of all the China specialists themselves—to regard China as essentially *sui generis,* a unique and in some respects exotic political phenomenon, which in the scholarly world should be the exclusive province of a few. The explanations for this fact have been many. An obvious one has been the extraordinary difficulty of mastering the basic tools for the study of China, of acquiring a knowledge of the Chinese language and even a minimal acquaintance with China's rich cultural background and long history.

Social scientists have been inhibited from attempting to incorporate the study of China into the mainstream of their intellectual interests for other reasons as well. The complex legacy of sinology—consisting largely of humanistic and historical studies conducted by tradition-oriented scholars—while contributing invaluable background for the study of contemporary society, tended until recently to cast doubt on the legitimacy of social science research on new types of problems. Even more important, the difficulty of studying a relatively closed society has created enormous obstacles to research. In the nineteen years since the Communist takeover in China, no American social scientists have been able to travel or conduct research in that country, and the difficulties of gathering information from documentary sources have been immense. While the published material flowing out of China has been voluminous, the officially selected information that it contains is fragmentary and obscured by the esoteric terminology of Marxism-Leninism. These and other problems have clearly delayed the development of social science research on China.

Despite all these problems and difficulties, however, recent years have seen significant progress in political science research on China. This progress has been especially notable in the past decade. During the years immediately after the establishment of the Peking regime in 1949, most political analyses of Communist China tended, perhaps understandably, to be general, descriptive surveys of the over-all political structure. These were useful, as far as they went, and they laid an essential foundation for subsequent work. But few of them dealt in detail with the kinds of questions that students of comparative politics have been raising in recent years.

Now, however, an increasing number of political scientists doing research on contemporary China are turning their attention to questions about the basic nature of the political system and the course of its political development, questions about the nature of the leadership, the character of the political culture, the functions performed by varied political structures, the processes of policy formulation and policy implementation, the techniques of social mobilization, the role of the military, the system of communications, the operation of the bureaucracy, and so on.

During the past decade a new generation of younger China specialists has begun to emerge. It consists of scholars who are committed both to mastering the linguistic and other special skills required to study China and to incorporating Chinese studies into the mainstream of political science. Increasingly, they are analyzing Chinese politics in terms of questions directly relevant to the broader concerns of the evolving field of comparative politics.

One interesting and significant trend in the work of these younger scholars has been their strong interest in microsocietal studies of the Chinese Communist political system, studies which attempt to probe the characteristics of the political system at the subnational level, as it affects local areas and particular groups. This effort to analyze, in greater detail than previously and with increasing sophistication, particularized aspects of the political system should, over time, lay the basis for a deeper understanding of the nature and functioning of the system as a whole.

The conference which produced this volume commissioned eleven papers by scholars engaged in such studies, and the drafts of these papers were subsequently revised on the basis of suggestions and criticisms offered at the conference by a number of leading China scholars who served as discussants. The meaning of "microsocietal" was interpreted broadly, but it was agreed that the main emphasis would be on "particularized or local studies, involving a variety of methods—documentary analysis, interviews, field work—that focus on small units in the society and polity and can contribute to our understanding of political structure, behavior, and processes in contemporary China and to the formulation of broader hypotheses and generalizations."

The range of potentially useful microsocietal studies which might have been considered for such a conference was, of course, extremely broad. Consequently, it was not possible—and in fact no attempt was made—to include studies that would cover, or even illustrate, all the many areas of research that would be needed for a comprehensive study of the political system as a whole. The aim was more limited: to throw new light on a few important aspects of the political system.

The studies included in this volume do exactly that. Several of them are pioneering efforts, both substantively and methodologically, which break new ground in areas previously neglected by political scientists concerned with China. Many of the authors had done field research in Hong Kong and Taiwan; and, significantly, more than half of the studies include information gathered from mainland China refugees—an important source of information which until recently has tended to be neglected.

The studies fall into several categories. Three examine the historical roots of important aspects of the Chinese Communist political system, two analyze the characteristics of leadership and leadership problems at the local level, one is focused on problems of personality and politics in China's changing political culture, two deal with the regime's techniques of control and mobilization in rural areas, and three analyze aspects of Chinese Communist policies toward key social groups which are of special political importance in urban areas—the youth, the urban bourgeoisie, and the workers.

It has been widely recognized that the Chinese Communists' experience during their struggle for power helped to shape the character of the regime they established after 1949. But there has been relatively little systematic social science analysis of the factors underlying their success or of the way in which some of the Chinese Communists' most distinctive patterns of organization and behavior evolved in the revolutionary bases which they ruled in the 1930's and 1940's. The studies by Roy Hofheinz, Ilpyong Kim, and Mark Selden fill some important gaps in this respect.

Hofheinz begins his study with a critical examination of various general theories which scholars have propounded in the past as explanations for Communist success in China—theories specifying certain social conditions or attitudes as basic causes of revolution—and he finds them unsupported by case study data on the growth of the Communist movement in specific areas. He proceeds to outline a general framework for analyzing basic social factors and ecological conditions relevant for any thorough assessment of factors influencing Communist failures and successes in China. On this basis, he examines available Chinese data on some of these factors—including causes of peasant grievances, levels of political and cultural development, the impact of modernizing forces, and others.

One must question, Hofheinz asserts, the validity of many current assumptions about the correlation between these factors and actual "revolutionary potential" or susceptibility to Communist influence. Some of the generalizations made in the past to explain Communist success in China simply are not supportable, he argues, on the basis of the data available on specific local areas where the Chinese Communist movement grew. The factors contributing to Communist success in China were not only extremely complex, he suggests, but varied significantly from place to place and from one period to another. He concludes that before more sophisticated and valid general explanations of the Chinese Communists' rise to power can be formulated, there will have to be a greater number of more detailed, systematic, microsocietal studies of the development of the Chinese Communist movement and the social environment in which it grew, in specific local areas—most particularly in specific counties (*hsien*) in China. In sum, generalizations about the causes and character of the revolution in China must take greater account, he argues, of the varieties of local conditions and the congeries of local experiences involved. The kinds of questions Hofheinz raises have a relevance for the study of revolutions elsewhere than in China, and his analysis suggests a number of fruitful possibilities for future research.

Kim and Selden both focus their attention on the evolution, in the pre-1949 period, of distinctive patterns of political organization and behavior which have greatly affected the character of the Chinese Communist regime since 1949. Both provide valuable insights into the ways in which experiences during a revolutionary party's struggle for power can shape the nature of the regime established after a seizure of power.

Special attention is devoted, in both studies, to the evolution of effective methods of political and social mobilization—a subject recognized to be of great importance by most students of political development. Specialists on China have long had an interest in the distinctiveness of the so-called "mass line" techniques developed by the Chinese Communists and have been impressed by the way in which the regime since 1949 has employed such techniques to carry out an unprecedented mobilization of the population. But there has been relatively little systematic investigation of the pre-1949 origins of the "mass line." Kim and Selden help to fill this gap by analyzing the evolution of mass mobilization policies in two extremely important early periods of Chinese Communist growth—the Kiangsi Soviet period and the Yenan period.

Kim shows that already by the early 1930's, in the Kiangsi period, Mao Tse-tung and other Chinese Communist leaders had concluded that it was essential "to mobilize the masses" in rural areas. Moreover, in their program of land confiscation and class warfare during that period, they had begun to evolve the kinds of mobilization techniques that were later to be refined and codified in the "mass line." Rural mass campaigns and mass organizations, with wide peasant participation, became an established pattern.

As Selden's extremely revealing study indicates, full maturation of the "mass line" and the organizational techniques associated with it then took place during the Yenan period, especially in the early 1940's. Selden analyzes the concrete organizational problems which the Chinese Communists faced in the Yenan region at that time and shows how, in response to these problems, they developed many of their "mass line" techniques—including "rectification" (cheng-feng) campaigns, campaigns to combat bureaucratism, decentralize administrative authority, and reinforce local Party initiative and control, and campaigns to send cadres to the villages, attack land problems, encourage collectivism (mutual aid) in agriculture, spur increased production, expand mass education, and so on.

All of these pre-1949 efforts involved mobilization of a fairly impressive sort. It is striking to see the degree to which the regime's post-1949 "mass line" mobilizational efforts were foreshadowed by these earlier developments. It is clear, in fact, that if in 1949 the outside world had had a better knowledge of the Chinese Communists' earlier patterns of behavior, it would have better understood the pattern of mass mobilization efforts which unfolded in China in the 1950's.

The importance of elite studies, and studies of leadership characteristics, in analyses of political development is generally recognized. Over the years there have been several such studies focused on Communist China's leaders, but most have concentrated on analysis of the characteristics of the new elite at the national or provincial level. Until recently, there has been very little detailed or systematic examination of leadership characteristics at the local level, in either rural or urban areas.

Lacking detailed data, students of contemporary China have, perforce, tended to view local leaders throughout that vast country as a relatively homogenous mass of seemingly undifferentiated cadres. We have been only dimly aware of the significant patterns of differentiation which have in fact developed among local elites, or of the serious problems that emerged as a result of such factors as changing mobility rates.

The studies by Michel Oksenberg and Ying-mao Kau deal with problems of elite development and local leadership in China since 1949, and both add significantly to our knowledge of the characteristics of the political system at the local level.

Oksenberg, whose analysis deals with rural local leaders (at the county level and below), starts by attempting to define who the local leaders actually are. He then develops a typology of various groupings of local leaders differentiated on the basis of a multiplicity of relevant factors, including the administrative levels at which they work, the functional responsibilities which they carry, the topographical, social, economic, and other characteristics of the areas in which they work, the ratings given these areas by higher level leaders, and the particular patterns of Communist takeover in their areas. With this typology as a basis, and using data gathered from a variety of sources (including interviews with refugees and reports made by visitors to China as well as information from official Chinese Communist publications), he outlines profiles of the characteristics of various groups of rural local leaders. He also analyzes trends over time affecting such factors as the ages of cadres, their educational levels, the roles of Party and non-Party cadres, the ratio of "outsiders" to local cadres, and the degree of stability or turnover in cadre positions.

Oksenberg's conclusions indicate that rural local leadership in Communist China is far less homogeneous, and more differentiated, than has commonly been assumed. He also suggests the existence of significant tensions and problems within the local elite which are highly relevant to any understanding of the forces for change that have been operating in China in recent years. (In an appendix to his study, on "Sources and Methodological Problems in the Study of Contemporary China," he analyzes both the utility and the limitations of the different types of sources that he has used.)

Kau's study of the top bureaucratic elite in a major Chinese Communist municipality also draws a revealing profile of the elite's characteristics and then traces recent trends affecting its composition and nature. The factors he analyzes include the ratio of men and women, the relative importance of those with urban as contrasted with rural backgrounds, the role of "outsiders" versus local cadres, the relationship of Party to non-Party members, the significance of past revolutionary careers, the importance of class background and education, and patterns of bureaucratic experience and technical training. Kau pays special attention to levels of functional expertise, career mobility, stability of job tenure, and changing recruitment patterns. With the Weberian model of modern bureaucracy providing his criteria, he assays some general judgments about the degree to which the Chinese Communists have created an effective modern bureaucracy in the city he studied. His analysis highlights certain problems which, like those described by Oksenberg, are clearly relevant to broader analysis of leadership in modernizing nations—including the conflict between leaders selected on the basis of political criteria and those with specialized or technical qualifications, and the problem of ensuring opportunities for career mobility in a revolutionary regime after its initial takeover of power.

Interest in the relationship between personality and politics is a relatively new development within the broad field of comparative politics, and it has yet to affect studies of the Chinese political system in any significant fashion. Richard Solomon, in a pioneering effort in this respect, uses psychological techniques of analysis to examine attitudinal and behavioral changes in China as they affect the problem of political and social integration.

Solomon's main concern is to determine, through studies of Chinese personality (based on interviews with refugees as well as analysis of written sources), what some of the most fundamental aspects of social motivation in China are. More specifically, he focuses his attention on attitudes toward authority, one of the most basic attitudes affecting the nature of political systems. He concludes that, traditionally, an attitude of dependency in social relations in general and in orientations toward political authority in particular was deeply imbedded in Chinese culture and society. Transmitted from generation to generation through well-established patterns of childhood socialization, this basic orientation, he argues, involved tight control over all urges toward aggression and interpersonal conflict. This, Solomon maintains, in normal times reinforced the hierarchical, authoritarian structures characteristic of the society, but it also resulted, during periods of social breakdown and disintegration, in violent outbursts and disorder.

Solomon also concludes that in the revolution in China since 1949 Mao Tse-tung has attempted to create new attitudes, to provide a new basis for social integration. Mao, he maintains, has tried to make controlled or mediated conflict a legitimate element in social processes and to create a new conception of social authority, one in which personal responsibility and activism replace traditional attitudes of dependency and in which the impersonal authority of ideology replaces traditional personalized authority.

The evidence suggests, however, according to Solomon, that while some significant attitude changes have occurred, Mao's aim to transform the basic outlook of ordinary Chinese is still, not surprisingly, far from being achieved. Apparently youth—perhaps even more than their elders—are still inclined to accept a dominant, personalized authority. And the current Cultural Revolution demonstrates, he says, "the shallowness of change, relative to Mao's revolutionary objectives, that in fact has occurred in China since 1949."

This study attempts to apply new concepts and research techniques to the study of China and makes broad generalizations, based on selective interviewing, about basic elements in China's political culture. Its conclusions are inevitably controversial, but as perhaps the first study of its kind on China, it raises important questions, demonstrates imaginative approaches to studying Chinese politics, puts forth provocative hypotheses, and suggests new ideas for research in the future.

In the study of political systems, analysis of organizational structures is essential, but even more important is the need to understand political functions and processes. Two studies in this volume, by Thomas Bernstein and Robert Birrell, throw light on processes of policy implementation in rural China. Both focus on the implementation of particular policies during specified time periods. They illuminate many facets of the political process in China—the way in which political power penetrates to the grass-roots level in rural areas, the problems faced by China's leaders in getting the peasants to comply, the varieties of social controls employed, and the complex mixture of negative controls and positive mobilization methods involved in policy implementation in rural areas. In sum, both papers are concerned with the interaction of state and society (or perhaps one should say, in the Chinese case, Party and society) in the vast rural hinterland where a majority of all Chinese live.

Bernstein analyzes the Chinese grain-supply crisis of early 1955 and the regime's response to it. His study reveals how, even in a relatively monolithic totalitarian society such as that existing in China in the 1950's, the actual shape of policy as it evolved was determined by a complicated process of interaction involving the mass of ordinary peasants and the local cadres responsible for implementing policy at a grass-roots level as well as the top leaders who defined the main lines of policy. The central leadership, despite its enormous power, clearly did not have an unlimited capacity to ensure implementation of all its policy directives. Peasant pressure, operating through the local cadres, created serious problems which had to be acknowledged by the central leadership.

Bernstein highlights the key role which local cadres play in the operation of the entire political system, and underlines the difficulties they face as links between the higher authorities and the masses. He provides a revealing picture of the mechanisms of mass mobilization employed in rural China. He also analyzes the shifting mixture of persuasion, pressure, and coercion involved in mobilizational policies directed at the peasants. His study demonstrates, by detailed analysis of one concrete case, that to understand the reality of political processes in Communist China it is not enough simply to examine the policies promulgated by the central leadership. One must also determine how policies evolve and are modified or adapted during the process of policy implementation, a process in which both popular attitudes and the behavior of local cadres influence the final results.

Birrell also focuses his attention on how policy has evolved in rural areas. More specifically, he analyzes—using Amitai Etzioni's threefold division of social controls as his framework—the particular mixture of remunerative, normative, and coercive controls employed by the Chinese Communist regime when it moved to restructure the rural communes in the post-Great Leap crisis of the early 1960's.

Birrell discusses in some detail the problems which local cadres faced in attempting to manage the newly formed communes (and especially their lowest subunits, the production teams) in that period. He maintains that, because of the deficiencies of the regime's initial efforts to improve the communes' performance primarily by remunerative controls (greater material incentives), from 1962 on the tendency was to increase the use of normative and coercive controls (including more centralized direction and more control of commune affairs by outside agencies).

Of particular interest is Birrell's analysis of basic management problems in the communes (for example, the problems of calculating members' work points, allocating net income to members, and so on). And his study, like Bernstein's, highlights the important role which local cadres play in the interaction that takes place between higher policy-making authorities and the masses. Both studies demonstrate the need for microsocietal studies of how policy implementation actually takes place at the local level if one is to have more than a superficial understanding of the dynamics of political processes, even in totalitarian societies.

The last three studies in this volume deal with aspects of the relationships between the Chinese Communist regime and particular groups within Chinese society. They focus primarily on problems in urban areas and highlight both the dynamics of social change affecting these special groups and the evolution of the regime's policies toward them.

James Townsend examines the changing message to youth contained in one of the Chinese Communists' principal youth journals, *Chung-kuo Ch'ing-nien* (Chinese Youth). His study suggests not only that serious difficulties have faced the regime as it has tried to indoctrinate and socialize a new generation in the revolutionary values promoted by the Party, but that youth itself has found it difficult to cope with the great and constantly changing demands imposed on the younger generation by the regime. Over time, it is clear, the attitudes of youth in China have changed, and so too have the regime's images of them.

One central question, according to Townsend, that has constantly arisen in the Chinese Communist leaders' minds in the years since political takeover has been: How long a period of intense revolutionary struggle will be required before the new values can be thoroughly imbedded in the youth of the country and the basic socialization goals of the leadership achieved?

The expectations of the regime in this regard have significantly changed over the years, Townsend concludes. He argues that the period 1956–58 represented an important turning point in regard to the elite's expectations relating to youth. Prior to that time, he says, the Chinese Communist leaders were optimistic and believed that ideological reform could be accomplished in a relatively short period of time, after which the emphasis in the regime's policies could be shifted from a primary focus on class struggle against clearly defined enemies to the broader tasks of institutional transformation and "socialist construction." However, in the late 1950's, Townsend indicates, there came a realization that the youth had not, in fact, been successfully socialized to accept the regime's values in the way the leaders had believed or hoped. Consequently the easy optimism of earlier years evaporated. China's leaders, now recognizing that the development of "socialist consciousness" would at best be a long and arduous process, even after basic changes had taken place in the nation's institutions, began thinking in terms of prolonged, virtually indefinite, revolutionary struggle to obtain acceptance of the regime's values. And the consequent change in its approaches to youth emphasized struggle and conflict rather than unity, and class differences rather than national consensus.

John Gardner examines, in his paper, the problems which the Chinese Communist Party faced, and the policies it pursued, when it moved at the time of political takeover from its rural bases of power into the alien environment of China's major cities. In specific terms he analyzes the *wu-fan* (five anti) campaign, directed primarily against the urban bourgeoisie, as it unfolded in Shanghai in the early 1950's.

The concerns of the Party at that time were numerous. Corruption was a threatening danger. The Communists feared a decline in revolutionary morale and standards among their own cadres. The urban working class had yet to be organized into militant revolutionary bodies and, in fact, did not appear to be motivated primarily by revolutionary class antagonisms directed against the urban bourgeoisie. And the members of the bourgeoisie possessed, on the one hand, status and influence which made them a potential opposition group, and on the other hand, scarce skills which were clearly needed by China's new Communist rulers.

Gardner shows how in the *wu-fan* campaign the Communists not only eliminated the potential danger that the urban bourgeoisie might develop into a political opposition group, but also went far in organizing and politicizing the masses, in creating an effective communications and propaganda apparatus to penetrate the entire society, and in applying "mass line" mobilizational techniques to their new urban environment. The campaign was designed to clarify lines of class demarcation and intensify class conflict, atomize and intimidate the business class, create a new subelite of lower-class origin, organize, mobilize, and regiment the urban masses, weaken traditional pluralistic social ties, and create new political and social values and patterns of behavior. At the same time, the regime recognized the need to continue using the essential skills of the urban bourgeoisie.

While Gardner's study focuses on one campaign as it affected one city in China, it throws light on the general characteristics of the Chinese Communists' mobilizational techniques, the kinds of aims and methods underlying many of their subsequent mass campaigns, and the dynamics of engineered social change in China since 1949.

Joyce Kallgren's study of the social welfare programs which the Communists have established for Chinese workers since 1949 deals with aspects of modernization and social change in China and their possible political implications. She analyzes the rationale underlying the Chinese Communists' welfare policies, and devotes special attention to the labor insurance system, which applies primarily to organized workers in large industrial enterprises. The system is designed, she indicates, to support the general value system promoted by the regime; for example, it reinforces the high value which the Communists place upon increased productivity as a goal. It contributes to the regime's aim of restructuring social relationships and altering patterns of urban life, and it helps to weaken the social and economic role of the family in society. It also exacerbates some of the social and economic problems facing the regime, for example, by inhibiting labor mobility among those enjoying labor insurance benefits.

Mrs. Kallgren's most provocative and interesting hypothesis is that the labor insurance system (together with other policies which benefit selected groups of urban workers) may also have helped to create among certain industrial workers in Communist China new attitudes which are now a source of concern to the Maoist leadership. These workers, Mrs. Kallgren suggests, appear to have developed—at least to a certain extent, and in contrast with other groups who are less well off —both a feeling of separate identity and a kind of conservatism, a sense of having some tangible stake in a new *status quo* under which they are comparatively well treated. As a consequence, whereas the presently dominant Maoist leaders insist upon continued revolutionary upheaval and self-sacrificing dedication to long-range goals, certain groups of industrial workers may now be more preoccupied with the desire to preserve the gains and advantages they have already achieved. This may help to explain, Mrs. Kallgren feels, the recent indications that at least some workers have been unresponsive to the Maoist slogans in China's Great Proletarian Cultural Revolution and have clashed with militant groups of Red Guard youths. In sum, she suggests, the successes of the modernizing process, as it has affected key groups of industrial workers, appear in this instance to have created new problems for the Maoist leadership, and the process of social change may have significantly affected the social base of the regime's present revolutionary policies.

All of the studies in this volume add to our knowledge of the political system in Communist China. Moreover, they illustrate the value of microsocietal studies involving detailed analysis of particular areas, institutions, groups, processes, attitudes, and behavior patterns, which can provide new insights into the nature of the system as a whole. There is clearly a need for many additional studies of a comparable sort. The authors of the studies included in this volume would be the first to recognize that the work they have done represents only a preliminary exploration of even those questions which they have dealt with, and that many important areas of inquiry—for example, the role of the military, the nature of the communications system, the functions of ideology, the operation of the bureaucracy, the processes of decision making—are hardly dealt with at all here. In the past, perhaps a majority of studies of this sort have tended to focus on geographical areas and particular institutions as units of inquiry. These will continue to be important, but in the future there should be more which analyze functions and processes. There is also a need for more studies of changes over time, since rapid, dynamic development is one of the most notable characteristics of contemporary China.

The question of how to relate microsocietal data to macrosocietal generalizations needs careful consideration, although no simple answer is likely to be forthcoming. (The authors of these studies discussed the problem at their conference but have not dealt with it in their papers.) Obviously, broad generalizations about the over-all political system cannot be based on a handful of studies which concentrate on detailed portions or aspects of it. It is equally obvious, however, that the prevailing conceptions of the nature of the system as a whole cannot really be sustained unless they are consistent with, take into account, and are at least partially based on the data that emerge from microsocietal studies.

To provide a basis for generalizing, there is a need, therefore, for a representative range of microsocietal studies which will reveal both the varieties and the uniformities of structure and behavior in the system as a whole. This need is particularly great in the case of a country as vast and complex as China, where both variety and uniformity are extremely important and are difficult to understand on the basis of studies which focus solely on the national level. There is also a need for close and continuous interaction between knowledge of the particular and concepts of the more general in China, an interaction in which broad concepts provide the guidelines for inquiry into particular patterns of organization and behavior, and in which microsocietal studies provide a sounder basis for generalizations about the system as a whole.

Microsocietal analysis of China requires a wide variety of methodologies and sources of data, as the studies in this volume illustrate. The data problem is a particularly difficult and vexing one in the China field, in part because the student of Chinese politics has so little individual control over the accessibility of information. It is clear that over the years the data base for research on contemporary China has periodically changed, as the availability and utility of various sources —official Chinese publications, radio broadcasts, refugees who can be interviewed, visitors' reports on China, "wall newspapers," and so on—have changed.

What is necessary, therefore, is flexible and imaginative use of varying mixtures of sources and methods. (Equally important, scholars must be fully aware of the limitations as well as the potentialities of various sources, and sensitive to the fact that interpretations of Chinese politics over time can be affected by the changing data base as well as by real changes in China.) Some of the studies in this volume illustrate the kinds of creative and original approaches that deserve further exploration.

Many of the authors who contributed to this volume also strongly believe in the desirability of increased cooperation in gathering, compiling, and organizing basic data on the Chinese Communist political system. Such cooperation could include the organization of "data banks" of various kinds, the systematic pooling and exchange of research data, and at least experimental use of computer technology in handling and processing certain types of information.

Whatever sources and methods are used, a major task ahead is one which scholars such as the authors of these studies have begun, but only begun, to tackle, namely, that of more effectively integrating China studies into the mainstream of political scientists' current interests. As was stated earlier, these studies deal with many questions which are directly relevant to the broader concerns of the field of comparative politics to an extent that was not true of many studies of Chinese politics in earlier years. Scholars concerned broadly with processes of revolutionary change, elite characteristics and problems in developing nations, social mobilization, problems of value formation and political integration, and the relationship of political authority to potential "interest groups" in totalitarian societies—to cite just a few examples—will find in these studies data and ideas which should be of great interest to them.

For the most part, however, the relevance of these studies to broader comparative analysis and theory is implicit rather than explicit. In general, the authors do not address themselves directly to problems of comparison, nor do they attempt to deal directly with broad theoretical questions. The task of determining, in regard to the phenomena they have studied, what is uniquely Chinese, what is distinctively Communist or totalitarian, and what is related to more universal processes of modernization and development is left to a considerable degree to others.

In some respects this is not surprising. In practical terms, the skills required and demands imposed by empirical "area studies" of China, comparative studies of varied nations, and theory building in the field of comparative politics are by no means identical. Even though in intellectual terms they should be complementary and interacting, in practice they are often competitive.

There is a need, however, for at least some of the emerging generation of China specialists in political science to apply themselves more self-consciously and explicitly to the task of combining specialized research on China with comparative studies and theory building. This does not mean that empirical analyses of China alone should be considered any less valuable, as long as they address themselves to significant questions of broader relevance, as the studies in this volume do. However, it does mean that a very special, continuing effort will be required not only to understand the Chinese Communist political system in its own terms but also to ensure that evolving political science theory and generalizations about comparative politics are informed and shaped by knowledge of China as well as by knowledge of other societies which are more accessible and easier to study. This volume makes a valuable contribution to this task, but much of the work required lies ahead.

PART I

Historical Roots of Organizational and Behavioral Patterns

ROY HOFHEINZ, JR.

The Ecology of Chinese Communist Success: Rural Influence Patterns, 1923–45*

Chinese communism began, at least in its present form, in the villages of China. Despite its pretensions to represent the "proletariat" of China, it was a predominantly rural phenomenon, and its history, psychology, and etiology are inextricably enmeshed in Chinese country life. Chinese communism as a social movement and a political force must be seen first as a part of a complex rural political process before its wider implications and later evolution can be examined.

Yet despite this obvious point, such a view is seldom taken. Understandably, in the face of a powerful and sweeping historical movement, the tendency is to leap to the grand causes that "explain" the revolution. It is far easier to provide broad explanatory formulas or to impute monochromatic energies than it is to examine social reality in all its complexity. But full understanding of this revolution, like that of all the others, will have to wait until the details are known and examined.

Meanwhile, we are confronted with two distinguishable genres of theory, both of which seek to explain the "revolution" in China as a whole. First, is the genre of what we might call "contextual theories" —explanations which assert that the rise of Chinese communism in the villages must be understood as a product of the over-all social environment. The simplest and least convincing examples of this genre are the mechanical theories of revolutionary causation: those which postulate an action-reaction relationship between impinging forces—be they

* The generous support of the East Asian Research Center at Harvard University helped to make this paper possible.

3

"imperialism," "bureaucratic capitalism," or "agrarian feudalism"—
and reputed consequences, such as urban decay, rural impoverishment,
and organized indignation.[1] Then there are theories which work from
the biomedical analogy of organic systems: the rise of communism is
regarded as part of a process resembling cancerous growth in a mori-
bund social body.[2] Finally there are theories which attempt to relate
Chinese Communist influence to the process of "modernization" of
Chinese society and politics, holding that there is some kind of necessary relationship between changes in Chinese society, social structure,
popular attitudes, and individual psychology—wrought by the growth
of nontraditional technology, industry, and communication—and the
conditions which gave Chinese communism its opportunity.[3]

The second major genre seeks to explain the growth of Chinese
communism by referring to patterns of individual attitudes. We might
call these "motivational theories" because they treat dominant human
motives as the key explanatory variable. We might boil them down to
four: the "grievance theory," that the Chinese peasant, immersed in
the injustices of a corrupt and oppressive social system, joined the
revolutionary movement to satisfy his sense of right and his need to
pao pu p'ing—give debit where debit was due;[4] the "ambition theory,"
that the peasant joined the revolution in an attempt to find a channel
for advancement and self-expression, having been deprived of other,
more traditional outlets;[5] the "hatred theory," that without the fortuitous evocation of powerful emotions of hostility toward the Japanese
invasion after 1937 the Chinese Communists would have had little real
opportunity;[6] and finally the "terror theory," that the Communist
Party's hold on China's countryside can only be explained by reference

[1] The chapter on China in Barrington Moore, Jr., *The Social Origins of Dictatorship and Democracy* (Boston: Beacon Press, 1966), is perhaps the most recent example of a mechanical theory of what happened in China.

[2] For a version of the organic theory explicitly comprehending the Chinese case, see Chalmers Johnson, *Revolution and the Social System* (Stanford, Calif.: Hoover Institu-tion, 1966), and *Revolutionary Change* (Boston: Little, Brown, 1967).

[3] There is no comprehensive "modernization" theorist, but some suggestive insights are developed by John W. Lewis in "The Study of Chinese Political Culture," *World Politics,* XVIII, No. 3 (April, 1966), 503–24.

[4] R. H. Tawney's *Land and Labour in China* is the classic statement (Boston: Beacon, 1966; paperback).

[5] Not yet developed for mainland China, but Lucian Pye's *Guerrilla Communism in Malaya* (Princeton, N.J.: Princeton University Press, 1956), might, *mutatis mutandis,* be applied to the Malayan Chinese ethnic brethren at home.

[6] Though Chalmers Johnson's theory of "peasant nationalism" at times seems to include nonattitudinal elements, the ethnocentric theme seems dominant. See *Peasant Nationalism and Communist Power: The Emergence of Revolutionary China, 1937–1945* (Stanford, Calif.: Stanford University Press, 1962; paper, 1966).

to a ruthless application of *force majeure*.[7] Whatever the operative motive, each example of this genre relies on the force of an analogy between individual attitudes and collective behavior.

There is clearly some merit in both these broad genres of theoretical approach to the Chinese revolution. And within each of the genres there is an element of truth in most of the more specialized "explanations" that have been offered. Faced with such a confused chorus of argumentation, it is tempting to shrug one's shoulders, confess ignorance, and conclude that the ultimate choice of how to weigh the various factors depends on one's "point of view." To take such an agnostic position, however, is not only to abandon the tenets of a responsible social science; it amounts to leaving the interpretation of one of the world's most explosive and divisive phenomena—that of rural revolution—in the hands of apologists and special pleaders. Somewhere between the Maoist pseudo science of revolution and the more recent pseudo science of counter insurrection, is there no general theoretical explanation of phenomena such as the Chinese Communist rural victory?

There is, of course, one major obstacle in the way of any such general theory, and that is the striking variability of the Communist movement in China itself. It might be argued that the place to begin in order to understand the Chinese revolution is in case studies of a well-selected number of different villages or counties over a thirty-year period of time. In a sense each experience, each area, each phase in the Chinese revolution is sufficiently different from the next to give the historian plenty of room to "thrill to the unique event," and good reason can be given why the case study strategy must be a preliminary to any more general treatment.

But despite the variety, we should pause before throwing ourselves headlong into the local newspapers, pamphlets, and intelligence reports which are slowly becoming available, to ask ourselves what we are looking for, and to try to get a picture of the movement as a whole. This is so if only for the reason that the Chinese Communist leadership itself tends to generalize liberally about its earlier relationships with the villages. From the viewpoint of the Chinese Communists, there is a sense of coherence, of collective mission, of the historical unity of struggle which we ignore at our peril: they might well be right!

---

[7] Fortunately, there are few serious proponents of this theory, but the interested reader might consult Chiang Kai-shek, *Soviet Russia in China* (New York: Farrar, Strauss, and Cudahy, 1957).

Moreover, our own hopefully more objective eyes see underlying patterns in the relationship which inexorably shaped the subtle variations in type of influence, policy, and power exercised in different situations. Each and every attempt by the Communists to create a viable power base in the countryside had to deal with at least three constant factors: (1) the villages were Chinese, not African or American, and thus shared certain more or less culturally common characteristics of social structure, economic system, and political attitude which differentiated them from those in other parts of the world; (2) the villages were at one end of a rural-urban continuum and thus were only part of a greater political situation: the weaker, peripheral, rustic share of Chinese political society; (3) the Communists, despite the variation in their strategies, personnel, and "style," were a phenomenon unique in the Chinese countryside. They shared certain types of appeal and modes of operation with antecedent "movements"—such as the Taipings, the Nien, the Boxers, or even the warlords—and thousands of other less well-known "social bandits." But from their very earliest contacts they brought to the villages a breath of new air, a firmness of organizational discipline, a sense of nationwide purpose, *and* an ability to capitalize on newly acquired "modern" facilities, such as weaponry and communications, which their predecessors lacked. The very novelty of the Chinese Communist movement in the countryside is one of the constant parameters in its shifting but increasingly successful affair with the hinterland.

It can be argued on a priori grounds that there are enough constants in the Communist relationship with the villages to make a generalized assault on the available aggregate data interesting. This study is an attempt to test a research strategy based on this idea. It proceeds from the hope that at least some of the macrotheories about the Communist movement's strength can be tested with macrodata. Just as in the study of political development the comparison of the characteristics of a large number of nation-states can be used to analyze the relation between political phenomena and underlying "explanatory" measures, the rise of the Communist movement in China can be, I suggest, put in perspective by examining the background of the regions in which the movement was most successful. I propose to begin a treatment of Chinese Communist success by an examination of the environment or "ecology" of that success.

The question of what kind of data to employ in such a study is highly problematic. There is a school of thought which would reject

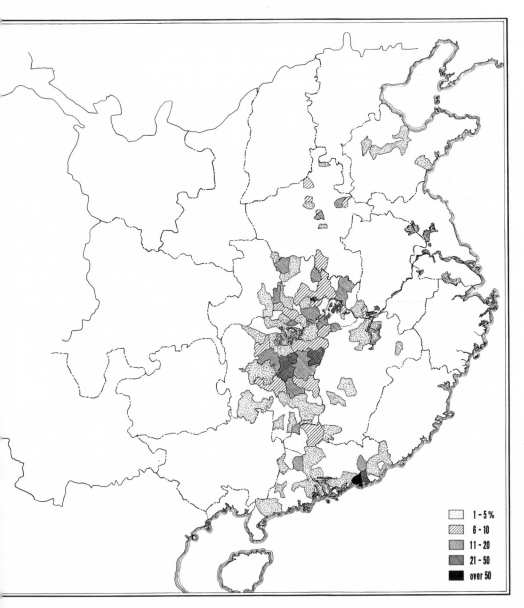

MAP 1. Communist Influence, 1926–27: Percentage of Rural Population in Peasant Associations

COMMUNIST
INFLUENCE
KIANGSI
PROVINCE

PERCENT OF AREA OCCUPIED

1 - 14 %	▨
15 - 49	▨
50 - 79	▨
80 - 100	▬

Miles

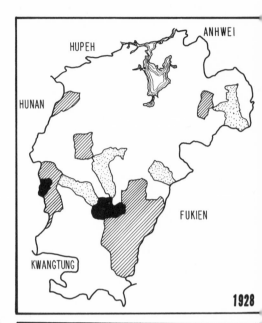

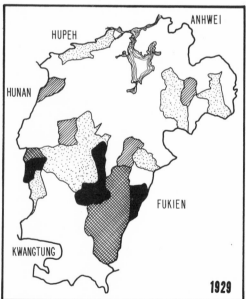

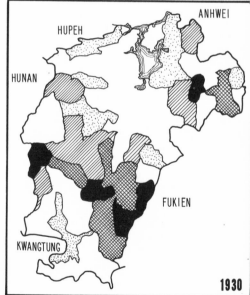

MAP 2

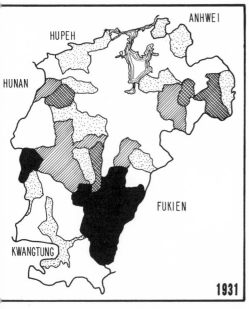

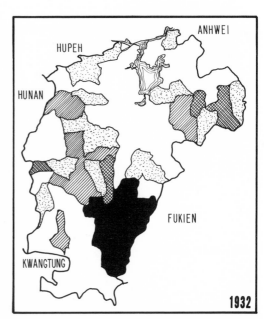

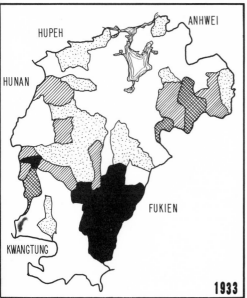

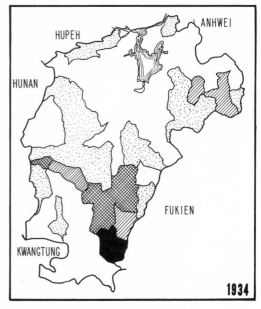

MAP 2

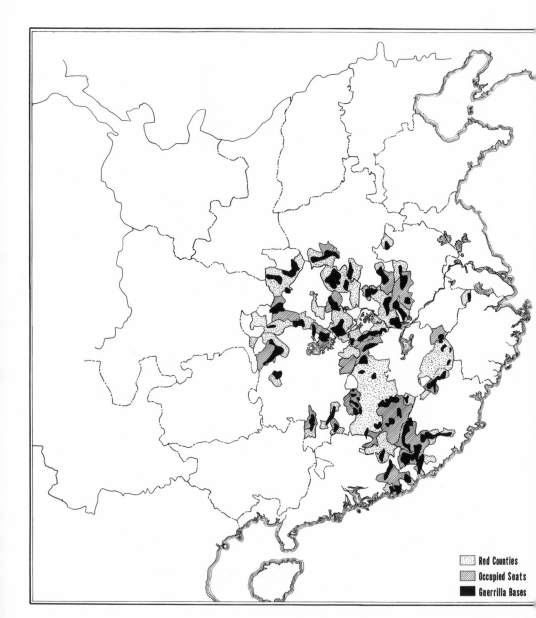

MAP 3. Communist Influence, 1932

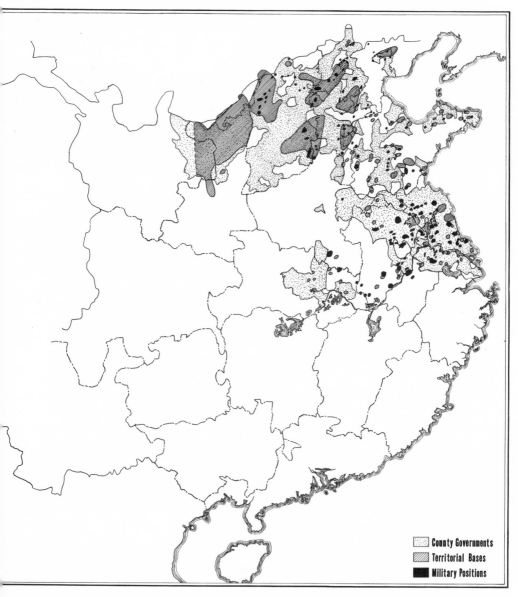

MAP 4. Communist Influence, 1938–41

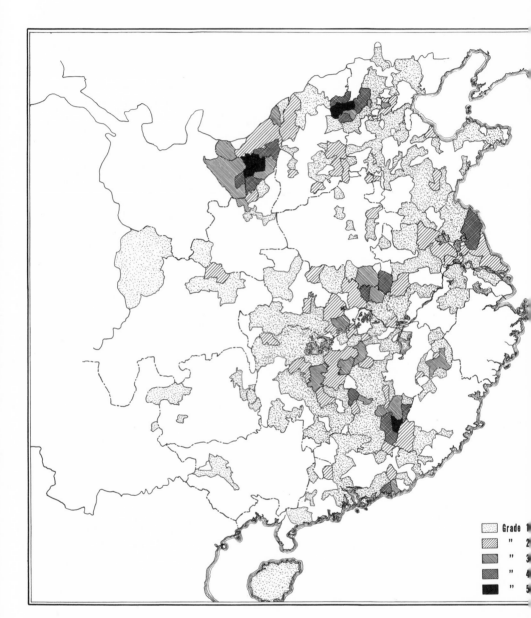

MAP 5. Communist Influence, A Composite Map, 1923–45

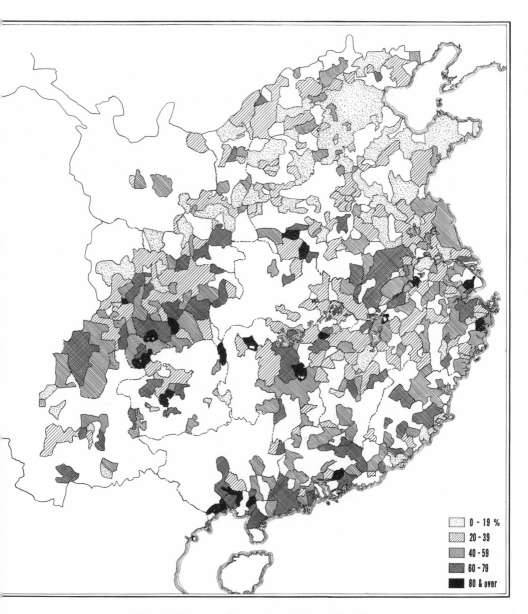

MAP 6. Tenancy: Percentage of Farm Families

0 - 19 %
20 - 39
40 - 59
60 - 79
80 & over

PERCENT OF CROP PAID IN RENT

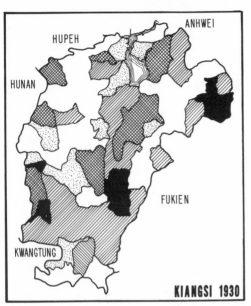

KIANGSI 1930

CONVERSION RATE
CHRISTIANS / MILLION / MISSIONARY MAN-YEAR

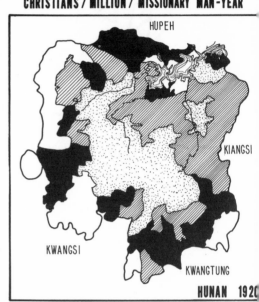

HUNAN 1920

under 50 ▨
50 - 59 ▨
60 - 69 ▨
70 and over ■
no data ☐

under 1.5 ▨
1.5 - 3.3 ▨
3.3 and over ■
no data ☐

PERCENT OF FIREARMS PRIVATELY OWNED

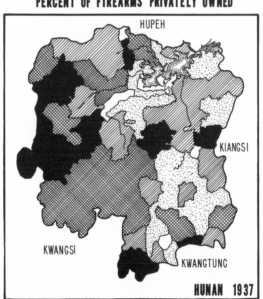

HUNAN 1937

0 - 19 ▨
20 - 49 ▨
50 - 79 ▨
80 and over ■
no data ☐

MAP 7A, above left; Map 7B, above right; Map 7C, below

SIZE OF BANDIT BAND

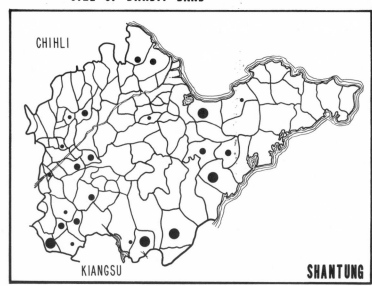

100 - 400 men ·
401 - 1000 ·
1000 and over ●

CHIHLI

KIANGSU

SHANTUNG

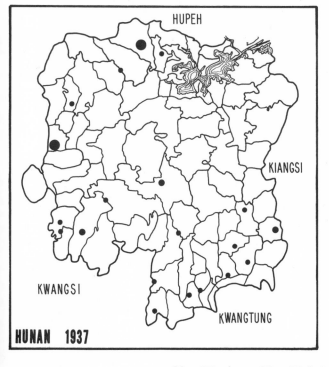

HUPEH

KIANGSI

10 - 100 men ·
101 - 1000 ·
1001 and over ●

KWANGSI

KWANGTUNG

HUNAN 1937

Map 7D, above; Map 7E, below

KMT MEMBERS PER 10,000 POPULATION

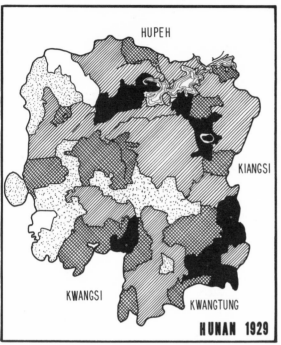

HUPEH

KIANGSI

KWANGSI

KWANGTUNG

HUNAN 1929

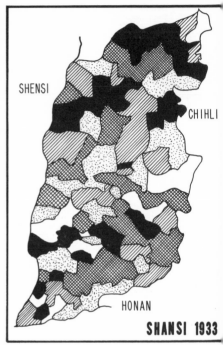

SHENSI

CHIHLI

HONAN

SHANSI 1933

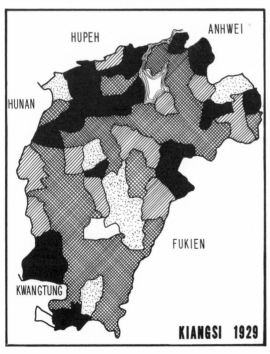

HUPEH

ANHWEI

HUNAN

FUKIEN

KWANGTUNG

KIANGSI 1929

under 2
2 - 7
7 -14
over 14
no data

0   50   100

Miles

MAP 8A

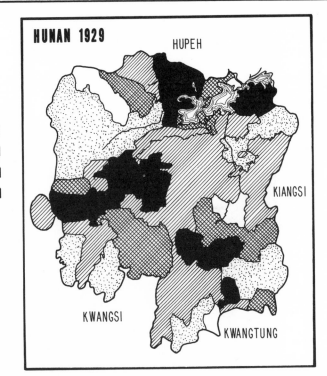

HUNAN 1929

HUPEH

KIANGSI

KWANGSI

KWANGTUNG

under 3%
3 - 10 %
10- 18 %
18% and over

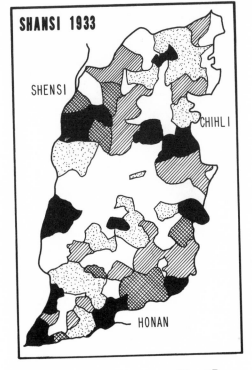

SHANSI 1933

SHENSI

CHIHLI

HONAN

under 4 %
4 - 10 %
10 - 15 %
15% and over
no data

MAP 8B

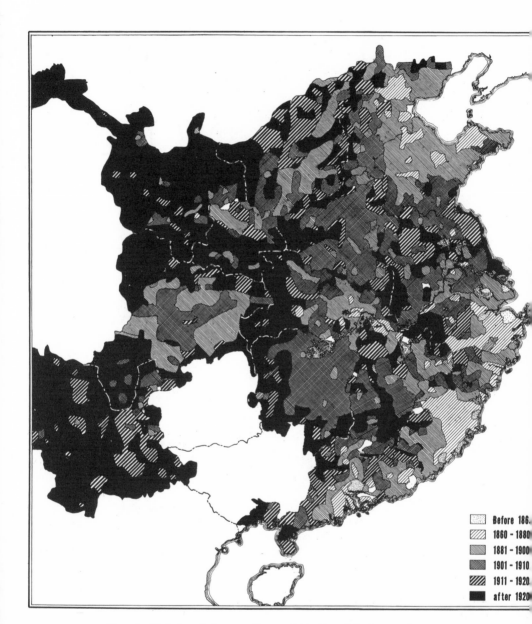

	Before 186.
	1860 – 1880
	1881 – 1900
	1901 – 1910
	1911 – 1920
	after 1920

MAP 9. Christian Influence: Date of Earliest Missionary Penetration

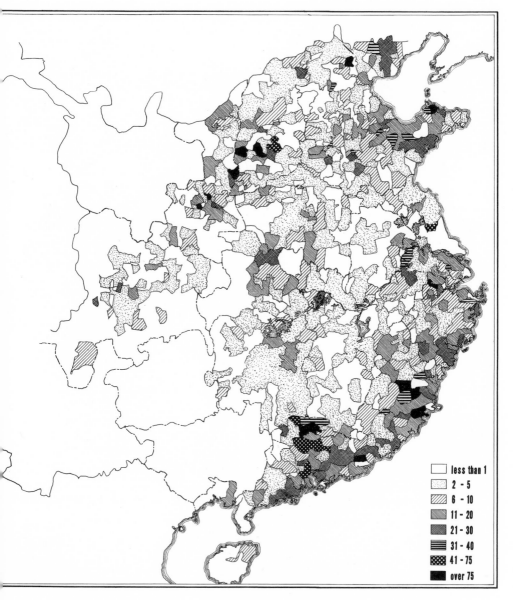

Map 10. Christian Success, 1919: Christian Converts per 10,000 Population

less than 1
2 - 5
6 - 10
11 - 20
21 - 30
31 - 40
41 - 75
over 75

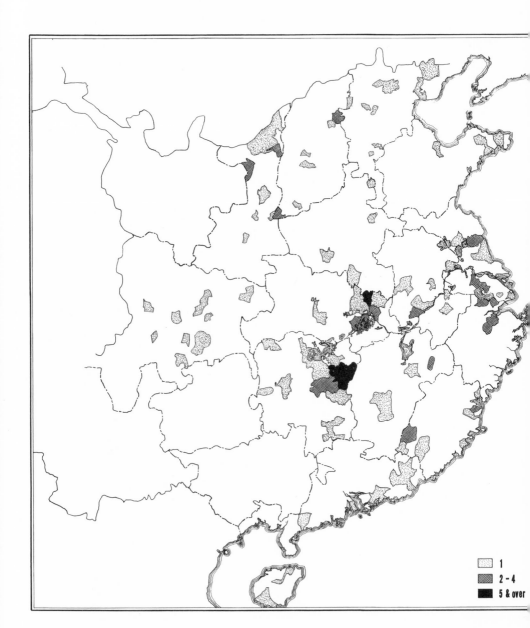

Map 11. Chinese Communist Elite Origins: Distribution of Home Counties of 375 Present Leaders

Legend:
- 1
- 2 – 4
- 5 & over

any Chinese numbers as fundamentally worthless. I do not share this view, but for the moment I must forego discussing the problem of reliability. Although I have been forced on occasion to fall back on cross-provincial data, the twenty-odd provinces are far too large to do justice to the analysis. Should the provinces alone be compared, there is a real danger that important relationships between background factors and Communist success might be obscured, or that spurious ones might appear. That such an ecological correlation error can easily occur will become clear in the later analysis. Villages (or the next highest administrative unit, the district or *hsiang*—of which there were some forty-eight thousand in 1947) would be much better, but there are no data to speak of for that level. I have for the most part, therefore, relied on the county (*hsien—N* = about two thousand) as the main unit of analysis. Although no attempt has been made in this paper to go beyond a rough eyeball estimate (the reasoning is largely based on my own hand-drawn maps, some of which are reproduced here), the basic concept will ultimately lend itself to statistical analysis. Just as the politics of the world can be viewed in cross-national perspective, China will be viewed in this study from the vantage point of a "cross-county" survey.

A Measure of Success

The analysis of political radicalism in the Western world has profited greatly from an accident. The spread of universal voting in this century, while not necessarily favorable to radical causes, has made the measure of their influence considerably easier. Analysts have been able to assume comfortably that either votes for or membership in a political party are sufficiently clear indications of strength or influence that there is no need to probe further.[8] Given that the vote or membership figures are available, the well-developed techniques of opinion sampling,[9] or of ecological correlation[10] could be applied directly to the analysis of "causes."

But in China we are several steps removed from such work. Not only

[8] A recent example of work based on this assumption is Glaucio Soares and Robert Hamblin, "Socio-economic Variables and Voting for the Radical Left: Chile, 1952," *American Political Science Review*, LXI, No. 4 (December, 1967), 1053–65.

[9] Gabriel Almond, *The Appeals of Communism* (Princeton, N.J.: Princeton University Press, 1954).

[10] Rudolf Heberle, *From Democracy to Nazism* (Baton Rouge: Louisiana State University Press, 1945). Eric Allardt, "Social Sources of Finnish Communism: Traditional and Emerging Radicalism," *International Journal of Comparative Sociology*, V (1964), 49–72.

do we have little of the background statistical data (not to mention access to interview subjects for the pre-1949 period), we are hard pressed to establish a measure of Communist strength. How are we to draw an "electoral geography" of Chinese communism when either there were no elections, or the equivalent of electoral or membership data is unavailable below the grossest level? Is it possible to establish some indicator or indicators of "success" which will serve the same purpose as election data in traditional American "political science"— that is, areally and temporally compatible information on the extent of Chinese Communist influence at the *hsien* level and below? If not, are we forced to abandon the attempt to grasp the Communist phenomenon in China and revert to theories reminiscent of Divine Right?

The concept of winning over the masses is to Communist activists somewhat like that of "works" is to missionaries. To both, they are the only visible signs of rectitude—whether in the faith or in the judgment of history. There is no more damning imprecation to the Leninist than the semimagical phrase, "failed to have faith in the power of the masses." Convinced Communists have perhaps as much difficulty dealing with the problem of defeat as the Christians since Augustine have had dealing with that of evil. The question of whether the Chinese Communists were good organizers of the masses or successful politicians thus cannot be dealt with simply on the grounds of their own claims. Verily, by their own works shall we know them.

But how are we to begin to measure the extent of Chinese Communist success? In the absence of detailed election data we are forced to rely on the gross indicators of growth. There are basically two main approaches to the gross measures: either we can compile what is available in the way of quantified information about the number of individuals involved in the Communist movement—the total membership of the Party, of the Red Armies, the front organizations, and so forth; or we can describe and analyze the geographic spread of the movement. On the one hand we deal with a numerical constituency, and on the other with a spatial one.

The conception of numerical growth is one which plays an important part in Mao Tse-tung's personal view of political warfare. A preoccupation with the phenomenon of numerical expansion shaped the expectations of a long series of Chinese Communist misadventures: the extravagant hopes of the peasant movement of the 1920's was based on a belief that expansion of membership in the peasant associations was an accurate indication of the "strength of the forces of revolution." A similar conception inspired the vision of the people's communes and influenced any number of other nationwide campaigns, from collectivization to the Red Guards. "Movements" are in large part judged on the basis of the percentages, and Mao is not happy unless he can see membership or participation graphs rising.

This is as it should be. Karl W. Deutsch, who has remarked on this peculiar propensity of Mao's, suggests that we would be wise to follow his example. Crude growth and decay patterns are useful to the observer as well as to the politician, since "rates of recruitment and attrition may . . . serve as indicators of the morale and the intensity of motivation of each side."[11]

Indeed, some observers have done remarkable things with the crude growth-rate figures for Chinese communism. Chalmers Johnson, for example, in his *Peasant Nationalism and Communist Power,* develops at length what we might call the *ex crescendo* argument. By studying Japanese intelligence estimates of the growth figures of the Chinese Communist forces from 1937 to 1941, he concludes that these figures were "enormous" and "fantastic," and that their magnitude can only be explained by reference to a factor which he calls "peasant mobilization." Had not the "war-mobilized peasantry" responded to the Japanese invasion by offering themselves to the Communists, Mao's armies could not have grown so rapidly.

We will deal with some problems in this thesis later. But it is worth noting at this point that in terms of crude growth rates the resistance period was not markedly superior to other periods in the rise of Chinese communism (see Fig. 1). In at least two periods, 1925–26 and 1928–29, the rates of growth of the Party organization as a whole exceeded even the most fruitful years of the early Anti-Japanese War.[12] It is true that in absolute terms the movement made a break-through in 1940 when it reached the one million figure, but long before that it had demonstrated a capacity to achieve rapid increments in size over sustained periods. From this point of view alone the early peasant movement and soviet periods can hardly be considered failures, and explanations of their numerical success will have to consider other factors than resentment of the Japanese.

It would, however, clearly be wrong to think that each of the periods

---

[11] K. W. Deutsch, "External Involvement in Internal War," in Harry Eckstein (ed.), *Internal War* (Glencoe, Ill.: The Free Press, 1964), p. 105.

[12] Growth rate figures for mass organizations, as contrasted with the Party, during the 1924–27 period are even more spectacular.

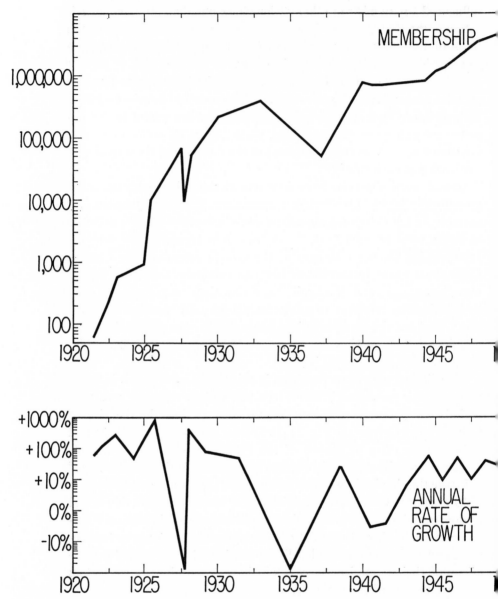

FIGURE 1. Membership and Annual Rate of Growth of the Chinese Communist Party

of maximum growth in the movement represented somehow identical processes of accretion. The apparently monotonic increase in total Communist allegiance hides a great diversity in styles of growth. At least four different phases in the numerical expansion of the movement up to 1949 stand out, each characterized by its own mix of appeals, types of protective cover, and dimension of growth.

TABLE 1

RURAL EXPANSION PERIODS

Periods	Main Growth Dimensions	Protective Cover	Recruitment Appeal
Peasant movement period, 1923–27	Geographical and organizational	Political	Remunerative
Soviet period, 1928–35	Pre-emptive and geographical	Military	Coercive
Resistance period, 1936–45	Geographical and pre-emptive and organizational	Political and military	Normative and remunerative
Civil war period, 1945–49	Geographical and pre-emptive	Military and political	Mixed

THE PEASANT MOVEMENT EXPANSION

From 1923 to 1927 the Communist peasant leadership, operating under the wing of the Kuomintang (KMT) in South China, tended to play down the growth of the Chinese Communist Party (CCP) and especially of Communist-controlled military units in favor of the expansion of bloated front organizations called "peasant associations." The growth of these associations, which far outpaced the growth of the Communist Party itself, was largely attributed to (1) the geographical expansion of the "national revolution" under the Kuomintang, and (2) the organizational efforts of the CCP at the lowest village level. Great hopes were placed, at least by Mao Tse-tung and his entourage, on the military conquest of geographic space as a prime means of expanding Communist influence. The Peasant Movement Institute oriented its training of local operatives, in much the same way as the Whampoa

Academy, toward the organization of newly captured areas.[13] Building the "organization" during the peasant movement period meant largely establishing from scratch village level mass membership associations, often without benefit of military or political protection. The main focus of their propaganda and the crux of their appeal to new members was the private interest of the peasantry in reduced rent and tax burdens. Land ownership was not yet held out as bait. Despite some grumbling by more realistic CCP cadres, the Communist leadership during this period dispensed with its own military organization and relied instead on the political pressure it hoped to be able to exercise through sympathetic members of the Kuomintang leadership.

THE SOVIET EXPANSION

During 1928–34 the Communists sought to pick up the remains of the shattered great revolution. Shorn of the political cover of the KMT, Communist influence in the countryside had to be protected entirely by military force.[14] The remarkable growth rates of 1928–34 are due to two separate trends. First, a sizable portion of the new members of the movement during the early period were defectors from the KMT cause. Considerably more than half the Communist military strength in 1931 came from preorganized units which switched sides. The Chingkangshan base survived until 1929 only through the defection of P'eng Teh-huai in June, 1928. The last major example of large-scale defection during the period was the Ningtu uprising of December, 1931, which brought sixteen to seventeen thousand troops and more than twenty thousand rifles to the Red Army.[15] From 1931 on, the growth of the army and the Party resulted mostly from intensive recruitment within areas already occupied or newly occupied. There was considerable experimentation in the type of appeal used to win over converts, but the high pressure tactics necessary to squeeze the soviet areas of their available manpower made the disputes over the "correct" land policy somewhat academic.

THE RESISTANCE PERIOD EXPANSION

During 1937–45 the Chinese Communists put to use a combination of the patterns which had been successful in earlier years. The peasant

---

[13] The term "liberated" dates from about 1945.

[14] There were, of course, some small-scale political deals of mutual nonaggression with certain warlords—with, for example, KMT figures in Hupeh before 1932 to protect the young Oyuwan Soviet Area, and the short-lived truce with the Fukien "revolutionary government" in 1933.

[15] *Hung-se Chung-hua* (Red China), Juichin, No. 2 (December 18, 1931).

association form of mass organization was resuscitated, but this time its use was preceded by secure military control of occupied areas. Co-option of pre-existing military forces was widely practiced on the model of the earlier era, which had demonstrated the necessity of thorough political indoctrination to ensure that the new recruits would not quickly defect in reverse. And the acquisition of large portions of the Chinese countryside, some exploited with an intensity approaching that of the Kiangsi Soviet, enlarged the ranks of the movement. Both military protection in the form of the Eighth Route and New Fourth Armies and political insulation in the form of standoff agreements with the Kuomintang and institutions incorporating non-Communist personages were employed in a varying mix. The main themes used for recruitment stressed normative appeals to patriotism and ethnic solidarity, but there were also conscious and powerful remunerative rewards held out to many who joined the resistance forces.

THE CIVIL WAR EXPANSION

In their march south from Manchuria in the "liberation" of the late 1940's, the CCP used the entire panoply of political devices for winning over villages which it had developed in the resistance. Certainly all the organizational skills of rural takeover—the propaganda teams, struggle meetings, night-time governments, and military administrations—were as fully employed as earlier.[16] But the overwhelming fact of the war was the sweep of Communist military forces to the Yangtze and beyond—a process in which all villages, whether successfully organized or not, fell under Communist rule. In the following account I will omit discussion of the Civil War of 1945–49, not because relevant issues do not arise, but for practical reasons: first, the military factors operating in this period seem to dominate the others so much that the crude measuring devices I hope to use for the earlier periods are rendered useless for the period of the Communist march to the south. Second, the basic research material—intelligence archives and captured documentation—is simply not at hand.

I stress here the clear differences in the characteristics of Communist expansion during these several periods not because I feel we are dealing with unbridgeable qualitative gaps between them but because the nature of the difference is not always clearly understood. It is tempting to argue that there are phase states or "takeoff points" in the

---

[16] By far the most fascinating account of village takeover during this period is William Hinton's *Fanshen* (New York: Monthly Review Press, 1966).

development of an insurgent movement such as Chinese communism. Mao himself expressed such a belief when he told Edgar Snow that, once the Communists controlled eighty million Chinese, victory would be "almost won."[17] Similarly, if somewhat more optimistically, during the peasant movement period he believed that the national revolution would have achieved a "secure victory" if and when 10 per cent of China's three hundred million peasants—especially those in the "politically more important provinces"—could be organized into peasant associations.[18]

Mao's reasoning was probably based on what analysts of crowd or election psychology might term the "band-wagon effect": a movement of considerable size which can successfully claim a constant rate of expansion and promise triumph within the foreseeable future is in an excellent position to enlist new followers. But the history of the Chinese Communist movement leads us to believe that there may have been conflicting forces at work: the secular trend in the *rate* of growth of the movement is downward from the beginning, not upward. The final years of the periods I have listed do not consistently demonstrate higher growth percentages than the beginning. The "band-wagon effect" is most evident in the months of rapid growth in 1926–27 and 1948–49, when Communist efforts were thrown into massive military expeditions, the first sweeping from south to north, the second from north to south across wide expanses of the subcontinent.

There are a number of reasons why rates of growth, except for periods of the "band-wagon effect," should show a downward trend. First, it is possible that large-scale political organizations suffer from the same sort of diseconomies that plague corporations. Each additional member recruited or each new territory added presented the leaders of the movement with more problems of training, coordination, and supervision which absorbed energies earlier available for recruitment and growth. This phenomenon—what we might call "scale diseconomy effect"—was in large part the motivation behind the "crack troops and simple administration" (*ching-ping chien-cheng*) reforms of the late resistance period. Second, pre-emptions of large units of population, which earlier would have been phenomenal increments, in later periods proved to be only small additions to the total movement membership. An excellent example of this is given by the KMT intel-

[17] Edgar Snow, *Red Star over China* (New York: Random House, 1938), p. 68.

[18] See my "Peasant Movement and Rural Revolution: Chinese Communists in the Countryside 1923–1927" (Ph.D. dissertation, Harvard, 1966), p. 80.

ligence records for Anhwei Province during the entry of Liu Po-ch'eng's army in 1947. Despite the pedestrian over-all growth rate of CCP units in 1947, the Anhwei spearhead apparently increased its strength by a factor of twenty in twelve months![19] Finally, what we might call a "vacuum effect" seemed to operate. It is easier to score gains in an early period of growth than in a later one because of the element of surprise and the absence of determined opposition. Thus Communists were able to organize rapidly in situations where the political, administrative, or military framework left openings for penetration. The KMT expanded too rapidly in 1924–27 and left the CCP to organize behind the lines and in the villages; the warlord-territorial system of the thirties permitted Mao's "Red Political Power" to expand in the no-man's land between the various satrapies; the Japanese military administration of the "points and lines" of North China left the villages beyond the fringe of rule. Into each of these vacuums the CCP was able to inject its power rapidly, at least until it began to generate its own natural enemies.

The "break-through" of 1937–40, then, may be seen as a product of these two trends: the accelerated ecological vacuum effect—accelerated because the North China plain was an area in which the CCP had not yet generated its own "natural enemies"—and the band-wagon effect. It may well be that both these effects are as important in explaining Communist growth during the period as shifts in individual attitudes toward the Japanese.

THE RED HSIEN DATA: INADEQUACY OF PRESENT MAPS

Since so much of our circumstantial data about rural China is based on the *hsien* as the operative unit, it would be desirable to translate our information about Communist influence into maps showing which *hsien* were "communized" in any given year. For the peasant movement period of the 1920's, the membership figures issued by the Kuomintang Peasant Bureau provide one indication of Chinese Communist success. For each of the four or five most important provinces in South China where the Communist-led peasant associations had large constituencies we have provincial membership totals. But since these totals obscure the more interesting intraprovincial variations in Communist influence during the period, they are less useful than the available *hsien* level data. The three provinces in which the peasant movement was

---

[19] Documents in the Bureau of Investigation, Ministry of Justice, Taipei, Taiwan.

most successful—Kwangtung, Hunan, and Hupeh—did in fact produce *hsien* breakdowns of the membership totals. The main problem with these figures is that they represent membership at different stages of the development of the movement and are not fully commensurate across provinces. For example, figures on Kwangtung Province in late 1926, during a period when anti-Communist forces had already begun to strangle the peasant movement, would naturally show a lower figure for membership in proportion to total population than those for, say, Hupeh six months later, when the Wuhan government swung to the left, the anti-Communist reaction had not yet occurred, and the Party needed inflated figures. Furthermore, the type of peasant association (even during the height of Communist influence in Hunan and Hupeh some associations remained under non-Communist control) would also have to be taken into account to assess these figures as an index of Communist influence. But despite these drawbacks, figures on the *hsien* association membership, as a proportion of total population, adjusted slightly to take account of the different dates for each provincial set, provide the best indication we have for the period. Map 1 is based on these figures.[20]

For the subsequent soviet period the Nationalist compilers of the *Kiangsi Yearbook* have given us an intriguing set of data for that province.[21] Map 2, drawn from these statistics, purports to show the percentage of the total area of each *hsien* occupied by the Communist Red Armies in a given year. Were it accurate, this areal measure might be converted rather easily, making certain assumptions about population distribution within *hsien,* into a figure comparable to the earlier peasant movement data. Unfortunately, the Kuomintang authorities, despite their attempt at precision, appear not to have known exactly where the Communists were. The 1928 figures, for example, greatly exaggerate the size of the CCP forces in southwest Kiangsi; Communist penetration in the extreme south of the province in 1929 is not indicated; and the county of Hsunwu in the southern tip, known to have been one of the strongly held "central *hsien*" of the soviet from 1932 to 1934, appears to be completely lacking in Communists. But even with these aberrations, the Kiangsi maps constitute a better time series of data tracing the expansion and contraction of a Communist base than we have for any other area or time.

[20] For a discussion of the measure of success during the peasant movement period, see my "Peasant Movement and Rural Revolution," chaps. iii, v, and vi.

[21] *Chiang-hsi Nien-chien* (Kiangsi Yearbook) (Nanch'ang: Statistical Office of the Kiangsi Provincial Government, 1936), pp. 1265–70.

For those parts of China other than Kiangsi which were under Communist influence during the soviet period, we are forced to fall back on Japanese intelligence estimates. Hatano Ken'ichi, a Japanese Foreign Office historian of the Communist movement, has provided us with some examples of this genre, though he himself took a rather skeptical view of trying to measure Communist strength by counting *hsien*.[22] An instructive example of his efforts is the map he prepared for presentation to the Diet in 1932, which we reproduce here in modified form as Map 3.[23] It contains three different measures of Communist influence as of July, 1931: (a) *hsien* in which Communist activity was reported; (b) *hsien* in which the county seat was overrun or occupied during the year by the Red Armies; and (c) *hsien* known to be Red Army guerrilla bases.

These three measures, which we may think of as ascending in order of Communist strength and capability, provide us with a crude geographic scale of influence. The "activity" measure, extensively used in Hatano's voluminous written reports, is perhaps the least valuable, since it gives little indication of relative strength. The measure indicating Communist "occupation" of central places (here Hatano has given the struggling movement every benefit of the doubt; if the East River *hsien* seats in Kwangtung were captured from the bristling Cantonese militarists in 1931, it must have been in the dead of night) is more enlightening, since it demonstrates where the Communists had sufficient military strength to overcome an urban garrison. The measure indicating what areas were "guerrilla bases," founded as it is on a very rough guess about territorial control, is approximate at best, but it probably comes closer than the other two in reflecting the extent of long-term Communist presence.

For the resistance period, our mapping problems are even more severe. There are no adequate KMT maps of Communist-controlled areas in this period, as far as is known, and the Japanese ones are less informative than Hatano's early efforts. In addition, to confound the picture a new indicator of influence appears: "Anti-Japanese *hsien* Governments." These institutions were almost automatically established after the entry of a Communist political work unit into an area.

[22] See Hatano Ken'ichi, "Shina Sekishoku Chiku no Kenkyū" (A Study of China's Red Areas), *Tōa Mondai Kenkyū* (Studies on East Asian Problems), No. 2 (Tokyo, 1941), p. 91.

[23] Gaimushō, *Shina oyobi Manshū ni okeru Kyōsan Undō Gaisetsu* (Outline of the Communist Movement in China and Manchuria) (Tokyo: Japanese Foreign Office, 1933). Hatano Collection, Microfilm 942.10.

Largely because CCP policy in the resistance period favored establishing *hsien* governments even in relatively insecure areas, and because the war permitted such governments to exist longer than they might have in an earlier era, the number of these *hsien* "political organs" proliferated. As a result, when used as a measure of Communist influence, they tend to overstate the true geographical extent of Communist power. A Communist *"hsien* government" was often only one of two or three rival (including Kuomintang, pro-Japanese, or both) local political organs, and might continue to exist whatever the strength of the Communist Party, army, or mass organizations.[24] To cite an example, the multiplication of *hsien* level Communist "governments" in the central Hopei flood lands in the late thirties has been treated as a remarkable example of Communist geographical expansion.[25] Certainly the maps of *hsien* governments indicate a phenomenal concentration of CCP influence in the area. As we shall see below, however, other indicators of Communist presence in the North China plain during the period reveal that these governments lacked the backbone of support found in better established Communist bases.

Map 4 is a composite of the "Communist *hsien* government" maps of the Japanese and two additional depictions drawn by Japanese intelligence personnel for the period of maximum Communist growth rates in 1938–41. Estimates made by the Kōain (the Asia Development Board —the special branch of the Gaimushō concerned with the "China incident") are more lenient in defining areas of Communist influence than are those of the military intelligence organs of the North China Area Army. (The army map data indicate, perhaps too accurately, the location of anti-Japanese armed units.) But there is sufficient overlap in the information from the three sources to give us a certain confidence that they reflect the same reality.

None of the "influence maps," however, really provides the kind of quantitative scale of success that we need; nor does any map give

[24] See the construction of "governments" in P'ingchiali, eastern Hopei. *Li-shih Yen-chiu* (Historical Studies), No. 5 (1965). So far as can be told, it was only the larger bases during the soviet period, such as in the Central and Oyuwan regions, that went to the trouble of establishing *hsien* level political organs. It was the mark of the resistance period that governments were set up in regions only nominally secure from the military viewpoint. This stress on village governmental organs as devices for gaining support was one which Mao personally advocated during his turn as chairman of the Kiangsi Central Soviet (see his untranslated reports on soviet work in Ts'aihsi—Ch'en Ch'eng Microfilms).

[25] See Johnson, *Peasant Nationalism*, pp. 117–19. The appearance of higher CCP concentration in the Hopei lowlands results from an accident of administrative geography: there were more *hsien* in the region.

much indication of the qualitative differences between various areas under Communist control. We know, for example, that the Communist expansion across North China in 1937–41 was characterized by a great variety of patterns of activity involving varied relationships between the CCP and the villages. The most authoritative work on the period, Chalmers Johnson's *Peasant Nationalism and Communist Power*, despite its main message that peasants throughout North and Central China reacted in essentially the same mobilized, nationalistic way, still betrays hints of considerable variety in patterns of Communist success within the over-all pattern. It differentiates, for example, "main military strongholds," "base areas," "war areas," and "guerrilla territory." These distinctions are, of course, part of the vocabulary developed by the Communists themselves to describe nonuniform spatial control.[26] Whether the distinction was between the "great rear area" of Shen-Kan-Ning and the regions of more direct contact with the enemy, or between a small handful of villages within a few square kilometers of territory which were fimly in CCP hands and those neighboring villages which were not, the Communists' own sense of gradation in the extent and degree of their power was highly sophisticated. Without further development of our measures of influence beyond what crude maps provide, we will not be in a position to appreciate these subtleties.

It should be evident from inspection of Maps 1–4 that, first, there is almost no geographical correspondence between the three periods of Chinese Communist success. It is almost as though once a Communist movement had been successfully developed in a particular area and then that movement was suppressed, the area became in some sense immune to further easy inroads by Communist organizers.[27] This point will be discussed later when we try to analyze the factors behind the rise and fall of Communist influence. But it should also be clear that the criteria for determining "success" in each of the three periods are extremely diverse. Before we can attempt to create a composite map of

[26] The development of a geographical sense of influence by Mao and his group is worth more extensive treatment. In 1927 "peasant areas" were contrasted with "counterrevolutionary," in 1933 "central areas" with "border areas" and "white areas," and by 1938 the "base-guerrilla-enemy" vocabulary had emerged.

[27] Robert W. McColl's assertion that the location of guerrilla bases in the 1927–34 period "was the result of the earlier concentration of party activities in the same area" is mistaken, as his own maps reveal. See his "The Oyuwan Soviet Area, 1927–1932," *Journal of Asian Studies,"* XXVII, No. 1 (November, 1967), 42–45. The quotation is from Robert W. McColl, "A Political Geography of Revolution: China, Vietnam and Thailand," *Journal of Conflict Resolution*, XI, No. 2 (June, 1967), 157.

"success" which transcends historical periodization, we will have to discuss the ambiguities of the notion of influence itself.

A Measure of Influence

The Chinese Communists were everywhere and nowhere, depending on the sources. Estimates of the numbers of Communists involved in a given incident, or stationed in a given area, could and often did vary by factors of ten. Estimates of Communist forces, however defined, suffered from the inherent inaccuracy of intelligence reporting (at least in the early thirties the KMT information was poor indeed) or from the deliberate distortion of figures for political purposes (of this the Russian Communists were even more guilty than the Chinese). The claim that there were nineteen anti-Japanese "liberated areas" on V-J Day at the end of World War II has been repeated often by Chinese and Western historians. Yet the source for such a figure is obscure. It could have been either the enumeration given by the Yenan newspaper *Chieh-fang Jih-pao* (Liberation Daily) in its July 7, 1945, editorial, or a speech by Mao the next month.[28] Both of these did use the number nineteen, but even they disagree as to the identity of *four* of the "bases."

But beyond establishing the presence of CCP forces, the problem of defining their influence also poses formidable difficulties. There is no question about the extent of Communist control in such distinct areas as the one around Yenan, but we can doubt whether local areas through which the Long March passed, or where a small band of renegades operated underground hundreds of miles from a Communist power source—as, for example, in a number of areas in South China after 1934[29]—might be legitimately regarded as areas of Communist strength. Clearly we are not dealing with a situation analogous to that of voting, in which attitudes and influence can be defined and measured in terms of a solitary, specific act.

But the problems of estimation from limited data may be less formidable if we first attempt to deal with certain conceptual ambiguities in the notion of "Communist influence." In fact there are two separate types of ambiguity that make the concept a tricky one to deal with— whether it be in our present endeavor or in dealing with a complicated

---

[28] Mao Tse-tung, *Selected Works* (Peking: Foreign Languages Press, 1961), IV, 38. As of October, 1945, Mao mentioned only eighteen "liberated areas." *Ibid.*, IV, 61.

[29] See Yang Shang-k'uei, *The Red Kiangsi-Kwangtung Border Region* (Peking: Foreign Languages Press, 1961), for an account of some ridiculously small units which kept the prairie fire alive during this period.

situation such as that in contemporary Vietnam. The first ambiguity centers around the problem of who should count as a Communist. In view of the fact that, particularly during periods of rapid expansion of the revolutionary movement, a large number of new recruits and marginal converts may join, should we not attempt to distinguish the true Communists from what might be called the "rice" Communists?

To cite some examples, during the peasant movement period the line between the Kuomintang and the Communist party was deliberately obscured for all except those most privy to the secrets of both parties. The peasant associations in Kwangtung and Hunan were led for the most part by Communists, but the exceptions provided CCP leaders with no end of headaches. The remarkable growth of the Red Army from 1928 to 1930 brought in thousands of troops whose leaders could not be considered wholly reliable—a fact which explains the origin of such incidents as the Fut'ien mutiny of 1930 and the great "AB Corps" purge in Oyuwan in 1931–32.[30] During the resistance period, Japanese maps of anti-Japanese forces show a nevoid pattern of multicolored blotches representing small units of extremely varied loyalty. The Communist "Central" itself was often in doubt about the ultimate allegiance of such units.[31] Such ambiguity as this could easily become a severe problem in periods when the fortunes of the Party appeared to be falling. The questions that have been raised about the loyalty either of Mao Tse-tung in Kiangsi (to the CCP Central Committee in Shanghai in 1931–33) or of the leaders of the New Fourth Army prior to the south Anhwei incident of January, 1941 (to the new Maoist leadership in Yenan), are legitimate. A series of disastrous mutinies punctuated Chinese Communist history from the late twenties to the early forties, and the leadership itself developed a clear sense of who were its enemies and friends only in the course of these struggles. A professed affiliation, an ability to use the proper slogans, a known and disciplined organizational connection, or the proven willingness to sacrifice everything in the name of the current Communist Party leadership—all became criteria to distinguish the real Communist from the impostor.

But our purposes are not to pass judgment on the crimes of errant

---

[30] For a reference to this purge, see McColl's "Oyuwan Soviet Area." Basing his assumption largely on the scanty English sources, McColl accepts the standard Communist interpretation that the victims were planning a *coup d'état.*

[31] For example, the guerrilla force of such a staunch Communist as Wu Chih-p'u (later of Honan people's commune fame, but in 1938–40 one of the founders of the New Fourth Army's Sixth Detachment) was under a shadow until his superiors printed a public announcement that he had not been dropped from the Party rolls during a long period of silence in the 1930's.

comrades, any more than they are to label as "Communist" any group which sought to alter the status quo by resort to violence or heterodox propaganda. I would suggest that for the most part the Communist "Central's" criteria for who is a Communist are sufficiently candid that we can accept them as a solution. While it may be that the leadership's claims at any given time distort the reality of allegiances for political purposes, I have found that when these claims are viewed in hindsight by us and the Communists themselves a more accurate picture can be pieced together.

The second type of ambiguity, however, cannot be so easily resolved. Our ordinary language notion of the word "influence" is extraordinarily imprecise. It may be used to denote the effect on one's judgment of a drug, the subtle pressures of friendly advice, or the brute power of a ruthless politician. The influence of one nation upon another likewise ranges from the frivolous commercial impact implied by the French word "Coca-colonization" to the late-nineteenth-century notion of "spheres of influence" which became the conceptual cover for international larceny. The argument that the struggle in Vietnam is necessary to limit Chinese "influence" often rages around the great variety of roles China might play in Southeast Asia. If we are to analyze the sources of Chinese Communist strength within China during the revolution, then we have every right to insist on a precise definition of "influence." Basically five types of influence, in increasing order of seriousness, can and should be distinguished.

1. Influence is presence. People on the ground—a man in the village, whether schoolteacher or student or relative of a Red Army soldier— were the first wielders of Communist influence. Propaganda teams, perhaps armed, perhaps only visiting young radicals, arrived from outside the village. Red Army troops were stationed in the area, perhaps within a day's walk. In a land of face-to-face communication, the mere existence of committed revolutionaries in the villages and towns of a county was the first stage in influence building.

2. Influence is impact. Demonstrations, disturbances, mass meetings (for festivity or hostility), assassinations or public executions of landlords and traitors first brought home the reality of Communist presence. Distribution of confiscated property or elimination of unpopular "oppressors" fixed the impression. These evidences, constructive or destructive, of organized power marked a second stage of advance.

3. Influence is control. Security from outside attack, protection against internal enemies, the monopoly over trade, business, and travel

were all signs of the CCP's increasing ability to command the environment of the village. The administration, however crude, of the coercive and financial reins of local power initiated a third stage of influence.

4. Influence is mobilization. Increasing numbers of men and women were recruited for activity outside the county; a broader segment of the population was exposed to propaganda and brought into agitation; joining began—starting with the relatively inoffensive mass organizations such as peasant associations and women's associations, then spreading to organized economic activity such as cooperatives, or political activity such as elections, or paramilitary activity such as the militia, then finally to disciplined military and political systems such as the Red Army and the Chinese Communist Party itself. Gradually an enormous web of associations was created to harness the energies of every able-bodied individual. This mobilization marked the fourth phase of influence building.

5. Influence is participation. A new stress on active rather than passive membership in organizations, on normative rather than coercive appeals, on ethical pressures to make sacrifices and to criticize oneself and others is the sign that a final stage of influence has begun, the ultimate aim of which is the creation of a totally committed and unquestioningly loyal population.

In a hypothetical Chinese village these five types of influence might have succeeded one another in a roughly chronological fashion. But the reality was vastly more complicated. Counties, towns, and even villages were often sharply divided between Communist and non-Communist areas or even families.[32] Areas in close proximity within a county might be at radically different points on this five-point scale of influence. The alternation between day and night itself brought sudden changes in the presence and influence of the Communists in many areas, especially during the Anti-Japanese War period. Finally the entire order of the types of influence might be reshuffled in an almost random manner: commitment of a small but powerful group of converts might precede military presence, as, for example, in Haifeng in 1923. Control and security might precede visible impact on an area into which Communist armies moved quietly and surreptitiously, as, for example, in parts of south Kiangsi in the late twenties. Participation in its fullest sense in the Red Army, though involving only a minority of the population, might precede mobilization of any sizable portion of the uncommitted,

---

[32] As for example in the important south Kiangsi *hsien* of Ningtu in 1932.

as, for example, in the Oyuwan Soviet in the early thirties, and so on. There were even cases of counties which had known all the degrees of Communist influence yet whose population revolted against the CCP leaders.[33] The inherent ambiguity in the notion of influence, regardless of the apparent clarity of our typology, remains a key stumbling block in the path to a usable indicator.

SOME SUGGESTED INFLUENCE INDICATORS

Despite the indeterminacies, in principle it should still be possible to categorize roughly the extent of Communist influence in a given *hsien*. The following analysis of useful indices for *hsien* rank ordering make the assumption that even though any given *hsien* may be divided into Communist-influenced and non-Communist areas, if a reasonable portion of the *hsien* appears to have been in CCP hands, the entire *hsien* has to be regarded, for our purposes, as an analytically significant unit.

1. *Security.* One useful indication of Communist influence is the length of time a given *hsien* was in Communist hands (however defined) without succumbing either to (a) defeat by external forces, or (b) collapse from internal rebellion. Obviously, no direct causal connection can automatically be assumed to exist between defeat and popular disaffection or any other broad-based sentiment or attitude. Even the most deeply committed population, such as that of Haifeng, for example, could be turned from its attachment to the Communist movement by the application of sufficiently brutal force. Nevertheless, victories in "encirclement and suppression" campaigns often did rest in no small part on the participation of anti-Communist local forces. To cite one example, the CCP attempts to establish a base in eastern Hopei during the early forties failed not solely (as has been sometimes claimed[34]) because of the application of harsh military pressure. There were important local organized elements—including a politico-religious sect called the Hsien T'ien Tao (Ancient Heaven Society)—reminis-

---

[33] See the "Trotskyite" mutinies in the West Lake region of Shantung in 1939 (discussed by the CCP Central in *Tang-te Sheng-huo* [Party Life], No. 4 [April, 1941], Bureau of Investigation Collection, Taipei) and the "two or three uprisings" in north Kiangsu ("Directive on Preventing Counterrevolutionary Uprisings," of the CCP Mid-China Sub-Bureau, in *Hua-Chung T'ung-hsun* [Central China Bulletin], No. 4 [July 5, 1946], pp. 23–25, Bureau of Investigation Collection). Johnson cites one rebellion in central Anhwei in 1941, which he treats as an isolated "defection" caused by failures of individual CCP cadres who lacked "talent and incorruptibility." But never before or after this incident did the Shouhsien region of Anhwei become one of sizable Communist influence—until its capture in 1947 by Liu Po-ch'eng's armies. The Shantung and Kiangsu rebellions were significant in that they did occur in areas of high apparent "success."

[34] See Johnson, *Peasant Nationalism*, p. 113–15.

cent to present-day newspaper readers of the Hoa Hao in Vietnam—
which contributed to its defeat and which had to be crushed by the
Eighth Route Army before a guerrilla base could be constructed.[35] In
Oyuwan, so-called "landlord armed forces" actually adopted guerrilla
tactics and retreated to the hills to sweep down and plunder the never
too well-established soviet government installations,[36] and their presence made the task of the KMT suppressing armies easier. The security of an area thus reflected to a considerable extent the ability of the
Communist forces to generate loyalties and mobilize energies.

The amount of time a given *hsien* was controlled by Communists
provides another crude indication of the extent of CCP impact on local
society. The difference between "newly liberated areas" and "central
areas" (some *hsien* were called "central *hsien*" to distinguish them
from their newly acquired neighbors) was clear-cut to the Red Army
organizers, who recognized that time was generally their ally in consolidating their control. Mobilization proceeded at a finite pace, and care
was usually taken to ensure that the population was fully prepared for
each successive campaign. The internal enemy was always "waiting for
the autumn harvest to settle accounts," but his patience had a limit. By
the second or third year of occupation, even under adverse circumstances, the greater portion of the internal threat had usually been
eliminated, and the local population could be pushed to greater feats
of commitment, contribution, or participation. Each new *hsien* occupied, by a process of outward expansion from a central *hsien*—for
example, the outlying areas around Juichin in west Fukien in 1932, or
the Michih-Kuangshan region in northeast Shensi in 1939–40—would
have to undergo the same process, but they would in all likelihood
remain several stages behind the original base in the extent or degree of
mobilization, internal security, and commitment to the cause. Hence,
we need to divide border regions and soviet areas into several grades of
hsien according to the dates on which each *hsien* was acquired.

2. *Social Mobilization.* Ideally an analysis of the success of Chinese
communism should include more than indicators of control and security. For each established base area we might hope eventually to
supply the type of information desired by Karl Deutsch in his treatment of "social mobilization."[37] That is to say, we might search for

---

[35] See "The Revolutionary Struggle of the P'ingchiali People," *Li-shih Yen-chiu,* No. 5
(1965).

[36] See *Hung Ch'i Chou-pao* (Red Flag Weekly), No. 10 (May, 1931).

[37] See K. W. Deutsch, "Social Mobilization and Political Development," *American
Political Science Review,* LV, No. 3 (September, 1961), 493–514.

indices of rates and extent of "development" measured by, for example, exposure to modernity, the extent of contact with the mass media, literacy, urbanism, linguistic assimilation, per capita income, and so on. Our present level of information is so low that even a rough estimate of such an "M index" would be hazardous. But still, a beginning can be made.

a. *Newspapers*. One important indicator of the extent of Communist influence is the relative size, complexity, and efficacy of a mass media network.[38] Since radios were not available for mass communication in the guerrilla areas (the transistor radio of the 1960's may have transformed insurgent politics in this sense), the chief vehicle for one-way communication from the leadership to the villages was the newspaper.

Printed media were not an important part of the earliest Communist village efforts during the peasant movement period. There was an element of truth in Trotsky's charge that the CCP had failed to develop its own newspaper system.[39] The peasant movement leadership during the revolution of the twenties did try to produce a periodical literature, under the aegis of the Kuomintang, which we may regard as the embryo of later publication work. Such peasant movement magazines as *Li-t'ou Chou-pao* (The Plow Weekly) which was produced in Canton by P'eng P'ai's Communist-led Provincial Peasant Association was sophisticated and slick in format, but it was obviously not adapted to the needs of reaching a semiliterate village population. Propaganda workers during the Northern Expedition concentrated more on word of mouth and "armed propaganda" than on the distribution of leaflets and newspapers.[40]

After the collapse of the great revolution, there was little attempt to generate a regularized press network until after the formal establishment of the Central Soviet Republic in Kiangsi in 1931. The movable-

[38] Curiously, the only work to date on the subject, Barton Whaley's *Guerrilla Communications* (Cambridge, Mass.: M.I.T. Center of International Studies, 1967), pointedly excludes this type of indicator (p. 10).

[39] See his speech to the Seventh Plenum of the Executive Committee of the Communist International: "The Communist party of China was in the preceding period a party bound. It lacked even its own periodical. Imagine just what this means at any time, but especially what it means during a revolution! Why does it have to this day not yet its own daily newspaper? Because the Kuomintang will not allow it." *Die Chinesische Frage Auf dem 8 Plenum der Executive der Kommunistischen Internationale* (Hamburg: Verlag Carl Hoym Nachf., 1928), p. 39.

[40] See the numerous stories of how slickly printed literature was "distributed" simply by tossing it in bundles out the windows of trains rapidly moving northward. E.g., in Chu Ch'i-hua (alias Li Ang), *1927-Nien te Hui-i* (My Reminiscences of the Year 1927) (Shanghai: Hsin-hsin Ch'u-pan She, 1933).

type press at Juichin in south Kiangsi was fairly prolific, and the Ch'en Ch'eng collection of documents captured from this area in the early thirties includes a wide assortment of pamphlets, magazines, and journals that probably received widespread circulation. Other soviet areas appear to have lacked such modern technology: I have seen only one other "lead print" product for the period—a newspaper from west Hupeh (the Hunghu base) in the Gaimushō files in Tokyo. The use of mimeographed local publication designed for local consumption was begun during this period, as a number of items in the Ch'en Ch'eng collection reveal, but my general impression is that the number of newspapers produced as well as the circulation of each title remained quite small until well into the Anti-Japanese War.

During the stay in Kiangsi, however, the CCP began to develop extensively the tradition of mimeographed local publication for local consumption. Although they had much smaller runs than the central newspapers such as *Hung-se Chung-hua* (Red China) in Juichin and later the *Chieh-fang Jih-pao* in Yenan, the miniature "oil presses" such as were carried along on the Long March and scattered throughout North and Central China during the resistance could and did become major bearers of the written word and promoters of literacy. Even the main documents of the Central Committee during the early Yenan period were elegantly printed on paper clearly marked "Horii Myriagraph"—not the least contribution of the Japanese to the Communist effort.

By the early 1940's the mimeograph machine and movable presses under Communist control had proliferated in step with the expansion across North China. One Japanese source for the period gives some indication of the growth of an extensive press network in the region occupied by the New Fourth Army in Central China. The Japanese were unable to obtain reliable circulation figures for these newspapers, but their estimate that the main organs of the south Anhwei base (*Huai-nan Jih-pao* [South Huai Daily]) and of the headquarters of the new Fourth Army at Yench'eng (*Chiang-huai Jih-pao* [Yangtze and Huai Daily]) had runs of 3,000 and 7,000, respectively, seem reasonable. Such figures are commensurate with estimates[41] that *K'ang-ti Pao* (The Resistance), the party organ of the Shansi-Chahar-Hopei base in North China, which was edited by Teng T'o (the recent victim of the Cultural Revolution), circulated in an edition of about 2,500 copies.

[41] Johnson, *Peasant Nationalism*, p. 101.

Even though these figures probably indicate a considerable advance over Kiangsi days, the total exposure to these main journals remained small when compared with the situation after takeover in 1949. In these three guerrilla areas there was one copy of the main paper for each 930, 500, and 7,500 persons, respectively, whereas the corresponding figure for China in 1955 is on the order of one newspaper for 50 persons. But even though by comparison with what followed, the exposure rate of Communist papers remained low, by contrast with the

TABLE 2

NEWSPAPERS IN CENTRAL CHINA (NUMBER OF TITLES)*

Area	1940 and Before	1941	1942	1943	1944
Central Kiangsu		1	7	10	10
Yench'eng-Founing	2	2	2	2	2
Huai-Hai	1	1	4	4	5
South Kiangsu		2	4	4	4
East Chekiang					1
Central Anhwei			1	1	1
South Huai-Kiangsu/Anhwei	2	5	5	5	6
North Huai-Kiangsu/Anhwei	1	4	4	4	4
Honan-Hupeh Border		3	9	10	10
Total	6	18	36	40	43

* Source: "Kachū ni okeru Chūkyōkei Shimbun" (Chinese Communist Newspapers in Central China), signed Shanghai, May 20 [1944], in *Jōhō* (Intelligence Report), published by Dai Tō-a Shō.

Kiangsi period and certainly with the nonexistent mass media in Japanese- and Kuomintang-controlled areas, the newspaper system during the resistance demonstrated noteworthy success.

In fact the available information suggests that the mass media themselves might be treated as one measure of Communist influence: a measure of the extent of what we might call "literary mobilization." It should be possible to derive a crude weighting factor for Communist influence based on a judgmental assessment of the quality and quantity of Communist publications—including the type of press used, the quality of newsprint, the extent of circulation, the frequency of publication, the number of titles, and so on. The materials for this assessment, unlike those for many others, are readily available in the libraries of America, Japan, Taiwan, and elsewhere. Counties with a high output of books, periodicals, and the regular "lead print" press should rank higher on the scale of literary mobilization than those in which only mimeograph publication was available. For example, in the data on the New Fourth Army area in the Japanese study cited above, twenty-two of the forty-three titles were printed in movable type, but the twenty-two were concentrated in two of the nine locations: namely, the Yench'eng-Founing headquarters of the New Fourth Army and in the north Anhwei base. Consequently, I have made a vernier adjustment in my estimate of Communist "influence" in those two areas.

b. *Schools*. Practically every commentator on Chinese communism during the Anti-Japanese War period remarks on the immense efforts put into education—both of the young and of the old. It is true, of course, that from the beginning of the peasant movement the Communists placed great stress on education and training. Along with hospitals and arsenals, schools were part of the indispensable institutional framework of a viable rural base during the Kiangsi era. But as in the field of literary mobilization, the resistance period seems to have marked a break-through on the educational front as well.

The war—and the united front—provided an even better opportunity to build "grey colored" schools than it did to build ambivalent governments. In certain areas informal Communist-run schools were, in some respects, more important than other institutions, including even the army, Party, and government, because they were not forced underground. The Japanese considered this educational network so important that their intelligence services drew maps of its distribution.[42] Counties such as Chinhsien in Hopei, which were not noted by Japanese intelligence for their "insecurity" or for their active Communist political activity, might still reveal a rival system of village level, part-time schools under CCP influence or control.

But how do we measure different degrees of educational mobilization? We might begin by examining the nature and extent of the system of higher education established by Communist governments and armies. Of course, for the peasant movement period, information on the classes of the Peasant Movement Training Institute as well as of the different KMT party schools and military academies in which

---

[42] See the Japanese intelligence map of Chinhsien in central Hopei, a *hsien* which was not completely Communist—it had a total CCP cadre count of just under one thousand in 1940, or 0.5 per cent of a population of over two hundred thousand—and which lay within an area of poor military security (the railroad bisected it). Yet there were Communist schools, grain levy posts, and grain storehouses in over half the nearly two hundred villages. Tada Corps, *Chūgoku Kyōsantō Undō no Kaisetsu* (An Explanation of the Communist Movement) (Peiping, February 17, 1941).

the Communists played a role is available. However, since these schools—which were important training grounds for the future educational efforts of the CCP—were largely located in the major cities or followed the expeditionary armies, it is difficult to develop a sense of varying spatial impact on the fortunes of the peasant movement. Likewise, in the soviet period we know only of the names of some of the major cadre and officer training schools, but have little indication of the distribution of higher educational efforts. Fortunately, information on the resistance period is much richer, and one Japanese intelligence map helps us to visualize the spread of Communist institutions of higher education across the countryside in the late thirties.[43]

Compiled by the North China Area Army in 1941, this map shows nearly a hundred schools established within Communist-held bases at that date. In addition to more than ten "branches" of Resistance University, spread across North China, there were three other universities and several "academies," a central Party School, and the Academy of Marxism-Leninism (the latter two established in Yenan). Though there is doubtless some undercounting, the Japanese listed and located more than twenty Communist middle schools. But more than half the "higher institutions" of education shown on the Japanese map were "Military-Political Cadres Schools" or "Officers' Training Institutes." These last two types of school, numbering more than fifty installations in all, were spread far more widely across the countryside than were the purely academic institutions.

One can, of course, raise doubts about what the presence of higher educational institutions actually indicates. Is it a measure of the existence of a body of eager cadres ready to learn and advance, or merely an indication of the intent of the leadership to "cultivate" new leaders in a given area? In this Japanese map of Communist schools, for example, the ill-fated Honan-Anhwei-Kiangsu base is shown to have a well-developed educational system—but in this case there clearly was not a sizable base of popular support or a notable group of potential leaders. The same could be said for eastern Shantung, where schools were set up by Hsu Hsiang-ch'ien in the early forties; they were established (and show on Japanese map) to meet an anticipated need for large numbers of new cadres, a need that never materialized. A similar map prepared for the earlier soviet period would no doubt reveal far fewer higher cadre training schools than were set up in North China during the resistance. Does this mean the educational

[43] *Ibid.*

needs were less pressing, or that they were taken care of in a less institutional way (through "on the job training" in the army and the like), or that there simply was neither the time nor the manpower to devote to training schools?

Despite these queries, there is good reason to make use of our information about higher education in the base areas. Certainly a base which was able to support a number of military cadre training classes as well as public universities to attract the intellectual youth and specialized academies (such as the medical schools and technological institutes found in the Yenan base) was one in which the educational impact of Communist rule would be more widely felt. Our indicator of educational mobilization, then, should include considerations of the extent of nonmilitary, specialized, and higher training in addition to the quantity of schools.

It is much more difficult to find a measure of the impact of Communist education on the mass, as opposed to the elite, population. Ideally we would like to find some indication of the percentage of school-age children enrolled in Communist schools in each county or each base area. Unfortunately, such information is not available except for a few scattered instances. But what exists suggests that mass education developed at a much slower rate than elite education, and that the Anti-Japanese War period saw considerably more extensive work with the school-age population than the earlier periods.

A case in point is the north Kiangsu base, the formation of which is described in Chalmers Johnson's study.[44] Johnson describes how the Communists under Liu Shao-ch'i acted to turn this region into a viable base before 1941. As we noted above, this area (situated at Yench'-eng-Founing) did establish a considerable press and higher educational system during the early years of the resistance. But Japanese sources reveal that the spread of mass education took place only in the years after the base had already been established.

Assuming the population of the six-*hsien* region to be around 2.5 million, the net result of four years' work was that a little under 3 per cent of the population (around 8 per cent the school-age population) was receiving Communist education.[45] Several of the older, more estab-

---

[44] Johnson, *Peasant Nationalism*, pp. 153–54.

[45] In 1944 the six *hsien* were Pinhai, Sheyang, Foutung, Founing, Lientung, and Huaian, each of which had Communist *hsien* governments and *hsien* Party committees. The assumption is that 15 per cent of the population fell in the six- to twelve-year age range. For support of this assumption see Leo A. Orleans, *Professional Manpower and Education in Communist China* (Washington, D.C.: National Science Foundation, 1961), p. 157.

lished bases during the resistance were reported by Communist sources to have a higher percentage: the Shansi-Chahar-Hopei Border Region in 1946 boasted an enrollment of over a million pupils in primary schools, something over 24 per cent of the school-age population, and

TABLE 3

GROWTH OF ELEMENTARY SCHOOLS IN YENCH'ENG-FOUNING*

	1940	1941	1942	1943	1944
Elementary schools	500	465	773	950	1,186
Elementary pupils		21,365	25,265	44,077	67,452
Teachers		83	128	1,466	2,064
Middle schools	24	3	9	8	13
Middle students	1,200	300	1,200	1,453	1,873
Teachers	100		95	115	207

* Source: "En-Fu-ku Shin Shigun no Gakkō Kyōiku Hatten Kaikyō" (The Expansion of School Education by the New Fourth Army in Yen-Fou), *Jōhō*, No. 38 (December 15, 1944), p. 65.

the most secure and established subregion of that base claimed the amazing figure of two-thirds.[46] Surprisingly, however, the Shen-Kan-Ning Border Region appears to have been less successful with primary education. Although Table 4 shows the same steady growth in mass education during the years of base building experienced in other areas, the 1944 total percentage of school-age population remained relatively low compared with North and Central China during the same period. Perhaps these figures suggest the difficulty of mobilizing and educating

TABLE 4

GROWTH OF PRIMARY EDUCATION IN SHEN-KAN-NING BORDER REGION

	Primary Students	Estimated Percentage of School-Age Population
Early 1937	5,600	5.3%
Late 1939	22,000	10.5%
Early 1944	29,500	13.1%

Source: Primary school students from Mark Selden, "Yenan Communism: Revolution in the Shensi-Kansu-Ninghsia Border Region, 1927–1945" (Ph.D. dissertation, Yale University, 1967), p. 306. Population estimates are my own and assume 15 per cent of total population is school age.

[46] See Michael Lindsay, *Notes on Educational Problems in Communist China* (New York: Institute of Pacific Relations, 1950), pp. 38–39. I adjusted Lindsay's estimate of 28 per cent downward to conform to the demographic assumption above.

a population with much higher illiteracy and lower contact with the affairs of the modern world. But whatever the results, it seems plausible to assume that data on mass education, when they are available, will be useful indicators of the relative influence of the Communist leadership in a given area.

3. *Participation Mobilization.* It may be argued, however, that the hallmark of the Chinese Communists' success in mobilizing the energies of the population was not so much that they brought modern media and education (though these played an ancillary role), but that they were able to draw the masses into one form or another of active commitment by including them in political organizations. We should therefore seek data on the percentage of the population organized into various types of Communist-controlled political and military groupings. But the question must arise, to which type of grouping should we give the greatest weight in our index of Communist mobilization success?

a. *Party Membership.* It might be suggested that the membership of the Chinese Communist Party in a given locality is in the final analysis the best indicator of the mobilization success of the movement, since the Party constituted the elite of the elite, and the final source of power in a given region. But Party membership per capita is a less reliable indicator than we might expect. Even after 1949 when the Communists had a free field of recruitment, the size of the Chinese Communist Party has generally not exceeded 3 per cent of the population. Resistance within the leadership to admitting unreliable elements, and the desire to keep the Party small and exclusive, both contribute to a low threshold on membership. It is worth noting that before 1949 it was rare indeed for an area to have as much as 2 per cent of its population enrolled in the CCP. This was true despite Mao's well-known dictum that at least one-third of the army ought to be composed of Party members.

Although the reasons were somewhat different, even during the peasant movement period a low threshold on membership was rigidly imposed: collaboration with the KMT required deliberate efforts to restrain the growth of a CCP organization that might rival the fraternal party. The figures on CCP membership during the mid-twenties clearly reflect that restraint. Total Party membership during the period peaked at under sixty thousand for all China, and much of this was concentrated in urban areas (50 per cent were classified as "workers" and only 18.7 per cent as "peasants").

TABLE 5

DISTRIBUTION OF COMMUNIST PARTY MEMBERS, MAY, 1927*

Area	Members	Percentage of Population
Hupeh	13,000	.047%
Hunan	13,000	.03%
Kiangsu-Chekiang	13,000	.02%
Kiangsi	3,000	.02%
Kwangtung-Kwangsi	9,027	.017%
Chihli–Shansi–Mongolia	3,109	.005%
Honan	1,300	.003%
Shantung	1,025	.002%
Shensi–Kansu	388	.002%
Anhwei	323	.001%
Southern Manchuria	308	.001%
Fukien	168	.001%
Northern Manchuria	137	.001%
Szechwan	200	.0005%

* Source for Party membership figures: *What One Must Know About China* (Moscow: Workers Publishing House, 1927). Cited in Kuwajima Jukei, *Chū-nan Shi Kyōsantō oyobi Kyōsanhi no Kōdō Jōkyō* (The Operations Situation of the Communist Party and Communist Bandits in Central and South China) (Tokyo: n.p., 1930), pp. 70–71. The population figures used in calculations of percentages are those of the 1953 census, without adjustment.

However, by the time of the soviet period the deficiency in Party membership was a problem the Communists recognized and tried to remedy. By 1933, for example, the Communist leadership was able to claim that there were 40,000 Party members in the Hupeh-Honan-Anhwei Border Region (2 per cent of the claimed population of 2,000,000) and 97,451 in the Kiangsi Provincial Soviet (somewhere around 4 per cent of the estimated population).[47] Even though it may be argued that these high percentage figures were less an indication of significant mobilization than of high pressure policies aimed at Party expansion, they cannot be dismissed as indicators of mobilization. It is true that "Party construction" received a great deal of stress during this period, largely in the form of exhortation to recruit more "industrial workers" into a predominantly rural organization. But it was not the case that all soviet bases responded to this call by announcing

[47] CCP Kiangsi Provincial Committee, "The Organizational State of the Party—Item No. 4 of Materials Prepared for the All-Province Party Congress" (mimeographed; dated September 20, 1933), Ch'en Ch'eng Microfilm, Reel 3, Item 49. Li Chen-nung in December, 1932, gave a figure of 4.2 per cent for his northeast Kiangsi Soviet District—Hatano, Ken'ichi, *Chūgoku Kyōsantō-Shi* (History of the Chinese Communist Party) (Tokyo: Jiji Press, 1962), III, 312, 335.

TABLE 6

CCP PARTY MEMBERSHIP BY HSIEN, HSIANG-O
HSI, SUMMER, 1932 (THE HUNGHU SOVIET BASE) *

Hsien	Members	Percentage of 1931 Population
Chienli	4,468	.93%
Mienyang	2,920	.31%
Chiangling	2,834	.35%
Ch'ienchiang	1,931	.48%
Hanch'uan	1,406	.26%
T'ienmen	1,400	.17%
Yingch'eng	805	.30%
Chingmen	785	.12%
Chingshan	705	.12%
Chiangnan	472	?
Hsiaokan	188	.02%
Chunghsiang	120	.02%

* Source: Shanghai Imperial Consulate of Japan, *Chūgoku Kyōsantō no Kinjō* (The Present Situation of the Chinese Communist Party) (Shanghai, July, 1944), p. 143. The percentage figures are somewhat deflated in this figure by the use of the total 1931 population of the dozen counties instead of an estimate of the controlled population. But the error is less for Chienli, which was nearly 100 per cent Communist, than for the less mobilized counties.

large per capita membership. For example, the Hunghu base in south Hupeh, where Ho Lung, Teng Chung-hsia, and Tuan Te-ch'ang invested many years in base building and cultivation of manpower resources, showed considerably less success in generating Party membership than the two other soviet regions mentioned above. Table 6 reveals that only in Chienli *hsien,* the headquarters of the base, did the Party percentage approach even 1 per cent of the population.

By the peak of the resistance period there seems to have been an almost unwritten law in the CCP that secure base areas were to try to incorporate roughly 1 per cent of the population in the Party. In highly secure, established, and well-mobilized villages the figure might run as high as 7 per cent,[48] but 1–2 per cent appears to have been the average. It was only after a year of severe struggle within the village described

[48] An example here is the model village of Third Township discussed in Mark Selden's dissertation. During three years of "land revolution" before 1937, and in the course of two years of consolidation in which Third Township became the administrative center of the local subdistrict, some 134 residents joined the party out of a total population of around 1,700. "Yenan Communism: Revolution in the Shensi-Kansu-Ninghsia Border Region, 1937–1945" (Ph.D. dissertation, Yale University, 1967), pp. 91, 100.

by William Hinton that the Communist Party broke through the 1 per cent barrier.[49] This fact suggests that those areas in which CCP membership during the soviet and resistance periods approached 1 per cent of the total *hsien* population should be treated as under strong Communist influence, while areas with a smaller ratio were under lesser degrees of control.[50]

b. *Military Membership.* The size of that portion of the population induced to join nonregular military forces provides another useful indicator of Communist influence. It may for certain purposes even be superior as a measuring device to the size of the regular army force recruited in the area, since it reflects an impact on the broad population and suggests that the Communists had proceeded beyond mere warlord-style impressment of troops. Table 7 represents an attempt to piece together some scanty statistics of population, militia, and professional military manpower in a number of the most important Communist bases during the soviet and the resistance periods.

This chart of percentages should give pause to those who claim that the Kiangsi Soviet collapsed because of its failure to "mobilize" the population. Even if one recognizes that there may well have been subtle differences in the quality of popular participation in militia forces during the Kiangsi period as compared with the years of the Anti-Japanese War, it cannot be denied that in Kiangsi the Communists managed to recruit a large number of persons into paramilitary organizations as well as the full-time army. Societies with a military mobilization rate of from 3–5 per cent of the population are rare indeed in the modern world: such a rate is achieved in the militarized 1960's only by such nations as Taiwan, Korea, Israel, and Jordan.[51] Yet during the soviet period in Kiangsi and in Hupeh-Honan-Anhwei these rates, which exceed those of all the later anti-Japanese bases save the Maoist fastness of Shen-Kan-Ning, were readily achieved. We may estimate that all the soviet areas put together totaled only nine million in population, and yet they supplied the Red Armies with over three hundred thousand armed men—most of whom perished or disappeared

[49] Hinton, *Fanshen,* p. 174. Thirty people, mostly "poor peasants," in the village of a thousand joined the Party in the first year of land reform.

[50] There is evidence that Communist cadres regarded this as a good rule of thumb. Documents from the north Huai (Kiangsu-Anhwei) Border Area during the Party construction drive of 1943–44 indicate that *ch'ü* (the sub-*hsien* administrative units) which demonstrated a figure lower than 1 per cent—almost always newly acquired areas —were regarded as the main focus of the drive.

[51] See Bruce M. Russett, "Measures of Military Effort," *American Behavioral Scientist,* VII, No. 6 (February, 1964), 26–27.

TABLE 7

MILITARY MOBILIZATION

Area	Population (in millions)	Militia	Percentage	Regular Army	Percentage
Soviet Bases (1933–34)					
Kiangsi Soviet	3.0*	266,345†	8.9%	150,000*	5.0%
Hupeh-Honan-Anhwei Soviet	2.0*	?	?	60,000‡	3.0%
North China Resistance Bases (1943–44)					
Shensi-Kansu-Ninghsia Border Area	1.4§	224,355§	16.0%	80,000§	5.7%
Shansi-Hopei-Honan Border Area	6.0‖	320,000#	5.3%	40,000**	0.7%
Shansi-Chahar-Hopei Border Area	19.0‖	630,000#	3.3%	45,000**	0.2%
Shantung guerrilla area	18.0‖	500,000#	2.8%	30,000**	0.1%
Shansi-Suiyuan Border Area	2.0‖	50,000#	2.5%	?	?
Central China Resistance Bases (1943–44)					
North Kiangsu	3.5‖	85,000#	2.4%		
South Huai (Anhwei)	2.8	55,000#	2.0%		
Central Kiangsu	8.1	130,000#	1.6%		
Central Anhwei	1.6	25,000#	1.6%	55,000**	0.2%
North Huai (Anhwei)	5.5‖	70,000#	1.3%		
South Kiangsu (Kiangsu-Chekiang)	2.7	25,000#	0.9%		
East Chekiang	2.0‖	10,000#	0.5%		

* My estimate.
† Li Kuang-yuan, *Chung-Kuo Kung-ch'an-chün Fa-chan Shih* (History of the Growth of the Chinese Communist Army [in Japanese translation]) (Shanghai Japanese Imperial Consulate, January, 1943), p. 116.
‡ McColl, "Oyuwan Soviet Area," *Journal of Asian Studies*, XXVII, No. 1 (November, 1967), 56.
§ Mark Selden, "Yenan Communism," pp. 145, 146, 154.
‖ *CFJP*, July 7, 1945.
Hsü Yung-ying, *A Survey of Shensi-Kansu-Ninghsia Border Region* (New York: Institute of Pacific Relations, 1945), II, 151.
** Kachū Chū Kyō no Kōsaku jōkyō" (Situation of Chinese Communist Activity in Central China), *Jōhō*, No. 14 (December 15, 1943), p. 49.

during the Long March. By contrast, the immensely larger anti-Japanese population base (Mao in 1945 estimated that one hundred million persons were under Communist rule) was able to produce an armed force of around a million. Although the People's Liberation Army which issued from the resistance armies in 1945 was large in absolute terms, its relative cost to the parent population in able-bodied manpower was smaller than that of the army of the Long March.[52]

A second point worth noting about the military mobilization percentages is the great variety among the different wartime resistance bases themselves. In estimating the degree of influence measured by these figures, it helps to realize that Shantung, while enjoying a high degree of irregular militia mobilization, never managed to give birth to large-scale Communist armed forces. It is possible that Shantung's notorious propensity for banditry made organization of irregular guerrillas relatively easy, but the failure to produce a disciplined armed force of any size meant that Shantung could not become a "base area" with the same order of security as the border regions to her north and west. It is curious, I might add, that an effective Communist army should fail to appear in a province which since World War I had been garrisoned steadily by Japanese troops. In this case, a simple "peasant nationalism" thesis must yield to the analysis of more complicated factors. But whatever the explanation of this particular anomaly, the measure of rates of military mobilization does clearly indicate differential Communist influence over the local population.

A MAP OF COMMUNIST INFLUENCE

Map 5 represents an attempt to grapple with all the indeterminacies discussed above. It shows all the *hsien* of mainland China, excluding Manchuria and the far western provinces, ranked along a six-valued scale (from 0 to 5) of "maximum Chinese Communist influence." The judgments about which rank a given *hsien* should be given were based on a large number of considerations, and no simple formula seemed to emerge from the mass of different cases. Particularly open to question is the relative weight to be given each of the three main periods: clearly the type of power or influence exercised by the Communists in Hsiangt'an (Hunan, 1927), Kuangshan (Honan, 1932), and Jench'iu

[52] Ch'en Yün admitted that military recruitment during the resistance was "more difficult" than during the "period of agrarian revolution." "Expanding Mass Work Is the Core of Present Local Work," *Kung-ch'an-tang-jen* (Communist Party Member), No. 2, pp. 2–8, Bureau of Investigation Collection.

(Hopei, 1942) was not exactly the same, yet in Map 5 they fall within the same rank. It may be argued that the rankings for the peasant movement period consistently overstate the true power of the Communists (as opposed to the Kuomintang), since in only one county (Haifeng) did the CCP come close to establishing an independent regime and an independent army during the era. It may further seem that the criteria to qualify as a "successful" Communist county during the Anti-Japanese War period are too severe, and that perhaps the entirety of the North China plain should be placed at least in Rank 1 in order to reflect what we know to have been a massive infiltration. Finally, there may be argument about the relative importance of one county over another, or one base area over another during a single time period, since the criteria used to distinguish them may have been arbitrary and lacking in commonality.

I would argue, however, that, first, we should be less interested in the absolute rank of counties than we are in relative rank; second, we are less interested in comparing across periods than in comparing periods and explaining variety within periods; and third, in the final analysis the basic geographic pattern of Chinese Communist influence will approximate that of Map 5 regardless of the need to make certain adjustments in the ranking. But to lay all my cards on the table, the following are the main criteria I used to arrive at the present ranking.

For the 1923–27 peasant movement period, the principal criterion was the figures for maximum *hsien* peasant association membership in the provinces of Kwangtung, Hunan, Hupeh, and Honan. Grades 1–4 represent the following percentages of peasant association membership as a proportion of total population:

$$1 = \ \ 1-10 \text{ per cent}$$
$$2 = 11-20 \text{ per cent}$$
$$3 = 21-50 \text{ per cent}$$
$$4 = 51+ \ \ \ \text{ per cent}$$

In addition, certain counties in other provinces which were known to have had sizable peasant association membership (though perhaps amounting to less than 1 per cent of the population) have been awarded Rank 1 status. These include the Wei Valley in Shensi and the Poyang Lake region in north Kiangsi.

For the 1928–35 soviet period, the following rank criteria were used:
1 = Any "red *hsien*" in Japanese estimates.
2 = A "red *hsien*" which had a prolonged history of guerrilla

activity, or which had the county seat occupied by the Communists for a prolonged period of time, or which served as a center of military administration for a larger region.[53]

3 = The above, plus more than three years of Communist occupation and control.

4 = The above, plus evidence of a high degree of mobilization.

5 = The above, plus having served as the capital of the Central Soviet, the headquarters of the Party, the site of higher educational institutions, and so forth.

It may seem arbitrary to assign a special rank to a county simply because it happened to be the seat of administration, but in view of the massive investment in local institutions in Juichin and Yenan, as well as the influx of large numbers of activists from outside, there is good reason to count Communist influence there a cut above that in other places. In Map 5 it may be that there should be more counties in Rank 2 than appear there: all the Rank 1 counties of western Kwangsi Province in fact met most of the criteria for the higher status in early 1930, but they were abandoned on orders of the Central Committee. Rank 1 itself might have been expanded by several dozen counties if the scattered guerrilla operations of 1934–37 had been taken into account. But the microscopic size of the Communist units in these *hsien* after the collapse of the Kiangsi Soviet led me to treat them as insignificant.

For the 1937–45 anti-Japanese period, the following criteria were used to rank counties:

1 = Counties which supported both an anti-Japanese government and a sizable military force, whether guerrilla or regular.[54] Had the only criterion been the existence of *hsien* governments, the result would have been a larger number of areas in Rank 1.

2 = In Shantung, Anhwei, Honan, and northwest and southeast Shansi, those *hsien* described by the Communists in 1944 as "completely" under CCP control;[55] in central Hopei, counties with a history of Communist presence dating from 1938; and in Shensi

---

[53] Some sources: for Kwangsi, Hsieh Fu-min, *Wei Pa-ch'un* (Peking: Chung-hua Shu-chu, 1960). For Szechwan, Hatano, *Chūgoku Kyōsantō-Shi*, III, 135; and for southwest Hunan, Kweichow, and west Szechwan, Japanese Ministry of the Army, *Shina Kyōsangun ni tsuite* (Concerning the Chinese Communist Military) (Tokyo: Rikugunsho Shimbun-han, 1936).

[54] The Koain and Tada Corps maps are the main source, supplemented by *hsien* mentioned in Johnson, *Peasant Nationalism*, appendix.

[55] E.g., in *Chieh-fang-ch'ü Kai-k'uang* (An Outline of the Liberated Areas) (Yenan: Chieh-fang She, 1944), and local border region reports.

those whose Communist takeover dated from the late resistance period.

3 = In Shensi-Kansu, counties taken over in the Communist expansion of 1939–40; in Hopei, those which were main operations centers for the Eighth Route Army as well as areas with a long history of CCP activity.

4 = The original core *hsien* of the main border regions, marked by a high degree of security and mobilization.

5 = Counties at the Party center in the Shen-Kan-Ning Border Region, with higher security and mobilization than Rank 4 centers.

SOME EXPLANATORY VARIABLES

If and when we establish an adequate measure of "Communist influence" in the hundred-score counties of China, what then? Are adequate data available for Republican China, or for any other period for that matter, which might reveal underlying patterns? Did all *hsien* which at one time or another became Communist strongholds exhibit certain common characteristics independent of their connection with the movement? Given the nature of information on Chinese local areas, despair is perhaps the safest reaction. The journalist's dream, in John Fairbank's words, turns rapidly into the statistician's nightmare.

Not only do we lack an electoral geography of Chinese communism, we have even less of a geography of Chinese society at the local level. With the exception of J. L. Buck's massive study of the utilization of land throughout China proper, there have been no attempts to generate comprehensive measures that penetrate to the *hsien* level. Not only do we have no data bank that might provide a "handbook of political and social indicators" along the lines of Bruce Russett's volume for the world's nations, we do not even have reliable crude population figures for the *hsien* of China,[56] and so for the middle Republican period I have been forced to rely on the highly approximate estimates of the Ministry of the Interior of 1931.[57]

Perhaps it is not very helpful to list the types of data which we do *not* have for China's counties. But the first step in any process of enlightenment is to discover where the gaps in our knowledge are. I would suggest that the analysis of China at the county level ideally

---

[56] The 1953 census surely developed estimates at the *hsien* level, but I have seen no published series. The single exception seems to be Hunan, for which *hsien* level population figures as of 1958 are found in *JPRS*, No. 16387 (November 27, 1962).

[57] Ministry of the Interior, *Nei-cheng Nien-chien* (Internal Affairs Yearbook) (Nanking, 1935), II, 415ff.

ought to be based on a wide variety of social indicators, of which the following list might be illustrative:[58]

I. Demographic data
    A. Total population
    B. Density of population
    C. Percentage of population in cities
    D. Percentage of population in agriculture
    E. Percentage of population unemployed
II. Wealth data
    A. Social product
    B. Growth of social product (or decline)
    C. Calories of daily food consumption per capita
III. Distribution data
    A. Distribution of agricultural landholding
    B. Percentage land rented
    C. Income distribution
IV. Communications and education data
    A. Literacy
    B. Newspaper circulation
    C. Volume of domestic mail
    D. Railroad density, utilization, or "population distance"
    E. Percentage of school-age children in school
V. Governmental activity data
    A. Tax revenue
    B. Military participation (in KMT armies, warlord armies, and the like)
    C. Participation in political parties
    D. Policing expenditures
    E. Deaths or property losses due to domestic violence or invasion

Compared with the information available about practically every other large country in the world, data of this variety for China are remarkably lacking. In fact, I have found nationwide *hsien* level estimates (admittedly partial and arbitrary) for only three or four of the items listed (IA, IB, IIC, and IIIB). The rest will require much greater effort.

On the basis of the limited data that I have so far been able to

---

[58] Taken largely from Norton Ginsburg, *Atlas of Economic Development* (Chicago: University of Chicago Press, 1961), and Bruce Russett *et al.*, *World Handbook of Political and Social Indicators* (New Haven, Conn.: Yale University Press, 1964).

collect, what can be said about the way various social factors relate to our county level index of Communist success?

POTENTIAL GRIEVANCE MEASURES

Some idea of the complexity of the notion of rural injustice and peasant dissatisfaction in China can be gained by examining the complaints listed in an authoritative work on the subject which deals with the critical years of the 1930's. The various Chinese authors who contributed to the Institute of Pacific Relations' volume on *Agrarian China*[59] deal with at least six different measures of rural decline, which can be categorized in the following way:

1. Inequality of landholding, either traditional or resulting in or from:
   a. extensive or increasing corporate ownership;
   b. a rise in nonagricultural employment;
   c. an increase in out-migration or work outside the villages.
2. High, or rising, or inequitably distributed percentages of crop paid in rent.
3. Declining *or* rising land prices.
4. High, rising, or overly complicated taxes, surtaxes, or military assessments.
5. High, rising, or unduly complicated interest rates.
6. The use of unfair weights and measures, "exploitative" subleasing, excessive rent deposits, the loss of *kan-ch'ing* (empathy between owner and tenant), and other noneconomic injustices (including various "feudal" obligations).

With such a bewildering array of potential causes for dissatisfaction, there is little wonder that no adequate conception of "grievance potential" has yet been developed. I have some hope, however, that additional data relevant to at least some of these indicators can be assembled. For example, the national government did collect statistics during the early thirties on interest rates, land prices, and taxes at the county level, and some of Buck's work deals precisely with certain of the indicators listed above, including tenancy and rent rates.

Inequality of landholding is one measure of grievance which is very popular with present-day Chinese Communist historians. It has become, in fact, a matter of ritual in Peking accounts to invoke injustices

[59] *Agrarian China* (London: Institute of Pacific Relations, 1939). The great majority of articles originally appeared in the Shanghai journal, *Chung-kuo Nung-ts'un* (The Chinese Villages).

of land distribution in introducing the story of any particular guerrilla movement. Yet by all accounts China in the pre-1949 era did not suffer, by world standards, from an unusual degree of land concentration, even in the worst of areas. Using the figures for land concentration introduced by the Soviet mission to China in the twenties, Bruce Russett has estimated that China ranked in the highest third of all nations on a scale of equality of land ownership.[60] Furthermore, the geography of land maldistribution within China itself casts further doubt on a thesis which stresses landholding. The Communists achieved some of their most notable successes in the North China plain, an area of remarkably equitable distribution of the ownership of land.

Kuomintang Ministry of Internal Affairs data illustrate this fact clearly for the provincial level.[61] From its estimates of the percentage of total land owned by rich, middle, and poor peasants, we can rank the provinces along a scale running from low to high concentration or inequality.

A calculation of the "equal share percentage"—that is to say, of the percentage of all farmers in each province who together owned half the total land owned[62]—reveals the following ranking for the provinces in 1934:

TABLE 8

INEQUALITY OF LAND DISTRIBUTION, 1933

Province	Equal Share Percentage
Shansi	67%
Honan	68%
Kansu	68%
Shensi	69%
Shantung	70%
Kiangsu	72%
Hopei	73%
Suiyuan	73%
Kwangtung	76%
Hunan	76%
Chahar	78%
Anhwei	79%
Yunnan	79%
Chekiang	80%
Hupeh	81%
Chinghai	83%
Kwangsi	84%

[60] Bruce Russett, "Inequality and Instability: The Relation of Land Tenure to Politics," *World Politics*, XVI, No. 3 (April, 1964), 450–52.

[61] *Nei-cheng Nien-chien*, III, 422–25.

[62] For an explanation of the value of this measure, see Bruce Russett, "Indices for Comparing Inequality," in Richard L. Merritt and Stein Rokkan (ed.), *Comparing Nations* (New Haven, Conn.: Yale University Press, 1966), pp. 363–64. Russett suggests that this coefficient may be regarded as indicating the size of the lower classes.

What is notable about this ranking is that there appears to be a negative relationship between areas of unequal land distribution and areas where the Communist movement blossomed. The south coastal and remote southwestern provinces (Chekiang, Kwangsi, Yunnan, Chinghai), the least fertile for Communist growth, suffered from the highest inequality percentages. The northern provinces of Hopei, Honan, Shansi, and Shantung, into which the Communist movement expanded so rapidly after 1938, reveal rates of land concentration from 5 to 15 per cent lower than in the southern areas where the Communists were less successful.

It is, of course, possible and correct to argue that within provinces there were wide variations in distribution patterns. It might well be that within-province variation in land concentration correlates in some instances with Communist success. But it is interesting to note that some county level data on land concentration for the important province of Kiangsu demonstrates a negative correlation similar to the provincial data. Figures on land distribution obtained by the Rural Rehabilitation Commission in the thirties in three *hsien* of north Kiangsu show the following equal share percentages[63] and ranks in my map of Communist influence:

	Equal Share Percentage	Influence Rank
P'eihsien	83%	0
Ch'itung	80%	1
Yench'eng	78%	4

That Yench'eng, the headquarters of the entire New Fourth Army during the resistance, shows a lower degree of land concentration than other counties in north Kiangsu suggests that land concentration in the area had little to do with its selection as a site for Communist activity.[64]

I would not suggest that a high degree of maldistribution of the land was a guarantee against Communist influence. North Shensi, the area of the Yenan base, allegedly suffered from a relatively high degree of

[63] See *Agrarian China*, p. 14, and *Chiang-su sheng Nung-ts'un Tiao-ch'a* (Rural Survey of Kiangsu Province), comp. by Rural Recovery Commission of the Executive Yuan (Shanghai: Commercial Press, 1934), p. 12.

[64] For a suggestion that the negative correlation between land concentration and Communist activity shows strongly in present-day Vietnam, see Edward J. Mitchell, "The Significance of Land Tenure in the Vietnamese Insurgency," *Asian Survey*, VII, No. 8 (August, 1967), 577–80; and Edward J. Mitchell, "Inequality and Insurgency: A Statistical Study of South Vietnam," *World Politics*, XX, No. 3 (April, 1968), pp. 421–38.

landlord monopoly: the Communists claimed a distribution with an equal percentage of around 85 per cent in 1935. Their land reform in north Shensi succeeded in reducing this inequality to the remarkably low level of 52 per cent by 1938, a fact which may help explain the rapid consolidation of Communist power in the Shensi-Kansu-Ninghsia Border Region.[65] But the fact remains that large areas of North China —including such model villages as the Long Bow in Shansi described by William Hinton (equal share percentage = 70) and the east Hopei village of P'ingchiali recently extolled in the Peking journal *Li-shih Yen-chiu* (Historical Studies) (equal share percentage = 73), both of which fell rather easily under Communist influence—were not characterized by an unusual malapportionment of land rights.

We may assume that grievances created by extortionate rents might be different from and more acute than the pressures of land inequality. Of course, in those areas of North China where little land was rented such a question is not very relevant. But what about South China?

The left-wing Japanese journalist Tanaka Tadao[66] attempted to explain the rise of communism in Kiangsi by analyzing the average percentage of the yearly crop paid in rent. His results, however, are far from convincing, even though Kiangsi was a province with a tradition of rather high rent rates. A map of his data (Map 7A), when compared with my map of Communist influence, does indicate that counties in which an average of more than 70 per cent of the annual crop was paid in rent tended to fall under some Communist influence. But they were not, as a rule, those counties which ranked highest on our influence scale. The heartland of the Kiangsi Soviet area, the counties of Juichin, Huich'ang and Yutu, reported rates of only 50 per cent—considerably lower than the rates in the nearby Kan River Valley counties that never developed a sizable CCP force.

It may be that the rent data for other provinces, which I am now studying, will reveal a more convincing pattern. Meanwhile, the only reasonably comprehensive county level data that might relate to the grievance theory of Chinese Communist influence is a measure of the prevalence of tenancy. Given the complexity of Chinese landholding patterns, the percentage of village population which rents the land it tills may or may not correlate with the variables of rent rate and

[65] Hsu Ti-hsin, "Shen-Kan-Ning Henku—Tekigo Konkyochi no Zaisei Keizai," *Jōhō*, No. 69 (July 1, 1942), p. 3. On the "land revolution" in Shen-Kan-Ning, see also Selden's "Yenan Communism."

[66] Tanaka Tadao, *Kakumei Shina Nōson no Jisshō-teki Kenkyū* (A Concrete Study of Revolutionary Rural China) (Tokyo: Shujinsha, 1930), pp. 312–14.

inequality. But since land tenure is often an important part of the argument for a grievance-based explanation of the rise of communism, I have attempted to create a map of the distribution of tenancy at the county level in China in the 1930's. Pieced together from three independent estimates (John Lossing Buck's atlas of land use, a Nanking University study of the Yangtze Valley, and the Agricultural Bank study of tenancy in Szechwan),[67] Map 6 shows clearly the tremendous variety in agrarian patterns in pre-Communist China: the counties are spread remarkably evenly across the entire range from darkest (over 80 per cent of the population renting someone else's land) to lightest (less than 20 per cent).

The over-all distribution of the pattern of tenancy shown in Map 6 comes as no surprise. Tenancy appears to be correlated rather highly with land maldistribution: North China, and especially the North China plain, is an area of quite low tenancy rates. Tenancy in north Kiangsu Province, for example, is lower in Yench'eng and higher in P'eihsien, just as we found the land inequality measure to be. But the additional detail in the tenancy map suggests a subtlety which was missing when we discussed inequality—missing perhaps because we do not have comprehensive *hsien* level data for the latter variable. That is that *within-province* variations in tenancy may in some cases yield a positive correlation with Communist influence. For example, not only does the county of Fushih (Yenan) appear darker than the surrounding areas (as we would expect from its rather high equal share percentage), other counties in other base areas show a similar tendency. Foup'ing in northwest Hopei (a county central to the Shansi-Chahar-Hopei base), Hoshun in southeast Shansi (the first county developed for the Shansi-Hopei-Shantung-Honan Border Region), and several of the counties in the north Anhwei bases stand out from their immediate background. In Szechwan, not a province of notable Chinese Communist influence, the northernmost tier of counties is generally low in tenancy, but the exceptions to this rule were the centers of the short-lived Szechwan-Shensi Soviet Area. Likewise, Mach'eng in northeast Hupeh, Shangch'eng in south Honan, and Liuan in west Anhwei, three of the counties which constituted the Hupeh-Honan-Anhwei Soviet in

[67] John Lossing Buck, *Land Utilization in China: Atlas* and *Land Utilization* in *China: Statistics* (Nanking: University of Nanking, 1937), index maps 4 and 5; University of Nanking, *Konan, Kohoku, Anki, Kōsei Shi-shō Kosaku Seido* (The Tenancy System of the Four Provinces of Honan, Hupeh, Anhwei, and Kiangsi) (Tokyo: Seikatsusha, 1940); and Central Bank of China (comp.), *Shisen-shō Kosaku Seido* (The Tenancy System of Szechwan) (Shanghai: Japanese Imperial Consulate, 1943).

the early thirties, appear to have a higher tenancy rate than the surrounding counties.

The patterns, therefore, suggest that it was not the absolute level of the tenancy percentage, but its intensity relative to the immediately surrounding counties which contributed to Communist influence. A question can immediately be raised, of course, as to whether we might not be measuring something else entirely. Most of the relatively high tenancy areas mentioned above are located in remote, rather sparsely populated border districts situated on the boundary of two or more provinces. By contrast, the densely settled plains of Hopei and Shantung, despite some variety in tenancy rates, do not seem to show a pattern of relationship between tenancy and Communist influence.

POLITICAL DEVELOPMENT MEASURES

It might seem to those familiar with recent theoretical work on the politics of "underdeveloped countries" that a more profitable approach to explaining the variance in Communist influence would be to analyze the political and institutional makeup of the various counties. Was there any correlation between Communist influence and the level of governmental activity in a particular locality; or the level and type of unofficial, informal political activity carried out by the gentry, secret societies, and clans; or the degree of political instability at the county level? Just how effective was the Kuomintang, for example, as an integrative force in China's villages, and how did this affect the Communists' prospects?

It is sometimes claimed that Chinese communism drew its recruits largely from those areas with a high incidence of traditional-style banditry, that the "bandit lairs" of past history were ideal places for the development of CCP bases. There is some merit in this notion, particularly for such out of the way localities as Chingkangshan, where we know Mao's entry in 1927 was facilitated by a deal with local bandit leaders. But certainly Communist recruitment of guerrillas was also in competition with bandit recruitment in much of China. Areas with traditionally large bandit populations, such as certain counties in Shantung and south Honan, might have been extremely difficult for the Communists to penetrate successfully because of the solidarity of the traditional bandit bands. And to the extent that local paramilitary forces had firm connections with secret societies of gentry or urban leadership, they would be even less inclined to ally themselves with a weaker Communist force. Nevertheless, the relationship between banditry and communism deserves examination.

There seems to be little hope, however, of devising reliable measures of the strength of banditry or secret societies for more than a few areas. But suggestive maps can be drawn for Shantung in the late twenties and Hunan in the late thirties.

A comparison of Maps 7D and 7E, which show the location and strength of bandit bands during those time periods, with our map of Communist influence suggests that there was scant connection between the two phenomena. In Hunan, there is little sign of overlapping territory between bandits and Communists for either the peasant movement or the soviet period: banditry appears to have been endemic in the southwest of the province, even in the 1920's, as it was in the nineteenth century. Of course, the absence of bandits in the Ch'angsha area, which had been such a hotbed of peasant movement activity, might be explained by the severe pacification imposed by the KMT on these counties, but if so then the soviets in eastern Hunan, which were created after 1927, would have had little bandit support. The information on banditry in Shantung Province, which dates from a decade earlier, is similarly inconclusive. In fact, with few exceptions counties which were host to bandit bands of any size in 1928 were not localities of considerable Communist guerrilla activity in the early 1940's, and counties with large bandit bands (such as in the extreme south and southwest of the province) were quite remote from the centers of Communist anti-Japanese activity.

These data should not, in my opinion, be given undue significance. The size and location of a bandit force (and indeed the definition of a bandit force, given the complexity of the rural Chinese military scene) would not have been easy for an observer to determine. Moreover, the years that separate these data from the periods of maximum Communist influence may well have seen radical changes in the bandit picture. But they do suggest that if local bandits became important recruits to the Communist guerrilla forces, they were probably small, disorganized, and relatively poorly established bandits. Rivalry may have been a more typical relationship between banditry and communism than collaboration.

Could we then entertain a thesis that certain types of political institutions, such as banditry, secret societies, and what Robert Scalapino has called "private government," were more potent opponents of

Communist incursion than were the rudimentary instrumentalities of
the modern state in China? Such a thesis would gain some support in
one province from statistics on the distribution of firearms. The Hunan
provincial government published data on the number of weapons in
public and private hands in 1937, and we may assume that areas with a
high proportion of guns in private hands might have been subject to a
greater degree of influence of informal political or paramilitary forces.
In 1937 Hunan was in fact divided into two regions of high and low
degree of public (that is, KMT) mastery over fire power. Map 7C
shows that those regions which supported an active peasant movement
in the 1920's tend to fall in the high public ownership sector. The
exceptions—Liling and Hsianghsiang counties—were both areas of important secret society membership (the Kolaohui) in the 1920's, and
there is reason to believe that the CCP was more successful in winning
over these particular societies than any others. As for the soviet period
in Hunan, those counties which fell under Communist influence—such
as Sangchih, where Ho Lung operated, Huajung in the Hunghu base,
and P'ingchiang, where P'eng Teh-huai was active—were all areas of
relatively good public control of firearms, according to this information. In Hunan, at least, it appears that a high concentration of weapons in the hands of the Kuomintang government and police correlates
positively with Communist influence. It might prove to be the case that
counties with modernizing military administrations, such as those in
Hunan, were more susceptible (at least to the peasant movement type
of influence) than were more backward districts where physical force
was still controlled by "traditional" groups. My own view, however, is
that this phenomenon was much more important in Hunan than in any
other province, for reasons that have to do with the strength of traditional local gentry groups and with the peculiar development of the
peasant movement in that province. Still, the assumption that Chinese
communism fed only on relatively backward, unmodernized, traditional areas needs to be re-examined.

But what of the Kuomintang itself? Those who regard political
parties as the most noteworthy bearers of political institutionalization
might suggest that we examine the distribution of the KMT membership. There are two possible conflicting hypotheses about the KMT we
might propose to test: either (1) high Kuomintang membership might
be correlated with high rates of urbanization, "social mobilization,"
modernization, and thus with susceptibility to revolutionary radicalism

(that is, the KMT and CCP could be regarded as drawing on similar social and economic bases), or (2) high KMT membership might represent a strongly traditionalist orientation, and thus correlate with low modernization and low "social mobilization" (that is, the KMT and CCP might draw upon radically different populations).

Map 8A depicts the per capita membership of the KMT for three separate provinces, each of which was important for the rise of the Communist movement. Unfortunately, the time periods covered by the data stand in varied relationships to the time periods of maximum Communist influence in each province. In Hunan they date from after, and in Kiangsi and Shansi from before, the time of peak Communist power. The purges of the KMT organization in Hunan after 1927 may have been especially severe in those counties, such as P'ingchiang and Liuyang, where Communists were influential during the great revolution.[68] But in the main they do reflect the relative strength of the Kuomintang during the mid-Republican period.

The explanation of the variance of KMT membership is a subject for another essay. But it is curious to note how random the geographic distribution seems to the eye. The high concentration of membership in the administrative centers and large cities of Ch'angsha, Nanch'ang, and T'aiyuan is to be expected. The Kuomintang did expand outward from the urban centers, and a large portion of its members consisted of leading provincial bureaucrats. But *non*administrative cities such as Hengyang in south Hunan, Kanchow in south Kiangsi, and Yangch'uan in east Shansi ranked quite low in per capita membership. Moreover, there are curious concentrations of KMT members in places where we would not, on the basis of our crude hunches about the rural-urban continuum, expect to find them. In extreme southeast Hunan and neighboring southwest Kiangsi, or in northeast Shensi, there are far more KMT members than in a number of other counties of equal distance from the main cities or of roughly equivalent social and economic conditions. Are we justified in assuming that the distribution of KMT recruitment (which averaged only a few tenths of a per cent of the population in these provinces) resulted mainly from the importance of personal ties rather than basic social conditions?

Whatever the reason (or lack of reason), the apparent randomness

[68] See *Min-kuo 19 Nien Hu-nan Sheng Cheng-chih Nien-chien* (Hunan Provincial Political Yearbook for 1930) (Ch'angsha: Secretariat of Hunan Provincial Secretariat, 1931), which usually mentions those *hsien* with high CCP infiltration in 1927, along with those purged afterward.

of KMT membership renders correlation with Communist success not very profitable. An eyeball comparison of Map 8A with our map of Communist success (Map 5) suggests a slight negative correlation between the impact of the two parties, and it certainly can be said that the counties with the highest concentration of KMT and CCP influence do not at all coincide. At least we may conclude that, without introducing new evidence or some important intervening variables, it will be difficult to make a clear case for the strength of the Kuomintang as an explanation for differential Communist success.

A final measure of political development we might introduce is that of rural cooperatives. The cooperatives built by the Nationalist government in the 1930's were widely regarded as a vehicle for the rural reforms necessary to combat Communist influence. We might assume that the measure of cooperative membership would indicate the degree of success of rural "rehabilitation" as well as of the impact of the national government on village life.

Significantly, the data on the 1930's show that only an extremely small number of these cooperatives were established: the membership of all KMT cooperatives as a proportion of the total rural population remained around one-quarter of 1 per cent, only slightly higher than KMT membership per capita. The contrast with the mobilization rates of the Communists is thus overwhelming.

Nonetheless, some interesting patterns emerge from the data on cooperatives. First, the distribution of cooperatives by province suggests that it was not the strongholds of the Kuomintang which enjoyed the highest degree of mobilization in cooperatives: Kiangsu, Chekiang, and Kwangtung provinces appear rather far down on the list. By contrast, Kiangsi (immediately after the defeat of the Chinese Communist movement in that province) demonstrated the highest rates of cooperativization. The most plausible explanation for this is probably that the cooperatives were used as a part of Chiang Kai-shek's "New Life" movement designed to consolidate the new victory. It is not so easy to explain the relatively high cooperative membership in the North China provinces of Anhwei, Shensi, Honan, and Hopei, since these areas were latecomers to the KMT movement and did not receive much attention from KMT "pacification" experts.

One possible explanation of the broad influence of cooperatives in North China is intriguing: village conditions in the northern tier of provinces were much more amenable to cooperative-type activity—by virtue of the long-standing traditional practices of communal cropwatching.[69] Japanese researchers, notably Hatada Takashi, acquainted us long ago with the differences between the major regions of China in this respect, but their "theory of village collectivity" (*nōson kyōdōtai ron*) has not received the attention it deserves. It is possible that the North China area, despite its apparent "backwardness," was in fact a region more receptive to collectivist policies and organizations by virtue of its indigenous village structure than were the central and southern provinces of the country.[70]

The second pattern of interest to emerge from the data on cooperatives is that they do not appear to demonstrate a positive correlation with our distribution of Communist influence. In fact, with the exception of the counties in central Hopei which contributed considerable support both to the CCP in 1937–40 and to the KMT cooperatives in 1937, areas of maximum Communist influence appear to have been only very sparsely organized by the rural cooperative movement. The central Hopei example suggests that the successful penetration of Communist forces, under Lü Cheng-ts'ao, into the region after 1937 was an anomaly when considered in the light of the movement as a whole.

CULTURAL MEASURES

Backwardness. Impressionistic accounts of village life recorded by early twentieth-century travelers in China usually begin with estimates of the extent of "cultural" progress in the area. Opium smoking, footbinding, and even the wearing of the old Manchu-style queues were still to be seen in the mid-thirties in some villages. Provincial authorities of the Republican period who were interested in bringing such villages into the modern age sometimes recorded their own information on such practices. Can this information be used to shed light on the distribution of Communist influence? We might consider two hypotheses: that the Communists were able to take advantage of the oppressive quality of traditional practices, and that measures of such practices should therefore correlate positively with CCP influence. Or that such practices were signs of the strength of "backwardness," of traditional customs, social patterns, and political organizations, and that there should therefore be a negative correlation.

[69] On these customs see Sidney D. Gamble, *North China Villages* (Berkeley and Los Angeles: University of California Press, 1963).

[70] See Hatada Takashi, "Chūgoku ni okeru sensei shugi to 'Sonraku Kyōdōtai riron'" (Absolutism in China and the Theory of Village Community), *Chūgoku Kenkyū* (China Studies), XIII (September, 1950), 2–12.

Map 8B represents the results of one set of such data: the proportion of the population with bound feet for Hunan and Shansi (actually the figures for Shansi give a ratio of footbinding to the total number of households, and thus slightly understates the per capita incidence). It should be noted that areas of extreme "backwardness," according to this measure, were not the areas of prime CCP strength. The northeastern portion of Hunan, which supported the peasant movement, and the northeastern counties of Shansi, which were host to the Shansi-Chahar-Hopei Border Region government, appear in the third or fourth quartiles of all counties ranked according to footbinding per capita. They thus do not appear to have been areas with relatively high cultural holdovers from the past. The exceptions to this statement—Menghsien in the northern part of Shansi, and Liaohsien in the southeastern part of the same province—though they did rank rather high on the "backwardness" scale, were not the centers of Communist activity in their respective areas. Without more precise analysis it is impossible to say whether the over-all correlation between Communist influence is negative or positive. In either case it will not be an indication of strong association. There is, however, one other use for the footbinding data that has interesting possibilities: as an explanation not of CCP but of KMT strength. There is in both these provincial surveys of footbinding (conducted quite independently) a rather strong negative correlation between Kuomintang membership and this measure of backwardness. Such a relationship leads us to suspect that KMT membership in the counties and county towns of China may have gone hand in hand with the extent of acceptance of the "new culture" of the post–May Fourth generation.

Western Impact. A variety of theories hold that Chinese communism fed on a hatred of foreign aggression on Chinese soil, or at least profited from resentment at the intrusion of the bearers of Western culture. Both the authors who stress "imperialism" and those who emphasize the "impact of Western ideas" suggest that the rise of Chinese communism ought to be closely related to Western influence. If we attempt to translate this notion into the terms of our research strategy, the Western impact hypothesis asserts that areas which felt the greatest effect of foreign trade, ideas, and personnel were most likely to produce devoted Communists. To test this rather crudely stated hypothesis, I have compiled maps of one type of Western influence on the counties of China: that of Protestant Christian missionaries who flooded the continent after the mid-nineteenth century.

Fortunately for our purposes, the Protestant missionaries were far better social accountants than most other actors on the Chinese stage during the Republican period. A "general survey of the numerical strength and geographical distribution of the Christian forces in China," conducted by the Protestant China Continuation Committee in 1918–1919,[71] provides us with some suggestive maps of Christian activity. Map 9 shows the time differential of missionary penetration; areas of older Christian work are light in color, while areas of recent incursion are dark. Map 10 indicates the number of Chinese converted to Christianity by the time of the survey, and thus may be regarded as a rough indication of the distribution of missionary success. The portion of the total Chinese population which had been Christianized by 1920 (approximately one-tenth of 1 per cent), we should note, was of the same order of magnitude as the total Kuomintang strength, as well as of cooperative membership.

As we might have suspected, these maps do not support any simple hypothesis that there was a direct correlation between Christianity and communism. The data show that *no hsien* settled by missionaries before 1860 developed into a seedbed for communism, and practically none which was "occupied" before 1880 did. The exceptions are marginal ones; certain *hsien* with a long history of missionary activity— such as Yingshan-Hsiaokan and Tayeh-Kuangchi in Hupeh, Iyang-Kueich'i-Shangjao in northeast Kiangsi, and the counties around Peking—all supported a moderate level of CCP activity at one time or another, but never were hard-core CCP areas. Conversely, areas which had not been touched by Christianity in 1920 also were not overly susceptible to Communist blandishments. Important exceptions to this rule were the hinterland to the northwest of Yenan, which formed part of the Shen-Kan-Ning region, and the Central Soviet in Kiangsi; however, the *capitals* of both these Communist bases, Fushih and Juichin, had been settled by missionaries for some time. The great majority of counties which show high levels of Communist influence fall, curiously enough, in regions which were Christianized between 1880 and 1920. In some provinces this correlation is startling. In Hopei and Kiangsu, for example, the areas of CCP influence during the Anti-Japanese War coincide almost exactly with areas which Christianity penetrated during 1880–1920.

[71] Milton T. Stauffer, *The Christian Occupation of China* (Shanghai: China Continuation Committee, 1922). Understandably from the title, the publication of this book became a *cause célèbre* among post-May Fourth nationalistic students. The committee was unable to obtain Catholic statistics at the county level.

Conversion Susceptibility. The map showing Christian converts does not add much to this picture, except to suggest the possibility of a measure of "susceptibility to foreign ideas," which might indicate whether some *hsien* or regions were more easily converted to the Christian faith than others. To achieve this, a measure of missionary effort would have to be devised that would take into account (1) the strength of the foreign religious contingent; (2) the length of time it had been working the area; and (3) the number of Chinese co-workers trained and used—as well as other important imponderables, such as style of work (for example, one sect might be known to be more diligent about inscribing new souls than another; or certain *hsien* may have had a higher percentage of nonworking missionaries, and so on). One such formula, extremely crude, I applied to the figures for Hunan Province, as follows:

$$\frac{\text{Chinese converts}}{\text{missionary man-years} \times \text{total population}}$$

Map 7B shows the results of this calculation. Aside from producing the sobering conclusion that in 1920 Protestant missionaries were converting on the average fewer than five souls per million for every man-year of missionary time they invested, there is an interesting geographical pattern revealed.

As seen in Map 7C, Hunan could be divided roughly into three distinct regions according to this measure of susceptibility to Christian conversion. The highest conversion rates were found in those counties which were on the outer periphery of the province. Inside this ring of readily convertible populations was a broad area in which the smallest number of converts were obtained; and in the northeast of the province, in an area surrounding the capital city of Ch'angsha but not including it, were a number of counties which fell in the middle range on the scale. This distribution suggests a hypothesis that the missionaries were most successful in areas having weak connections with modern administration, trade, and culture (a phenomenon not unknown in other parts of Asia), and secondarily successful in the regions of maximum urbanization and modernization. The broad areas that lay between these two poles, that is, the transitional areas between traditional and modern societies, were the least susceptible to Christianization.

But susceptibility to Christianity, as measured by this calculation, is not very helpful in explaining the distribution of Communist influence.

If the backlands of Hunan were the most susceptible to Christianity, they were the least susceptible to communism, at least during the peasant movement period. Those relatively remote counties which after 1927 did become soviet bases (that is, those on the eastern edge of the province bordering Kiangsi) tended to fall in the middle range of Christian susceptibility. Although in Hunan both communism and Christianity, as we have measured them, seem to be related to the backward-modern variable, the shape of the relationship is quite different: for Christianity it is a U-shaped curve, for communism (in Hunan) a rising straight line.

MODERNIZATION MEASURES

John Lewis has suggested that it should be possible to devise a "scale of potential revolution and mobilization" or a "modern revolutionary scale"[72] which might help us analyze the growth of communism in rural areas. He notes particularly that Hunan Province in 1927 appears to bear out a thesis that revolution (defined in terms of peasant association membership) and modernization (defined in terms of William Skinner's criteria of transformations in marketing structures) are closely correlated.

The main difficulty with this hypothesis is that from the beginning to the end of the Communist rise to power, Hunan appears to be the only province which demonstrates any such relationship. Even during the peasant movement period, when CCP activities were closely connected with the power of the Kuomintang in the great urban centers of the south, it was not possible to generate substantial peasant movement strength in the regions close to any of the other cities, such as Canton or Shanghai. This fact is revealed in our map of Communist influence. Skinner's work to date does not provide us with material for a nation-wide map based on his index of modernization, but his partial maps strongly suggest a negative, or at best an indeterminate, correlation during all of the periods of Communist growth—except in Hunan. His map of village-to-market ratios in Kwangtung[73] shows that maximum CCP influence lies in areas of low to medium modernization. For Szechwan the Communist impact (occurring in the desperate period prior to and during the Long March) lay in those parts of the province at the least advanced stage of Skinner's "traditional intensification

---

[72] Lewis, "Study of Chinese Political Culture," p. 510.
[73] G. William Skinner, "Marketing and Social Structure in Rural China," Part 2, *Journal of Asian Studies*, XXIV, No. 2 (February, 1964), 195–228.

cycle."[74] For Shantung, although Skinner does not provide us with a map, he mentions three areas which he regards as having undergone modernization.[75] Of these, at least two (the Chiaochou and Tzu-Po regions) were not known to have supported notable resistance forces.

In this light, Lewis' suggestion that "modernization" and revolutionary potential may be synonyms requires further study. Lewis recognizes that the highly modernized conurbations of Southeast China did not contribute much to Mao's power, but he postulates that their "potential" was blunted by (1) the brute application of counterrevolutionary force, and (2) lineage conflict which produced a chaos that "helped disable revolutionary organization in the southeast." We can accept that these factors—along with a considerable number of others —help to explain why the peasant movement failed to take root. But if so many qualifications are necessary, then why try to salvage a notion of "revolutionary potential" that seems to fit only one province?

This is not to say, however, that Skinner's measure of modernization is of no value to us. To cite one example, the Japanese intelligence map of Communist installations in Chinhsien, Hopei, in 1939 (mentioned above, note 42) suggests that their distribution among the villages of the *hsien* was probably related inversely to Skinner's measure. Chinhsien, traversed by a railroad, divides sharply into a northern half, which had an extensive road structure and a number of medium-sized walled (presumably market centers) villages, and a southern half, which had clearly inferior transportation and sparser settlement. It was the latter area which had the greatest ratio of Communist to non-Communist villages in the Japanese survey. Even though Chinhsien had a high population density and was being transformed by modern communications, the main support for her strong Communist minority came from the less modernized, less densely populated villages. Even counties, it may be surmised, might have their own "border regions," and as an instrument to measure subcounty variation the Skinner index may yet prove to be of considerable worth.

CONCLUSION

There was no single pattern of Communist success or influence in China. Theories of the "political geography" of the Communist movement which claim that the location of a point of maximum influence might have been predicted from a generalized model of background

[74] *Ibid.*, p. 225.
[75] *Ibid.*, p. 219.

factors have yet to explain the great variety in the relationships between Communist forces and the villages.[76] This is not to say, however, that there were no discernible constant patterns visible during the time span we have been considering. There are nonrandom alternatives to propositions of complete uniformity, and a crude typology of the sorts of counties which sustained considerable Communist influence does appear to emerge. The CCP was able to develop three quite different types of relationship with the countryside. Counties could be classified according to whether they fell into one or another of the three following categories of base.

1. The *radical hotbed* type of county included areas in which the movement obtained the intense commitment of a significant minority. The converts were often younger intellectuals, such as schoolteachers, or native peasant leaders. A number of historical factors, such as a tradition of gentry independence from central authority (Hunan) or of peasant intransigeance (Haifeng), or a fortuitous concentration of young revolutionary leaders (parts of Kwangtung or Shensi), contributed to the early success of the Communist organizers. A map of the place of origin of the present Chinese Communist top leadership, such as Map 11, shows clearly that these radical hotbeds produced more than their share of future leaders of the Chinese Communist Party.

The background social factors in hotbed counties played an important role in the movement's future. The apparent ease of the spread of mass organizations through the broad population, the rapid growth of CCP groups, underground networks, and guerrilla activity—often in the face of difficult odds, poor security, and a strong potential opposition—all require some reference to background characteristics.

Hotbed counties appear in each of the three time periods. We may regard Mao's own home counties in Hunan (Liuyang, Hsiangt'an), Lin Piao's home county in Hupeh (Huangp'o), Ho Lung's famous lacustrine base of the early thirties (Hunghu), and Lü Cheng-ts'ao's anti-Japanese headquarters *hsien* in Hopei (Jench'iu) as prototypes of the hotbed county. The rapid spread and prolonged success of the Communist movement in such counties as Haifeng in Kwangtung and Huan-gan-Mach'eng in Hupeh suggest that they too should be regarded as hotbeds, despite their relative remoteness and sparse population.

For the most part hotbed counties were characterized by low security from outside attack—their proximity to cities and to high-density population areas meant that KMT or other anti-Communist military

[76] See, for example, McColl, "Political Geography of Revolution."

or police forces had relatively easy access. On scales of modernization or of Western cultural impact these counties would have ranked in the moderate to high range, although counties with the highest modernization or Westernization did not as a rule become hotbed areas. Perhaps the concept of a transitional county might have a certain value in explaining why some counties became hotbeds and others did not. Often hotbed counties measured high on the crude scale of "grievance potential": considerable tenancy and high rent rates were characteristic of all the prototype counties except Jench'iu in Hopei. There were, of course, many counties in China which fell into the broad category defined by these background characteristics. Particularly puzzling is the failure of the broad areas around Shanghai-Ningpo in East China and in the Szechwan Basin to develop any Communist hotbed areas. Clearly, background social factors, though to some extent necessary, were not sufficient conditions for a hotbed of Communist activity. Our explanations of this fact must either allude to more subtle variations in background social conditions, or place greater stress on the importance of local political institutions. I would suggest that the Shanghai and Chungking regions did not become hotbeds for two political reasons, both difficult to measure quantitatively: first, historical circumstances prevented the Communists from appearing in the regions as the vanguard of a popular mass movement; second, the strength of local level opposition to the Communists in the area was considerably greater than in, say, Hunan and Kwangtung in the 1920's, or central Hopei in the 1940's. Exactly how these variations in political environment affected developments is a subject requiring longer treatment, but that they were important in determining the location of Communist hotbeds is undeniable.

2. The *border area base* county was a type that was consciously sought by Mao Tse-tung during his search for a place to rest the "buttocks" of his revolutionary movement. The analogy he used in this search was apt: border bases, more ephemeral than hotbeds, served largely as places of rest for the revolutionary armies. Yet counties which were protected largely by their location between conflicting provincial authorities were not secure enough for long-term occupation. Constant attention to the problem of military security in these bases prevented any extensive attempt to mobilize the population. The overt trappings of political and military power were themselves like red flags in the face of the anti-Communist bull, and so border area counties were unable to achieve long-term permanent political rule.

The prototype counties of the border area base might be the three Chingkangshan *hsien* of 1927–29, P'eng Teh-huai's bailiwick in northwest Kiangsi of the early thirties, the two Huai River Valley bases in north Anhwei, and the complex and late-developing border base at the juncture of Shansi, Hopei, Shantung, and Honan during the Anti-Japanese War. All these bases were characterized by a strategic location between relatively distant centers of anti-Communist administration. Generally remote from modernized or Westernized sectors, border area bases tended nonetheless to rank relatively high on scales of grievance potential, such as that of tenancy. At least part of the decision to settle in an area to create a border base was nonstrategic, and the ability to hold it depended as often on the strength of local opposition as on that of the external threat. Border bases, unlike the great rear areas, were not complete power and population vacuums. Certain provincial borders never could, despite effort, be transformed into a secure base: the Honan-Anhwei-Kiangsu border and the southern sector of the Shansi-Shensi border proved for local reasons to be unproductive soil. Social and political background factors, such as low grievance potential, well-developed opposition (KMT party organization in southwest Shansi), or local village structure (native and KMT cooperatives in Honan-Anhwei-Kiangsu, for example), clearly made a difference in these areas.

3. Background social factors seem the least relevant in the location of the third category of Communist base: the *great rear area*. The chief characteristic of counties which served as such bases was that they must be clearly defensible against massive attack for a long period of time. Naturally, very few areas in China proper could qualify. The prototypes of rear area counties were Yenan in north Shensi and Juichin in south Kiangsi, both the capitals of Communist Central regimes. The high tenancy rates in both counties may have been significant in their selection as the headquarters of the Party-army within the base, but a far more important determinant of the location of the rear area county was its logistical distance from centers of opposing power. The low population density of these counties was a blessing, since it meant less attention was required for work with the local people, and fewer administrative problems. The almost total lack of contact with the Westernized or modernized parts of China in such areas was far from being an unqualified asset. On the one hand it made the Red Army, with all its primitive limitations, appear to be strikingly modern and attractive to a certain segment of the local population (the

Communist counterpart to relatively high Christian success in the far hinterland). But on the other hand the backwardness of the rear areas made the training, arming, and feeding of the population of these counties a much more difficult task. Nonetheless, because of the security provided by terrain and distance, the rear area base counties were able to achieve the highest rates of mobilization and participation in Communist politics.

But what of the broader explanations of the rise of communism in China with which we began this essay? Has our examination of the "ecology" of the successful Communist base counties brought us any closer to a general theory of the rise of the movement? I think the answer is a qualified yes. Insofar as the first step in theory building is the questioning of established notions or paradigms of thought, we have made some progress.

By examining the variance in certain background factors which some theories have held to be important, we have been able to cast considerable doubt on a number of the larger explanations of Chinese Communist success. For example, peasant nationalistic hatred could hardly have been the main factor in the remarkable spread of Communist power in the peasant movement period or in the soviet era. "Modern revolutionary potential" is not a satisfactory explanation for the high Communist success in the rear areas or even in the North China plain. The grievance theory, insofar as it can be tested by the crude indices we have suggested, explains only a limited portion of the variance in Communist success.

This is not to say that all the theories have been put to the test. I have been unable, for example, to develop indicators of the mix between persuasive and coercive tactics to test the "terror theory," or of the uses or effects of channels of upward mobility to test theories emphasizing "ambition." The more plausible of the broader contextual theories, the one which treats Chinese society as an organic whole, is particularly difficult to test against quantified facts: I have been able to think of no index of "organic decay" which might confirm or dispel this notion.

But to go beyond the destructive to the constructive phases of theory building is a more difficult step. It is clear that no single-factor explanation is satisfactory for a phenomenon as complicated as the Chinese Communist revolution. But what is the proper mixture of contextual and motivational factors that seems most satisfactory when the Communist movement in China is seen as a whole? I would suggest that the contextual and motivational theories lie at the two poles of a continuum of explanations which centers on what is perhaps the most important and least examined of all the possible explanations of Chinese Communist success: the behavior of the Chinese Communists themselves. It seems almost impossible to develop quantifiable indicators of such imponderables as the viability and vitality of the movement itself, its organizational dynamism, the quality of its personnel, the vigor of its recruitment. But as we reconstruct it, the sense of forward movement, or at least of an alternative way out of present dilemmas, must have seemed as important an "appeal" to recruits as personal interest or patriotism. An important part of the motivation to join the movement depended on the very presence within the local context of a Communist political structure. Thus, motivation depended on context and context on motivation, and at the center of the interaction was the vital core of committed individuals that made the movement into a political force in the villages.

To say that the Chinese revolution was a "rural revolution" is a half truth: at least half of Chinese rural society did not participate in it, and at least half of the credit for the revolution belongs to the Communists themselves. The expansion of Communist forces in any area during any period was likely to be better correlated with Communist presence in the vicinity than with any other social phenomenon. Part band-wagon, part demonstration, part mobility opportunity, part the path of least frustration, the Chinese Communist movement tended to appeal to nonmembers by its very presence and to grow by its known capacity to expand. Once a foothold in a county was gained, within primary communication distance of the county's population, these forces began to work, and combined with the proper mix of symbol manipulation, skills, threats, appeals, cajoleries, and acts of independent bravery, unquestionable honesty, and unusual competence, produced the potential for recruitment and for the establishment of legitimacy that placed the county effectively under Communist control. In the final analysis, any general theory of the rise of Chinese communism that omits the importance of organizational presence and vitality will remain only a partial explanation.

ILPYONG J. KIM

Mass Mobilization Policies and Techniques Developed in the Period of the Chinese Soviet Republic

One of the most important organizational goals of the Chinese Communist movement during the Kiangsi Soviet period (1931–34) was mobilization of the broadest possible mass participation in the revolutionary processes of the Chinese Soviet Republic. The principal economic and social policies of the Central Soviet Government were formulated with the aim not only of preserving the Kiangsi political system but also of expanding the revolutionary base to other areas of China and strengthening the Red Army to guard against external attacks, and mass mobilization was viewed as essential to this end.*

By emphasizing the central concept of "mass participation," the soviet government achieved considerable success in mobilizing the population in the process of implementing its newly formulated social and economic policies in the soviet areas. One can discover in Chinese Communist concepts and practices during the Kiangsi period, therefore, the roots of "mass line" politics, which have been so important in China since 1949. Thus, the first moves toward evolving the "mass line" can be seen in the political style and organizational techniques by which the Chinese Soviet Republic was able to implement its policy of

* This paper focuses on the role of certain mass organizations in relation to agrarian policy to support my main proposition about the development of the mass mobilization techniques in the Kiangsi period. The available data on local government in the Kiangsi period also support this proposition. (See my unpublished Ph.D. dissertation, "Communist Politics in China: A Study of the Development of Organizational Concepts, Behavior, and Techniques of the Chinese Soviet Movement during the Kiangsi Period" (Columbia University, 1968).

mass mobilization in the early 1930's, even though the concepts involved were not fully developed and refined until the Yenan period and even later.

The structure of the Kiangsi Soviet system can be viewed, in one sense, as consisting of three major groups: (1) the militant vanguard made up of leading Party and soviet government personnel; (2) auxiliaries, consisting of the mass organizations that paralleled the soviet government at all levels; and (3) subordinate administrative cadres who worked in the lower level units of the soviet system of government. To understand fully the mobilization policy and organizational techniques characteristic of the Kiangsi political system, we must pay special attention to the structure and operations of mass organizations, which served as administrative auxiliaries; among the most important of these were the poor peasant corps and the farm labor union, which were developed within the general framework of the Party's over-all mobilization policy.

The Kiangsi Soviet period is particularly important in the history of the Chinese Communist movement, because it was then that the Chinese Communist leaders acquired, for the first time in their struggle for power, control over a definite geographic area and population consisting of approximately three hundred *hsien* (counties) and thirty million people.[1] The Central Soviet Government in Juichin experimented with a variety of economic and social programs, and, as already stated, the institutional theories and administrative practices which have subsequently developed in China have deep roots in the programs evolved in the Kiangsi period.

Mao Tse-tung had already begun to formulate and articulate the concepts underlying his distinctive style and techniques of mass mobilization when he was head of the Central Soviet Government. Already he placed primary stress on the need to arouse and organize the masses. For example, in 1934 Mao declared:

The central task of [the soviet government] is to mobilize the broad masses to take part in the revolutionary war, overthrow imperialism and the Kuomintang by

[1] The geographic areas and population of the soviet area during the Kiangsi period varied from time to time, and no two writers agreed on the extent and population of the Chinese Soviet Republic. For example, in an interview with Edgar Snow in 1936, Mao Tse-tung estimated that the maximum 1934 population of the central soviet area was nine million. However, Hatano Ken'ichi argued that the area and population of the entire soviet area, at their peaks, were three hundred *hsien* and thirty million, respectively; see his seven-volume *Chūgoku Kyōsantō Shi* (History of the Chinese Communist Party) (Tokyo: Jiji Press, 1961), I, 635. Many of the three hundred *hsien* claimed may have had only small pockets of guerrillas in them.

means of such war, spread the revolution throughout the country, and drive imperialism out of China. Anyone who does not attach enough importance to this
central task is not a good revolutionary cadre. If our comrades really comprehend
this task and understand that the revolution must at all costs be spread throughout
the country, then they should in no way neglect or underestimate the question of
the immediate interests, the well-being, of the broad masses. For revolutionary war
is a war of masses; it can be waged only by mobilizing the masses and relying on
them.[2]

It was on the basis of this concept that Mao adopted a variety of
social and economic policies—in collaboration with the Soviet-trained
student group which then controlled the central organs of the Chinese
Communist Party (CCP). Even though the Soviet-trained student
group based their views on the Russian model as they had observed it,
while Mao Tse-tung built his theories from his personal experiences in
Kiangsi, the evidence suggests that the Soviet-trained Party leaders
who were in control of the central Party operations and Mao Tse-tung,
who led the Central Soviet Government, were in essential agreement on
basic organizational approaches and cooperated in the process of implementing them.

It is true, of course, that there were ideological debates and power
struggles between factions in the Chinese Communist movement, and
within the central leadership itself, following the debacle of 1927. They
centered on two major policy issues: the relation of guerrilla tactics to
the revolution in the urban centers, and the question of what agrarian
policy to follow. These two issues were interchangeably utilized by
factions competing against each other. It is also true that Mao and the
Party's Central Committee were at times in disagreement concerning
these two issues, during the period between 1927 and 1930. However,
in the end, the views which prevailed were Mao's.

The discussion which follows will focus on aspects of the evolution
of agrarian policy during the Kiangsi period, since the question of the
relation between guerrilla tactics and revolutionary strategy in the
urban areas has already been explored in some detail by other scholars.
And an attempt will be made to relate the evolution of agrarian policy
to the development of the Party's mass mobilization concepts.

To understand the issues involved in the development of agrarian
policy during the Kiangsi period, one must start by analyzing the content of more than a dozen resolutions adopted by the CCP on the

---

[2] Mao Tse-tung, *Selected Works* (Peking: Foreign Languages Press, 1961), I, 147. The
words in brackets were altered by the Peking authorities. When Mao actually spoke at
the Second National Soviet Congress in January, 1934, he used the term "the soviet
government."

agrarian question, as well as the official documents published by the Central Soviet Government for the period of 1927–35.[3] These documents indicate that one of the major concepts underlying the development of agrarian policy was the idea of "mass mobilization." The policy was designed to create a psychological atmosphere and conditions under which the peasant masses would feel, for the first time, that they were actually involved not only in the process of land confiscation and distribution, but also in the political processes of managing local affairs.

It is difficult in some respects to generalize glibly about Mao's agrarian policy, since he was not wholly consistent in stating his views about the various issues involved. In fact, at first he oscillated between "left" and "right" positions, before he finally decided to base his agrarian policy on the fundamental concept of mass mobilization.

When he was at Chingkangshan, Mao's agrarian policy was at first radical and "leftist," and he believed at that time that all *tzu-keng-nung* (peasant proprietors) should be viewed as potential enemies; in fact, he even advocated executions of present proprietors.[4] However, his position had shifted greatly by February, 1930, when he drafted the February 7 land law which stressed the goal of obtaining broad mass support. According to the February 7 law, the principle underlying land distribution was that only the land and capital owned by landlords, plus the land which rich peasants rented to tenants, was to be confiscated, and this land was to be distributed to farm laborers and poor and middle peasants, under the slogan "Distribute All Land Equally to the Peasants."[5] Since the farm laborers and the poor and middle peasants constituted more than 85 per cent of the rural population of China in the 1930's,[6] and since even rich peasants were to be

---

[3] These documents include: the Resolution on the Land Question adopted by the Sixth Party Congress on July 9, 1928; the Draft Land Law passed by the Conference of Delegates from the Soviet Area in May, 1930; the Land Law of the Chinese Soviet Republic adopted at its First National Congress on November 7, 1931; Circular No. 9 of the CCP Central Bureau on the land question and the anti-rich peasant policy; the Resolution on the Slogan of "Distribute All Land Equally" adopted by the CCP Central Committee; the Procedures of Land Confiscation published by the Kiangsi provincial soviet government; the Resolution adopted by the Conference of the Leaders of the Hsien Soviet Governments in Hupeh, Honan, and Anhwei; and the Directive of the Hunan-Hupeh-Kiangsi provincial soviet government on the land question. All these documents are available in the Ch'en Ch'eng Microfilms.

[4] For this interpretation, see John E. Rue, *Mao Tse-tung in Opposition, 1927–1935* (Stanford, Calif.: Stanford University Press, 1966), pp. 194–96.

[5] *Ibid.*, pp. 196–202.

[6] Wang Chien-min, *Chung-kuo Kung-ch'an tang shih-kao* (Historical Materials of the Chinese Communist Party) (Taipei: National Cheng-chih University, 1965), I, 187–90.

allowed to keep land which they themselves tilled, Mao's agrarian policy at that time clearly aimed at creating a very broad base of mass support.

Essentially, the same aims and principles underlay the draft land law passed soon afterward by the National Conference of Delegates from the soviet area in May, 1930; this law, which was sponsored by the Party's central leadership under Li Li-san, became the basis of the major agrarian reform program of the Chinese Soviet Republic in the subsequent years.

Both Mao's February law and the revised May program stipulated that "only the land rented from the rich peasants by the tenant farmers was to be confiscated";[7] thus, both Mao and the central leadership now advocated similar land policies—even though Mao had previously disagreed with the CCP Central Committee on the question of land confiscation.[8] Both now stressed mass mobilization on a broad base. (As will be indicated later, in 1932 the regime started an anti-rich peasant struggle which tended to narrow the base of mass mobilization somewhat, but this campaign itself provided the basis for continuing efforts to mobilize the majority of ordinary peasants.)

The key change involved in Mao's new policy as of 1930 was the fact that it permitted the rich peasants to keep their own land, if they were willing to cultivate the land by themselves. This replaced the previous policy (just before 1930) of forcing "rich peasants" to accept less fertile land in exchange for their richest acreage.

The criteria for drawing class lines varied from region to region, and they depended to some degree on local economic conditions and on the perceptions of the local administrators of the land reform program. However, the Sixth Party Congress in July did establish criteria for classifying various categories of peasants, including the "rich peasants." It stipulated that "those who maintained a superior economic position by profits from renting land to tenant farmers" were to be regarded as "rich peasants"; the land which they rented to tenants was to be confiscated. Peasants who owned only a small amount of land were to be considered "middle peasants"; they were permitted to accumulate some capital for investment purposes. Peasants who owned a very small fraction of land, which did not produce sufficient crops to support their families, and who therefore had to rent additional land from landlords or rich peasants to produce food, were considered

---

[7] For the text of this law, see *ibid.*, II, 357–62.
[8] See Rue, *Mao Tse-tung in Opposition*, pp. 195–203.

"small farmers" (*hsiao-nung*). Peasants who owned no land and whose livelihood therefore depended entirely on the income from rented land were to be classified as "poor peasants." Those whose livelihood depended entirely on income from manual labor, especially individuals employed in small agrarian enterprises (such as tea manufacturing establishments, oil refineries, and flour mills), were to be classified as "farm laborers."[9]

In the actual process of implementing the program of land distribution during this period, the peasants in some instances were simply divided into three categories: the "poor," "middle," and "rich" peasants. According to reports on the work of land distribution in Anhwei Province, submitted by a CCP agent to the Central Committee, peasants who owned land and also made profits from renting out land were in practice classified as rich peasants, while peasants who cultivated their own land and produced just enough crops to support their families, but not enough to make profits, were regarded as the middle peasants. Industrial workers and the soldiers who owned no land were classified as poor peasants.[10]

The Kiangsi provincial soviet government, following at this time Mao's relatively lenient attitude toward the rich peasants, declared that:

The agrarian policy in the soviet area at the current stage of revolution is to continue the traditional form of the small farm unit as a consequence of the agrarian conditions found in the soviet area. Therefore, it resolutely opposed the policy of socialist collectivization advocated by Trotsky. A country which still has a backward and semi-feudal form of agrarian economy should go through the processes of land reform under the principle of equal distribution of land. It is therefore unthinkable to raise the question of collectivization because all land in the province has already been distributed equally to many millions of peasants.[11]

The main objective of the land distribution at that time, according to the resolutions adopted by the CCP as well as documents published by the Central Soviet Government, was to obtain as broad support as

[9] Quoted in Li Chün-lung, "Chung-kuo Kung-ch'an tang ti t'u-ti cheng chih kai-kuan" (Survey of the Land Policy of the Chinese Communist Party), *Chung-kuo ching-chi* (Chinese Economy), I, Nos. 4 and 5 (Shanghai, 1933).

[10] This document may be found in Himori Torao, "Shina sekigun oyobi sovieto kuiki no hatsuten chokyo" (The Chinese Red Army and the Development of the Soviet Area), Part 1, *Mantetsu chosa geppo* (Monthly Research Report of the South Manchurian Railway Company), XII, No. 8 (August, 1932), 94–119.

[11] "Resolution adopted by the Joint Conference of the General Department of the First Army and the Kiangsi Provincial Soviet Government," quoted in Hatano, *Chūgoku Kyōsantō Shi*, V, 174–75.

possible from the peasant masses by providing them with a sense of participation, not only in the revolutionary cause, but also in direct management of land distribution. The available evidence indicates that it was because the leaders of both the Party and the government were concerned with obtaining as broad mass support as possible in this period, that they tolerated the continued existence of the rich peasants in the land distribution program, in order not to antagonize or alienate them. (By 1932, when the anti-rich peasant struggle was begun, this attitude had obviously undergone some change, but even then the stated aim was to "transform" the rich peasants rather than to eliminate them.)

This relatively moderate policy clearly had an effect on the rich peasants, and one report submitted by a CCP agent in northeast Kiangsi to the CCP Central Committee in Shanghai[12] claims that some of them even sought refuge in the soviet border areas after escaping from the white (non-communist) areas. The question of policy toward rich peasants continued to be a focus of policy debate and a source of tensions among Communist policy makers, but the policy now implemented was the moderate one specified in May and July, 1930.

What were the organizational techniques by which the program of land confiscation and distribution were carried out in this period? According to Mao Tse-tung, the implementation was actually carried out in three stages: (1) land confiscation and distribution; (2) land classification; and (3) land improvement (or construction). Whenever a Red Army unit first occupied a rural region, it immediately established three new bodies to carry out the land policy: a land committee, a confiscation committee, and a workers' and peasants' inspection team (*kung-nung chien-ch'a tui*), with the active participation of the local peasants.[13]

The confiscation committee first conducted a general census covering all households and classified the population of the occupied region into five major classes: the landlords, the rich, middle, and poor peasants, and the farm laborers. This preliminary survey included information on the number of individuals in each household—indicating the sex, age, occupation, and class status of each—and data on the quantity and quality of each land holding. The results of this survey were

[12] Ma Lo, "Report to the CCP Central Committee on the Situation of the Northeast Kiangsi Soviet Area," collected in Himori, "Shina sekigun oyobi sovieto kuiki no hatsuten chokyo," Part 2, *Mantetsu chosa geppo*, XII, No. 9 (September, 1932), 57–66.

[13] Mao Tse-tung, "Ch'a-t'ien yün-tung ch'u-pao tsung-chieh" (Preliminary Summary of the Land Classification Campaign), *Tou Cheng* (Struggle), No. 24 (August 29, 1933).

announced on a large wall poster erected in a public place in each village so that everyone in the community would be able to see it.

The posting of the survey results was designed to convince the peasant population that there was to be no secrecy in the administration of local affairs and, furthermore, to give them the impression that they had the power to make final decisions on important matters. They were invited to contribute suggestions for improvement and to make criticisms. The decision to follow these "democratic" processes meant that more than two months usually elapsed from the time of the general survey to the actual implementation of land distribution. (The confiscation committee also stressed the concept of mass participation and tried to obtain popular support when it carried out the complicated processes of conducting land surveys and distributing the land.)

Following the preliminary survey of land and population, carried out by the confiscation committee, the task of distributing land was usually turned over to the land committee. As mentioned earlier, such committees were organized in every village and *hsiang* ("administrative village" or "township," including several "natural villages") in a newly occupied region. Each committee included the chairman of the local soviet government, the leaders of the poor peasant corps and the farm labor unions, and family representatives of the Red Army. This emphasis on providing representation for as many people as possible in the local mass organizations was designed to create a sense of real popular participation. However, the actual management of the land distribution was carried out by professional cadres assigned this task by the land departments of the village and *hsiang* soviet governments. All of these cadres attended Party schools to receive professional training on how to handle the administration of the land reform program.

The size of the land committees varied from region to region; it depended largely on the size of the occupied area and its population. However, the average land committee in a *hsiang* was reported to have thirteen or seventeen members, while each village land committee generally had five or seven members. The organizational structure of these committees followed the general pattern of the committees set up by soviet governments at all levels. Each committee elected a chairman to convene the meetings and supervise the committee's work. In addition to the chairman, each *hsiang* land committee maintained two clerical staff members, two research and statistical cadres, and an executive secretary. In a village committee, the committee members performed all functions of administration without the aid of any standing committees.

The central task of a land committee was to supervise and manage all aspects of the distribution process in the land reform program. It also was responsible for land improvement. The land committees at the grass-roots level reportedly continued in existence even after the completion of their initial functions, and served as the administrative bodies of local governments to handle the second and third stages of the land reform program.[14]

The workers' and peasants' inspection teams investigated complaints made by peasants, especially claims that mistakes had been made concerning their class status. They also evaluated general peasant opinions and attitudes toward land distribution. Each of these committees included almost all the leading citizens of a village. In many respects, the committees served as the eyes and ears of the local soviet government and helped the soviets determine whether economic equality and social justice had resulted from land confiscation and distribution.

The methods of land distribution varied. One of the simplest procedures was that established by the Oyuwan (Honan-Hupeh-Anhwei) Soviet government, which is described in a booklet that it published entitled, "How to Distribute Land." According to this booklet, land distribution in the soviet area at that time followed the principle of "all land to the peasants based on the number of individuals and the strength of the labor force of each household."[15] In describing how land distribution was actually carried out, the booklet stated that each land committee began its work by apportioning twenty to thirty *mou*[16] of good land in each *hsiang* to support the Red Army. Such land was generally called public land (*kung-t'ien*) and was directly managed by the *hsiang* soviet government, with the help of the village level soviet governments, which contributed the necessary labor and implements to cultivate it. The produce from the public land was used to support the Red Army; approximately 70 per cent was for direct use by the army units, and the other 30 per cent was deposited in a retirement fund, the profits from which were used to support retired Red Army personnel.

---

[14] Ch'i Ch'i-sheng, "Chih-ch'u ti nung-yeh cheng-chih" (Agrarian Policy of the Red Areas), was originally published in *Kuo-wen Chou pao* (National News Weekly) and collected in Hatano, *Chūgoku Kyōsantō Shi*, V, 169–95.

[15] *Ibid.*, p. 186.

[16] A Chinese land measure of area; it varied in different provinces, but generally 6.6 *mou* equaled one acre.

(According to a detailed report on the work of the Hupeh–West Hunan Soviet government, which was made to the CCP Central Committee in Shanghai, it was the *hsiang* soviet governments which were responsible for managing public land and keeping a record of the annual production and the status of the retirement fund.[17])

Each land committee, after collecting statistical data on all land in its jurisdiction, classified it into three categories—the "best" (*shang*), "good" (*chung*), and "poor" (*hsia*) land, and then divided it for distribution to farm laborers and poor and middle peasants. The fertility of land, which was taken into account in the distribution, was determined on the basis of its annual yield as well as its location and quality. The location factor took into account accessibility to transportation facilities and also the topography.

Part of the land in each of the above-mentioned three categories was assigned to each household, in accordance with the number of individuals in the household. According to one report made by the Anhwei Soviet government, the amount of land actually distributed was allocated on the following basis: five *mou* to each adult; three *mou* to each child between the ages of nine and fifteen; two and a half *mou* to each child under the age of nine.

In some areas, however, the division was based on the amount of the harvested rice produced by the land. Under this system, each adult received land yielding five piculs of rice per year;[18] each child in the age group between nine and fifteen received land yielding three piculs of rice per year; and each child under nine received land yielding two and a half piculs.[19]

In either case, the rich peasants preserved the land that they cultivated at this time, on the same basis as others, if they expressed the desire to cultivate it with their own labor. The middle peasants kept the land they already owned and cultivated.

After completing the plan for allocating land to the receiving peasant families, the land committee would announce the plan on a wall poster erected in a public place so that the peasants in the community had an opportunity to make suggestions and present complaints if they

---

[17] "Hu-pei Hu-nan nan-hsi pu su-wei-ai kung-tso" (The Soviet Work in the Hupeh and Southwest Hunan Areas), collected in Himori, "Shina sekigun oyobi sovieto kuiki no hatsuten chokyo," Part 2, pp. 111–23.

[18] A picul is approximately equivalent to 133 pounds.

[19] *Ta Wan Pao* (The Evening News), "Chih-se ch'ü ti tsu-chih yü chien-she" (The Organization and Construction of the Red Areas), published in Shanghai on May 15, 1932; collected in Himori, "Shina sekigun oyobi sovieto kuiki no hatsuten chokyo," Part 2, pp. 140–49.

felt the plan contained any injustices. During this period of adjustment, not only could the peasants air their grievances, but the government could observe the general attitudes and behavior of the peasants
toward the land distribution program. If no one objected to the proposed plan of land distribution, or, if there were complaints, after
necessary adjustments had been made, the land committee proceeded
to register the land and issue land ownership certificates.

Both the poor peasants and farm laborers who acquired new land,
and the middle peasants or rich peasants who kept the land they
previously cultivated, were required formally to register their land
with the land committee and to obtain land ownership certificates,
which contained information on the size, boundaries, and yield of the
allocated land. These certificates provided legal evidence that the peasants actually owned the land,[20] and since this was the first time that
many of them had ever owned land, the certificates were psychologically important to them.

The *hsiang* soviet district generally functioned as the basic unit in
the process of land confiscation and distribution. However, a village
could serve as the basic administrative unit if the peasants in that
village decided at a mass rally that they wished to carry out the land
reform program.

The peasants were actively involved, in fact as well as in theory, in
the processes of land confiscation and distribution, in part as a result of
creation of two auxiliary organizations under the *hsiang* soviet government's jurisdiction: the poor peasant corps and the farm labor union.
These mass organizations achieved considerable success in arousing
class consciousness and a sense of participation on the part of the
ordinary peasant masses.[21] This was one of the few times in Chinese
history that any serious attempt was made to involve the mass of
ordinary peasants in significant activities aimed at social change and
modernization.

The poor peasant corps was established in 1932, in the period when
the Chinese Communists adopted (as will be noted below) a new

[20] The form of the land ownership certificates varied from province to province. I saw
several types of these certificates collected in the display room of the Bureau of
Investigation of the Ministry of Judicial Administration in Ch'ingtan, Taiwan. An
interesting aspect of the certificates was the fact that the Kiangsi provincial soviet
government issued three sets of certificates: one for the rich peasants, one for the middle
peasants, and another for the poor peasants.

[21] For a discussion of the participation of the masses in the administrative processes of
the society, see James R. Townsend, *Political Participation in Communist China* (Berkeley and Los Angeles: University of California Press, 1967), p. 46.

anti-rich peasant policy. The prime purpose was to arouse the class consciousness of the peasant masses and to stimulate "class struggle" in rural China. The units of this corps were organizations through which the peasant masses could express their views, find outlets for their psychological frustrations, and to some extent participate directly in the decision-making processes of the local soviet government and administration. The membership of the poor peasant corps included not only poor peasants but also all farm workers, coolies (laborers), and handicraft workers. Anyone in these categories above the age of sixteen, regardless of sex, who lived in a rural village was invited to participate. The poor peasant corps clearly attempted to involve as many peasants as possible, to have them participate in the processes of land reform and engage in class struggle against rich peasants.

At the *hsiang* level, each corps was organized as follows: A mass meeting elected an executive body of seven or nine members. This committee in turn elected a four-member standing committee consisting of the chairman, an organization director, a propaganda director, and a secretary. The members of both the executive committee and the standing committee were elected at three-month intervals to allow as many peasants as possible to acquire administrative and managerial experience.

Wherever the *hsiang* executive committee of a poor peasant corps was established, it dispatched cadres to organize mass meetings in all the villages of the area and to establish a poor peasant corps in each village. The leadership of each village peasant corps was chosen in a way similar to that of the *hsiang* and consisted of a three- to five-member executive committee. Each village level poor peasant corps was further divided into smaller teams (*hsiao-tsu*), based on occupations; these could be farm laborers' teams, handicraft workers' teams, and coolies' teams.

One of the important functions of the poor peasant corps in general was to serve as an administrative auxiliary of the local soviet government in the process of implementing the land reform policy. Conversely, it was the local soviet governments which sent the cadres who initially helped to establish the poor peasant corps. The local *hsiang* soviet government led all of the poor peasant corps in its area, and the leaders of the poor peasant corps often served as a reservoir from which personnel were drawn for the administrative committees of the *hsiang* soviet government.

Whenever a *hsiang* or village soviet government initiated a new program, it generally invited one leader from each of the village peasant corps to participate in the discussions of the council meeting. Upon returning to his own village, this representative was charged with the responsibility of organizing mass meetings to discuss how to implement the policy. These discussion sessions generally resulted in a resolution in support of the policy adopted by the general membership of the poor peasant corps.

Each *ch'ü* (district) soviet government called a meeting at least once a week for the leaders of the peasant corps under its jurisdiction. These meetings were designed to explain the administrative directives of the Central Soviet Government, to solicit the views and opinions of the poor peasant corps leaders, and to determine peasant attitudes toward the government policy and land reform program. They provided an opportunity for the leaders of every poor peasant corps to visit and attend meetings at the capital of the *ch'ü* soviet government and to make suggestions on how to implement policy.

Each *hsien* soviet government also maintained a close link with the poor peasant corps by dispatching its representatives to attend the meetings of the corps' leadership. Thus, the leaders of the poor peasant corps functioned as an important transmission belt for the diffusion of the central government's policy at the grass-roots level, and to some extent they also served as a channel for "feedback" from the peasants.

In theory at least, the poor peasant corps operated on a strictly voluntary basis and were enjoined not to use coercion in dealing with the mass of peasants.[22] They were not tightly controlled, and the majority of peasants and workers in the villages could join and participate in their operations. They attempted to function as fairly spontaneous organizations, and the basic units did not meet regularly, because it was felt that regular meetings would be too mechanical. There were no membership dues. They did not maintain a rigid hierarchical structure at the provincial, *hsien,* and *ch'ü* level, such as those maintained by the farm labor union, which will be discussed below. The "basic" units existed only at the level of the lowest governmental units, such as the *hsiang* and the village, where they could best mobilize the peasant masses (although, as noted above, their leaders did meet regularly with higher level soviet governments).

[22] Chung-hua su-wei-ai chung-yang cheng-fu, "Kuan-yü ch'a-t'ien yün-tung ti hsün-ling" (Directive on the Land Classification Campaign), *Hung-se Chung-hua* (Red China [an official organ of the Chinese Soviet Government]), Juichin, No. 87 (June 20, 1933).

Therefore, the poor peasant corps were firmly rooted in the idea of mass participation at the basic level. And they provided a channel through which the peasants could express their opinions or grievances to the proper authorities.[23]

The farm labor union (or the tenant farmers union) was different in one basic way. It did maintain a hierarchical structure of organization at all levels of the governmental system. At the bottom of the hierarchy, each farm labor team was usually made up of three or four farm laborers (tenant farmers). "Subunits" of the village farm labor union consisted of approximately three teams, and three or four "subunits" together generally formed one village union. Each *hsiang* farm labor union was formed by grouping together three or four village farm labor unions. Thus, a hierarchical structure was set up, directly parallel to the various levels of the soviet governments. Mass meetings of the farm labor union were normally convened at three-month intervals, at which time the leadership organs of the executive committee and its standing committees were chosen. Otherwise the farm labor union was very similar to the poor peasant corps. Thus, the main organizational difference, as noted, was that the former maintained a vertically hierarchical structure while the latter had a looser horizontal structure.[24]

Once these mass organizations were organized they were used to mobilize the majority of peasants in the soviet areas to participate in class struggle. In fact, in 1932 (after the switch to a harsher policy toward rich peasants), the Kiangsi provincial soviet government stated that the primary purpose of the poor peasant corps was "to oppose the rich peasants and exterminate their reactionary attitudes by establishing the closest possible alliance between the poor peasants and the middle peasants."[25] In some respects, however, policy toward the rich peasants continued to be relatively restrained, at least by comparison with the violent policies directed against landlords. The rich peasants were still not to be executed, but rather they were to be transformed into "revolutionary" peasants through education and the use of the

[23] Hara Masaru, "Chūgoku soveto ni okeru hinnō oyobi konō no soshiki to sono tōsō kōryō" (Organizations and Their Programs for Poor Peasant Corps and Farm Labor Union in the Chinese Soviet Areas), *Mantetsu chosa geppo*, XV, No. 5 (May, 1935).

[24] Political Department, Central Revolutionary Military Committee, *Ku-nung kung-hui ti kang-yao* (A Summary of the Farm Labor Union), dated February, 1931, in the Ch'en Ch'eng Microfilms.

[25] "Resolution on the Work of the Poor Peasant Corps" adopted by the Kiangsi provincial soviet government on July 14, 1932, cited in Hara, "Chūgoku soveto ni okeru hinnō oyobi konō no soshiki to sono tōsō kōryō."

"class struggle." In carrying out this newly defined anti-rich peasant policy, the poor peasant corps emerged in mid-1932 as the most powerful force.

The development of this anti-rich peasant policy is a complex story. All available documents and official pronouncements lead one to believe that the launching of the policy was not primarily motivated by economic considerations, nor was it primarily the result of factional struggles in the leadership organs of the Party and government.[26] The available evidence suggests that, in a basic sense, the anti-rich peasant policy was a logical development and extension of the policy of mass mobilization. In short, this new form of class struggle was apparently adopted by the CCP leadership and by Mao Tse-tung as a new means to try to mobilize mass support among the majority of the peasantry (other than rich peasants).

This was the period in which the Japanese Army was expanding its control to include not only the coastal areas of China but also the important cities in the interior of the country. In this situation the Central Soviet Government "declared war" on Japan (on April 15, 1932), apparently in order to try to capitalize on the growing force of Chinese nationalism to help support its mass mobilization program.[27] At this time also the Fourth Encirclement campaign was launched by the Kuomintang Army against the Kiangsi Soviet area. Because of these circumstances, the Chinese Communist leadership (including both the Central Party leaders and the leaders of the Central Soviet Government) launched an all-out campaign to mobilize the population of the soviet areas.

The establishment of the poor peasant corps and the initiation of a "land classification campaign" were designed to be the main instruments in the peasant mobilization program, and these were linked to the new anti-rich peasant policy in order to try to arouse the masses.

The situation within the Kiangsi Soviet area was somewhat different

---

[26] Some scholars contend that the initiation of the anti-rich peasant policy was closely associated with the consolidation by the twenty-eight Bolsheviks of their position as the most powerful leadership of the CCP. For this interpretation, see Hsiao Tso-liang, *Power Relations within the Chinese Communist Movement, 1930–1934: A Study of Documents* (Seattle: University of Washington Press, 1961); Rue, *Mao Tse-tung in Opposition;* and Shanti Swarup, *A Study of the Chinese Communist Movement, 1927–1934* (Oxford: Clarendon Press, 1966).

[27] The evidence now available on the Kiangsi Soviet period indicates that Chalmers A. Johnson's thesis that nationalism probably played a minimum role in mobilizing the mass support during the Kiangsi Soviet period is incorrect. See his *Peasant Nationalism and Communist Power: The Emergence of Revolutionary China, 1937–1945* (Stanford, Calif.: Stanford University Press, 1962).

in 1932 from what it had been in 1930–31, because of the results of the land distribution campaign that had been carried out since 1930. The first stage of land confiscation and distribution had improved, at least to some extent, the economic position of the lower-middle peasant class in the area and had resulted in some increased socioeconomic mobility. Thus, some former poor peasants had moved toward the status of the middle peasant, and some members of the former middle peasant class had moved toward rich peasant status. As a result, a new policy issue was posed: how to treat the newly created rich peasant class. Should the Central Soviet Government treat them as it had previously treated rich peasants during the first stage of land distribution? Should it indiscriminately attack all rich peasants? Or should it try to devise new approaches by which not only middle peasants but also new rich peasants who did not exploit others (that is, those who cultivated all their own land) could be mobilized to meet the external pressures of the time? The leaders of the CCP and the Central Soviet Government seem to have decided on the latter course, a fact which was reflected both in the new poor peasant corps and the land classification campaign (*ch'a-t'ien yün-tung*) initiated at this time.

The new policy called for class warfare against rich peasants, but it was still restricted to those rich peasants who "exploited" others. However, the basis for determining which rich peasants were guilty of such "exploitation" was clearly broadened. "The anti-rich peasant struggle (*fan fu-nung tou-cheng*) is not only to oppose the exploiting rich peasants left over from the pre-revolutionary period but also to struggle against the rich peasants emerging as a new class under the soviet government," declared Circular Number 9 of the CCP.[28] Moreover, under the new policy, the criterion for determining who was to be classified as a rich peasant was not simply "how much exploitation the peasants committed." It was stated that "if a peasant rented his land to others, used others' labor power, earned profits on his rent, engaged in speculation, and exploited the people, he must be classified as a rich peasant regardless of whether he economically was prosperous or not."[29] At the same time, however, it was clearly specified that a peasant "should not be classified as a rich peasant" just because he was prosperous.[30] If he relied on his own muscle and skill, and did not exploit others, he should not be attacked.

[28] For the text of Circular Number 9, see Li, "Chung-kuo Kung-ch'an tang ti t'u-ti cheng-chih kai-kuan," p. 196.

[29] *Ibid.*

[30] *Ibid.*

The anti-rich peasant campaign is not an empty slogan nor a device through which the soviet government intends to collect the economic resources of the peasantry [the Party circular asserted], but it is truly a technique by which the soviet government plans to mobilize the broadest possible mass support in order to conduct the struggle not only against the feudal and exploitative elements of the soviet society but also the external enemy which is waging war on the soviet areas.[31]

The main objective of the anti-rich peasant policy, therefore, was to mobilize and educate the majority of the entire population, and to focus attack on the minority who were the exploiting rich peasants.[32]

In the process of implementing this new anti-rich peasant policy, with the aim of improving mass mobilization, both the Central CCP leadership headed by Ch'in Pang-hsien (Po Ku), and the leadership of the Central Soviet Government under Mao Tse-tung, collaborated in devising new organizational techniques: they decided that the poor peasant corps should be developed to function as the vanguard of the peasant masses and to establish a powerful alliance between the poor peasants and the middle peasants, and on this organizational basis to carry out the new anti-rich peasant struggle. The cadres at all levels of the soviet government were thus directed "to take seriously the anti-rich peasant policy as the form of class struggle and as the means to generate the latent power of peasant masses in the struggle of carrying out the Chinese revolution."[33]

The organizational activities of the poor peasant corps were also closely related to the land classification campaign which the Central Soviet Government launched in 1933. In fact, the poor peasant corps was the main instrument for implementing the land classification campaign and for carrying out land reclassification and redistribution at this time, and it performed many of the functions that had previously been performed by the land committees of the local soviet governments.

The land classification campaign was launched by Mao Tse-tung himself on June 1, 1933. In his speech inaugurating the campaign, Mao declared that the central tasks were to survey the current status of land distribution and determine who had emerged as members of a new class of rich peasants (as currently defined) after the first stage of land distribution.[34]

[31] *Ibid.,* p. 197.

[32] This interpretation of the anti-rich peasant policy differs from that in recent studies by Rue and Swarup, cited in note 26.

[33] Li, "Chung-kuo Kung-ch'an tang ti t'u-ti cheng-chih kai-kuan," p. 197.

[34] See *Tou Cheng,* an official organ of the CCP Central Committee in the soviet area, No. 24 (August 29, 1933).

In analyzing the current status of the land distribution program in the central soviet area, Mao stated that approximately 80 per cent of the area had not yet completely resolved the problems involved in the land distribution. He, therefore, called on the leaders of the local soviet governments, the poor peasant corps, and the farm labor unions throughout the region to launch the land classification campaign as soon as possible. "The land classification campaign should be able to light the flames of class struggle among the two million peasants in the area," Mao asserted, "and eliminate completely the remainder of the feudal elements."[35]

The important questions to answer in this drive, Mao said, were: whether the land had been equally distributed, whether the first stage of confiscation had achieved the objectives of the land law of the Chinese Soviet Republic, and whether the former landlords and exploiting rich peasants had been able to continue in existence and had continued to accumulate wealth after the first stage of land confiscation and distribution had been carried out.

After Mao's speech concerning the land classification campaign, the Central Soviet Government called a conference of the leaders of the eight *hsien* governments, which was convened from June 17 to June 21 to discuss the new policy. This conference adopted a resolution which stated that "the purpose of launching the land classification campaign is to eliminate the landlord and feudal forces, and to further strengthen and improve the work of soviet governments through the mobilization of the peasant masses in the soviet areas."[36] It was followed by another conference, held from June 25 to July 1, which brought together the poor peasant corps' leadership to discuss the reasons for instituting the land classification campaign and to establish procedures for carrying out the campaign in the soviet areas. At this meeting it was argued that certain landlords had disguised themselves as rich or middle peasants during the first stages of land distribution, thereby infiltrating the local soviet governments in order to receive land, and that the new campaign was necessary to eliminate these elements through intensified class struggle.[37]

[35] *Ibid.*

[36] Mao Tse-tung, "Chung-hua su-wei-ai kung-ho-kuo chung-yang chih-hsing wei-yüan hui yü jen-min wei-yüan hui tui ti erh-tz'u ch'uan-kuo su-wei-ai tai-piao ta-hui ti pao-kao" (Report of the Central Executive Committee and People's Commissars of the Chinese Soviet Republic to the Second National Soviet Congress), *Hung-se Chung-hua*, No. 148 (February 12, 1934) and the special issue, No. 7. Also in Hatano, *Chūgoku Kyōsantō Shi*, IV, 131–221. *Hung-se Chung-hua*, No. 87 (June 10, 1933), p. 3.

[37] *Ibid.*

"The land classification campaign is unquestionably one of the most extraordinary and severest forms of class struggle," Mao declared, "we must mobilize the broadest possible mass support from the poor peasants and farm laborers, and make them our foundation and vanguard for the land classification campaign." Mao urged the leaders of the local soviet governments to strengthen their alliance with the poor and middle peasants and the farm laborers, and to mobilize them in order to utilize their power. He also proposed that local soviet governments recruit new cadres from the most ardent revolutionary cadres in the poor peasant corps.

The land classification campaign was not the responsibility of the poor peasant corps alone; in fact, an effort was made to involve the entire bureaucracy of the soviet governments in it. The leaders of the various soviet governments were to serve as the organizers of the campaign. At the *hsien,* the *ch'ü,* and the *hsiang* levels, the local soviet governments were directed to establish land classification committees, in cooperation with the poor peasant corps, and these committees therefore included both the department heads of the soviet governments and the leaders of the nongovernmental mass organizations.

The *hsien* soviet governments were instructed to establish plans for carrying out the land classification plans within the month, and each plan was to be reviewed every month to determine whether the campaign within the *hsien* soviet area had been carried out according to the original concept. At least once a week the *ch'ü* and *hsiang* soviet governments were to call meetings of the chairmen of the local soviet governments and the leaders of the poor peasant corps to draft concrete schedules and establish inspection systems to check on the progress of the campaign. At the level of the *hsiang* soviet governments, efforts were made to generate maximum support from all the members of the *hsiang* delegate council, the poor peasant corps, the labor unions, and the other mass organizations, in order to create the broadest possible participation in the campaign.

The *hsien* soviet governments were also charged with the responsibility of organizing training programs for the cadres who would carry the major burden of implementing the campaign. These training programs, held during July, August, and September, generally involved ten days of specialized training for the leaders recruited from each *hsiang* within the *hsien* district; the most revolutionary members of the poor peasant corps, the farm labor union, and the *hsiang* delegate council (the soviet) were also given specialized training at the *hsien* soviet government headquarters. After completion of the training, they returned to their own villages to serve as the organizers and leaders of the land classification campaign.

The *hsiang* soviet governments revived their confiscation and distribution committees, which now generally included the leaders of the local poor peasant corps in the area. These committees, under the supervision and direction of the *hsiang* soviet governments, performed the actual tasks of confiscating and redistributing the land owned and operated by the landlords and rich peasants. Directives from the CCP Central Bureau urged these land classification committees to pay special attention to strengthening the alliance with the middle peasants, since "the middle peasants are the vanguard of the revolutionary masses, and the administration and success of our policies greatly depend on the support and participation of the middle peasants."[38]

All the decisions made by the poor peasant corps and the *hsiang* soviet governments were carefully explained to the middle peasants in the effort to gain their support. The poor peasant corps and the soviet governments "must listen to the voice of the middle peasants," it was said. Moreover, "any attempt to exterminate the rich peasants should be stopped," because they, unlike the members of the landlord class, possessed a revolutionary potential.[39] However, the policy toward rich peasants now became more radical and harsh. In the actual distribution of land, the exploiting rich peasants (defined in the fashion described above) were no longer allowed to keep any land that they tilled themselves. Thus, in effect, the pre-1930 policy was revived; as a consequence, part of the rich peasants' land was confiscated.

Reading through the Party directives, the resolutions of the various conferences, and the speeches made by Mao Tse-tung about the land campaigns in the Kiangsi period, it seems clear that the aim of the campaigns was not simply to classify and redistribute land, and to differentiate the various peasant classes. Underlying these objectives was the broader basic goal of developing an effective mass mobilization strategy.

The great achievements of the land classification campaigns sufficiently proved that it was still necessary to pay attention to the class struggle in the rural areas of the local soviet government, and the land classification campaigns were our most important techniques for conducting the continuous class struggle in the rural areas, and method of completely exterminating the remainder of the feudal forces.[40]

[38] This quotation from Ch'i, "Chih-ch'u ti nung-yeh cheng-chih," p. 205.
[39] *Ibid.*
[40] Mao Tse-tung's speech to the Second National Soviet Congress, see note 36.

The land campaigns, and the establishment of the poor peasant corps and the farm labor union, were expressions of the determination to carry out widespread mass mobilization during the Kiangsi Soviet period, a determination that was shared by Mao and the "Twenty-eight Bolsheviks" who were then in control of the Party's Central Committee. The concepts and techniques of mass revolutionary struggle which were evolved at that time have greatly influenced the means subsequently used to mobilize the masses in China, in the Yenan period and ever since the Communists achieved nationwide power in 1949. Mao's concepts of mass mobilization, which in time were codified as the so-called "mass line," not only continue to be important in China today, they also serve as a powerful model influencing many revolutionaries in the underdeveloped regions of the world.

MARK SELDEN

The Yenan Legacy: The Mass Line*

In the rise of the Chinese Communist Party there have been three periods of crippling defeat, each of them bringing the movement close to annihilation, and each leading to radical innovation in the Party's approach to war and revolution. In all three instances Mao Tse-tung eventually emerged as the leading architect of the new line after fierce intra-Party strife. The Kuomintang's anti-Communist coup of 1927 destroyed the first united front and paved the way for new overtures to the peasantry stressing a combination of guerrilla warfare and land revolution. The annihilation of the Kiangsi Soviet and other Communist bases in 1934 created conditions for abandoning agrarian revolution and armed insurrection in favor of the Anti-Japanese National United Front and the New Democracy. Finally, out of the devastation and hardship wrought by Japanese offensives coupled with the Kuomintang blockade against Communist-led base areas during 1941–42, emerged a constellation of policies associated with the "mass line."

This paper concerns the last of these major turning points, specifically the mass line as it emerged and took shape in the Shensi-Kansu-Ninghsia Border Region, whose capital Yenan served as the Party's headquarters throughout the War of Resistance Against Japan. The mass line politics of 1943 represented a synthesis of policies developed initially during the Kiangsi period and experience culled from the subsequent guerrilla resistance against Japan in Communist-sponsored

* I am indebted to the participants in the Conference on the Microsocietal Study of the Chinese Political System for valuable suggestions, many of which have been incorporated in this paper.

se areas. That synthesis contained in a developed form virtually every significant element of the Chinese Communist Party's distinctive approach to war and rural modernization. No wonder then that in the years after 1949 the leadership would repeatedly evoke the name and spirit of Yenan—the Party's most creative epoch and an era that culminated in the smashing defeat of the enemy Japan.

THE REVOLUTIONARY HISTORY OF THE SHEN-KAN-NING BORDER REGION

The loess hills of northern Shensi below the Great Wall rank among China's most desolate and inaccessible areas. In the declining years of the Ch'ing dynasty and subsequently under warlord rule, the region was notorious as a bandit lair, and its primitive agrarian economy disintegrated. However, when revolutionary currents swept Shensi in the 1920's, its remote northern reaches and the Shensi-Kansu Border Area were little affected. It was rather in the rich and populous lands of the Wei River Valley near Sian that the presence of revolutionary forces of the Northern Expedition permitted the formation of worker and peasant associations and political agitation among students and soldiers during 1926 and 1927.

These movements and the fledgling Communist Party were shattered by the counterrevolutionary crackdown of 1927. Although subsequent efforts were made to rebuild the movement in the Wei Valley area, it was in the rugged terrain of the north, an ideal guerrilla sanctuary, that local partisans led by Liu Chih-tan and Kao Kang eventually united guerrilla tactics with agrarian revolution to create the Shen-Kan-Ning Soviet area.[1] By 1935, after nearly a decade of fighting in the countryside and constant friction with higher Party authorities critical of the heterodox composition and "mountain stronghold" tactics of the partisans, land revolution was completed in approximately twenty counties (*hsien*) comprising the embattled soviet area.

A peripheral and weak soviet on the Shensi-Kansu border became the focus of the Communist movement and Kuomintang efforts to crush it in the fall of 1935 with the arrival of Mao Tse-tung and the Party Central at the head of the first wave of battered troops completing the Long March. Shen-Kan-Ning as the lone surviving Communist base was designated a "model area," symbolic of Communist policies

---

[1] I have discussed the early history of the border region in an article on "The Guerrilla Movement in Northwest China: The Origins of the Shensi-Kansu-Ninghsia Border Region," *China Quarterly*, Nos. 28–29 (1966–67).

as the Party halted agrarian revolution and mounted a vigorous nation-wide campaign for a national united front against Japan. The tacit recognition by the Nationalists of the base area, and its transformation from a soviet to a special region of the national government in the fall of 1937, completed the transformation from rebels to rulers of a stable area comprised of 23 counties with a population of 1,400,000, and from violent class revolution to a politics of class cooperation in the interest of national unity.

Prominent political features stressed by the leaders of the Shen-Kan-Ning Border Region and other base areas after 1937 were the united front, class harmony, bureaucratic administration, and moderate reform. The basis for the united front in the border region (*pien-ch'ü*) was the restoration of political and economic rights (but not confiscated property) to former landlords and rich peasants, including many who had fled during the land revolution. Land revolution had destroyed the economic basis of landlord power and introduced a high degree of economic equality, but it had done nothing to transform the system of private family farming, or to prevent the resurgence of former landlords or domination by a new land-based elite. Moreover, in the years after 1937 the mass mobilization techniques applied effectively to rouse the peasantry in the land revolution and during the creation of a soviet yielded steadily to bureaucratic administration directed by an educated cadre elite which was remote from the problems of village life. Former local partisans, including peasant activists, remained prominent in Communist politics at the local level, but as armed revolution gave way to emphasis on stability and gradual reform, the initiative passed to a rapidly growing bureaucracy.[2]

The Rectification Movement of 1942–44

The rectification (*cheng-feng*) campaign of 1942 to 1944 marked a significant turning point in the development of the Chinese Communist movement. Six years earlier, in 1936, the Party adopted a program in which the idea of a united front was the basis for limited economic reform and political mobilization. In the years 1937 to 1940 that policy was spectacularly successful nationally. Starting from a tenuous and isolated position in remote northern Shensi, by 1940 the Communists dominated important areas throughout North China and posed the

---

[2] The transformation from revolutionary to bureaucratic rule is treated at length in my unpublished dissertation, "Yenan Communism: Revolution in the Shensi-Kansu-Ninghsia Border Region, 1937–1945" (Yale, 1967).

dominant threat to Japanese aspirations for conquest. But the very success of that program undermined its basis: rapid expansion precipitated sharp clashes with the Japanese and the Kuomintang. In 1941, following the Communists' successful Hundred Regiments offensive in North China, the brunt of the Japanese attack shifted to the Communists. Under this assault, the population in Communist areas shrank by almost half, from forty-four million to twenty-five million, and the Eighth Route Army from four hundred thousand to three hundred thousand men.[3] The breakdown of the united front with the Kuomintang was felt acutely in Shen-Kan-Ning. The Kuomintang blockade of the border region, initiated in 1939, was tightened in 1941 following the clash of Communist and Kuomintang forces in the New Fourth Army incident. Moreover, just as the Communists were feeling the pinch of blockade and military defeat, the central government cut off the subsidy provided since 1937 for the Eighth Route Army and administration of the border region.

The reverses of 1941 and 1942 revealed the weaknesses and limitations of the movement to that time. Without outside financial support from the central government, in 1941 the Communists were forced to impose a crushing burden of taxation and military conscription on the people in Shen-Kan-Ning. As blockade contributed to economic strangulation and rampant inflation, the regional government announced an all-time high tax levy of two hundred thousand piculs[4] of millet—more than doubling the previous year's total and compounding difficulties for the beleaguered peasant, including the poor and the new middle peasants who were the bulwark of Communist support. The crises of these years intensified the tensions and contradictions in Communist policy in governing the border region.

Since 1937 two conceptions of politics—one revolutionary and one bureaucratic—had uneasily coexisted in the border region. The administrators included both students and intellectuals drawn to Yenan from outside the area and traditional landlord-officials, many of whom returned to the border region after the land revolution. Both were members of the educated elite. The students had been exposed to modern

---

[3] Chalmers A. Johnson, *Peasant Nationalism and Communist Power: The Emergence of Revolutionary China, 1937–1945* (Stanford, Calif.: Stanford University Press, 1962), pp. 56–60. Cf. Ho Kan-chih, *A History of the Modern Chinese Revolution* (Peking: Foreign Language Press, 1960), pp. 373–74. Ho states that during 1941 the population in base areas in the entire country was reduced from 100,000,000 to 50,000,000 people and the Eighth Route Army from 400,000 to 303,000.

[4] A picul is approximately equivalent to 133 pounds.

ideas and imbued with the united front spirit which initially motivated their participation in Communist-sponsored governments. The local elite was skilled in the politics and administration of the warlord era, and willing in many cases to cooperate with the Communist government out of a combination of altruism and self-interest—that is, a combination of acceptance of the united front and a desire to preserve the remnants of their economic and political power in the border region. In Shen-Kan-Ning these groups formed the bulwark of the regional and county bureaucracy whose powers steadily increased in the years 1937 to 1941. On the other hand, most county magistrates and virtually all lower level cadres working at the district (*ch'ü*) and township (*hsiang*, also translated as "administrative village") levels were local revolutionaries, predominantly illiterate peasant youths who had earlier demonstrated leadership in the course of the armed struggle and land upheaval. Their primary commitment was to a social revolution which would eliminate oppression and bring equality and hope to the poor in the desolate villages of the border region.

There was little common ideological ground uniting cadres of varying background and experience beyond anti-Japanese nationalist ideals and a vision of a strong and free China. With the exception of the highest level Party cadres and intellectuals, there had been virtually no exposure to Marxist-Leninist thought or any other systematic ideological training. Modern and reformist ideas prevalent among outside cadre administrators and intellectuals, most of them new to the Party, were conceptions developed in the eastern cities during and after the May Fourth movement. Local revolutionaries, on the other hand, despite their commitment to land revolution, remained deeply imbued with traditional rural values and bound by complex social relationships and village loyalties. By 1941, at a time of nationwide military setbacks and blockade, increased tensions between the peasantry and the government confronted the Communists with fundamental problems concerning the adequacy of their administration in the border region. Had the traditional elite merely been replaced by a new cadre elite, leaving basic elements of rural poverty and oppression unresolved? Were local cadres capable of carrying out rural reforms and permanently superseding the traditional landlord elite as the dominant power in village life? Could the border regions' isolated villages be effectively linked with over-all policy emanating from higher levels of Party and government? Was a costly and remote bureaucracy with a monopoly on educated and experienced administrators the most effective means for governing and politicizing the border region? These problems were not new. They had been developing since 1937 with the adoption of the united front line and the influx of new members uncommitted to the Party's vision of rural revolution. But from 1941 they became the focus of intense intra-Party debate in the *cheng-feng* movement.

Cheng-feng was directed toward building a unified Party with common ideas, ideology, and goals. The heterodox composition of the Party, government, and army, all of whose ranks had grown rapidly since 1937, required education and ideological training to instill primary loyalty to the Party in the face of powerful enemy forces and conflicting personal bonds. The magnitude of the problem is suggested by the twenty-fold increase in Party membership from forty thousand to eight hundred thousand in the three years after the outbreak of war in 1937. Under conditions of guerrilla warfare throughout North China and isolation of many villages in the border region, the ideal was not blind obedience to party directives, though *cheng-feng* did attempt to strengthen the chain of command. Guerrilla conditions in particular involved a high degree of flexibility and autonomy, and a minimum of central direction and control, making it all the more imperative that local military units and particularly their commanders share the goals and outlook of the larger movement. As Stuart Schram has aptly observed, the goal of the rectification campaign was to "harmonize the two conflicting imperatives of 'conscious action' by individuals and impeccable social discipline."[5] Toward this end the Party launched a cadre education campaign of unprecedented proportions. In the 1942 *cheng-feng* movement, Marxism-Leninism and examples of its application in China provided the tools, and a basic rectification methodology —consisting of intensive education, small group study, criticism and self-criticism, and thought reform—was developed toward a full analysis of the past and present problems confronting the Party and its individual cadres.

In two speeches of February 1, 1942, officially launching *cheng-feng,* Mao set forth guidelines which were followed during the next two years. His major theme was the role of ideology in the Chinese revolution, specifically in "the study of current affairs . . . historical re-

---

[5] Stuart Schram, *Mao Tse-tung* (Harmondsworth, Eng.: Penguin, 1966), p. 269. For a lucid official expression of these twin goals, cf. the September 1, 1942, "Central Committee Resolution on the Unification of Leadership in the Anti-Japanese War Bases" in Boyd Compton, *Mao's China: Party Reform Documents, 1942–44* (Seattle: University of Washington Press, 1952), pp. 161–75, especially p. 162.

search, and . . . the application of Marxism-Leninism."[6] Although a variety of errors, including "subjectivism," "sectarianism" and "commandism," came under Mao's scathing attack, his harshest comments were reserved for those who "study the theories of Marx, Engels, Lenin, and Stalin abstractly and aimlessly, and do not inquire about their connection with the Chinese revolution . . . it's merely theory for the sake of theory."[7] In that biting sarcasm of which he was a master, Mao insisted that:

We do not study Marxism-Leninism because it is pleasing to the eye, or because it has some mystical value, like the doctrines of the Taoist priests who ascend Mao Shan to learn how to subdue devils and evil spirits. Marxism-Leninism has no beauty, nor has it any mystical value. It is only extremely useful. It seems that right up to the present quite a few have regarded Marxism-Leninism as a ready-made panacea: once you have it, you can cure all your ills with little effort. This is a type of childish blindness and we must start a movement to enlighten these people. Those who regard Marxism-Leninism as religious dogma show this type of blind ignorance. We must tell them openly, "Your dogma is of no use," or to use an impolite phrase, "Your dogma is less useful than excrement." We see that dog excrement can fertilize the fields, and man's can feed the dog. And dogmas? They can't fertilize the fields, nor can they feed a dog. Of what use are they? (Laughter).[8]

The *cheng-feng* campaign was concerned with defining a basic corpus of Marxist texts, particularly the interpretations of Mao Tse-tung, whose principles could be directly and readily applied by diverse Party and government cadres to resolving problems in their own work.

Cheng-feng was not a purge in the conventional sense. All cadres, particularly those accused of serious errors, were subjected to "struggle" under conditions of psychological stress. However, the goal clearly was to reconstruct and reincorporate them within the movement rather than to eliminate them as enemies. Mao's own metaphor for this process was that of curing a sick man.

Our object in exposing errors and criticizing shortcomings is like that of a doctor in curing a disease. The whole purpose is to save people, not to cure them to death. . . . If a person who commits an error, no matter how great, does not bring his disease to an incurable state by concealing it and persisting in his error, and if in addition he is genuinely and honestly willing to be cured, willing to make corrections, we will welcome him so that his disease may be cured and he may become a

---

[6] Mao Tse-tung, "Reconstruction of Our Studies," in Compton, *Mao's China,* p. 62.
[7] *Ibid.,* p. 64.
[8] "Reform in Learning, the Party and Literature," in *ibid.,* pp. 21–22.

good comrade. . . . We cannot adopt a brash attitude toward diseases in thought and politics, but an attitude of "saving men by curing their ills."[9]

On February 8, 1942, directing himself specifically to foreign formalism and dogmatism in the Party, Mao elaborated on this theme, suggesting that the cure of sick men involved psychological techniques other than those of ordinary education.

It is necessary to destroy these conditions and sweep them away, but it is not easy. The task must be performed properly, which means that a reasonable explanation must be given. If the explanation is very reasonable, if it is to the point, it can be effective. The first step in reasoning is to give the patient a powerful stimulus: yell at him, "You're sick!" so the patient will have a fright and break out in an over-all sweat: then he can actually be started on the road to recovery.[10]

Recent studies of group dynamics suggest the immense psychological power certain groups are able to wield over their members. In particular, one is impressed by the awesome pressures to conform to group norms of individuals who are unanimously declared "sick" or insane. The "patient" is able to save himself, in the sense of restoring his own self-esteem as well as being reincorporated in the group, only by demonstrating complete acceptance of group demands, that is, by giving up his individuality. These pressures were effectively increased by methods of small group study and discussion, including both the criticism of every cadre by his peers and searching self-criticism.[11]

I am familiar with no cases of cadres imprisoned or excluded from the Party in the course of the intensive study and criticism which began in the spring of 1942. In the midst of a brutal war the services of every individual willing to commit himself to the Party's leadership were valued. Even so prominent a "sick man" as Mao Tse-tung's former rival, Wang Ming, continued to serve as president of the Women's University in Yenan, a minor post to be sure, while retaining his Central Committee membership. The writer Wang Shih-wei, object of unquestionably the most virulent public campaign of denunciation, and a man adamant in his refusal to admit his "errors" and to reform at Party behest, renounced his Party membership and was eventually

---

[9] *Ibid.*, pp. 31–32. James Townsend has observed that Lenin too viewed intra-Party disputes as a "sickness that could be cured." *Political Participation in Communist China* (Berkeley and Los Angeles: University of California Press, 1967), p. 39. There is no evidence, however, that Lenin ever considered or devised a rectification methodology.

[10] "In Opposition to Party Formalism," in Compton, *Mao's China*, p. 37.

[11] I am indebted for a number of insights on group behavior to Boris Astrachan and David Musto and members of the psycho-history group at Yale University in 1966–67. Cf. Robert J. Lifton, *Thought Reform and the Psychology of Totalism: A Study of "Brainwashing" in China* (New York: Norton, 1961.)

sent to "reform through labor" in a factory after the failure of intensive efforts at re-education.[12] Individual cadres were virulently criticized, ideally with a view to reforming them, but in some cases from
deep personal antagonisms. Public criticism in the Communist press of
a few individuals provided negative examples for cadres to apply in
eliminating shortcomings in their own work. However, for the thousands of cadres and students participating in *cheng-feng*, the emphasis
throughout the campaign was on overcoming incorrect methods of
administration and leadership, or erroneous policies in their own work,
rather than criticism of individuals per se.

In 1942 Mao and his colleagues devised a viable means for dealing
with the intense frictions, contradictions, policy disputes, and hetero-
doxy within the Party and government. As Mao would recall fifteen
years later, at the height of the Hundred Flowers campaign,

In 1942 we worked out the formula "unity-criticism-unity" to describe this democratic method of resolving contradictions among the people. To elaborate, this
means to start off with a desire for unity and resolve contradictions through
criticism or struggle so as to achieve a new unity on a new basis. . . . In 1942 we
used this method to resolve contradictions inside the Communist Party, namely
contradictions between the doctrinaires and the rank-and-file membership, between
doctrinairism and Marxism.[13]

Few were expelled from the Party or received demotions as a result of
the campaign. Rectification not only replaced expulsion, imprisonment,
or death, which had commonly occurred in earlier intra-Party struggles, but established a procedure of group criticism which generated a
high degree of unity and cohesion and provided an effective means of
leadership training and testing. Significantly, both Mao Tse-tung and
Kao Kang, who respectively took the lead in this movement nationally
and at the regional level, had themselves been participants in and
victims of the old method of arrest and purge.

The rectification must be evaluated in the perspective of traditional
Chinese leadership values and methods, grounded in face-to-face relationships, obedience to personal authority, and a variety of face-saving
techniques to shield leadership from criticism or embarrassment. These
values were perceived as threatening by Communist leaders intent on

[12] See Merle Goldman, *Literary Dissent in Communist China* (Cambridge, Mass.:
Harvard University Press, 1967), pp. 18–50, for a full discussion of the case of Wang
Shih-wei and other Communist writers during the rectification campaign.

[13] Mao Tse-tung, "On the Correct Handling of Contradictions among the People," in
Communist China, 1955–1959: Policy Documents with Analysis (Cambridge, Mass.:
Harvard University Press, 1962), p. 278.

forging strong Party loyalties which would override personal ties. This was particularly significant as the Communists were about to embark on a radical shift in policy, including the reorganization of village life, which could undermine the entire basis of personal relationships both within and outside the Party, and create disaffection among cadres with a strong united front orientation. Hierarchical relationships based on mutual interest and personal loyalty, which had provided a basis for leadership within many isolated hamlets of the border area, posed an obstacle to the new goals. Intense criticism and self-criticism was an extraordinarily effective method for breaking down traditional leadership conceptions, overcoming differences in values between outside and local, educated and uneducated cadres. In the process of group study and criticism, cadres were educated in and committed to group norms while leadership dedicated to the Party and its principles was identified and rewarded. The leadership which emerged in the course of *cheng-feng* had demonstrated its ability to persuade and motivate peers in intense group sessions where status and face were scorned as dangerous and deviant. To set oneself above the group, to rely on rank or office, implied rejection of the power of the group to evaluate each individual's criticism and self-criticism. In small group meetings it was difficult for a leader to remain a distant exalted figure. Rather, leaders were forced repeatedly to renew their "mandate" by articulating and defending both their policy line and its implementation.[14]

At the same time, from 1942 a related leadership phenomenon of a very different kind developed. In the *cheng-feng* campaign the prestige of Mao Tse-tung as a Party and national leader sharply increased, and for the first time the image of his thought and personality was widely projected as the embodiment of Communist Party policy and spirit.[15] In part this represented Mao's growing stature within the Communist movement as exemplified by the extensive use of his writings in the rectification campaign. In part, in the tradition of Chinese rebel movements, it was a deliberate effort to present a leader and personality as a rallying point for the nation at a time of greater friction and increasingly overt competition with the Kuomintang. Moreover, as the partic-

---

[14] Richard Solomon's study on "Mao's Effort to Reintegrate the Chinese Polity: Problems of Authority and Conflict in Chinese Social Processes," included in this volume, further illuminates the characteristics and the tenacity of the traditional leadership style of rigid hierarchical relationships, dependency on personalized authority, fear of conflict, and the resultant problems of communication and interaction between superiors and inferiors. The *cheng-feng* movement was the first of a continuing series of Communist assaults on these patterns of leadership.

[15] See, for example, the party organ, *CFJP*, Yenan, July 17, August 7, 1943.

ularistic basis of leadership ties came under attack in the *cheng-feng* campaign, it was vital for the cohesion of the Communist movement to have a single personalized leader to whom all cadres owed allegiance.

With the Central Committee directive of April 3, 1942, cadres throughout the border region began an elaborate program of study and a thorough examination and revaluation of the work of every organ and individual. Under the close supervision of the Central Committee and the Northwest Bureau, special committees were set up at all levels of the Party, government, and army to direct the study campaign. All cadres were ordered to devote two hours per day to study, including group discussion and criticism, preparation of study notes, and finally examination on designated texts. Extended study of the rectification documents preceded a thorough investigation of each organization's work, applying the newly assimilated principles to one's concrete duties and to evaluation of the performance of every cadre.[16]

The eighteen documents originally selected for study (their number was shortly increased to twenty-two with the addition of four more documents from the Soviet Union) clearly reflected Mao Tse-tung's dominance within the Party. Mao was identified as the author of seven, and he may personally have written as many as six of the remaining items, the latter being mainly Central Committee resolutions and Propaganda Bureau documents entirely consonant with his views. With one selection each, Liu Shao-ch'i, K'ang Sheng, and Ch'en Yün were the only other Chinese authors represented by name in the original collection. By including only two Soviet documents in the original eighteen (one from Stalin's pen), the Chinese Communist Party asserted its independence in the area of ideological training. Henceforth Party education would stress the realities of the Chinese revolution, and particularly problems of organization, cadre training, and concrete investigation of the Party's past and present work.[17]

During the years 1942 to 1944 substantial progress was made toward many of the rectification goals. Tens of thousands of recent Party recruits received their first extended exposure to Marxist ideology and particulary to the writings of Mao Tse-tung in an atmosphere of

[16] "Report of the Propaganda Bureau of the Central Committee on the Cheng Feng Reform Movement," Compton, *Mao's China*, pp. 3–8. The report was printed as an editorial in *CFJP*, April 7, 1942.

[17] The original eighteen documents and the four additional Soviet documents are listed in *ibid.*, pp. 6–7. Compton's translation of the rectification documents also includes those subsequently added to the study curriculum by the Central Committee, including other writings by Mao Tse-tung and Liu Shao-ch'i.

critical self-examination. The disparate elements which comprised the Party's ranks were welded into a more unified and effective organization, though the Party's heterogeneity remained a problem requiring continued attention. In addition, *cheng-feng* provided the occasion for a major re-examination of the Party's history and its present condition, leading to new directions in Communist policy. The rectification movement of 1942 brought together and developed the major principles of Chinese Communist cadre education and reform, and provided a model for all subsequent campaigns.

Out of the *cheng-feng* campaign emerged a new strategy cognizant of the shortcomings of prevailing policies, and cadres in the Party, government, and army were trained and prepared for its implementation in the border region. From this time the latent energies of the masses were to be unleashed and directed, not toward destruction of a class as in the land upheaval, but primarily toward reconstruction of the economy, reordering of social and political relationships, and the struggle against an inhospitable terrain which impeded economic progress. Development of the stagnant agrarian economy was seen as the key to the success of all other programs and ultimately to mass support and wartime victory. After five years of emphasis on united front harmony and creation of stable base area governments, the Communist Party turned to the task of revolutionizing the fabric of social and particularly economic life at the village level in Shen-Kan-Ning and in the base areas of North China.

The scope and intent of the policies implemented at the time of the *cheng-feng* movement are suggested by the major campaigns launched simultaneously by the Party and government. Here we may briefly enumerate them and observe their interrelationship before analyzing each in greater detail:

1. The campaign for crack troops and simple administration (*ching-ping chien-cheng*), 1941 to 1943, consolidated and reduced organs and personnel in the army and particularly in the government bureaucracy. In government the independent power of the bureaucracy was curbed by increasing Party controls and the prerogatives of district magistrates and other officials, who were given broad new coordinating powers. The focus of government work shifted downward from regional and county offices to the township and the village. Reductions in military and administrative personnel were designed to reduce costs for the taxpayer.

2. The first "to the village" campaign (*hsia-hsiang*, later more

widely known as *hsia-fang*), 1941 and 1942, sent many "outside" or "intellectual" cadres to serve in the countryside, providing an influx of new leadership to hundreds of isolated communities and for the first time directly involving large numbers of cadres in production. The campaign was designed to destroy barriers between outside and local cadres, between bureaucrats and village cadres, and between administration and production, while strengthening the lower levels of government.

3. The campaign for the reduction of rent and interest, 1942 to 1944, roused the peasantry in areas where there had been little or no land revolution. By guaranteeing the producer an increased share of the crop, this policy would raise productive enthusiasm and increase support for the Communist Party and its program. In the struggle against landlord economic power, new peasant leadership would emerge, and village social and political relationships would be restructured.

4. The cooperative movement, 1942 to 1944, was the heart of the Party's first major effort to reorganize the village economy. It developed and modified numerous traditional forms of mutual aid previously practised on a limited scale. Mutual aid had important implications not only for increasing agricultural production, but for the reorientation of village social and political relations.

5. The production movement of 1943 introduced a variety of new approaches to the political economy of the border region, including:

a. "Organizational economy." Labor by all cadres in the Party, government, army, and schools was designed to increase production, reduce the tax burden, stimulate new attitudes toward manual labor, and provide experience in management of the economy.

b. Labor hero campaigns provided economic and political incentives for peasant and worker producers. Labor heroes not only served as models in their local communities, they also received special training and encouragement to lead the transition to a cooperative agricultural economy.

6. The education movement of 1944 expanded the scope and modified the forms and content of education, spreading literacy and introducing new ideas to many villages for the first time.

These programs—many of them new, others pioneered in various forms in Kiangsi and later in anti-Japanese base areas—culminated in a conception of leadership in which mobilization of the masses was enshrined as the Party's fundamental approach to the problems of war, revolution, politics, and production. This was the mass line. To trace its development and assess its significance, we begin with the policy innovations of 1942.

THE MOVEMENT FOR CRACK TROOPS AND SIMPLE ADMINISTRATION

The border region's economic and financial crisis, following the tightening of Kuomintang blockade and the cutoff of central government subsidies in late 1941, precipitated the movement for crack troops and simple administration. Material difficulties—the shortage of supplies and funds to maintain the large administrative establishment—necessitated sweeping economy moves in all organs and particularly in government.

The campaign for the simplification of government produced a fundamental administrative reorganization. In its early stages, the basic goals were these:

a. To reduce the size and cost and increase the efficiency of administration, particularly by streamlining the organizational structure and reducing the number of cadres in the bureaucracy at the county and regional levels.

b. To strengthen lower echelons of government, particularly the township and district, by transferring cadres, mainly outside intellectuals, from higher bureaucratic organs. This was related to the concurrent "to the village" movement, which will be discussed below.

As the campaign proceeded, the second of these goals became predominant, and an additional aim was delineated:

c. To curb independent bureaucratic power by increasing the coordinating functions of the Party, county magistrates, and interdepartmental committees over individual branch-type (*pu-men*) bureaucratic organs.

As conceived in December, 1941, full-time cadres at all levels of the government, Party, self-defense forces, and mass organizations were to be reduced by 20 per cent, from 7,900 to 6,300.[18] At the regional level, the "more than 1,000 cadres" were to be decreased by one-third, and

---

[18] The original program is described in detail in *CFJP*, December 13, 1941. Cf. Lin Po-ch'ü, *Chien-cheng wen-t'i* (Problems in the Rectification of Government) (Yenan, 1943). These and other sources are frequently ambiguous concerning whether Party, local military, or mass organization cadres are included in personnel figures. I believe that seventy-nine hundred full-time cadres included all of these but neither Public Security nor Eighth Route Army forces defending the border region.

the 4,021 cadres serving at the subregion, county, and district levels were to be reduced by 625 (about 15 per cent) to 3,396. Limited reductions were planned in the military. Five hundred regular army men (*ching-wei tui*) were to be demobilized and sent to work in factories. One thousand militia (*tzu-wei chün*) leaders, formerly full-time cadres, retained their posts, but without salary, as they were ordered to participate in production. Finally, the 1,100 cadres in mass organizations were to be cut by almost half to 600. Those whose positions were eliminated were transferred directly to other posts, sent to school prior to reassignment, or put to work in factories or farming. Thus many former administrative cadres, such as those dispatched to schools, continued to be supported at public expense.

The initial reduction of cadres was combined with an effort to increase administrative efficiency and eliminate the "top-heavy" structure of government, whose trained personnel was overwhelmingly concentrated at higher levels in regional and district offices. Bureaucratic organization was consolidated by amalgamating departments and sending personnel from the county and regional levels to expand and fortify district and township governments. For the first time, outside cadres served extensively at lower levels. Many bureaucrats were transferred to head district and township governments. A full-time secretary (*wen-shu*), usually a student but occasionally a former bureaucrat, was dispatched to assist every township head in governing at this basic administrative level. In many instances, secretaries were assigned to district governments, and in some cases county governments, in which the level of literacy and administrative efficiency were exceptionally low. Local cadres such as township and district heads typically were illiterate peasant revolutionaries. For example, in 1942, two-thirds of the fifty-one township heads in Yen-ch'uan County were completely illiterate.[19] Consequently secretaries performed such important tasks as maintaining the flow of directives and reports to and from higher echelons, and training local cadres to perform administrative functions. Outside cadres were supposed to inject new ideas into the isolated rural communities. Moreover, they were committed in their careers to furthering the government program and were unfettered by local personal relations, an important factor when official policy provoked local resistance. This would become crucial as the focus of government work shifted to production and other tasks vitally affecting the economic and

[19] *CFJP*, June 20, 1942.

political infra-structure of the village. Reciprocally, it was believed that former bureaucrats and students would benefit from extensive contact with the masses in their new tasks.

These were the goals of the first campaign for crack troops and simple administration carried out in the border region in early 1942. No comprehensive information is available to indicate the extent to which the numerical quotas were fulfilled, but in April a second campaign was launched to carry the movement further. Throughout 1942 many more cadres were sent to work at lower echelons. In May, for instance, it was reported that 200 cadres from the regional bureaucracy were being transferred down to the district and township levels. Of these, 80 per cent were to serve in the districts and 20 per cent in the townships. By early June, at least 150 of the planned 200 had already been sent down.[20] In the course of the campaign, the most highly educated and trained cadres, those who had served in the county and regional bureaucracy, were almost invariably reassigned to strengthen lower levels of administration; a small number went to schools for further training. These men, some of whose work had been severely criticized during the rectification movement, rarely were deprived of official position. From 1942 their new jobs, although lower in the status hierarchy, nonetheless formed the major thrust in the administration of the border region as the tasks of revolutionizing rural life received highest priority. On the other hand, many local cadres were removed from district and township payrolls to return to production, and a few were sent to schools for basic education. In eight districts of Yench'uan the number of cadres was reduced by 17 to a total of 38. Among these 17 cadres, 11 resumed full-time productive work, 4 became township heads, and 2 were sent to Yenan for study.[21] By the summer of 1942 the effort to provide a secretary in each township had been completed in many counties and was continuing elsewhere.

These changes suggest the tensions engendered by transfer of cadres to lower levels. Not only were these new men "outsiders" to the local population and to the prevailing network of ties and loyalties, but by education and experience they frequently were modern in outlook and invariably possessed administrative skills and ties to higher authority. Many were contemptuous of village mores. Moreover, their arrival frequently meant that a local cadre lost his official position and even in

[20] *Ibid.,* May 20, 25, June 4, 9, 1942.
[21] *Ibid.,* June 20, 1942.

some cases was demoted from cadre status to become a farmer once again.

By the conclusion of the second campaign for crack troops and simple administration in December, 1942, many cadres and students had been sent to new posts. However, the goal of substantially reducing the number of persons on the government payroll was apparently unrealized. As a third campaign was about to be launched in early 1943, Lin Po-ch'ü reported that 8,200 cadres were serving in all levels of government and its subsidiary organs. This actually exceeded the estimated 7,900 at the beginning of the movement in December, 1941! In addition, the government supported 3,300 students at middle level schools (excluding military schools and schools for cadres' dependents). Including all dependents (but exclusive of Eighth Route Army forces), 22,500 persons were supported at public expense. Lin reiterated the call for a reduction in cadres and middle school students from 11,500 to 7,500, a slash of about one-third. At the same time he stressed the need for a continued effort to raise the quality and discipline of cadres, particularly by sending intellectual cadres to the lower levels.[22] By the completion of the campaign for crack troops and simple administration in January, 1944, the number of organs directly subsidiary to the regional government was reportedly reduced from 35 to 22; one-fourth of all bureaucratic departments at the regional level were eliminated by processes of amalgamation, and those at the subregion (*fen-ch'ü*) and county reduced from 8 or 9 to 4 or 5.[23]

The importance of the series of campaigns for administrative simplification lay neither in dramatic budget cuts nor in substantial reductions of "surplus" bureaucrats. Efforts to reduce substantially the number of cadres on the public payroll apparently proved inconclusive; no final statistics were issued. Their significance lay rather in the profound changes in the structure, composition, and conception of government. Lower level administration, particularly the township, was strengthened, and its responsiveness to directives from above increased by the presence of outside cadres, either experienced administrators or students, unfettered by local ties and committed to government policy. Many former local officials who had manifested leadership ability during the land revolution but lacked administrative experience re-

---

[22] Lin, *Chien-cheng wen-t'i*, pp. 13–19; *CFJP*, December 13, 1941.

[23] *CFJP*, February 8, 1944, contains the official summary of the results of the campaign in a report by Li Ting-ming.

turned to their villages where they frequently assumed informal leadership roles during the production drive of 1943.

VERTICAL AND DUAL RULE

In the course of the campaign for crack troops and simple administration, lines of power were redrawn to reduce the independence of bureaucratic departments of government. These changes strengthened controls over individual departments by extradepartmental officials and agencies of government, such as county magistrates and governing committees, with broad coordinating powers. They also increased the leverage of the Party with respect to government.

From the early years of the united front and relative peace after 1937, government decision making and planning were centralized in the regional bureaucracy, and administration was concentrated in its district sections. Staffed almost exclusively by outside intellectual cadres, these bureaucratic organs established powerful branch or vertical networks penetrating downward from the regional level. Prior to 1942, departments such as finance, education, reconstruction, and civil affairs, with a virtual monopoly of the expertise for stable and efficient administration, enjoyed broad autonomy in fulfilling their specialized functions. This was vertical rule. For example, educational policy was drafted in the Department of Education of the regional government, and orders for its execution were channeled directly to the education section in each district and eventually to lower level education offices or schools for implementation. In this vertical organization, there were few checks on departmental autonomy by Party or government cadres outside the department. In particular, at the district level there was little influence which either the magistrate or the Party could bring to bear on these organs, whose cadres felt primary allegiance and responsibility to departmental superiors. The system enabled bureaucratic procedures to become regularized within each department on the basis of a clear-cut chain of responsibility and command, with power concentrated at the regional level. On the other hand, this centralization of authority in regional departments made it extremely difficult to coordinate the work of the several functional departments at the county and lower levels, or to respond creatively to local variations and emergencies. In addition, as in traditional Chinese governments, resources were monopolized at the county seat and at higher levels where the administrative efficiency and controls were greatest, but with the result that most townships and villages remained remote from schools or new publicly financed industry.

These patterns of bureaucracy were modified in the campaign for crack troops and simple administration, when dual rule superseded branch or vertical rule as the dominant administrative pattern, and the leadership of the Party and of government officials with coordinating functions increased in importance.[24] The classic statement for the implementation of dual rule is contained in Mao Tse-tung's "On Methods of Leadership," a resolution written in 1943 for the Central Committee.

In assigning a task (such as prosecution of the revolutionary war, production, education, the rectification campaign, checking up work, examining cadres, propaganda, organizational or anti-espionage work, etc.) to a subordinate unit, the higher leading organization and its departments should act through the leader who has overall responsibility for the lower organization concerned, so that he can undertake the assignment with a full sense of responsibility, thereby achieving a division of duties under unified leadership (centralized authority). It is inadvisable for one department of a higher organization to have contacts only with its counterpart in lower organizations (for example, the organizational, propaganda or anti-espionage departments of a higher organization to have contacts only with the corresponding departments of lower organizations), leaving the responsible head of a lower organization (for example, the secretary, chairman, director or school principal, etc.) uninformed and unable to answer for the work assigned. It is essential that the leader of a lower organization concerned as well as the heads of its particular departments should be informed of the assigned task and held answerable for its fulfillment. Such a centralized authority, i.e., division of duties under unified leadership, permits the leader at the top to mobilize a large number of people—on occasion even the entire personnel of an organization—to carry out a particular task; in this way, shortage of workers in particular units can be remedied and a large number of people can be drawn in as active participants in a given task. This is also a form of linking up the leadership with the masses.[25]

The dynamic conception of politics outlined in this resolution conflicted directly with tendencies toward stabilization and bureaucratization. It placed a premium on the coordinating and mobilizing roles best exemplified by the Party, and suggested a campaign style of politics in which cadres and the masses alike would be mobilized to attack the most pressing problems. Narrow specialization and monopolization of power by an administrative elite were discouraged.

[24] The terms "vertical" and "dual rule" are discussed by Franz Schurmann in *Ideology and Organization in Communist China* (Berkeley and Los Angeles: University of California Press, 1966), pp. 88–89, 102, 188–210.

[25] Mao Tse-tung, *Selected Works* (New York: International Publishers, 1954), IV, 115 (hereafter *SW*). Cf. Boyd Compton's translation in *Mao's China,* p. 181.

In Shen-Kan-Ning the immediate repercussions of this approach are best observed at the county level, where the interaction between bureaucratic sections and local governments clearly reflected the shift to dual rule. From 1942 a section head was responsible not only to his superiors within the department at the regional level but also to a coordinating committee of the county government, and to the magistrate. Moreover, the chain of command was altered, and the flow of directives to county sections of the bureaucracy was rerouted. For example, the county section of the Education Department no longer received orders directly from its superiors within the department at the regional level. These orders were transmitted first to the governing committee or to the county affairs committee, headed by the magistrate, before being passed on to the educational section. Likewise directives from a section of the Education Department down to lower offices or schools as well as up to the regional department once again passed through the governing committee.

The advent of dual rule placed the county affairs committee and magistrate in a pivotal role. Directives and communications to and from higher level departments of the bureaucracy had to pass through and secure the approval of the magistrate; likewise with the flow of information to subordinate organizations. This was the first step toward making the magistrate master of all government work within his county, and toward curbing the independence of bureaucratic sections at the district level.

Several other measures were taken simultaneously. The magistrate increased his power over personnel matters. The appointment and transfer of the county political affairs secretary, bureaucratic section chiefs, and the commander of the county self-defense army remained the prerogative of the regional government, but all their subordinates were henceforth to be hired and transferred at the discretion of the magistrate.[26] The magistrate's position was strengthened by the addition of a minimum of two intellectual cadres as subordinates on his staff, serving respectively as general affairs secretary and political affairs secretary. As many magistrates were illiterate or semiliterate, this action increased their ability to deal effectively with bureaucratic

---

[26] *CFJP,* June 13, 14, July 9, 1942; Lin, *Chien-cheng wen-t'i,* pp. 2, 3, 14–16; "Draft of the Revised Shen-Kan-Ning Border Region District Government Provisional Organizational Laws," proclaimed April 25, 1943, pp. 85–88 in Shen-kan-ning pien-ch'ü ts'an-i-hui wen-hsien hui-chi, pan-kung-t'ing (ed.), *Shen-kan-ning pien-ch'ü cheng-ts'e t'iao-li hui-chi hsü-p'ien* (Policies and Statutes of the Shensi-Kansu-Ninghsia Border Region: A Supplement) (1944) (hereafter *CTHP*).

organs operating in their districts, at least to the extent that they were able to control the activities of their new secretaries.[27]

One additional important step in consolidating dual rule was the development of a system of committees with extensive power to coordinate policy at each level of administration. At the regional and subregional levels these were called political affairs conferences (*cheng-wu hui-i*), and at the county level they were known as county affairs committees (*hsien-wu wei-yüan-hui*). County affairs committees met each week under the chairmanship of the magistrate to plan and coordinate the full range of government policy. Membership included the head of each bureaucratic section, the judge, security chief, and in some cases Party and military representatives.[28]

The increased power of the county magistrate and the creation of political affairs conferences substantially reduced the independence of individual departments within the bureaucracy. Moreover, within bureaucratic departments, power which had been highly centralized at the regional level now shifted downward to the county. Once interdepartmental coordination of all work at the county level became essential, it was impossible to monopolize decision-making powers within each department at the regional level. Increasingly, important decisions were made on the spot in bureaucratic sections and interdepartmental meetings at the county level. Bureaucratic sections thus won greater autonomy vis-à-vis departmental superiors but were subject to more integration and control by the county magistrate and coordinating committees. The tasks of the official working in a county section of the bureaucracy under dual rule involved more than routine enactment of policies handed down from above; he was required to modify and adapt policy, and above all to articulate and defend it in the competitive environment of the county affairs conference. It was precisely these qualities which the Party sought to foster in small group criticism in the *cheng-feng* movement. The cadre with a broad grasp of local conditions and the ability to coordinate and unify diverse

[27] "A Summary of the Implementation of Policies of Simplification of Government in the Shen-Kan-Ning Border Region," in *CTHP*, p. 9.

[28] The work of district affairs committees is discussed in the "Provisional Organization Laws for District Affairs Committees in the Shen-Kan-Ning Border Region," passed June 30, 1942 by the Border Region Political Affairs Conference, pp. 59–62 in *K'ang-jih ken-chü-ti cheng-ts'e t'iao-li hui-chi* (Policies and Statutes of the Anti-Japanese Bases: Shensi-Kansu-Ninghsia) (1942). The powers of political affairs conferences at all levels of government are defined and their importance stressed in the "Draft Summary of Political Regulations in the Shen-Kan-Ning Border Region," pp. 72–76 in *CTHP*. Cf. Hsü Yung-ying, *A Survey of Shensi-Kansu-Ninghsia Border Region* (New York: Institute of Pacific Relations, 1945), I, 52.

policies was at a premium. These qualities were critically important for the effective functioning of the magistrate. In his expanded role he was authorized and expected to mobilize cadres from all departments as well as the masses to participate in campaigns which were designed to achieve a swift break-through in a critical problem area. This, of course, was the very antithesis of regularized bureaucratic procedure. The rising power of the magistrate was a direct function of the increased emphasis on the campaign style of politics.

The shift from vertical to dual rule also increased the power of the Party at all levels of administration, particularly at the county and below. As the independence of the bureaucracy was weakened by dual rule, there was an increased stress on Party leadership of government, particularly through the use of disciplined Party fractions. A Party fraction in any non-Party organization, such as a government agency or an army company, performed important watchdog functions of insuring the disciplined implementation of the Party's policy by its members and others within that organization. In addition, it served in a liaison capacity, informing the Party of actions planned and executed by other organizations, and keeping those organizations abreast of current Party policy. As a united "bloc within," the Party fraction enabled Party members to increase their leverage within all organizations, without (ideally) resorting to dictatorial methods of flaunting the authority of the Party to insure support for their actions in other organizations.[29] Even more than political affairs committees of government, the Party, whose members held positions among the leadership and rank-and-file in all government agencies as well as the army and mass organizations, was eminently suited for the task of coordinating diverse activities and providing over-all leadership of the government and army.

In politics and administration at the county level, the emphasis under dual rule was policy coordination, not Party usurpation of the government's routine administrative tasks or authority. The Communists continued to seek the participation in government of non-Party persons, particularly those with administrative skills. But, in concert with the district affairs committee, the Party increasingly provided coordination and leadership of all cadres and of the people in the series

---

[29] References to Party fractions in Shen-Kan-Ning are rare even in intra-Party directives. One of the most explicit is a secret document distributed by the Lung-tung subregion Party propaganda department. *Cheng-ch'uan chung ti "tang-t'uan" chiang-shou ta-kang* (Teaching Outline of "Party Fractions" in Government) (1942 [?]).

of campaigns launched during and after 1942. Before turning to those campaigns, we must consider the parallel and related changes occurring in the village politics of the border region.

THE "TO THE VILLAGE" (HSIA-HSIANG) MOVEMENT AND GOVERNMENT REORGANIZATION

As county government was restructured in accord with principles of dual rule, basic changes were occurring in the townships and villages. To understand the altered dimensions of village life after 1941, we must turn first to conditions produced by the land revolution carried out in much of the border region in 1935 and 1936. That revolution had undermined or destroyed the landlord elite, and replaced some of the most oppressive forms of "feudal exploitation" by an unprecedented degree of economic equality among the peasantry. Radical new leadership had developed primarily among poor peasant youths, who served as the backbone of the revolution during years of guerrilla activity and eventually in land redistribution. Many of these cadres continued to dominate local government and Party organization after the termination of the land revolution and the formation of a united front government in 1937. But the united front also permitted and encouraged the return of former elite elements who had fled the revolution. After 1937, in villages where Party organization was weak and in areas where land redistribution had not occurred, the landlord elite often retained or restored its grip on the economic and political life of the community. Encouraged by the Communists to cooperate, many landlords and former landlords served prominently in all levels of the government, and some even became Party members.

By 1941, both in counties which had experienced the land revolution and in the new areas which had not, local power was shared between revolutionary peasant cadres and the traditional elite. Despite land revolution and periodic political mobilization of the peasantry, the official emphasis on unity and stability after 1937 allowed economic and social life in the isolated rural villages of the border region to revert increasingly to prerevolutionary patterns. Work teams from the outside occasionally penetrated to the villages. However, their temporary presence had a minimal effect, particularly since their major functions—like those of traditional Chinese governments—were to collect taxes and recruit soldiers. No method had been devised to maintain and develop the organized strength and enthusiasm of the aroused peasantry after peace was restored, and attention shifted to

routine farming, local administration, and war preparations.[30] Under
the crisis conditions of 1941, Communist leaders came to realize their
failure effectively to break the isolation and economic stagnation of
village life. This was attributed principally to the fact that the village
economy remained virtually untouched; if tenancy had been largely
eliminated by the land revolution in many districts, "feudal" productive methods still prevailed, and the pattern of landlord oppression
(particularly where land revolution had not occurred) continued. In
the years after 1937, despite the existence of an elaborate organizational structure of locally elected township and village governments,
and a variety of mass political and military organizations and local
party units, village life had not been fundamentally altered.

The reorganization of village politics was aimed at developing more
effective leadership in terms of new production-oriented and other
socio-political goals formulated during 1942 and 1943, and at returning
expendable cadres to the economy. One of the first signs of the Communists' renewed preoccupation with village government was the "to
the village" movement. "To the village" began quietly in July, 1941,
with reports of Party, government, and army cadres as well as students
proceeding to the countryside to aid in the wheat harvest. This aspect
of the movement, the short-term use of cadres to assist during peak
production periods such as planting and harvesting, continued in subsequent years, but other more significant departures were soon incorporated under the slogan "to the village."[31] Shortly, the pragmatic and
short-run goals of using "nonproductive labor" to overcome shortages
in periods of intense economic activity gave way to a conception of
mutual benefit from the interaction of outside cadres and intellectuals
with peasants and local cadres.

This second phase of *hsia-hsiang* was inaugurated in the spring of
1942 in connection with the rectification movement. Students and
intellectuals studied in Yenan, preparatory to being sent down to the

[30] This suggests one of the significant ways in which the rear area bases differed from
Shen-Kan-Ning, particularly prior to the introduction of mass line politics in 1943. In
such areas as Chin-Ch'a-Chi (the Shansi-Chahar-Hopei Border Region), which were
repeatedly subject to enemy attack, active village militia organizations, imperative for
local defense, could also provide the nucleus for socioeconomic reorganization of village
life. These units simultaneously retained strong village ties while increasingly serving to
link individual villages with the outside world, and provided the channel for introduction
of outside cadres. The history of Shen-Kan-Ning—it alone of the Communist bases had
experienced land revolution and was exempt from Japanese attack—also helps to account
for the relatively small role played by the army and the preponderance of the Communist
Party in local politics.

[31] *CFJP*, July 3, 15, 1941. Cf. *CFJP*, June 24, 1944, March 31, 1945.

villages. The sequence was significant, for it was believed that without prior assimilation of new goals and attitudes toward the people, intellectuals were likely to remain alienated from the peasant masses, regardless of extensive contact with village life. In a number of instances the basic assignment of the intellectuals was to engage in agricultural production. However, *hsia-hsiang* neither always nor primarily involved physical labor. In the majority of cases, intellectuals sent to the village served as teachers or as cadres assisting in the tasks of the local Party and government organizations. The campaign was designed to overcome the mutual ignorance and prejudice of intellectuals and peasants through sharing and observing a common experience, and to overcome psychological barriers separating mental and manual labor. Insights gathered by painters and writers in the countryside would subsequently appear in their art, an art to be devoted to the Party's cause of achieving victory in the resistance war and improving and modernizing rural life. As K'ai Feng, head of the Propaganda Department of the Central Committee, remarked in a speech to Party intellectuals, the purpose of *hsia-hsiang* is that "intellectuals truly serve the workers, peasants, and soldiers, reflect their livelihood and work. . . ."[32]

The skills of intellectuals would be utilized, but in the context of village life rather than in the regional or county capitals where their bureaucratic offices and schools were concentrated. One report relates how seven intellectuals from Yenan were dispatched to Fu-hsien where they subsequently served as directors of the subdistrict propaganda departments of the Party. Another typical example is that of 178 middle school students who left Yenan to establish and teach winter schools for the peasants in remote villages.[33]

Hsia-hsiang of the intellectuals was related to the movement for crack troops and simple administration carried out simultaneously in 1942. Not only artists, writers, and students but also cadres from the upper strata of the regional and district bureaucracy were dispatched

[32] *Ibid.,* March 28, 1943.

[33] *Ibid.,* April 15, October 7, 24, 1942. Niijima Junryō, *Gendai chūgoku no kakumei ninshiki. Chūsō ronsō e no sekkin* (Modern China's Revolutionary Perception) (Tokyo: Ochanomizu Shobō, 1964), pp. 123–43, provides the fullest and most perceptive account of the goals and achievements of the intellectuals' *hsia-hsiang* experience in Shen-Kan-Ning. An excellent discussion of the Communist conception of "to the village," emphasizing its role in economic development in the years after 1949, is Rensselaer W. Lee, III, "The *Hsia Fang* System: Marxism and Modernization," *China Quarterly,* No. 28 (October–December, 1966), pp. 40–62. A. Doak Barnett and Ezra Vogel present a more critical view of *hsia-fang* as practiced in recent years. See *Cadres, Bureaucracy, and Political Power in Communist China* (New York: Columbia University Press, 1967), pp. 51, 60–61, 174–76.

to strengthen politics and administration below. In the "to the village" movement new positions, such as township secretaries, as well as those of township and district heads of government were filled by outside cadres. The transfer of trained cadres to lower levels of administration reduced the isolation of the villages by linking local governments more effectively with higher levels through written budgets and reports, and introduced new conceptions of leadership, particularly those developed and learned during the *cheng-feng* movement. In addition, they increased the literacy of the local cadres and students and taught them administrative skills, training them for an independent and expanded leadership role.[34]

What did *hsia-hsiang* mean to the cadres and students sent down to spearhead the production movement, overcome "feudal remnants" of village life, and in the process educate themselves? There can be no question that for some, particularly older and more experienced cadres securely settled in their bureaucratic routines, the new tasks represented a jarring form of punishment or demotion in status as well as a blow to effective administration. But for the youthful majority, especially the students, the experience was apparently an exhilarating and moving one which must be perceived in terms of war-induced patriotism and a faith in the compelling ideology of national salvation and public service. During the *cheng-feng* movement, cadres and students learned that the crucial problems facing China and specifically the border region could not be resolved in bureaucratic offices or in their schools, but only by going to the villages, to the "production front," to arouse and organize the peasant masses. The outpouring of cadres and students from Yenan was by and large the exciting odyssey of young men and women off to conquer new worlds of experience, and in the process to save their country. The idealism and crusading spirit of wartime Chinese youth was directed in *hsia-hsiang* not only to bringing the message of civilization (and revolution) to a backward people, but to sharing in and learning from the experience of the masses as well.

The spirit of *hsia-hsiang* and some of the goals as seen by its youthful participants strikingly resemble those of the United States Peace Corps in its earliest and most idealistic years. In both cases youth, drawn primarily from the privileged and highly educated classes, grasped not only a new perception of urgent problems, but a feeling that they might *now* contribute meaningfully to their resolu-

[34] Lin, *Chien-cheng wen-t'i,* p. 17; *CFJP,* April 23, May 20, June 9, 20, 1942.

tion. Involved was more of a vision of progress than a detailed plan of the concrete steps to be taken; indeed, both were characterized by the "creative disorder" of an experimental situation. The participants sensed the necessity of reaching out directly to help (and, in the process, to learn from) the poor and oppressed; they were conscious of the futility of previous official or organized attempts by elders and bureaucrats to achieve these goals. There was a sense of participation in an historic mission, a feeling that nothing quite like this had ever before been attempted. Part of the exhilaration of the experience lay precisely in the spartan life, in shared hardship. Both the Peace Corps and the "to the village" movements established officially sanctioned channels for the rebellious energies of youth, and a means for expressing youth's consciousness that poverty and oppression might and must be eliminated. However, unlike the Peace Corps, whose volunteers went abroad as representatives of an advanced power, the problems to which *hsia-hsiang* was directed were immediately at hand in the poverty-stricken villages of the border region.[35]

Enthusiasm in itself could not insure success. Friction and difficulties arose as students and cadres, the elite of the Party, attempted simultaneously to reform and share in village life. The position of outsiders could be a tenuous one. In many cases there was intense resistance to change. Often *hsia-hsiang* precipitated power struggles in villages whose leadership felt threatened by cadres who remained aloof from local ties and loyalties and who, in some instances, replaced local cadres in positions of authority. Party leaders found it necessary constantly to reiterate that outsiders came to aid, not to usurp, the position of local cadres, that the secretary to the township head was an assistant, rather than the boss, of local government, and so on.[36] Finally, a clash of ideas was inevitable, as these cadres—trained and educated outside the border region or in Yenan—brought a vision of modern society which conflicted with many deep-rooted village values. We shall attempt to assess the degree of success and failure of the "to the village" movement in terms of the concrete programs of reform developed during the years 1942 to 1944, in which outside cadres played so important a role.

[35] For a vivid if occasionally stereotyped description of the excitement of her first "to the village" experience by a young urban intellectual who served near Yenan shortly after the Great Leap Forward, see Jan Myrdal, *Report from a Chinese Village* (New York: Pantheon, 1965), pp. 321–28.

[36] See, for example, the editorial in *CFJP*, July 9, 1942.

THE CAMPAIGN FOR THE REDUCTION OF RENT

The Communist Party's approach to the peasantry during the Kiangsi period was based on land revolution. In 1937, when the united front against Japan officially replaced class conflict as the focus of Party policy in the Shen-Kan-Ning Border Region, land redistribution yielded to the slogan of reduction of rent and interest. Included among "The Ten Great Policies" proclaiming the Communist's wartime program on August 15, 1937, was the succinct statement, "Reduce rent and interest rates."[37]

However, in Shen-Kan-Ning, in the period immediately after 1937 no effort was made to implement reduction of rent. Beyond the strong official commitment to preserve the revolutionary gains of land distribution and to guarantee private ownership of land, it might almost be said that from 1937 to 1940 there was no land policy. Since landlordism was assumed to have been eliminated in most of the area under Communist control, and united front policies were being stressed, problems of land tenure were rarely mentioned. Neither in the laws and documents of the first regional council (1939) nor in the extensive Party and government publications of this period was rent reduction an issue.

However, in 1939 and 1940, following the initial stages of the breakdown of the united front, fighting between Communists and Kuomintang forces brought substantial territories of Sui-te and Lung-tung subregions under the effective control of the regional government. In most of these areas, land redistribution had not occurred; in some, where it had taken place in 1935 and 1936, the revolution was subsequently reversed following recovery by the Kuomintang. In short, particularly in Sui-te, landlord power was entrenched in 1940, at the time of its incorporation in the border region. Moreover, the Kuomintang blockade after 1939 and the general decline of the united front rendered the Communists less hesitant to introduce such policies as the reduction of rent, which generated friction between classes.

Although occasional references to rent reduction appear in 1941 documents of the border region, the Party was not yet prepared to make the issue the focus of a mass campaign. However, on January 28,

---

[37] "The Ten Great Policies of the Chinese Communist Party for Anti-Japanese Resistance and National Salvation" is translated in Conrad Brandt *et al.* (ed.), *A Documentary History of Chinese Communism* (Cambridge: Harvard University Press, 1959), pp. 242–45.

1942, three days prior to the start of the *cheng-feng* campaign, the Politburo issued the Party's first major statement on land policy since the outbreak of the War of Resistance. Written by Mao Tse-tung, "The Decision of the Central Committee on Land Policy in the Anti-Japanese Base Areas" established basic guidelines which remained in effect in all Communist-led areas until 1946.[38]

These principles, reappraising the relationship between the united front and rural revolution, provided the basis both for the campaign for the reduction of rent and for the new political economy which was to develop subsequently in Shen-Kan-Ning and other Communist bases. The land resolution of January, 1942, did not explicitly contravene earlier Party formulations of the wartime period concerning the united front or the land question. However, it departed from previous official statements in two respects. First, it introduced the theme of the "production battle," placing it virtually on a par with the War of Resistance against Japan. The battle for production would shortly become the preoccupation of Party and government in Shen-Kan-Ning; from 1942 their major task was defined as increasing production, particularly in agriculture. Second, the Party, after five years of consistent homage to the ideal of *national* unity, tentatively reintroduced the *class* rhetoric of landlord "feudal exploitation," and re-emphasized its primary commitment to the oppressed peasantry. Although the guidelines stressed that the Party "should not take a one-sided stand either for the landlord or for the peasant," it marked the onset of a more militant phase of Communist politics designed to break the social and economic grip of the landlords through organized peasant power, and to increase Communist independence within the united front against Japan.

The January, 1942, "Decision on Land Policy" has frequently been cited to illustrate the Communists' moderate wartime land policy in contrast both to the land revolution of the Kiangsi period and its policy after the total collapse of the united front in 1946.[39] However, in the context of evolving wartime policy it should be viewed as a signal that initiated mass campaigns to reduce rent and challenge landlord su-

[38] The document is attributed to Mao in Political and Economic Research Office of Hupeh University (ed.), *Chung-kuo chin-tai kuo-min ching-chi shih chiang-i* (Lectures on China's Modern National Economic History) (Peking: Kao-teng chiao-yü ch'u-pan-she, 1958), p. 460. The text is translated in Brandt *et al.* (ed.), *Documentary History*, pp. 276–85.

[39] Cf. Brandt *et al.* (ed.), *Documentary History*, pp. 275–76; Chao Kuo-chün, *Agrarian Policy of the Chinese Communist Party* (New York: Asia Publishing House, 1960), pp. 38–44.

premacy, and in this sense it was a step toward a more radical class position.

The effort to link land revolution, in its limited form as rent reduction, with the drive to increase production suggests new concerns and greater sophistication in the Party's approach to the peasantry and the economy. Land revolution during the Kiangsi period held out a vision of prosperity and equality to stimulate the peasant masses to radical action. However, a frequent by-product of land upheaval was severe economic disruption resulting from war devastation, commercial expropriation, fear of further confiscations, and uncertainty on the part of peasants and merchants concerning the new economic ground rules. In 1942 the Communists in Shen-Kan-Ning, facing an economic crisis, devised a program to combine limited rural revolution with economic reorganization and modernization of rural life. By then it had become possible to exert a degree of control over peasant revolution that would previously have been unattainable. Not only had Party and government organizations been consolidated, particularly during the *cheng-feng* movement, but *hsia-hsiang* enabled hundreds of outside cadres to play an active role at the grass-roots level.

Extensive land investigations in the spring and summer of 1942 led to a drive for the reduction of rent in approximately ten districts, most of them in the Sui-te or Lung-tung subregions. The explicit goals of the campaign were moderate: the reduction of rent by 25 per cent and a rent ceiling set at 37.5 per cent of the crop. As in a number of their wartime programs, the Communists deliberately adopted legislation which had remained dormant on the books of the national government. "I want to remind you," Mao Tse-tung told a visiting foreign correspondent in 1944, "that in 1930 the Kuomintang government in Nanking issued an agrarian law restricting land rents to 37.5 per cent of the tenant's main crops while no rent was to be paid on secondary crops. But the Kuomintang has proved unable and unwilling to carry it out in practice."[40]

The 1942 campaign for reduction of rent was launched on a note of class cooperation. A considerable effort was made in the early stages to obtain the voluntary support of landlords on the basis of aiding the war effort. Statements urging cooperation in the reduction of rent by prominent gentry such as An Wen-ch'in, a wealthy Sui-te landlord and

[40] Gunther Stein, *The Challenge of Red China* (New York: McGraw-Hill, 1945), p. 113.

vice-president of the regional council, were widely publicized.[41] However, pressures on the landlords soon increased. Recalcitrant landlords, including two who headed subdistrict governments in Mi-chih, were prosecuted and punished for violations of the rent reduction laws, and their cases widely publicized.[42]

Increasingly in the latter part of 1942, as the campaign was intensified, its focus became mobilization of peasant associations and other organizations to demand and enforce rent reduction. After four years in which the emphasis was on stability and unity, peasant activists were encouraged to rouse the masses; if their goals and means were more limited (there was, for instance, virtually no physical violence reported), the excitement and promise of a new order based on equality were reminiscent of the earlier land revolution. Through group meetings peasant fears were allayed, and a militant spirit stirred. A crucial step was taken when peasant associations and local governments firmly guaranteed tenant rights and enjoined landlords from arbitrarily repossessing land.

Peasant fears were well grounded. Landlords of the Ma clan, the most powerful in northern Shensi, had previously evicted a number of tenants who pressed claims for reduction of rent. In 1940, Ma Jui-t'ang's tenants demanded that rent be lowered to 30 per cent, but threats of eviction eventually led them to pay 50 per cent. In campaigns conducted during 1942, and again in 1943 and 1944, however, more militant and effective peasant organizations produced significant victories in the struggle over rent. In 1943 Ma Wei-hsin was confronted en masse by his tenant families vociferously demanding reduction in rent, and agreement was reached. Nonetheless, the fact that the campaign against the Ma landlords and others had to be repeated in some districts both in 1943 and in 1944 suggests the complexity of fully resolving the problem without eliminating tenancy entirely. Many tenants who vigorously and outspokenly supported the peasant associations secretly made supplementary payments of rent. Such abuses were exceedingly difficult to remedy while awe of landlord power lingered.[43]

The difficulties of enforcing reduced rentals continued to plague peasant organizers as long as the landlords and fear of them remained.

---

[41] *CFJP*, November 9, 1942.

[42] *Ibid.*, November 28, December 18, 23, 27, 1942.

[43] *Ibid.*, October 30, 1943, December 20, 1944; Yenan nung-ts'un tiao-ch'a-t'uan, *Mi-chih hsien yang-chia-k'ou tiao-ch'a* (Investigation of Yang-chia-k'ou in Michih District) (Peking: San-lien shu-tien, 1957), p. 86.

The psychological impact of an agreement to reduce rent was obviously not comparable to the complete humiliation, flight, or killing of landlords and the attempt to achieve total destruction of the system of tenancy, which had earlier occurred in the land revolution. Nonetheless, successive annual campaigns after 1942 gradually eroded landlord power, and without the disruptive side effects which had accompanied violent land revolution. In addition, rent reduction contributed to easing the economic and psychological burdens of tenancy, and to developing organization among the peasantry. The peasant associations formed in connection with the movement for rent reduction subsequently played a new role in attempts to organize rural economic life through the production drive and cooperative movement launched in 1943.

The Cooperative Movement

The essential decision reached during the *cheng-feng* movement was to embark on the fundamental restructuring of life—in all its social, economic, political, and military configurations—at the village level. The core of the program was a new approach to the central problem of rural life: agricultural production. Previous Communist attempts to alter radically village life had involved violent land upheaval and attack on the local elite but had left unaffected the system of individual small-scale farming based on the family unit.

In 1942 the Communists determined once again to assault the problems of rural isolation, poverty, and oppression in the border region. The formation of mutual-aid teams as the basic units for agricultural production was to revolutionize the rural economy; mutual-aid teams also provided the nucleus for new forms of social and political life. This program was grounded in the belief that, in the absence of outside financial or technical resources, a "production war" offered the only resolution of the economic crisis of a desperately poor area facing economic stagnation and blockade-induced strangulation. Land revolution and reduction of rent were perceived as the initial campaigns, but in themselves incapable of fully mobilizing popular forces for the final victory. As Mao Tse-tung pointed out in an address of October, 1943,

In the past, feudal exploitive relations restricted the border region's productive power and prevented its development. Half of the region, through land revolution, has destroyed these feudal bonds, and half, through reduction of rent and interest, has weakened the feudal bonds. Taken together, the great majority of feudal relations in the border region have been destroyed. This is the first revolution.

However, if we cannot change the methods of production from individual to collective labor, then productive power still cannot develop. For this reason, it is essential to create labor mutual-aid organization on the basis of the individual economy (do not destroy the individual private base), that is the peasants' agricultural production cooperatives. Only thus can productive power be greatly raised.[44]

Communist concern with the economy and efforts to organize it did not begin with the cooperative movement of 1943. Various forms of cooperative enterprise, particularly consumer and transportation cooperatives, had been introduced in the Kiangsi Soviet. Within weeks of the arrival of the first wave of troops after the Long March, cooperatives of a similar kind were introduced in northern Shensi. However, the cooperatives developed prior to 1943 were organized almost entirely from above by Party and government officials at the district and township levels, and were (correctly) viewed by the peasants as agencies of government. With a few exceptions, these first cooperatives had only a peripheral effect on the economic life of the region and certainly did not affect agricultural production, being concerned primarily with commercial transactions. By 1940 the Communists recognized the failure of the movement as it had developed to that time, and therefore abolished virtually all existing cooperative organizations in the border region, with the exception of a small number of successful transport and consumer cooperatives.[45]

Despite the long history of cooperative experiments beginning in Kiangsi and continuing in Shen-Kan-Ning, in the years 1937 to 1942 the available Party literature contains virtually no discussion of applying cooperative methods to the long-term resolution of problems of agricultural production. However, from early 1943, organization of agricultural mutual-aid teams on an unprecedented scale throughout the border region became the heart of Communist strategy in the production campaign.

Two basic types of mutual aid (and dozens of variations) had long been practised by the peasants of northern Shensi. In *pien-kung* (labor exchange) a small number of families, usually two or three, exchanged labor and sometimes draft animals during periods of peak agricultural activity, such as planting and harvesting. Because absolute trust was

---

[44] Mao Tse-tung, "Lun ho-tso-she" (On Cooperatives), in *Mao Tse-tung hsüan-chi* (Selected Works of Mao Tse-tung) (Chin-ch'a-chi: Hsin-hua shu-tien, 1944), V, 207 (hereafter *HC*).

[45] *CFJP*, February 10, 1944. Mao Tse-tung, "Ching-chi wen-t'i yü ts'ai-cheng wen-t'i" (Economic and Financial Problems), *HC*, V, 56.

essential, *pien-kung* was traditionally based on long-standing personal relationships and in many cases limited to kinship groups. In the *cha-kung* (labor gang) form of collective labor, a group of workers, often ten or more, hired out as a team. These were actually work gangs, usually operating locally in the service of a patron (*kung-chu*), who was invariably a rich peasant or landlord. *Cha-kung* teams were organized and led by a boss (*kung-t'ou*), who acted as intermediary with the patron or other landlords who employed the team. *Cha-kung* was highly organized and disciplined but contained obvious elements of exploitation in the roles of the boss and patron.[46]

In launching the cooperative movement in the border region, the Party committed itself to the most formidable organizational hurdle it had yet undertaken. To be sure, in the land revolution the individual risks had been far greater, but the rewards of victory were obvious and the Party's millennial appeal was a familiar one to the poverty-stricken peasantry. In 1943 Party cadres returned once again to the villages of the border region, this time to persuade the peasantry that a fundamental reorganization of the agrarian economy along new and unfamiliar lines held the key to prosperity. The Communists were keenly aware that the initial stimulus for mutal aid would have to come from outside the village, from Party and government cadres sent down to educate and organize. But the long-range success of the cooperative movement was predicated on the development of local peasant leadership committed to its development. And in the final analysis, unless mutual aid shortly produced visible returns in terms of increased production, no amount of adept leadership could overcome peasant skepticism and resistance. As the cooperative movement developed in 1943, official literature reveals a keen awareness of these problems.

> But there we must take heed: labor mutual-aid organization must be grounded on a basis of voluntarism of the masses, in order to prevent formalisms, in whatever way they may arise, such as forcibly organize them into *pien-kung* or *cha-kung* brigades, make up name lists thinking that thus "all will turn out well," then not only will production efficiency and work morale not rise, but on the contrary will be lowered.

[46] A full description of traditional forms of *pien-kung* and *cha-kung* is given in the report of the Northwest Bureau on "Various Old Forms of Agricultural Mutual-Aid in the Villages of the Shen-Kan-Ning Border Region," pp. 3–14 in Shih Ching-t'ang (ed.), *Chung-kuo nung-yeh ho-tso-hua yün-tung shih-liao* (Materials on the Agricultural Cooperativization Movement in China) (Peking: San-lien shu-tien, 1957) (hereafter *HTHSL*). Cf. Ajiya Keizai Kenkyūjo, *Chūgoku kyōsantō no nōgyō shudanka seisaku* (Chinese Communist Agricultural Collectivization Policy) (Tokyo: Ajiya Keizai Kenkyūjo, 1961), pp. 5–25.

Moreover, in organizing labor mutual-aid we must remember that it is something active and concrete; we must absolutely give heed to concrete conditions in the areas concerned and not regard them as uniform. Thus if we today strive to expand one kind of mutual-aid labor organization among the people, the *pien-kung* brigades organized must not be too large. Neither the township nor the administrative village (*hsing-cheng ts'un*) must be taken as production units. Because if organization is too large, it can waste a great deal of labor power and a lot of time. It is best to take the natural village as a unit. . . .

In regard to leadership of mutual-aid in labor, one must proceed through the masses and select and promote as leaders individuals who are respected by the masses, positive in production and capable.[47]

The basic principles—flexibility in adapting to local variations, limiting the size of productive units, and selection of the village or subdivision of it rather than any artificial administrative unit as the organizational basis for mutual aid—indicate a sensitivity to the problem of winning genuine mass support. Large units—particularly multivillage units—for mutual aid would have compounded production problems, greatly increased the administrative burden, and above all involved the peasant in alien relationships far beyond the scope of his experience.

The drive to make mutual aid the basis for agricultural production was launched prior to spring planting in 1943. Official reports estimate that 15 per cent of the border region's full-time labor power of 300,000 people was organized into mutual-aid teams at that time. During the summer months 25 to 40 per cent, or more than 75,000 people, participated in mutual-aid teams. Reports for 1944 claimed 50 to 75 per cent participation in at least some mutual-aid activity, compared to 28 to 45 per cent the following year when the campaign entered a period of retrenchment and consolidation. In the early stages, many mutual-aid teams existed in name only, as overzealous cadres reported the formation of teams which never actually functioned. One investigation revealed that of 6,794 persons officially enrolled in *pien-kung* teams for spring planting in Ch'ü-tzu County in 1943, only 2,700 actually participated.[48] Although statistics remain problematical, during the years 1943 to 1945, for tens of thousands of peasant proprietors throughout the border region, agricultural production was fundamentally restructured along cooperative lines.

We cannot explore fully the complex reorganization of production on

[47] "Let's Organize the Labor Force," Schurmann, *Ideology and Organization in Communist China,* pp. 421–22. Minor changes have been made in orthography and terminology.

[48] *HTHSL,* p. 244. Statistics on participation in mutual aid are given in *CFJP,* April 24, 1944, and December 21, 1945, *HTHSL,* pp. 211, 216.

the basis of mutual aid, involving experimentation with various improvised and modified old forms of cooperative and collective labor, leadership techniques, and economic and ideological incentives. We shall instead focus on two central problems, analyzing contradictory tendencies within the movement and how the Communists ultimately dealt with them: first, the issue of voluntarism and independence from government control, of pressures from above as opposed to leadership generated within the village; second, the conflicting goals of the cooperatives, which were designed to ensure member profits, increase overall production, and provide services to the community or government.

The issues of discipline and organization versus spontaneous labor enthusiasm were embedded in the very virtues and limitations of the traditional forms upon which the new mutual aid would be based: thus *cha-kung* was valued for the former and *pien-kung* for the latter. The modified forms of *pien-kung* and *cha-kung* which the Communists ultimately favored suggest that compromises between a predisposition for maximum collectivization and the necessity for individual land ownership were necessary to form a practical basis for increasing production. Although *pien-kung* groups involving seventy-five or more persons or even whole villages were tried, optimum results were attained with about ten workers. An effort was made to overcome the lack of organization characteristic of former *pien-kung* groups by insisting on obedience to an elected leader, and by expanding them beyond the narrow limits of friends and relatives, particularly to include poor peasants. *Pien-kung* groups were encouraged to operate on a long-term basis throughout the production cycle rather than disbanding after the planting or harvesting season.

Cha-kung was frequently used to open new lands. Efforts were made to eliminate the oppression inherent in the system of bosses and patrons. Rather than work for a rich peasant, the new *cha-kung* teams often labored for themselves by dividing the land which they had collectively opened. In addition, loans from cooperatives or the government sometimes enabled the poor to hire *cha-kung* teams—prerogatives formerly limited to the wealthy.[49]

A crucial problem for the cooperative movement lay in establishing criteria for income distribution. The issue centered on ambivalent Communist attitudes toward the rich peasants. On the one hand rich peasants with plentiful lands and draft animals were valued for their contributions in material resources and skills, but there remained the

[49] *HTHSL*, pp. 25, 84, 217–69.

fear of rich peasant domination at the expense of the poor. By 1943, it was determined that rich peasants would be encouraged to participate in mutual-aid teams, and that the success of the movement required the preservation of private ownership rights.

The mutual-aid teams represented a new Communist approach to the peasant and the village with the creation of organizations embedded in the production activities within the village. Mutual-aid teams were not organs of the state, though they received official encouragement. In the large numbers of villages where mutual aid successfully took root, it not only led to a basic restructuring of economic patterns and increased possibilities for production gains, it also created opportunities for social and political change within villages long isolated from modernizing and reform currents. Mutual aid was a key element in the 1943 drive to overcome peasant particularism and in the process to modernize and bring prosperity to the border area.

THE 1943 PRODUCTION MOVEMENT

The year 1943 marked a shift in Communist policy in the border region from political and military to economic preoccupations. The new goal toward which a series of campaigns was launched was the creation of a self-sufficient economy and a more prosperous peasantry. This was the production war. The mutual-aid movement was the heart of that struggle, and it was reinforced by a number of innovations introduced on a large scale for the first time in 1943. The most important of these were the development of "organizational production," and new material and ideological incentives centering on the movement for emulation of labor heroes.

From 1943 all organizations became deeply engaged in production and played an increasingly significant role both in agriculture and in the primitive industrial and commercial sectors of the economy. This use of troops and civilian cadres was not a new one. In 1936 Edgar Snow reported on a system of "Saturday brigades" in which "every Soviet official, Red partisan, Red guard, women's organization, and any Red Army detachment that happened to be nearby, were mobilized to work at least one day a week at farming tasks."[50] However, the system of "Saturday brigades" soon fell into disuse; at least no more is heard of it. Before long, though, selected army units became deeply involved in agricultural production.

Mao Tse-tung's description of these earliest experiments vividly

[50] Edgar Snow, *Red Star over China* (New York: Grove Press, 1961), p. 241.

reveals how an *ad hoc* emergency measure eventually led to a fundamental departure in the Party's conception of production and leadership. In Kiangsi, Mao related, the military had taken no part in
production because grain had been plentiful. In 1938 in northern
Shensi, army units first experimented with production of grain, caring
for animals, and making their own shoes. When the Communists
launched the first region-wide production campaign to counter the
Kuomintang blockade in 1939, they seem suddenly to have become
aware of the immense but as yet "unproductive" reservoir of labor in
the army and other organizations. Why should these able-bodied men
not support themselves in addition to performing their duties as soldiers, Party and government cadres, or students? Thus began the effort
by the military to engage in and direct productive enterprises.[51] To the
goal of improving the livelihood of its members was added a realization
that its burden on the strained financial resources of government and
the hard-pressed peasantry could be correspondingly lightened. But
prior to 1942, although increasing in scope, organizational production
was still far from universal. Its impact on the agrarian economy
remained marginal. Out of the economic and financial crisis of 1941
and the *cheng-feng* movement, however, came the firm commitment to
achieve economic self-sufficiency in the border region.

In the 1943 production drive an attempt was made to realize the full
potential of the organizational sector of the economy. Henceforth *all*
cadres participated extensively in productive labor and management as
an integral part of the new role of the cadre in political *and* economic
activity, as leader *and* participant.

We may briefly examine the production process which developed
under the auspices of the military, both as representative and as the
leading sector of the organizational economy. By 1943 all military
units were extensively engaged in production, according precedence to
agriculture but operating and managing commercial and small-scale
industrial enterprises as well. Indeed, by that time, and increasingly in
1944, military budgets were predicated upon reduced government subsidy, assuming that the units had achieved partial self-sufficiency. The
outstanding example was Wang Chen's model 359th Brigade, which
since 1938 had been the leader in military production at Nan-ni-wan, a
mountainous area bordering on the counties of Yenan, Yen-ch'ang, and
I-ch'uan. The brigade submitted a 1943 budget in which its own

---

[51] "Economic and Financial Problems," *HC*, V, 93–98.

production provided 82 per cent of the required revenue.[52] Mao's 1943 injunction to all troop units to achieve 80 per cent self-sufficiency was never fulfilled, but the military succeeded both in supplying an increasing share of its own needs (perhaps one-third to one-half by 1944) and in spurring the economy of the entire region.[53] In January, 1945, Mao Tse-tung told a conference of labor heroes that the 1944 budget for troops and all public agencies was the equivalent of 260,000 piculs of millet. Of this total, 160,000 was supplied by the people in taxes and the remainder, approximately 40 per cent, was produced by the units and agencies themselves.[54]

The earliest productive efforts of the 359th Brigade at Nan-ni-wan were explicitly modeled on the *t'un-t'ien* or "camp field" system of frontier military colonies, which originated and developed two millennia earlier during the Han and Six dynasties periods. Sent to one of the poorest and most sparsely inhabited wasteland areas of the border region, which had been devastated in the Muslim Rebellion almost a century earlier, the 359th Brigade was given title to a large tract of barren, uncultivated terrain to open and farm.

Here is Commander Wang Chen's description of the initial endeavors of his troops to achieve self-sufficiency:

When I led my troops here to start our first army-production project four years ago, there were no caves or houses for us to live in, there was no food to buy, there were no tools, and no farmers whom we could ask to work for us.

The Border Region as a whole was so poor at that time that we could not bring enough food and scarcely any implements. We received little money from the government in Yenan. Right from the beginning we had to provide for ourselves almost everything we needed. . . . To have something to exchange for the goods we needed most urgently we cut hard pines, which the people in the adjoining areas like for coffins, and sold them to the villagers. . . .

Our tool problem was solved at last when one of my soldiers, young Company Commander Liu, discovered a big, old iron bell on the top of a hill in a long-abandoned temple. It was too heavy to bring down and I don't know how it ever got up there. Liu dug a big hole underneath and smelted it on the spot, and we found some blacksmiths who were willing to teach our men how to make tools from the two thousand pounds of iron we got from the bell and from scrap we collected in the distant villages.[55]

Such feats were the stuff of which legend was made. The exploits of Wang Chen and other heroic production warriors were embellished and

[52] *Ibid.*, p. 123.
[53] *Ibid.*, pp. 155–56.
[54] Mao, "We Must Learn to do Economic Work," *SW*, IV, 231–32.
[55] Stein, *Challenge of Red China*, pp. 67–68. A full report on the early productive efforts of the 359th Brigade is in "Economic and Financial Problems," *HC*, V, 123–44.

told over and over again in the form of stories, songs, and dances, and above all plays, which dramatized the fact that soldiers throughout the border region were deeply immersed in the production struggle. Wang Chen's description suggests two of the major themes of the production campaign in the military. First, the theme of self-reliance and self-sufficiency, of conquering nature with little more to work with than the labor of one's hands. The 359th Brigade was sent out with no tools, virtually without funds, and with no "experts" on economic development. It had no choice but to rely on its own manpower resources and available peasant help. Its success was also related to a second theme: that of ingenuity, of discovering and devising new techniques requiring little or no capital to meet the needs of production. Melting down the iron bell was such a feat. By 1944 Nan-ni-wan had long been a showpiece for visitors to the border region and the model for military production which had become an integral feature of life in all army units.

Industrial Development

In agriculture, organizational production played a significant but subordinate role, overshadowed by the private sector. However, in industry and to a lesser extent commerce, organizational and government-financed production was a dominant factor in initial efforts to achieve development and self-sufficiency. Prior to the creation of a Communist base, there had been virtually no industry or handicrafts, and little commercial development, in the border area. The region's primitive economy had depended on the import of yarn and cloth, in return for which salt was the major export. After the arrival of Communist forces at the end of the Long March, such items as printing presses, paper, military supplies, and agricultural implements were required. At the height of the united front nearly all were imported. However, from 1939, the blockade forced the leadership to turn inward to improvise the production of these necessities. Lacking a tradition of industry and with few people available with technical and entrepreneurial skills, the Communists naturally relied on officially sponsored and managed industry. Deep-seated suspicion of the bourgeoisie and the necessity to control strategic resources in wartime reinforced this decision.

The pattern of textile development in the border region is illustrative of the basic innovations of 1943. In that year the Communists extensively applied two principles which were to characterize their distinctive approach to economic development. These were "centralized leadership and dispersed management" (*chi-chung ling-tao, fen-san ching-ying*) and absorption of unutilized or under-utilized persons into the labor force. Centralized leadership and dispersed management, meaning unified planning and decentralized production, represented an effort to "resolve the contradiction between production and distribution." In an area of primitive communications and widely scattered population, the concentration of industrial production in a few centers necessitated heavy transportation costs both for raw materials and distribution of the finished product. Specifically in the case of cloth, after 1941 cotton was grown in widely scattered parts of the border area and cloth woven and sold nearby. In 1943 the Communists abandoned a policy of industrial centralization in order to take advantage of reduced transportation costs.[56]

The development of household production was an integral part of the drive for decentralization. In 1942, Communist planners became acutely aware of problems created by a labor shortage (partially attributable to the high percentage of able-bodied men serving in the army) in attempting to develop the economy of the border region. Their solution was to mobilize all available nonproducers. We have already noted the introduction of the army, as well as Party and government cadres and students, to extensive productive activity. In the case of the textile industry, the Communists built on the remnants of a tradition of women's home weaving. As with mutual-aid teams, their effort was to expand from a traditional base, utilizing available native expertise to develop the textile industry. During 1943 and subsequently, thousands of peasant women were successfully mobilized for part-time weaving on simple home looms.

There were two additional factors in the decision to decentralize industry. One of these was the tactical consideration that dispersed industry was less vulnerable to enemy attack. The other, which will be discussed below, was the desire to spread new ideas, both economic and political, throughout the border region in an effort to break down stubborn traditional values which were viewed as impeding development. Bringing industry to the villages, even in the form of household production, was viewed as an important step in this direction. This was

[56] "Economic and Financial Problems," *HC*, V, 107–8 analyzes and defends the theory of "centralized leadership and dispersed management."

the economic corollary of "to the village" and the movement to strengthen local government.

The textile industry exemplifies the basic patterns of industrial development during the War of Resistance. With little available capital and technical skill, the industrial drive was pushed initially through organs with the most extensive administrative skills—the government and army. Eventually, in 1943 and after, rapid expansion was coupled with decentralization, and women were incorporated on a large scale through home industry.

Certain other important facets of the border region's industrial development are best revealed in the primitive efforts to produce iron and to fashion arms and munitions. No iron had ever before been produced in the area, the small quantities required being imported. However, in 1941, using iron ore and coal mined in the border region, the first crude pig iron was smelted. Lacking experienced technicians and modern equipment, the Communists improvised and were eventually able to produce desperately needed iron for weapons and tools.[57] Particularly after 1943, there was frenetic experimentation on the basis of the primitive human and natural resources available, and a determined effort to crack the powerful psychological barrier of peasant fatalism. Crude iron produced in this context was important not only because it provided the best available raw material for certain weapons and implements, but because it symbolized man's conquest of nature and developed a new sense of the possible.

We have seen that from 1943 the Communists focused the financial and manpower resources of the border region on economic problems. The effort was made to maximize the economic contribution of all individuals, particularly former nonproducers, including cadres in the Party and government, soldiers defending the border area, students, women, immigrants, and idlers. In an intensive series of campaigns, political pressures and economic incentives were directed toward involving all of these groups in production. In the organizational economy, in the "to the village" and cooperative movements, and in the dispersion of industry, organizational forms evolved to give substance to a new conception of developing the border region's primitive and troubled economy.

[57] Stein, *Challenge of Red China*, pp. 174–75. The development of iron production is discussed in Shen-kan-ning pien-ch'ü cheng-fu pan-kung-t'ing (ed.), *Wei kung-yeh p'in ti ch'uan-mien tzu-chi erh fen-tou* (Struggle for Complete Industrial Self-sufficiency) (Yenan [?], 1944), p. 55, and Harrison Forman, *Report from Red China* (New York: Holt, 1945), p. 78.

LABOR HEROES

In the production and cooperative movements, the Communists embarked on a new approach to the peasantry. One significant technique employed widely after 1943 was the use of the labor hero as leader and model. Building on a Chinese tradition of emulation of models of filial piety and loyalty to the state as well as the experience of the Russian Stakhanovite movement, the Communists added their own innovative flair. The border region's first labor hero campaign was launched in the summer of 1943 with a vigorous propaganda drive linked to the production movement of that year. In every village, township, and district, outstanding workers were selected, honored, and rewarded.

Mao Tse-tung's welcoming talk to the first regional conference of labor heroes held in November, 1943, suggests both the contemporary mood and the direction of the production drive. After dwelling on the accomplishments of the past year and the importance of the organizational economy, Mao turned to the many types of cooperative labor which had begun to revolutionize production in the border region.

With these four types of cooperatives of the masses of the people and the collective labor cooperatives in the armed forces, offices and schools, we can organize all the forces of the masses into a huge army of working people. This is the only road to lead the masses of the people to liberation, to lead them from poverty to prosperity and to the victory of the War of Resistance. . . . Among the Chinese people there are in fact thousands upon thousands of "Chukeh Liangs," every village, every town having its own. We should go into the midst of the masses, learn from them, sum up their experiences so that these experiences will become well-defined principles and methods, and then explain them to the masses (through agitation work), and call upon the masses to put them into practice in order to solve their problems and lead them to liberation and happiness.[58]

It was in 1943 that the Communist Party developed and applied a variety of organizational techniques for effectively grounding its leadership at the local level in the productive process. The Communists thus became deeply involved in the most crucial concern of village life, the peasants' struggle to eke out a livelihood. In 1943 a full-scale attack on "feudal" conditions in the villages of the border region was being carried forward through a series of vigorous, interrelated political and economic campaigns which attempted, as in the case of mutual

[58] Mao Tse-tung, "Let Us Get Organized," *SW,* IV, 152–53. Chukeh Liang was a military strategist of the Three Kingdoms period, subsequently immortalized as a popular hero in the novel *The Romance of the Three Kingdoms Period.* His ingenuity was legendary.

aid and home weaving, to build on local forms and traditions. Labor heroes were natural leaders whose intimate knowledge of village life enabled them to discover creative means for resolving the complex and intractable problems of production and to lead in transforming rural society from within. Mao's invocation of the name of Chukeh Liang symbolized the new importance accorded production and the peasantry. As a *Liberation Daily* editorial pointed out, "Hitherto, the only heroes were warriors or political figures, but now laborers also can become heroes."[59]

The labor hero movement was more than a publicity campaign to spur peasant and worker production by praise and material reward; it provided an opportunity for identifying, training, and motivating potential leaders. Those chosen as labor heroes within their villages or townships, as well as the select few who made the trip to Yenan as the most honored workers in the entire border region, were prepared to return to their villages or factories with new ideas, incentives, and the prestige to carry forward the production revolution. Labor heroes also spearheaded the competitions waged between individuals, factories, army units, cooperatives, and whole districts which became a distinctive feature of the regional economy in 1943.[60]

Along with leadership which emerged in the land revolution and later in the campaign for reduction of rent, labor heroes provided a leadership core within the villages to carry forward the reorganization and development of the economy.

THE YENAN MODEL FOR ECONOMIC DEVELOPMENT

The production war launched by the Party in 1943 represented more than a crisis reaction to straitened circumstances: viewed as a whole it marked a major synthesis in the approach to social and economic development of rural China. Moreover, it is clear that the innovations of this period form the basis for the most distinctive features of subsequent Chinese Communist approaches to development and modernization. At the 1942 Senior Cadres Conference, Mao pointed out the

[59] *CFJP*, April 8, 1943.

[60] A vast body of contemporary literature is devoted to the labor hero campaigns. See for example, Chao Yüan-ming, *Shen-kan-ning pien-ch'ü ti lao-tung ying-hsiung* (Labor Heroes of the Shensi-Kansu-Ninghsia Border Region) (n.p., 1946). Numerous volumes, each describing the activities of an individual labor hero, are collected at the Hoover Institution, Stanford University. Also, cf. *CFJP*, February 18, April 30, September 13, 1942, February 3, July 5, November 25, 1943, July 12, 1944.

historical significance of the policies upon which the Party was about to embark as he compared the new conception with other models of economic development:

The publicly managed economic enterprises begun in the past five years are an extremely great accomplishment. This accomplishment is precious both for us and for our nation. That is, we have created a new model for the national economy. This is a new form since it is neither the old Bismarckian form of national economy nor the Soviet Union's newest form of national economy; rather it is a New Democratic or Three People's Principles' national economy. . . . The people's needs can as yet only be met through the impetus to organize provided by the Party and government and by the action of the masses themselves.[61]

In the same address, Mao denounced those who insisted that economic resources be channeled immediately into heavy industry or who designed grandiose but empty development schemes. In the virtual absence of capital, he proposed a labor-intensive development program involving the introduction of new forms of organization at the village level. All available material and human resources, including former nonproducers were mobilized. Their labor was channeled in new and rationalized forms, the most important of which were cooperatives and mutual-aid groups. The initial impetus and direction in the production movement was provided by the Party and government, but the financing, adaptation to diverse conditions, and subsequent development depended heavily on local material, and above all on the mobilization of all available manpower resources.

In defending this program, Mao Tse-tung lashed out at defeatists who saw economic development in the backward border area as hopeless or who considered it irrelevant to the immediate task of winning the War of Resistance. He was equally critical of those who favored development approaches based exclusively on foreign experience under totally different conditions. Once again Mao aligned himself squarely with the seminal figure of Chinese nationalism, Sun Yat-sen, in describing the path to development as the Three People's Principles or New Democracy. In fact, neither Sun's economic pronouncements nor Mao's own *On New Democracy*, written in late 1939, provided the basis for the departures of 1943. The brief and rather abstract section on the economy in *On New Democracy* provides no hint of the reforms introduced just three years later.[62] The Yenan model for economic development emerged only gradually from the bitter experience of

[61] "Economic and Financial Problems," *HC*, V, 99.
[62] Mao, "On New Democracy," *SW*, III, 122–23.

war-induced privation and blockade in the barren wastes of Shen-Kan-Ning.

In discussing the mass mobilization model of development applied in the border region during and after 1943, we have described the full range of changes planned and implemented, and the underlying philosophy which produced them. We must now attempt to evaluate the entire movement in terms of its actual contribution to economic development in Shen-Kan-Ning. The task is a formidable one, compounded by the fact that the period in which the experience may be judged was brief (the Communists were driven from Shen-Kan-Ning in early 1947) and by the dearth of empirical data. If earlier production statistics for the agrarian sector were little more than gross estimates or projections, later statistics are still more problematical. Decentralization of government and the economy, a key feature of the 1943 program for rural development, compounded the difficulties both of statisticians and of central planners. However, the shortage of reliable statistics should be taken not as a sign of economic breakdown, but as an inevitable and foreseen consequence of a decentralized model. For example, statistical control over textile production declined when the bulk of production shifted from a small number of government factories to looms in thousands of private homes.

The following points may be suggested, in any preliminary assessment, noting that they are inevitably based heavily on qualitative indicators drawn primarily from the Communist press. The Communists' 1943 approach to economic development in the border area's blockaded and primitive rural economy was a labor-intensive one based on mass mobilization and decentralization. At the very least, the ambitious attempts to restructure the rural economy on a cooperative basis and to mobilize tens of thousands of nonproducers did not result in large-scale disruption. Although many peasants remained outside the mutual-aid network, the transition from an individual economy seems to have been relatively smooth, in part because it was built upon traditional cooperative practices. Grain production, the basic economic indicator, apparently continued to develop steadily, though without spectacular growth, through the period of change. Impressive production gains were reported in 1943 for textiles, the border region's major industry; however, statistics for subsequent years are unavailable. "Organizational production," particularly the contribution of the fifty thousand regular army men, seems to me to have been an unqualified success under conditions of economic crisis. The army and some government cadres were able to provide not only a valuable manpower supply, but, more important, industrial, commercial, and managerial skills lacking in the border area. From 1943 they were widely and effectively used to bolster the economy. The use of mass mobilization techniques coupled with revival of traditional cooperative and other economic practices, such as home weaving, represented an astute appraisal of the possibilities for smoothly and rapidly developing production at the village level. Whatever the actual results in statistical terms, the production war was clearly viewed by the leadership as a resounding success, providing an organizational model and inspiration for the Party's subsequent approaches to economic development.

EDUCATION AND RURAL MODERNIZATION

The political and economic innovations of 1942 and 1943 were part of a larger vision of rural modernization. The drive for rapid modernization at this time was tempered by the realization that long-term progress had to rest on firm popular support for the Party's program within the village. The Communists attempted to minimize dislocation by building on traditional forms and developing indigenous village leadership rather than relying exclusively on outside cadres. In the cooperative movement, the ideal of mutual-aid teams run by and for the people (*min-pan*) replaced government-controlled and -financed cooperatives. The *min-pan* concept, embodying increasing popular control and participation in activities formerly monopolized by officials or experts, rapidly spread to many other areas vitally affecting village life.

During 1944 the concept of the *min-pan* school was widely implemented to meet the growing demand for education throughout the border region. Responsibility was vested in local cadres, labor heroes, and village heads to create appropriate forms for local education. The same principles, involving expanded local responsibility, were applied to spread knowledge of health and hygiene to remote villages. Finally, a variation on this theme was the new dimension of the culture movement which grew out of the *cheng-feng* campaign. From 1942 the symbol of mass culture in the border region was the *yang-ko* (native folk songs and dances), which the Communists combined with dramatic programs illustrating contemporary problems and policies. Throughout the border region *yang-ko* teams toured the villages and performed for the peasants. The goal was to link culture more closely with rural life by developing traditional popular themes to entertain and educate the peasantry.[63]

We cannot here elaborate on each of these movements. The evolution of the Communist conception of education, however, adds such significant dimensions to the new conception of rural modernization that we may briefly examine its most salient features. The critique of border region education developed during the *cheng-feng* movement paralleled contemporary analyses of the shortcomings of government and the cooperative movement. By 1942, the education system, despite rapid development under Communist rule, had barely begun to resolve the overwhelming problems of illiteracy and ignorance. Education remained elite education in that it was centered in district capitals, catered largely to families who could afford to send children there for study, and left most of the border region villages without schools or convenient access to them. Although the number of primary school students rose impressively from 5,600 in early 1937 to 22,000 by late 1939 and 29,500 in early 1944, this still affected only a small fraction of the school-age youth, estimated in 1944 at 165,000.[64] Despite adaptation of the curriculum, it was found to have little relevance to peasant life. Students, rather than being prepared to serve as the vanguard of the rural revolution in their villages, tended to disdain productive labor and to inject divisive influences into the family and village when they returned home. Traditional views of education as the first step on the ladder of success proved tenacious. Educated children were expected to assist their families, but by entering the elite and being successful as officials rather than by tilling the soil at home. From 1943 as official attention focused on production and other village problems, these failings posed dilemmas of the first magnitude. To integrate education with the production war required an educational system physically and intellectually closer to rural life, that is, located within the villages and responsive to their problems. But where were the teachers and material resources to be found? And would not village mores prove triumphant in a contest with the plan to introduce

[63] Concerning the application of *min-pan* principles to health and hygiene, see, for example, *CFJP*, November 20, 1944; on mass culture and the *yang-ko*, cf. *CFJP*, April 11, May 27, 1944; Stein, *Challenge of Red China*, pp. 219–21.

[64] Shen-kan-ning pien-ch'ü cheng-fu wei-yüan-hui, *Shen-kan-ning pien-ch'ü cheng-fu kung-tso pao-kao (1939–41)* (1939–41 Work Report of the Shensi-Kansu-Ninghsia Border Region Government) (Yenan, 1941), p. 63.

modern ideas to the people? Would the results at best simply dilute the quality of education already woefully inadequate?

In 1944 when the popular education movement became the focus of Communist policy in Shen-Kan-Ning, solutions to these and other problems were worked out. While formal cadre education retained priority in regular higher level schools, the basic direction of the movement was to stress rudimentary literacy and productive skills. Education was closely linked with the cooperative and production drives. Primary schools located in the county capitals and administered by the county government and education department were frequently divided and placed under the jurisdiction of district, township, or even village governments. Many new *min-pan* schools were designed for part-time education. They included large numbers of night schools, half-day schools, winter schools, and literacy groups, in many cases directly linked to production units. The curriculum was often determined by the students and teachers in each school, sometimes with the advice of cadres from the education department. Often the school principal or teacher was a prominent labor hero or local cadre, perhaps himself illiterate but imbued with new hopes and convictions about education and production. These teachers were frequently joined by cadres or students sent to the village from higher levels to assist in the drive to eliminate illiteracy and create a foundation for the economic and social changes which were currently revolutionizing rural life.

The *min-pan* school was predicated on principles of total education. Education could not be divorced from social movements, from the goals of Party and government, or from the concrete problems of the village. In *min-pan* schools, most students remained in their home villages, and all participated regularly in production and other tasks to assist the family and village. Simultaneously the curriculum in regular and cadre schools in the towns was modified to place increased stress on participation in and education for production and other local problems. The emphasis was on practical knowledge, on analysis of contemporary and historical conditions, and on service. The new education was integrated with the economic and political movements sweeping the border region during the years 1942 to 1944.[65]

[65] Among the most important items in the voluminous literature on education and the 1944 reform are the following: Chiao-yü chen-ti-she (ed.), *Ken-chü-ti p'u-t'ung chiao-yü ti kai-ko wen-t'i* (Problems in the Reform of Ordinary Education in the Base Area) (Kalgan: Hsin-hua shu-tien, 1946) ; Shen-kan-ning pien-ch'ü cheng-fu, pan-kung-t'ing (ed.), *Ssu-ko min-pan hsiao-hsüeh* (Four People's Elementary Schools) (Yenan [?],

In 1944 education in the border region assumed many of the characteristics of other mass movements of that period: transfer of authority from professional educators at the district and higher levels to cadres and labor heroes working and living in the villages; decentralization; stress on mass rather than elite education; integration of education with the social and economic life of the village. The Party did not entirely abandon regular forms or deliberately sacrifice quality, though educational resources were strained to the limit, priorities were reordered, and the teaching in some of the most advanced centers was diluted. The 1944 educational goals were sweeping in scope; every man, woman, and child was involved in forms of education ranging from formal schooling to spare-time study or reading groups among the members of mutual-aid teams, everywhere linked to concrete problems of production and social revolution. Just as the ambitious aims of the production movement had heightened the awareness of a labor shortage, in 1944 the number of teachers was found insufficient for the task. And again the solution rested on dual development, combining advanced and rudimentary techniques. Teachers were drawn not only from the educated elite, including former teachers and students, but also from among natural village leaders, many of them labor heroes or mutual-aid team leaders who could scarcely sign their names. If much of the new teaching was extremely primitive and irregular, and if some of the new experiments undoubtedly proved short-lived, the first glimmerings of education were brought to hundreds of isolated villages at a time when new skills and ideas could be effectively utilized in carrying forward the modernization process.

THE MASS LINE

The radical departures in Party policy developed during the *cheng-feng* movement led beyond a new conception of economic development to a broader vision of state and society in revolution. It was precisely at this time that the leadership principles of the mass line, elements of which may be traced to the Kiangsi period, were fully articulated by Mao Tse-tung. The June 1, 1943, resolution of the Politburo on "The Methods of Leadership" represents the classic statement of mass line leadership principles which the Party developed during the rectifica-

---

1944); Shen-kan-ning pien-ch'ü cheng-fu, pan-kung-t'ing (ed.), *Shen-kan-ning pien-ch'ü chiao-yü fang-chen* (The Educational Policy of the Shensi-Kansu-Ninghsia Border Region) (Yenan [?], 1944). Cf. *CFJP,* March 11, 22, April 17, May 27, August 10, 1944.

tion and production movements of 1942–43 and which have subsequently been enshrined as orthodoxy.

The two methods which we Communists should employ in carrying out any tasks are, first, the linking of the general with the specific and, second, the linking of the leadership with the masses. . . . In all practical work of our Party, correct leadership can only be developed on the principle of "from the masses, to the masses.". . . The basic method of leadership is to sum up the views of the masses, take the results back to the masses so that the masses give them their firm support and so work out sound ideas for leading the work on hand. In summing up the opinions of the masses and mobilising them to uphold the ideas so adopted, the leadership should use the method of combining general directives with specific guidance, which is an organic part of the method "from the masses, to the masses." On the basis of numerous cases of giving specific guidance we work out general ideas (general directives) for action, then put these general ideas to the test in many individual units (not only by ourselves, but by others acting on our advice), and finally generalise (i.e., sum up) the new experience so gained so as to work out new directives for the general guidance of the masses.[66]

The significance of the mass line becomes clearer when we contrast previous leadership techniques developed during the periods of land revolution and the early united front with those which succeeded them. In the land revolution of the Kiangsi period the Communists roused the peasantry to destroy the landlord-dominated order and create a new society based on equality. From 1937, united front principles directed at winning support of the traditional and new student elite underlay the effort to create a stable bureaucratic administration as the basis for reform in Shen-Kan-Ning.

Despite substantial Communist successes in both of these phases, it is fair to say that by 1942 little visible headway had been made in overcoming the stubborn problems of modernization and production stagnation throughout the border area. During the land revolution the Party had been able to appeal to deep-rooted passions and ideas in an oppressed and alienated peasantry. In the early united front, with the exception of the collection of taxes and military conscription, there was little government impact on village life. By 1942 it had become clear that on the basis of prevailing policies land revolution would not eliminate the isolation of the village or overcome economic stagnation. Reform efforts which were attempted—such as initiating textile pro-

---

[66] "On Methods of Leadership," *SW*, IV, 111–14. Cf. the translation in Compton, *Mao's China*, pp. 176–80. For a full discussion of the mass line in Chinese Communist ideology and practice, see John W. Lewis, *Leadership in Communist China* (Ithaca, N.Y.: Cornell University Press, 1963), pp. 70–100; Townsend, *Political Participation in Communist China*, pp. 57, 72–74, 94–95, 101–2.

duction or expanding education—tended to be concentrated in Yenan or in the district capitals, where the bureaucracy functioned most effectively. On the other hand, the program of economic development and rural modernization which emerged from the 1942 *cheng-feng* campaign was founded on the introduction of new ideas and programs directly to the villages. If success depended in part on effective measures designed and implemented by Party and government cadres in Yenan, it ultimately rested on the ability to develop enthusiastic support and indigenous leadership within the villages. It was at this time that the Party developed the distinctive economic, political, and social innovations which spread throughout the base area in successive mass movements during 1942 to 1944. In every case the goal was to build from an existing institutional base—such as traditional forms of mutual aid, culture, and medicine—toward economic and social institutions which would provide the basis for development and eliminate oppression. In this context the intellectual or bureaucrat familiar exclusively with modern Western or Marxist approaches to development was no longer an undisputed expert. His knowledge assumed importance only when supplemented by a thoroughgoing understanding of local economic and social patterns and the ability to win active local support for Party policies. It was in part to provide outside cadres with such knowledge and experience that the "to the village" movement was initiated; and it was to overcome traditional conceptions of officials as superior beings remote from the people, imposing policy by fiat from above, that the mass line became the cardinal principle of Communist leadership.

During the rectification and production movements of 1942 and 1943 a new conception of the Communist ideal man emerged. It was an ideal which transcended barriers of specialization and status to combine in a single individual the values and accomplishments of the laborer, the leader of men, the soldier, and the student. In mass line leadership, these qualities were best exemplified by the labor hero, who became a model both for his fellow workers and for cadres as well. He took the initiative not only in introducing and persuading others of the utility of new methods in his own village or factory, but organized and participated in the local militia and struggled to learn and to educate others in his "spare time." The gulf which separated the leadership from the led was thus appreciably narrowed. The labor hero or outstanding local cadre was an intermediary between higher levels of officialdom and the village, committed at once to Party guidelines, and to finding creative approaches for their implementation on the basis of prevailing village practices and values.

The mass line conception of leadership brought honor and status within the grasp of every youth or adult who was prepared to devote himself totally to the Communist cause, regardless of his class, skills, or family background. If peasants could "rise" to leadership through struggle and self-education, students, bureaucrats, and traditional elite elements could "descend" by means of "to the village" and production campaigns to unite with and lead the people within the confines of the natural village. In either case, leadership implied a break with the past and the acceptance of a multiplicity of roles which traditionally had been separate and distinct.

A number of distinctive features of the Yenan period and the border region help to account for the Party's dramatic success in achieving military victory against Japan and at the same time making impressive strides toward rural modernization. First, the war itself provided a crisis situation in which Communist authority and prestige in spearheading the national resistance struggle was enhanced. The urgency of internal reform could be effectively dramatized for all classes in terms of supporting the war effort. Second, many of the reforms associated with the mass line, most notably the new forms of mutual aid, were carefully developed to harmonize with prevailing practices, and with an astute eye to fostering peasant welfare. As a result they often won widespread initial acceptance, eliminating the necessity for an alien modernizing elite to coerce an unwilling populace. Third, the small size of many base areas, and particularly Shen-Kan-Ning, may have contributed to the development of a particularly effective style of leadership based on deep familiarity with local problems and mores, and highly responsive to the popular will as prescribed in the mass line.

The great contribution of the Yenan period in the Chinese Communist movement was the discovery of concrete methods for linking the military effort and rural social and economic problems in a single program of wartime mobilization penetrating to every village and every family, and involving every individual. This required new organizational and leadership techniques which were developed and raised to the level of theory as the mass line. In the final triumphant years of the War of Resistance against Japan, the mass line took root in base areas and battlefields throughout China as the fundamental leadership doctrine of the Communist Party. It remains so to this day.

PART II

*Leadership Characteristics
and Problems at the Local Level*

MICHEL OKSENBERG

Local Leaders in Rural China, 1962-65: Individual Attributes, Bureaucratic Positions, and Political Recruitment

What factors have affected the recruitment of local leaders into specific bureaucratic positions in rural China? And what have been the broader implications of the recruitment process? These are the central questions in this study of local leaders in rural areas of Communist China, in the period 1962–65.

While a study of the backgrounds and career patterns of leaders cannot alone provide a basis for predicting the policies they are likely to pursue after they attain office,[1] such a study can reveal much about the characteristics and underlying processes in a society, including the opportunities for social mobility enjoyed by different segments of the population, the individual attributes that are rewarded, and the power of particular organizations to advance their men.

The indicators of an effective recruitment process—which is a key to the smooth functioning of a political system—are clear.[2] The supply

[1] For discussion of this problem, see Lewis Edinger and Donald Searing, "Social Background in Elite Analysis: A Methodological Inquiry," *American Political Science Review*, LXI, No. 2 (June, 1967), 428–45. Also Dankwart Rustow, "The Study of Elites: Who's Who, When, and How," *World Politics*, XVIII, No. 4 (July, 1966), 690–717.

[2] See Lester G. Seligman, "Elite Recruitment and Political Development," *Journal of Politics*, XXVI (August, 1964), 612–26; David Apter, "Nationalism, Government, and Economic Growth," *Economic Development and Cultural Change*, VII, No. 2 (January. 1959), 117–36; and Ralf Dahrendorf, *Class and Class Conflict in Industrial Society* (Stanford, Calif.: Stanford University Press, 1959), esp. chap. vi. The notion of recruit-

and demand of talent should be balanced. Career aspirations by and large should be met; expectations should not outrace career opportunities. Moreover, the right men should end up in the right jobs. Talent should flow into positions where it is needed. In addition, an effective recruitment process should reduce what might be called the "civil war potential" of society; it should cut across the cleavages in society. Finally, in a society led by a modernizing elite, traditional recruitment patterns should give way to patterns more suited to the needs of an industrializing, modernizing nation.

When matched against these criteria, China's recruitment process prior to the Cultural Revolution of 1966–67 was partially but by no means fully effective. In rural areas, new skill groups appeared, and many people with the appropriate skills were recruited into the right jobs. The top leaders of China wrested control of the recruitment process from traditional groups and institutions. In other respects, however, the recruitment process has shortcomings which added to the problems facing the regime. For example, over time it produced growing disenchantment among the youth and intensified the generational conflicts that inevitably accompany industrialization. The generation of officeholders who came to power in 1949–53 clung tenaciously to their positions, while youths did not find the opportunities for rapid advancement which they hoped for. Moreover, the jobs available to youth—primarily in the fields of transportation, communication, finance, trade, education, and science—did not confer the anticipated rewards.

In addition the recruitment process seemed to intensify interagency conflicts in the bureaucracy. Institutions tended to recruit their officials from separate sources. Thus, differences in the individual attributes of local leaders tended to acquire organizational identity, with the result that conflicts among bureaucratic agencies seemed to be exacerbated.

Finally, political recruitment continued to be based to a large extent upon ascription and particularist attributes. The persistence of these traditional criteria undoubtedly retarded industrialization, at least to some extent. The existence of problems such as these suggests that China's recruitment process is likely to undergo further change in the years ahead.

To understand the recruitment process affecting China's local lead-

---

ment criteria employed in this paper comes from Amitai Etzioni, *A Comparative Analysis of Complex Organizations* (New York: The Free Press of Glencoe, 1961), pp. 151–57.

ers it is necessary to analyze a number of questions. Can local leaders be typed according to their backgrounds and career patterns? If so, in the period examined, how were these types distributed among various bureaucratic positions? Further, what factors affected the recruitment of particular types into different positions? Once the key determinants of recruitment into local leadership positions are identified, a final question can be asked: How efficient was the process?

The answers to questions such as these illuminate some of the problems which China's rulers are likely to face in the years ahead. They also make possible an identification of some of the factors which produced the Cultural Revolution that erupted in China in late 1965 and 1966.

DEFINITION OF "LOCAL LEADERS"

Before discussing the conclusions which emerge from this study, we must stipulate some basic definitions. For the purposes of this paper, "local leaders" are defined as those persons with power and influence at administrative levels up to and including the county (*hsien*).

Since the seat of county government often was not easily reached by peasants in many villages, particularly those in the more remote areas of a county, we should make explicit the three principal reasons which exist for including county level leaders in a study of "local" leadership. (There are approximately two thousand counties in China, with populations generally between three hundred thousand and eight hundred thousand.) First, in the period studied there was a great deal of leadership mobility within the county. County level leaders spent a considerable portion of their time at lower levels, in communes and villages, particularly when they were charged with running various campaigns. Commune officials frequently lived for months in villages, especially in the less productive ones, to try to increase local production.

Second, leaders frequently held positions simultaneously on two or three levels: a member of a Chinese Communist Party (CCP) county committee might also be the first secretary of the Party organization in his commune. The head of the production brigade almost always was a member of his commune's management committee. The circulation of officials, and the multiple positions held by many of them, were important aspects of local leadership. Only by studying leadership in the county as a whole is one sensitized to this aspect of local leadership.

A third reason to include the county leaders as part of "local" leadership in this study is that, in order to gather data from many areas which could be compared through time, the levels of government selected for analysis had to be relatively stable ones. While subcounty units in China were the objects of constant reorganization throughout the 1950's and early 1960's, the counties were in a basic sense stable territorial units. The use of counties as units of analysis therefore facilitated the charting of trends.

Below the county, in China since 1949, there usually have been four organizational tiers (although the organizational forms at each tier have changed frequently): the district, the multivillage, the village, and the subvillage units. The available biographical information on local leaders suggests that the leaders serving on each of these levels tended to be different in their characteristics. Therefore, while the term "local leaders" is used in this study to refer to all people with power and influence from the county level to the subvillage level, distinctions must be made between leaders who served on different levels.

To define "leaders" simply as those with power and influence also involves complicated conceptual and methodological problems. What, after all, distinguished those who were powerful from those who were near powerful? At what levels in the bureaucratic apparatus did office-holders have—or lack—real authority? Community studies in the United States, based on great amounts of data, do not provide entirely satisfactory answers to such questions. The problems are much more complex in the study of power in China, a nation which has a different culture and is closed to field research.

A satisfactory definition of "leaders" should include both formal and informal leaders. But without the opportunity to engage in field research, how can students of China identify the informal leaders who, lacking official titles, nonetheless wield a certain amount of influence? Some might argue that, to simplify matters, data should be gathered only on the holders of specific official positions, such as brigade directors and team accountants. But there are strong arguments against such an approach. It would preclude the possibility of investigating one of the more interesting questions about local leaders: To what extent does their power stem from specific positions, and to what extent does it inhere in individuals independent of the position they hold? Moreover, the titles of jobs tell little about the real roles and functions actually performed; the responsibilities of accountants, for example, varied enormously from brigade to brigade in China.

One must also distinguish between *active* and *potential* leaders.

Potential leaders include those who have access to the locus of power and periodically may influence policy; they also form a group from which the active leaders are drawn. Ideally, a study of mobility and recruitment patterns should attempt to identify potential leaders and analyze the circumstances under which they become active. Because of the nature of the data available, however, this study concentrates upon the active leaders—that is, those who actually exercised power and influence.

According to the definition of "leaders" used in this study, some state employees in China were leaders and others were not, while many who were not state employees were leaders. (Village and subvillage leaders were not state employees; they were on the payroll of their local units—production brigades, production teams, credit cooperatives, and so on. These nonstate or local cadres did not have a fixed income, but received an annual wage allocated from the income and production of their unit.) Most Chinese Communist Party members exercised power, but a few less active members did not. An accountant in one brigade might be able to affect policy and hence was a "leader"; in another brigade, the accountant might be politically impotent. Informal leaders may have emerged whose names were not carried on any list of officials. The potential leaders and the amorphous groups, such as the elder peasants (*lao-nung*) and those engaged in newly created occupations in the countryside (technicians, communications personnel, and so on), played political roles and occasionally exerted unorganized influence upon national policy. Unfortunately, however, firm data on informal or potential leaders are hard to obtain. In sum, the definition of "local leaders" used in this study enables one to deal with important questions, but it also means that these questions will have to be answered with considerable imprecision.

EIGHT TYPES OF LOCAL LEADERS

On the basis of two main factors—the date of a leader's recruitment into a position of political importance, and his institutional background—eight different but somewhat overlapping categories or types of local leaders serving in rural China during 1962–65 can be identified: old cadres, land reform cadres, collectivization cadres, demobilized members of the People's Liberation Army (PLA), middle school graduates, cadres sent to local areas from higher levels, influential individuals whose leadership credentials were established under the pre-Communist political system, and retired cadres.[3] These categories were recognized by the Chinese themselves, and colloquial terms were used to describe each group. Moreover, each type tended to have different skills and expectations. Let us examine each type more closely.

Old Cadres. "Old cadres" were local leaders who had joined the Communist movement during its guerrilla days. To a large extent, it was the ability to enlist these people that enabled the CCP to come to power. Most of the old cadres (*lao kan pu*) who served in the rural areas after 1949 were persons who had received only a rudimentary formal education and came from a poor peasant background. By 1962–65, most of them were over forty-five years of age, which in the context of rural China meant that many of them were nearing retirement from active careers.

Two biographical sketches, one of a county level official and another of a village leader, illustrate this type. Chiao Yu-lü was born into a poor peasant family in Shantung Province in 1922, and received little formal education before having to work in the fields.[4] When the Japanese captured his native village in 1938, he was sixteen years old and was drafted to work in a Japanese coal mine in Manchuria. He escaped from the mines, returned home briefly, and then fled to Kiangsu Province to escape arrest. There he worked as a hired hand from 1943 to 1945. A victim of poverty and foreign aggression, the youth was apparently attracted by the economic appeals and antiforeign stance of the Chinese Communist Party, which he joined in 1946. He became one of the thousands of Communist cadres who were charged with pacifying areas captured by the People's Liberation Army in its rapid sweep to victory. From 1947 to 1951, this Shantung youth worked in rural areas in Honan Province. By 1953, he had been transferred to an urban area, serving as section chief and Party secretary of a workshop in Honan's Loyang mining machinery factory. He apparently worked in urban areas until 1962, but during the economic depression follow-

---

[3] Categories based primarily upon interviews. For some case histories of local officials, see also: CCP Central Committee (ed.), *Chung-kuo Nung-ts'un ti She-hui-chu-yi Kao-ch'ao* (Socialist Hightide in the Chinese Countryside) (Peking: People's Press, 1956), 3 vols. CCP Chekiang Party Committee (ed.), *1955 Che-chiang Nung-ts'un Kung-tso Ching-yen Hui-pien* (Compendium of 1955 Rural Work Experience in Chekiang) (Hangchow: Chekiang People's Press, 1956). Shensi Party Committee (ed.), *Shen-hsi Nung-ts'un ti She-hui-chu-yi Chien-she* (Socialist Construction in the Shensi Countryside) (Sian: Shensi People's Press, 1956 and 1958), 2 vols. Chinese novels and short stories also provide clues about career patterns of local level officials.

[4] *JMJP*, February 7, 1966; NCNA, Peking, February 13, 1966.

ing the Great Leap Forward, the forty-year-old Chiao Yu-lü was posted first to Weishih County and then to Lankao County in rural Honan as Party first secretary, the most important office in the county. He subsequently died of cancer of the liver, while serving in Lankao County.

Another example of an "old cadre," this one a man who served at the commune level, was Fu Yung-chih.[5] Born in 1919 in a village near the Yellow Sea in northern Kiangsu, Fu was a hired laborer in pre-1949 China. Elements of the Communist New Fourth Army came to Fu's village in 1941, where they organized and developed a local militia corps. Typical of the marginal man recruited by the CCP, Fu, who was still a hired hand, assumed leadership of the local militia, and then he sparked opposition to the Japanese in this area from 1941 to 1945 and to Chiang Kai-shek from 1946 to 1948. After the CCP consolidated its control over northern Kiangsu, Fu became an established local leader. In 1965, he was deputy political commissar of his commune's militia regiment, and deputy Party secretary of the commune.

Old cadres such as these were the backbone of the Communist revolution, and consequently many of them thought that the fruits of victory rightfully belonged to them. Many stories in the Chinese Communist press describe the privileges which the old cadres expected. Some of them were distrustful of people who joined, or wanted to join, the Party after 1949, believing the late-comers to be opportunists. At the same time, a strong feeling of nativistic anti-intellectualism apparently characterized many of these old cadres. Not surprisingly, therefore, local Chinese newspapers contain many stories of old cadres refusing to admit younger, better educated youths to Party membership, and revealing their resentment about the more rapid promotions won by better educated cadres with less seniority.[6]

Land Reform Cadres. Soon after it moved into any rural area, the CCP implemented its land reform program. Implementation of this program required the cooperation of some natives of an area; they were needed to act as informants, identifying the landlords and listing the grievances against them. Many of these "land reform activists," frequently uneducated poor peasants, subsequently were recruited to

---

[5] NCNA, Nanking, May 27, 1966, in *SCMP,* No. 3709 (June 1, 1966), pp. 32–35.

[6] For example, see *Szu-ch'uan Jih-pao,* January 8, 1955; *Chiang-hsi Jih-pao,* July 17, 1955, and August 11, 1956; *Kan-su Jih-pao,* October 22, 1955, and July 1, 1956; *Hsin-hua Jih-pao* (New China Daily), October 23, 1955; *Hsi-k'ang Jih-pao,* February 10, 1955; *Che-chiang Jih-pao,* May 30, 1956; *Shan-hsi Jih-pao,* October 24, 1956; *Hsi-an Jih-pao,* November 6, 1956.

serve as local leaders. In later years, the land reform activists had diverse fates, but by 1954 many had become township (*hsiang*) leaders. (*Hsiang* is sometimes translated as "administrative village.")

From 1955 to 1958, the organization of the *hsiang* underwent considerable changes, and many of the land reform cadres serving at this level were transferred. Some were promoted to the district and county levels, while others were demoted and returned to their native villages. Some land reform activists became village leaders after land reform, and then led the collectivization drive in their villages in 1955–56. Others, having acquired land and increased stature as a result of land reform, apparently resisted the collectivization movement; they were attacked for their "spontaneous capitalist tendencies."

Finally, a few land reform activists never received any important political positions. Not long after land reform, higher level authorities placed the blame for excessive violence upon some of them, perhaps using them as scapegoats, and they were purged. Although as a group the land reform activists met a mixed fate, in 1962–65 many of them continued to play major political roles, particularly at the district and township levels.

Yen Wei-chuan in some respects was typical of such cadres.[7] Chairman of a commune located twenty-five miles from Peking, he had only two years of formal education. At age twenty-one he was a land reform activist. Then he became a leader of the first mutual-aid team (MAT) formed in his village, in response to a request made by a higher level CCP cadre. In 1952, Yen became the chairman of the lower stage agricultural producers' cooperative (APC) established in his village, and in 1955 he retained his position when his cooperative was reorganized into an advanced type cooperative. When his cooperative was merged with the neighboring ones, he became chairman of the resulting commune. This land reform cadre, and tens of thousands of others like him, joined the revolution at an opportune moment and consequently played an important leadership role during the following fifteen years. By 1962–65, such cadres were generally between thirty-five and forty-five years of age and could look forward to another five to ten years of active leadership.

Collectivization Cadres and Post-1955 Peasant Recruits. A number of activists were recruited into the CCP during the Party's intensive campaign to expand its membership during 1955. Many of these

---

[7] Edgar Snow, *The Other Side of the River: Red China Today* (New York: Random House, 1961), pp. 440–44.

cadres, often from poor peasant families, had not played a major role in the land reform period of the early 1950's but enthusiastically enlisted in the CCP's effort to collectivize agriculture. Most of them apparently retained leadership positions when the communes and production brigades were formed in 1958. In 1962–65, cadres in this category averaged between thirty and forty years of age.

Cadre Chou, the Party branch secretary of a production brigade in coastal Kwangtung Province, was an example of this type.[8] Sixteen or seventeen years old at the time of the Communist takeover, he did not play a major role in the land reform program. By 1955, however, perhaps in part because of his parents' class status (they were hired hands), Chou had attracted the attention of higher level Party authorities and was recruited into the CCP. He became a secretary of the Party branch in his APC, and then in 1958 became the branch secretary of his production brigade. He served in this post until 1965, when he was dispatched to a neighboring county to help run the "Four Clearance" movement. For the most part, however, such cadres remained in their native locality, and did not enjoy much upward mobility.

The "post-1955 peasant recruits" closely resembled the collectivization cadres. Poorly educated and often from impoverished backgrounds, they usually served in their native locality and enjoyed very limited career opportunities following their initial appointments. By 1962–65, they generally were over thirty-five years old. Most post-1955 peasant recruits acquired positions either in 1958, when the communes were formed, or in 1962–65, during the socialist education campaign.

These post-1955 peasant recruits, it should be noted, were not the only type of persons assuming positions of leadership after 1955. As will be pointed out below, young middle school graduates and ex-servicemen were other important sources for new leaders. In a sense, the post-1955 peasant recruits and the young middle school graduates and ex-PLA members competed for local leadership posts, and there were some tensions among them.

Army Veterans.[9] China's pool of over seven million men who had

---

[8] See my protocols from Brigade Interviews, Informant 10, Question 24; APC Interviews, Informant 10, Question 18. (These and other protocols cited are available upon request.)

[9] For discussion of the role of the veteran in underdeveloped societies, see Lucian Pye, "Armies in the Process of Political Development," in his *Aspects of Political Development* (Boston: Little, Brown, 1966), p. 181. Also Nobutaka Ike, "War and Modernization," in

served in the PLA was another major source of local leadership. Perhaps as many as seven hundred thousand or more men were mustered out of military service annually in the early 1960's. The number demobilized in the mid-1950's was even higher, for in those years the overall size of the PLA was reduced from five million to less than three million men.[10] Veterans were demobilized in two different ways. Some were transferred to specific organizations and enterprises (*chuan-yeh chün-jen*); others were simply returned to civilian life (*fu-yüan chün-jen*). The transferred veterans became state cadres in the county, district, and township. The returnees often became village and subvillage leaders, many holding posts in the militia, the village protection committees, and the local public security organizations. For example, in Heilungkiang, over 70 per cent of the militia leaders were demobilized PLA members. In Chekiang, according to incomplete statistics, more than 117,000 of over 180,000 ex-PLA members served as cadres in the militia.[11] Large numbers of the demobilized soldiers also staffed the political work departments established in various governmental agencies in 1964–65.[12]

A detailed report by the Management Bureau of Kiangsi Province's Post and Tele-Communications Department reveals the importance of army veterans as a source of local leaders.[13] From 1956 to 1958, this department added 1,407 demobilized soldiers to its payroll (this was 42 per cent of the total number of new personnel). Of these veterans 61 per cent were Party and Youth League members. Twenty-two per cent of the total became either directors of post and tele-communications stations at the district level (*yu-tien-so chu-jen*), heads of production groups (*sheng-ch'an-pan tsu-chang*), or administrative management workers (*hsing-cheng kuan-li kung-tso jen*), while 52 per cent of them became technical workers (*chi-shu-yüan*).

The report observed that many of the other cadres in the Post and Tele-Communications Department were unhappy about the transfer of so many veterans to their agency. Because some of the demobilized

Robert E. Ward (ed.), *Political Development in Modern Japan* (Princeton, N.J.: Princeton University Press, 1968), pp. 189–212. These important articles underline the political significance of this source.

[10] John Gittings, *The Role of the Chinese Army* (New York: Oxford University Press, 1967), p. 305; *Nei-wu-pu t'ung-hsün* (Bulletin of the Ministry of Internal Affairs), No. 11 (November, 1958), p. 3 (hereafter *NWPTH*).

[11] *NWPTH*, No. 1 (January, 1959), p. 31, and No. 4 (April, 1959), pp. 5ff. Also Radio Chang-sha, January 14, 1966, for Hunan.

[12] Chalmers Johnson, "Lin Piao's Army and Its Role in Chinese Society," Part 2, *Current Scene*, IV, No. 14 (July 15, 1966), 6.

[13] *NWPTH*, No. 6 (June, 1959), p. 36.

PLA members were dissatisfied with their wages, the article stated, some other cadres believed that the veterans gave them only trouble. Compared with the other employees, the former soldiers were described as having a higher level of class consciousness, stronger organizational skills, and greater determination in the pursuit of revolutionary activities. On the other hand, their educational level was rather low, and many suffered from bad health, the result of injury and disease incurred while in the army. As a result, the article noted, many post and tele-communications cadres believed that "technical matters in post and tele-communications are complicated, and therefore other departments should be the ones to absorb the veterans." In short, the article revealed that significant tensions existed between veterans and nonveterans.

Indeed, the educational level of the average demobilized soldier mustered out in the 1950's was probably quite low. For example, a report from a county in Liaoning Province gave the educational background of 114 former officers in the county.[14] Of the 114, 27 were illiterate, 15 had less than two years of formal education, 58 had the equivalent of elementary school education, and 14 had completed eight years of school. (As the PLA modernized, however, presumably the training within the army became more rigorous, and the average educational level of those mustered out had probably increased by the 1960's.)

The demobilized soldiers were overwhelmingly Party or Communist Youth League (CYL) members. Nearly 60,000 soldiers were demobilized in Hunan Province in 1957, and 80 per cent of these were Party members. Eighty-nine per cent of the 24,600 soldiers who returned to Chekiang Province from January to June of 1957 were members of the CCP and CYL.[15]

Many important questions about the veterans remain unanswered. For example, we do not know to what extent their experiences in the PLA produced profound changes in their loyalties and aspirations. But it is known that many PLA veterans, who usually were Party members as well as the recipients of some advanced technical training, played important leadership roles in rural China.

Young Middle School Graduates. Another source of local leaders in China was the graduates of the nation's lower and higher middle schools, which have greatly increased in number in the past twenty

[14] *Ibid.*, No. 8 (August, 1959), p. 18.
[15] *Che-chiang Jih-pao,* August 14, 1957; *Hsin Hu-nan Pao,* February 16, 1957.

years.[16] Only a small percentage of middle school graduates could go on to college. The overwhelming majority were employed by state enterprises, administrative units, and the commune's production brigades. The oldest of this type of local leader—those youths who graduated in the mid-1950's—were nearing thirty years of age in the early 1960's. The youngest were still in their teens.

A relatively recent article in *Chung-kuo Ch'ing-nien* (Chinese Youth), describing the roles that middle school graduates played in China's rural areas, stated that among China's one hundred million rural youth over forty million had more than six years of schooling.[17] The article noted that these educated youth played important roles in the spread of advanced scientific techniques, such as those relating to soil improvement, seed selection, pest control, tool improvement, and so on. The article mentioned that over 80 per cent of China's tractor drivers and mechanics of various kinds were educated youths. Educated youths were deeply involved in directing the collective economy, the article continued; in fact, ten million of the forty million educated youths served as accountants, wage-point recorders, and protection members in production brigades. Finally, the article noted that educated youths were an important force for raising the cultural level of the peasantry. Under the leadership of the CCP, they ran night schools, organized workers clubs, promoted art troops, and so on.

Two examples of such educated youths were Wang Wen-po and Wang Wei-tseng (not related). Wang Wen-po was a Shantung girl born in 1941.[18] She graduated from elementary school in 1954 and by 1957 was serving as a livestock tender in her advanced type agricultural producers' cooperative. In 1958, after attending a short training course at the county level, she returned to her village and was put in charge of seed distribution work. From 1959 to 1961, she served in the seed distribution station of her commune, but in 1961 she returned to her village where she once again became the livestock tender. By 1963, Mrs. Wang—then the mother of two children—had won the provincial Communist Youth League Red Flag prize, was a "Three-Eight Red Flag" winner in the provincial women's federation contest, and was a representative to the Party provincial congress. She earned such recognition by overcoming the existing resentment against women (her job

[16] See Robert D. Barendsen, "The Agricultural Middle School in Communist China," *China Quarterly*, No. 8 (October–December, 1961), pp. 106–34.

[17] "On Knowledgeable Youth Participating in Agricultural Production" (in Chinese), *CKCN*, No. 18 (1963), p. 4.

[18] *Ibid.*, No. 4 (1965), pp. 10–11.

was not generally considered to be a female occupation) and doggedly pursuing her career despite the fact that she had two children at home.

Wang Wei-tseng was a mail carrier in Shantung Province.[19] Born in 1946, he evidently had received a middle school education. In April, 1964, Wang was assigned to become a mailman in a rural area which previously had been without regular mail service. His diverse tasks included helping production teams to organize reading groups, organizing the intellectual youth and schoolteachers in his area to read newspapers to the peasants, and enlisting subscribers to various journals. As a result of his aggressive salesmanship, all of the 106 production teams under his jurisdiction subscribed to the journal *Agricultural Knowledge* (*Nung-yeh Chih-shih*), and the number of subscriptions to *Chinese Youth* increased from four to twenty-seven.

These, then, were an important category of local leaders in China: young graduates of the middle schools serving primarily in occupations related to industry, communications, transportation, propaganda, education, and science.

Cadres Sent Down from Higher Levels. A number of the Chinese Communists' personnel programs called for the dispatch of higher level cadres to serve at lower administrative levels for varying lengths of time.[20] Small groups of cadres or work teams (*kung-tso tui*) were sent to local levels, particularly during campaigns, for a variety of purposes: to educate the masses, direct local affairs, and inspect local conditions. Individual cadres were sent as "envoys" to townships and communes (*chu-hsiang kan-pu* or *chu-she kan-pu*) to assist the native cadres in many of their tasks. In the early 1960's, the central government sponsored a program for higher level cadres to remain at lower levels for extended periods of time; cadres doing this were said to be "squatting at a point" (*tun-t'ien*). China's top leaders hoped that this program would increase the social awareness of the higher level cadres "sent down" and improve relations between the masses and the central government. The *tun-t'ien* program was an extension of the earlier programs to send cadres to the countryside (variously called *hsia-hsiang* in the early 1950's and *hsia-fang* in the late 1950's and early

---

[19] *Ibid.*, No. 3 (1965).

[20] See A. Doak Barnett (with a contribution by Ezra Vogel), *Cadres, Bureaucracy, and Political Power in Communist China* (New York: Columbia University Press, 1967), pp. 174–76; Rensselaer W. Lee III, "The *Hsia Fang* System: Marxism and Modernization," *China Quarterly*, No. 28 (October–December, 1966), pp. 40–62; and Hermia Chen, "The *Xiafang* of Cadres: A Means of Mass Communication," *China Mainland Review*, II No. 4 (March, 1967), 257–61.

1960's). These programs resulted in millions of students, cadres, and industrial workers living in China's countryside for periods ranging from a few weeks to over a year.

Mutual suspicion and distrust frequently marked the relationship between the cadres sent down and the permanent local leaders.[21] Local leaders tended to fear the investigatory power of the higher level cadres, who were expected to report local malpractices to the higher levels. (Sometimes, local leaders also suspected that the higher level cadres had made political mistakes which resulted in their dispatch to the lower levels.) The higher level cadres, on the other hand, also had reason to feel uneasy and to tread lightly. If they acted too vigorously, they were vulnerable to the charge that they were "dogmatic" and guilty of "commandism" (barking out orders instead of convincing the masses of their wisdom). Moreover, higher level cadres sent down to lower levels generally wished to enjoy good relationships with the villagers among whom they lived, and they often lived in the homes of the very leaders they were supposed to investigate. The mutual realization that each was vulnerable to the other frequently led to tacit bargains between the higher level cadres and the local leaders in which each in effect agreed to avoid pressing his advantage.

Influential Individuals from the Old Regime. Although the Communist revolution brought about an almost complete turnover in the local power holders in rural China, nonetheless several kinds of influential individuals survived. A few former Kuomintang (KMT) officials continued to serve at the county level until the *wu-fan* campaign of 1955. During the Hundred Flowers campaign of 1956–57 they enjoyed a brief renaissance, but by 1962–65, former KMT officials were no longer influential in county level government.

In the villages, on the other hand, there were still several influential types whose leadership credentials predated Communist rule. First, there were some local leaders who possessed scarce skills demanded by their community. Often, old farmers with special agricultural skills exerted considerable influence. When the government's rural policy allowed free markets to flourish, well-educated old villagers with commercial skills and special connections at higher levels acted as advisors in planning and marketing crops. Old peasants familiar with water tables, springs, and patterns of water flow were consulted during water

---

[21] The following is based on the author's interviews on *hsia-fang* with both cadres who had been sent down and villagers who received cadres. The informants all came from different villages, however.

conservancy campaigns. Their value was heightened when government policy placed the more professionally trained water technicians under suspicion; lacking skills in water conservancy themselves, and unable to draw upon the knowledge of the technicians, local Party leaders had to turn to the old peasants for help.

A second group of influential individuals—perhaps they should be called informal opinion leaders—were the old ladies (*lao-p'o-p'o*), who formed the core of the informal gossip network in villages. Upon occasion, these old ladies sparked resistance to such government policies as those fostering birth control, delayed marriages, and women's participation in work. The *lao-p'o-p'o*, refugee informants suggest, were almost impervious to government controls. If the Party had tried to subject them to self-criticism or public criticism, it would have exposed itself to mockery. Old ladies in China's rural villages, in short, seemed to play the same kind of maverick roles which they had in pre-1949 China.

Finally, a third group of influential persons surviving from the old regime at the village level included some of those who guarded and spread the belief systems of pre-1949 China. To the extent that old beliefs remained alive, their purveyors retained traces of influence. For example, the mainland press and captured CCP documents from rural Fukien and Kwangtung have despairingly noted the continued role in China's villages of geomancers, marriage counselors, and a number of other traditional specialists in ritual.[22]

Retired Cadres. In the years ahead, an increasingly important source of informal local leaders may be the growing number of retired cadre officials who either return to their native places or remain in one of the areas in which they have served. There are some indications already that such officials (*t'ui-wu-yüan* if retired from the army, *t'ui-chih-yüan* if retired from the state apparatus) can become influential locally. This category is particularly worth noting in view of its importance in traditional China, where retired officials used their connections with higher level officialdom in order to further the interests of their local communities. If this type of local leader increases in importance in Communist China, it will be a sign that the government has not yet fully succeeded in institutionalizing its power and influence. To the extent that retired officials retain power and influence, these become personal attributes not easily controlled by the government.

---

[22] See Maurice Freedman, *Chinese Lineage and Society* (London: Athlone Press, 1966), pp. 173–84.

Two examples of retired cadres exerting significant influence in local areas illustrate the point. Kuang Chang-ta was born in 1900 in Yung-hsin County of Kiangsi Province. He joined Mao's forces when they came to his area in 1928, and became a member of the CCP in 1929. A veteran of the Long March, Kuang served in several guerrilla bases from 1937 to 1949, and then assumed higher level positions in the Chinese People's Republic (CPR). Because of poor health, he retired to his native county in 1958. The peasants there referred to him as they would have referred to a retired official during the Ch'ing dynasty, that is, as an "official who had stepped down from his chair." A story describing Kuang's activity after his return home accorded him the respect and status due to an old public servant. The story mentioned that Kuang was consulted continually by the county officials, and represented his native township in county level affairs.

Another example of an influential retired official was K'an Tsu-ch'ang, an old revolutionary from Kiangsi Province who had joined the revolution in 1929.[23] A veteran of the Long March and of many military campaigns, by 1952 he headed the Logistics Department of the Sinkiang military command. In September, 1957, he was injured, and returned to his native Kiangsi village. An article describing K'an's activity observed that after his return home he inspected every commune in the county and most of its production brigades. K'an was said to enjoy a deep affection and high prestige among the local people.

More typical, perhaps, of influential retired officials were those aging village leaders who yielded their positions to younger kin. In some cases, such retired village officials continued to intervene in village affairs when crucial decisions were made.

Since the student of China cannot engage in field research, he is unable to ascertain the frequency, circumstances, and consequences of retired officials retaining informal influence. But the available information indicates that, as in traditional China, at least some retired Communist officials have enjoyed special influence because of their age, contacts, and experience.

Summary. Thus, eight types of local leaders existed in rural China in the 1962–65 period covered by this study: old cadres, land reform cadres, collectivization cadres and post-1955 recruits, army veterans, young graduates of middle schools, leaders whose credentials were established under the old regime, and retired informal leaders. Re-

---

[23] *NWPTH*, No. 8 (August, 1959), pp. 22–23; also NCNA, Nanchang, March 14, 1966, in *SCMP*, No. 3659 (March 17, 1966), p. 25.

cruited into the political system at different times and possessing distinct skills, these eight types had somewhat dissimilar career patterns under Communist rule, and, conscious of their identities, they tended to be slightly antagonistic toward one another.

BUREAUCRATIC POSITIONS

Further light is thrown on patterns of local leadership in China by examining the individual attributes of local leaders serving at different levels of government, in different functional positions, and in different geographical areas. It is useful to identify the levels at which members of the eight categories of local leaders served and to analyze the differences among local leaders in terms of their Party affiliations, educational attainments, ages, and places of origin.

The Chinese Communists do not systematically provide aggregate data on the education, Party affiliation, birthplace, age, income, socioeconomic status, and career patterns of their local leaders. Most information and impressions come from interviews with former residents of the CPR, from scattered articles in the Chinese press about the general problems involved in recruiting and assigning local leaders, and from brief individual biographies of rural leaders. These sources provide the principal data on which this study is based.

The study also draws upon brief biographical sketches of 353 local leaders which have been compiled by the author. Data on 125 leaders were derived from an interview project conducted in Macao;[24] 84

[24] The Macao interviews were based upon a set of eight lengthy questionnaires on such topics as the production team, the brigade, village organization, *hsia-fang* cadres, communications, technical change, water conservancy, and agricultural producer's cooperatives. The set of questionnaires, which took about ten hours to administer, was designed to elicit information about the informant's village officials. Sixteen informants, all from Kwangtung and mostly young peasants, were interviewed in 1965–66, before the Macao riots and problems of obtaining reliable research assistance called an unfortunate halt to the project. Many of the respondents were unable to provide much information about their commune officials, an interesting fact in itself. We consider the data to be, as the Chinese say, "basically reliable." The one exception might be the reliability of data derived from the APC questionnaire; memories of that period have grown dim, and many of the informants were too young to recall the mid-1950's. Biographical data from the APC questionnaire therefore have not been included. The questionnaires had built-in checks to aid in assessing reliability. Moreover, two of the informants came from the same production brigade, and their responses were, with a few exceptions, the same. In short, we consider the data from the interviews to provide a rough profile of subcommune level leaders in coastal Kwangtung during the mid-1960's.

Information was recorded on the following aspects of an individual's life: position; native place (i.e., was he a native or outsider, and if an outsider, from outside the village, commune, county, or province); age; education; Party affiliation; kinship; prior career; and, if no longer holding a particular post, subsequent career. Data on the economic class background of local officials were not aggregated, since the reporting of

biographical sketches were gleaned from the mainland China press;[25] information on 63 local leaders was obtained from short stories and novels;[26] and 81 were sketched by visitors to the mainland.[27] The

---

this data was highly unreliable. In interviews, however, we inquired into the parental occupations and economic positions of local officials. Only the interviews yielded all this information for most individuals. Data on local officials derived from the press, fiction, and tourists' accounts tended to be very fragmentary.

[25] Data from the mainland press come mainly from the U. S. Consulate General translation series for the years 1955–57 and 1964–65. *Hsin-hua Yüeh-pao* (New China Monthly) and *Hsin-hua Pan-yüeh-k'an* (New China Fortnightly) for the mid-1950's, and books such as the widely publicized *Chung-kuo Nung-ts'un ti She-hui-chu-yi Kao-ch'ao* (Socialist Hightide in Rural China). Data were also collected from *Chinese Youth* (in Chinese) for 1955–57 and 1963–64, a journal rich in biographical information. The data were not aggregated, however, since they would have skewed the press data in favor of youth. The press data clearly do not provide a representative sample of China's local leaders. The data are not geographically representative. For example, the old guerrilla base areas in Shensi, Shansi, Hopei, and Shantung are overrepresented; Szechwan goes virtually unreported. The data deal primarily with administrative and political personnel; few data are available on military and public security officials. Moreover, in contrast to the interview data, the press data include biographies of county and commune officials, but do not include descriptions of team officials. Comparisons between the interview data and the press data must therefore be handled with care.

[26] Short stories and novels yielded data on sixty-three officials from the county level to the village level. A research assistant sifted through the English-language journal, *Chinese Literature,* and several novels, such as those by Chao Shu-li and Chou Li-po. Chinese fiction was used, since the authors, committed to "socialist realism," often write about villages they have actually visited. In terms of the levels and functions of the officials described, fiction yields data comparable to information derived from journals, newspapers, and nonfiction books. However, since few short stories indicate the locality of the "real" village upon which the story is based, we have no idea about the geographical sample represented. The old guerrilla base areas once again may be overrepresented.

[27] Data on eighty-one local officials were derived from the travelogues and village studies conducted by Westerners: Boyd Orr and Peter Townsend, *What's Happening in China* (New York: Doubleday, 1959); Simone de Beauvoir, *The Long March* (New York: World Publishing Company, 1958); Julio Del Vayo Alvarez, *China Triumphs* (New York: Monthly Press, 1964); Edgar Faure, *The Serpent and the Tortoise* (London: Macmillan, 1958); G. S. Gale, *No Flies in China* (London: Allen and Unwin, 1955); Felix Greene, *Awakened China* (New York: Doubleday, 1961); Robert Guillian, *Six Hundred Million Chinese* (New York: Criterion Books, 1967); Robert Guillian, *When China Wakes* (New York: Walker, 1966); Harry Hamm, *China: Empire of the 700 Million* (New York: Doubleday, 1966); Leslie Haylen, *Chinese Journey* (Sydney: Angus and Robertson, 1959); Lisa Hobbs, *I Saw Red China* (New York: McGraw-Hill, 1966); Indian Government Planning Commission, *Report of the Indian Delegation to China on Agrarian Co-operatives* (New Delhi, May, 1957); Hewlett Johnson, *China's New Creative Age* (London: Lawrence and Wishart, 1953); K. S. Karol, *China: The Other Communism* (New York: Hill and Wang, 1967); Sven Lindquist, *China in Crisis* (New York: Crowell, 1963); Jan Myrdal, *Report from a Chinese Village* (London: Heinemann, 1964); Tibor Mende, *China and Her Shadow* (New York: Coward-McCann, 1962); Hugh Portisch, *Red China Today* (Chicago: Quadrangle, 1966); Myra Roper, *China: The Surprising Country* (New York: Doubleday, 1966); Peter Schmid, *New Face of China* (New York: Pitman, 1959); Snow, *The Other Side of the River;* William Stevenson, *The Yellow Wind* (Boston: Houghton-Mifflin, 1959); Isabel and David Crook, *The First Years of Yangyi Commune* (New York: Humanities Press, 1966); William Geddes, *Peasant Life in China* (Ithaca, N.Y.: Cornell University Society for Applied Anthropology, 1963).

last-mentioned category also includes information obtained from the writings of Rewi Alley and Anna Louise Strong.[28] A comparison of the data from these four sources shows that each source yielded somewhat different impressions of the backgrounds of local leaders (for detailed discussion of sources, see "Sources and Methodological Problems in the Study of Contemporary China," pp. 577–606).

One problem with the data is that they do not cover equally the local leaders holding various jobs at different administrative levels. Most of the sketches of county officials describe persons performing political and general administrative tasks. The sketches of village and subvillage leaders, on the other hand, describe many persons performing financial or educational tasks. Care in the use of the data is required, therefore, to eliminate interpretive errors arising from this difficulty.

The data in no sense represent a random sample of the total community of local leaders in China. Therefore, in the discussion which follows, when I state that 29 per cent of the village leaders were "outsiders" or 100 per cent of the county level leaders were CCP members, *I certainly do not imply* that these figures represent the actual percentage of village leaders who are outsiders or of county leaders holding CCP membership. The figures are simply those which emerge from the very limited data available. Rather than yielding precise and valid information on local leaders in China as a whole, therefore, the data are suggestive, and are used mainly for general comparisons of the attributes of local leaders serving in different sorts of positions.

COMPARISON OF LEADERS ON DIFFERENT LEVELS

As a general rule, as one ascended the ladder of government in rural China, from subvillage organizations to the village, township, district, and county levels, both the proportion of Party members and outsiders among local leaders and the age of the leaders increased. The tenure of officials at each level also appeared to differ, the tenure of subvillage leaders being especially short.

The Levels. The organizational complexities of local government in China, the bewildering terminology for local units, and the existence of

---

[28] Rewi Alley, *China's Hinterland in the Leap Forward* (Peking: New World Press, 1961); Rewi Alley, *Land and Folk in Kiangsi* (Peking: New World Press, 1962); Rewi Alley, *Amongst Hills and Streams of Hunan* (Peking: New World Press, 1963); Anna Louise Strong, *Letters from China*, Nos. 1–30 (Peking: New World Press, 1963–65), 3 vols.; Anna Louise Strong, *The Rise of the Chinese People's Communes—and Six Years After* (Peking: New World Press, 1964).

regional differences made it difficult to develop suitable analytical categories to distinguish among cadres serving at different administrative levels. Territorial units with the same title could be quite dissimilar in size, structure, and function. For example, in 1965, mountainous Kweichow's 4,200 communes probably tended to be quite different from Kwangtung's 1,724 communes.[29] The aggregate figures suggest that Kweichow's communes usually embraced only a few villages, while the larger Kwangtung communes frequently may have coincided with a "standard marketing area."[30] Moreover, because of frequent reorganizations, administrative units even within a single province occupied different positions in the government hierarchy at different times. The history of the communes in Kweichow illustrates the point. Shortly after their organization, the 537 communes in Kweichow seemed comparable in size to the province's 487 *ch'ü* (districts) that had existed in early 1958. As a result of a subsequent reduction in their size, by 1965 Kweichow's communes had increased in number to 4,200, and they were comparable in size to the 4,261 *hsiang* which had existed in the province in 1958.

An additional problem was created by the fact that cadres did not always serve at the level designated by their title. Besides his civil service rank, each rural administrative cadre on the government payroll was designated a "county level cadre" (*hsien-chi kan-pu*), "district level cadre" (*ch'ü-chi kan-pu*), or "township level cadre" (*hsiang-chi kan-pu*). Some district level cadres actually were in the employ of the county and worked at the county seat; others were sent to townships and held offices there. Similarly, county and township level cadres could actually work at any of several levels. Chinese organizational terms, in short, were imprecise and covered such a diversity of practices that they could not always be employed for analytical purposes.

Instead, it seemed necessary to define categories somewhat independent of Chinese terms. For this analysis, therefore, local government has been analyzed in terms of five tiers—county, district, multivillage, village, and subvillage. The county coincides with the Chinese *hsien* unit. The district refers to all units below the county but above

[29] Figures on Kweichow from the series, *Chung-hua Jen-min Kung-ho-kuo Hsing-cheng Ch'ü-hua Chien-ts'e* (Handbook on Administrative Subdivisions in the Chinese People's Republic) (Peking: Ministry of Internal Affairs, 1957 and 1960), and *JMJP*, March 14, 1967. Figure on Kwangtung communes from *Yang-ch'eng Wan-pao*, August 19, 1965.

[30] Compare the number of communes in 1965—1,724—to the 1,691 markets that existed in Kwangtung in 1890. The later figure is from G. William Skinner, "Marketing and Social Structure in Rural China," *Journal of Asian Studies*, XXIV, No. 2 (February, 1965), note 109.

units that embraced only a few villages. The term "multivillage" refers to administrative groups of several (roughly four or five) villages.[31] The term "village" refers to such Chinese units as *chen, ts'un, chuang,* or *k'ou.* Finally, subvillage units include all groupings of families and individuals within a village. Better data might yield a more refined set of categories which would distinguish between districts of varying sizes and villages which differ not only in size but also in economic roles. But the available data only enable one to identify local leaders as serving on one of the five levels specified above.

Distribution of Cadres with Different Backgrounds. The differences among the backgrounds of leaders serving at various levels is suggested by the data derived from the biographical sketches (Table 9). In-

TABLE 9

BACKGROUNDS OF CADRES SERVING ON DIFFERENT
LEVELS OF GOVERNMENT, 1962–65*

Level	N	Old Cadres	Land Reform Cadres	Collectivization and Post-1955 Peasant Recruits	Ex-PLA Cadres	Young Middle School Graduates
County	37	*57%*†	19%	14%	5%	5%
District	35	20%	*46%*	14%	11%	9%
Multivillage	35	14%	11%	*31%*	*26%*	*17%*
Village	88	9%	14%	36%	9%	*31%*
Subvillage	45	0%	0%	*56%*	7%	*38%*

* The data derived from these tables have not been tested for their statistical significance; to do so would suggest greater precision than they deserve. I want only to employ quantitative data to formulate suggestive hypotheses.

† Italicized numbers in this and subsequent tables refer to those figures which especially substantiate the point made in the text.

depth interviewing of former local cadres and articles in the Chinese Communist press point in the same direction.[32] All these sources yield the strong impression that the eight types of local leaders already described were spread unevenly among the different administrative levels. The county level apparently tended to be dominated by old cadres, although a few land reform cadres and an even smaller number

---

[31] In Professor Skinner's terms, the multivillage is any unit that is *part* of one or more standard marketing areas. For a discussion of this concept, see his "Marketing and Social Structure."

[32] "The People Who Run China's Rural Communes," NCNA, Peking, March 22, 1966, in *SCMP,* No. 3665 (December 28, 1964), p. 29.

of collectivization cadres were found in jobs at this level. Demobilized PLA cadres also occupied many county level positions, and a few young middle school graduates were found in some of the technically demanding county level posts. At the district level, there were significant numbers of land reform cadres, collectivization cadres, veterans, and middle school graduates. At the multivillage level, there were substantial numbers of collectivization cadres and ex-servicemen. This level also frequently had a number of *hsia-fang* cadres. The villages defied easy generalizations, since considerable differences existed among them. In villages in the former guerrilla areas, old cadres seemed to dominate the top leadership, while land reform and collectivization

TABLE 10

BACKGROUNDS OF POLITICAL WORKERS SERVING ON
DIFFERENT LEVELS OF GOVERNMENT, 1962–65

Level	N	Old Cadres	Land Reform Cadres	Collectivization and Post-1955 Peasant Recruits	Ex-PLA Cadres	Young Middle School Graduates
County	20	60%	15%	20%	5%	0%
District	19	32%	42%	16%	11%	0%
Multivillage	13	23%	15%	46%	15%	0%
Village	25	20%	28%	32%	8%	12%
Subvillage	11	0%	0%	54%	27%	18%

cadres dominated in the south. Also at the village level were found those categorized as influential persons from the old regime and retired cadres. Numerous *hsia-fang* cadres, as well as young middle school graduates in technical jobs, were also found at the village level. Finally, the leadership of subvillage organizations seemed to consist mainly of post-1955 peasant recruits and middle school graduates.

Since the data on leaders of the five levels are not strictly comparable, Table 10 shows the backgrounds of cadres in one occupation—political workers—and the same general conclusions emerge. The county level tended to be led by old cadres, the district by land reform cadres, the multivillage by collectivization and post-1955 peasant recruit cadres, and the subvillage by the middle-aged, poorly educated peasants recruited after 1955.

Natives and Outsiders. The data suggest that the higher the level of government, the greater was the percentage of outsiders who served as local officials. This fact is particularly significant in China, because the traditional Chinese governmental system had elaborate regulations to prevent certain officials—especially at the county level and above—from serving in their native area or developing close ties to the area they served. Students of contemporary China are interested in knowing whether similar practices still exist.

The analytical problem is complex, however, for the question arises: what exactly is meant by "native" and "outsider"? The definitions used in this study are purposefully vague. A "native" is defined as one born in or having close ties to the area he serves. An "outsider" is defined as one born outside and having no close ties to the area he serves. But what are the criteria for close ties? And whose perception counts? When determining who is an "outsider" or a "native," three different perspectives can be applied: those of the local leader himself, those of his superiors, and those of his subordinates. Take the case of a recently appointed village leader who, though not from that village, comes from the county seat of the area in which that village is located. The county officials perceive the newly dispatched village leader as a native sent to another area of the county. The members of the village tend to perceive him as an outsider, although less of an outsider than if he had come from a different county or province. The village leader probably perceives himself ambivalently, as an outsider among the villagers, but sharing the ties that arise from their being natives of the same county.

Adding to the problem is the fact that a leader initially perceived to be an outsider can gradually acquire ties that, for all practical purposes, make him a native. The Chinese describe this as changing from *wai-hang* (outsider) to *nei-hang* (insider). Becoming familiar with the area, developing a rapport with the populace, perhaps marrying a local girl, and moving the location of one's household registry are some of the acts that can signify the change from being an outsider to being a native. The process is subtle and gradual.

Because of the complexity of factors involved, to classify local leaders into native and outsider categories and then aggregate the data probably oversimplifies matters. Nonetheless, this was done, and the results are presented in Table 11A (which covers all leaders for whom data are available) and Table 11B (which reports data for political workers and administrators on each level).

The data clearly reveal a pattern in which there are more outsiders at higher levels. (The one exception is, in fact, a theoretically interesting one. The multivillage level had more natives than did the village

MICHEL OKSENBERG

TABLE 11A

NATIVES AND OUTSIDERS BY LEVELS
OF GOVERNMENT, 1962–65

Level	N	Native	Outsider
County	27	41%	59%
District	35	58%	42%
Multivillage	21	86%	14%
Village	99	70%	29%
Subvillage	60	93%	7%

TABLE 11B

NATIVES AND OUTSIDERS ACCORDING TO FUNCTION, BY LEVELS, 1962–65

Level	POLITICAL OFFICERS			ADMINISTRATORS		
	N	Native	Outsider	N	Native	Outsider
County	20	40%	60%	10	60%	40%
District	14	50%	50%	16	75%	25%
Multivillage	10	80%	20%	3	100%	0%
Village	16	74%	26%	26	88%	12%
Subvillage	8	100%	0%	27	93%	7%

level. The implications of this are discussed later, in an analysis of the factors determining deployment of personnel.)

Among the twenty-seven county leaders for whom data were available, seventeen, or 59 per cent, were identified as outsiders. The native place of fifteen of these seventeen was ascertained. Thirteen came from outside the province while two served in counties located in their native provinces. The fragmentary data were nationwide in origin, including examples of outsiders serving in counties in the old guerrilla base areas of Honan, Hopei, Shensi, and Kansu provinces. Data on county leaders derived from other sources re-enforce the observation that there was a significant presence of outsiders on the *hsien* level. Interviews with refugees concerning county level organizations conducted by A. Doak Barnett and Ezra Vogel revealed the importance at this level of northerners, and particularly former members of the PLA and the so-called "south bound work teams" who became county officials in the south as their units captured and organized *hsien* in the provinces of Fukien and Kwangtung.[33] A report from Tanleng County in Szechwan Province stated that of the seven members of the standing committee of the county Party committee, over half came from outside the county.[34] And

[33] Barnett (with Vogel), *Cadres, Bureaucracy, and Political Power in China*, p. 130.
[34] *JMJP*, January 21, 1966, p. 2.

from Chekiang Province in the East came a similar report. The December, 1957, purge of Ch'en Hsiu-liang, deputy director of the Chekiang Party Propaganda Department, detailed the charges against her. One was that, on a visit to Haining County in Chekiang, Miss Ch'en stated: "Shantung people on the county committee are many; natives are few."[35] Although the data are scattered, they point in the same direction. Outsiders have clearly played an important role in directing the affairs of county level organizations.[36]

Most of the village level "outsiders" covered by the data used in this study came from outside the villages' "standard marketing areas." The origins of twenty of the twenty-nine outsiders identified at the village level (Table 11A) were determined. Three came from another village in the same marketing area, five from another standard marketing area in the same county, and twelve from another county in the same province. None came from another province. (Figures on the number of outsiders in village government would have been even higher if women officials who married into the village were counted as outsiders, but somewhat arbitrarily it was decided that these should be classified as natives.) The actual percentage of village leaders in China who were outsiders was probably less than the 29 per cent figure shown in Table 11A. But the appearance of even a few outsiders in top village posts was a new phenomenon,[37] and it indicated the penetration of state power to the village level.

Party Membership. As anticipated, the data also suggest that the percentage of Party or Youth League members among local officials increased at each higher level in the administrative hierarchy.[38] Table

---

[35] *Che-chiang Jih-pao*, December 1, 1957, p. 1.

[36] One of the clearest statements of Peking's policy with respect to the systematic appointment of outsiders was Teng Hsiao-p'ing, "Kuan-yu cheng-feng yün-tung ti pao-kao" (Report on the Rectification Campaign), *1958 Jen-min Shou-ts'e* (Peking: Ta Kung Pao Press, 1958), p. 40.

[37] Based on the biographical information contained in A. Doak Barnett, *China on the Eve of Communist Takeover* (New York: Praeger, 1963), pp. 103–57; David Crook, *Revolution in a Chinese Village* (London: Routledge and Kegan Paul, 1959); Fei Hsiao-t'ung, *Peasant Life in China* (London: Routledge and Kegan Paul, 1939); Fei Hsiao-t'ung, *China's Gentry* (Chicago: University of Chicago Press, 1953); Sidney D. Gamble, *Ting Hsien* (New York: Institute of Pacific Relations, 1954); Sidney D. Gamble, *North China Villages* (Berkeley and Los Angeles: University of California Press, 1963); Daniel Kulp, *Country Life in South China* (New York: Columbia University Press, 1925); Cornelius Osgood, *Village Life in Old China* (New York: Ronald Press, 1963); C. K. Yang, *A Chinese Village in Early Communist Transition* (Cambridge, Mass.: M.I.T. Press, 1959); and Martin Yang, *A Chinese Village: Taitou, Shantung Province* (New York: Columbia University Press, 1945).

[38] The same point is made in Peter Tang, *Communist China Today* (Washington, D.C.: Sino-Soviet Research Institute, 1961), p. 217.

12A includes all the data (with their unavoidable biases), while Table 12B provides a more precise but limited comparison. To repeat, the data are not a representative sample of all local officials in China; and therefore the figures cited do not reveal the real percentages of Party officials serving at each level with accuracy. Rather, the data are used

TABLE 12A

PARTY AFFILIATIONS OF LOCAL
LEADERS BY LEVEL, 1962–65

Level	N	CCP or CYL Members
County	20	100%
District	26	100%
Multivillage	21	90%
Village	90	83%
Subvillage	67	60%

TABLE 12B

PARTY AFFILIATIONS OF LOCAL LEADERS BY
LEVEL, ACCORDING TO FUNCTION, 1962–65*

Level	FINANCE AND TRADE		ADMINISTRATORS	
	N	CCP or CYL Members	N	CCP or CYL Members
Multivillage	5	60%	3	100%
Village	20	60%	15	93%
Subvillage	33	48%	23	52%

* The data are derived from the same source—interviews— and apply to workers in the same functions, thereby making them rigorously comparable. The data cannot be manipulated to yield more complete and equally rigorous comparisons.

to suggest patterns affecting different levels and functions. They indicate clearly that there was an increasing preponderance of CCP and CYL members among local officials as one ascended the levels of government. This phenomenon was no doubt the result, at least in part, of the preference in promotions enjoyed by Party members, as well as of the rapid recruitment into the Party of those non-CCP members who were promoted to higher level posts.

Age and Tenure in Office. In Table 13, the levels of local government are compared with respect to the age of officials and their tenure in office. Charting the average age of officials through time provides a rough indicator of generational change. There are four possible trends which would be of interest. First, the average age of officials could drop; this would result from younger men rapidly replacing older men. Second, the average age could remain the same. Then, tenure in office would be sufficiently short and the newcomers sufficiently young to keep the average age constant. Third, the average age could increase gradually; in this situation, an undeterminable combination of two factors might be at work. The turnover might not be sufficiently high or the replacements might be too old to keep the average age constant. In this instance, one could speak of generational stability, for the average age of officeholders would be increasing, with the same generation remaining in office. Fourth, the average age could increase rapidly; in such a case, an older generation would be replacing a younger generation. In the most general terms, it is the third case which is evident from the data available on leaders at the country, district, and village levels in China.

The aggregate data are difficult to interpret, but they suggest some interesting hypotheses. They show considerable differences among the various levels for the average age of local officials in 1962–65 and also differences in the changes in average age from 1955–57. Table 13 makes this clearer:

TABLE 13

COMPARISON OF AVERAGE AGE OF LOCAL OFFICIALS,
BY LEVEL, 1955–57 AND 1962–65

Level	N	Average Age 1955–57	N	Average Age 1962–65	Change in Age 1955–57 to 1962–65
County	7	32	20	45	plus 13
District	6	31	39	40	plus 9
Multivillage	14	33	17	33	no change
Village	51	26	82	34	plus 8
Subvillage	6	41	61	34	minus 7

The data, together with the more impressionistic information derived from the Chinese press and from interviews with refugees, lead to the following observations. First, leadership at the county, district, and village level displayed greater generational stability than leadership at the multivillage and subvillage levels in the decade from 1955 to 1965. The best indicator of this is the fact that, according to the data, the average age of county, district, and village level leaders went up by thirteen, nine, and eight years, respectively, from 1955–57 to 1962–65; in contrast, the average age of multivillage leaders remained constant, and the average age of subvillage officials dropped seven years. Second, by 1962–65, leaders at the county level tended to be somewhat older than those on the district level, who in turn tended to be somewhat older than those at the multivillage level. In 1962–65, the average ages of officials at these levels, according to our fragmentary data, were forty-five, forty, and thirty-three, respectively. This reflects the fact, noted already, that old cadres dominated at the county level, land reform cadres at the district level, and collectivization and ex-PLA cadres at the multivillage level. Third, subvillage organizations had begun to give many official posts to younger leaders. Only at this level did the average age of local leadership drop.

The increase in the average age of local leaders as a group, however, does not mean that the leaders as individuals enjoyed long tenure in office. At the county level, in fact, the evidence suggests that there were instances of high turnover rates, with the new appointees in the same age group as the replaced officials. A 1957 Hunan newspaper article on this subject is worth quoting at length:

> In the past few years, many cadres have been promoted and transferred. Of the 92 counties and municipalities in the entire province, 62 have had their secretary changed over four times. Among the current county secretaries, 66% have not served in their present post for over two years; among them, 28% have not been in their post for a year. As to the average cadre, the phenomenon of excessive transfers also exists.[39]

Although this article called for a longer tenure in office in order to consolidate leadership, news from the same province seven months later disclosed that the high turnover rate persisted. A New China News Agency dispatch from Ch'angsha stated:

> The Hunan Provincial Party Committee has recently decided to detail 61 cadres, on or above the rank of CCP *chuan-ch'ü* (special district) level (*ti-chi*), from organs under the provincial committee and *chuan-ch'ü* committees to take up leadership tasks at the lower levels. Most of them will be working as *hsien* committee secretaries, in order to strengthen leadership over agricultural production. In this way, the posts of Party committee first secretaries in 52 *hsien* or over 61% of all *hsien* within Hunan will be taken over by cadres whose rank is equal to or above *chuan-ch'ü* level.[40]

[39] *Hsin Hu-nan Pao,* April 15, 1957.
[40] NCNA, Ch'angsha, November 26, 1957, in *SCMP,* No. 1668 (December 10, 1957), p. 13.

Other data on Hunan leaders tended to support these reports.[41] Moreover, biographies of county secretaries in other provinces suggest that the high turnover rate persisted into the 1960's.[42]

Although the tenure of district and multivillage leaders is basically unknown, some inferences can be made from the data available. Between the county level and the village, the intermediate units of government underwent almost continual reorganization, which reduced the size of *ch'ü* and *hsiang* (1951), abolished *ch'ü* and merged *hsiang* (1956–57), combined the three cooperatives (agricultural, credit, and supply and marketing) into one (1957–58), merged the *hsiang* with cooperatives and formed communes (1958), reduced the size of communes (1961–64), and so on. In addition, local leaders have been the target of frequent rectification campaigns, such as the antirightist campaign of 1957–58, the "Four Clearance" movement of 1963–65, and the "Revolutionize the County Committee" effort of 1965. As a result of both the frequent reorganizations and the rectification campaigns, district and multivillage leaders lacked job security and continuity in office.

At the village level there was some turnover in leadership, but less than at the district and multivillage levels. In the existing literature on the subject, the generalization is often made that the village (production brigade) leaders of the 1960's tended to be the APC leaders of the 1950's and the land reform enthusiasts of the 1940's. Indeed, there were many villages in which this was the pattern. But more accurately, the top leaders in the villages mostly emerged either during land reform, collectivization, communalization, or the "Four Clearance" movement. (The percentages of village leaders who fell into each of these categories are unknown.) Each of the major movements that swept rural China included a re-evaluation of village leaders. When higher authorities discovered that the village leader's loyalty to the regime and its policies was doubtful, they removed him, and he became an ordinary peasant. Therefore, even though both the press and interviews with refugees suggest that many village leaders had long tenure in office, by 1962–65 there had been a considerable turnover among the village leaders who achieved their positions during the early revolutionary years.

[41] Data on Hunan leaders in my files.

[42] The tenure of county level leaders in the Fukien *hsien* studied by Barnett and Vogel appeared considerably longer than the tenure in Hunan. Until the discrepancies between the Hunan information and the Barnett-Vogel data can be explained, our conclusions must remain tentative.

The subvillage, in comparison to the other levels, appeared to have the highest turnover rate. Interviews with refugees pointed overwhelmingly to a short tenure in office at this level, and to the appointment of youths below twenty-five to subvillage leadership posts. The drop in the average age of subvillage leaders (Table 13) also suggests a rapid replacement of subvillage leaders between the mid-1950's and mid-1960's by younger men. Moreover, although the press does not frequently describe subvillage leaders, the evidence it presents substantiates the data obtained from refugee interviews.[43] As many as 70 to 80 per cent of subvillage leaders, for example, may have been removed from office in some provinces during the "Four Clearance" movement. Nor is this large turnover surprising. The leaders at higher administrative levels had reasons to maintain a rapid rate of turnover. Moreover, the jobs were so difficult, and unrewarding, that many incumbents probably grew weary of their burdens.

Subvillage leaders were cast in roles similar to those of factory foremen or noncommissioned officers. They generally bore the brunt of peasant hostility, deflecting discontent that otherwise might have been directed toward higher levels. By removing the subvillage leaders from office, the higher level authorities might reduce the level of discontent for a short period of time. In addition, subvillage leaders were not rewarded, as were cadres at higher levels, with regular salaries, total exemption from physical labor, high upward mobility into village and multivillage posts—or even opportunity to exercise much local discretion. Moreover, during campaigns, subvillage leaders were expected to work harder than anyone else, to "take the lead," and to do more than the average peasant. Interviews with refugees suggest that most people did not want to become subvillage leaders; many considered the jobs very undesirable. All these factors produced a high turnover rate among subvillage leaders.

Summary. The attributes of leaders who served on each level tended to be different. The higher the level of local government, the more likely it was that the top officials were senior Party members, outsiders, and over thirty-five years old. Opportunities for upward mobility seem to have been limited for persons at all levels, but they were particularly so for those at the multivillage, village, and subvillage levels. While the

---

[43] This has also been mentioned during the Cultural Revolution. See Richard Baum and Frederick Teiwes, "Who Was Right?" *Far Eastern Economic Review,* LVII, No. 12 (September 17–23, 1967), 564; also Radio Peking, International Service, September 3, 1967.

precise differences in tenure at various levels could not be ascertained, it appeared that the subvillage had, comparatively, the highest turn-over rates.

COMPARISON OF LEADERS IN DIFFERENT FUNCTIONS

An important aspect of local government in 1962–65 was its organi-zation into broad functional "systems" (*hsi-t'ung* or *chan-hsien*).[44] These systems, which included both Party and government institu-tions, grouped agencies that were engaged in related functions into one hierarchy. Presiding over the functional hierarchy was a CCP agency responsible for that function.

In rural counties, the main functional systems were: (1) political-le-gal activities (*cheng-fa*); (2) culture and education (*wen-chiao*); (3) agriculture, forestry, and water conservancy (*nung-lin-shui*); (4) finance and trade (*ts'ai-mao*); and (5) industry and communication (*kung-chiao*).

The emergence of these systems in the mid-1950's and their growing importance in subsequent years reflected the increasing specialization of a developing society. To perform new and complex tasks, the bu-reaucracy had to become more differentiated. An important question, therefore, is whether the attributes of officials in each functional sys-tem tended to be different. One should also ask whether the attributes of officials in each system become *increasingly* different through time.

Unfortunately, however, the data available for this study do not shed very much light on these questions. For example, the biographical sketches compiled do not include enough cases even to attempt a comparison of all systems. However, there were data on a sufficiently large number of cadres in finance and trade work, and in the coercive or political-legal apparatus, to permit an analysis of these categories. But the cases available for the other three systems—agriculture, indus-try, and culture—were so few that one can only treat them as a single category, which I will call educational and technical work, a rough description that embraces all three of them.

A few cadres, it should be noted, were independent of the functional systems; these included some in the following categories: (1) political cadres—those in charge of formulating policy and managing interper-

[44] For a more extensive discussion of "systems" in China, see Barnett (with Vogel), *Cadres, Bureaucracy, and Political Power,* pp. 6–9. Also my "Local Government and Politics in Communist China, 1955–58," in Andrew Cordier (ed.), *The Dean's Papers* (New York: Columbia University Press, 1967), pp. 266–67.

sonal relations—and (2) administrative cadres—those generalists in charge of coordinating and supervising day-to-day policy implementation. The analysis which follows therefore compares local leaders in five broad categories: politics, administration, finance and trade, coercion, and education and technology.

Distribution of Types. Officials performing various functions tended to have been recruited from different places and at different times. This hypothesis is suggested by the data in Table 14. Political workers

TABLE 14

BACKGROUNDS OF CADRES PERFORMING DIFFERENT FUNCTIONS, 1962–65

Function	N	Old Cadres	Land Reform Cadres	Collectivization and Post-1955 Peasant Recruits	Ex-PLA Cadres	Young Middle School Graduates
Politics	87	30%	23%	29%	11%	6%
Administration	57	19%	25%	43%	4%	11%
Finance and trade	46	0%	5%	28%	9%	58%
Coercion	19	11%	16%	37%	37%	0%
Education and technology	16	0%	0%	6%	6%	88%

tended to have long-established credentials in political activity; that is, they were more likely to be old cadres and land reform cadres. Administrators appeared to include more officials recruited in the recent past. Leaders in finance and trade work and educational and technical work apparently included a high percentage of young middle school graduates. And the coercive apparatus, the data suggest, was heavily staffed by former members of the PLA.[45] Table 14 aggregates data for all levels of local government; when analyzed separately, by level, the data yield similar patterns.[46]

[45] This is made clear in articles on Party strength in different functions. See *URI Clipping Files, Party and Government, Building Party Work* (1955–56), Vol. I, 13154–1315422.

[46] Each category included the following positions: (1) Political—Party secretaries on each level, Youth League secretaries on each level, chairmen of the Women's Federation on each level (*fu-lien-hui chu-jen*), propaganda workers, and political representatives to higher levels (*tai-piao*); (2) Administrative—chairmen and vice-chairmen of government and production units, general service personnel (*tsung-wu-yüan*), recording secretaries (*mi-shu*), and grain supervisors; (3) Finance and Trade—supply and marketing officials (*kung-hsiao-she*), work point recorders, bursars, accountants, and economic managers in production units; (4) Coercive—militia officials, armed forces department officials (*wu-chuang pu-men*), local security personnel (*ti-an-yüan* or *pao-an-yüan*), and political and legal department personnel (*cheng-fa-pu*); (5) Educational and Scientific Workers—teachers and technicians.

Native-Outsider. Some functions showed a higher percentage of outsiders than others. The data in Table 15 rank the functional fields in order of decreasing percentage of outsiders, as follows: education and science, coercion, politics, administration, and finance and trade. In short, education and science had the highest percentage of outsiders, while finance and trade had the lowest.

Moreover, if we analyze separately each level for which we have data, the same pattern holds. For example, on the county, district, multivillage, and village levels, the percentage of outsiders among

TABLE 15

NATIVES AND OUTSIDERS, BY FUNCTION, 1962–65

Function	N	Native	Outsider
Politics	90	69%	31%
Administration	47	87%	13%
Finance and trade	51	88%	12%
Coercion	10	60%	40%
Education and technology	19	21%	79%

political workers exceeded the percentage among administrators (see Table 11B). And, for the three levels for which data were available (multivillage, village, and subvillage), the difference in percentage of outsiders among the administrators and the finance and trade workers was negligible.

The tendency for there to be more outsiders among political workers, as we have defined them (primarily Party secretaries in our data), than among administrators (primarily heads of the government apparatus) can be independently confirmed. Several studies have noted that the leading government officials in the provinces and larger municipalities tended to be natives, and the top Party leaders tended to be outsiders.[47] The fragmentary data available on county leaders present a similar picture. Of the ten county magistrates (*hsien chang*) for whom we have data, six were natives and four were outsiders. In contrast, nine of twelve first secretaries for whom we have data were outsiders, while only three were serving in their native county.

There is also support for the conclusion that there tends to be a high percentage of outsiders among educational and technical workers. Marie Sieh's useful discussion of schoolteachers in China notes that

[47] Frederick Teiwes, *Provincial Party Personnel in Mainland China, 1956–1966* (New York: East Asian Institute, Columbia University, 1967), p. 17; Ezra Vogel, private papers.

school principals were usually persons transferred from another local-ity. Among the many sources of China's teachers, Mrs. Sieh states, were the "raw recruits arbitrarily assigned to teaching jobs after grad-uation from school."[48] A number of such raw recruits, many of them outsiders, taught in the primary schools in my refugee informants' villages; they also are mentioned in the Shensi village described by Jan Myrdal.[49] Many technicians were also assigned to non-native areas, and one refugee informant who had experience in agricultural exten-sion work in Shansi Province states that this was a matter of deliberate policy.[50]

Although few data were available for persons in the political-legal field, the high percentage of outsiders among these wielders of the instruments of coercion fits into the larger pattern. As might be ex-pected, those responsible for engineering social change seem to have included a higher proportion of outsiders.[51] The officials responsible for securing attitudinal change included those who exercised normative powers (political officers), those who were involved in the sociali-zation of youth (teachers), and those who controlled the instru-ments of violence (public security personnel). Peking apparently cal-culated that persons with few ties to the areas they served could discharge their responsibilities more effectively than those with stronger local ties.

The high percentage of outsiders among those in certain functions also may have reflected problems of recruitment. Not only did Peking seem purposefully to assign outsiders to those tasks related to social change, as noted above, but natives may actually have been less willing to serve in the sensitive posts in these fields. In other words, the task of trying to change the behavioral patterns of one's neighbors may have been consciously avoided by many local leaders. We will return later to the implications of these findings.

Average Age of Officials in Each Function. The data suggest that the average age of leaders in different functional fields differed signifi-cantly, with administrators the oldest, followed in the age scale by those in politics, coercion, finance and trade, and education and tech-

---

[48] Marie Sieh, "The School Teacher: A Link to China's Future," *Current Scene,* III, No. 18 (May 1, 1965), 4, 6.

[49] Myrdal, *Report from a Chinese Village,* pp. 293–317.

[50] See protocol from Informant C, September 29, 1965, p. 5.

[51] The postulate is derived from organizational theory. A classic discussion is in Philip Selznick, *TVA and the Grass Roots* (Berkeley and Los Angeles: University of California Press, 1953).

nology (Table 16). Moreover, a comparison between the average ages of leaders in separate functions in 1962–65 and 1955–57 shows that the average ages of some functional groups increased more rapidly than others. The comparison also tentatively indicates that the differences among the functions increased from 1955–57 to 1962–65. In 1955–57, the oldest group—the administrators—were on the average eleven years older than the educators and technicians. By 1962–65, the gap had increased to nineteen years. These findings suggest interesting hypotheses about different recruitment patterns among the various functions.

Generational stability appeared to characterize the holders of jobs in the political and coercive fields. That is, in the approximately seven

TABLE 16

Average Age of Local Leaders, by Function, 1955–57 and 1962–65

Function		Average Age			
	N	1955–57	N	1962–65	Change
Politics	36	33	70	39	+ 6
Administration	29	35	72	46	+11
Finance and trade	21	27	49	30	+ 3
Coercion	4	29	11	34	+ 5
Education and technology	9	24	16	27	+ 3

years from 1955–57 to 1962–65, the average ages of these two groups increased six and five years, respectively. These statistics and the individual cases they represent indicate that the same age groups have held on to these positions. The average ages of the finance and trade workers and the educators and technicians, on the other hand, increased by only three years. These figures suggest that youth found more attractive employment opportunities in these lines of work, a conclusion supported by in-depth interviews with refugees.

Finally, the rapid increase in the average age of administrators—up eleven years from 1955–57 to 1962–65—may highlight a potentially significant development. The individual cases behind these aggregate statistics fall into two patterns. First, on the village and subvillage levels, while young middle school graduates tended to replace aging leaders in finance and trade and education and technology (a phenomenon also reflected in the data in Table 14), the poorly educated, over thirty-five years old, "post-1955 recruit" tended to replace the retiring administrator. On the village and subvillage level, an age and education gap has developed between the administrators and the other leaders whom they direct—bookkeepers, water conservancy technicians, and so on. Second, in several instances, a man who was an older Party secretary in 1955 had, by 1965, dropped his Party post to become the head of the government apparatus on that level. Several 1959 Party branch secretaries became brigade heads in communes; and several men who were commune heads in 1962–65 had previously been higher ranking Party secretaries. The early signs of a phased retirement pattern may be emerging here, with older leaders first withdrawing from the more arduous political (Party) posts to become administrators, and then perhaps later retiring in a full sense. One important question this raises (unanswerable on the basis of available information) is whether former political workers retain influence after leaving their political posts. Do they become the equivalent of the elders in traditional China—men without formal political position but retaining influence and much of the substance of power?

Educational Levels. Important differences emerge in a comparison of the educational levels of officials in different functional fields (Table 17). As might be expected, those in education and technology rank

TABLE 17

DISTRIBUTION OF LOCAL LEADERS IN DIFFERENT FUNCTIONS,
ACCORDING TO FORMAL EDUCATION, 1962–65

Function	N	Average Formal Education	YEARS OF FORMAL EDUCATION		
			0–2	3–6	7–12
Politics	43	3.6	42%	44%	14%
Administration	50	4.0	40%	42%	18%
Finance and Trade	42	5.6	10%	67%	24%
Coercion	9	2.8	44%	55%	0%
Education and technology	11	10.5	0%	0%	100%

first, with an average of 10.5 years of formal schooling. Behind them come finance and trade workers with 5.6 years, administrators with 4.0 years, political workers with 3.6 years, and coercive agents with 2.8 years.

Here the data appear to shed light on the conflict between the "reds" and the "experts." The data clearly show the higher level of education enjoyed by the "expert" educators and the technicians, compared to the "red" political workers.

Party Affiliation. Because of data problems, one cannot be confident of the accuracy of the available information on Party and CYL membership of persons in various functional fields. Elsewhere, I discuss the general upward bias in the reporting of CCP and CYL affiliations.[52] Comparisons are made difficult, moreover, because the available data on the political, coercive, and administrative officials relate to individuals working at all levels of local government, while the data on workers in the finance and trade field and on educational and technical workers relate only to persons working at the multivillage, village, and subvillage levels. It will be recalled that the proportion of Party members among local officials apparently increases at each level. Thus, the available figures on Party membership of finance and trade workers and educational and technical personnel, which indicate a lower proportion of Party and CYL members, may be slightly misleading when compared with persons in other functional fields.

Recognizing these problems, we still report that the highest percentage of CCP members existed among coercive agents (100 per cent, $N = 7$) and political workers (99 per cent, $N = 83$), followed by administrators (88 per cent, $N = 65$) and education and technical personnel (88 per cent, $N = 9$). The lowest percentage of Party membership was among finance and trade workers (58 per cent, $N = 64$). While this pattern conforms to what one might expect, the biases in the data make their interpretation difficult.

Summary. Different types of leaders tended to serve in separate functional positions. Old cadres and land reform cadres provided the bulk of political workers, especially above the village level. While administrators also were predominantly old and land reform cadres, they appeared to include both a greater number of post-1955 recruits and a number of semiretired former political workers. Finance and trade workers and educators and technicians were recruited to a considerable degree after 1955 from among young middle school graduates. In contrast, personnel in the coercive apparatus seem to have been drawn in large part from the ranks of demobilized PLA members. The data also suggest differences among leaders in regard to age, education, origins (natives or outsiders), and Party membership. As a result of these differences, finance and trade personnel and the education and technical workers tended to be quite different in many respects from the political workers and the coercive agents; the former tended to be

[52] See my "Sources and Methodological Problems in the Study of Communist China," in the Appendix to this volume.

younger, better educated, and natives (except for educators), while the latter tended to be older, less well educated, and outsiders.

COMPARISON OF LEADERS ON THE BASIS OF PARTY AFFILIATION

Thus far, the characteristics of different groups of local leaders have been examined according to the levels of government on which they served and the functions they performed. It is also of interest to analyze differences among three other groupings: those who were CCP members, those who were CYL members, and those who were not affiliated with either the CCP or CYL. In examining these groups, one notes significant variations in educational background and place of origin, which re-enforce the observations made earlier about the red-expert problem and about the use of outsiders as loyal agents of social change.

Education. The red-expert dilemma is reflected in the data which show that Party members were less educated than non-Party local leaders (Table 18). In spite of an upward bias in press reporting of the

TABLE 18

DISTRIBUTION OF LOCAL LEADERS BY PARTY AFFILIATION, ACCORDING
TO FORMAL EDUCATION, 1962–65

Party Affiliation	N	Average Years Formal Education	YEARS OF FORMAL SCHOOLING		
			0–2	3–6	7–12
CCP	82	4.5	41%	47%	12%
CYL	38	5.4	13%	40%	48%
None	39	5.4	21%	49%	30%

educational level of Party members, educational differences are evident. The available data show that the number of years of formal education enjoyed by Party members averaged 4.5 ($N = 82$), while the formal education of non-Party members ($N = 39$) averaged 5.4 years. Youth League members also averaged 5.4 years of education. However, in contrast to non-Party officials, CYL officials included fewer who were either very poorly educated or very well educated. Whereas 15 per cent of the non-Party officials had over ten years of formal education, only 3 per cent of the CYL members had attained this level. On the other hand, all CYL members had received at least one year of formal education, while 15 per cent of the unaffiliated local leaders had never attended school.

The biographies of non-Party officials with varying levels of formal education—including six with no formal education and six with an upper middle school (high school) education—suggest one of the significant differences between Party or CYL and non-Party personnel. Two important criteria were employed by Peking in evaluating personnel: political reliability or "virtue" (*te*) and skill or talent (*ts'ai*). What the non-Party personnel lacked in political reliability was balanced by the special skills they offered, and this was true regardless of their level of formal education. All six of the uneducated non-Party officials were older men who brought to their jobs extraordinary experience, wide personal contacts, or both. All six of the very well-educated non-Party officials either brought rare skills to their job or had personal attributes which encouraged the regime to overlook their deficiencies in terms of political "virtue." (In two cases the well-educated non-Party officials were from overseas Chinese families, and received remittances from abroad. In 1962–65 Peking did not wish to jeopardize the flow of these remittances and therefore allowed these Chinese to enjoy successful careers.[53]) In short, the data suggest that non-Party members compensated for their lack of political reliability by offering the regime either skills or other values which it considered to be important. But this exacerbated the differences between the reds and the experts.

Native Place. Were Party members or non-Party members more likely to serve as outsiders? The data from the biographical sketches (Table 19) suggest that Party and Youth League members were more

TABLE 19

NATIVES AND OUTSIDERS AS A FUNCTION OF PARTY AFFILIATION

	N	Natives	Outsiders
Party and CYL	180	79%	21%
Non-Party	44	95%	5%

likely to serve as outsiders than leaders unaffiliated with the CCP or CYL were. The reason for this may be related to the earlier observation that Peking apparently is inclined to assign outsiders to undertake many tasks related to the implementation of social change. Outsiders

[53] For further discussion, see John C. Pelzel, "Production Brigade and Team Management" (paper for the Columbia University Seminar on Modern East Asia: China; February 16, 1966); Franz Schurmann, *Ideology and Organization in Communist China* (Berkeley and Los Angeles: University of California Press, 1966), chap. vii.

perhaps are more likely to remain loyal to Peking; similarly, Party and CYL members perhaps are more likely to owe their allegiance to the nation. For sensitive local positions demanding the unquestioned loyalty of the officeholder, then, the incumbent is more likely to be both an outsider and a Party or CYL member. If the job is sensitive enough to require an outsider, the data in Table 19 suggest, it possibly also requires a Party or CYL member. Despite this fact, however, non-Party officials were in many instances dispatched to lower levels (that is, many were subject to *hsia-fang,* or "transfer downward"). The data suggest, though, that in comparison with Party officials, non-Party officials were more likely, when sent to the local level, to be sent to their native place. (While the available data suggest that this was probably true, however, more adequate documentation would be required to assert that this was a standard practice.)

COMPARISON OF LEADERS IN DIFFERENT GEOGRAPHICAL AREAS

Not surprisingly, given the diversity and complexity of Chinese society, the fragmentary and impressionistic information available suggests that the individual attributes of local leaders varied according to the localities in which they served. Unfortunately, the data only permit an analysis of the regional differences among those local leaders who worked at the multivillage level and below, and information is lacking on possible regional variations in the traits of leaders at the county and district levels. It is perhaps fair to assume, however, that the causes of differences among village leaders also operated at the county and district levels. Three general factors seemed to explain many of the variations among village leaders in separate areas: local socioeconomic conditions, the ratings given local political units by higher authorities, and distinctive revolutionary histories. Let us look at each of these in greater detail.

Socioeconomic conditions. A number of geographic, economic, and social factors affected both the tasks facing village governments in rural areas and their capabilities to perform these tasks.[54] Village government and politics acquired a distinctive flavor, depending upon

---

[54] Several recent articles have correctly pointed out that unqualified generalizations which claim validity for the entire Chinese society and polity are oversimplified and misleading. Attempts to explain Chinese politics must include analysis of regional differences. See Skinner, "Marketing and Social Structure in Rural China"; John W. Lewis, "The Study of Chinese Political Culture," *World Politics,* XVIII, No. 3 (April, 1966), 503–24; and John K. Fairbank, "The State That Mao Built," *World Politics,* XIX, No. 4 (July, 1967), 664–78.

whether the village was in a mountain area or on the plains; in an old revolutionary base or in a newly liberated area; in a coastal or "border" region or in an inland region; in an area with extensive ties to overseas Chinese or with significant minority groups or in an area with a population that was exclusively "Han" with no links overseas; in a market town, in a village with easy access to a market town, or in a village remote from a market town. Villages differed, also, according to whether they had easy access to an urban center or were in an isolated area; in a prosperous area which yielded a high tax revenue or in an impoverished area that required a budget subsidy from higher administrative levels; in an area that required the massing of large numbers of laborers at one site for irrigation projects, or one where less concentration of mobilized laborers was the pattern; in a region where rice was double cropped or in an area where it was single cropped. Differences were also related to whether Mandarin or a local dialect was the native tongue; whether the village was in a newly reclaimed area settled under Communist rule or in an old agricultural region; whether traditional lineage and sublineage organizations had been strong or weak in the pre-1949 period, whether the area had single-lineage villages, multilineage villages, or no villages at all but only scattered housing; whether or not there were modern transportation facilities. Because of such variations, every type of village had its own set of problems and drew upon a different set of resources to meet these problems. Moreover, the central government had different expectations concerning the performance of villages with varying characteristics. The distinct problems, resources, and expectations characteristic of different types of villages, in turn, seem to have produced differences in leadership patterns.

While the information about these differences is merely suggestive, and not conclusive, the following tentative observations can be made. Mountain villages appeared to receive a large number of young middle school graduates, sent from areas with better school systems, who were assigned to local educational and technical posts.[55] The militia and public security forces seemed to be more highly developed and important in coastal and border regions, with the probable result that the leaders of these organizations—often demobilized members of the PLA —played especially significant political roles there.[56]

[55] Derived from *CKCN*.
[56] Lang Yi, *Kung-an Pu-tui* (The Public Security Forces) (Peking: Chinese Youth Press, 1958), pp. 4–12. Statistics on PLA troop deployment are in Ministry of Defense

Villages from which sizable numbers of persons migrated overseas presented special problems and opportunities to Peking.[57] On the one hand, the CCP feared that the villagers in these areas might be corrupted by the pernicious influence of their relatives abroad, many of whom periodically visited their old villages and regularly sent remittances home. On the other hand, such villages clearly benefited from the flow of remittances. When its primary concern was the possible corrupting influence of the overseas Chinese, the CCP apparently attempted to reduce the ties of such villages with their overseas Chinese relatives, and in such instances it seems to have relied more heavily upon outsiders to lead such villages. When its primary concern was to increase the flow of remittances, the CCP appeared to rely heavily on village leaders (many of them not Party members) whose influence among overseas Chinese predated the establishment of Communist rule in China.

Linguistic patterns also affected the characteristics of leaders at the local level. Some problems were involved in sending cadres who did not speak the native tongue to villages where a distinctive local dialect or language was spoken. On the other hand, precisely because such villages were not composed of native speakers of Mandarin (*kuo-yü*), there were strong arguments for sending in outsiders to break down localism and to try to integrate these villages more fully into the national community.[58]

There were significant differences between old guerrilla base areas, which came under Communist rule in the 1930's and 1940's, and areas that saw little of the Communists until the late 1940's. Not surprisingly, old cadres seemed to be particularly strong in the villages in old guerrilla base areas. In contrast, land reform cadres appeared to be more numerous and influential in the villages of provinces such as

---

Security Bureau (ed.), *Ti-ch'u Tzu-liao* (Materials on Provincial Areas) (Taipei, January, 1965).

[57] For some of the problems and opportunities which areas with overseas Chinese faced, see five fascinating pamphlets. Three of them were published by the Communists and are intended to encourage overseas Chinese to remit money to their old home: *Nan-hai-hsiang hsün* (Bulletin of Nan-hai Township), No. 1 (Nanhai County, Kwangtung, April, 1959); *Ch'ao-shan Ch'iao-hsiang hsüng* (Bulletin of Ch'ao-shan-ch'iao Township) (Hong Kong: Chi-wen Press, 1955); *Sha-tung-ch'iao-hsiang yüeh-k'an* (Sha-tung-ch'iao Township Monthly Gazette), No. 1 (December, 1958). Two were published by anti-Communists: *Chin-jih ti Kuang-tung* (Kwangtung Today) (Hong Kong, April, 1957); *T'ai-shan Ch'iao-hsiang Hsueh-lui Shih* (A History of the Bloodbath in Tai-shan County Ch'iao Township) (n.p., January, 1952).

[58] See "Fu-chien yi-ke hsiang ti chi-chi" (Miracle in a Fukien Township), *Hung Ch'i* (Red Flag), No. 4 (July 16, 1958), p. 35.

Kwangtung, Hunan, and Szechwan, which came under CCP control in later years. Army veterans constituted a higher percentage of the population, and appeared to make up a higher proportion of the local leadership in the old guerrilla base areas (where the PLA recruited so many of its members in the 1940's) and in some border provinces (to which many demobilized soldiers were dispatched after being mustered out of the PLA). For example, in late 1962, 30 per cent of all basic level cadres in Shantung Province were veterans, but in the old base areas, the figure was 60 per cent.[59] The concentration of former soldiers in these areas is suggested by the fragmentary statistics presented in Table 20, which is a compilation of scattered figures on demobilized

TABLE 20

NUMBER OF DEMOBILIZED SOLDIERS IN EIGHT PROVINCES*

Province	Total Population (Million)	Year	Number of Veterans (Thousand)	Percentage of Total Population	Type of Province
Chekiang	22.9	1957	190	0.81%	liberated post-1947
Heilungkiang	11.9	1959	307†	2.58%	border
Honan	44.2	1958	310‡	0.70%	mostly liberated post-1947
Hunan	33.2	1959	210‡	0.66%	liberated post-1947
Kiangsi	16.8	1958	78	0.46%	liberated post-1947
Kiangsu	41.3	1957	283	0.69%	partly liberated post-1947
Shansi	14.3	1959	200+	1.40%§	old base area
Shantung	48.9	1957	610	1.31%	old base area

* Figures were obtained from the following sources: population statistics from 1957 *Jen-min Shou-ts'e;* Statistics on veterans from Chekiang: *Chekiang Jih-pao,* June 5, 1957; Heilungkiang: *NWPTS,* No. 7 (July, 1959), p. 4; Honan: *SCMP,* No. 1786 (June 6, 1958), p. 5; Hunan: *NWPTS,* No. 5 (May, 1959), p. 10; Kiangsi, *SCMP,* No. 1780 (May 28, 1958), p. 47; Kiangsu: *SCMP,* No. 1653 (November 18, 1957), p. 29; Shansi: *NWPTS,* No. 10 (Oct., 1959), p. 9; Shantung: *SCMP,* No. 1588 (August 12, 1957), p. 13.

† This figure does not include another hundred thousand veterans serving in state farms.

‡ This is a minimum estimate; the actual figure is probably higher.

§ In Shansi fully 12 per cent of the total population were either natives in service, veterans, dependents of servicemen and veterans, or survivors of those who died while in the service. *SCMP,* No. 1780 (May 28, 1958), p. 5.

soldiers in several different provinces. (To the best of my knowledge, the CPR has not published more complete statistics on this.)

The biographical sketches compiled for this study also suggest that in the early 1960's retired Party cadres were appearing in large num-

[59] *SCMP,* No. 2915 (February 8, 1963), p. 10.

bers in the old guerrilla base areas, which can be explained in part by the fact that these were the areas from which the CCP had recruited the bulk of its members a generation before.

Differences between new settlements and villages in older agricultural areas also deserve attention. In the years after 1949 the government built a large number of new settlements on former waste and marshland. These new settlements became the homes of demobilized soldiers, young middle school graduates sent from the cities, some cadres sent down from higher levels, convicts and former convicts, and peasants resettled by the government. Among the leaders of these settlements were many older veterans, young middle school graduates, and higher level cadres.

Thus, it appears that a number of socioeconomic and historical factors have affected village leadership patterns. Analysis of these variables must, at present, be somewhat impressionistic, in view of a paucity of firm data, but unquestionably they have been significant in helping to shape the character of political life at the local level.

Rating System. Local leadership patterns were also affected by the CPR's rating system. It is quite clear from a reading of the Chinese Communist press that local political and administrative units—at the county, *ch'ü,* commune, brigade, and team levels—were rated on a three-point scale: "grade one" (*ti-yi-teng*); "grade two" (*ti-erh-teng*); and "grade three" (*ti-san-teng*). Grade three units were labeled "backward" (*lo-hou-ti*), while grade one units usually were labeled "progressive" (*chin-pu-ti*). In addition, superior units were given praiseworthy titles, such as "model (*mo-fan*) unit" or "red flag unit." Moreover, some local units were used as centers for experimentation in Peking's "ink-blot" approach to rural development. Leadership patterns differed in each category of unit.

The concept of "key points" (*chung-tien*) was an important element in the CCP's approach to local leadership problems. When higher authorities decided to implement a particular policy or program, local leaders were gathered together at a "key point," where the new practice was being tried out for demonstration and experimental purposes. The experience gained in this "key point" became the basis for wider implementation of the new policy. Since higher authorities invested substantial resources in the "key point" and had a large stake in its outcome, they took an intense interest in its development. Some "key point" experiments were financed entirely by appropriations from the administrative unit at the next higher level rather than by a local unit's own funds. There is evidence to suggest that the higher authorities involved often acquired a strong vested interest in the success of such "key point" activities.

Consequently, "key points" were tightly controlled by higher levels. A quotation from one revealing article which discusses "key points" makes this clear:

> In the past few years, the vast majority of counties in the nation have established key-point *hsiang*. Each level Party committee employs this locality for developing experiments, cultivating models, and improving leadership techniques. Although this facilitates the socialist transformation of agriculture, not a few localities have weaknesses in leading the key-point *hsiang* itself. . . .
>
> Here is the situation in Yangshangk'ou *hsiang,* the key point for Wuhsiang county in Shansi Province. In order to cultivate well this key-point *hsiang,* not only did the county [Party] committee dispatch important *ch'ü* level cadres to this *hsiang* to serve as the *hsiang* head and [Party] branch secretary, but it also dispatched a large number of cadres to reside for a long time at the *hsiang* to help in work. Last year, the number of long residing cadres had in this *hsiang* reached over 20. [At this time, the average *hsiang* had three to five cadres.] On the average, every small cultivation team (each team has about 10 households) in a cooperative has a cadre. This year, the county committee has also dispatched ten cadres—led by such important cadres as a *hsien* committee member, deputy *hsien* magistrate, and deputy chief of the agriculture and forestry office—to reside for a long time at this *hsiang* to assist in work.
>
> Because the number of cadres dispatched to this *hsiang* was so large and their capacity was so strong, last year the *hsiang* displayed a rather satisfactory work experience. . . .[60]

The result, however, was that no work was done by local cadres, according to the article. They did not have a chance to develop their own skills, the article stated; instead, all work was directed by the "envoy to the *hsiang* cadres" (*chu-hsiang kan-pu*).

Undoubtedly, this article selected an extreme example to make a point, but the tendencies it describes seem to hold for other "key points" as well. Leadership patterns in the "key points" (there were "key point" counties as well as "key point" *ch'ü,* cooperatives, brigades, and so on) were therefore unique. It is clear that "key point" areas had more outsiders in leadership positions. More impressionistically, it appears that "key point" leaders included a higher percentage of Party members and cadres with a relatively good education, as

---

[60] Tien Liu, "Kai-shan chung-tien-hsiang ti ling-tao" (Improve Leadership over Key Points), *Hsin-hua Yüeh-pao* (New China Monthly), No. 68 (June 28, 1955), pp. 20–21. See also Thomas Bernstein, "Leadership and Mass Mobilization in the Soviet and Chinese Collectivization Campaigns of 1929–30 and 1955–56: A Comparison," *China Quarterly,* No. 31 (July-September, 1967), pp. 31–33.

well as persons with technical skills. (Tenure in office in "key point" units may have been relatively short.)

There is also little doubt that the patterns of leadership prevailing in any unit were affected by whether the unit was classified "grade one," "grade two," or "grade three." The following quotation makes this clear:

> Comrade Ch'en Chan-chao was sent down to Hohsin *hsiang,* Ank'ang county in the spring of 1957. Prior to being sent down he was production executive secretary (*sheng-ch'an kan'shih*) in Liushu *ch'ü.* He was dispatched to reside in Tingta APC. In the past, this co-operative was a grade one co-op (*yi-teng-she*). Subsequently, owing to a relaxation in leadership, various kinds of work lagged behind other co-ops. Especially after entering the spring season, owing to the reduced production from last year's natural disaster, 88 of the co-op's 101 households did not have money to buy grain.[61]

The story goes on to describe how Comrade Ch'en's exploits assisted the villagers to make their cooperative a superior one again.

As this story suggests, if a "grade one" unit lost its ranking, outsiders were likely to be dispatched to the area. Other articles indicate that generally leaders of "grade three" units were susceptible to removal and replacement by outsiders sent on either a temporary or a permanent basis to remedy the situation. If a cadre was able quickly to boost the ranking of his unit from "three" to "one," his chances of recognition and promotion were enhanced. "Grade one," "red flag," and "model unit" areas were less likely to have outside cadres assigned to them. In fact, cadres from such advanced units frequently were reassigned to the backward units. The mainland press suggests, therefore, that cadres in "grade one" units enjoyed greater mobility, both lateral and vertical.

In short, higher authorities often made decisions concerning the deployment of local officials on the basis of the ratings given to local units, and leadership patterns were also affected by whether or not a unit was a "key point." However, until further information is available on the process by which units were chosen to be "key points" and on the criteria used to rate units, the effects of these factors upon leadership patterns can only be partially understood.

Patterns of Revolutionary Change. The Communist revolution in China involved the seizure of power by certain groups and the forceful

---

[61] Teng Chün-yang, "Ling-tao she-yüan k'e-fu k'un-nan fa-chan sheng-ch'an" (Leading Co-op Members to Overcome Difficulties and to Develop Production), in CCP Shensi Committee Office (ed.), *Socialist Construction in Rural Shensi* (Sian: Shensi People's Press, 1958), p. 11.

removal from power of other groups. This seizure of power (which in any particular area took a period of time and therefore was in a sense gradual) occurred at all levels, including the village. In any case, at least by 1955, the revolution had effectively removed power from the hands of those groups which had wielded it under the old regime, including the leaders of lineages, village headmen, and other intermediaries between the village and the formal governmental apparatus, as well as the local officials of the Republican government. To replace them, new local leaders emerged. Obviously, these new leaders were major beneficiaries of the revolution, for it gave them increased power, wealth, and—as the revolution acquired legitimacy—authority.

While this general statement gives some idea of the impact of the revolution upon local leadership, it does not capture the diversity in the revolutionary process. In reality, the political changes engendered by the Communist revolution varied considerably among villages—a fact often overlooked by students of contemporary China. Moreover, the few reliable village histories available for the post-1949 period suggest that differences in revolutionary experiences in the early years continued to be reflected, in later years, in the varied characteristics of village leaders in different types of villages.

In analyzing revolutionary experiences in different villages, it is useful to note the types of cadres who became the new leaders of the villages during the Communist revolution. As indicated earlier in this article, all leaders who emerged in the takeover period can be classified as old cadres or land reform cadres. But these cadres can also be differentiated according to the type of change that brought them to positions of leadership in their villages. In some villages, the effects of the revolution on leadership were primarily of a class nature, and it was the landless and poor peasants who became the new leaders. In other villages, however, the revolution involved different sorts of social changes, in which one lineage replaced another lineage (or a sublineage replaced another sublineage) as the most influential group. In some other villages, one of the main effects of the revolution appeared to be generational change. There the youth, including the kin of the old village leaders, banded together to lead land reform.

In yet other villages, a combination of family and class change occurred. In the late 1920's and 1930's the destitution wrought by the famines that swept North and Central China caused considerable population movement. From the biographies of recent village leaders in Shantung, southern Shensi, and Shansi, it appears that many were migrants who came to villages in these provinces from Honan and northern Shensi. They settled on marginal land and were employed as hired hands; if they could eke out a living, they were sometimes subsequently joined by other members of their impoverished families. Before the revolution, many were still very poor. Then the revolution provided them the opportunity to become the new leaders of the villages to which they had only recently moved. Revolution in these villages thus entailed both class and family change.

Finally, in a few villages, the revolution apparently was in part a sham, at least at the start. Despite *pro forma* changes in leadership, in reality the old elite continued to have a powerful voice in village affairs.

In Maoist terminology, each village had its own set of contradictions, cleavages, and conflicts; these included class conflicts, kinship rivalries, generational tensions, and native-outsider strife. Mao believed that it was necessary to manipulate these tensions for the CCP's ends, and the Party's rural policy apparently permitted enough flexibility to allow this to be done in a variety of effective ways, depending on the local situation. Thus, in villages where class conflict could be effectively manipulated, a new economic class was brought to power. In other situations, though, the CCP manipulated kinship rivalries. This very flexibility in revolutionary method, in short, meant that the process of revolution varied as it unfolded in China's villages.

One can ask a variety of questions about the distinctiveness of the legacy of each type of revolutionary change. Exactly how, and to what extent, did patterns of local leadership in the 1960's reflect the type of change which a locality had experienced during the early years of the revolution? Did a locality where the effects of change appeared to be primarily generational, for example, have different leadership patterns from a locality in which the revolution mainly involved the rise of individuals from the poorer classes to positions of power?

The paucity of information makes it difficult to give clear answers to such questions, but several hypotheses are suggested by the available village histories.[62] First, in those villages where the revolution was primarily characterized by generational change and the new leadership group was uniformly young, the new leaders tended to stay in office through the 1950's and early 1960's. Many of these villages, in other

---

[62] The following discussion is based upon information gathered from sources cited in footnotes 24, 25, 26, 27, and 28 above. The interviews, Myrdal's *Report from a Chinese Village,* and Crook, *First Years of Yangyi Commune* were particularly valuable.

words, probably continued to be led by the original group of old cadres and land reform cadres; as a result, younger potential leaders, such as demobilized PLA veterans and middle school graduates, may have found it more difficult in later years to win leadership posts there. Second, in villages where the revolution brought familial change, it seems likely that by the 1960's the old and land reform cadres who first came to power had retired in greater numbers, partly because at the time of their recruitment they were already middle-aged and partly because they were willing to step aside in favor of their younger relatives. One may hypothesize, therefore, that by the 1960's such villages may have had more young middle school graduates and former soldiers as leaders. They may also have had a larger number of retired, informal leaders who continued to advise their younger kin. Third, in many villages where class conflicts and economic motivations provided the principal force for revolutionary change, many of the original land reform cadres were doubtless loath to loose their economic gains through collectivization and communalization. Posing obstacles to further social change, such cadres were often removed and replaced by ex-PLA cadres as well as by peasants recruited during the collectivization and communalization drives. Fourth, in those villages where the Communists found no deep cleavages or "contradictions" that could be effectively exploited, revolutionary change was minimal. To induce change in such villages, greater numbers of cadres had to be sent from higher levels, and despite the presence of such cadres, village affairs probably continued to be heavily influenced by informal leaders left over from the old regime. Finally, since the revolutionary change experienced by most villages involved a combination of generational, familial, and economic class conflict, subsequent leadership patterns reflected a combination of the first, second, and third patterns described above.

BUREAUCRATIC POSITIONS: SUMMARY

To summarize, distinctions can be made among local leaders in China who serve on different levels of government (county, district, multivillage, village, and subvillage), who perform different functions (politics, administration, finance and trade, coercion, and education and technology), and who work in different kinds of geographical areas (classified according to the area's socioeconomic characteristics, ratings by higher authorities, and revolutionary experience). The available data make possible fairly precise comparisons among leaders serving on different levels of government, less precise comparisons among those with different functions, and only tentative observations about the characteristics of local leaders serving in different types of geographical areas.

However, one conclusion is clear, on the basis of this analysis. The individual attributes of different groups of local leaders varied, no matter on what basis they are compared. Recruitment of local leaders into bureaucratic positions, it follows, was governed by some identifiable underlying principles; it was not a haphazard process. A recruitment process that worked at random would have resulted in a more even distribution of the eight distinguishable types of local leaders among the available bureaucratic positions.

FACTORS AFFECTING RECRUITMENT AND THEIR EFFECTS UPON THE GOVERNMENTAL SYSTEM

To what extent, on the basis of the data already cited, is it possible to identify some of the more important factors governing the recruitment process?

Seniority, political reliability, the premium placed on certain skills, attitudes on the relative desirability of various jobs, the emphasis of current government policy, and the legacies of the early years of the revolution all seemed to be determinants affecting the recruitment of local leaders into specific positions.[63] These determinants (with the exception of the revolutionary heritage) are typical factors affecting political recruitment anywhere. What is necessary is to determine the relative importance placed upon each factor at various periods and in varying circumstances.

Seniority and Availability of Jobs. All the available data point to the great importance of seniority in determining local job assignments in China. Old cadres and land reform cadres who had filled positions at an early date continued, at least until recently, to occupy them, with the more important vacancies frequently being filled by men of comparable ages. This conclusion is supported by previously cited data on the backgrounds of all cadres and political workers serving at different levels of local government (Tables 9 and 10) and the backgrounds of cadres performing different functions (Table 14), as well as by the average age of local leaders at different levels (Table 13) and in

[63] Similar conclusions are reached in the penetrating article by Ezra Vogel, "From Revolutionary to Semi Bureaucrat: The 'Regularisation' of Cadres," *China Quarterly*, No. 29 (January–March, 1967), pp. 39–48.

different functions (Table 16) in 1955–57 and 1962–65. All these data strongly indicate that the generation which seized power during the early years of the revolution continued to monopolize the centers of power at the local level, at least until the start of the Cultural Revolution.

The reverse side of the coin was the fact that youth enjoyed limited job opportunities. Tables 21 and 22 below lend weight to this interpretation. A comparison of the percentage of leaders at each level who were over thirty-five years old, presented in Table 21, suggests that

TABLE 21

COMPARISON OF PERCENTAGE OF LOCAL LEADERS OVER 35, BY LEVEL, 1955–57 AND 1962–65

Level	N	Age	
		Over 35	Under 35
County, 1955–57	7	28%	72%
1962–65	20	85%	15%
District, 1955–57	6	33%	66%
1962–65	39	64%	36%
Multivillage, 1955–57	14	35%	65%
1962–65	17	36%	64%
Village, 1955–57	51	34%	67%
1962–65	82	45%	55%
Subvillage, 1955–57	6	83%	17%
1962–65	61	43%	57%

leaders below thirty-five years of age found their greatest career opportunities at the less desirable lower levels. Indeed, among the leaders covered by the data, the percentage of leaders under thirty-five at both the county and district levels dropped considerably from 1955–57 to 1962–65.

A comparison of the percentage of leaders over thirty-five in each functional field (Table 22) further documents the same trend. People under thirty-five, these statistics suggest, were most likely to find jobs in finance and trade and education and technology (occupational lines having the greatest number of new openings), although many young army veterans were also able to find employment in the coercive functions. (A large number of the 64 per cent of workers in coercive fields who were under thirty-five were army veterans between twenty-

TABLE 22

COMPARISON OF PERCENTAGE OF LOCAL LEADERS OVER 35, BY FUNCTION
1955–57 AND 1962–65

Function	N	AGE	
		Over 35	Under 35
Politics, 1955–57	36	42%	58%
1962–65	70	60%	40%
Administration, 1955–57	29	52%	48%
1962–65	72	70%	31%
Finance and trade 1955–57	21	14%	86%
1962–65	49	26%	74%
Coercion, 1955–57	4	25%	75%
1962–65	11	37%	64%
Education and Technology, 1955–57	9	0%	100%
1962–65	16	12%	88%

five and thirty-five years of age.) The data also indicate that the percentage of local leaders under thirty-five may have decreased in all functional fields over the past decade, with the most noticeable drop in the pivotal political and administrative functions. The principle of seniority has clearly been a powerful factor governing recruitment in China.

Political Loyalty and Reliability. Another factor that significantly affected patterns of recruitment was the regime's attitudes toward the political reliability of job candidates. The more sensitive and vital the job, the more important was political loyalty to the CCP and Peking. Seniority, Party membership, and degree of identification with the national government were three criteria which the higher levels of authority in China apparently stressed in evaluating the reliability of job candidates.[64] As already noted, senior officials generally occupied the more sensitive positions. The evidence also indicates, not surprisingly, that the percentage of Party members increased in the politically more important jobs. The higher the level of local officialdom (Table 12), and the more political the function, the greater was the percentage of Party members filling the available posts. Outside cadres, who generally were dispatched to a locality to solve particular problems and whose dedication to the central government was considered to be

[64] *Ibid.*

particularly important, were especially likely to be Party members (Table 19). And evidently Party members predominated in leadership posts in the important "key point" areas.

Peking apparently felt that outsiders tended to be more loyal than natives. As stated earlier, the outsider was less vulnerable to the pressures generated by the local community, since he had fewer ties to it. According to the data from the available biographical sketches, more outsiders served at the higher levels of local government (Table 11) and in relatively sensitive political functions (Table 15).

The data revealed two apparent exceptions. At the multivillage level there were proportionately more native leaders than in the villages (Tables 11A and 11B), while the educators and technicians (holding jobs not usually considered particularly sensitive in political terms in the West) had the highest percentage of outsiders (Table 15). Actually, however, these instances also reflected the importance of political considerations. Frequent reorganizations of administrative units at the multivillage level created artificial groupings of villages, which were not naturally cohesive socioeconomic units. In contrast, the villages were traditional units which tended to be relatively unified and cohesive as a result of kinship ties and common economic interests. According to several organizational theorists, it is easier to retain the loyalty of officials serving in artificially designed administrative units, particularly if they are subject to periodic reorganization, than to retain the loyalty of those serving in "naturally cohesive" institutions.[65] Concerned as they were about the political loyalty of local leaders, the higher level authorities in China may have felt that they could safely assign more natives at the multivillage level than at the village level, since at the village level they were more likely to articulate and identify with local interests.

The higher percentage of outsiders among the educators and technicians also reflected the importance of political loyalty and reliability as criteria for job assignments. As noted previously, in China the educators shared with the political and coercive workers the task of engineering social change. In contrast with the West, therefore, educators in China did hold politically sensitive jobs. They daily battled the values of the old society. In this wearying struggle, outsiders, who were

---

[65] This approach to administration, which has been labeled "ecological control," is briefly discussed in Dorwin Cartwright, "Influence, Leadership, Control," in James March (ed.), *Handbook of Organizations* (Chicago: Rand McNally, 1965), pp. 19–21. Although Etzioni qualifies this notion, he comes to essentially the same conclusion. See his *Complex Organizations,* chap. viii, esp. p. 195.

more dependent upon the higher level authorities for support, were probably viewed as being more reliable than natives. A native, serving among persons he knew, was perhaps more susceptible to local pressures and influences. Thus, because the roles of local educators demanded strict loyalty to Peking, there were strong arguments for using many outsiders.

Skills Demanded. Obviously, job assignments were also affected by the skills required for specific positions, and people with special talents were recruited into jobs demanding those talents. Political and administrative skills were very important for some tasks, while technical skills were important for others. Guerrilla warfare, essentially a political struggle, endows the good guerrilla fighter with skills in leading men and managing interpersonal relations, and after 1949 ex-guerrilla fighters were assigned positions that demanded these leadership skills. The PLA taught soldiers to use weapons, and upon discharge veterans were often recruited into the coercive apparatus. In the border and coastal areas, where national defense considerations were important, ex-servicemen played more important roles. The young middle school students, who had acquired arithmetic, agronomy, meteorology, veterinary medicine, and similar skills, were recruited into finance and trade and education and technical work (see Table 14). There was a tendency to fill many jobs demanding higher education with better educated officials (Table 17).

In short, China's recruitment process clearly was responsive in some respects to the needs of the society for a variety of skills. And yet, the evidence suggests that this determinant in recruitment was not given as much weight in assignments as cadres' seniority or judgments about their political loyalty. Well-trained youths were not absorbed into the bureaucracy as quickly as their educational attainment seemed to merit, and non-Party members apparently had to display special skills to find good employment opportunities (Table 18). (Careful studies of the use of manpower in China as a whole also conclude that the nation's skills could have been more effectively employed.[66]) In short, although the demand for skills definitely affected recruitment, other criteria seem to have been at least as important, and in many instances more so.

Government Policy. The relative weighting of the various recruit-

---

[66] For example, see Cheng Chu-yuan, *Scientific and Engineering Manpower in Communist China, 1949–1963* (Washington, D.C.: National Science Foundation, 1965), pp. 276–79.

ment criteria in China seemed to reflect shifts in Party and government policy. Some students of China argue, for example, that Peking relied more heavily upon outsiders when its policy emphasized social change, and stressed the role of natives when it wished to stimulate economic production.[67] While support for this assertion requires better documentation, several instances in which policy shifts affected recruitment patterns have already been noted. Local leaders who had been influential under the old regime, and who possessed marketing skills, came to the fore when free markets flourished. Mass campaigns, especially those stressing production, drew upon the native wisdom of old peasants. The turnover rate of village and subvillage leaders increased during periodic rectification campaigns. The criteria employed to rate local units (with important effects, noted earlier, on the type of cadres deployed there) seemingly reflected broader policy changes. More impressionistically, it appears that the rulers relied more on coercion in securing compliance at the local level in the 1960's, in comparison with the 1950's, and this subtle shift in policy seems to have been accompanied by a rise in the importance of those local leaders associated with coercion, such as army veterans.

All of these shifts in personnel policies reflected a basic dilemma faced by the leaders of the Chinese People's Republic. They were pursuing multiple goals, and these goals often came into conflict, at least in the short run. A particularly acute short-run conflict occurred between the goal of securing attitudinal change, which required destruction of traditional institutions, and the goal of increasing production, which required securing maximum economic output and state revenue from existing institutions. The history of the CPR could be written in terms of the continual shifts in the priorities assigned to these goals. Personnel policy reflected these changes. At times the importance of those most skilled in securing social change (such as the old cadres) was stressed, while at other times the importance of those skilled in increasing production (such as economic experts or rural middle school graduates) was emphasized.

The Desirability of Jobs. The criteria for recruitment discussed thus far are those determined by the employer, namely, the Party and government. But local leaders in China appeared to be selective, to a

---

[67] In particular, see G. William Skinner, "Compliance and Leadership in Rural Communist China" (paper read to the annual meeting of the American Political Science Association, September 8–11, 1965). Also John W. Lewis, "The Leadership Doctrine of the Chinese Communist Party: The Lesson of the People's Commune," *Asian Survey,* III, No. 10 (October, 1963), 457–64.

limited extent, in their responses to the recruitment efforts of higher authorities. Recruitment, in other words, reflected both the priorities and standards set by higher levels of authority and the selective responses of the potential recruits.[68] For example, the turnover rate of personnel appeared highest for those jobs considered to be the least desirable, especially those at the subvillage level. Local positions which required action to try to alter existing institutions and values may have been more difficult to fill with local recruits.

The over-all impression one gets, however, through interviewing former residents of the CPR and reading the Chinese Communist press (rather than from any quantifiable data), is that recruits for political posts in China had relatively few options. In short, even though the recruitment process did involve an interaction between the recruiters and those recruited, the advantages rested primarily with the recruiter. The key determinants affecting political recruitment in China were basically either the impersonal products of the system or a reflection of policies consciously adopted by higher level authorities.

Revolutionary History. One special factor which strikingly affected recruitment patterns in China was the legacy of the revolution. Actually, it is not surprising that only fifteen to twenty years after Communist takeover, Chinese society continues to bear the marks of one of the greatest political upheavals in history. Of the eight identifiable categories of cadres, only the young middle school graduates, the post-1955 peasant recruits, and the demobilized soldiers who had joined the army after 1955 acquired their positions of political leadership through relatively routinized, postrevolutionary recruitment channels. As of 1962–65, all the other leaders were persons who had emerged from the turmoil of the revolution.

More specifically, the effects of the revolutionary legacy were apparent in various ways. First, cadres who participated in the early years of the revolution were singled out for special treatment. Second, many political workers serving at the county level tended to be outsiders who had come from old guerrilla base areas. Third, the old guerrilla base areas had a higher percentage of ex-PLA members, many of whom served as local leaders. Fourth, it appeared that the way the early stages of the revolution unfolded in each of China's hundreds of thou-

---

[68] One of the better descriptions of the tactics employed by a Chinese youth to secure a job he wants is in Teng Chi-p'ing, *The Thought Revolution* (New York: Coward-McCann, 1966).

sands of villages continued to affect the recruitment patterns in those villages in various ways which have already been discussed.

Finally, the timing of the revolutionary takeover of power (the revolution came to some villages in the 1930's, to others in the 1940's, and to still others in the early 1950's) was a factor which helped to explain continuing differences among China's villages. By the early 1960's, those villages which had been under Communist rule the longest began to experience a significant process of leadership change, a kind of generational succession, whereas those villages which came under Communist rule in the early 1950's had not yet begun to experience this process. It is impossible to predict with any accuracy what changes will occur in the years ahead, but it seems likely that the revolutionary legacy will persist and influence leadership patterns for years to come.

THE CONSEQUENCES OF THE RECRUITMENT CRITERIA AND THE CULTURAL REVOLUTION

The criteria for recruitment of local leaders had important consequences for the Chinese political system, three of which merit particular mention. The recruitment process promoted intense generational and bureaucratic tensions. In addition, as the criteria became part of routine practice, "rules of the game" developed for pursuing cadre careers. Finally, the criteria displayed considerable continuity with traditional recruitment patterns. All of these are crucial to an understanding of the Great Proletarian Cultural Revolution which swept China in 1966–67.

GENERATIONAL AND BUREAUCRATIC TENSIONS

The importance attached to seniority and political reliability limited job opportunities for younger aspirants to power. So too did the economic crisis in China in the early 1960's, since the economy was not expanding rapidly enough to provide the kinds of jobs which the increasing numbers of educated youth in China expected.[69] Instead, as stated earlier, the greatest employment opportunities for youth were now in relatively unattractive fields; they had to be satisfied with such

---

[69] See Edwin Jones, "The Emerging Patterns of China's Economic Revolution," in U.S. Congress, Joint Economic Committee (ed.), *An Economic Profile of Mainland China* (Washington, D.C.: U.S. Government Printing Office, 1967), I, 91. Also John Emerson, "Employment in Mainland China: Problems and Prospects," in *ibid.,* II, 403–69.

positions as accountants of production brigades or elementary school teachers in mountain villages. As a result, youths became antagonistic toward those whom they held responsible for their increasing frustration. The most obvious targets for their hostility were the old cadres in political and administrative work. The grievances of youth against these cadres were twofold. First, the old cadres were responsible for the recruitment process and therefore were blamed for the lack of desirable job opportunities. Second, they themselves held the very jobs which youth had the greatest difficulty attaining.[70] Not surprisingly, the old cadres were the people who bore the brunt of Red Guard attacks during the Cultural Revolution.

The nature of the recruitment process had also intensified inter-agency rivalry. It was noted earlier how individuals with different backgrounds and characteristics tended to gravitate toward different organizations and fields of work. The recruitment process gave organizational identity to the differences among local leaders. Several observers of the China scene have noted the bureaucratic nature of Chinese politics, which they attribute both to the governmental structure and to the structure of society itself.[71] But in recent years this natural proclivity for bureaucratic infighting appears to have been nourished by a recruitment process that produced contending bureaucrats who differed in individual characteristics as well as in organizational interests. The eight types of local leaders that emerged after 1949 were quite conscious of their identities. Once conflict became manifest in the Cultural Revolution, tensions were difficult to mediate, and many conflicts took on dimensions of personal animosity.

In Mao's view, these generational and bureaucratic tensions posed some fundamental problems, but also presented tempting opportunities. In oversimplified terms, what he decided to do was to forge alliances with those aggrieved groups in China who could be induced to

---

[70] Indeed, the *People's Daily* felt the promotions of six men under thirty-five years of age to the posts of county Party secretaries were events deserving front-page coverage. See *JMJP,* January 21, 1966.

[71] This is a major theme in Barnett (with Vogel), *Cadres, Bureaucracy, and Political Power,* and Franz Schurmann, "Politics and Economics in Russia and China," in Donald W. Treadgold (ed.), *Soviet and Chinese Communism: Similarities and Differences* (Seattle: University of Washington Press, 1967), pp. 297–326. For articles relating Chinese bureaucratic practices to the structure and values of the society, see Etienne Balazs, "China as a Permanently Bureaucratic Society," in Balazs, *Chinese Civilization and Bureaucracy* (New Haven, Conn.: Yale University Press, 1964), pp. 13–27; and C. K. Yang, "Some Characteristics of Chinese Bureaucratic Behavior" in David Nivison and Arthur Wright (ed.), *Confucianism in Action* (Stanford, Calif.: Stanford University Press, 1959), pp. 134–64.

identify their interests with his own, use the PLA to give them protection and support, and allow them to direct the force of their frustrations against the old cadres in the bureaucracy. As a result, these groups, through their aggressive acts, attacked and attempted to destroy the elements in society which Mao believed were the obstacles to progress. Far from considering the existing tensions a bane, therefore, Mao saw them as the basis on which he could change the course of history. It was precisely these generational and bureaucratic tensions which Mao sought to manipulate during the Cultural Revolution.

UNWRITTEN "RULES OF THE GAME"

Another consequence of the recruitment patterns and processes that emerged in China was the gradual evolution of unwritten rules which greatly affected the way in which youths planned their careers. These "rules" (plus the increasing importance of standardized admissions procedures and examinations in the educational system) helped to produce a "mentality" among many youths and officials which Mao and his colleagues labeled "careerism." Mao wanted Chinese society to be a society in permanent revolution, and because of his antibureaucratic bias he had a deep-seated distrust of routine, stability, and predictability. In the society Mao envisioned, people would not be concerned about "careers"; indeed, as the term is ordinarily understood, career lines would cease to exist. Totally selfless individuals would place their lives in the hands of the regime, which would deploy them wherever needed in its programs to develop an industrialized, socialist China.

But by 1962–65, definite and predictable recruitment patterns and career lines had emerged in China. Joining the Party enhanced a person's chances for upward mobility. Volunteering for the PLA increased the chances that one would become a state cadre; it also maximized the chance that, when a soldier returned home, he would be involved in influential or prestigious activities, such as political-legal work. Graduation from middle school became the best route for those desiring to enter the fields of education and technology or finance and trade. Someone with "careerist" notions avoided—if possible—returning to his native village to become a subvillage leader. The chances of promotion from this position were almost nil. These and many other unwritten rules guided the behavior of those who wanted to plot their own careers and achieve success under the system. The crucial point is that the system had already developed established unwritten rules of this sort, and to this extent Chinese society was no longer revolution-ary.

Understandably, given Mao's goals, the Cultural Revolution at-tempted to reduce the predictability of the lives of ordinary citizens. Attempts were made not so much to rewrite but rather to erase the "rules of the career game." For example, examinations in the educa-tional system were abolished, but no new criteria for admission to colleges were elaborated. The more ardent supporters of Mao opposed admission standards of all kinds, for they believed that as soon as standards were set, individuals would begin to make career plans. With no standards or rules to guide them, individuals would be unable to plot careers, and in the view of the radicals supporting Mao, they therefore would have to place their fates entirely in the regime's hands.

But the attempt to eliminate recruitment criteria inevitably encoun-tered resistance. Many had profited from these criteria, particularly the old cadres; they were understandably inclined to defend a system which had rewarded them. Moreover, in spite of some problems, the recruitment criteria basically were in accord with Chinese realities. They helped to direct the flow of talent to the places and positions where it was needed. Any outright attack upon these criteria (as contrasted with efforts to reform them) faced opposition from "moder-ates," who placed higher priority upon the need to achieve orderly economic growth than upon the goal of building a revolutionary society such as that envisaged by Mao.

As of the autumn of 1967, the unfolding of the Cultural Revolution reflected an intense struggle among these three groups—radicals, old cadres, and moderates—and one of the many basic issues was the issue of recruitment criteria. The radicals pursued their aim of building a society without structured bureaucratic careers. The old cadres de-fended a system which they believed was essential for the development of China. And the moderates sought to make use of the Cultural Revolution to bring about improvement in the system—including im-provements in the regime's methods of recruitment.

PERSISTENCE OF TRADITIONAL CRITERIA

Finally, any study of local leadership in China must note the persist-ence of some traditional Chinese recruitment criteria. The importance attached to seniority and "virtue" echoed traditional criteria, though admittedly the standards of virtuous conduct had changed greatly. It still seemed necessary to take into account a leader's native place in job assignments. Moreover, there was evidence that family and other particularist ties continued to affect recruitment. (Unfortunately, it is not possible to discuss this complex subject here.) Moreover, the Chinese leaders had not, by 1962–65, solved the old problem of establishing a retirement process in which aging leaders exited from the political stage, rather than withdrawing from formal roles only to assume influential informal roles. Power and influence still appeared to be vested as much in individuals as in bureaucratic positions. Purging —with public denunciations—appeared to be almost the only way to destroy the influence of many aging leaders.[72]

The Great Proletarian Cultural Revolution can also be seen, in part, therefore, as a response to the persistence of traditionalism. The purge eliminated officials whom the system did not seem to be able to eliminate by other means. It also attacked those officials who gave primacy to the interests of their local communities, persons who had, in effect, become "local" rather than "outside" leaders. In addition, it involved a conscious effort to destroy traditional recruitment patterns based upon seniority and other ascriptive criteria.

Mao's attempt to establish a society in which people would not plan careers seems totally unrealistic. In addition, his willingness to tap deep-rooted generational and bureaucratic tensions proved dangerous, for the generational and bureaucratic conflicts that he tried to manipulate rapidly escaped his control. But these dysfunctional elements of the Cultural Revolution are not what merit attention in this study.

More important is the fact that the Cultural Revolution was in many respects a response to real tensions and problems which had arisen, in part because of the local leadership patterns that had emerged. The attack upon seniority, the search for adequate retirement processes, and the attempt to alleviate some of the sources of discontent among youth were attempts to solve acute problems. The harsh, frenzied methods of the Cultural Revolution proved disastrous. But it is predictable that in the future other attempts will be made to grapple with problems of such a fundamental sort. Likewise, as long as recruitment patterns intensify generational and bureaucratic tensions, it is predictable that generational and bureaucratic conflict will be hallmarks of Chinese politics.

---

[72] This argument was made for the USSR under Stalin. See Zbigniew Brzezinski, *The Permanent Purge: Politics in Soviet Totalitarianism* (Cambridge, Mass.: Harvard University Press, 1955).

YING-MAO KAU

The Urban Bureaucratic Elite in Communist China: A Case Study of Wuhan, 1949-65*

INTRODUCTION

Max Weber described modern bureaucracy as a legal-rational system of authority characteristic of modern society.[1] In contrast to traditional and charismatic bureaucracies with diffuse, ascriptive, and personal orientations, modern bureaucracy, he maintained, is marked by a high degree of structural differentiation and functional specialization. A major concern of a modern bureaucracy is to mobilize organizational resources for efficient task performance and goal achievement based on secular and rational principles. Its system of personnel recruitment, assignment, transfer, and promotion is governed by pre-established, universalistic, impersonal, and achievement-oriented standards.[2]

* I wish to thank John W. Lewis, Lea E. Williams, Robert M. Marsh, and Paul Harper for their comments and suggestions. For research, computer programing, and other assistance, I am indebted to Pierre Perrolle, Peter Chi, Phil Ginsburg, Carl Thayer, and Stanley Griffith. Finally, I wish to thank the Social Science Research Council for support which made the tabulation and computer analysis of data possible.

[1] For Max Weber's theory of bureaucracy, see Talcott Parsons (ed.), *Max Weber: The Theory of Social and Economic Organizations* (New York: The Free Press of Glencoe, 1964; paperback), chap. iii.

[2] Examination and elaboration of the Weberian theory of bureaucracy and modern complex organization may be found in Peter M. Blau, *Bureaucracy in Modern Society* (New York: Random House, 1956); Amitai Etzioni (ed.), *Complex Organizations: A Sociological Reader* (New York: Holt, Rinehart and Winston, 1961); Amitai Etzioni, *Modern Organizations* (Englewood Cliffs, N.J.: Prentice-Hall, 1964).

Though empirical research cannot be expected to confirm fully the existence of such an "ideal type,"[3] the development of modern bureaucracy following the emergence of complex industrial society in the West has lent significant support to the general validity of this model. The increasing professionalization and specialization of modern bureaucracy, resulting from the growing intake of specialists and professionals, has strongly confirmed the key characteristics that Weber identified. Despite criticism of specific aspects of his model, Weber is essentially correct in hypothesizing that as bureaucracy modernizes, its charismatic and traditional elements tend to decline, while rational-secular orientations emerge.[4]

Max Weber observed:

When there are very urgent economic or administrative needs for precise action . . . government by amateurs [is] technically inadequate, on the one hand, in organization beyond a certain limit of size . . . or, on the other hand, where functions are involved which require technical training or continuity of policy.[5]

A quick look at some government bureaucracies in modern societies will convince us of the accuracy of his observation. Take the government bureaucracy of New York City, for example. An analysis of 1,191 cabinet appointees during 1898–1957 reveals that at the turn of the century only about 60 per cent of the cabinet members ($N = 62$) were equipped with job-oriented training or experience. A quarter of a century later, the proportion had increased to 72 per cent ($N = 90$); and by the 1950's it had risen to 85 per cent ($N = 87$).[6] The limited

---

[3] As Weber explained his views, "In its conceptual purity, this mental construct [of an ideal type] cannot be found empirically anywhere in reality. It is a utopia. Historical research faces the task of determining in each individual case, the extent to which this ideal-construct approximates to or diverges from reality. . . ." Max Weber, *The Methodology of the Social Sciences,* trans. and ed. by Edward A. Shils and Henry A. Finch (Glencoe, Ill.: The Free Press, 1949), p. 90.

[4] An excellent summary of the development of modern bureaucracy in the Western world may be found in Fritz Morstein Marx, "The Higher Civil Service as an Action Group in Western Political Development," in Joseph LaPalombara (ed.), *Bureaucracy and Political Development* (Princeton, N.J.: Princeton University Press, 1963), pp. 62–95. For a brief discussion of the theory and development of modern bureaucracy, see Blau, *Bureaucracy in Modern Society,* pp. 27–44.

[5] Parsons (ed.), *Max Weber,* p. 415.

[6] Data taken from Theodore J. Lowi, *At the Pleasure of the Mayor* (New York: The Free Press of Glencoe, 1964), pp. 10, 60. It has often been noted that bureaucracies in the United States tend to be dominated by lawyers. However, this general notion needs to be qualified. It should be noted, first of all, that many of these lawyers are also highly trained or experienced in other occupational fields, such as finance, accounting, taxation, construction, and so on, and that they are often recruited into the government, particularly the civil service, not because of their legal education, but rather because of their expertise and skills in other fields. Secondly, it should be noted that there is a steady

data available on the bureaucratic elite of the Soviet Union demon-strate a similar trend toward bureaucratic professionalization in that country.[7] A recent study of the backgrounds of Party first secretaries of the twenty most industrialized *oblasts* shows that in 1961 fifteen of them (75 per cent) had an engineering education and seven (35 per cent) were former enterprise directors. In 1966, of the sixteen Party first secretaries whose background data were available, thirteen (81 per cent) were highly specialized engineers, and eight (50 per cent) were former enterprise managers.[8]

In other, less developed parts of the world there is also a growing awareness of the importance of a professionalized bureaucracy and of its long-range implications for modernization.[9] Increasing emphasis on professional knowledge and skills in government bureaucracy, as re-flected in the widespread adoption of the "merit bureaucratic system" or "modern civil service," has become virtually a universal trend.[10]

In developing countries, especially those under authoritarian rule, bureaucracy has a particularly crucial role to play. In order to achieve industrialization and modernization as rapidly as possible, govern-ments in these countries perform not only political but also economic functions. The state becomes deeply involved in virtually all aspects of economic planning and operation. In these cases the significance of the quality of the official bureaucracy can scarcely be overemphasized: How the bureaucracy is organized, staffed, and run will inevitably have a great effect on the process of political and economic development in these countries.[11]

---

decline in the proportion of men with law degrees in civil service. See, for example, David T. Stanley, *The Higher Civil Service: An Evaluation of Federal Personnel Practices* (Washington, D.C.: The Brookings Institute, 1964).

[7] See, for example, Jerry Hough, "Groups and Individuals," *Problems of Communism,* XVI, No. 1 (January–February, 1967), 28–35; Jerry Hough, "In Whose Hands the Future?" *Problems of Communism,* XVI, No. 2 (March–April, 1967), 18–25; John A. Armstrong, "Party Bifurcation and Elite Interests," *Soviet Studies,* XVII, No. 4 (April, 1966), 417–28; George K. Schueller, "The Politburo," in *World Revolutionary Elites,* ed. by Harold D. Lasswell and Daniel Lerner (Cambridge, Mass.: M.I.T. Press, 1965), pp. 97–178.

[8] According to this study at least three of the other four were once secretaries of the primary Party organization in a giant plant; and they, too, are almost surely graduate engineers with managerial experience in the plant. Hough, "In Whose Hands the Future?" pp. 22–23.

[9] The problems of bureaucracy and modernization in the underdeveloped countries are dealt with in depth in LaPalombara (ed.), *Bureaucracy and Political Development.*

[10] See note 4 above.

[11] Political and economic development is defined narrowly here to mean the growth and expansion of administrative and economic "output." Most reservations about developing strong bureaucracies in the underdeveloped countries are related to the questions of

Since it assumed power in 1949, the new Communist leadership in China has given priority to modernization and industrialization among its major national goals. These priorities have helped sustain a rationale by which the state instituted and maintained an extensive system of totalitarian control over China's national life. Replaced by that system, private organizations and enterprises in China were systematically emasculated from 1949 on, and virtually disappeared after the 1956 "upsurge" of socialist transformation. Since then, the entire nation has come under the control of a unified system of official bureaucracies and their semiofficial agents; and the responsibility for achieving national goals has fallen entirely on the state and Party bureaucracies. Thus, before the Great Proletarian Cultural Revolution and its violent assault on the bureaucracies in 1966, it was not an exaggeration to say that the bureaucracies held the key to China's future development.

Important as the Chinese bureaucracy may be, however, our knowledge of it, based on empirical data and scientific research, has been very limited.[12] This is particularly true in our understanding of lower level bureaucracies. The monumental work by A. Doak Barnett (with a contribution by Ezra Vogel), published in 1967, remains the only major source of information on the Chinese bureaucracy.[13] Even though systematic research has been conducted by other scholars, the results of their work are not yet fully available.[14] To help fill this gap, this study will examine selectively, within a limited scope, one particular segment of the urban bureaucracy in China, namely, the top bureaucratic elite of Wuhan city. First, I will identify some salient

---

democratic values and the development of a Western-type democracy in these countries. See, for example, Joseph LaPalombara, "Bureaucracy and Political Development: Notes, Queries, and Dilemmas," in LaPalombara (ed.), *Bureaucracy and Political Development,* pp. 34–61. This kind of concern is obviously irrelevant in the case of China.

[12] Several major articles dealing with China's bureaucracy and cadres have been published recently: John W. Lewis, "Political Aspects of Mobility in China's Urban Development," *American Political Science Review,* LX, No. 4 (December, 1966), 899–912; A. Doak Barnett, "Social Stratification and Aspects of Personnel Management in the Chinese Communist Bureaucracy," *China Quarterly,* No. 28 (October–December, 1966), pp. 8–39; Michel Oksenberg, "Paths to Leadership in Communist China," *Current Scene,* III, No. 24 (August 1, 1965), 1–11. Recent books relevant to the subject include: Franz Schurmann, *Ideology and Organization in Communist China* (Berkeley and Los Angeles: University of California Press, 1966); Frederick C. Teiwes, *Provincial Party Personnel in Mainland China, 1956–1966* (New York: East Asian Institute, Columbia University, 1967).

[13] A. Doak Barnett (with a contribution by Ezra Vogel), *Cadres, Bureaucracy, and Political Power in Communist China* (New York: Columbia University Press, 1967).

[14] Major studies using extensive empirical data, for example, are now being prepared by John W. Lewis on Tangshan city and by Ezra Vogel on Canton city.

socio-political characteristics of that elite and assess the extent to which this bureaucratic elite approximates or deviates from the Weberian model. Next, I will examine the changing patterns of the structure of this elite over time. And, finally, I will speculate, on the basis of our findings, on the impact that bureaucracy may have exerted on China's efforts to modernize.[15] Because of the chaotic state of recent events in the ongoing Cultural Revolution, no attempt will be made to deal with changes which may have occurred after 1965.

The primary focus of the study will be on leaders in formal organizational roles within the urban setting of Wuhan. A Weberian assumption implicit here is that in a highly differentiated and specialized bureaucracy (of which the Wuhan bureaucracy will be shown to be an example), bureaucrats' actions are shaped by the formal roles to which they are assigned, so that an analysis of men in such roles will help to illuminate various operational aspects of the bureaucratic organization. This approach, focusing on the formal elites, is chosen with the awareness that informal or latent leaders in Wuhan may have played political and bureaucratic roles of equal importance. However, given the circumstances in Communist China today—a tightly closed society allowing no access to field research and issue-oriented data—study of such additional factors is clearly out of question at the present.[16]

In this study particular attention will be given to patterns of elite recruitment and mobility. Evidence is clear that, in coping with cadre recruitment and mobility, the leadership was vitally concerned with bureaucratic efficiency; but, of equal importance, it also desired to maintain maximum political control over the bureaucracy.[17] For the sake of bureaucratic efficiency, the Party found it necessary to recruit men of ability and talent; but for the sake of political control the leadership needed cadres of unquestioned loyalty and submission.

[15] This exercise of comparing the Wuhan bureaucracy with the Weberian "ideal type" does not necessarily imply the value judgment that the "ideal type" will be the best for Wuhan. The purpose is primarily to use the Weberian model as a convenient yardstick for measuring.

[16] This drawback is somewhat compensated for by the fact that most of the informal organizations and groupings in Communist China have been suppressed or rooted out by the regime through various campaigns against "sectarianism," "localism," "favoritism," and so on, in the past eighteen years.

[17] The best evidence may be found in major policy statements such as An Tze-wen, "Chung-hua Jen-min Kung-ho-kuo San-nien-lai ti Kan-pu Kung-tso" (Cadre Operations in the People's Republic of China over the Last Three Years), *JMJP*, September 30, 1952; and Ch'en Yi, "Tui Pei-ching-shih Kao-teng Hsüeh-hsiao Ying-chieh Pi-yeh Hsüeh-sheng ti Chiang-hua" (Address Before the Graduates of Higher Institutes in Peking), in *Jen-min Shou-ts'e, 1961* (People's Handbook) (Peking: Ta-kung Pao She, 1961), pp. 319–21.

Ideally the Party would have liked to recruit only men who were both "red" and "expert," combining "virtue" and "ability." Unfortunately, men with this combination of qualities were not easily available; the leadership had to face the difficult task of establishing priorities between "red" and "expert," and had to recruit from among individuals who were either "red" or "expert." As a result, two broad types of cadres seem to have emerged within the bureaucracy: one representing those who were recruited mainly because of their political "redness"; the other representing those who were recruited for their professional "expertness." How to balance the two so that the leadership could maintain maximum political control over the bureaucracy without seriously obstructing the intake of expertise and damaging the efficiency of bureaucracy is the dilemma that has beset the leadership since it took over the administration of the nation in 1949. It appears that that dilemma has been both aggravated and postponed by the events of the Cultural Revolution since 1966.

BACKGROUND TO THE DEVELOPMENT
OF THE BUREAUCRACY OF WUHAN

Since I will attempt to examine the structure of a bureaucratic elite in one of the most advanced industrial sectors in China, a note on the modernization process of Wuhan is in order. Western influence began to affect Wuhan as early as 1861, when the British established the first foreign concession in the city; and thereafter five other foreign powers obtained matching arrangements.[18] Under the leadership of Chang Chih-tung, then governor-general of Hupeh and Hunan, industrialization started in Wuhan in the 1890's with the opening of modern iron and steel works and textile mills.[19] Supported by the rich supply of iron ore and coal from the neighboring towns of Tayeh and Huangshih, a major industrial complex had grown up by the 1930's. The city enjoyed fame for its output of machine tools, chemicals, shipbuilding, and food processing, in addition to the steel and textiles. Located in the heart of China, Wuhan geographically linked the north (Peking) and the south (Canton) by railroads, and the east (Shanghai) and the west (Chung-

[18] The other five powers which also established concessions in Wuhan were Germany, France, Russia, Japan, and Belgium. The Japanese Army invaded and controlled the city in 1938–45. P'an Hsin-tsao, *Wu-han-shih Chien-chih Yen-ko* (History of the Development of Wuhan Municipality) (Wuhan: Hu-pei Jen-min, 1956), pp. 62–69.

[19] William Edgar Geil, *Eighteen Capitals of China* (London: Constable, 1911), pp. 248–65. See also Arthur W. Hummel (ed.), *Eminent Chinese of the Ch'ing Period* (Washington, D.C.: Government Printing Office, 1943), I, 27–31.

king) by the Yangtze waterway. It has continued to be a major commercial and communication center, a position it has enjoyed since ancient times.

Originally the name "Wuhan" was the compound word designating the three separate cities of Wuchang, Hankow, and Hanyang, but rapid urbanization gradually linked the three cities into a sprawling metropolitan area. Immediately after the Communists entered the area on May 16, 1949, these three separate cities were formally incorporated into the single municipality of Wuhan.[20] In the succeeding eight years the population of Wuhan increased from roughly 1.4 million to 2.2 million (the latest population figure available, for 1957), making Wuhan the fourth largest city in China.[21] Under Communist rule the city has been designated as one of the nation's major centers for industrial development. The completion of the Yangtze Bridge in 1957 and the probable completion of the Wuhan Iron and Steel Complex in the early 1960's made Wuhan a national symbol of China's industrial progress.[22]

If the number of occupational groups and educational institutions in any area can serve as an approximate measure of modernization, it is worth noting that Wuhan in 1952 had at least 87 formally organized trade associations and 102 educational institutions beyond the primary school level, including 12 colleges and universities.[23] In conjunction with its physical growth Wuhan also developed a complex governmental bureaucracy. As elsewhere in urban China, the organizational

[20] For the takeover of the city by the Communists and their early rule, see *JMJP* (Peking), May 18, 19, 22, 27, June 5, September 14, 1949, May 20, September 19, 1950; *Jen-min Shou-ts'e, 1950*, pp. 12–13. See also P'an, *Wu-han-shih Chien-chih*, pp. 68–69. According to a report in *JMJP* May 19, 1949, a municipal people's government and a Military Control Commission were established for the Wuhan municipality three days after the Communists took over control of the city.

[21] *JMJP* May 18, 1949. Also *Shin Chūgoku Nenkan, 1962* (New China Yearbook for 1962) (Tokyo: Chūgoku Kenkyūjo, 1962), p. 40.

[22] "Ch'ing-chu Wu-kang K'ai-shih chien-ch'ang" (Celebrate the Commencement of the Construction of the Wuhan Steel Works), *Hsin-hua Pan-yüeh-k'an* (New China Fortnightly), IX (1957), 68–69 (also appeared in *JMJP,* April 9, 1957). See also Jan Yu-li, *A Concise Geography of China* (Peking: Foreign Languages Press, 1964), pp. 139–42. *Shin Chūgoku Nenkan* (1962), pp. 109–10; *Gendia Chūgoku Jiten* (Lexicon of Modern China) (Tokyo: Chūgoku Kenkyūjo, 1959), pp. 631–33. The construction of the Yangtze Bridge was started in September, 1955, and completed in September, 1957. Information on the Wuhan Steel and Iron Works is fragmentary. The construction appears to have proceeded in two stages. The second stage was originally scheduled to be completed in 1961. But because of the withdrawal of the Russian technicians, who possibly took their blueprints with them, the target date seems to have been postponed.

[23] *Hsin Wu-han Pao* (New Wuhan News), March 21, 1952, p. 1. For other reports on occupational groups and educational institutions, see *Ch'ang-chiang Jih-pao* (Yangtze Daily), September 30, 1951. *JMJP* (Peking), May 18, 22, 1949.

patterns of Wuhan's bureaucratic system were extremely complex. In the mid-1950's, for example, the municipal government included not only the offices of mayor and eight deputy mayors, the People's Congress, the People's Council, the People's Court, and the People's Procuracy, but the administrative apparatus under the Municipal People's Council, which consisted of eight staff offices *(pan-kung-shih)*,[24] thirty-seven functional bureaus *(chü)* and independent divisions *(ch'u)*,[25] and numerous subordinate offices such as *k'o* (sections), *ku* (units), *tsu* (groups), and the like. In addition, there were twelve permanent committees and commissions in charge of a wide range of long-term policy-planning and supervision functions.[26]

The top officials in this administrative hierarchy from 1949 through 1965 may be broken down as follows:

1. Mayor and deputy mayors;
2. heads of general administrative organs and specialized functional bureaus (including directors of staff offices, chairmen of commissions and committees, and presidents of the court and the procuracy);
3. members of the Municipal People's Council (MPC) (known as the Municipal People's Government Council before 1954).

[24] In the 1950's the eight major staff offices, organized along functional lines, were the following: (1) Political and Legal Affairs, (2) Capital Construction, (3) Communications and Transportation, (4) Industry, (5) Agriculture, Forestry and Water Conservancy, (6) Finance and Trade, (7) Culture and Education, and (8) Transformation of Capitalist Industry and Commerce.

[25] The thirty-seven bureaus and independent divisions reported in the local press were as follows, in alphabetical order: Agriculture, Building Construction, Building Materials, Civil Affairs, Commerce (First and Second), Communications and Transportation, Construction, Control, Cooperative Enterprises, Culture, Education, Electric Power, Finance, Food, Foreign Trade, Forestry and Marine Products, Handicrafts, Housing and Real Estate, Industry, Justice, Labor, Machine-building, Material Supply, Military Service, Nationalities Affairs, People's Parks Administration, Public Health, Public Relations, Public Security, Public Utilities, Religious Affairs, Statistics, Tax Administration, Textile Industry, Trade, Water Conservancy, and Workers and Peasants' Spare-Time Education. Information on all these offices is in this writer's files. Four extensive lists of Wuhan's bureaus and committees may be found in *Tu-pao Shou-ts'e* (Newspaper Reader's Handbook) (Wuhan: Ch'ang-chiang Jih-pao She, 1950), pp. 156–57. *JMJP*, March 30, 1950. *Ch'ang-chiang Jih-pao,* July 23, 1954, January 24, 1957. Each of these bureaus and independent divisions was responsible for a highly specialized and differentiated area of government work. They were normally grouped along various functional lines under the supervision of the staff offices listed in note 24. For an excellent and detailed analysis of the division of labor among bureaus at the *hsien* level, see Barnett, (with Vogel), *Cadres, Bureaucracy, and Political Power,* pp. 205–310.

[26] The twelve permanent committees and commissions reported in the press were Archives, City Planning, Economic Planning, Finance and Economics, Housing Adjustment, International Trade Promotion, Narcotics Control, People's Control, Physical Culture and Sports, Rehabilitation and Construction, Science and Technology, and Urban-Rural Coordination.

In this study, a total of 157 leaders holding these key posts during 1949–65 are considered to be the "bureaucratic elite" of Wuhan and are sampled for analysis. The members of this top elite, by virtue of the authority officially vested in their government offices, are treated as formal leaders of strategic importance in Wuhan's bureaucratic system. Ideally the sample should also have included for analysis the leaders who occupied key Party posts, including the Party secretaries and department directors and members of the Standing Committee of the Municipal Party Committee. Unfortunately, the limited data available on these categories of leaders were not sufficient to justify their inclusion. This drawback, however, was somewhat compensated for by the fact that a large number of senior Party leaders (mainly the secretaries and key department heads) also held membership in the MPC concurrently, and thus were included in the sample (see discussion below on the role composition of the MPC).

The offices of mayor and deputy mayor and the top posts in specialized organs are politically and administratively important, both because of the strategic organizational positions they occupy within the bureaucracy, and because of the stature of the men who hold these offices. Generally, cadres in these offices are men of power, prestige, or expertise, whose authority and influence in the bureaucracy can hardly be questioned.

The case of the MPC, however, is not so clear. Composed of the mayor and deputy mayors (all ex officio members) and more than thirty members elected by the local People's Congress, the MPC performs in theory executive and administrative functions comparable to those carried out by both the State Council and the Standing Committee of the National People's Congress at the national level.[27] Constitutionally it is the MPC, as the highest organ of executive authority and collective leadership of the city government, and not the mayor, which exercises the powers of policy making and supervision.[28] Actual political and bureaucratic processes in China, however, appear to be rather different from these constitutional arrangements. The fact that the MPC meets very infrequently, and then only holds brief sessions, leads one to doubt strongly whether the MPC really functions as the center

---

[27] See Articles 62–63 of the Constitution of the People's Republic and Chapter III of the Organic Law of the Local People's Congresses and Local People's Councils of the People's Republic of China, available in Albert P. Blaustein (ed.), *Fundamental Legal Documents of Communist China* (South Hackensack, N.J.: Fred B. Rothman, 1962).

[28] Chou Fang, *Wo-kuo Kuo-chia Chi-kou* (The State Organ of Our Country) (Peking: Chung-kuo Ch'ing-nien, 1955), pp. 84–90.

of administrative power. In spite of this doubt, the composition of the MPC reveals some highly significant features. For example, among the forty-three members elected in 1961 were twelve secretaries and department heads of the Municipal Committee of the Chinese Communist Party and two local military district commanders. Also included were seventeen key administrators (the mayor, deputy mayors, and bureau heads of the city government), eight mass organization heads, and three high level intellectuals (*kao-chi chih-shih fen-tzu*).[29] Although the power of the MPC as a collective organ may be questionable, the importance of the individual leaders represented in that organization can hardly be challenged. In fact, it included persons drawn from several elite groups; moreover it included those who occupied the most influential posts in the key sectors of the Wuhan community, in which they held the largest amount of power, prestige, status, or expertise.[30] Indeed, one may equate membership in the MPC with formal recognition of a leader's elite status in the community.[31]

Another salient characteristic of the composition of the MPC was the presence of a considerable number of mass organization and "democratic party" leaders. It should be noted that the representation of these groups, though designed largely for the purposes of the united front, was by no means entirely ceremonial. The admission of these nongovernmental leaders into the MPC constituted a crucial formal link of communication and political control between the governmental bureaucracies and nongovernmental organizations, such as the municipal trade union, the Federation of Industry and Commerce, and various "democratic parties." It was through these kinds of formal personnel and organization links that nonofficial organizations were incorporated into the unified system of government control, and nongovernmental leaders were converted into government officials.

Methodologically, the MPC—a solid group of persons belonging to

[29] A complete list of the members of the 1961 MPC may be found in *Wu-han Wan-pao* (Wuhan Evening News), June 6, 1961. The institutional affiliation of one member was not ascertained.

[30] For a discussion on this concept of elite, see Harold D. Lasswell, Daniel Lerner, and C. Easton Rothwell, *The Comparative Study of Elites* (Stanford, Calif.: Stanford University Press, 1952), p. 6.

[31] Representing many of the arenas of power in the Wuhan community, this group of MPC members may even be identified as a "community elite" in the city. However, in view of the highly centralized nature of the Chinese political system and the fact that this elite is hierarchically dominated from above and by the Party, and lacks local autonomy of its own, it would be more proper to label it a "bureaucratic" rather than a "political" or "community" elite. Moreover, since no attempt will be made here to identify the real center of power, the terms "power elite" and "ruling elite" will not be used.

the bureaucratic elite, officially identified by the leadership—serves as a convenient focus for elite analysis. Examination of the composition, turnover rate, and other characteristics of its membership over time will help illuminate the process of elite formation and changing patterns of the elite structure in Wuhan.

Since this study relies heavily on biographic and organizational data, a word on sources is in order. The data used in this study, unless otherwise noted, were drawn mainly from four local Wuhan newspapers, *Ch'ang-chiang Jih-pao* (Yangtze Daily), *Hu-pei Jih-pao* (Hupeh Daily), *Hsin Wu-han Pao* (New Wuhan News), and *Wu-han Wan-pao* (Wuhan Evening News.)[32] Extensive biographical files on Chinese Communist leaders, available in Hong Kong, provided the second set of primary sources. In addition, a number of valuable interviews which the author conducted with Chinese refugees from the Wuhan area were also used. These interviews helped to clarify informational ambiguities and bridge many critical gaps in the published data.

Major Characteristics of the Elite

Let me begin the examination of the bureaucratic elite of Wuhan by pointing out some of its more obvious characteristics. The upper part of Figure 2 shows three major sociological attributes of the 157 senior bureaucrats in the samples used for this study.[33] First, males were predominant; second, the elite members were recruited primarily from men with extensive urban backgrounds; and, third, the overwhelming majority of the members of the elite sampled were "outsiders," in the sense that they were not born and brought up in Wuhan.[34]

It is not surprising to find only a small proportion of women leaders in any Chinese group. In Wuhan 10 out of 156 senior bureaucrats tabulated (6 per cent) were women. However, the data will become more meaningful if put in historical and comparative perspective. In

---

[32] Other newspapers published in the Wuhan area also used in this study include: *Hu-pei Ch'ing-nien Pao* (Hupeh Youth News), *Chung-nan Cheng-yüan* ([Journal of] the Political Institute of the Central-South), and *Chung-nan Kung-jen* (Workers of the Central-South). Major biographic works such as *Who's Who in Communist China* (Hong Kong: Union Research Institute, 1966) and *Gendai Chūgoku Jimmei Jiten* (Biographic Dictionary of Modern China) (Tokyo: Kazan Kai, 1966) were also consulted.

[33] The total number tabulated for each category includes only those on whom information on that specific category is available, so the figure is ordinarily smaller than the total sample of 157.

[34] Many other major socioeconomic characteristics of the elite, such as age, geographical mobility, associational membership, and so on, which are obviously important for any elite analysis, are not discussed here, mainly because the data available are so fragmentary that no meaningful statistical analysis can be made.

pre-modern China, even during the Ch'ing and Nationalist periods, virtually no women ever occupied any top bureaucratic offices (even at the local levels).[35] Under Communist rule it is now common to find women making up about 10 per cent of the cadres.[36] This suggests that women in China are now playing a more active and significant role in

FIGURE 2

SOCIO-POLITICAL CHARACTERISTICS OF THE ELITE

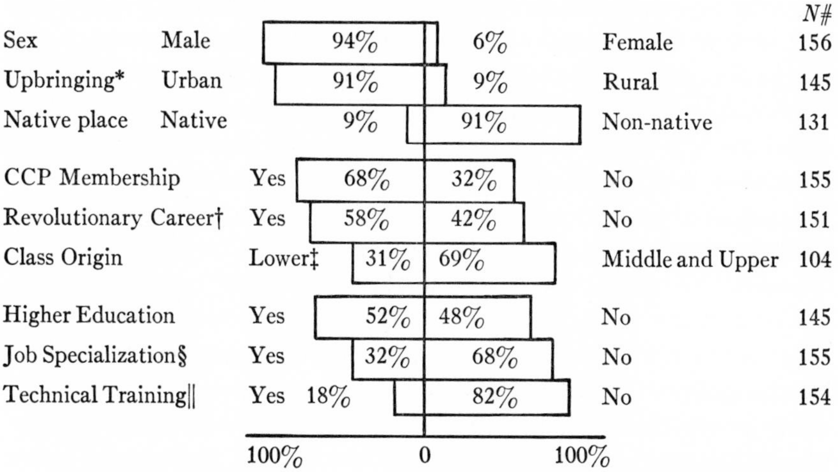

					N#
Sex	Male	94%	6%	Female	156
Upbringing*	Urban	91%	9%	Rural	145
Native place	Native	9%	91%	Non-native	131
CCP Membership	Yes	68%	32%	No	155
Revolutionary Career†	Yes	58%	42%	No	151
Class Origin	Lower‡	31%	69%	Middle and Upper	104
Higher Education	Yes	52%	48%	No	145
Job Specialization§	Yes	32%	68%	No	155
Technical Training‖	Yes 18%		82%	No	154

100%   0   100%

* Upbringing refers to the urban or rural setting in which leaders spent their youth.
† Those who joined the Communist movement before 1945 are considered to have had a revolutionary career.
‡ Lower class origin includes both worker and peasant family origins.
§ Eight years or more of consistent service in one functional area of political or administrative activity is considered to represent job specialization for the purpose of this study.
‖ Technical training refers to technical training at, or equivalent to, the college level.
Numbers for each category include only those on whom information is available. Thus they are smaller than the total of 157 in the sample.

politics than they were before. Although half of the women cadres in the sample specialized in work related mainly to women's organizations, some did occupy other posts of power and importance. Hsia Chih-yü, for instance, once held the directorship of the powerful Organization Department of the Municipal Party Committee; and Ling

[35] See, for example, various studies of traditional China's bureaucratic mobility, in Johanna M. Menzel (ed.), *The Chinese Civil Service: Career Open to Talent?* (Boston: Heath, 1963).

[36] For example, women constituted roughly 10 per cent of the entire Chinese Communist Party membership in 1956.

Sha for a time headed the Bureau of Culture and Education of the municipal government.[37]

The pattern of elite socialization experiences in terms of an urban-rural dichotomy reveals that an extremely high proportion of the sample (90.8 per cent of 145) had grown up in an urban environment —they had received either their secondary or higher education in the cities or had worked in the cities for an extensive period of time during their youth.[38] The data thus imply that some degree of "urbanism" was virtually a prerequisite for an urban bureaucratic career. In view of the fact that Wuhan is one of the most advanced urban centers in China, this finding should not surprise us. What appear to be important are its implications. The data call our attention to the popular hypothesis about the "ruralism" of the Chinese Communist leadership. It is often contended that the Communist leaders were strongly rural oriented because of their protracted rural-based guerrilla activities and thus were not "qualified" to rule the cities. There was, however, little sign of "ruralism" in the top bureaucratic elite of Wuhan.[39]

Urban living provides education, skills, and know-how which have now become the key prerequisites for entering highly professionalized bureaucracies in the cities. A lack of urban socialization experiences in youth would therefore tend to block access to modern education and training, and, as a result, would block access to professional urban careers. The finding that only an extremely small proportion of the members of Wuhan's bureaucratic elite (9 per cent) were drawn from the rural sector would appear to support this hypothesis.

The current Chinese Communist policy of discouraging rural youth from seeking schooling and careers in the cities, effective since the latter 1950's, will undoubtedly have a very far-reaching impact by limiting the opportunities of rural youth for advancement and mobility.[40] Furthermore, as will be shown below, since the urban bureauc-

[37] In the mid-1950's Hsia was first promoted to the post of assistant to the minister of light industry and later named deputy minister of food industry. Ling became president of Peking Normal College in 1955.

[38] For comparison with urban-rural mobility in the Ch'ing period, see P'an Kuang-tan and Fei Hsiao-t'ung, "City and Village: The Inequality of Opportunity," in Menzel (ed.), *Chinese Civil Service,* pp. 9–21.

[39] In his study of Tangshan city, John W. Lewis has found that the Communists recruited continuously from the urban area during the thirties and forties. Lewis, "Political Aspects of Mobility."

[40] See, for example, the directive of the State Council of December 18, 1957, banning unauthorized migration to the cities. *Kuang-ming Jih-pao* (Bright Daily), December 19, 1957.

racy constitutes a major channel of upward mobility to provincial and national leadership, a rural cadre will clearly have far less chance than his urban counterpart in competing for the upper rungs of the bureaucratic ladder.

Another important finding revealed in Figure 2 is that only 12 out of a total of 131 leading cadres whose native places (*chi kuan*) could be ascertained were natives of Wuhan in the sense that their parents or ancestors had established permanent residence there before their birth. If six "democratic personages" and two intellectuals are subtracted from this tiny group of twelve native cadres, there were only four natives in the entire sample who could be ranked as real political and administrative leaders in Wuhan. Among these four, none had advanced beyond the level of bureau head. In contrast, there were many cases where "outsiders" were assigned from other cities or provinces directly to bureaucratic posts in Wuhan, including such formally elective offices as the mayoralty or deputy mayoralties.[41] Being a native of Wuhan, it appeared, in no way constituted an asset in placement or advancement in the city.

This finding inevitably raises the question as to why so few ranking native cadres of Wuhan were assigned to work in their own native place. The sociological maxim that urban population, particularly that of a rapidly industrializing and urbanizing city, is generally composed of immigrant "outsiders" may provide a partial explanation. But perhaps a more pertinent reason can be found in the deep-rooted traditions of China's bureaucratic system. Beginning in imperial days, officials were in principle not to be assigned to posts in their own native *hsien* or provinces. Briefly, two reasons may have accounted for this. In the first place, working in his home district, an official could more easily be induced to commit bureaucratically undesirable acts because of extensive kin ties and personal obligations. Secondly, the imperial court was ever suspicious that a mandarin could more easily conspire against the imperial authorities in his own home base, because of these same ties and obligations.[42] Although there is no way to test empirically the extent to which "traditionalism" still exists in China today, such

---

[41] One of the most striking cases was the transfer of Hsüeh Pu-jo in 1961 from the Honan Provincial Government to the post of deputy mayor of Wuhan, which was formally an elective office.

[42] Cf. Ch'ü T'ung-tsu, *Local Government in China under the Ch'ing* (Cambridge. Mass.: Harvard University Press, 1962), pp. 14–35.

reasoning, in slightly altered forms, appears to influence Communist behavior.[43]

The small number of senior cadres recruited from the native populace, however, was compensated for by a larger number of leaders (29 per cent) drawn from the surrounding province of Hupeh. Approximately one-third of the non-native members of the Wuhan elite were from China's coastal provinces; and another third came from the northern and central regions. Only three were from the border areas and vast regions of the West. These data reveal that the overwhelming majority of those belonging to the elite were recruited from the coastal provinces and Central China, the most modernized sector of the nation.[44] This pattern of distribution presents a striking parallel with our earlier finding on the "urbanism" of the elite. Both findings tend to validate the conclusion that senior members of the bureaucratic elite in China were recruited predominantly from individuals who were from the urban sector or had urban backgrounds.

The middle section of Figure 2 sets forth the characteristics of the 157 leaders sampled in terms of three variables which may be considered political in nature. The data indicate that, first of all, the elite was strongly dominated by Chinese Communist Party (CCP) members (68 per cent); next, over one-half of the members of the elite (58 per cent) were career revolutionists in the sense that they had made their career in the Communist movement before the beginning of the Third Revolutionary Civil War (1946–49); and, finally, a minority of 30 per cent of the 104 leaders in the sample on whom information on family backgrounds was available were from worker or peasant families.

The characteristics deserve further comment. The dominance of Communist Party members was, of course, to be expected. What appeared to be significant, however, was the predominance of old cadres among the 108 Party members in the sample (see Table 23). Ranked according to the standard periods of Party seniority, over 82 per cent of the members of the elite who were Party members had Party seniority at least equivalent to "liberation cadre" level (1946–49). Only 15 per cent joined the Party during the Third Revolutionary Civil War (1946–49), while only three leaders (roughly 3 per cent of

[43] The periodic campaigns against localism, sectarianism, and "independent kingdoms" serve as a clear indication of the leadership's suspicion of local power. See Oksenberg, "Paths to Leadership," pp. 3–4.

[44] John W. Lewis has pointed out the significance of the influence of the level of socioeconomic development on Chinese politics in his article, "The Study of Chinese Political Culture," *World Politics*, XVIII, No. 3 (April, 1966), 503–24.

the 108 Party cadres) were men who joined the Party after 1949. In the early 1950's, all Party members who held posts at the level of bureau chief and above were at least "Yenan cadres." These and similar findings lend strong support to the long-standing impression of scholars in the field that Party seniority was indeed a major criterion in assignment and advancement to high-ranking posts in the government.[45]

TABLE 23

PARTY MEMBERS AMONG MEMBERS OF THE ELITE RANKED
BY PARTY SENIORITY

Party Seniority	N	Percentage
Long March cadres (1921–35)	30	27.8%
Yenan cadres (1935–40)	43	39.8%
Anti-Japanese cadres (1941–45)	16	14.8%
Liberation cadres (1946–49)	16	14.8%
Post-Liberation cadres (1949)	3	2.8%
Total	108	100.0%

The proportion of non-Communists within the bureaucratic elite (32 per cent), small as it might appear to be, highlights some important features of Wuhan's political recruitment. In the first place, the data suggest that the monopoly of high ranking posts by the CCP was not so complete as generally believed. At least until 1965, non-Communists with talent and ambition could find their way into senior bureaucratic positions in Wuhan. It is clear that talent was needed by the bureaucracy for efficiency just as much as political loyalty was desired by the Party for control. Secondly, the distribution of the forty-nine non-Communist members of the elite by political affiliation reveals that just over two-thirds of them (67.3 per cent) belonged to "democratic parties," while the remaining one-third were non-party affiliated personages (*wu-tang-p'ai jen-shih*). Leaving aside for the moment the political impotence of the "democratic parties" and the uncertain role of mass organizations in Communist China, the fact remains that "democratic" leaders and non-party-affiliated persons were normally selected from various important occupational groups and professional organizations to represent these groups and organizations. This suggests that

[45] In his case study of the bureaucracy of a ministry, A. Doak Barnett has also found that Party seniority played a significant role in assignment. See Barnett, "Social Stratification," pp. 23–25.

"interest groups," whether in the form of mass organizations or "democratic parties," were not completely eliminated. They continued to play some roles, though highly circumscribed, in politics under Communist rule.

The mass organizations and "democratic parties" served as channels of political recruitment and were used as means for advancement by those highly trained professionals and formal social and business leaders who for one reason or another remained outside the Communist Party. As such, the mass organizations and "democratic parties" were among the few legitimate channels of mobility still open to non-Party leaders. Take Ch'en Ching-yü, for example. As a member of the na-

TABLE 24

DISTRIBUTION OF NON-COMMUNIST LEADERS

Party Affiliation	N	Percentage
"Democratic party" leaders	33	67.3%
Non-party affiliated leaders	16	32.7%
Total	49	100.0%

tional bourgeoisie, he apparently was not eligible for CCP membership. However, being chairman of both the local Democratic Construction Association and the Federation of Industry and Commerce of Wuhan, he steadily ascended the ladder of the city's bureaucratic hierarchy and, finally, in 1957 was promoted to become deputy governor of Hupeh Province.

For others, the "democratic parties" and mass organizations served as a stepping stone into the CCP hierarchy. Yü Chin-t'ang and Yüan Wen were typical of these cases. Yü and Yüan originally belonged to the local Democratic Construction Association and the Revolutionary Committee of the Kuomintang, respectively. Their leadership among the intellectuals and apparent devotion to the new government seem to have won them membership in the CCP in the mid-fifties. They were subsequently elected to the Municipal Party Committee, in 1959, and were even put in charge of the Party's United Front Work Department and the city's Civil Affairs Bureau. In the light of cases such as these, it would be a mistake to dismiss entirely the political function of the "democratic parties" and mass organizations in China. (See also the discussion below on the contributions of functional expertise by the non-Party leaders.)

Another finding of considerable importance derived from the same middle section of Figure 2 discloses that slightly over two-thirds (69 per cent) of the 104 members of the elite tabulated for class background were from the middle and upper socioeconomic strata. Even within the group of leaders who were also CCP members, the proportion of those with middle- and upper-class origin still stood at 62 per cent.

In comparison with the situation during the Ch'ing and Kuomintang (KMT) periods, the data show that, under Communist rule, men of lower-class origin appear to have better access to elite status.[46] Yet, the data also demonstrate that the Communist recruitment system in Wuhan did not work as much as one might have expected in favor of cadres with lower-class background. In other words, the leadership of Wuhan was by no means drawn mainly from what Sigmund Neumann called the "marginal men" belonging to "marginal groups" of society.[47] Class origin, important as it may have been (particularly in the recruitment of new cadres at lower levels in the post-1949 period), clearly did not carry as much weight as other political attributes, such as Party membership and seniority.

Drawing from the data in Figure 2 again, we can analyze (from the data in the lower section) the members of the elite in terms of whether they had higher education, job specialization, and technical training. These three variables were chosen as rough indicators of the elite's nonpolitically oriented achievement and expertise.

The data show that slightly over half of the 145 members of the elite tabulated (52 per cent) had some education beyond the secondary school level. According to present-day Chinese standards, the top elite as a whole might be considered well educated.[48] In contrast to this better than average educational background, the Wuhan elite appears

[46] For the Ch'ing period, Robert M. Marsh has found that only 13.7 per cent of the officials listed in *T'ung Kuan Lu* were from the commoner families. See his article, "Formal Organization and Promotion in a Pre-Industrial Society," *American Sociological Review*, XXVI, No. 4 (August, 1961), 550. Robert C. North has shown that only 6 to 19 per cent of the members of the Central Executive Committee of the Kuomintang, during 1924–31, were of poor merchant and peasant origin. See Robert C. North, "Kuomintang and Chinese Communist Elites," in Lasswell and Lerner (ed.), *World Revolutionary Elites*, p. 453. See also Menzel (ed.), *Chinese Civil Service*, pp. 20–45.

[47] Sigmund Neumann, *Permanent Revolution* (2nd. ed.; New York: Praeger, 1965), p. 62.

[48] For example, of the ninety-seven Central Committee members of the CCP in 1958, seventy-three of them (74 per cent) appear to have received education at the college level, including training in military academies. Chao Kuo-chün, "Leadership in the Chinese Communist Party," *Annals of the American Academy of Political and Social Science*, CCCXXI (January, 1959), 47.

to have had a relatively low degree of job specialization, measured in terms of the length of uninterrupted service in one of the major functional areas of government administration. Only 32 per cent of the 155 bureaucrats tabulated, for example, had stayed in one of the regime's five main functional areas of work (namely, political and legal work, education and culture, industry and communications, finance and trade, and agriculture and forestry) for more than eight years.[49] Limited comparable data available on the senior bureaucrats of other countries would seem to support the impression, stated above,[50] that this suggests a relatively low degree of job specialization.

The last part of Figure 2 further indicates that the Wuhan elite as a whole was also poorly trained professionally and technically: only 18 per cent of the 154 tabulated had technical training at college level. This figure, together with earlier findings, strongly suggests that a large proportion of the Wuhan bureaucratic corps was composed of political "generalists" (as opposed to job-experienced or job-trained "specialists"), a proportion larger than one would ordinarily expect in a highly modernized bureaucracy.[51]

This combination of a reasonably high level education with a relatively low level of professionalism is probably attributable to two major factors. First, the "higher education" which many of these Communist leaders received appears to have been primarily of the type offered by institutions such as the Anti-Japanese War College under the auspices of the CCP during World War II, or in higher Party schools in the post-1949 period, both of which were fundamentally

---

[49] The percentage would presumably have been different if we had had more complete information on the career history of every member of the elite covering the entire eighteen-year period under study.

[50] Studies of the federal bureaucrats of the United States government (GS-15 and above), for instance, show that approximately 70 to 85 per cent of the top bureaucrats have served in only one of the thirty-odd standard functional (organizational) fields throughout their entire government career, which normally has ranged from twenty to thirty years. It should be further noted that the functional fields as defined in the United States Civil Service are much more refined than the five to eight broad areas used in Communist China. Stanley, *The Higher Civil Service*, pp. 31–34, 137. John J. Corson and R. Shale Paul, *Men Near the Top* (Baltimore: The Johns Hopkins Press, 1966), pp. 116–18, 175–76.

[51] For comparable data available on the United States and Soviet elites, see Lowi, *At the Pleasure of the Mayor;* Stanley, *Higher Civil Service;* Hough, "In Whose Hands the Future?" For the elites of other countries, see, for example, Thom Kerstiens, *The New Elite in Asia and Africa* (New York: Praeger, 1966); Clement H. Moore, *Tunisia Since Independence* (Victoria, Australia: Longmans, 1965); Wendell Bell, *Jamaican Leaders* (Berkeley and Los Angeles: University of California Press, 1964); Robert A. Scalapino and Junnosuke Masume, *Parties and Politics in Contemporary Japan* (Berkeley and Los Angeles: University of California Press, 1962).

designed for general political education and revolutionary training. Thus, even though on paper they appeared to be highly educated, they were not really technically trained. Second, the lack of an effective assignment and transfer system after the Communist takeover of the government apparently further reduced the opportunities available to bureaucrats to specialize and accumulate functional expertise (a fact which will be considered further in the discussion on the personnel transfer system, below).

DISTRIBUTION OF FUNCTIONAL EXPERTISE

The sociology of Wuhan's bureaucratic elite analyzed in the preceding section focuses primarily on the elite as a whole. This analysis tells us little, however, about differences between the Communist and non-Communist leadership elements in terms of their relative levels of technical expertise and job specialization.

Table 25 presents the distribution of Party and non-Party members

TABLE 25

DISTRIBUTION OF FUNCTIONAL EXPERTISE BETWEEN PARTY AND
NON-PARTY GROUPS

Political Affiliation	TOTAL		E+		S+		T+	
	N	Percentage	N	Percentage	N	Percentage	N	Percentage
Party members	106	68%	34	45%	17	35%	2	7%
Non-Party members	49	32%	41	55%	32	65%	26	93%
Total	155	100%	75	100%	49	100%	28	100%

E+ = Leaders with higher education.
S+ = Leaders with job specialization.
T+ = Leaders with technical training.

of the elite by higher education, job specialization, and technical training. Although the data indicate that the highly educated were almost equally divided between the Party and non-Party groups (45 per cent to 55 per cent), the breakdown of leaders with job specialization stood clearly in favor of the non-Party group by approximately two to one (65 per cent to 35 per cent). What seemed most striking of all was the one-sided distribution of technical skills in favor of the non-Party group; in fact; virtually all professional skills (93 per cent) were supplied by this group. This finding strongly reinforces the speculation that the Communist members of the elite may have received higher level education without being professionally and technically trained. Table 25 also shows a slightly higher degree of job specialization among Party leaders, a finding which results from the number of cadres who started a specialized bureaucratic trade in the post-1949 period. These findings demonstrate clearly that in spite of the fact that there were twice as many Party cadres as non-Party cadres among the Wuhan elite, the latter as a whole disproportionately contributed the technical skills and expertise which the bureaucracy needed.

Using the same set of data as shown in Table 25, Table 26 presents a

TABLE 26

DISTRIBUTION OF FUNCTIONAL EXPERTISE AMONG PARTY
AND NON-PARTY MEMBERS

106 PARTY MEMBERS			49 NON-PARTY MEMBERS		
P+	N	Percentage of P+	P−	N	Percentage of P−
P + E +	34	32.0%	P − E +	41	83.6%
P + S +	17	16.0%	P − S +	32	67.0%
P + T +	2	1.8%	P − T +	26	53.0%

P+ = Party members.
P− = Non-Party members.
E+ = Leaders with higher education.
S+ = Leaders with job specialization.
T+ = Leaders with technical training.

different set of percentages to show the distribution of functional expertise between Party and non-Party leaders in each achievement category. The table indicates that non-Party bureaucrats as a group were clearly much better educated, specialized, and trained (84, 67, and 53 per cent for the non-Party elites in each category as opposed to 32, 16, and 2 per cent for the Communists). This finding is complementary with that in Table 25. The non-Party bureaucrats achieved greater technical expertise not only because a larger proportion of them were more professionally and technically trained but also because they served more consistently in one functional area for a longer period of time.

To shift the focus of analysis from the relative strength of technical expertise of the Party and non-Party groups to the question of recruitment criteria, a less obvious characteristic of Wuhan's bureaucratic system may be detected from the data in Table 26; the fact that the overwhelming majority of non-Party members of the elite were better educated, were more specialized, and had greater technical skill implies that they may have been recruited because of these technical qualifications.[52] In contrast, the fact that only a very small minority of the skilled and specialized leaders were Communist cadres would seem to suggest that most of the Party members may have been recruited for reasons other than their technical qualifications and competence. Political qualifications such as seniority, loyalty, and Party membership must have been the key factors that operated in their favor. Moreover, the data in Table 26 also show that as many as seventy-two Communist cadres in the sample (68 per cent) had none of the three technical achievement attributes. This means that the non-job-trained or non-job-experienced Communist cadres constituted a group far exceeding in numbers the total number of all non-Communist leaders in the sample. This pattern of distribution strongly suggests that political attributes as determinants of bureaucratic recruitment seemed to carry much greater weight than technical achievements. To state this finding differently, it seems clear that political criteria in general took priority over achievement criteria in recruitment. This appears to be particularly true in cases where conflict occurred between these two sets of criteria, and the leadership had to choose.

The dominance of political attributes was equally apparent in job assignments. Cross tabulation of the Party seniority of members of the elite and the types of jobs they held, as shown in Table 27, yields a relatively high contingency coefficient of 0.666, with the chi-square significance value and its corresponding probability standing at 63.006 and .001 respectively.[53] These figures suggest a fairly high degree of correlation between the two variables measured. In other words, with technical expertise held constant, the more political seniority a cadre possessed, the more likely he was to receive a post of political importance and power. In fact, the powerful and politically sensitive jobs, such as those in public security, personnel, and education, were virtually monopolized by cadres with high Party seniority, while non-Party officials were normally assigned to offices of lower political sensitivity and power, such as those in forestry, public health, and construction.

---

[52] This speculation, however, does not neccessarily preclude other possible motivations of a political nature. As noted earlier, in the period immediately following the takeover, the Party recruited a considerable number of non-Party intellectuals and personages for united front purposes.

[53] A note on the meaning of Karl Pearson's contingency coefficient may be found in note 68 below.

If we assume that the order of political sensitivity from high to low would be roughly equivalent to the order of technical complexity from low to high, the data in Table 27 also show that most non-Communist members of the elite held posts on a high technical level, while the Communists filled jobs of low technical orientation. This finding indicates that the non-Party leaders' higher level of technical competence

TABLE 27

POLITICAL SENIORITY AND JOB ASSIGNMENT

Political Sensitivity of Jobs	POLITICAL SENIORITY							
	Long March and Yenan Cadres		Anti-Japanese and Liberation Cadres		Non-Party Cadres		Total	
	N	Percentage	N	Percentage	N	Percentage	N	Percentage
Highly sensitive	54	75.0%	21	60.0%	7	16.3%	82	54.7%
Sensitive	18	25.0%	12	34.3%	15	34.9%	45	30.0%
Not sensitive	0	0.0	2	5.7%	21	48.8%	23	15.3%
Total	72	100.0%	35	100.0%	43	100.0%	150	100.0%

Chi sq. = 63.006   NDF   = 4
CC   = 0.544   CC/max. CC = 0.666

may have played a part in their assignment to technical jobs. However, the fact that many Communist leaders in Wuhan who—on the basis of the available evidence—had no technical expertise or job-oriented skills were also found in jobs with a high technological orientation would seem to suggest that, in these cases, political considerations outweighed technical considerations.[54] This disparity between political and achievement attributes, and possible tensions stemming from it, will become even more apparent when we examine these attributes in terms of their influence on bureaucratic mobility.

PATTERNS OF BUREAUCRATIC MOBILITY

Among the 157 members of the bureaucratic elite of Wuhan studied, 104 (66 per cent) showed definite records of job promotions over the years—that is, advancement from lower to higher posts, such as a promotion from section chief to bureau director, or from deputy mayor

[54] It should be noted that using Party seniority as the indicator of political qualification alone may be questionable in some cases. A. Doak Barnett, for example, has pointed out in his study that Party seniority may suggest degrees of organizational skills and administrative ability. Barnett, "Social Stratification," p. 16.

to department head at the provincial level, and the like.[55] For 23 per cent of the sample there was no clear evidence of job promotion (that is, they seemed to have stayed at roughly the same level of bureaucratic hierarchy at which they first entered).[56] The remaining 10 per cent of the leaders (16 cadres) had been either demoted or dismissed from office because of administrative negligence, misconduct, or political crimes.

Among those promoted (105 cadres), over half of the leaders had impressive and successful career records indeed: 24 per cent (25 leaders) reached the level of provincial governor or minister of the national government, and 43 per cent (45 officials) attained offices equivalent to mayor or department director at the provincial level (*t'ing-chang*) by 1965. This category included men such as Wang Jen-chung (deputy mayor and acting mayor, 1952–54), Chang P'ing-hua (Party secretary, 1949–55), and Hsieh Pang-chih (chairman of the Control Commission and Party secretary, 1949–52).[57] All three started building their bureaucratic careers in Wuhan in the early 1950's. By 1966, they were reported to have occupied the posts of first secretary of the Central-South Bureau of the Central Committee, deputy director of the Central Committee's Propaganda Department, and Ambassador to Bulgaria, respectively. Findings such as these on career mobility highlight two significant features regarding upward mobility patterns. First, members of the urban bureaucratic elite such as those of Wuhan appear to have had abundant opportunities for advancing upward into the provincial, regional, and even national bureaucratic hierarchies.[58] Second, the finding also suggests that urban bureaucracy constituted an important channel of upward mobility for local cadres and a major source of trained manpower for recruitment into the national leadership.

[55] A complete classification table of the job (rank) hierarchies and their salary grades for all government organs and cadres may be found in Chung-hua Jen-min Kung-ho-kuo, Ts'ai-cheng-pu (comp.), *Chung-yang Ts'ai-cheng Fa-kui Hui-pien, 1955* (Compendium of Financial Regulations of the Central Government for 1955) (Peking: Ts'ai-cheng Ch'u-pan She, 1957), pp. 464–71.

[56] Although some cadres in this category may have obtained raises in salary grades, moving, say, from grade eighteen to sixteen, data of this sort were normally not available. As a result, it is virtually impossible to tell the degree of promotion for cadres who failed to attain any clear job (rank) promotion.

[57] Biographical information on these three leaders is available in *Who's Who in Communist China*.

[58] Powerful figures like Li Hsien-nien, T'an Cheng, and T'ao Chu were also associated with Wuhan's bureaucracy in the early fifties. Li was mayor in 1952–54; while T'an and T'ao were chairman and vice-chairman, respectively, of the Wuhan Military Control Commission in 1949–52.

In contrast to the reasonably high upward mobility rate, the downward mobility in Wuhan appears far lower. In spite of periodic "rectification" campaigns and political purges, such as the *san-fan* (three anti, 1951–52), *ching-chien* (streamlining organizations, 1955–57), *hsia-fang* (sending cadres downward, 1955–58), and *fan-yu* (antirightist, 1957–58) movements, the top members of the bureaucratic elite as a whole do not appear to have been seriously affected. Although the *san-fan* hit hard at the leadership corps of Wuhan, most of the purged leaders managed to return later (see below for further analysis of this). In Wuhan a total of twenty-nine leading cadres showed records of demotion, dismissal, or other punishment of varying degrees, but thirteen of these (46 per cent) quickly regained their standing. Thus, only sixteen cadres (10 per cent of the total sample) were permanently purged or demoted (see Table 30, p. 244).

Some behavioral patterns of the "fast runners" among these promoted members of the elite are worth noting. The "fast runners" tended to have transferred more frequently than their less successful comrades, with generally shorter tenures in each job. They normally moved vertically in the bureaucratic hierarchy rather than horizontally. Furthermore, the "fast runners" appear to have held jobs in a wide variety of functional areas and to have displayed little technical expertise or job specialization.

The case of Hsieh Pang-chih typifies the career pattern of the "fast mover." Hsieh was first assigned to Wuhan as a deputy Party secretary in 1949 and was soon put in charge of the People's Control Commission. In spite of the official demotion and disgrace he suffered during the *san-fan* campaign, he recovered quickly and became director of the Minsheng Shipping Company in 1953. Two years later he moved into the Ministry of Communications as an assistant to the minister, and then moved on to the Control Ministry as deputy minister. In 1958 he shifted again to a new post, deputy minister of justice. Shortly afterward, in 1960, he was reported to have been named commander and political commissioner of the militia of Chiaotung University. A few months later, he moved into the Municipal Party Committee of Shanghai as its secretary general, and in 1961 he became Ambassador to Bulgaria.[59] In sharp contrast were some bureaucrats like Lei T'ung, Li Leng, and Sung T'se, who were known specialists, respectively, in the fields of industry, public security, and statistics. All these men served

---

[59] See also *Who's Who in Communist China,* pp. 228–29.

more than ten consecutive years in their assignments and appear to have accumulated considerable expertise and experience in their respective functional fields. Nevertheless, all three remained at the rank of deputy director or director throughout the period under study; and none of them seems to have advanced to levels higher than the Wuhan municipal government by 1965.

This pattern of mobility brings to light a serious bureaucratic dilemma in Communist China. A considerable number of "fast runners" seem to lack the technical expertise and specialization urgently needed by China's modernizing bureaucracy; but they often move sooner than others to senior positions of responsibility and power. In contrast, some professional specialists, who spend long years mastering their bureaucratic functions and become highly trained and experienced in their fields of specialization, seem to end up as "slow runners" in the bureaucratic race.[60]

Determinants of Mobility: Political versus Achievement Qualifications

The preceding paragraphs have sketched a general balance sheet of factors affecting bureaucratic mobility in Wuhan. The discussion now turns to the task of identifying and assessing the determinants that may be held responsible for mobility in the Wuhan elite. We will again focus on the relative influence of the political and achievement qualifications,[61] so that a comparative evaluation with respect to the earlier findings on the criteria of recruitment can be made.

[60] Analysis of the career patterns of twenty-seven Politburo members of the Communist Party of the Soviet Union (CPSU), 1917–51, reveals a similar paradox. They appear to have high interorganizational and interoccupational mobility. See Schueller, "The Politburo," Appendix C: "Career Lines of Politburo Members," pp. 145–71. Pending further research, the tentative conclusion derived from the Wuhan case should not be overstated. Statistical analysis based on Tables 31 and 32 (see below) suggests a somewhat optimistic picture, however. Job specialization shows a stronger influence on the promotion rate than other achievement qualifications. It is interesting to note in passing that Lenin is quoted as having said, "capable leaders should be promoted to responsible posts only after a ten-year testing period." *Zaria Vostoka* (May 5, 1966), quoted in Hough, "In Whose Hands the Future?" p. 19.

[61] The concept of political versus achievement qualifications is developed on the basis of the dichotomy between *te* (virtue) and *neng* (ability), or "red" and "expert," that the Communists themselves formulated. Party literature often treats such qualifications as Party membership, revolutionary career, and peasant and worker class origin as objective indicators of political "virtue," which should be taken into consideration in recruitment and promotion. Education, professional expertise, and special technical skills, on the other hand, are seen as objective indicators of achievement "ability." In the West, party affiliation, class origin, and political background are in general excluded from the list of civil servant qualification requirements by law. See also note 54.

Holding the achievement qualifications constant, Table 28 is designed to be a rough measure of the relative influence on promotion of three indicators of political qualification: namely, CCP membership, revolutionary career, and lower-class origin.

TABLE 28

POLITICAL QUALIFICATIONS AND UPWARD MOBILITY

	CADRES WITH POLITICAL QUALIFICATIONS				CADRES WITHOUT POLITICAL QUALIFICATIONS		
	Total	Promoted			Total	Promoted	
	N1	n1	Percentage $\left(\dfrac{n1}{N1}\right)$		N2	n2	Percentage $\left(\dfrac{n2}{N2}\right)$
P+	106	89	83.9%	P−	49	14	28.5%
R+	90	75	83.3%	R−	63	27	42.7%
C+	32	28	87.5%	C−	72	39	54.1%

P+ = Party members.
R+ = Elite members with revolutionary careers.
C+ = Elite members of lower-class origin.

P− = Non-party members.
R− = Elite members without revolutionary careers.
C− = Elite members of middle- and upper-class origin.

The first row of figures in the table shows that among the 106 leaders who were CCP members, 89 had records of promotion, which accounted for approximately 84 per cent of the entire group of Communist elite members in the sample. Of the 49 non-Communist leaders, only 14 (29 per cent) were promoted. The table further reveals that while well over 80 per cent of those with revolutionary careers or working-class origin were promoted, only 43 to 54 per cent of leaders without such political attributes were promoted. The table thus clearly indicates that men with political qualifications had decisive advantages for promotion over those without such qualifications, by about two to one.

On the other hand, holding constant the political qualifications, Table 29 contrasts the proportion, among those promoted, of cadres who had achievement attributes and those who had none. The results suggest that those who had achievement orientations—as measured by higher education, job specialization, and technical training—had a lower rate of upward mobility (53, 41, and 25 per cent in each category) than those who lacked such orientations (77, 73, and 72 per cent in each category).

TABLE 29

ACHIEVEMENT QUALIFICATIONS AND UPWARD MOBILITY

CADRES WITH ACHIEVEMENT QUALIFICATIONS				CADRES WITHOUT ACHIEVEMENT QUALIFICATIONS			
Total	Promoted				Total	Promoted	
$N1$	$n1$	Percentage $\left(\dfrac{n1}{N1}\right)$			$N2$	$n2$	Percentage $\left(\dfrac{n2}{N2}\right)$
E+	75	40	53%	E−	70	54	77%
S+	49	20	41%	S−	106	77	73%
T+	28	7	25%	T−	132	95	72%

E+ = Elite members with higher education.
S+ = Elite members with job specialization.
T+ = Elite members with technical training.

E− = Elite members without higher education.
S− = Elite members without job specialization.
T− = Elite members without technical training.

The findings of these two tables combined reveal two striking features of the pattern of upward mobility among the Wuhan elite. First, men with a high level of political qualification clearly had a better chance of upward mobility than those without such qualification. In fact, the data show not only that a higher ratio of the politically qualified cadres obtained promotion (84 per cent) but also that a larger number of them were promoted (eighty-nine persons). Second, in terms of the mobility criteria, the data demonstrate that, as a determinant of promotion, political qualifications carried more weight than achievement qualifications. Political qualifications alone seem to have provided a cadre better than a four-to-one (83–88 per cent; see Table 28) chance of promotion; while achievement qualifications offered only even odds for promotion at best (25–53 per cent; see Table 29).

The influence of political qualifications appears to have been equally significant in the downward mobility of the Wuhan elite. If we use only CCP membership as a measure of political qualifications, Table 30 shows that while only 9 per cent of the 106 Communist cadres failed to move upward (that is, they remained roughly at the same level throughout the period under study), the percentage for the non-Communists stands at 51 per cent. However, the proportions of elite members with records of demotion or purge (dismissal) in the two categories, Communist and non-Communist, appear to be fairly close (17

TABLE 30

Downward Mobility: Party vs. Non-Party Leaders

Political Affiliation	Total N	Remained $n1$	Percentage $\left(\dfrac{n1}{N}\right)$	Showed Demotion Records $n2$	Percentage $\left(\dfrac{n2}{N}\right)$	Rehabilitated $n3$	Percentage $\left(\dfrac{n3}{n2}\right)$	Demoted $n4$	Percentage $\left(\dfrac{n4}{N}\right)$
Party leaders	106	10	9.4%	18	16.9%	11	61.1%	7	6.5%
Non-Party leaders	49	25	51.0%	11	22.4%	2	18.1%	9	18.3%

per cent versus 22 per cent). This may suggest that the Communists were as vulnerable as the non-Communists to administrative and political disciplinary action, and that non-Communist cadres were no more likely to be targets of purge than Communists. The significant difference between them seems to be that the Communists tend to have had a greater possibility of recovering from their period of disgrace than the non-Communists. The data on rehabilitation demonstrate this point vividly. As high as 61 per cent of the Communists who had been formally disciplined (as opposed to 18 per cent of the non-Communists) survived their demotions or temporary purges. Thus, over the long run, the Communist leaders in the sample showed a net demotion rate two and one-half times lower than that of the non-Communist leaders (6.5 per cent versus 18.3 per cent).

The Party members' greater ability to survive in the bureaucracy was probably best illustrated by the purge of Wuhan's top leadership corps in connection with the purge of Liu Ching and Sung Ying during the *san-fan* period.[62] The top leadership, including the mayor himself, was found guilty of corruption and political deviation and was severely punished in 1952. Leading cadres such as Mayor Wu Te-feng, Deputy Mayors I Chi-kuang and Chu Ti-hsin (concurrently head of Public Security), and President of the People's Court Wang Chih-chun were all dismissed from their offices. Three bureau heads were officially demoted.[63] Also on the list of those punished were Party secretaries Chang P'ing-hua and Hsieh Pang-chih. Nevertheless, all but two of the

[62] Detailed reports on the case may be found in *Ch'ang-chiang Jih-pao,* December 15, 1951, January 13, April 16, 1952.

[63] The three bureau heads purged were Ch'en Hsiu-shan (Labor), Yüan Wen (Personnel), and Lu Ching-ch'eng (Public Health).

Party leaders involved recovered from the purge within one or two years. Four of them were later even promoted to ministerial level posts. In sharp contrast, two non-Communist leaders also involved in the case disappeared permanently from the political scene. During the 1957–58 *fan-yu* campaign, seven non-Communist bureaucrats were reported to have been identified as "rightists" and were violently criticized.[64] Only one of them appears to have survived the antirightist purge. These cases seem to indicate that leading Party cadres, by virtue of their political credentials, tended to have a greater ability to survive than the non-Communists (at least until the launching of the Cultural Revolution). These findings also lead one to suspect that functional experts were quickly dispensed with when they openly challenged the Party's legitimacy and its established political priorities.

The relative influence of political and achievement attributes may also be measured in terms of the leaders' promotion rates, calculated on the basis of the number of years taken to advance one salary grade.[65] Analysis of the promotion rate of the 157 Wuhan bureaucrats shows that 15 per cent of the sample advanced one salary grade (also popu- larly known as cadre rank) approximately every two years while 34 per cent took roughly three to four years to advance one grade.[66] These two groups, which constitute roughly half of the sample, might be considered as "fast runners" in the bureaucratic race.

Who were these fast runners in Wuhan? Were they political cadres or technical experts? Table 31 tells us, first of all, that the fast runners

[64] Among the leading figures attacked were Wang I-ming (deputy mayor), Li Jui, Li Wu-chin, Ma Tse-ming, T'ien Chu-tseng, and Yen Hsün-fu.

[65] The promotion rate is calculated on the basis of the length of service, divided by the number of salary grades (also popularly known as cadre grades) advanced. As already mentioned, information on salary grades of cadres is very difficult to find. It is possible, however, to estimate the approximate number of grades advanced on the basis of job ranks a cadre held at different points of time, by consulting the standard classification table of job ranks and their corresponding salary grades for state cadres, issued by the State Council on July 6, 1956. See *Chung-yang Ts'ai-cheng Fa-kuei Hui-pien, 1955*, pp. 464–71. For this study, the following classification scheme adapted from the official table is used: premier level (grades 2–3), minister level (grades 4–6), provincial governor level (grades 5–7), mayor level (grades 7–9), bureau director level (grades 10–12), divi- sion head level (grades 13–15), section chief level (grades 15–17), subsection head level (grades 17–19), group leader level (grades 19–21), staff member level (*pan-shih-yüan*) (grades 21–24). The promotion rate is a better measure than the highest rank or the total number of grades attained, because the leaders obviously started their careers at different points of time and rank, and also because the great majority of them were still in the process of climbing the bureaucratic ladder.

[66] The average federal bureaucrat of the United States government, for example, advances about one grade (in an eighteen-grade hierarchy) every three years. For this and other comparable data on the United States bureaucrats, see Stanley, *Higher Civil Service*, pp. 34–38, 99–100.

were predominantly Party members (88 per cent). The proportion of fast runners among the Communist members stands at a high 61 per cent, as opposed to 18 per cent among the non-Communists. Even granting the fact that Party membership was always crucial as a determinant of the promotion rate, one would still not necessarily rule out the possibility that achievement attributes might also play an important role, in which case one would expect to find that for the more educated, specialized, and experienced bureaucrats, CCP membership would make little difference with respect to the rate of promotion. However, the data in Table 31 indicate that this was not the case. The

TABLE 31

FAST RUNNERS AMONG PARTY AND NON-PARTY MEMBERS WITH VARIOUS
ACHIEVEMENT QUALIFICATIONS*

	TOTAL	FAST RUNNERS			TOTAL	FAST RUNNERS	
Party Members	N1	n1	Percentage $\left(\dfrac{n1}{N1}\right)$	Non-Party Members	N2	n2	Percentage $\left(\dfrac{n2}{N2}\right)$
P+	106	65	61.3%	P−	49	9	18.3
P+E+	34	22	64.7%	P−E+	41	7	17.0
P+S+	17	12	70.6%	P−S+	32	12	37.5
P+T+	2	1	50.0%	P−T+	26	4	15.3

* For the symbols used, see the explanatory key to Table 26, p. 236.

ratio of fast runners to the total number of Communist members in all three achievement categories (65, 71, and 50 per cent) is decisively higher than that for the non-Communist group (17, 38, and 15 per cent). It is instructive to note that in no achievement category, with the exception of job specialization,[67] was the ratio significantly higher than those for the two group totals, Communist and non-Communist. (The ratio of 65 per cent for the Party members with higher education was not significantly higher than that of 61 per cent for all the Party members as a group regardless of their achievement qualifications. In the case of the ratio of 17 per cent for the non-Communist leaders with higher education, it was even lower than that of 18 per cent for the entire non-Communist group.) One may thus conclude that the pres-

[67] It is worth noting that job specialization, as shown in Table 31, stands out as a more important determinant of promotion than the other two achievement qualifications. This pattern is also clearly indicated in Table 32.

ence or absence of achievement qualifications could hardly be regarded as a crucial variable affecting a cadre's promotion rate, for the data reveal little association between the achievement attributes and the promotion rate. The presence or absence of political qualifications, as shown in the test of Party membership, was obviously much more crucial.

The preceding assessment of the relative influence of political and achievement qualifications is partly statistical and partly interpretive. A more precise approach would be to rely more heavily on statistical data and reduce interpretive speculation. One way to do this is to use Karl Pearson's coefficient of contingency (usually abbreviated to C or C-Coefficient) to test the degree of correlation between various qualifications and the promotion rate of members of the elite.[68] An implicit assumption here is that since the promotion rate must have been determined by qualifications of some kind, reflecting political or achievement criteria, the degree of correlation (in terms of the value of C-Coefficient) between a particular qualification and the promotion rate may serve as a numerical measure of the influence of that criterion on promotion. For this test, we have used data on Party membership, political seniority, revolutionary career, and social class origin as indicators of political qualification, and data on education level, job specialization, and technical training as indices of achievement qualifications. Cross tabulation of the distribution of each of these factors as an independent variable against that of the promotion rate as a common dependent variable produces seven contingency tables (see the Appendix, pp. 265–67). Each table is then subjected to the chi-square test to see whether the paired variables are serially correlated and whether our null hypotheses should be rejected. The results of the chi-square test reveal that all the independent variables are serially correlated with the dependent variable at a high significance of probability ranging from .001 to .02, with only one exception for the educational

[68] Karl Pearson's coefficient of contingency (C) is designed to measure the degree of contingency, or correlation, between two variables. Like many other measures, Pearson's C ranges from 0 to 1, representing a continuum of correlation from noncorrelation to perfect correlation. It is calculated on the basis of the deviations of the observed frequencies (O) from the expected frequencies (E) as measured by chi square (X^2). The formulas used for computation are:

$$\chi^2 = \sum \frac{(O-E)^2}{E} \qquad C = \sqrt{\frac{\chi^2}{\chi^2 + N}}.$$

For a good discussion of this statistical tool, see, for example, John H. Mueller and Karl F. Schuessler, *Statistical Reasoning in Sociology* (Boston: Houghton Mifflin, 1961). Also, V. O. Key, Jr., *A Primer of Statistics for Political Scientists* (New York: Crowell, 1966).

variable table, whose significance value falls slightly lower to the .05 level.

Table 32 summarizes the chi-square values (χ^2) obtained, their corresponding probabilities (P), and corrected contingency coefficients (C) of the seven contingency tables, one for each of the seven independent variables. As can be seen from the table, the C-Coefficients obtained for the political variables (ranging from .554 to .711) without

TABLE 32

DEGREE OF CORRELATION BETWEEN SELECTED
QUALIFICATIONS AND PROMOTION RATE*

	Qualification Variables	χ^2 (Chi-square)	P (Probability)	C (Contingency Coefficient)
Political	Party membership	51.436	.001	.711
	Political seniority	60.598	.001	.660
	Revolutionary career	38.882	.001	.642
	Class origin	26.531	.001	.554
Achievement	Education	13.152	.05	.357
	Bureaucratic seniority	14.952	.02	.454
	Technical specialization	29.959	.001	.497

* For the contingency tables, see the Appendix, pp. 265–67.

exception are higher than those for the achievement variables (ranging from .357 to .497). This finding, thus, demonstrates conclusively that political qualifications were considerably stronger than achievement qualifications as determining factors of bureaucratic advancement in Wuhan.

PATTERNS OF TENURE, TURNOVER, AND TRANSFER

The stability and efficiency of a modern bureaucracy depend on a system of well-balanced leadership tenure and transfer. Both an excessive rate of personnel turnover and a nonspecialization-oriented system of assignment and transfer[69] jeopardize the manpower training and leadership stability of bureaucracy.

[69] The specialization-oriented system of assignment and transfer stresses in principle that a bureaucrat should be assigned and transferred to jobs to which his professional training or experience is oriented.

An analysis of the mean tenure of Wuhan's 157 top bureaucrats (based on the length of service in each principal job), using the data in Figure 3, shows that roughly 50 per cent of the elite changed their primary jobs once every 4 years. The median tenure of 47.4 months (approximately 4 years), means that the average bureaucrat was normally transferred at intervals of 4 years.[70] Or, during the years 1949–65, the average leader changed jobs about 4 times. Moreover, he often found himself transferred to jobs in different functional areas

FIGURE 3. DISTRIBUTION OF AVERAGE TENURE
(IN PERCENTAGE OF THE TOTAL NUMBER BY YEAR)

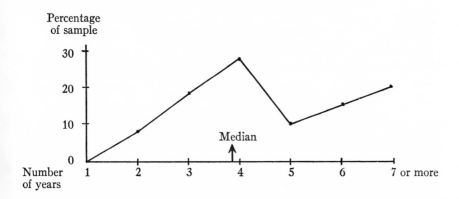

(see further discussion below). The data also reveal that 48 per cent of the sample served with the Wuhan government less than 6 years, while only 10 per cent (15 officials) stayed with the city for more than 15 years.

In the absence of comparable data from other bureaucracies, the consequence of such a pattern of tenure is hard to assess. Judging from the frequent complaints in the Communist press about the excessive turnover of personnel at local levels in the 1950's, however, one is led to suspect that the leadership feared that the then typical length of

[70] The formula used for calculating the median tenure is

$$Md = L + \left(\frac{\frac{N}{2} - cf}{f} \times i \right)$$

(L: the lower limit of the class interval in which the median is located; N: the total frequency; cf: the cumulated frequency up to the median class interval; f: the frequency of the median class interval; and i: class width).

tenure was not sufficiently long for building leadership stability and promoting professionalization.[71]

Analysis of the membership continuity of five sessions of the Municipal People's Council of Wuhan between 1950 and 1961 reveals some features which help to explain the fear expressed by the leadership in the 1950's. As shown in Tables 33 and 34, the MPC registered in 1950–61 a varying annual turnover rate ranging from 7 per cent to 19 per cent, with a mean rate standing at 14 per cent. This mean rate implies that every year 14 per cent of the leading cadres left the city bureaucracy and were replaced by an equal number of new members of the elite who moved in. At this rate, it was possible (though not likely)

TABLE 33

LEADERSHIP CONTINUITY OF THE MPC:
NUMBER OF MEMBERS RE-ELECTED*

Year	1950	1952	1955	1958	1961
1950	51				
1952	21	38			
1955	12	21	37		
1958	8	15	24	47	
1961	6	10	17	36	43

* Top figures in each column denote the total number of MPC members elected in the years listed. The remaining figures below represent numbers of members re-elected in each session.

that the whole slate of original bureaucrats in 1949 could have been replaced in just seven years. Comparison of the membership of the 1950 MPC against that of the 1958, in fact, shows that only 26 per cent of the 1950 members were still in the 1958 MPC (see Table 33).

By 1961 the percentage was further reduced to only 19 per cent. In other words, as much as 80 per cent of the 1950 leadership corps had left the council by 1961. Comparing the Wuhan case with some data available for the bureaucracies in the Soviet Union and other countries, one may conclude that the Wuhan rate was relatively high.[72]

[71] See, for example, Ch'en Shu, "Ching-chien Shang-ts'eng Chung-shih Hsia-ts'eng" (Streamline the Upper Level to Strengthen the Lower Level) *JMJP,* June 24, 1955. Also, *Hsin Hu-nan Pao* (New Hunan News), April 15, 1957, on the excessively high turnover rate of county Party secretaries.

[72] The Central Committee of the CPSU, for example, registered an annual turnover rate of 4.2 per cent during 1961–66 (17 per cent of the old members were replaced by new members who constituted 25.1 per cent of the total membership). A slightly higher rate was recorded in the earlier years: 8.4 per cent in 1956–61 and 10.8 per cent in 1952–

The problem of leadership continuity and specialization in Wuhan seems to have been aggravated by a confusing system of personnel transfer and assignment in the 1950's. Cadres were not consistently transferred or reassigned to jobs involving their technical specialization and experience. Instead, in many cases, men were transferred to jobs outside their fields of specialization or to posts unrelated to their previous experience. Chang Hsüeh-t'ao was a typical example. He first served as director of the Civil Affairs Bureau in 1949. In the following year he was appointed chief judge of the People's Court. Two years later he was reassigned as secretary-general of the MPC. In 1963 he was named deputy mayor of Sian, Shensi. Similar cases of transfers of this sort were common within the sample.

Statistical analysis of the transfer data available does not suggest that the patterns of transfer would facilitate effective training of professional manpower either. Nor does it indicate that the system was carefully designed to make optimal use of the already scarce professional skills. Among the 157 bureaucrats studied, 23 per cent had been assigned and transferred to a wide variety of different functional areas, showing career patterns similar to that of Chang Hsüeh-t'ao illustrated above. (In fact, the variety of interdepartmental shifts was such that it was virtually impossible in many cases to identify an individual's principal areas of specialization or institutional identification.) Nineteen per cent had been transferred out of their broad functional area of service 25–50 per cent of the time,[73] while the remaining 58 per cent of the elite were transferred within one of the five standard functional fields over 75 per cent of the time.[74]

---

56. Even during these post-Stalin purge and destalinization periods, the rates were still lower than the average rate of Wuhan. It is instructive to note that the 1961 rules of the CPSU officially set a compulsory "renewal" rate of 25 per cent for each session of the Central Committee, CPSU, and 33 per cent for each session of the Republican central committees. On the assumption that these organs are re-elected every four years, the required annual "renewal" rates will be 6.2 per cent and 8.2 per cent, respectively.

In his study of the Chinese leadership group in Bangkok, G. William Skinner has found that the average annual turnover rate for a group of Chinese elite members was 8.6 per cent in 1952–55. In comparison with this rate, the rate for the Wuhan bureaucratic elite was relatively high. Armstrong, "Party Bifurcation," p. 420; Hough, "In Whose Hands the Future?" pp. 19–21; G. William Skinner, *Leadership and Power in the Chinese Community of Thailand* (Ithaca, N.Y.: Cornell University Press, 1958), pp. 252–54.

[73] If a person was transferred out of his specialized area one out of four times he was considered to have been transferred out of his area of specialization 25 per cent of the time.

[74] As mentioned earlier, comparable data on the United States federal bureaucracy suggest that 70–85 per cent of the top bureaucrats have never been transferred out of their field of specialization in their entire career. Stanley, *Higher Civil Service*, pp. 31–34, 137.

Changing Patterns of Elite Recruitment and Mobility

The profile of the bureaucratic elite of Wuhan analyzed in the preceding sections is derived primarily from the aggregate data, which covered the entire time span of sixteen years under study. This profile reveals some highly significant characteristics which, as expected, do not fully conform to the "ideal-type" modern bureaucracy that Max Weber conceptualizes. Although the Wuhan bureaucracy had recruited some men with needed talents and expertise, and showed some signs of professionalism, the structure and process of its recruitment and mobility were still under the strong influence of political priorities. The profile also shows that a relatively high rate of elite turnover and interorganizational transfer prevailed in this bureaucracy, and that the leadership has apparently not succeeded in developing a personnel system which could effectively build up a pool of professional manpower to expedite bureaucratic modernization. This over-all portrait, one should hasten to add, is basically "static" in nature. It does not convey the dynamics of its development or highlight the changes that have taken place and the direction in which this bureaucracy has been evolving.

In this section we shall attempt to examine the Wuhan bureaucracy from a time-series perspective, so that we can assess the major changes and trends of development since the Communist takeover. For this task, the Municipal People's Council may again serve as a convenient focus of analysis. Comparison of the membership composition of the MPC over time in terms of its members' major qualifications and institutional roles will highlight the changing patterns of recruitment and mobility. Moreover, changes in tenure and turnover rate of the MPC membership over time may be used to measure the trend of leadership continuity and professionalization.

Figure 4 presents the distribution of the major qualifications of MPC members elected during the five sessions of the MPC in the period from 1950 to 1961. The qualifications chosen for analysis here, as before, include Party membership, revolutionary career, and worker and peasant class origin—representing political attributes—on the one hand, and higher education, job specialization, and technical training —representing achievement attributes (of a nonpolitical nature)—on the other. Close examination of this graph reveals a very significant pattern of change over the years. The importance of political attributes appears to have declined consistently from 1949 through 1958, with a

FIGURE 4. Political and Achievement Attributes of
Members of the MPC, 1950-61
(in Percentage of the Total Members in Each Category)

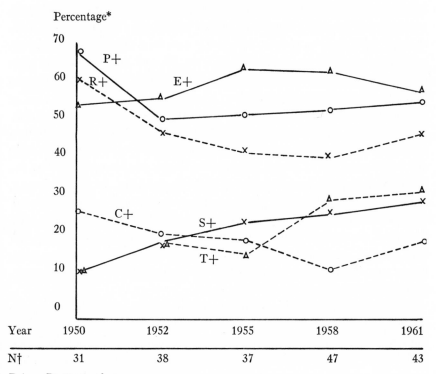

Percentage*

Year	1950	1952	1955	1958	1961
N†	31	38	37	47	43

P+ = Party members.
R+ = Leaders with revolutionary career.
E+ = Leaders with higher education.
C+ = Leaders of worker and peasant class origin.
T+ = Leaders with technical training.
S + = Leaders with job specialization.
  * Percentages represent the proportion of members in each attribute category to the total membership in each session. Since each member normally exhibits more than one attribute, and they are counted for each one, the combined total of percentages for each selected session exceeds 100 per cent.
  † The total number of MPC members in each session.

sharp drop in 1952. Though this trend of decline was slightly reversed in 1961, the gain was not significant. In contrast, the importance of achievement attributes showed a gradual over-all rise over time. This was particularly evident in the areas of job specialization and technical training. The level of education declined somewhat after 1955, yet, it should be noted, its 1961 percentage was not only still higher than that for 1950–52 but also at the top of all attributes. The significance of an increase in educational qualifications becomes more meaningful if considered in conjunction with the decrease in the number of Party members and those with revolutionary careers. In 1950 there were more MPC members with Party membership (68 per cent) or revolutionary careers (61 per cent) than with higher education (55 per cent). This pattern was sharply reversed in 1952, however. The level of higher education reached its peak in 1955, at 65 per cent, well over the respective percentages of 41 per cent and 43 per cent for Party membership and revolutionary careers.

The contrast between the distribution pattern for 1950 and that for 1961 in each attribute category reveals that the political attributes, without exception, showed signs of decline, while all the achievement attributes emerged stronger. Though the degree of difference was by no means striking, the trend itself was highly significant. In the Weberian sense, this trend testified to some improvement of the professional quality of the bureaucracy during the years studied. More men with technical expertise, professional experience, and better educational background, instead of men with political qualifications only, were being recruited, though very slowly, into the senior bureaucratic positions in Wuhan.

Although the analysis of major qualifications of MPC members reveals some tendencies of the Weberian type, further examination of the composition of the MPC in terms of members' major political and social roles (or institutional identifications) fails to show the same trend. The MPC, as suggested earlier, brought together local leaders who played various formal leadership roles; and membership in the council was a symbol of elite status. The primary institutional roles that each of the MPC members played outside of the council may be divided into five basic categories: (1) Party elite members, (2) leading government administrators, (3) "democratic party" personages, (4) mass organization leaders, and (5) high level technical experts and intellectuals. Figure 5 presents the role composition of the MPC between 1950 and 1961, indicating the number of elite members in each role category in proportion to the total membership of the MPC. The figure demonstrates a striking growth of the Party's representation over the years, which expanded from an initial 19 per cent in 1950 to 33 per cent in 1961. This increase seems to imply that the Party, by virtue of its ever-expanding representation, played an ever-increasing role in the city's bureaucratic and administrative processes. In other words, there was a clear trend toward Party dominance of the bureauc-

FIGURE 5. ROLE COMPOSITION OF THE MPC, 1950–61
(IN PERCENTAGE OF THE TOTAL MEMBERS IN EACH ROLE CATEGORY)*

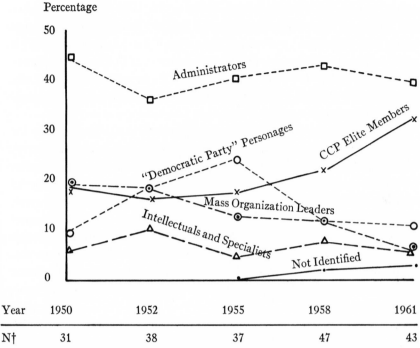

Year	1950	1952	1955	1958	1961
N†	31	38	37	47	43

* Each member is classified only once by his most salient official role. Thus, the combined total of percentages for each session stands at 100 per cent.
† The total number of MPC members in each session.

racy. If the presence of military leaders in the MPC could also be interpreted as a sign of political control, then the formal reappearance of two local military leaders in the MPC following 1958, after a lapse of seven years, could also be cited as an indication of this trend.[75] In contrast to the expansion of the Party's representation, it should be noted, the representation of administrators and professional specialists remained at about the same level, with some signs of fluctuation and minor decline.

Another conspicuous trend shown in Figure 5 was the decline of the

[75] The immediate reasons for the reappearance of military leaders in municipal posts might have been related to the political unrest caused by the Hundred Flowers movement and the Anti-Rightist campaign in 1957–58, and to the ascendence of the People's Liberation Army's political role following Lin Piao's takeover of control of the military in 1959.

representation in the bureaucracy of leaders of the "democratic parties" and mass organizations. This decline might be attributable partly to the increasing professionalization of the urban government and partly to the diminishing function of the "united front" organizations for purposes of power legitimization.[76] In conjunction with the trend of Party dominance, as discussed above, it is instructive to note that the decline of the representation of mass organization and "democratic parties" failed to boost that of professional administrators and experts. Instead, it was the Party that filled the positions given up by leaders of the mass organizations and "democratic parties."

The trend of bureaucratic development in Wuhan, in short, showed a somewhat mixed pattern, involving simultaneously the rise of professionalization and increased Party control. More qualified and specialized bureaucrats were recruited into positions of authority and power in the sixties than in the fifties. However, a countertrend of intensification of Party control over government administration appears to have been accelerated also. If a bureaucracy of both "red" and "expert" was what the Communist leadership had consciously planned to achieve, the findings would seem to confirm that the Party had made progress in that general direction.[77]

In contrast to the above findings, which suggest that the bureaucracy of Wuhan achieved only a limited gain in the intake of professional expertise and the expansion of administrative authority, progress in other areas appears to have been rather more impressive. Let us again take the MPC as the point of departure. The membership turnover of the MPC during 1950–61, as presented in Table 34, showed a remarkably steady decline over the years. The high annual turnover rate of 19.3 per cent in 1950–52 was reduced by two-thirds, to 6.6 per cent per year, in the 1958–61 period. The high rate in 1950–52 may have resulted from the *san-fan* purge, yet that purge was by no means the only contributing factor. Take the 1955–58 rate of 13.6 per cent for example. In spite of the heavy toll among the non-Party members of the elite during the *fan-yu* movement (1957–58), the turnover rate was still lower than that of the preceding period (14.7 per

---

[76] One indication of the trend was the elimination of the representation of model workers after 1955.

[77] The current upheaval of the Cultural Revolution has raised serious doubt as to whether the leadership is still strongly concerned about the building of a bureaucracy balanced with both "reds" and "experts." Violent attacks on the Party as well as state bureaucracies by the Maoists and Red Guards suggest that the leadership in charge is determined to put the "reds" in absolute command at the expense of the "experts."

TABLE 34

MEMBERSHIP TURNOVER OF THE MPC, 1950–61

Year	Total Number of Leaders	NUMBER OF LEADERS LEFT		NUMBER OF LEADERS ENTERED		AVERAGE ANNUAL RATE OF TURNOVER*
		N	Percentage	N	Percentage	Percentage
1950	31					
		10	32.3%	17	44.7%	19.3%
1952	38					
		17	44.7%	16	43.3%	14.7%
1955	37					
		13	35.1%	22	46.7%	13.6%
1958	47					
		11	23.4%	7	16.3%	6.6%
1961	43					

* Average annual rate of turnover for the entire period: 13.5 per cent.

cent). Thus, it is reasonable to assume that if it were not for the fact that the trend of decline was already in progress then, the net rate for this period would have been as high as that for the early 1950's.

A survey of the patterns of mobility year by year from 1949 through 1965 also demonstrates a trend toward leadership stabilization in Wuhan. Figure 6 summarizes the annual distribution in percentages of those promoted, those demoted, and those remaining at the same rank (unchanged). It indicates that 1949 was clearly a year of "collective" upward mobility for many Communists and their supporters who started their government careers following the Communist victory. Of those for whom 1949 career information was available, 79 per cent appear to have received their first governmental assignment or to have been promoted in that year. This group of "collectively" promoted leaders, contrary to the popularly held impression, was not necessarily confined to the Communist cadres. In fact, a considerable number of democratic personages were also recruited into the Wuhan government in this period. Motivated by a variety of considerations and desiring to create an attractive image of the new government and the united front, the Communist leadership in the early period of takeover seems to have preferred recruiting fresh "democratic" personages and leading intellectuals into government rather than promoting the officials left over from the Nationalist government.[78]

[78] The best indication of this, of course, was the fact that only a small number of the "retained" personnel attained the ranks of the elite.

FIGURE 6. PATTERN OF MOBILITY, 1949–65
(IN PERCENTAGE OF THE TOTAL MEMBERS BY YEAR)

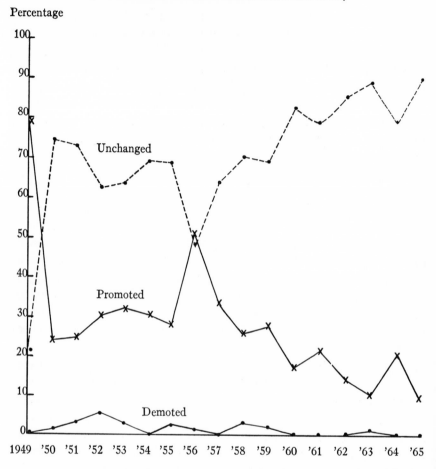

After the 1949 "mobility boom," the upward mobility rate in 1950
dropped sharply, to 25 per cent of the sample. In the next six years a
trend of upward mobility persisted, showing a moderate increase during 1950–55 and a startling leap up to 51 per cent in 1956. After that, a
reverse trend emerged. The rate of upward mobility began to fall
consistently, though it fluctuated from time to time. This new trend of
over-all decline implies that after 1956 fewer leaders were constantly
on the move in the bureaucratic hierarchy, and that a trend toward
manpower stabilization had emerged. This decline in upward mobility
was also clearly reflected in the corresponding rise in the proportion of
leaders remaining in the same rank. In short, statistical analysis of

mobility patterns over the years reveals that the Wuhan bureaucracy has tended toward leadership stabilization since 1957.

The actual stabilization of the top administrative and Party leadership in Wuhan provided the most convincing evidence of this trend. In the first eight years of Communist rule, 1949–56, Wuhan had four mayors and ten deputy mayors. This means that the average tenures for mayors and deputy mayors in this period were only twenty-two and twenty-four months, respectively, representing a turnover rate of approximately 50 per cent per year through 1956.[79] In sharp contrast Liu Hui-nung, the fifth mayor of Wuhan under Communist rule, has remained in office ever since November, 1956. (If he has not been purged during the current Cultural Revolution, his tenure is now over ten years.) At the same time, it should be noted that the average tenure of the deputy mayors increased from two years to seven years after 1956.

Moreover, leadership stabilization occurred not only in the municipal government but also in the city's Party leadership, in a similar pattern. In the first eight years, the top leadership of the Party also changed hands four times, registering an average tenure of twenty-one months for the Party secretary (or first secretary) and thirty-two months for the deputy secretaries (including second and third secretaries, or first, second, and third deputy secretaries). These figures represented, repectively, turnover rates of 57 per cent and 38 per cent per year. Nevertheless, Sung K'an-fu took over as first secretary in 1956, and he appears to have remained in that post through 1966.[80] Furthermore, the average tenure for the other Party secretaries since 1956 has stretched to six years. The parallel between the stabilization pattern affecting government leadership and that affecting Party leadership in Wuhan strongly suggests that the leadership stabilization was a significant trend, rather than a random development.[81]

[79] Data on the Soviet bureaucracy suggest that in the last two decades directors in the vast majority of important plants have held their posts for five to ten years or even longer. Jerry Hough, "The Soviet Concept of the Relationship between the Lower Party Organs and the State Administration," *Slavic Review*, XXIV, No. 2 (June, 1965), 227. For other comparable data on the Soviet Union, see note 72 above.

[80] It is not clear whether Sung has been purged during the Cultural Revolution. At any rate, his name has not been mentioned in the press since mid-1966.

[81] The trend toward leadership stabilization appears also to have been evident in the mass organizations, such as the Communist Youth League and the Federation of Industry and Commerce. Structural and organizational stabilization appears also to have emerged in this period. Structural changes within the bureaucracy were greatly reduced. It should be noted, however, that the long average tenure of seven to ten years that senior bureaucrats were enjoying by the mid-1960's may have created problems of different types, namely, lack of mobility for younger cadres, recruitment stagnation, and generational tensions.

CONCLUSION

In his theory of modern bureaucracy, Max Weber predicted two major trends of bureaucratic development: an increase in structural differentiation and specialization of bureaucracy, and a growing intake of professional talent and expertise.[82] These trends, as aspects of the modernization process, both reflect and facilitate government and administrative efficiency.

In a formal structural sense the bureaucratic system of Wuhan appears to have been fully equipped for many years with the features of the "ideal type." Like many other modern bureaucracies, it has developed highly differentiated, specialized structures. However, conclusions derived from an analysis of this formal structure alone, without careful examination of the personnel and operational aspects of the system, will be superficial and even misleading.

As found in the course of this analysis, the prevailing recruitment and mobility system of the Wuhan bureaucracy did not, as of 1965, appear to have made fully operational its elaborate and differentiated structures in the direction that Weber predicted.[83] The composition of the leadership corps was biased in favor of "political generalists" rather than "professional specialists." The majority of the members of the elite appear to have been recruited and moved up the bureaucratic hierarchy mainly by virtue of their political merits and qualifications, rather than because of professional training and expertise. This phenomenon, however, does not imply that the leadership was totally unaware of the importance of professional expertise to the bureaucratic outputs and administrative efficiency. Periodic debates in China over the contradiction between "red" and "expert," and between "politics in command" and "professionalism in command," indicate clearly that the leadership was quite aware of the stakes involved. Yet, preoccupation with the desire to preserve its monopoly of political power and

[82] Parsons (ed.), *Max Weber;* Victor Thompson, *Modern Organization* (New York: Knopf, 1961), pp. 10–57.

[83] Readers are reminded again that the preceding analysis represents a case study of a specific urban bureaucracy and its senior elite. Thus many generalizations drawn from this study are not intended to apply uniformly to the bureaucracies in all sectors and at all levels in China. Lower level cadres in the countryside, for example, may exhibit features quite different from what we have found in Wuhan. However, some comments regarding the general impact of Communist policies on the Wuhan bureaucracy may be valid for the Chinese bureaucracy as a whole. Needless to say, a complete and accurate knowledge of the Chinese bureaucratic system will require more comparative and microscopic studies which cut across sectors and levels.

other political concerns have apparently prevented the leadership from developing a recruitment and mobility system oriented toward maximizing the intake of professional expertise, on the one hand, and using manpower in the most rational way possible to support bureaucratic modernization, on the other. As long as the charismatic Mao and his militant followers retain their rigid outlook, as they do in the current Cultural Revolution, maintaining that "politics is the soul, the supreme commander," and that it is not only worthless but also incorrect to "get one's job done without letting politics take command,"[84] it is not likely that the basic characteristics of the contemporary Chinese bureaucracy will be changed.

The trend of development as highlighted in the time-series analysis of this study, however, has revealed highly significant features of change. In the first place, the bureaucracy of Wuhan has shown over the years some positive, though still quite feeble, signs of professionalization, as measured by its increasing intake of expertise and talent. But a trend toward intensification of political control over the bureaucracy has also emerged since the late fifties.

Political campaigns—whether in the name of *cheng-chih kua-shuai* (put politics in command), or of *cheng-chih t'u-ch'u* (give politics prominence)—were all directed toward enhancing the power of militant revolutionaries vis-à-vis the authority of professional bureaucrats. Nothing illustrated this trend better than the systematic introduction, since 1962, of the political work departments (*cheng-shih kung-tso-pu*) and the appointment of a large number of military personnel in nonmilitary organizations.[85] Modeled on the operation of the People's Liberation Army's (PLA) political department system, this group of new political commissars, with exclusive control of political and personnel matters, began to overshadow, if not totally destroy, the authority of professional administrators.[86] Under these circumstances the division of labor between "political" and "technical" work, naturally, became extremely difficult, if not completely impossible, to maintain. No administrator could possibly insist that his work was purely techni-

---

[84] NCNA, Peking, 1729 GMT, May 17, 1966.

[85] An excellent account of the "political work department" system may be found in Chalmers Johnson, "Lin Piao's Army and Its Role in Chinese Society," Part 2, *Current Scene*, IV, No. 14 (July 15, 1966), 1–11.

[86] Detailed information on the power, structure, and operational process of the political department system within the PLA may be found in a collection of Communist documents under the title *Fei-chün Cheng-chih Kung-tso T'iao-li* (Regulations on Political Work of the Bandit Army) (Taipei: Ch'ing-pao-chü, 1965).

cal and, as such, should not be subject to political intervention. Moreover, the launching of the Cultural Revolution and the violent assault on the bureaucracy and on "bourgeois" professionalism amounted to a declaration of "war" against the bureaucracy by the militant Maoists. This "war" obviously is going to have a most destructive effect on the moderate gains that the Chinese bureaucracy has achieved the hard way over the past seventeen years.

Second, the study also indicates that 1957 was a landmark year in Wuhan's bureaucratic development. The relatively high rate of cadre mobility and turnover characteristic of the post-liberation period began to slow down after that year; and the top leadership of Wuhan began to stabilize. High personnel mobility and turnover, of course, tends to create a faster rate of political recruitment, more active political participation by the populace, and broader sharing of political power. Thus, political mobility, as John W. Lewis has pointed out, tends to play the important function of generating political support and legitimacy for a new government.[87] However, fostering high political mobility without giving due attention to such bureaucratic problems as personnel staffing, the training of manpower, and the continuity of leadership may easily lead to overstaffing, manpower waste, and leadership instability. These troubles may be compounded if high mobility is accompanied by a system of transfer and assignment not carefully designed to facilitate manpower training and specialization.

During the first eight years of Communist rule, the bureaucracy in Wuhan appears to have developed these symptoms. The rapid political recruitment and upward mobility following the seizure of power seem to have strongly boosted the prestige and legitimacy of the Communist leadership. But by the mid-fifties the problems of overstaffing and manpower waste in the bureaucracies began to create difficulties for the leadership and eventually forced it to resort to drastic measures such as the *ching-chien* and *hsia-fang* movements during the second half of the fifties. By the end of the 1950's these drastic measures had succeeded in correcting the previous excesses, and a new trend toward stabilization began to set in. As a result of the leadership's strong push to reduce mobility, and even to promote downward mobility, the government apparently traded one evil for another. Judging from the long tenure (seven to ten years) which many top members of the elite had enjoyed in the mid-1960's, one suspects that the high turnover of the

[87] Lewis, "Political Aspects of Mobility," pp. 908–10.

early fifties slowed down because of the need for a short stage of stabilization in the late fifties, which was followed by a swing to the other extreme of excessively long tenure, low mobility, and stagnation in the sixties. This stagnation, in fact, may have been one of the major causes of the widespread criticism of the regime, political resentment, and discontent which steadily grew within various key sectors of population; it may also have been responsible for tensions between the old guards and new cadres and even for the emergence of "localism" which has occurred in the 1960's.[88] How to maintain a moderate rate of political mobility so that the leadership can attain a high degree of both political legitimacy and bureaucratic efficiency is, of course, a task of supreme importance to China's bureaucratic development. This task will be particularly crucial in the period following the Cultural Revolution.

Third, the analysis of the recruitment and mobility processes in Wuhan clearly reveals that the leadership commanded tremendous power to influence the course of bureaucratic development. The powerful Organization Department of the Party, through its systematic control of personnel offices in all the government bureaucracies and mass organizations, had a virtual monopoly of control over cadre recruitment, mobility, and transfer.[89] It had the power not only to dictate over-all policies and priorities regarding criteria and rate of recruitment, but also to examine, approve, or reject each individual candidate. This power has been evident in the Party's membership recruitment campaigns in the past, for example. The Party has repeatedly demonstrated its ability to designate specific membership qualifications, rates of recruitment, and even sectors of the population to be recruited from over specified periods of time. Moreover, the Party has

---

[88] Tensions of these sorts were vividly seen in Communist documents such as *Kung-tso T'ung-hsün* (Bulletin of Activities) for the period between January 1 and August 26, 1961; and *Fan-kung Yu-chi-tui T'u-chi Fu-chien Lien-chiang Lu-huo Fei-fang Wen-chien Hui-pien* (Collected Documents Captured During an Anti-Communist Raid on Lien-chiang Hsien, Fukien Province) (Taipei: Ch'ing-pao-chü, 1964). Particularly relevant to our study are the tensions between the old and new cadres, which may have stemmed from three major sources: (1) the old cadres, acting out of their instinct of self-preservation, tried to hold on to their positions, while the new ones aspired to advance; (2) the existence of a wide gap of experience, education, and training between the old guards and the new recruits; and (3) the lack of support and respect for the superior cadres from the subordinates because of the former's failure to show knowledge and expertise commensurate with their positions and superior to that of the latter.

[89] An excellent discussion of personnel control by the Party may be found in Barnett, "Social Stratification," pp. 18–20, 29–34.

also shown an indisputable power to rectify and purge cadres selectively, under Party guidance.[90]

The centralized character of recruitment and mobility processes in China and the Party's ability to monopolize control suggest that the leadership was wholly responsible for the course of China's bureaucratic development. The influence of social and economic trends on the course of the development of bureaucracy, important as it may be, is primarily a factor of long-term significance. As this study of the Wuhan bureaucracy indicates, there have been few signs of the emergence of a new generation of "technocrats" able to give a fresh outlook to those operating the system. As of 1965, there was little doubt that the nature of the system was primarily a product of the leadership's deliberate policy choices.

If there is to be a sharp change in the direction of China's bureaucratic development, obviously the initiative will have to come from the leadership. If the leadership were to decide today to moderate its fanatic drive toward *cheng-chih t'u ch'u* (giving prominence to politics) and re-establish the balance of priorities between "red" and "expert," it would be reasonable to expect that such a decision would have an immediate and direct effect on the patterns of cadre recruitment and mobility and, thus, in the long run on the outlook of the entire bureaucratic system. Such a decision (which is extremely unlikely to take place so long as the "Maoists" are in charge) would obviously be the most crucial factor in determining whether the modernization and professionalization of China's bureaucracy is to be achieved in a comparatively short time or to be delayed for another one or two generations. Furthermore, any change in the direction of bureaucratic development in China would certainly in turn exert an impact of strategic importance on China's long-term economic and technological modernization.[91] In this regard, the significance and im-

[90] The ability to control recruitment is best illustrated by the large-scale recruitment of urban industrial workers in 1950–52 and that of intellectuals in 1955–56. The *san-fan* in 1951–52 and the *fan-yu* in 1957–58 are probably the best examples of purges.

[91] This observation does not necessarily imply that political leadership is always dysfunctional and should be completely eliminated from bureaucracy. Even Max Weber himself admitted that the continued existence of political leadership is not only inevitable but to some degree essential for meaningful development of political order. What appears to be particularly critical today in China's bureaucratic system is the regime's excessive emphasis on political priorities and hostility toward bureaucratic authority and professionalism. A more balanced system which pays equal attention to political leadership and to professional authority is probably what China needs most in its quest for modernization. For a succinct discussion of Weber's view on the need for political leadership in bureaucracy, see Alfred Diamant, "The Bureaucratic Model: Max Weber

plications of the current Great Proletarian Cultural Revolution as a power struggle between Mao's charismatic leadership and the bureaucracies' institutionalized authority, and between the "radical revolutionists" and the "pragmatic bureaucrats," cannot be overemphasized.

APPENDIX: PROMOTION RATE AND SELECTED QUALIFICATIONS

TABLE 35

PROMOTION RATE AND PARTY AFFILIATION

Promotion Rate*	Party Members		Non-Party Members		Total	
	N	Percentage	N	Percentage	N	Percentage
Very fast	22	21.2%	0	0	22	14.5%
Fast	43	41.3%	9	18.8%	52	34.2%
Slow	27	26.0%	7	14.6%	34	22.4%
Very slow	12	11.5%	32	66.7%	44	28.9%
Total	104	100.0%	48	100.1%	152	100.0%

Chi sq. = 51.436   NDF   = 3
CC   = 0.503   CC/max. CC = 0.711

* Very fast = promoted one grade every 1–2 years.
  Fast   = promoted one grade every 3–4 years.
  Slow   = promoted one grade every 5–8 years.
  Very slow = promoted one grade in 8 years or more.

TABLE 36

PROMOTION RATE AND PARTY SENIORITY

Promotion Rate	Yenan Cadre		Liberation Cadre		Non-Party Cadre		Total	
	N	Percentage	N	Percentage	N	Percentage	N	Percentage
Very fast	18	25.7%	4	11.4%	0	0	22	14.9%
Fast	29	41.4%	15	42.9%	6	14.0%	50	33.8%
Slow	17	24.3%	10	28.6%	6	14.0%	33	22.3%
Very slow	6	8.6%	6	17.1%	31	72.1%	43	29.1%
Total	70	100.0%	35	100.0%	43	100.1%	148	100.1%

Chi sq. = 60.598   NDF   = 6
CC   = 0.539   CC/max. CC = 0.660

Rejected, Rediscovered, Reformed," in *Papers in Comparative Public Administration,* ed. by Ferrel Heady and Sybil L. Stokes (Ann Arbor: Institute of Public Administration, University of Michigan, 1962), pp. 67–69.

TABLE 37

PROMOTION RATE AND REVOLUTIONARY CAREER

Promotion Rate	With Revolutionary Career		Without Revolutionary Career		Total	
	N	Percentage	N	Percentage	N	Percentage
Very fast	21	23.3%	1	1.7%	22	14.7%
Fast	35	38.9%	16	26.7%	51	34.0%
Slow	24	26.7%	10	16.7%	34	22.7%
Very slow	10	11.1%	33	55.0%	43	28.7%
Total	90	100.0%	60	100.1%	150	100.1%

Chi sq. = 38.882   NDF   = 3
CC   = 0.454   CC/max. CC = 0.642

TABLE 38

PROMOTION RATE AND CLASS ORIGIN

Promotion Rate	Worker and Peasant Class		Petty Bourgeois Class		Bourgeois Class		Total	
	N	Percentage	N	Percentage	N	Percentage	N	Percentage
Very fast	8	25.8%	2	7.7%	3	6.5%	13	12.6%
Fast	13	41.9%	13	50.0%	9	19.6%	35	34.0%
Slow	7	22.6%	7	26.9%	9	19.6%	23	22.3%
Very slow	3	9.7%	4	15.4%	25	54.3%	32	31.1%
Total	31	100.0%	26	100.0%	46	100.0%	103	100.0%

Chi sq. = 26.532   NDF   = 6
CC   = 0.453   CC/max. CC = 0.554

TABLE 39

PROMOTION RATE AND EDUCATION

Promotion Rate	Higher Education		Secondary Education		Elementary Education		Total	
	N	Percentage	N	Percentage	N	Percentage	N	Percentage
Very fast	8	10.7%	6	13.0%	4	19.0%	18	12.7%
Fast	21	28.0%	18	39.1%	10	47.6%	49	34.5%
Slow	14	18.7%	14	30.4%	4	19.0%	32	22.5%
Very slow	32	42.7%	8	17.4%	3	14.3%	43	30.3%
Total	75	100.1%	46	99.9%	21	99.9%	142	100.0%

Chi sq. = 13.151   NDF   = 6
CC   = 0.291   CC/max. CC = 0.357

TABLE 40

PROMOTION RATE AND BUREAUCRATIC SENIORITY

Promotion Rate	Over 13 Years		7–12 Years		Under 6 Years		Total	
	N	Percentage	N	Percentage	N	Percentage	N	Percentage
Very fast	10	15.4%	3	21.4%	1	6.7%	14	14.9%
Fast	29	44.6%	4	28.6%	4	26.7%	37	39.4%
Slow	18	27.7%	5	35.7%	2	13.3%	25	26.6%
Very slow	8	12.3%	2	14.3%	8	53.3%	18	19.1%
Total	65	100.0%	14	100.0%	15	100.0%	94	100.0%

Chi sq. = 14.952   NDF   = 6
CC   = 0.370   CC/max. CC = 0.454

TABLE 41

PROMOTION RATE AND JOB SPECIALIZATION

Promotion Rate	No Specialization		Low Specialization		High Specialization		Total	
	N	Percentage	N	Percentage	N	Percentage	N	Percentage
Very fast	1	3.1%	9	13.6%	12	22.2%	22	14.5%
Fast	9	28.1%	25	37.9%	18	33.3%	52	34.2%
Slow	5	15.6%	24	36.4%	5	9.3%	34	22.4%
Very slow	17	53.1%	8	12.1%	19	35.2%	44	28.9%
Total	32	99.9%	66	100.0%	54	100.0%	152	100.0%

Chi sq. = 29.959   NDF   = 6
CC   = 0.406   CC/max. CC = 0.497

PART III

Personality and Politics

RICHARD H. SOLOMON

Mao's Effort to Reintegrate the Chinese Polity: Problems of Authority and Conflict in Chinese Social Processes

Empires wax and wane; states cleave asunder and coalesce. When the rule of Chou weakened seven contending principalities sprang up, warring one with another til they settled down as Ts'in and when its destiny had been fulfilled arose Ch'u and Han to contend for the mastery. And Han was the victor.

The Romance of the Three Kingdoms

In the past our adult citizens have been unable to unite on a large scale or for a long period. They have been derisively compared to "a heap of loose sand" or spoken of as having "only five-minutes' enthusiasm." Now, incapacity to unite is a result of selfishness, and the best antidote for selfishness is public spirit.

Chiang Kai-shek, *China's Destiny*

Destroy selfishness; establish the collective (*p'o-szu, li-kung*).
Maoist political slogan from the
"Great Proletarian Cultural Revolution"

INTRODUCTION

The attainment of a new and stable level of political integration in many ways has been the essential problem underlying the turmoil of China's twentieth-century political history. This particular problem is not new to China, however. Seen in a broader time perspective *re*integration has been the problem, at least if we adopt the historian's notion of the "dynastic cycle"; of phases of centralized political control alternating with episodes of regional fragmentation and chaotic violence—a rhythm of their history and social life that Chinese express in

271

the polar concepts of *ho-p'ing* and *luan,* tranquillity and confusion. The most powerful and enduring symbols of the Confucian political tradition reflect this polarity of ordered peace and violent social disintegration: the "warring states" as opposed to the universal empire and "the great unity" (*ta-t'ung*). And it needs no elaboration that the vitality of these symbols has been all too painfully renewed in the twentieth century, in the machinations of regional warlords and the uncompromising struggle to re-establish a unitary political structure.

Within the altered world political context of foreign nations now crowding in upon her, however, China's twentieth-century political problem has been to rise above the decentralized integrity of an agrarian society—a condition that Sun Yat-sen and Chiang Kai-shek could only balefully compare to a "heap of loose sand"—to attain the higher level of cohesiveness, and power, of an industrialized nation-state.

Approaching the analysis of China's difficulties in achieving a new level of political integration presents both conceptual problems and comparative challenges. One of the only partly answered questions of recent Asian political history is why Japan, a "feudal" society in the cultural shadow of the Chinese empire, was able to attain the reality of nation-state status with apparent ease and rapidity, while the parent polity remained fragmented despite a long tradition of centralized bureaucratic political authority. Has the mere geographical factor of size been a major contributing element? Or are there significant underlying social factors not apparent to the foreign observer?

A key assumption underlying this study is that a fruitful perspective on problems of social and political integration is to be found in the social attitudes and political orientation of the individuals who comprise a given society.[1] The notion of "political culture"—of the attitudes and emotions affecting political behavior which a society teaches

---

[1] Most recent theoretical work on the problem of political integration has focused at a macroscopic level of analysis: the selection and quantified evaluation of indexes of social transaction that reveal *existing* levels of national or supranational social cohesion; the study of state or regional processes that help realize the "mutual interests" of various political groups; and the qualitative study of normative social values that promote or hinder group cooperation. Almost all of this work has proceeded within the context of Western and national political processes; and only a minimum of effort has been devoted to the study of what would seem to be the most basic element affecting social and political integration, the individual personality. It is telling that a recent review of research on integrative political processes devoted only passing notice to this microscopic level of analysis, before moving on to more traveled paths of inquiry. (See Philip E. Jacob and James V. Toscano [ed.], *Integration of Political Communities* [Philadelphia: J. B. Lippincott, 1964], p. 14, and *passim.*)

its members—has provided an orientation to data gathering;[2] and the research techniques developed by David C. McClelland for the study of psychological "needs" has provided both tools of analysis and insight into social motivation.[3]

The primary objective of this study is to set forth an interpretation of why the attainment of a higher level of social integration has been so difficult for the Chinese. Our political point of departure is the continuing concern expressed by Chinese leaders for the attainment of a state of national unity, and the past century's history of political fragmentation even in the face of foreign manipulation and the Japanese invasion. Our analytical focus, however, is at the level of individual motivation and perception. In particular, we have tried to identify the structure of attitudes and emotions in terms of which Chinese perceive social relations, and to relate this orientation to the realm of political action. And, by comparing the political attitudes of "anonymous" Chinese citizens with the expressed concerns of their political leaders, we have tried to identify the areas of tension and common expectation linking leader and led.

The major interpretation developed in the following pages is that Chinese social attitudes form a pattern which we choose to call the "dependency" orientation toward interpersonal relations. This orientation includes a hierarchical conception of authority and great concern about interpersonal conflict. These two attitude dimensions paradoxically seem to account for both the sense of order and stability which could characterize the enduring Confucian polity, and also the episodes of unrestrained conflict and violence which periodically fragmented the society.

When we compare the leadership conceptions of traditionally ori-

---

[2] The "political culture" concept is a refinement of earlier formulations of "national character" or "political ethos." This analytical framework was first articulated by Gabriel Almond in an article, "Comparative Political Systems," *Journal of Politics*, XVIII (1956), 391–409. Among subsequent studies based on this concept are: Gabriel Almond and Sidney Verba, *The Civic Culture: Political Attitudes and Democracy in Five Nations* (Princeton, N.J.: Princeton University Press, 1963), and Lucian W. Pye and Sidney Verba (ed.), *Political Culture and Political Development* (Princeton, N..J: Princeton University Press, 1965).

[3] Virtually the only methodologically disciplined and comparative work to go beyond earlier, and none too successful, efforts at unstructured "national character" analyses has been David C. McClelland's research on *need achievement, need power,* and *need affiliation.* For a description of these analytical categories and some of his research findings see, in particular, *The Achieving Society* (Princeton, N.J.: D. Van Nostrand, 1961).

ented Chinese with those of Communist Party Chairman Mao Tse-tung, it appears that two of the main dimensions of attitude change promoted by the Communists in post-1949 China have been in the areas of rejecting this "dependency" orientation toward authority, and altering attitudes toward criticism and conflict.

In the following analysis we identify three social concerns, three attitude polarities or "contradictions," which seem to give continuity to problems of social integration in traditional and Communist China: the tension between a unitary, hierarchical conception of authority, and the subordinate individual's efforts to balance his dependence on authority with a striving for a degree of personal autonomy; the contradictory demands in Chinese society between group life and the private, between collective interests and the personal; and the tension between hostility and aggressive impulses which are denied legitimate expression, or which burst forth to produce social "complications" and to "confuse" the proper ordering of human relationships which are seen as giving stability to society.

These three dimensions of tension in social attitudes not only suggest areas of continuity between China's pre- and post-Communist political history; they also help to establish the links between individual social attitudes and larger social processes.

The data from which the present interpretation is developed are a set of ninety-two intensive interviews with literate Chinese émigrés of three generations who come from a broad range of mainland provinces. While this group cannot be said to represent China's peasants, it does include a variety of urban occupational backgrounds and educational levels. And perhaps most meaningfully, this sample does seem to reflect the attitudes of those who have been most directly participant in China's twentieth-century political life.

Each interview was carried out recently in either Hong Kong or Taiwan, and consisted of approximately ten hours of discussion structured around a series of open-ended questions concerning family life, social perceptions, and personal concerns. Certain data were gathered during each interview in a more formal manner through the use of an attitude scale and a set of nine Thematic Apperception Test (TAT) pictures, which were used to elicit respondents' expectations about certain types of social interaction.[4]

This is without question a small base of data from which to try to

---

[4] The attitude scale and TAT pictures are reproduced in Appendix A at the end of this paper, on pp. 352–58.

generalize about the social attitudes and political orientations of nearly a quarter of mankind. Moreover, the fact that these respondents are émigrés raises further questions about the reliability of our data. And the inevitable need to use such shorthand identifying labels for attitudes or individuals as "traditional" or "modern" may create concern in the minds of some readers. These various methodological points will be given more detailed consideration at appropriate points in the following discussion.

As a general perspective on this analysis, however, it should be stressed that in developing an interpretation our general analytical rule of thumb has been to use only those social perceptions and emotional concerns which clearly are shared by this particular interview group (and where possible, we have handled the data in a quantified manner, as will be indicated below). But most importantly, we have tried to relate the themes found in our interviews to the concerns of China's political leadership, as revealed in a variety of public documents. Hence, our interpretation is based on a reinforcing *pattern* of data rather than on the unique interview response or on material collected from only one source. In sum, however, it should be stressed that the interpretation developed here remains at the level of hypothesis until more extensive data, or studies from a variety of perspectives, have added depth and independent evaluation to our preliminary findings.

The following discussion naturally structures itself into two sections; indeed, Parts I and II could almost be considered separate studies. The first section is an exploration of the manner in which traditional Chinese society was bound together. Through the interpretation of interview data, and historical and sociological materials, we try to give a sense of the interplay between individual attitudes and forms of social organization in giving structure and process to the traditional society. This initial section makes explicit those aspects of the traditional Chinese political culture which have influenced the pattern of integration characteristic of a history of "dynastic cycles" or alternating phases of centralized order and regional conflict; and it underscores political themes which turn out to be of continuing concern to the Chinese Communists in their efforts to create a new level of social integration.

The second part is an analysis of certain political measures that the Chinese Communists have implemented which appear to be a direct response to the strengths and tensions of the traditional social order: their effort to maintain the unitary quality of the Confucian polity; yet their concern with creating an "active" society in which change is an accepted and ongoing process, and where cooperative social relations have knitted the entire society together.

In conclusion, we will relate the themes and interpretations developed in Parts I and II to more recent events in Communist China, for in a number of ways the "Great Proletarian Cultural Revolution" now convulsing this society is a test both of the validity of the present analysis, and of the durability of China's new system of political integration.

I. TRADITIONAL CHINA: THE INTEGRATION OF PERSONAL DEPENDENCE AND GROUP INTERDEPENDENCE

One of the simplicities that continues to limit our understanding of traditional Chinese social processes is the notion that "family loyalty" was the basis of stability of a society and culture with more than three millennia of continuity. The very reasonableness of this assertion, however, masks a much more complex reality. By way of illustration, on the basis of one attitudinal indicator of relative commitment to family or nation, "modern" Americans turn out to be more family oriented than Chinese of largely conservative upbringing.[5]

Responses to this one attitude survey statement, as summarized in

[5] In the following analysis a number of comparisons are drawn between the attitudes of an American sample and those of the Chinese respondents. We have tried to match these two groups so that they represent samples drawn from similar places in the social structures of their respective societies; that is, both have a high educational level relative to the rest of their countrymen, they are largely urbanized individuals, and can be considered "middle to upper-middle class" bearers of the value system of the most politically mobilized strata of their societies (in the case of the Chinese, representative of the groups who ruled during the Nationalist era). In addition they have been selected so as to represent a broad distribution of geographical origins within their respective countries.

This matching effort should not obscure the fact, however, that these two groups have not been randomly selected, are not large enough to represent fully reliable data bases, and that the Chinese are émigrés, while the Americans are not. The precise nature of any biases which might be built into—in particular—the Chinese sample, is difficult to estimate, but it is at least worth making explicit to the reader just how we have interpreted and weighted these data: Beyond viewing these two groups as representative of the particular social strata just mentioned (and not necessarily representative of their entire societies), we have compared the attitude distributions of these two groups primarily to provide a point of *contrast* for analytical clarity. The American data, if nothing else, help to make explicit the cultural biases of the author; and the points of attitude similarity and difference between these two groups are at least helpful in a heuristic sense, underscoring what seem to be really distinctive cultural attitudes, and forcing us to refine interpretive hypotheses.

It should be stressed, however, that we realize that these two samples may not be ideally comparable for a number of reasons; and we view the present analysis as the source of interpretations requiring further validation.

FIGURE 7. Responses to the Attitude Survey Statement, "The Nation Naturally Has Its Importance; but Family Life Is More Important"

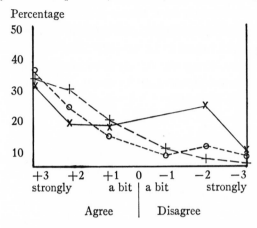

Percentage

+3	+2	+1	0	−1	−2	−3
strongly		a bit		a bit	strongly	

Agree | Disagree

Symbol	Group Tested	Mean	Standard Deviation	Sample Size
+ − −	American males*	+1.45	1.76	269
O − − −	"Conservative" Chinese males†	+1.24	1.96	136
X ——	"Communist" Chinese males‡	+0.81	2.19	32

* This sample consists of 226 college students from the University of Michigan and Parsons College, and 43 adults of white collar employment and high education from a Detroit suburb. The students were selected to represent a broad geographical distribution of places of socialization.

† This sample consists of fifty-nine adult Chinese émigrés from a broad range of mainland provinces, and seventy-seven college students in Taiwan of a variety of family "native places."

‡ This sample consists of émigré Chinese, predominantly from southern and coastal provinces, most of whom were in their twenties when interviewed and who received secondary education in Communist-run schools, or who were in the Communist Party or Youth League.

Figure 7, must be handled with considerable caution, particularly when cross-cultural comparisons are involved, for the symbols to which these groups respond—"nation" and *kuo-chia;* "family" and *chia-t'ing*—are obviously less than equivalent in meaning. But such a crude comparison does convey a sense that, when asked to indicate the relative importance in their lives of nation or family, Americans and Chinese are far from poles apart.[6] The problem is to proceed beyond the simple notion of "family loyalty" as being the essential element affecting the

[6] In Part II of this analysis we will have more to say about the social orientation of young Chinese refugees educated by the Communists, who at least on this one item rather clearly reveal significant attitude changes.

level of social integration, and to explore the reality of interpersonal relationships which lies behind the phrase.

In our interview research on Chinese attitudes toward social relations, one of the most meaningful indicators of a whole complex of personal attitudes was found to be an individual's conception of that period of his life cycle which was felt to be most satisfying. Here again a comparison between Chinese and American groups is most suggestive, as can be seen in Table 42.

TABLE 42

RESPONSES TO THE INTERVIEW QUESTION, "Which Is a Happier Time of Life, Childhood or Adulthood?"

Group Tested	"Childhood"	"Adulthood"	Undecided*	N
American student males	45.3%	52.0%	2.6%	225
American adult males	23.1%	74.4%	2.5%	39
Chinese émigré males, 20–29 years of age	65.4%	15.4%	19.2%	26
Chinese émigré males, over 29 years of age	66.7%	20.6%	12.7%	63

* The "undecided" responses are probably not comparable: the Americans were given the attitude survey in a group administration and had no opportunity to qualify their responses; while the Chinese, interviewed individually, could give a verbal qualification even though they were encouraged to make a choice between the "childhood" and "adulthood" responses.

The sample of American college students is about evenly divided as to whether childhood or adulthood is the happiest time of life. But as the distribution of attitudes for the adult sample suggests, after struggling with the adolescent identity problems that are of such emotional concern to many of our culture, American adults are able to find self-realization in one of the many careers provided by our industrial society, and within the context of a newly formed nuclear family.[7] Within the Chinese sample, however, one finds neither the perception of adulthood as a happy time of life, nor the shift in attitude over the generations; childhood remains the most appealing phase of the life

[7] The significance of the American family as a social context for self-realization is suggested both by the data in Figure 7 and the material in Table 43, discussed on page 282.

cycle.[8] As one middle-aged refugee from the North China province of Hopei phrased it,

Youth years are happier than adulthood because you don't know or understand anything; all you do is play; you are without worries. When you become an adult then there are problems about studying, marriage, and your working future. All these can get you bothered. I think that life up until you are twenty is a relatively happy time; after you are thirty your superiors make trouble for you, and if you do not manage interpersonal relations well you can provoke people's hatred, so it is very annoying.

This response is rich in perceptions and emotional concerns expressed by most of our interviewees: the appeal of the unburdened innocence of youth, when "you don't know or understand anything" and, within the shelter of one's family, all needs are effortlessly gratified; a desire to avoid the responsibilities of adulthood that come with the establishment of a new family and career; and anxiety about dealings with manipulative superiors and "complicated" (*fu-tza*) and potentially conflict-laden social relations. We find in our interview records no indication that Chinese find personal independence and self-realization to be goals worth striving for; indeed, our respondents consistently expressed an attitude that has been observed as well by other students of China: ". . . the life of a single individual is an incomplete life." A Chinese of traditional social orientation finds in the Western stress on "individualism" a life style which "makes orphans out of children and makes lonely people out of parents by having the children live apart from their parents; . . . which values not companionship but separation . . . ."[9]

In such an attitude Chinese express the firm conviction that life is not realized as an individual, but only within the context of a group;

---

[8] An interpretation based solely on the responses of émigré Chinese does raise important questions of reliability. Are they not responding to the peculiar difficulties and circumstances of their disrupted lives? This kind of a distinctive bias cannot be fully ruled out; but it is worth pointing out a number of reasons why this group's glorification of childhood does not seem to be simply a reflection of their "refugee" status. The younger group was composed largely of students in Hong Kong or people gainfully employed in Taiwan, while the older respondents, most of whom had come to Taiwan in the late 1940's, had lived out their professional lives in the employ of the Nationalist government, or were active in one of the educational and cultural associations that continue to give a sense of community to mainland refugees on Taiwan. And perhaps more meaningfully, when asked to elaborate the reasons for their feeling childhood (or adulthood) to be a happier time of life, these people did not tend to stress either their refugee status or the obvious political turmoil surrounding their lives. As discussed in the text, their perceptions are related to very fundamental and enduring attitudes toward social relations.

[9] Cited in C. K. Yang, *Chinese Communist Society: The Family and the Village* (Cambridge, Mass.: M.I.T. Press, 1965), I, 166–67.

and that personal satisfaction is most fully attained in a condition of being cared for by others. Nothing is more fearful than the prospect of facing life alone, like "an orphan"; and the anticipation of interpersonal conflict produces an anxious longing for the sheltered life once known in the innocence of youth.

The best term to describe this most basic of Chinese orientations toward social relations seems to be "dependency"; and its full meaning for the problem of social integration will become fully clear only when we explore in some detail its implications for the Chinese conception of social authority, and of peer relations.

THE AMBIVALENCE OF DEALING WITH AUTHORITY

Traditional Chinese political documents, at least those of the dominant Confucian tradition, make it clear that family relationships were the core organizational pattern for the entire society. Of the five "cardinal social relationships" (wu-lun) through which the Confucianists sought to give structure and order to society—the bond of emotions and responsibilities linking father and son, elder and younger brother, husband and wife, friend and friend, ruler and his ministers —three are of the family. As well, it should be noted, all but one of these relationships are hierarchical in quality. They were the building blocks of the traditional social order; and it is within their highly personalized set of reciprocal obligations that the Chinese sought to give reality to a government of men, not laws.[10]

The attitude survey responses dealing with social authority make it very clear that Chinese still see political action in highly personalized terms—rather than in terms of issues, programs, or norms for mediating political conflict. They are highly consistent in the orientation,[11] and of one mind,[12] that social order should be based on the guidance of talented men (jents'ai) who, without opposition and unchecked by any-

[10] A number of Western observers have been impressed by the assertive manner in which Chinese seek to assure Westerners, and perhaps themselves, that a government of men is somehow more civilized than a government of laws. Such a point of view seems to be just one more example of the traditional Chinese "dependency" orientation toward social relations: the concern that there be a personalized authority on whom one can rely, and who will take responsibility and provide security for his dependents. Laws are cold, without kan-ch'ing (human feeling), and stimulate fears of being abandoned to the impersonality of self-reliance. See Jerome Alan Cohen, "The Criminal Process in The People's Republic of China: An Introduction," Harvard Law Review, LXXIX, No. 3 (January, 1966), 470.

[11] Consistency is indicated by very similar attitude distributions on the other attitude survey items dealing with social authority, especially items 11, 23, and 31.

[12] Group unanimity is inferred from the low standard deviations on these items.

FIGURE 8

RESPONSES TO THE ATTITUDE SURVEY STATEMENT, "Although Laws and Public Programs Have Their Place, What Our Country Needs Even More Is a Few Courageous, Firm, and Dedicated Leaders in Whom the People Can Put Their Trust"

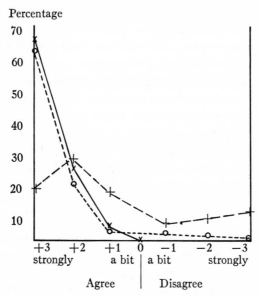

Symbol	Group Tested	Mean	Standard Deviation	N
+ − −	American males	+0.62	2.16	269
O − − − −	"Conservative" Chinese males	+2.29	1.33	136
X ——	"Communist" Chinese males	+2.56	0.70	32

thing beyond their own moral "cultivation," actively work to solve the people's problems and maintain social order.[13]

Here comparison with the American sample is highly suggestive. As is indicated in Figure 8, the Americans have what is roughly a U-shaped or bimodal distribution on this (and on the other) authority items. This bimodality seems to represent a tension between a majority of 60 or 70 per cent of the population which is willing to go along with the initiatives of their leaders, and a 30 or 40 per cent minority who feel that individual initiative is more important, or who are highly sensitive to any encroachments by public authority on their personal auton-

[13] A traditional view of the importance of *jen-ts'ai* in effective government is presented in Mary C. Wright, *The Last Stand of Chinese Conservatism* (New York: Atheneum, 1966), chap. v.

omy.[14] This tension seems to be the essence of the effective working of American democracy: a willingness on the part of the majority to go along with the decisions and initiatives of their elected leaders, with the concomitant pressure of a smaller "activist" element which seeks to circumscribe the actions of public authority, and who will openly criticize what they see as encroachments on their capacity for personal action and realization of their own interests.

Another way of conceptualizing this cultural difference in attitudes toward authority, particularly as it pertains to the problem of social integration, is that the Chinese have sought to insure social order and stability through popular acceptance of and passive dependence upon the initiatives and guidance of a few talented individuals entrusted with social authority. But in return for their "filial loyalty and respect" the Chinese expected authority to insure social order by enforcing universal commitment of their peers to the obligations of the *wu-lun,* and satisfaction of the needs of those who had given dependent loyalty. This type of integration through common acceptance of hierarchical social authority is underscored by our attitude survey data: if degree of dispersion of response on any one item, as measured by the standard deviation, is taken as an index of consensus, then the rank ordering of this statistic indicates that the four items dealing with social authority (attitude survey items 6, 11, 23, and 31) rank fourth through seventh,[15] and are all among the lowest 22 per cent of the ranked standard deviations; that is, the Chinese have high consensus on attitudes concerning acceptance of the guidance of a personalized authority. These are also items with some of the highest mean scores, indicating strong approval of the ideas expressed in the statements.

Here again comparison with the American sample is instructive. A similar rank ordering of standard deviations indicates that personal autonomy and self-realization by way of a career[16] are the issues on which the American group has the greatest unanimity. This suggests that American society is tied together through active common commitment to the economic structure which provides the opportunities for career development and hence self-realization; whereas the Chinese

---

[14] This attitude is in strong contrast to the firm conviction of the Chinese that the guidance of a personalized authority is basic to social order, rather than self-discipline. See responses to attitude survey items 6, 11, 23, and 31, in contrast to items 4, 12, 20, 22, and 32, in Table 43.

[15] It is intriguing to note that the first three items all deal with the matter of learning about "foreign ways," which raises questions about notions of Chinese "xenophobia"!

[16] These concepts are indexed by the attitude scale items 20, 4, 12, 22, and 32.

TABLE 43

RANK ORDERINGS OF STANDARD DEVIATIONS (AS A MEASURE OF ATTITUDE
CONSENSUS) OF ATTITUDE SURVEY RESPONSES FOR CHINESE AND AMERICAN
SUBSAMPLES

CHINESE MALES*			AMERICAN MALES†		
Attitude Survey Item Number and Code Name	Mean Score	Standard Deviation	Attitude Survey Item Number and Code Name	Mean Score	Standard Deviation
19 (Lessons)	2.59	0.85	20 (Live Apart)§	2.76	0.86
24 (Foreign Films)	1.90	1.03	04 (Pick Career)§	2.59	1.00
10 (Foreign Ways)	2.32	1.10	22 (Scientist)§	2.05	1.23
23 (Effective)‡	2.16	1.14	19 (Lessons)‖	2.18	1.23
31 (National Trouble)‡	2.04	1.24	01 (Have Fun)	2.07	1.32
06 (Leaders)‡	2.34	1.24	12 (Commerce)§	1.66	1.37
11 (Obedience)‡	2.26	1.29	10 (Foreign Ways)‖	1.80	1.49
28 (Help)	−2.13	1.34	25 (War)	1.91	1.50
04 (Pick Career)§	2.22	1.37	28 (Help)	−2.20	1.53
27 (Patience)	1.72	1.46	05 (Strangers)	−1.84	1.59
20 (Live Apart)§	1.78	1.50	18 (Criticize)	−1.49	1.65
29 (Friends)	1.76	1.51	07 (Astrology)	−1.89	1.66
15 (Strict)	1.69	1.57	32 (Marry)§	−1.78	1.70
01 (Have Fun)	1.23	1.60	02 (Family)	1.45	1.76
30 (Understand)	1.33	1.72	27 (Patience)	0.99	1.81
32 (Marry)§	−1.37	1.74	24 (Foreign Films)	0.81	1.83
05 (Strangers)	−1.45	1.76	16 (Nuisance)	−1.14	1.86
26 (Artist)	0.26	1.78	26 (Artist)	−0.84	1.89
25 (War)	1.26	1.80	31 (National Trouble)‡	1.11	1.98
03 (Calligraphy)	1.25	1.81	23 (Effective)‡	0.87	2.02
22 (Scientist)§	0.99	1.82	17 (Traditional Morals)‖	−0.18	2.03
14 (Operas)	−0.58	1.84	15 (Strict)	0.93	2.06
18 (Criticize)	−0.77	1.87	08 (Women Work)	−0.77	2.07
12 (Commerce)§	0.13	1.90	03 (Calligraphy)‖	−0.24	2.07
21 (No Foreigners)	−0.20	1.93	11 (Obedience)‡	0.87	2.10
17 (Traditional Morals)	0.64	1.94	09 (Confucius)‖	−0.68	2.15
16 (Nuisance)	−0.32	1.96	06 (Leaders)‡	0.62	2.16
07 (Astrology)	−0.48	1.99	30 (Understand)	0.61	2.17
02 (Family)	1.17	2.00	21 (No Foreigners)	−0.69	2.18
08 (Women Work)	0.28	2.01	13 (Prove Self)	0.41	2.19
13 (Prove Self)	1.11	2.02	29 (Friends)	0.63	2.31
09 (Confucius)	−0.07	2.11	14 (Operas)‖	−0.65	2.37

* A total sample of 167, consisting of college students from Taiwan, and the 91 mainland refugees of three generations.

† A total sample of 269, consisting of 43 adults and the rest college students, all of high educational level and middle or upper-middle class socioeconomic status.

‡ Items dealing with social authority.

§ Items concerned with personal autonomy and self-fulfillment via marriage and a career.

‖ These items were reworded slightly to be suitable for an American reader.

have tried to integrate their society through a more passive acceptance of a dominant authority. This cultural difference in conception of the individual's relation to society and authority seems to embody the essence of Emile Durkheim's distinction between societies of "mechanical" and "organic" solidarity.[17]

Basic to this Chinese social orientation to authority, which we have chosen to characterize as one of "dependency," was the assumption that security and social order could best be maintained through a noncompetitive vesting of authority in those with greatest social experience; and a concomitant expectation that those with this dominant authority were obligated to care for their loyal dependents. This conception grew from Chinese family life, where parents sought to insure for their security in dependent old age through the rearing of filial sons and daughters who would provide for their needs just as they had cared for the children in the dependency of childhood. This is the *interdependence* of the generations elaborated to its highest degree. Reciprocal support was seen as the particular genius of the system,[18] and the expectation that social ties were the basis of one's personal security and potential career advancement permeated not only authority relations but dealings with peers as well.

What was seen in a larger social context as interdependence, however, acquired a rather different perspective in the way these attitudes were inculcated in young Chinese. Traditional parents, seeing in their offspring the security of their later years, relied on time-tested social norms in the raising of children to insure that they would not simply grow up to move away and establish independent lives of their own. Expressions of indiviualistic behavior in a growing child were branded with the epithet of "selfishness" (*tzu-szu*), and inquisitive or exploring actions were firmly discouraged in a variety of ways.

Without detailing all the ways in which traditional Chinese developed in their children a sense of dependence on the family group and parental authority,[19] we can point out a few aspects of the process, because they seem to have great impact on the problem of social integration. Most basic is the fact that Chinese parents felt they could

[17] See Emile Durkheim, "On Mechanical and Organic Solidarity," in Talcott Parsons *et. al.* (ed.), *Theories of Society* (Glencoe, Ill.: The Free Press, 1961), I, 208–12.

[18] See Yang Lien-sheng, "The Concept of 'Pao' as a Basis for Social Relations in China," in John K. Fairbank (ed.), *Chinese Thought and Institutions* (Chicago: University of Chicago Press, 1957), pp. 291–309.

[19] This is being done in the author's more detailed study now in preparation, *Mao's Revolution and the Chinese Political Culture.*

only control their children by developing in them a sense of anxiety ("fear") about contravening parental instructions. The response of unconditional obedience was a goal to be strived for. As one elderly respondent from Chekiang stated about his relation to paternal authority: "You could say that father never was angry with me. If I did not obey him in the least way it would just take one look from his face, a blink of his eyes, or a few words of instruction, and we would not dare to disobey him. We just feared him and that was it. As a result we obeyed him."

Concomitant with this style of parent-child relations was the notion that children had no legitimate opinions of their own, nor the authority to criticize their elders. To be sure, the Confucian classics did not consider a submissively uncritical attitude on the part of a son as truly filial behavior,[20] but the child's anxieties about facing up to authority, and indeed the model of parental behavior from which he learned interpersonal relations, all told him that talking back to elders was a dangerous business:

We never had disagreements [within our family] because father and mother were just diligent farmers and had no experience. If they had some problem they would discuss it with grandfather. Father and mother were very honest people, they did not like to talk a lot. [Did they ever have differences of opinion with your grandfather?] No, no one would dare to oppose anything that grandfather said. [Why would they not dare?] Grandfather was very stern, everyone was afraid of him. . . .[21]

Related to the parents' feeling that strictness and the inculcation of fear were basic to raising proper children was the attitude that the expression of emotions, even within the family, was improper. Affection between parents and children was considered threatening to the development of "filiality"; and love was expressed indirectly through caring for the child's physical needs. The son of a traditional scholar from Chekiang Province observed, "Father loved his children with all

---

[20] As is stated in the "Classic of Filial Piety," "when a case of unrighteous conduct is concerned, a son must by no means keep from remonstrating with his father, nor a minister from remonstrating with his ruler. Hence, since remonstrance is required in the case of unrighteous conduct, how can simple obedience to the orders of a father be accounted filial piety?" *Hsiao Ching*, trans. James Legge, in Max F. Muller (ed.), *Sacred Books of the East* (Oxford: Clarendon Press, 1879–1910), III, 484.

[21] This respondent was a middle-aged former local government official from Anhwei Province.

A more detailed analysis of the interpersonal communication patterns characteristic of traditional Chinese society, and some of the ways they affected social integration, will be found in my article, "Communication Patterns and the Chinese Revolution," *China Quarterly*, No. 32 (October–December, 1967), pp. 88–110.

his heart, but his love was *in* his heart, he would not express it. He was concerned that we had enough to eat, that we were properly clothed, and whether we were hot or cold. Every time he would go away from home he would definitely bring something back for us to eat; but his attitude was very stern. . . ."

If expressions of affection were considered improper, the release of aggressive or hostile emotions, especially toward superiors, was absolutely abhorred. A child was taught that the frustrations or resentments stemming from the harshness of learning to be filial should be "swallowed," "put in one's stomach," or isolated from the perception of having been mistreated: "Father was very strict. As I was always being made to kneel as a punishment it would get my anger (*ch'i*) up. [How did you express your anger?] How could you express it?! He is your father! You can't scold (*ma*) him! [Where did your anger go then?] We just wouldn't dare say anything to him; you just don't talk as you please to your father."

A traditionally educated child learned, as well, that aggression was impermissible even in dealings with peers. When asked to recall the things for which they had punished when young, our respondents most frequently mentioned for having quarreled or fought with siblings or neighborhood children (44.5 per cent of a sample of seventy-five).[22] And as was frequently, and ironically, mentioned in elaboration, expressions of hostility would quite literally be beaten out of a growing child: ". . . if I fought with other children mother would pull us apart and hit me, and would then apologize to the parents of the other child. [Even if the other child had started the fight?] Even then; after all I had had contact with him and so the fighting started. [How would she punish you?] Pull me into the house by the ear, make me kneel down and then hit me with a stick. . . ." In short, a maturing child was

---

[22] The next most frequently recalled causes of parental punishment were for doing poorly in school (33.4 per cent), and for being disobedient of parental authority (30.6 per cent). Parental concern with children doing well in school seems closely related to the enduring Chinese respect for the educated man, and for the security and prestige which they expect will come to them if their children achieve social position and a good job.

Of a sample of fifty-seven middle-class American college students asked this same question, only 15.8 per cent recall being punished for fighting. One respondent was punished for running away from a fight. The most frequent responses for this group, 59.7 per cent, have to do with the individual not being self-disciplining or meeting personal responsibilities.

The pattern of punishments characteristic of a culture is an important index of social values. It reveals both parental anxieties and the areas of behavior where the younger generation is likely to have strong emotional concerns, given the pain or loss of love they associate with such behavior.

taught that it was both improper and dangerous to express emotions, be they sentiments of affection or aggression; he was given no sense that there were *legitimate* and *mediated* outlets for the public release of such feelings, except perhaps in the affection lavished on a new infant, or the venting of frustration on a hapless younger brother or some other status or power inferior.

It appears that one result of this attitude toward the handling of emotions was the development of a strong sense of distrust of an individual's ability to maintain self-control in the face of such emotions once mobilized. "Holding in" feelings, and avoiding contact ("after all I had had contact with him"), became the best ways of preventing an emotional mobilization which would only invoke "complications" and "confusion" in interpersonal relations.[23]

What are the effects of this style of authority relations on social integration, on the ability of people to cooperate in solving a variety of social problems? On the surface of things it would appear that the expectations of social interdependence, reinforced by a person's sense of the inability to act effectively as an individual in society, would provide a sound basis for social solidarity. At least this would seem to be the expectation in the minds of those socialized within the system. In actual practice, however, or at least as revealed in the *expectations*[24] held by our respondents about dealings with authority, the situation turns out to be rather different.

Responses to the TAT pictures were highly revealing of our respondents' expectations about social interaction; and interpretations of

[23] Lest this discussion sound unduly abstract, it is worth pointing out that both in interviews and public writings Chinese consistently describe potentially conflictive social relationships as "complicated" (*fu-tza*), and use the term "confused" (*luan*) to describe social misadventures of either a sexual or aggressive nature (*luan-kao nan-nü kuan-hsi; luan-ta; luan-sha,* and so forth). The underlying implication of this terminology seems to be that when emotions become mobilized, people lose self-control, and social relations and "order" (*chih-hsü*) become "confused."

[24] It should be underscored here that this analysis focuses on Chinese social *attitudes* and *expectations* about interpersonal relations. There is obviously not a one-to-one relationship between attitudes and action; yet attitudes are in part a summation of past social experience and education, and at the same time they help to shape the calculation of future behavior. Evaluation of the way in which the reality of situational factors, emotional and attitudinal elements, and the more universal calculi of political power and economic pay-off *combine* to affect actual behavior in any given situation is both a most complex and perhaps indeterminate matter.

For purposes of the present discussion, however, we want to stress that the attitudes discussed here are considered to be only *one* of a number of elements necessary for evaluating political behavior. And in Part II we will try to give more data on how the attitudes discussed here seem to have had their effect on Chinese political action in the past.

Card IV yield some consistent themes about dealings between superiors and subordinates.[25] An authoritative individual is *normatively* described as "experienced" and "understanding," helpful in "instructing" and "guiding" his subordinates. But as so frequently occurs in these interpretations, the normative "mask" of the way society says authority *should* be drops away as the story unfolds, revealing a manipulative and willful authority who leads innocent dependents into great difficulties.

As the story in Appendix B so clearly illustrates, the subordinate is overwhelmed by his sense of anxiety in the face of the older man, and ends up acting against his own better judgment: "The younger fellow is fearful; he is unwilling to do [what the older man wants him to do]. [What kind of a thing might it be?] Just not proper. . . . [What is the result of this situation?] He [the young man] goes and does it." The sense of impotence and anxiety in dealings with authority makes "filial remonstrance" a philosopher's dream.

If authority is seen as being both manipulative and anxiety provoking, however, it is also seen as a source of potential security. And as we have stressed earlier, people socialized in this cultural tradition were taught to expect that autonomous behavior was either ineffectual or dangerous; that they should look to authority for guidance and support. The sum of these contradictory aspects of an individual's orientation toward authority can best be described as a strong sense of ambivalence, as was so clearly revealed in the earlier cited evaluation of paternal authority by the son of a Chekiang *hsiu-ts'ai:*

Father loved his children with all his heart, but his love was *in* his heart, he would not express it. He was concerned that we had enough to eat, that we were properly clothed, and whether we were hot or cold. Every time he would go away from home he definitely would bring something back for us to eat; but his attitude was very stern. *When you saw him you would both fear him and want to get near him.* [Emphasis added.]

How individuals resolved this ambivalent orientation toward authority seems to be a function of both the qualities of a given superior and the particular personality of the subordinate. But the two "solutions" most frequently revealed in our interview materials were either submission to authority or a breakdown in the superior-subordinate relationship. Most frequently expressed was the notion that the subordinate

---

[25] A representative interpretation of TAT Card IV is given in Appendix B, p. 359.

individual should renounce his personal opinions for the sake of maintaining the relationship:

[What would you do if your point of view and that of your superior were not the same?] You definitely should sacrifice your opinions; a subordinate should not express his own opinions in front of a superior. He cannot contradict or contend with him. . . . [What if the superior is incorrect?] After the affair is over then you can slowly talk with him about it, but you don't want to oppose him in front of his face. You can't openly tell a superior that he is incorrect, it is best not to say anything or at the most slowly plead with him later on. *If you should say that the leader has made some error you will destroy his position. He will definitely be angry and will hate you, and will not want to use you again.* . . . [Emphasis added.]

For some of greater independence of spirit, however, the way to deal with potentially manipulative authority was described as maintaining a defensive distance:

[If a subordinate directly criticizes his superior, what kind of trouble might the subordinate run into?] The boss might misunderstand; he might think the subordinate was opposing him, or not obeying his orders. He might get angry and then conflict would develop; and possibly the outcome would be bad for the subordinate. . . . You have to understand the superior's degree of cultivation. If he is insufficiently cultivated, if his personality is too strong, then he will have no way of accepting criticism and it is best just for you to leave him of your own accord; just do not get near him.

It is fairly obvious that in a traditional society of low social mobility the opportunities for "going away" when authority was found to be harsh and manipulative were highly limited.[26] But the net effect of this defensive and ambivalent orientation toward authority seems to be a highly conditional commitment to any one authoritative individual. If a superior was just, and if he provided for the dependency needs of his subordinates, then submission would willingly be given; but if he proved to be harsh and manipulative, or failed to care for those who had depended on him, then "going away" bore no moral stigma. Indeed, this attitude seems to be the essential psychological spring behind the Mencian notion of the "right of rebellion." Generations of Confucian scholar-officials communicated to the Emperor this orientation of the conditional acceptance of political leadership for an otherwise inarticulate peasant mass: the "Mandate of Heaven" could be lost—

[26] Other than in the sense of an escape into a world of fantasy in which unjust authority would meet its comeuppance. Such would seem to be the appeals of such widely read traditional novels as *Water Margin, The Romance of the Three Kingdoms,* and even *The Dream of the Red Chamber.*

that is, the peasant masses would withdraw their passive support and go into rebellion—if imperial authority failed to provide for the minimal needs of the people.[27]

As far as social integration is concerned, this basic orientation of ambivalence toward authority produced a constant hierarchical tension; a pull between subordinates anxious to avoid overly intimate ties with manipulative authority, and superiors anxious to see the dependent tie (on which they themselves were dependent) maintained. As a result one finds in our respondents' perceptions of dealings with authority a constant feeling that great problems lie just below the surface of social relationships ready to explode; yet there is also a concomitant ability to endure tension and ambiguity over the resolution of these problems in the face of an even more fearful facing up to authority. This is clearly revealed in the following interpretation of TAT Card III:

A son is pleading with his father about something. [What kind of affair might this be?] *From their faces it looks as if they have already split apart; the problem can't be solved.* The father has already decided. . . . [Afterward, what will be the relation of the father to the son?] The son for a short period will not have anything to do with the father, as they cannot solve the problem. [Ultimately?] *They will get together as before, after all, it is a family.* [How will the father then feel toward the son?] *He will think the son should not bring up such problems.* [And how will the son feel toward the father?] The son thinks the father is too conservative; too stubborn. [Emphasis added.]

Here we see no real interaction between father and son: ". . . they have already split apart," "the problem can't be solved." Yet in conclusion family unity is maintained, albeit without the problem being resolved, because, "after all, it is a family." In short, the problem and tensions are covered over for both practical and normative reasons, but the sources of tension remain unresolved below the surface of family relations.[28]

---

[27] The institutional manifestation of this desire to maintain a defensive distance between self and authority seems to be the highly introverted and protective clan, guild, or secret society forms of local associations characteristic of traditional China. As one recent analysis has emphasized, "They did not seek to influence the actions of the state in a positive way but only to establish the minimal connections necessary to avoid the harmful effects of state power." James R. Townsend, *Political Participation in Communist China* (Berkeley and Los Angeles: University of California Press, 1967), p. 19.

[28] Sanctions which family authority could apply, it should be stressed, also played an important role in holding the family together in the face of various group tensions. One of the most potent of these sanctions appears to be keyed in with the dependency theme which we have stressed: the fear of being cut off or isolated from family resources under the control of paternal authority. Punishments applied to a growing child—to one who

TABLE 44

<small>Perception of Conflict and Cooperative Outcomes in TAT Responses, Given as a Percentage of Total Responding*</small>

Group Tested	Family Relations (TAT III)		Superior-Subordinate Relations (TAT IV)		Peer Relations (TAT I)	
	Con-flict Out-come†	Coopera-tion Main-tained‡	Con-flict Out-come	Coopera-tion Main-tained	Con-flict Out-come	Coopera-tion Main-tained
Chinese émigré males, total sample, N = 88	76.3	25.0	34.5	57.7	79.5	27.4
"Traditional" Chinese males,§ N = 29	72.4	30.8	41.3	57.7	75.0	29.4
"Communist" Chinese males, N = 30	80.0	18.5	30.8	60.0	75.0	32.0
American student males,‖ N = 30	64.3	64.3	15.4	76.9	55.2	55.2

* Because of variations in the number of respondents in each sample who did not directly describe either immediate outcomes or future relationships, we have used only those responses which include a codable interpretation in making these calculations. This means there are some minor fluctuations in sample size for the various figures.

† This figure is calculated on the basis of those who attributed conflictive, hostile, or "splitting-up" outcomes to the *immediate* social situation they described.

‡ This figure is calculated on the basis of those who attributed cooperative or non-hostile competitive *future* relationships to the people in the social situations they described.

§ This sample consists of Chinese émigrés who had attended a traditional Confucian-style "home school" (*szu-shu*) when young. Their average age is 60.9 years.

‖ This sample consists of graduate students from the University of Michigan, selected to represent a broad distribution of places of geographical origin and areas of academic interest. They are about evenly divided between urban and small town or rural backgrounds, and come from a range of socioeconomic status families. Their average age is 25.5 years, very close to the "Communist" Chinese student group whose average age is 25.3 years.

Quantitative analysis of TAT responses, as summarized in Table 44 above, supports this qualitative interpretation. Chinese have a high

---

had already been taught that independent behavior was "selfish" and ineffectual—apparently reinforced fears of being *ku-li ti:*

> [What kinds of punishments did you frequently receive?] If I did not study well then I would be hit or isolated. [How would you be isolated?] They would not buy clothes for me, not give me presents. Or my parents would say, "All right, if your behavior is going to be that way then you won't be able to study any more. You can go out and work."

tendency to perceive conflict in family relations, and a low expectation of cooperation being maintained in the future. While an American student sample, in comparison with both the Chinese students and the entire émigré group, also perceives a relatively high level of conflict, the group has a much higher expectation of cooperative relations being maintained in the future.

This emotional unwillingness to face up to interpersonal problems openly within the family would appear to be the root of the larger pattern of social integration which historically has characterized China: the alternation of apparently tranquil periods of *ho-p'ing* with outbursts of violent *luan* when the accumulation of unresolved interpersonal problems and enduring resentments reached a point at which peaceful and reasoned resolutions were no longer humanly possible. As Lewis Coser has noted, "a greater intensity of conflict can be expected in those relationships in which the participants have been led to suppress hostile feelings. So the fear of intense conflict may lead to suppression of hostile feelings; and in turn, the accumulation of such feelings is likely to further intensify the conflict once it breaks out."[29]

The reluctance to attempt to resolve interpersonal disputes by direct contact seems to account in part for the outbreaks of social violence and disorder when political authority was weakened by internal disunity or corruption,[30] when it was disrupted by natural calamity or foreign invasion,[31] or when it used violence for its own purposes, thus implicitly legitimatizing its use for the solution of personal grudges.[32]

In superior-subordinate interaction beyond the family, our respondents perceived a lower level of conflict than they did in family relations. Their TAT responses suggest that this is related, rather paradox-

---

[29] Lewis Coser, *The Functions of Social Conflict* (Glencoe, Ill.: The Free Press, 1956), p. 68.

[30] The growth of violence, extortion, and piracy as imperial authority weakened along the China coast in the 1840's is described in John K. Fairbank, *Trade and Diplomacy on the China Coast* (Cambridge, Mass.: Harvard University Press, 1964), chaps. xviii and xix. A more general discussion of this phenomenon, based on internal Chinese sources, will be found in Hsiao Kung-chuan, *Rural China: Imperial Control in the Nineteenth Century* (Seattle: University of Washington Press, 1960), chap. x.

[31] During the 1840's, as British naval units invaded the China coast, foreign observers noted that as local political leaders fled before the foreign ships, the local populace would indulge in acts of personal violence and thievery having no relation to the foreign intervention. See Arthur Waley, *The Opium War Through Chinese Eyes* (London: George Allen and Unwin, 1958), Part 3, pp. 186–96.

[32] Both foreign and native observers of the "February 28" incident of 1947 in Taiwan, in verbal recollections given to the author, have noted the occurrence of violent "account settling" incidents unrelated to the politically-motivated military action of the Nationalist forces.

ically, both to the high level of power which superiors are seen to have over subordinates, and to a less intense or extensive degree of interaction. Again, in comparison with an American group, the Chinese perceive a higher level of conflict, and a lower expectation that cooperation will be maintained in the future.[33]

Part of the reason for the high frequency of breakdowns or "splitting-up"[34] outcomes in superior-subordinate relations seems to stem from a superior's dissatisfaction with the effectiveness of a subordinate in implementing his will. This is clearly stated in one respondent's interpretation of TAT Card IV:

The superior is criticizing his subordinate's work; he did not like the work of his underling. [What is the superior's attitude toward him?] He feels that his technical level isn't high. [What does he feel about the younger man?] He feels he isn't smart, isn't witty enough. [What does the younger man feel toward his superior?] He is expressing his difficulties. [But what does he feel or think about the superior?] From his facial expression he indicates that the work can't be done. [In the future, what about their relationship?] In the future they could split apart. [Why?] He is trying to teach the younger fellow, but the younger one thinks it cannot be done. [So what will happen in the future?] They split apart.

If from a subordinate's vantage point dealings with authority are anxiety laden and worth keeping at a distance, the superior finds problems of his own in dealing with dependent subordinates. They appear lazy, or unable to take initiative (which is not too surprising, inasmuch as they had been socialized to expect that responsibility and initiative lay with the superior individual), and hence must constantly be directed and disciplined or else they will act in a manner usually characterized as *luan*.

Parents, having raised children to be obedient to their authority, were subsequently faced with the problem of reassuring themselves that their offspring really had sufficient will power and self-discipline to fulfill the family obligations which were the essence of filial reciprocity.[35] Mao Tse-tung shared with many of his compatriots the sense of "exploitation" that came from parents who placed great pres-

---

[33] This is a figure based on content analysis of responses to TAT Card IV. These data are summarized in Table 44.

[34] The terminology indicating a breakdown in social relations, which occurs over and over again in these TAT responses in a truly remarkable manner, is usually: *fen-k'ai, fen-lieh, lieh-k'ai, fen-shou, fen-san.*

[35] The concern of many Chinese with the problems of laziness and will power has also been noted by Lucian Pye. He develops a somewhat different interpretation of the origins of this problem in his *The Spirit of Chinese Politics* (Cambridge, Mass.: M.I.T. Press, 1968), chap. viii.

sure on their children to "repay their debts." As he recalled to Edgar Snow:

My father wanted me to begin keeping the family books as soon as I had learned a few characters. . . . He was a severe taskmaster. He hated to see me idle, and if there were no books to be kept he put me to work at farm tasks. He was a hot-tempered man and frequently beat both me and my brothers. He gave us no money whatever, and the most meagre food.

But at the same time he noted, "My father denounced me . . . calling me lazy and useless. This infuriated me." Mao differed from many of his peers in having sufficient self-integrity to stand up to his father. "I cursed him and left the house. My mother ran after me and tried to persuade me to return. My father also pursued me, cursing at the same time that he demanded me to come back."[36]

It was from this incident, which Mao characterized as a youthful "rebellion," that he came to perceive his father's dependence on him and learned that he could manipulate authority by playing on its need to have loyal subordinates:

I reached the edge of a pond and threatened to jump in if he came any nearer. In this situation demands and counter demands were presented for cessation of the civil war. My father insisted that I apologize and k'ou-t'ou as a sign of submission. I agreed to give a one-knee k'ou-t'ou if he promised not to beat me. Thus the war ended, and from it I learned that when I defended my rights by open rebellion my father relented, but when I remained meek and submissive he only cursed and beat me the more.[37]

Related to authority's concern that its dependents have sufficient will power to fulfill filial obligations is the anxiety that lazy and self-indulgent behavior on the part of dependents will drain away scarce family or social resources. The problem of dependents "overeating" their superior's resources was rather poignantly revealed in the following parental evaluation by a wealthy Chinese from Shantung Province:

Father's weak point was that he was excessive strict with the children. [In what way was he excessively strict?] Take for example the son of my father's concubine: he went away to study, he was already twenty, and father gave him his tuition. But when he would return home father would make him account for the money he had spent. If things did not tally up then father would think that he had not used his money correctly and would beat him with a stick. Parents should be warmer than this, then you can have some emotional exchange; being so strict is not right, the children will just fear their parents. . . .

[36] Edgar Snow, *Red Star over China* (New York: Grove Press, 1961), pp. 125–26.
[37] *Ibid.*

The father fears that his concubine's son—rather obviously the fruit of his own sensual indulgence—will squander resources for lack of self-discipline. In theory the Confucianists saw parental behavior as a model to be emulated by the dependent children. Growing youngsters were not encouraged to be self-disciplining or autonomous. Hence it is not too surprising that they might seek to indulge themselves in the manner of their elders. The usual parental response to this concern that children might overconsume family resources was, as in this case, to apply the rod to the already "spoiled" child. Harshness was seen as the proper way to discipline even adult offspring who were still considered incapable of managing their own affairs through self-discipline.

It is clear from our interviews that most Chinese seem to have a strong expectation that it is a superior's duty to care for his dependents' needs; after all, this is an essential element of the filial relationship. And as one respondent explicitly indicated, the expectations of the filial son are writ large in attitudes toward political leadership:

[What is the most important thing a nation's leaders should do for their people?] They have to be all for the people; like a father, all for the younger generation. The nation is like a family, so the highest leaders have to take responsibility for doing things for the benefit of the people, working things out well for them. [What kinds of problems should they pay attention to?] Problems of the people's livelihood; education; jobs; science. All these things have an effect on the people's livelihood.

To an authority with limited resources, such expressions of the dependent tie—expectations that authority is to provide for the people's wants—can appear threatening. And the leader's recourse is to apply his authority with sufficient harshness to supply that discipline which he sees lacking in a dependent population.[38] If he thought that his dependents were lazy or tended to overconsume, an authority would

---

[38] This problem of a leader responding harshly to people's demands for support is all too clearly illustrated in the following episode recounted by Douglas Pike. During the days of the Diem regime in Vietnam, strategic hamlets were set up to provide an organizational framework whereby the central government could securely link itself to the people. Ngo Dinh Nhu, Diem's key advisor, was the prime mover behind these projects; and on the occasion of the establishment of a new hamlet he paid a visit to preside at a dedication ceremony. After the ceremony a group of village elders approached Nhu with a request for aid in constructing a school. Nhu brusquely rejected their request with the comment that, "the government's means are stretched now to their limit. Do not rely on outside aid." A group of American advisors, viewing this scene, not surprisingly felt that here was a blatant negation of the entire purpose of the strategic hamlet program. When they asked Nhu where he expected the villagers to be able to acquire the resources to build their own school, he brushed off their inquiry with the comment, "You do not understand these villagers. Satisfy one demand and they would return with ten more." Douglas Pike, *Viet Cong: The Organization and Techniques of the National Liberation Front of South Vietnam* (Cambridge, Mass.: M.I.T. Press, 1966), p. 67.

resort to a variety of methods of control: most notably a harsh or stern and unapproachable posture in dealings with his subordinates. This created problems of its own, however, if for no other reason than that such an attitude was unlikely to generate true sentiments of loyalty and commitment. And given the degree to which a superior was himself dependent upon the support of his subordinates, doubts about their loyalty could only make him more distrustful of their motives, and lead to even greater harshness in the relationship, thus compounding the subordinates' tendency to keep a defensive distance between themselves and authority.

We know from numerous historical studies that subordinates, anxious to maintain effective working relations with a superior, would frequently communicate up to him what they knew he wanted to hear —this being an indication of their loyal and diligent support of his cause—rather than what they knew a given situation to be "in reality." This could produce its own subversive impact on the effectiveness of a given leadership by quite literally cutting it off from reality. The ambivalence which characterized traditional dealings between superior and subordinate thus constituted a potential weak link in vertical communications. To use the current analytical jargon, the nonsecularized quality of traditional dealings with authority (resulting above all from the expectations of filial loyalty) produced a weak feedback process between leader and led. The harshness of authority, and the anxieties of authority's subordinates in the face of this harshness, could lead to a breakdown in effective communication between leader and led.[39] Or, to use the phrase currently in vogue on the mainland, leadership tended to "cut itself off from the masses" (*t'uo-li ch'ün-chung*).[40]

For a superior, when doubts arose about his subordinates' loyalty, there frequently was no more effective way to test the relationship than to resort to various ritualistic forms of behavior which, by their public and "voluntary" nature, could be used as tests of a subordinate's commitment. As we know from the rich linguistic and behavioral "deference patterns" which were so much a part of traditional Chinese

[39] This problem of interpersonal communication is explored in more detail in my study, "Communication Patterns and the Chinese Revolution."

[40] It should be noted that in addition to the psychological weaknesses which characterized elite-mass ties, a number of analysts have observed weak functional relationships of either an economic or a political nature, thus producing an institutional as well as a psychological point of cleavage between leaders and led. See Barrington Moore, Jr., *The Social Origins of Dictatorship and Democracy* (Boston: Beacon Press, 1966), pp. 202–3, 209–11, 224–25.

culture, the continuing use of ritualized manifestations of that inner sense of "filiality" represented efforts by those in authority (and their subordinates) to reassure themselves, and potential rivals, that the proper relationships were being maintained, that the "names" that defined the Confucian order were in fact properly rectified.[41]

PEER RELATIONS: PROBLEMS OF "HORIZONTAL" SOCIAL LINKAGES

Thus far our discussion has focused primarily upon the superior-subordinate tie, inasmuch as this was the central relational form by which the traditional social order was structured. But relations between peers, between those of approximately equal social status, had their own effect upon social integration, particularly in a lateral or "horizontal" sense. And as we shall now see, peer relations drew certain inspiration from the dominant hierarchical quality of the traditional social structure.

If the notion of "peer relations" is extended beyond its usual conception of interaction between those of similar age to include dealings among those of roughly equal social status, it is not too much of an exaggeration to say that there were few real "peer" relations in traditional Chinese society. It is at least obvious, as will be detailed below, that the traditional culture but weakly defined norms of behavior and methods of *direct* resolution of disputes between those of equal status. The predominant conception of the social structure was of mutually reinforcing hierarchies; and this conception, rooted in the model father-son tie, had an influence that pervaded all other social relations.

Within the family group a growing child learned that there were no status equals; no "brothers," only *ko-ko* (elder brothers) and *ti-ti* (younger brothers). The authority-deference pattern which he saw in relations between father and son was elaborated into a fully detailed pattern of deference and responsibility among blood relatives that was given manifest expression via a minutely articulated kinship terminology. This nomenclature of social interaction, the "names" by which the

[41] While it cannot be detailed in this abbreviated analysis, it should be obvious that the traditional educational system played a critical role in developing commitment to the ritualized behavioral patterns—and particularly verbal patterns—which played so dominant a role in social control. Be it the peasant's awe of the literate man—and indeed of the mystical qualities of just a scrap of paper containing a brushed character—or the scholar-official's use of Confucian maxims in rationalizing public policy, verbal or written communications played a key role in rituals of control. And as has been frequently observed, the open use of force was considered by the Chinese to be a sign of weakness rather than strength. To be able to effect a "voluntary" observance of proper social ritual (*li*) on the part of subordinates was the real test of a leader's potency (moral virtue?).

Confucianists sought to rectify social order, boxed the individual into a reinforcing pattern of hierarchical responsibility and deference which defined his social identity.[42]

The kinship group, however, acquired considerable authority of its own, inasmuch as it was through the maintenance of a "rectified" set of status relationships that paternal authority sought to attain social order and harmony. It was before the kin group that a growing child first learned the importance of being able to "face up" properly to his relatives, to fulfill those obligations which were his part of group interdependence—or face the threat of being cut off, isolated, from the group and its material and emotional support on which he had been taught to depend:

[Who punished in your family?] Father and mother both punished. They would hit our palms with a ruler, or for bigger problems we would have to kneel in front of the after dinner group and be scolded. Sometimes we would not be given our allowance money . . . or sometimes I would not get food to eat, and would have to sit on the side and watch everyone else eat.

As this and other interview responses imply, the potential sanctions of the peer group—the shame of a "loss of a face," and the more severe threat of being cut off from group material support—were strong psychological mechanisms which bound the individual to the group. But they were forms of control above all derived from the basic structural unit of paternal hierarchical authority, from which derived the sense of dependency which gave the emotional force to threats of being isolated.

Beyond the kin group, the one form of social interaction which partook most strongly of the quality of peer or status-equal relations was that between friend and friend. In a manner rather reminiscent of the way in which they stress the superior virtues of a society under the rule of men, Chinese will also frequently tell the foreign visitor: "We Chinese *really* know the meaning of friendship," or "We really know how to be friends!" In our interviews we tried to explore in some detail the set of expectations held by Chinese concerning relations among friends and why they felt their traditions had raised the quality of friendship to such a high level. Rather unexpectedly our data reveal that here too the dependency theme, which we have thus far explored in dealings with authority, comes through very strongly: "[What is the

---

[42] This "boxing in" quality of the traditional Chinese kinship system is clearly spelled out, and graphically conceptualized, in the study by Yang, *Chinese Communist Society,* Vol. I, chap. v, and especially the diagram on p. 88.

most important thing a person obtains from friends?] Their sympathy and support. A person can't take care of things all by himself. If he has friends who come and help him, encourage him and support him, then things can be dealt with effectively."

The effect of this set of expectations about friendship, with no little irony, however, seems to be one of in fact *dis*integrating or weakening ties among peers. As is clearly indicated in Figure 9, our respondents of relatively conservative upbringing display a high degree of consensus

FIGURE 9. Responses to the Attitude Survey Statement, "It Is an Unfortunate Thing That During One's Life It Is So Difficult to Find True Friends with Whom One Can Share the Thoughts and Feelings Deep in One's Heart"

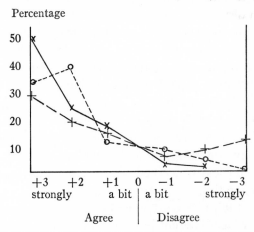

Symbol	Group Tested	Mean	Standard Deviation	N
+---	American males	+0.63	2.31	269
O---	"Conservative" Chinese males	+1.68	1.56	135
X—	"Communist" Chinese males	+2.09	1.29	32

that friendship is something quite difficult to attain. As a fifty-seven-year-old merchant's son from Hupeh elaborated:

[Why did you strongly agree that it is difficult to have true friends?] . . . It is difficult to explain: For instance, when you both are poor you are good friends; but once your friend makes money, becomes a big official, he just forgets his old friends. I once had a close friend. Then he became wealthy and the friendship gradually lost its flavor. [Why?] Because he had money, he was afraid that people would go and ask him for money—but I wouldn't do that. . . .

This defensive comment all too clearly indicates that the tension in friendship is rather similar to that which we observed in superior-subordinate relations: the more powerful, or in this case the more re-sourceful, member of the relationship fears the demands for assistance which normative expectations of friendship place upon him. Hence there is a desire to keep the "friend" at some distance if there is no expectation of reciprocity. The dependency orientation to social rela-tions, inculcated as the basis for creating social order and security through ties of loyalty and mutual aid, thus ironically works to a degree in the opposite manner to limit the development of such ties, particularly in terms of "lateral" or peer relations.

It is instructive here to compare the Chinese and American results on the attitude survey item dealing with friendship. As in the case of the attitude distributions concerning relations with authority, the American group displays what is roughly a bimodal or U-shaped pat-tern: about one-quarter of the group rather strongly disagrees with the notion that friendships are difficult to establish, while about half the sample (as do three-fourths of the Chinese respondents) feels that friendship is something difficult to attain. This bimodal or U-shaped distribution of attitudes among the Americans seems to represent a tension between those burdened with the now oft-discussed problem of alienation and loss of a sense of community in the mobile and urban life of modern-day America, and a concomitant effort on the part of others (perhaps no less concerned about a sense of community) to reach out for human ties.

Psychological studies have attempted to develop objective measures of the degree to which different individuals or cultures strive after the maintenance of positive emotional ties with others; and this concept, termed *need affiliation,* has been operationally defined as concern with "establishing, maintaining, or restoring a positive affective relationship with another person."[43] The use of the *need affiliation* concept in quan-tified content analysis studies has consistently revealed that Americans are rather high, relative to other national groups, in this emotional "need," whereas the Chinese have shown themselves to be relatively less concerned with the maintenance of positive emotional ties with others.[44]

These independently derived findings underline conclusions we have reached from our interivew materials: that Chinese have been taught that positive emotional interchange is neither appropriate nor to be expected in social relationships. The *need affiliation* data also suggest

---

[43] McClelland, *The Achieving Society,* p. 160.
[44] See these data in tabular form in Appendix C, p. 360.

that a motivational factor which has helped to integrate American society—the desire to establish positive emotional ties with other people—has not by tradition been such an important operative factor in China.

Chinese do indeed talk about the importance of "human feelings" or *jen-ch'ing* in interpersonal relations, and stress how important it is to *chiang jen-ch'ing* in dealings among friends. But the "emotions" that they seem to refer to by these oft-quoted phrases are those related to the interdependent quality of social life: the need to have an authoritative individual or friends who can be relied upon to give help or take responsibility in solving life's problems.[45] In a Western vocabulary the emotions that they imply by their conception of mutual help are those of sympathy and a sense of responsibility for one's dependents, and not so much those of affection or pleasure.

Beyond social interaction within the kinship group or a circle of intimate friends, our respondents indicate a number of concerns about dealings with unrelated individuals which are closely related to the themes of interpersonal relations which our analysis has stressed thus far, and which seem to work to limit lateral social integration. Consistent with the dependency theme is the expectation that people are not independent or autonomous social actors. The assumption is that an individual is always tied by loyalty or a web of obligations to some authority or group. Usually the first question asked by Chinese in evaluating an individual's social or political position concerns these ties: Who was the man's teacher? Under whose leadership did he get his early career training? In whose clique has he been active? The expectation is that an individual's loyalty and commitment are already heavily involved with some well-defined social grouping; and hence interpersonal relations can never proceed on a face-to-face or individual basis. The authority or group to whom the individual is tied must always be taken into account.

Apparently grown from this basic set of expectations is the elaborate set of social rituals for making commensurate differences in group prestige, authority, and responsibility. The language and social forms

---

[45] A middle-aged school teacher raised in Peking said:

"*Chiang jen-ch'ing*" means, for example, if you want to find a tenant to live in your house but you don't dare carelessly to let just anyone come to live with you, you should definitely find a third party who knows you both to "speak on both of your behalves," to introduce you. [Why, in Chinese society, is "*chiang jen-ch'ing*" so important?] In this way things will be peaceful; you won't have any disorder [*tao-tan*]. No difficulties [*mao-ping*] will develop. If there is someone to introduce you then you won't have any bad people coming in to make confusion [*kao-luan*].

associated with being *k'o-ch'i* (polite) and *li-mao* (mannerly) seem to be in essence interpersonal buffering devices intended to prevent a direct clash of interest and authority; accepted social norms by which different individuals, representing these groups or the authorities behind them, can resolve differences of status or interest. The frequent use of the intermediary or go-between in the resolution of interpersonal problems is one further effort at keeping interaction at a safe distance and providing a means by which the hierarchical authority and deference pattern which we have stressed as being the essential core of Chinese social structure could be made commensurate between different groups. But as one suggestive analysis has indicated, while the use of various intermediating techniques in social relations may "shield one from the direct impact of possible failure and rejection" or "inhibit direct rivalry," such indirection in resolving problems seems to work against compromise which might come through the "mutual adjustment of aim and desire."[46]

The open-ended questioning and TAT techniques in our interview procedure provided rich data which underline certain aspects of these general observations on difficulties of social interaction among those of approximately equal social status. As responses to TAT Card I[47] clearly and consistently indicate, situations in which a group finds itself of divided opinion result in a breakdown of effective group functioning: A group of men are holding a meeting and "they have put their heads together to discuss the situation and there are many opinions." One fellow feels that the group's opinions are nonsense.

He wants to support his own proposal but the others won't listen to him. [What is the outcome?] The fellow is very unhappy; and so he withdraws from the group—indicates his disapproval and goes. [In the future what relationship do the people in the group have with the fellow who left?] They have no mutual concern: you take care of yours, and I'll take care of mine.

In 79.5 per cent[48] of the cases in which our respondents describe peer group differences of opinion or conflict, the outcome is such a "splitting up" or breakdown in cooperative relations. There is virtually no expectation that peers, among themselves, can bargain and compromise their differences and maintain group solidarity. And compounding the

---

[46] See the suggestive analysis by John H. Weakland, "The Organization of Action in Chinese Culture," *Psychiatry*, XIII (1950), 361–70.

[47] See a sample interpretation of this TAT card in Appendix D, p. 361.

[48] This figure, based on content analysis of responses to TAT Card I, is included in Table 44 on p. 291 above.

problems of such a breakdown in relations is a residue of antagonism. As one respondent elaborated in his interpretation of TAT Card VIII: "[What happens when, as you have described, two people split apart?] They have resentment (*fan-kan*). [Why do they have resentment?] Because in their basic positions they are not alike."[49]

The traditional solution for dealing with such a situation of resentment and potential antagonism, at least as consistently revealed in our interview data, is to avoid interaction. Interpersonal conflict, the Confucian tradition stressed, should be handled through personal "cultivation," which, as the following interpretation reveals, means merely not facing up to the point of contention:

[What is meant by the term "cultivation" (*hsiu-yang*)?] . . . For example, if you are standing in line waiting for a bus and a man comes and steps to the front, most people who are "cultivated" won't say anything; but if you do say something to him then it could lead to a fight. We have a saying, "if you are not patient with the little things then there will be confusion and big plots" (*hsiao pu-jen, tse luan ta mou*). [Why would it lead to confusion (*luan*)?] There are many, many examples of people who get to quarreling over small things and this leads to the pulling out of knives. Or for example, if you step on someone's foot and do not excuse yourself the person could scold or hit you, or it might lead to the knives. [Why?] It is a matter of temperament (*p'i-ch'i*), of being hot tempered (*pao-tsao*), of not having any education, no knowledge. . . .[50]

This concern that aggression is always liable to burst forth in interpersonal relations, leading to "confusion" (*luan*), is a constant theme in our respondents' interpretations of social relations. And having been taught that the expression of aggression is neither socially permissible nor capable of *mediated* release, most of our respondents choose to solve situations of potential conflict by simply avoiding interaction:

[What kind of relationship did your family have with the neighbors?] Most of our neighbors were farmers. Those who got along well had contact rather often, and those who did not get along too well usually understood what the situation was and

---

[49] The data in Table 44 again indicate that Chinese have a significantly higher expectation of conflict in peer relations than Americans, and that they do not see cooperation maintained once conflict has occurred. Americans are taught that *limited* conflict is a natural aspect of ongoing social relations, whereas the Chinese tradition has stressed the elimination of conflict as necessary for the maintenance of group solidarity. In a world of rapid social change, this difference in attitude toward conflict is evidently critical in its effect on social integration.

[50] This respondent was a thirty-six-year-old son of a Confucian scholar-teacher from Honan. The traditional *ch'eng-yü* or saying which he cites is usually translated with the ending, "great plans will go awry." I have made the above translation on the basis of his apparent understanding and use of the phrase.

went out of their way to avoid having contact. [Why didn't some get along?] For instance, because of their children fighting. Everyone in general avoided contact so as to avoid quarrelsome situations.

It need not be emphasized that such an attitude toward interaction with one's peers, and the expectation that differences of opinion could lead to uncontrolled conflict and violence, worked to fragment lateral social ties and weaken integration of the society.

The manner in which our Chinese respondents see a resolution of problems of social conflict is also revealed in an interesting way by the attitude survey data. As can be seen in Figure 10, Chinese of a rela-

FIGURE 10. RESPONSES TO THE ATTITUDE SURVEY STATEMENT, "If a Neighbor Is Making a Public Nuisance of Himself, It Is Better Just to Try to Ignore Him or Avoid the Trouble of Involvement than to Attempt to Correct the Situation"

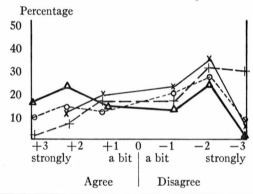

Symbol	Group Tested	Mean	Standard Deviation	N
+ – –	American males	−1.14	1.86	269
O – – – –	"Conservative" Chinese males	−0.21	2.01	136
X ——	"Communist" Chinese males	−0.81	1.64	32
△ ——	"Traditional" Chinese males*	+0.37	2.03	30

*This sample consists of Chinese émigrés who had attended a traditional Confucian-style "home school" (*szu-shu*) when young. This group is mostly in the fifty to sixty-five age bracket.

tively conservative upbringing are of divided opinion as to the best way to deal with a nuisance neighbor. The distribution of attitudes is much like the bimodal pattern we found in American attitudes toward authority and friendship.[51] In this instance about half the traditional

[51] This type of attitude distribution seems to illustrate rather clearly how various individuals, because of differences in personality and social status, may relate differently to an *issue* (in this case the handling of aggression) which is defined as problematical by a given society and culture. This is in contrast to other social issues, such as the proper way

Chinese choose to avoid dealings with the troublesome neighbor and thus prevent potential conflict, while the other group seems to favor rather strongly attempts to correct the neighbor's behavior. Unlike the American sample, which seems to have few reservations about criticizing peers, apparently because their traditions sanction critical interpersonal relationships and teach the individual that aggressive impulses are capable of mediated release and control, the more traditional Chinese group finds itself divided as to either avoidance or vigorous criticism.

The meaning of this polarization of attitudes is made clearer when we relate it to our respondents' expectations of authority. Underlying this polarity is the expectation that the only way that social order and harmony can be maintained is through the action of a strong and unitary authority who will impose order and unanimity upon potentially conflictive peers. A strong authority enables the individual to avoid the personal responsibility of facing up to points of contention, and at the same time ensures that "disorders" will be dealt with strictly:

I don't think laws have any usefulness [for dealing with social conflict], the only thing you can do is to have a highest leader. Having a good government includes the leader making an example of his own action, and having very strict punishments for his subordinates, because if the highest leader can promote good government then the subordinates below him would not dare but do the same thing.[52]

The only fearful thing is that this unitary authority, which imposes order, might itself become harsh, or, what is perhaps worse, that it might be removed. As an elderly teacher from Kiangsi Province rather self-consciously recalled,

I have a rather strange point of view. It was not too correct for the father of our country (Sun Yat-sen) to have overthrown the Ch'ing emperor. The people must have a symbol. We have had a dictatorial country for several thousand years, and then in a moment the Emperor was overthrown and everyone became confused (*luan le*). If there had been an emperor in those days then we would not have had the warlords.

Social problems are thus seen as capable of being resolved only within the hierarchical pattern which we have described as being central to Chinese conceptions of social order. There is no expectation

---

to relate to authority, or the importance of personal autonomy, about which there is very high attitude consensus.

[52] This respondent was a retired governmental office worker, the son of a Kwangtung merchant.

that peers, among themselves, can bargain and compromise differences of social opinion or interest. Interpersonal competition is seen as leading to an inevitable conflict to attain a position of dominance, for not only are security and social order conceived of as attainable only within the hierarchical pattern, but an individual's social identity is also seen as defined in terms of who is deferring to (or caring for) whom.[53] And as a former soldier from Honan elaborated in a most revealing response:

[What is the greatest effect of interpersonal competition on society?] There are several aspects to this: political competition; economic; and concerning "face." [What about political competition?] Everyone wants big power. There are only a few people in society like Sun Yat-sen who will give way (*jang-pu*); most are like Yüan Shih-k'ai. [What method could be used to deal with this kind of situation?] . . . Have a great leader stronger than anyone else to prevent competition for power . . . like President Chiang. Nowadays there are only a few who will compete for power; they do it in the dark. [Why does having President Chiang do away with competition?] . . . It is a matter of education: the leaders pay attention to the thinking [of potential competitors for power]. They make them study the "Three People's Principles" as if President Chiang were their teacher. You don't go against your teacher—after he dies maybe, but not before. . . .

[53] It is this tendency to struggle for the position of hierarchical dominance which seems to underlie much of the concern which Chinese express about "selfishness" (*tzu-szu*) and "individualism" (*ko-jen chu-yi*). Chiang Kai-shek (and now even Mao) joins a long tradition of Chinese political rulers who complain that "incapacity to unite is a result of selfishness, and the best antidote for selfishness is public spirit." (*China's Destiny*, trans. in William deBary [ed.], *Sources of Chinese Tradition* [New York: Columbia University Press, 1960], p. 810.) A vicious circle is thus set up in which submission to the group or public cause (*kung*) is seen as the best way to overcome the fragmentation and conflict which come with competition for unitary power—a submission, of course, under the guidance of a "highest leader."

It is not surprising that social authority should seek to overcome the *luan* of unrestrained conflict for unitary power via a stress on "public" or "collective" life and renunciation of "self"; but pressures for self-abnegation of the strength which have characterized Chinese society would seem to go against biologically and psychologically deep-seated human needs for a degree of personal autonomy. In seeking to sweep "selfishness" under the rug—just as they sought to cover over aggressive impulses—Chinese may have in fact made more inevitable and still stronger inclinations to be self-assertive. For some, as noted above, this urge to affirm the self took the form of a striving to achieve a position of dominance within the hierarchical structuring of society. For others a more anarchic withdrawal from society and dealings with any authority—as is so manifest in the strength of the Buddhist and Taoist traditions in China—would seem to represent an alternate strategy for attaining a position of self-integrity which was so strongly denied legitimacy by traditional Chinese social norms.

Hence, just as traditional Chinese efforts to order society by declaring conflict an illegitimate aspect of social relations may actually have made *luan* more inevitable, so the attempt to deny the individual a measure of autonomy may have contributed to the social fragmentation which was the result of efforts to achieve either dominance or social withdrawal.

SUMMARY

This revealing comment is an appropriate point from which to summarize some of the difficulties that have faced the Chinese in attaining a nationally integrated society, and for making explicit certain of the techniques that traditionally have been seen as appropriate for attaining a state of social integration. As the above interview response indicates, the expectation that competitive interpersonal relations will lead to a breakdown in social order requires that there be "a great leader stronger than anyone else to prevent competition for power"; a highest authority who can use his particular "ism" (*chu-yi*) to insure that there be a unanimity of opinion which is a guarantee of social order.

The Chinese yearn for a social condition which they term "the great unity" (*ta-t'ung*), a state in which their primary social concerns— which we have analyzed here in terms of the "dependency" concept, and great anxiety about interpersonal conflict—have been dealt with and society has evolved beyond the condition of a hierarchical structuring to a formless unanimity:

"The great unity" is mutual assistance; everyone has a spirit of mutual assistance and this causes there to be no conflict between the common people or no war between one nation and another. Everyone has enough food to eat, has clothing to wear and there can be unity in thinking among everyone. [How can we implement "the great unity"? Mankind can produce this if everyone has received an education and everyone's point of view will be the same. Then there will be no disorder (*luan*), there will be no war. [Are there any other things that can be done?] Education is most important, education must be universal, then everyone's knowledge will be about the same and then you can do away with much nonsensical bother. [What kind of "nonsensical bother"?] If everyone's opinion is not the same it can lead to quarreling and *luan*.[54]

"Education" thus becomes the mechanism by which authority maintains social order, assures that "everyone's opinion is the same" and that conflict and "confusion" are restrained within the confines of the pattern of deference and responsibility which is the essence of a society of filiality.

The particular "spatial" quality which was associated with the integration of traditional Chinese society was that of a reinforcing series of

[54] This interviewee was a sixty-eight-year-old teacher from Fukien. His father had been an imperial degree holder during the Ch'ing dynasty.

vertical, interlocking hierarchies, structurally analogous to a pyramid of gymnasts. Each individual was related to the social structure through expectations of dependent obedience from those below him, and deference to those above. Social integration was extended from the family or clan base of the society through commitment of loyalty and support to authorities at higher regional or state levels. This system had considerable stability in an agrarian society, where the demands of superiors on their subordinates, and vice versa, were relatively limited. There was a certain looseness in hierarchical relationships which allowed for a degree of autonomy within the various levels of the system. Yet lateral integration, as we have explored in detail above, was relatively weak: rituals of cooperation, of bargaining and compromise, among status peers in this system were slighted in favor of reliance upon superiors; and the "intermediary" performed the vital functions of buffering what were seen as potentially conflictive lateral interactions and making commensurate differences in expectation of social deference, of "face."

The particular vulnerability of this patterning of social relations was the loss of the "highest leader." The forcible removal or death of the man at the top eliminated a vital link of loyalty that held together the subordinate hierarchies; and the system could fragment into a series of highly competitive loyalty cliques composed of those who had been dependent on the "highest leader"—and who now sought to reintegrate the society through attainment of his position. Lest this characterization of the traditional pattern of Chinese social integration seem too abstract, it is only necessary to fit into the above-mentioned "gymnast pyramid" model the major actors of the warlord era—Yüan Shih-k'ai, Chang Tso-lin, Wu P'ei-fu, Tuan Ch'i-jui, Feng Kuo-chang, Ts'ao K'un, and others—to see that this spatial model could have considerable operational reality.

The two particular emotional drives which we have analyzed as underlying the pattern of Chinese social integration—the dependency orientation toward authority, and great concern with interpersonal conflict—seem to account, in part, for the temporal pattern of social integration in China, the alternation of periods of *luan* and *ho-p'ing*. It was the fearful destruction of such historical episodes as the "warring states" or the more recent Taiping and warlord periods which reaffirmed to Chinese that dependence on an all-powerful authority who could impose social order and restrain the *luan* of military or "bandit" violence was a social price worth paying. Harsh authority was welcomed as long as it restrained the aggressive impulses of distrusted peers and as long as it could maintain a degree of social order and provide for the expectations of material security of its dependents. But when the harshness of this hierarchical social order was not reciprocated with security or a minimal degree of justice, then the self-renunciation that characterized "filial" dependence could turn to great hatred for the authority that had "cheated," and lead to frightful violence as revenge was taken and power equals vied in a determined effort to impose a new hierarchical ordering of authority, one which would have the "mandate of heaven"—that is, the legitimacy of popular acceptance based on renewed fears of *luan* and concern for stability and material security.

The particular integrative devices which we have seen as characteristic of the traditional order were a highly specified structure of political relationships cemented together by the mutual expectations of loyalty and security which were the essence of "filiality," and defined by an elaborate set of social "names" or status positions. The individual was thus "boxed in" by a mutually reinforcing hierarchy of responsibility and deference, in which ritual became the unending test of acceptance of the deference pattern, and "education" a process by which individuals constantly affirmed their commitment to the established order.

Education had deeper psychological roots as well. The socialization of new generations with well-developed dependency needs made authority's control of resources (family land and wealth) a particularly potent way of insuring "filiality" in younger generations, for they had been trained to see no real alternative to dependence on family authority. Autonomous behavior was not only "selfish," but to attempt to make one's way in life as an individual was both ineffective and unthinkable. Great concern for one's social "face," developed through sensitivity to shame, further reinforced fears of social isolation, making acceptance of the norms of the interdependent group preferable to personal assertiveness.

The social attitudes and emotional needs which we have thus far analyzed as being central to integrative and disintegrative social processes in traditional China are not those that are easily swept away, for they are rooted in the socialization experiences of early life. The temporal framework for their change must be measured in the time of new generations, and not merely the passing of solar years. With the establishment of a Communist political order in China in 1949, however, some saw the end of the traditional culture—or at least the firm institutionalization of "revolutionary" change. Yet within the historically brief period of two decades certain leaders of the Chinese Communist Party were not so certain that their revolution was still making progress, or that the old culture was dead and gone. The Party's theoretical journal, *Red Flag,* noted with concern: "It need not take a very long period of time for the proletariat to seize power and overthrow the ownership of the exploiting classes. But it requires a very, very long period of time to eliminate the old ideas, culture, customs and habits left over by the exploiting classes for thousands of years."[55]

In the second part of this paper, to which we now turn, we will try to give some sense of the interplay between the traditional cultural elements affecting social integration which we have just detailed, and the conception of a new political order which the Communists have sought to institutionalize since they came to power.

II. The Image and the Reality of New Integrative Social Processes

INTRODUCTION

A society in revolution appears, at least to an outside observer, to have confused hope and reality. The way a revolutionary elite feels the world *ought* to be is often presented as the way things in fact *are.* Such a problem confronts us as we attempt to make some sense out of the apparently momentous social changes that have occurred in China during the last eighteen years. In this second part of the analysis we hope to provide some interpretive guidelines, and a limited amount of empirical evidence, which will enable us to evaluate more fully the relationship between elite goals and the remnants of old traditions and social processes.

The analysis in this part of the paper will attempt to preserve the distinction between what have been the revolutionary goals of the Chinese Communist Party leadership, and in particular of Party Chairman Mao Tse-tung, and the reality of popular attitudes and social processes inherited from the old society. It is obvious that the relationship between the "is" of the people and the "ought" of the Party has been one of tension, and the source of much of the conflict and turmoil that has characterized Chinese life for more than two decades. Indeed, as we will stress in the concluding section, this tension

[55] "A Great Revolution to Achieve the Complete Ascendancy of Mao Tse-tung's Thought," *Red Flag* editorial, No. 15 (1957), trans. in *Peking Review,* No. 42 (October 13, 1967), p. 11.

between goals and reality has now invaded even the Chinese Communist Party itself. The events of the current and continuing Great Proletarian Cultural Revolution have exposed some of the sources of tensions, and they provide a concluding framework within which to evaluate the impact of Party efforts to create new integrative social processes, to change China from an agrarian society into a unified and industrializing nation-state.

MAO'S IMAGE OF NEW INTEGRATIVE SOCIAL PROCESSES

The formative years of successful revolutionary movements represent one of the few historical situations where the unique individual is able to translate highly personal solutions to social problems into larger political processes, by virtue of his control over a growing organization and through popular receptivity to change. In time such movements become routinized; the impact of the charismatic leader is lost as new generations of leaders emerge to take the place of the innovator, and more deeply rooted social processes emerge once again. But for a short period of time at least, the visionary leader is able to leave his mark on human institutions.

Such is certainly the case with Mao Tse-tung, who brought to a floundering Communist movement in China a new image of political processes which in time and through struggle were legitimatized by their very successes. In terms of our central analytical problem, that of social integration, Mao's particular contribution to Chinese political life can be summed up in two points. First, *the attempt to make conflict a legitimate element in social processes* through its ability to bind people together and to provide the dynamic element to social change. Related to this is his conviction that the human capacity for aggression, manifest in the emotions of resentment and hatred, can provide both the emotional cement of a new social unity and the motive power of active social involvement. Second, Mao brought to the Chinese revolution *a new image of social authority,* one in which the dependency orientation to a personalized authority would be replaced with a sense of individual activism and responsibility, and where ideology, in the sense of a set of systematic general principles and objectives,[56] would replace the personal authority of the "cultivated individual."

[56] The most detailed and stimulating analysis of Mao's notion of "ideology" will be found in Franz Schurmann, *Ideology and Organization in Communist China* (Berkeley and Los Angeles: University of California Press, 1966), esp. chap. i.

Inasmuch as the attempt to repress all social conflict and to maintain a "harmonious" authority pattern of dependence upon a personalized hierarchy of "cultivated" leaders are the essential elements of China's traditional political order, Mao, I think, can be said to have made one of those truly insightful "great leaps" *of conception* in which the solution to existing social problems was seen to lie in a radical change in the existing order of things. It is Mao's determined effort to change such elemental aspects of China's traditional political culture that has made his rule truly revolutionary.[57]

Violent action is a thread common to almost all rebellious or revolutionary social movements, and Mao shares with revolutionary leaders the world over a capacity to rationalize the use of physical violence in terms of ultimate goals. The degree of Mao's innovation, however, must be evaluated within its own social milieu, within the Chinese tradition where, as we have elaborated in Part I, aggressive or conflictive behavior was considered by the political elite to be an illegitimate aspect of social relations.[58] Indeed, among our interview respondents we found the rather paradoxical orientation of a willingness to accept the use of state violence to make certain that conflict—as manifest in the behavior of "bandits" or *liu-mang*—would not occur. The pattern of social integration which we found characteristic of the traditional society had a polarized quality of either conflict and violence with little restraint, or apparent tranquillity; *ho-p'ing* alternating with *luan*.

Where Mao parts company with his compatriots is in seeing a middle ground between these two poles of peace and confusion, seeing both the possibility and virtue of making *controlled* and *mediated* conflict the dynamic element of a new political order. In his revealing "Hunan Report" of 1927, Mao—responding to those who reacted to the violent peasant uprisings of the mid-1920's with the anguish of "It's terrible!"—observed: "The peasants are clear-sighted. Who is bad and who is not, who is the worst and who is not quite so vicious, who deserves severe punishment and who deserves to be let off lightly —the peasants keep clear accounts, and very seldom has the punish-

[57] Yet, as we will stress in the conclusion, it is most ironical in both historical and psychological senses that Mao, having attained power, has found it necessary to resort to some of the very methods of leadership he opposes in order to maintain his power and his image of a proper future for Chinese society.

[58] This orientation was most obviously institutionalized in the Confucianists' depreciation of the military profession. There was in traditional China no *respected* social class skilled in the use of violence and tied to the formal or official moral order, such as *did* exist, for example, in the samurai of Japan.

ment exceeded the crime."[59] In short, Mao was saying to all those who panicked at the thought of violence, that it would not necessarily lead to *luan,* that aggression could find both meaning and limit within the context of a political organization and its objectives.

This is not to say, however, that all of Mao's cohorts agreed with his position. Indeed, we find that a constant theme in the development of the Party has been the effort to walk a proper course between the use of violence for its own sake and a reluctance to resort to any violence whatsoever. The Chinese Communist Party, at its Sixth National Congress in September, 1928, expressed concern about the "tendency to destroy cities and kill, burn, and rob purposelessly." The Congress communique noted that "this tendency is . . . a reflection of a lumpen-proletariat and peasant mentality" which can weaken the Party's influence among the masses. And while violence was seen as necessary, "what is opposed by the Party . . . is purposeless killing and burning which are irrelevant to our revolutionary mission. Burning and killing for their own sake and not for the real benefit of the revolution is objectionable."[60]

On the other side of the fence, Mao saw those among the Party leadership who were unable to cope with any violence whatsoever, and who, under the "right opportunist" leadership of Ch'en Tu-hsiu, had led the Party to near extinction: "Ch'en was really frightened of the workers and especially of the armed peasants. Confronted at last with the reality of armed insurrection he completely lost his senses. He could no longer see clearly what was happening, and his petty bourgeois instincts betrayed him into panic and defeat."[61]

[59] Mao Tse-tung, "Report on an Investigation of the Peasant Movement in Hunan," *Selected Works* (Peking: Foreign Languages Press, 1961–65), I, 28 (hereafter *SW*).

[60] Cited in Conrad Brandt, Benjamin Schwartz, and John K. Fairbank, *A Documentary History of Chinese Communism* (New York: Atheneum, 1966), p. 162. This Party Congress, held in Moscow, undoubtedly was anxious to account for, and perhaps to explain away, the Party's defeats of the previous year, beginning with the Nanchang uprising and concluding with the Canton Commune. Yet the problem of the undisciplined use of violence so clearly discussed in this Congress communique must be attributed to more than just Russian pressures to shift the blame for a bad policy. It is a question which comes up over and again in a variety of contexts. See, for example, Mao's criticism of what he calls "the purely military viewpoint" in his 1929 essay, "On Correcting Mistaken Ideas in the Party," *SW*, I, 105–16.

For a discussion of the tendency to alternate between *luan* and *ho-p'ing* in the area of "criticism and self-criticism," see the remarks by Mao and Liu Shao-ch'i on pp. 335–36.

[61] Snow, *Red Star over China,* p. 165. Mao's criticism of Ch'en must be handled with care, for this early Party leader perhaps has been singled out as a scapegoat where others are to blame. Yet the point of our interpretation of this passage is that Mao saw fear of violent revolutionary action as a problem; and the already discredited Ch'en, justly or

In sum, Mao saw the need for making conflict an integral part of the political process, for as he elaborated in his theoretical essay "On Contradiction," the resolution of *mao-tun* (contradiction) through mediated forms of social conflict provides the dynamic element to social change. But this conflict has to be both limited and purposeful in terms of higher revolutionary goals. As we shall see in Party efforts to institutionalize mediated conflict processes, largely in the form of "criticism–self-criticism" meetings, there has been a constant tension between the desires of some to see all conflict ended and the impulse in others which makes the release of aggression exceed the limits of ordered institutional political combat.

It should be stressed, however, that Mao saw in conflict not simply the dynamic element in revolutionary change, or even the more elemental quality of self-assertiveness.[62] Conflict could also contribute to social integration, at least in its mediated form of ideological struggle (as will be elaborated below). But at base Mao saw in hatred the emotional driving force behind political action, a motive power which could be used to create unity as well as dynamism. In his most revealing 1936 interview with Edgar Snow, Mao recalled of his family life: ". . . I think that in the end the strictness of my father defeated him. *I learned to hate him, and we created a real "United Front" against him*. At the same time it probably benefited me. It made me most diligent in my work; it made me keep my books carefully, so that he should have no basis for criticizing me."[63]

As this observation rather clearly suggests, it was a common hatred of authority which formed the basis of the family "United Front." And in time it was the hatred of a larger authority, manipulated through organizational controls, which became the motivational basis upon which the Party united and animated the People's Liberation Army (PLA). Mao made this explicit in a 1948 speech to a group of newspaper workers:

---

unjustly, was held up as a "negative example" to educate the Party to this problem. History used as a political weapon is perhaps more meaningful as an indicator of present problems than of the accuracy of what happened in the past. The symbols used and the interpretations given probably tell more about the concerns of the interpreter of past events, and about the anxieties of his audience, than they do about the motives of those who acted in days gone by.

[62] The development of self-integrity through combat, however, does seem to be an important element in Mao's conception of conflict, as is clearly revealed in his early essay, "A Study of Physical Education," translated in part in Stuart R. Schram, *The Political Thought of Mao Tse-tung* (New York: Praeger, 1963), pp. 94–102.

[63] Snow, *Red Star over China*, pp. 126–27. Emphasis added.

Once the masses know the truth and have a common aim, they will work together with one heart. This is like fighting a battle; *to win a battle the fighters as well as the officers must be of one heart. After the troops in northern Shensi went through training and consolidation and poured out their grievances (su-k'u) against the old social order, the fighters heightened their political consciousness and became clear on why they were fighting* and how they should fight; every one of them rolled up his sleeves for battle, their morale was very high and as soon as they went into action they won a victory. When the masses are of one heart, everything becomes easy.[64]

And with "liberation" the techniques developed by Party leaders for creating unity through common feelings of hatred, sentiments mobilized in grievance telling and struggle sessions, were to acquire elaborate organizational development.[65]

The second major element of Mao's image of a new political order in China focuses on questions of authority. Simply stated, Mao as a personality finds most repugnant the passive and dependent quality of traditional dealings with authority, and his constant stress on "activism" or "positive" (*chi-chi*) political participation—a style which others have termed "voluntarism"[66]—seems to represent an attempt to move away from the traditional style of social authority. Self-integrity, as opposed to the integrity of the filial hierarchical relationship, is something Mao clearly finds admirable. As he once observed in a tribute to Lu Hsün: "Lu Hsün was a man of unyielding integrity, free from all sycophancy or obsequiousness; this quality is invaluable among colonial and semi-colonial peoples."[67]

Out of the trials and failures of building a combat party, Mao discovered that greater organizational strength could come from a

---

[64] Mao Tse-tung, "A Talk to the Editorial Staff of the *Shansi-Suiyuan Daily,*" *SW,* IV, 241. Emphasis added.

[65] The place of hatred in Chinese political action has been explored in a most provocative paper by Lucian W. Pye, *The Dynamics of Hostility and Hate in the Chinese Political Culture* (Cambridge, Mass.: Center for International Studies, M.I.T., 1964), and in the present author's article, "America's Revolutionary Alliance with Communist China," *Asian Survey,* VII, No. 12 (December, 1967), 831–50. An interesting and succinct analysis of the organizational forms that have been developed in post-"liberation" China for emotional mobilization, and in particular the mass campaign or *yün-tung* technique, will be found in Frederick Yu, "With Banners and Drums: The Mass Campaign in China's Drive for Development," *Current Scene* (Hong Kong), IV, No. 9 (May 1, 1966), 1–13.

[66] The concept of voluntarism had been explored in an interesting paper by Ezra F. Vogel, "Voluntarism and Social Control," in Donald W. Treadgold (ed.), *Soviet and Chinese Communism: Similarities and Differences* (Seattle: University of Washington Press, 1967), pp. 168–84.

[67] Mao Tse-tung, "On New Democracy," *SW,* II, 372.

policy of "self reliance," of "regeneration through one's own efforts" (*tzu-li-keng-sheng*):

. . . We rely entirely on our own efforts, and our position is invincible; this is the very opposite of Chiang Kai-shek who depends entirely upon foreign countries. We live plainly and work hard, we take care of the needs of both the army and the people; this is the very opposite of the situation in Chiang Kai-shek's areas, where those at the top are corrupt and degenerate, while the people under them are destitute. Under these circumstances, we shall surely be victorious.[68]

If organizational self-reliance gave the Communist movement much of its strength, Mao also had discovered early in his career that organizational unity could be consolidated through delegation of responsibility (if not full authority). This attitude contrasts sharply with what, as we have seen in Part I, was the traditional expectation that those with authority keep all initiative and responsibility in their own hands. As Mao described in elaborating the organizational successes of the movement in South China:

Apart from the role played by the Party, *the reason why the Red Army has been able to carry on in spite of such poor material conditions and such frequent engagements is its practice of democracy. The officers do not beat the men; officers and men receive equal treatment; soldiers are free to hold meetings and to speak out; trivial formalities have been done away with; and the accounts are open for all to inspect. The soldiers handle the mess arrangements . . . all this gives great satisfaction to the soldiers.* The newly captured soldiers in particular feel that our army and the Kuomintang army are worlds apart. They feel spiritually liberated even though material conditions in the Red Army are not equal to those in the White Army. The very soldiers who had no courage in the White Army yesterday are brave in the Red Army today; such is the effect of democracy. . . . In China the army needs democracy as much as the people do. Democracy in our army is an important weapon for undermining the feudal mercenary armies.[69]

That Mao labels this altered style of the use of authority and delegation of responsibility as "democracy," when it clearly lacks the checks on the use of power which are basic to Western notions of that term, seems quite irrelevant within the social context of China. Simply the contrast of Mao's efforts to see the lower ranks of the army take certain responsibility upon their own shoulders, and to have the officers put an end to the physical brutality and denial of criticism which characterized traditional military life, was quite enough to produce a

---

[68] Mao Tse-tung, "Smash Chiang Kai-shek's Offensive by a War of Self-Defense," *SW*, IV, 91.

[69] Mao Tse-tung, "Struggle in the Chingkang Mountains," *SW*, I, 83. Emphasis added.

"spiritual liberation" and bind the individual into the organization through the sense of self-involvement which came from delegation of certain responsibility.[70]

However, the creation of a political structure in which the lower ranks were not simply told to depend on the guidance and initiative of their superiors was not an easy job. In the same analysis Mao commented on the difficulties of creating mass organizations in which people would be given a certain degree of initiative and responsibility:

People's political power has been established everywhere at county, district, and township levels, but more in name than in reality. Some places do have a council, but it is regarded merely as a temporary body for electing the executive committees; *once the election is over, authority is monopolized by the committee and the council is never heard of again. The evil feudal practice of arbitrary dictation is so deeply rooted in the minds of the people and even of the ordinary party members that it cannot be swept away at once;* when anything crops up, they choose the easy way and have no liking for the bothersome democratic system. Democratic centralism can be widely and effectively practiced in mass organizations only when its efficacy is demonstrated in revolutionary struggle and the masses understand that it is the best means of mobilizing their forces and is of the utmost help in their struggle.[71]

Mao's answer to how to deal with the tenacious persistence of traditional attitudes toward authority, and toward the use of authority, seems comprised of three elements: the attempt to depersonalize authority's image through the use of ideological norms; the attempt to subject to organized criticism, and in particular criticism from below, those who *apply* Party policies (an approach developed within the concept of the so-called "mass line"); and the attempt to shift a good deal of authority away from the individual Party operative into the workings of the peer group.

The depersonalization of authority seems to be an effort to move away from the highly personalized loyalties and factionalism which periodically fragmented the traditional political order. Within a framework of basic commitment to the Marxist view of the world and Party-created goals and strategies, Mao has seen the possibility of rising above the authority of the unique individual and restraining the *luan* of political conflict. But as he indicated in a document from one of the early "rectification" campaigns, this has not been easily done:

[70] This "innovation" of individual responsibility has been observed by Schurmann in the development of post-"liberation" techniques of industrial management. See *Ideology and Organization in Communist China,* p. 243.

[71] Mao, "Struggle in the Chingkang Mountains," pp. 90–91. Emphasis added.

The struggles which the Party waged in the course of its history against Chen Tu-hsiuism and Li Li-sanism were absolutely necessary. The defect in these struggles was that they were not undertaken consciously as serious steps for correcting petty-bourgeois ideology which existed on a serious scale in the party; consequently they neither clarified the ideological essence and roots of the errors thoroughly nor properly indicated the methods of correcting them, and so it was easy for these errors to recur. Moreover, *undue stress was placed on personal responsibility in the belief that once an erring comrade was attacked, the problem was solved. . . . So long as any comrade who has erred in the past understands his errors and has begun to correct them, we should welcome him without prejudice and unite with him to work for the party. . . . The task of the entire party from now on is to strengthen unity by clarifying thinking and holding fast to principle.* All our party's analyses, criticisms and controversies concerning questions of party history should start from the desire for unity and arrive at unity; any violation of this principle is wrong.[72]

Mao's efforts to see those who apply Party policies subject to mass criticism is a topic worthy of detailed analysis, for this form of political control has been applied by the Party leadership in a paradoxical manner. One might say that Mao and the Party hope to have their cake and eat it too, inasmuch as critical checks on authority have been restricted to those who *apply* Party policies, while the decision-making body has remained inviolate to criticism. Nonetheless, one can see in such *yün-tung* as the 1956–57 "Blooming and Contending" movement, or the more recent effort to build "congresses of poor and lower middle peasants," attempts not only to bind "the masses" into the political process by giving them a constructive and critical political role, but more basically an effort to check the authority of those who implement Party directives by trapping them between a "squeeze" of mass criticism from below and pressures for performance from top Party leadership. The notion of the "mass line" as a leadership style seems to be a direct response to the traditional weak linkage between leaders and led which we noted in Part I—an attempt to stave off through timely criticism the cleavage between mass and elite which in Chinese Communist jargon is known as "cutting oneself off from the masses" (*t'uo-li ch'ün-chung*).

In developing the authority of the peer group as a basis for strengthening social cohesion, Mao seems to have emphasized a traditional form of social control; for, as we noted in Part I, by tradition the peer group has had a re-enforcing role in maintaining the integrity

---

[72] Mao Tse-tung, "Our Study and the Current Situation. Appendix: Resolution on Questions in Party History," *SW*, III, 218–19. Emphasis added.

of hierarchical authority. Certainly the forms of group organization and activity which have become the hallmarks of the new political order in China—the use of the dunce-capped "object" (*tui-hsiang*) paraded before the struggle meeting, and *chien-t'ao* (self-criticism) within the context of the small study group—are activities which take their cue from and have limits set by top Party authority; yet they clearly seek to use peer relationships to control the individual's behavior. Such organizational forms seem designed to play upon the fears of isolation or alienation from the group which were such dominant themes in the traditional social order. And like his predecessors, Mao sees no place for the "self" or the private in the "people's" political order; the traditional norm is restated as *p'o-szu li-kung,* "destroy selfishness, establish the collective."

In stressing ideological uniformity as the basis for social unity, Mao seems fully to merge with Chinese political traditions dating back to the times of Li Szu. The current efforts to promote thought reform or "ideological remolding" (*szu-hsiang kai-tsao*) have given new life to the traditional stress on education as the basis of social control.

The almost compulsive Communist Chinese fascination with, and attention to, matters of organization gives evidence of the Party's continuity with the traditional inclination to achieve social solidarity through a proper structuring of interpersonal relations. Much of Mao's concern with problems of organization seems to focus on its capacity for mobilizing into political action those who by tradition have been passive and withdrawn from political involvement, and aggregating sufficient power to oppose the established order of things.[73] But as we shall suggest in the concluding section of this paper, the capacity of organization to be used predominantly as a restraining control mechanism to "box in" the individual within a system of interpersonal ties, such as characterized the traditional social order, seems to be highly repugnant to Mao as an individual. It does, however, seem to have particular appeal to many Chinese, and provides one of the points of conflict that has been exposed in the Great Proletarian Cultural Revolution.[74]

---

[73] These themes are explored in detail in the author's volume now in preparation, *Mao's Revolution and the Chinese Political Culture,* especially chaps. xii and xiv.

[74] The predominant image of organization as a device for restraining troublesome individuals was consistently revealed in our interview data. The notion of government and people having "intimate relations" (*mi-ch'ieh kuan-hsi*), and of people mutually involving themselves in each other's affairs as a way of preventing *luan,* was frequently voiced:

[What is the best way to improve a society and its customs?] The government has to have intimate relations with the people. [How should it do that?] Well, for example,

To summarize, Mao's image of how to achieve the reintegration of
the Chinese polity consists of four main elements: (1) *organization,* to
serve as the structure of unity; (2) *ideology* as the unifying content of
organizational transactions;[75] (3) stress on the *motives of hatred and
resentment* toward the revolution's enemies in order to give cohesion
and drive to the revolutionary organization, and manipulation of anxieties about being isolated (*ku-li ti*) from the peer group; and (4)
criticism to supply the dynamic to organizational transactions. These
elements of a new political order appear to have grown gradually and
through trial and error from the early defeats and constant difficulties
that have characterized the Communists' rise to power in China; but
on the eve of victory Mao could underline the fundamental importance
of this newly developed technique of political integration—and con-

---

now in a residential area there are not too many police; so if, for instance, a
Communist there does bad things people should interfere (*kan-she*) with his behavior
—the people have to have a sense of vigilance. [Should there be more police; is that
what you mean?] No, what I mean is the government and the people should have a
more intimate relationship. If ordinary people have vigilance and mutually involve
themselves in each other's behavior then it would not be easy for people to do bad
things. If people are disinterested (*san-man*) in social life, if they just sweep the snow
in front of their own doors, if they do not obstruct the bad behavior of others and do
not think about its long-term effects, then it will not be good for the nation.

And as a man who had been in positions of military leadership under both the
Communists and Nationalists explicitly observed in response to my question, "How can
you have *chih-an hao?*":

Everything has to be well organized. For example, if a person wants to steal, if you
know his motivation, you can prevent it. [What kind of organization do you have in
mind?] It is not a special, it cannot be a simple organization, it has to be united
with others. You have to know what a person is doing from the time he is small.
[What do you mean when you say, it cannot be a simple organization?] A person
cannot be isolated (*ku-li ti*), he cannot live alone. You have to have 4, 5, 6, 6,000
people around him. For example, if he gets sick you have to take him to a hospital
to get cured—so you have to have things well united. . . . They ought to have a file
on every person from the age of eight, so if, for example, he comes in for a job we
will know just what he has done. . . .

This observation clearly underscores the double-edged quality of organization in Chinese
eyes: being surrounded by all those people prevents isolation and alienation—"he cannot
live alone"—and insures the capacity of organization to take care of the individual's
needs, as in the case of getting sick and being taken to a hospital; but it also emphasizes
the control function of organization, for with all those people surrounding the individual,
with a dossier filled with information on the individual's personal life "from the age of
eight," a record filled with information from people who have "mutually involved
themselves in each other's behavior," then one's peers will not be able to make trouble.

In sum, Chinese have more than a little sympathy for the control function of
organization, for state or social encroachments on the life of the individual, if it will
insure social tranquillity.

[75] As Franz Schurmann has observed, the "cadre" (*kan-pu*) provides the activist and
leadership element in organizational transactions: "The cadre . . . is a leader who thinks
in terms of human solidarity. He knows how to 'solidarize' men so that goals can be
achieved; he can manipulate their thoughts and sentiments; he operates, not with ethos,
but with ideology . . ." (*Ideology and Organization in Communist China,* p. 167).

trast it with the disintegration that characterized the soon to be defeated enemy:

In the last few months almost all the People's Liberation Army has made use of the intervals between battles for large scale training and consolidation. This has been carried out in a fully guided, orderly and democratic way. It has therefore aroused the revolutionary fervor of the great masses of commanders and fighters, enabling them clearly to comprehend the aim of the [civil] war, eliminated certain incorrect ideological tendencies and undesirable manifestations in the army, educated the cadres and fighters and greatly enhanced the combat effectiveness of the army. From now on, we must continue to carry on this new type of ideological education movement in the army, a movement which has a democratic and mass character. You can see clearly that neither the Party consolidation nor the ideological education in the army . . . could be undertaken by our enemy, the Kuomintang. On our part, we have been very earnest in correcting our own shortcomings; we have united the Party and army virtually as one man and forged close ties between them and the masses of the people. . . . With our enemy, everything is just the opposite. They are so corrupt, so torn by ever increasing and irreconcilable internal quarrels, so spurned by the people and utterly isolated and so frequently defeated in battle that their doom is inevitable.[76]

PROBLEMS OF IMPLEMENTING THE MAOIST CONCEPTION

Evaluating the degree to which Mao's image of a new political order has in fact been realized on the Chinese mainland is no easy task. The existing information which might be used in such an evaluation is largely in the form of published Party documents, newspapers, or other heavily edited official publications—data which can be tested against only limited amounts of interview materials gathered from prisoners of war, émigrés, or visitors to the mainland. What we shall try to do in this section is to sketch out in rough form what appear to be the main areas of tension and resistance to the Party's efforts to institute a new political order, with the full awareness that this discussion is of a provisional and untested nature.

A second problem concerning the evaluation of political change on the mainland involves recognition that it has proceeded at two distinct levels: Mao has had to build his Party and army structures out of the existing human material, out of adults socialized within a social system that the Party has sought to destroy. Hence both the methods and the effectiveness of Party-sponsored change during the first years of full power represent attempts to alter in a radical manner the existing social orientations of adult Chinese. On the second level—that of

[76] Mao Tse-tung, "Speech at a Conference of Cadres in the Shansi-Suiyuan Liberated Area," *SW*, IV, 234.

raising new generations from early in life—the Party has made a concerted effort to effect a much more basic set of attitude changes among people in their formative years. The following discussion will attempt to take into account these two levels of change, first by focusing on the problems that the Party seems to have faced in realizing its new style of political participation during the period of its rise to national power and in the early years of national control, and then by making some estimates, through interview materials, of attitude changes among the younger generation.

STRUGGLE BRINGS UNITY

During the period of the Anti-Japanese War, Mao put forward a united front strategy which must have puzzled many Party members, for he wrote an article elaborating the notion that unity in the united front could come through "struggle":

The tactics required for [the extension and consolidation of the anti-Japanese united front] are to develop the progressive forces, win over the middle forces and combat the diehard forces; these are three inseparable links, and *the means to be used to unite all the anti-Japanese forces is struggle. In the period of the anti-Japanese united front, struggle is the means to unity and unity is the aim of struggle. If unity is sought through struggle, it will live; if unity is sought through yielding, it will perish. This truth is gradually being grasped by Party comrades. However, there are still many who do not understand it; some think that struggle will split the united front or that struggle can be employed without restraint,* and others use wrong tactics towards the middle forces or have mistaken notions about the diehard forces. All this must be corrected.[77]

This comment, in brief compass, summarizes Mao's approach to making conflict or "struggle" an integral part of the political process, a limited and mediated form of conflict designed to achieve political integration. How does this process appear to work in practice; and why have some comrades found it difficult to believe that unity comes through struggle? In this section we will try to develop some answers to these questions.

First, it should be clearly noted that in Mao's view unity is not achieved through the uniting of all; it is not a "politics of consensus." In the above quotation, as elsewhere, Mao breaks down the population into several groupings: the "progressive forces" (all too frequently in the minority), who are to be "encouraged" or "developed"; "middle

---

[77] Mao Tse-tung, "Current Problems of Tactics in the Anti-Japanese United Front," *SW*, II, 422. Emphasis added.

forces," a largely passive middle of the road element that is usually in the majority; and then a smaller "die-hard" or incorrigible core of opposition leadership. Mao's notion of unity is above all one achieved through the tension of conflict between the die-hard element and the progressives, a conflict in which a variety of techniques is used to shift the middle of the roaders off center, to encourage them to "unite" with the progressives. It is a unity of what is, hopefully, a majority achieved at the expense of a minority.

The form that political conflict takes varies with particular circumstances and with the strength of the "die-hard" elements; but for the most part—and certainly since the end of the civil war in China in 1949—Mao has sought to shift the ground of revolutionary action from the arena of military violence to that of ideological confrontation. It is the "struggle" of progressive versus reactionary ideas and behavior, carried out under the banner of "criticism–self-criticism" and promoted within the organizational contexts of the small study group (*hsüeh-hsi hsiao-tzu*), the investigation meeting (*chien-t'ao hui*), or the larger and more emotionally charged "struggle" meeting (*tou-cheng hui*).[78]

As we suggested earlier, the process of "criticism–self-criticism" is the dynamic aspect of Mao's efforts to create unity through mediated conflict. Yet consonant with his notion that unity is to be achieved for the majority at the expense of a small minority, the technique of ideological struggle becomes a two-edged sword, one that can be used to divide as well as to carve out a new unity.

Throughout its history the Party has attempted to expand its influence among "the masses" (and indeed among its own membership) through organizational devices of its own creation and control which will develop loyalty and commitment to its cause. This objective, however, has constantly been in "contradiction" with the personalized relationships (*jen-shih kuan-hsi*) that were so basic to the traditional Chinese social order—the particularistic obligations of loyalty and trust given to blood relatives, teacher, organizational superior, and friends.[79] To resolve this *mao-tun*, the Party has developed consider-

---

[78] A lively and detailed, if somewhat romanticized, account of the process of uniting poor and middle peasants in the land reform struggle against "reactionary" rich peasants and landlords in a Shansi village in 1948 will be found in William Hinton, *Fanshen* (New York: Monthly Review Press, 1966), chap. xlv, pp. 400–416, and *passim*.

[79] The effects of these particularistic personal relationships on the development of industrial organization in Communist China have been well explored by Franz Schurmann. See his *Ideology and Organization in Communist China*, pp. 225–38.

able skill in using the "criticism–self-criticism" technique as a divisive force in breaking down such "feudal" particularistic social ties. This was essentially the burden of Mao's 1937 attack on "liberalism," which, he said, meant to:

. . . let things slide for the sake of peace and friendship when a person has clearly gone wrong, and refrain from principled argument because he is an old acquaintance, a fellow townsman, a schoolmate, a close friend, a loved one, an old colleague or old subordinate. Or to touch on the matter lightly instead of going into it thoroughly, so as to keep on good terms. The result is that both the organization and the individual are harmed.[80]

The process used to combat these particularistic ties has been to encourage or coerce one or both parties in such relationships to criticize each other in public: most notably comes to mind the public attacks on parents by their children during the first years after "liberation," and the setting of friend against friend through criticism within the small group.[81] In short, Mao's notion that "there must be destruction before construction" finds practical application in Party efforts first to break down the personal ties which it finds competitive with its own organizational structures, and then to seek to rebuild social unity on its own terms.[82]

The unity that is constructed from the fragmented elements of more traditional social ties is one in which the Party seeks to embrace all but the most die-hard of the "enemy." It is a unity on the Party's own terms. And those terms, the style of involvement in the Party or mass organizations, are above all founded upon the notion of being "active" or "positive." Seen in a negative light, the Party has denied the individual in China the option of nonparticipation; he faces the alternatives

---

[80] Mao Tse-tung, "Combat Liberalism," *SW*, II, 31.

[81] The use of small group criticism to break down friendship ties has been explored in some detail in an analysis by Ezra Vogel, "From Friendship to Comradeship: The Change in Personal Relations in Communist China," *China Quarterly*, No. 21 (January–March, 1965), pp. 46–60. More detailed investigations of the Communists' use of "small group dynamics" to break down both interpersonal ties and self-respect will be found in Edgar H. Schein *et al., Coercive Persuasion* (New York: Norton, 1961), and Robert J. Lifton, *Thought Reform and the Psychology of Totalism: A Study of "Brainwashing" in China* (New York: Norton, 1961).

[82] The fact that Party history is full of efforts to combat a variety of "sectarian" tendencies ("unit-ism" [*pen-wei chu-yi*], the "guerrilla stronghold mentality," "closed-door-ism," and the like), in addition to the more traditional particularistic ties mentioned above, is some indication of just how difficult the Party has found the task of replacing the traditional notion of social relations cast in a framework of interpersonal commitments and personalized authority with the authority of ideological principles and the directives of the Party "Central."

of either alienated isolation or active commitment.[83] Yet Mao's ideal of participation is not of a passive and unquestioning variety, but rather one where ideology has "armed" the individual for self-initiated and spontaneous (yet coordinated) social action:

In order to get rid of the practice of acting blindly which is so common in our Party, we must encourage our comrades to think, to learn the method of analysis and to cultivate the habit of analysis. There is all too little of this habit in our Party. If we get rid of our baggage and start up the machinery [of our brains], if we march with light packs and know how to think hard, then we are sure to triumph.[84]

Also seen in a negative light, this emphasis on active involvement appears to be a reaction of the Party against the threat of a great dead weight of popular passive resistance (*hsiao-chi ti-k'ang*) which has been the traditional form of protest in China for those with no manifest and legitimate channels of political influence.

In a more positive view, however, the stress on "activism" is a recognition that the incredible capacity of the Chinese peasant or worker for sustained activity can be most effectively harnessed to Party causes where there is both personal commitment and a sense of personal responsibility. As can be seen in a variety of organizational activities developed during the post-"liberation" years, the Party leadership has sought controlled ways of giving a positive and critical role to those who by tradition have been politically passive. In addition, the Party has used a variety of positive appeals—the traditional incentives of prestige, power, and security associated with government office, the sentiment of nationalism, and the desire to participate in the excitement of building a new society—in enlisting popular support.

A measured judgment of the extent to which the Party has been successful in encouraging a degree of popular ego involvement in political goals and activities is something our limited and indirect data will not permit. It is worth noting, however, that refugee interviews reveal a very mixed picture, with certain activities inspiring a genuine degree of involvement and personal commitment, but others in which participation has become routine. The development of routinized forms of participation seems particularly notable in the critical interchanges of the small group. A number of respondents have directly compared

[83] A fine review and analysis of the factors which appear to *dilute* Party pressures for active commitment to the political process—giving a determined "passivist" a degree of escape—will be found in Townsend, *Political Participation in Communist China*, esp. pp. 185–209.

[84] Mao Tse-tung, "Our Study and the Current Situation," *SW*, III, 175.

participation in *chien-t'ao* to the workings of a theatrical performance: everyone knows the lines that are to be spoken; each member of the group knows the part he is to play; and the individual maintains a sense of "distance" between a core of his true "self" and the behavior he manifests before the group.

In balance with a variety of positive appeals associated with an active role in Party-directed organizational structures is the negative sanction of being "isolated" (*ku-li ti*). In Part I we explored in some detail how it has long been part of the Chinese cultural tradition to stress the individual's dependence upon group and authority for both material well-being and an emotional sense of identity. The Communists have taken these developed sensitivities to isolation and applied them in the service of discouraging passive withdrawal or opposition to Party-sponsored activities. How are the individual's feelings manipulated in order to make group participation preferable to withdrawal? In a succinct summary of the dynamics of the process, Franz Schurmann has written:

Essentially, the technique consists in the usually temporary alienation of a single member from the group through the application of collective criticism. One member is singled out for criticism, either because of faulty ideological understanding, poor work performance, or some other deviance. He is not only subjected to a barrage of criticism from the members, but also joins in and begins to criticize himself. The avowed purpose of the procedure is to "correct" (*kai-tsao*) the individual. Under normal circumstances, the individual is "reintegrated" into the group after the "temporary alienation." The experience of temporary alienation by the one criticized and collective criticism by the group members is, in theory, supposed to have the general effect of maintaining the group's cohesion and effectiveness. Great fear exists on the part of those potentially criticizable that they may become victims of a more permanent alienation. Fear of such a permanent alienation serves to strengthen the bonds within the group.[85]

As this interpretation suggests, the particular efficacy of the isolation procedure, in which one member of a group is singled out for criticism, is that the anxiety of alienation is felt not simply by the individual criticized, but empathically by *all* those who observe. The ability of the many to identify with the anxiety of the one singled out provides the group motivation to accept Party-defined norms of behavior. Thus, whether in the intimate surroundings of the small group or the more massive struggle meeting where, before thousands, a dunce-capped

---

[85] Franz Schurmann, "Organization and Response in Communist China," *Annals of the American Academy of Political and Social Science*, CCCXXI (January, 1959), 57.

"object" is made to bow his head, the Party seeks to propagate new norms and limits of behavior for the entire population.[86]

The Party leadership also views institutionalized criticism techniques as a way of combating the deeply rooted tendency to rely upon hierarchical patterns of authority and nondelegation of responsibility which formed the core of the traditional social structure. We explored in Part I how these traditional attitudes and habits tended to produce both lateral and vertical social fragmentation; and Mao, apparently in an effort to combat their disintegrating effects, has sought ways to shift greater authority away from the individual leader to the group:

In some (of course not all) leading bodies it is the habitual practice for one individual to monopolize the conduct of affairs and to decide important problems. Solutions to important problems are decided not by Party committee meetings but by one individual, and membership in the Party committee has become nominal. Differences of opinion among committee members cannot be resolved and are left unresolved for a long time. Members of the Party committee maintain only formal, not real, unity among themselves. This situation must be changed. From now on, a sound system of Party committee meetings must be instituted in all leading bodies.[87]

The search for organizational forms to prevent monopolization of decision-making power, and the concomitant tendency to form cliques, is something that has been a constant theme in Party history. As Schurmann has so effectively detailed, the struggle over hierarchical or decentralized systems of control has been a recurrent issue in political conflicts between Mao and his opponents. Perhaps the best documented of these is Kao Kang's attempt to create an "independent kingdom" in Manchuria within the framework of the "one man management" system of economic organization.[88]

The common element running through attempts to counteract individual monopolization of authority has been the effort to institutionalize forms of critical face-to-face interaction both vertically and horizontally. As our TAT materials indicated (and as was discussed in detail in Part I), Chinese seem to have little expectation that there can be active and open communication, bargaining, and compromise among either peers or superiors and subordinates in the solution of social

[86] An incisive and balanced analysis of the effectiveness of criticism meetings as a device for controlling individual behavior, based on interviews with Chinese prisoners of war during the Korean conflict, will be found in Alexander L. George, *The Chinese Community Army in Action* (New York and London: Columbia University Press, 1967), pp. 95–111.

[87] Mao Tse-tung, "On Strengthening the Party Committee System," *SW*, IV, 267.

[88] See Schurmann, *Ideology and Organization in Communist China*, pp. 263–96.

problems. The Party, in essence, has had to resort to nonvoluntary forms of communication and criticism—which to the outsider appear grotesque in their formality, and to the participant both anxiety provoking and repugnant—in order to counteract the traditional tendency to avoid critical relationships because of expectations of status, or anxiety about conflict. Thus we find published Party materials spelling out for cadres in the most detailed manner the methods by which joint solution of work problems should be pursued: "Place problems on the table . . . whenever problems arise, call a meeting, place the problems on the table for discussion, take some decisions and the problems will be solved. If problems exist and are not placed on the table, they will remain unsolved for a long time and even drag on for years."[89] Simple communication habits are clearly not a part of the traditional Chinese style of wielding authority:

Exchange information. This means that members of a Party committee should keep each other informed and exchange views on matters that have come to their attention. This is of great importance in achieving a common language. . . . Ask your subordinates about matters you don't understand or don't know, and do not lightly express your approval or disapproval.[90]

Estimating the effectiveness of Party efforts to develop habits of criticism and openness to communication through organizational measures is a major research problem in itself; but perhaps it is worth letting one Chinese with bureaucratic experience under both the Nationalist and Communist governments indicate his reactions to the work style (tso-feng) of the two systems. One émigré we interviewed had been a field grade officer during the Nationalist era, and had remained on the mainland where he served as a training cadre in the People's Liberation Army. We asked him about the effects of institutionalized criticism on cadres' ability to cooperate among themselves:

[High level cadres] have criticism meetings among themselves: they talk about their problems and develop a sense of unity. The Communists are always encouraging people to talk, to express their opinions. Originally there is no enmity among people, and if you talk about problems you can prevent misunderstanding and can maintain unity in work. During the Nationalist era things were not this way; you would hold back your opinions and they would continuously get greater. The distance between you would get greater and eventually you would become enemies. . . . [Does criticism lead to hating the other person?] People would not dare to develop hatred, or they would not dare to express it. If they did, they would just receive more criticism or eventually be punished. [Which do you think is a better

[89] Mao Tse-tung, "Methods of Work in Party Committees," SW, IV, 377–78.
[90] Ibid.

method, the Communist or the Nationalist method?] During the last hundred years China has been very *luan,* people did not obey the laws. This method enables everyone to understand the law and obey it.

This revealing response suggests that simply the lack of communication among organizational peers has been a major factor contributing to social fragmentation in China, and that Communist efforts to force lateral interaction may have a salutary effect because the problems, doubts, and sense of distrust are brought out in the open and seen to be a good deal less fearsome than imagined.[91]

For a people whose traditions, and indeed whose personalities shaped by those traditions, have laid great emphasis on the notion of ascriptive and hierarchical authority and on the virtue of avoiding conflict, the ability to face up to interpersonal criticism among peers, and to establish peer unity based on "openness," is more easily said than done. But a recent pamphlet discussing the theory of "criticism–self-criticism" asks:

Does criticism really obstruct unity among comrades? Is "group harmony" (*yi-t'uan ho-ch'i*) really unity? Our answer is: "group harmony" is not genuine solidarity. . . . Why do we say this? This is because the solidarity of our Party, the solidarity of the working class and the laboring people, is a solidarity constructed on the basis of correct political principles and correct organizational principles. . . . If some people go against [the principles of Marxism and working class interests upon which our Party is based], then we must promote criticism of them. This sort of principled criticism can do away with various sorts of unproletarian thinking that obstructs solidarity, can enable everyone to have unified thinking and understanding. When thinking and understanding are in agreement then there will be no mutual barriers (*ko-ho*) and naturally solidarity will be strengthened. . . .

On the other hand, if we cast aside this weapon of criticism and self-criticism, and deal with things by way of the rotten attitude of self-ism (*tzu-yu-chu-yi*); if we only want things to be nice and tranquil on the surface, if we knowingly don't face up to problems, if we don't want to open our mouths, if we don't firmly struggle with the influence of all sorts of unproletarian thinking, this is just unprincipled solidarity. . . . If in relations among comrades differences of opinion are not discussed then these differences cannot be done away with, it will be difficult to avoid mutual suspicion, doubt, and even displeasure, the distance in thinking will become greater and greater, and ultimately even this sort of superficial peace and harmony (*ho-hao*) will be difficult to maintain. This sort of relationship among comrades naturally cannot be good, and there can hardly be any talk about so-called solidarity.[92]

[91] This interpretation is supported by William Hinton's description of mutual criticism between Party and non-Party cadres in a Shansi village. See *Fanshen,* Parts IV and V, pp. 319–475, and *passim.*

[92] Ying Lin, *P'i-p'ing ho Tzu-wo-p'i-p'ing Shih Wo-men ti Wu-ch'i* (Criticism and Self-criticism Is Our Weapon) (Peking: Kung-jen Ch'u-pan She, 1956), pp. 19–20.

Beyond forcing the open airing of differences of opinion and disputes among Party members, "criticism–self-criticism" also provides a forum where, on the basis of Party objectives of rapid social and economic change, new policies and norms of behavior can be disseminated rapidly and discussed. In the traditional society, where social goals and norms of behavior were relatively unchanging over time, there was perhaps little need to discuss formally organizational objectives and styles of behavior. But now that tradition has been branded as "feudal" and the rapid change of both social organization and personal *tso-feng* (work style) are seen by the Party as the basis for progress, formal and participatory discussion of new goals and new forms of behavior obviously helps to maintain the mutuality of expectation which is one of the bases of coordinated social activity. It is worth noting that the Party, in its efforts to promote critical interpersonal relations, has laid great stress on the "scientific" and "proletarian" nature of "criticism–self-criticism" and has presented the technique as a method for overcoming backwardness and promoting progress. As an article in a 1951 study pamphlet designed to propagate the "criticism–self-criticism" technique exhorts: "Raise up the weapon of progress."[93]

A final aspect of the integrating qualities of this formalized encouragement of criticism concerns dealings with authority. As we saw in Part I, authority's image was consistently seen by our respondents as manipulative and anxiety provoking; and the consequent effort to maintain a defensive distance between self and authority produced a plane of potential cleavage which under certain circumstances could fragment the relationship between superior and subordinate. The Party leaders have few illusions about the well-entrenched traditions concerning both the use of, and expectations about, authority prevalent in their society; but they have tried to deal with this potential weakness in the tie between leadership and mass, between superior and subordinate, by using the technique of forced criticism as both a linking and a control function. A post-"liberation" Party resolution concerning the development of "criticism–self-criticism" in the mass media reveals the leadership's efforts to construct new forms of control over lower level Party operatives:

---

[93] See K'ang Chuang, "Ch'ing-chi Ch'ien-chin ti Wu-ch'i" (Raise Up the Weapon of Progress), in *Tzen-yang Chin-hsing P'i-p'ing Yü Tzu-wo-p'i-p'ing* (How to Promote Criticism and Self-criticism) (T'ien-ching: Ta-chung Shu-tien, 1951).

Because today the war on the mainland has been concluded, our Party already directs national political power; and hence errors and shortcomings in our work can easily harm the interests of the broad masses. And because the position and prestige of those directing political power has been raised high, it is very easy to produce feelings of arrogance, and both within and without the Party to prohibit or suppress criticism. With the creation of these new circumstances, if we do not develop criticism and self-criticism in an open and timely fashion concerning the short-comings and errors of the economic structures and mass organizations of our Party's People's Government, we will not be able to complete the task of constructing a new China because of the poisonous evil of bureaucratism.[94]

The techniques of mass criticism that were developed following "liberation" were well-grounded in Party and army traditions that had evolved through trial and error from the days in the Chingkang Mountains. As Mao noted just before the takeover: "The masses of soldiers should have the right to expose the errors and misdeeds of bad elements among the cadres. We should be confident that soldiers will cherish all good and comparatively good cadres. Moreover, the soldiers should have the right, when necessary, to nominate those whom they trust from their own ranks. . . ."[95]

The organizational devices for promoting "mass line" criticism of those with the authority to implement Party policies, however, have had constantly changing form and emphasis. Perhaps most revealing of the two-sided "control" and "integration" quality of Party-stimulated criticism of its lower level operatives was the 1956–57 "Hundred Flowers" period of *ta-ming ta-fang* (blooming and contending). Chou En-lai set the initial emphasis of this period by indicating that the Party leadership hoped to develop new forms of cooperation between Party and intelligentsia, "in a way that will stimulate their activity and enable them to apply their energies more fully to serve our great work of socialist construction. . . ."[96]

This relatively positive emphasis on enlisting the support of the intellectuals shifted in a negative direction, however, after Khrushchev's speech denouncing Stalin and the subsequent turmoil in Hun-

[94] Chung-kuo Kung-Ch'an-tang Chung-yang Wei-yüan-hui, *Kuan-yü tsai Pao-chih K'an-wu-shang Chan-k'ai P'i-p'ing ho Tzu-wo-p'i-p'ing ti Chüeh-ting* (Resolutions Concerning the Promotion of Criticism and Self-criticism in Newspapers and Publications) (Shanghai: Chieh-fang She, 1950), pp. 1–2.

[95] Mao Tse-tung, "The Democratic Movement in the Army," *SW*, IV, 191.

[96] Chou En-lai, "On the Question of Intellectuals," trans. in *Communist China, 1955–1959: Policy Documents with Analysis* (Cambridge, Mass.: Harvard University Press, 1962), p. 192.

gary and Poland. As revealed in a series of important Party documents published during 1956 and early 1957,[97] the emphasis shifted to one of "rectifying" abuses of power by Party cadres. As has been well documented,[98] the top Party leadership encouraged "the people," and largely the intellectual community, to express their grievances against those who *applied* Party policies. That this criticism in time began to exceed the Party-defined limit of acceptance of China's new "socialist order" should not obscure the fact that Party leaders were groping for some institutional formula through which they could limit cadre abuses of authority.[99] The "Hundred Flowers" period was not the first attempt in this direction, nor was it the last, as is obvious in such subsequent developments as the post-"Great Leap" promotion of "congresses of poor and lower middle peasants" and the associated "socialist education campaign" and "Four Clearance" (*szu-ch'ing*) movement.

It should not be ignored, however, that the Party leadership has consistently found itself caught in the self-created *mao-tun* of seeking to encourage criticism of those who apply Party policies, while attempting to hold immune from mass criticism the top decision-making authorities who are ultimately responsible for the policies themselves.

That the Party has faced great difficulties—many of which are of its own creation—in its efforts to develop a new level of social integration based on critical relationships between peers and within the authority-subordinate tie, should not lead us to ignore the fact that basically the Chinese revolution, like all others, represents a conflict over deeply entrenched attitudes, social values, and emotional concerns. "After the establishment of the dictatorship of the proletariat, even when the exploiting classes are eliminated, when small producer economy has been replaced by collective economy and the socialist society has been founded, certain rotten, poisonous ideological survivals of the old society may still remain in peoples' minds for a very long time."[100] These "poisonous ideological survivals" should be made explicit, both because they reveal the existence of many of the attitudes which we explored in Part I of this analysis, and because they indicate in part the dimen-

[97] These have been reproduced in *Communist China, 1955–1959*, chaps. iii, v, vi.

[98] See Roderick MacFarquhar, *The Hundred Flowers Campaign and the Chinese Intellectuals* (New York: Praeger, 1960), and Theodore Chen, *Thought Reform of the Chinese Intellectuals* (Hong Kong: Hong Kong University Press, 1960).

[99] And as well, perhaps, to develop a way of focusing popular resentments about Party programs on the operatives rather than the policy makers.

[100] "On the Historical Experience of the Dictatorship of the Proletariat," *People's Daily*, April 5, 1956, trans. in *CB*, No. 402 (July 25, 1956), p. 3.

sions of the difficulty which this revolutionary elite faces in trying to create a new political order.

Basic to the problem of attitude and behavioral change is the fact that traditional attitudes toward, and about the use of, authority are still deeply rooted in the personalities of the Chinese. As our attitude survey data indicate, authority is still seen as highly personalized, and hierarchical in quality. Despite Party efforts to shift the weight of authority onto ideological principles, and to play down personal ties, recent studies have indicated clearly that cadres within the state system are highly rank conscious and seek to create categories of expertise or experience which will give them hierarchical status within the governmental system.[101]

Despite Party efforts to stimulate mass criticism of its cadres, Chinese popular attitudes that authority should not be criticized, or that this is done at great personal risk, remain strong. Party leaders will frequently voice the opinion that cadres' unwillingness to accept mass criticism is simply an evil "bourgeois" remnant from the old society; but what information exists—and all that is known from Western studies of the "authoritarianism" of the working class— makes it seem extremely unlikely that Party efforts to recruit "progressive" cadres from among the workers and peasants will bring about much change. As one peasant revealed in describing his election to a position of leadership on a production team:

Fu Hai-tsao's place was to fall vacant because he was going to be elected deputy labor leader of the labor group for vegetable cultivation, and, besides, he had been proposed for election to the management of the labor brigade. So *I was asked: "Will you stand?" I said: "I'll stand. But only if I really am going to be elected, and if the voting is unanimous. I don't want to have any discussion about it. Either people have confidence in me or they don't have confidence in me.* If they have, then I shall be happy to have their trust and I shall do my best to be of service." Well, the meeting was held and I was elected, unanimously.[102]

Mainland newspapers continually reveal that Party efforts to foster criticism of those in lower level leadership positions meet obstructionist tactics among the cadres:

[101] This tendency of state cadres to create elaborate hierarchical categories, and to be highly status conscious, has been explored in a very revealing article, based on interviews with refugee cadres, by A. Doak Barnett: "Social Stratification and Aspects of Personnel Management in the Chinese Communist Bureaucracy," *China Quarterly*, No. 28 (October–December, 1966), pp. 8–39.

[102] Jan Myrdal, *Report from a Chinese Village* (London: Heinemann, 1965), p. 259. Emphasis added.

There are certain leadership cadres in our party who are still unable to comprehend the great significance of criticism and self-criticism in reality. . . . As soon as they meet with some success in work, they become vain and complacent. Gradually, they acquire the habit of detesting the criticism of their work by others. Some of them have even become so degraded as to practice the suppression of criticism and the framing of charges against the critics. . . .[103]

And at times the mainland press has carried reports of responsible officeholders who have even been dismissed for suppressing criticism.[104]

The opposite side of the coin of the unwillingness of those with authority to accept criticism is the continued reluctance of those in subordinate positions to be critical of their superiors.[105] Part of this reluctance seems attributable to the relative ease with which resentful cadres can "retaliate" against (*pao-fu*) those who subject them to criticism by a variety of subtle and indirect administrative measures. And the Party has proven itself either unwilling or unable to protect those who criticize. The constant undertone of hortatory articles in the press urging peasants to be "masters" (*chu-jen-weng*) in "People's China," and continuing efforts to devise organizational structures such as the previously mentioned "congresses of poor and lower middle peasants," seem to run afoul of the deeply entrenched anxiety about facing up to authority which we explored in Part I.[106]

It is interesting to note that our attitude survey data indicate rather mixed results concerning the matter of criticizing authority. As Figure 11 indicates, while the "conservative" Chinese are somewhat less likely than contemporary Americans to deny that criticism of superiors should be avoided, their average response is still on the "disagree" side. As indicated earlier, however, we found in the interview elaborations of

[103] "Firm Struggle Must Be Waged Against Acts of Suppression of Criticism," *People's Daily* editorial, September 11, 1954, trans. in *SCMP*, No. 911 (October 20, 1954), pp. 22–24.

[104] See, for example, "East China Communications Department Director Huang Yi-feng Expelled from Party for Suppression of Criticism," *CFJP*, Shanghai, January 19, 1953, trans. in *SCMP*, No. 502 (January 29, 1953), pp. 1–5.

[105] As James Townsend has noted in an analysis of Party-sponsored elections in China, "the masses tended to avoid criticizing candidates and to cite only their good points; moreover, they compared candidates on such grounds as cultural level, literacy, and number of children rather than on their ideology and political consciousness." *Political Participation in Communist China*, pp. 136–37.

Indeed, after the 1957 experience in which the Party promised to protect those who criticized its cadres, only to turn around and launch a vigorous 'antirightist' campaign against the critics, it seems likely that "the masses" have considerable doubt about Party *intentions* to protect them.

[106] See, for example, "Arouse the Enthusiasm of Poor and Lower Middle Peasants for Being the Master of the House," *NFJP*, Canton, October 14, 1964, trans. in *SCMP*, No. 3361 (December 21, 1964), pp. 4–6.

their responses that Chinese would constantly juxtapose a normative belief that superiors should be criticized with an affirmation of the attitude that criticism of superiors was a dangerous business, that it was something to be avoided, and if done at all should be carried out only in a "friendly" (*ho-ch'i*) or subservient manner. Inasmuch as this interview sample was a highly literate group, many of whom had had experience in positions of authority, it is reasonable to assume that

FIGURE 11. Responses to the Attitude Survey Statement, "Although Criticizing the Thoughts and Suggestions of Our Superiors Is Useful for Improving Work, It Can Lead to Much Trouble, and Hence Is Best Avoided"

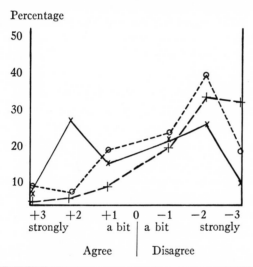

Symbol	Group Tested	Mean	Standard Deviation	N
+ ---	American males	−1.49	1.65	269
O ----	"Conservative" Chinese males	−0.90	1.85	136
X ———	"Communist" Chinese males	−0.25	1.88	32

semiliterate peasants would have a good deal less self-confidence in facing up to their superiors.

Efforts to develop critical integrative processes have foundered on more than just the traditional image of authority and of one's relation to it. As we detailed in Part I, the problem of controlling aggressive impulses has been a constant theme in the Chinese political culture: the tendency to alternate between extremes of apparent *ho-p'ing*, where all critical or aggressive impulses are kept below the surface, and the bursting forth of *luan*, of uncontrolled attacks. One finds this alternation clearly revealed in Party criticism of the manner in which "criticism–self-criticism" has been developed.

Mao's notable 1957 speech "On the Correct Handling of Contradictions Among the People" recalled early Party experience in the development of ideological struggle: "At one time in waging inner-Party struggle, the 'left' doctrinaires used the method of 'ruthless struggle and merciless blows.' "[107] And as Liu Shao-ch'i elaborated:

> Some comrades think that the more savage the intra-Party struggle, the better; the more serious the questions raised, the better; the more mistakes discovered, the more terms used, the more blame laid on others, the sharper the criticism, the more severe and rude the method and attitude of criticism, the better. . . . And if the words are louder, the expressions more violent, and the fangs longer . . . they consider this better and the "most revolutionary thing possible." In the intra-Party struggle and self-criticism, they do not endeavor to do what is proper, do not weigh their opinions, or stop when they have gone far enough; they struggle on with no limit.[108]

Liu went on to observe, however, that this undisciplined, or what he termed "unprincipled," struggle burst forth from a situation of apparent organizational peace:

> A formal kind of peace and unity have been manifest in the Party, for many comrades ordinarily do not dare to speak or criticize. But once the continued concealment of contradictions becomes impossible, once the situation becomes serious and the mistakes are exposed, they criticize and fight recklessly; opposition, schism, and organizational confusion develop in the Party, and it is difficult to reestablish order.[109]

Fear of offending other people's "face," of provoking their hatred or retaliation, and unwillingness to expose the shortcomings of others for fear of having one's own shortcomings exposed: these are constant themes in Party exhortations designed to break down enduring attitudes toward social relations which have made for the enduring polarity between *ho-p'ing* and *luan*.[110]

Mao has clearly spelled out the attitudes which he feels are necessary for establishing criticism as part of the political process, and at the same time keeping it within disciplined limits:

---

[107] *Communist China, 1955–1959*, p. 278.

[108] Liu Shao-ch'i, "On the Intra-Party Struggle," trans. in Boyd Compton, *Mao's China: Party Reform Documents, 1942–1944* (Seattle: University of Washington Press, 1952), p. 208.

[109] *Ibid.*, p. 214.

[110] See, for example, Wu Chiang, "Chih-shih-fen-tzu ti P'i-p'ing yü Tzu-wo-p'i-p'ing Wen-t'i" (Problems of Criticism and Self-criticism among the Intellectuals), *Hsüeh-hsi*, II, No. 9 (1950), 20–23.

First, "learn from past mistakes to avoid future ones," and second, "Cure the sickness to save the patient." The mistakes of the past must be exposed without sparing anyone's sensibilities; it is necessary to analyze and criticize what was bad in the past with a scientific attitude so that work in the future will be done more carefully and done better. . . . We can never succeed if we just let ourselves go and lash out (*luan-ta*) at him. . . .[111]

And again:

In 1942 we worked out the formula "unity–criticism–unity" to describe [the] democratic method of resolving contradictions among the people. To elaborate, this means to start off with a desire for unity and resolve contradictions through criticism or struggle so as to achieve a new unity on a new basis. . . . The essential thing is to start with a desire for unity. Without this subjective desire for unity, once the struggle starts it is liable to get out of hand (*tou-luan*).[112]

In sum, the image of a new political order, integrated through critical interpersonal processes and active participation—the whole set of elements of the Maoist formula for attaining an activist and nationally integrated society which we have elaborated above—provides the blueprint; but the limited evidence that does exist suggests that traditional attitudes firmly rooted in the personalities of adult Chinese raised before "liberation" continue to hamper efforts at social change.

ATTITUDE CHANGE AND CONTINUITY AMONG THE YOUNGER GENERATION

If the attitudes that Mao feels should be "remolded" in building a new social order in China have been slow to change among adults, what can be said for those of the younger generation socialized at least in part in "People's China"? Here we return to an evaluation of our attitude survey materials, which were gathered from a group of approximately thirty young émigrés of largely "bourgeois" background, from mainland China. This is obviously a pitifully small—and in terms of social background, unrepresentative—group from which to make interpretations. And it need not be overstressed that our findings here are highly provisional. But the differences that are revealed when we compare this group's attitudes to those of their elders are all the more interesting given their émigré and "bourgeois" status!

Perhaps the most striking aspect of attitude change in this group is related to Party efforts to break down the particularistic loyalties which characterized the traditional society, and to shift allegiance to

---

[111] Mao Tse-tung, "Rectify the Party's Style of Work," *SW*, III, 50.

[112] Mao Tse-tung, "On the Correct Handling of Contradictions among the People," *Communist China, 1955–1959*, p. 278.

Party and nation. As is clearly indicated by the attitude distribution in Figure 7,[113] in response to the statement that family life is more important than the nation, this younger group has on the average shifted quite remarkably in the direction of seeing the nation as more important than the family. The high standard deviation, however, and the percentage distributions themselves, reveal that the group is polarized, with over 30 per cent in strong agreement about the importance of nation over family, and another third of the group firmly identifying with the family. That young refugees should identify with their families is not surprising, but it does seem a remarkable indication of attitude change that so many of this younger group identify with the nation from which they have fled. This indication of a weakening in the role of the family is reinforced by the TAT data. In Table 44 it is clear that the younger Chinese are more inclined to see family relations as conflictive, and less likely to embody cooperation in the future, than their elders. In sum, it does seem that the Party has been rather successful in aligning the issue of nationalism to its cause, and has a considerable fund of potential support from the younger generation, from those whom they now seek to designate as "revolutionary successors" (*chieh-pan jen*).

Concerning attitudes toward authority, if we review the data in Figure 8,[114] we find that this young group is more consistent in accepting a dominant and personalized authority than is the older group. Their attitudes toward criticism of superiors,[115] in addition, suggest that they are if anything less emotionally willing to criticize those with authority than are their more traditional elders. This interpretation will perhaps help to explain the data from TAT Card IV, in Table 44 on page 291, in which the "Communist" group sees somewhat less conflict with superiors than does the older group, but also slightly more cooperation in the future. It does seem that this younger group continues to see authority as highly personalized and immune to criticism.

Concerning dealings with peers, one finds, in Figure 10 (p. 304), that the younger group has shifted away from the polarized attitudes of their elders, and exhibits a unimodal distribution skewed in the direction of criticizing peers in a manner rather similar to the American sample. This would imply that criticism of their peers has become

[113] See p. 277.
[114] See p. 281.
[115] See Figure 11, p. 335.

more fully integrated into their view of social relations. The data from TAT Card I, summarized in Table 44, indicates that while this young group is as likely to see conflict outcomes as their elders, they have a slightly higher expectation that cooperation will be maintained in the future.

When we look at the attitudes of this young group toward dealings with friends,[116] however, we find an even more pessimistic set of expectations about developing friendships than in the more conservative older group. Given the stress that the Party has placed on breaking down friendship ties in favor of "comradely" relations within organizations under its control,[117] it would appear that the Party has been more than a little successful in weakening the ties to friends and family which it finds threatening to its goal of national political unity.

An over-all interpretation of these data within the context of our focus on problems of social integration is not easily made; but the general impression is one of young people with weakened ties to friends and family, yet grasping for new social commitments and identity within the context of Party-directed tasks of building a new nation. That such attitude shifts as we have seen in these limited data have been found among young émigrés—among those who were explicitly singled out for their "bad" class backgrounds and in many cases denied access to education and a career consonant with their social skills and expectations—makes their plight all the more poignant, for they clearly have moved in some of the attitude directions that the Party has encouraged.

The manner in which the areas of attitude continuity and change which we see in this one group of younger Chinese relate to problems of social integration in Communist China, however, becomes most meaningful within the context of the recent development of the Cultural Revolution. This fantastic political confrontation with the "four olds" (*szu-chiu*) of China's enduring traditional "customs and habits, ideology and culture," and the manner in which Mao Tse-tung has sought to pit "revolutionary" young people against their "revisionist" elders in a surrogate class (or generational?) struggle, will help us to attempt a concluding analysis of the extent of cultural change and social integration in China today.

[116] See Figure 9, p. 299.
[117] This Party effort has been discussed in detail in the works of Vogel and Barnett cited earlier.

CONCLUSION: ONE PERSPECTIVE ON THE GREAT PROLETARIAN CULTURAL REVOLUTION

> In his recent instruction Chairman Mao has said:
> There is no fundamental clash of interests within the
> working class. Under the dictatorship of the prole-
> tariat, there is no reason whatsoever for the working
> class to split into two big irreconcilable organizations.
> —from a *Red Flag* editorial, July, 1967

The factional conflict and sporadic violence which have convulsed China since the summer of 1966 call into question many of our assumptions about the degree of national unity and political centralization which the Communists apparently had achieved after nearly two decades of control on the mainland. The full meaning of these events, however, is so profound and all encompassing in its implications regarding the changes that have, and have not, occurred in Chinese society in recent years that no one interpretation is likely to account for more than a facet of the whole. Furthermore, many of the data that would be necessary for a full understanding of Mao's efforts to "prevent a restoration of capitalism" in China, and to keep the Communist party from "changing its color," have yet to be made public. Hence, with the full awareness that the following remarks can be considered only provisional and incomplete, we nonetheless want to conclude this analysis of Communist Party attempts to restructure and unite Chinese society according to the Maoist conception with some hypotheses on the meaning of the Cultural Revolution for the matter of political integration.

To at least one seasoned observer of the Chinese political scene, the public conflict which erupted on the mainland in the late summer of 1966 is yet another bursting out of that condition of *luan* which has been so much a part of the rhythm of Chinese social life: "There is no real civil war. What is happening has happened many times before in the course of Chinese history. It is war welling up from below. It is disintegration."[118] Whatever general characterization is given to the present situation, it is clear that the basic issue of political integration has been brought to the fore; and Mao's conception of how "People's China" should be restructured and driven forward to modernity has been called into question.

[118] *China News Analysis,* Hong Kong, No. 667 (July 7, 1967), p. 1.

Probing the meaning of the Cultural Revolution as it affects the matter of social integration requires analysis at two distinct levels. It is clear that preceding the public manifestation of conflict in China, beginning with the mass Red Guard rallies in August of 1966, there was a breakdown in the ability of the top Party leaders to cooperate among themselves.[119] Subsequently, as a result of this breakdown in relations among the country's leaders, public conflict was initiated and expanded in scope, in time coming to encompass the most basic levels of social organization, and giving an increasing quality of regional fragmentation and local chaos to mainland political life. The following analysis will proceed within the framework of these two levels of the Cultural Revolution.

In the light of recent events it appears that at least since 1957—probably beginning with the failure of Mao's Hundred Flowers policy for dealing with the intellectuals—a series of fundamental policy miscalculations increasingly called into question the legitimacy of Mao's "revolutionary" style of leadership. The great costs of the dispute with the Soviet Union, the failure of the Great Leap Forward, and more recent foreign policy misadventures in the underdeveloped world undoubtedly created great strains among China's rulers, forcing a critical review of the country's most basic foreign and domestic policies. Yet for reasons that are only now becoming apparent, these tensions went well beyond dispute over specific policy issues; they shattered what so many observers of the mainland scene had come to see as a particular capacity of the Long March generation of leaders to resolve disputes with considerable give and take.

The critical factor contributing to this breakdown of the Party leadership seems to have been the issue of succession, of who in time will attain Mao's position as leader of the Party and nation. More exactly, it seems that Mao, in his uncompromising determination to see his own style of leadership and authority maintained despite the resistance of long-time colleagues, first reacted to criticism of his policies as attacks on his leading role; and then he himself raised the conflict to

---

[119] Several recent analyses have made important contributions to our understanding of the erosion of elite cohesiveness preceding the more recent period of public conflict. See, for example, Charles Neuhauser, "The Chinese Communist Party in the 1960's: Prelude to the Cultural Revolution," *China Quarterly*, No. 32 (October–December, 1967), pp. 3–36; Richard Baum and Frederick C. Teiwes, *Ssu-Ch'ing: The Socialist Education Movement of 1962–1966* (Berkeley: Center for Chinese Studies, University of California, China Research Monograph No. 2, 1968).

the level of status relations by attempting to designate a new "close comrade in arms" to implement his policies and then carry them on after his death.

That the Cultural Revolution has grown from a breakdown in elite relations, and embodies at its core the succession issue, is suggested by one of those ambiguous "esoteric" or Aesopian phrases found in an important political document which is as tantalizing in its implication as it is vague in its full meaning. In one of the major articles of the 1964 polemical exchanges with the Soviet Union occurs a detailed analysis of the conditions which Mao, or those writing in support of the Maoist position, saw as basic to maintaining proper revolutionary leadership in China.[120] Among the conditions specified for those who would be "revolutionary successors" (*chieh-pan jen*) to Party leadership are the following two:

> They [revolutionary successors] must be proletarian statesmen capable of uniting and working with the overwhelming majority. Not only must they unite with those who agree with them, *they must also be good at uniting with those who disagree and even with those who formerly opposed them and have since been proved wrong.* But they must especially watch out for careerists and conspirators like Khrushchev and prevent such bad elements from usurping the leadership of the Party and the government *at any level.*
>
> They must be models in applying the Party's democratic centralism, must master the method of leadership based on the principle of "from the masses, to the masses," and must cultivate a democratic style and be good at listening to the masses. *They must not be despotic like Khrushchev and violate the Party's centralism, make surprise attacks on comrades or act arbitrarily and dictatorially.*[121]

With the added clarity of hindsight, and on the basis of information subsequently revealed in the mainland press and in Red Guard newspapers, it seems that a likely interpretation of this ambiguous passage would run something as follows: Increasingly during the first five years of the decade of the sixties Mao found himself unable to translate his own will into implemented policy decisions. As a result of his establishment of what Red Guard newspapers have termed "first and second lines" of leadership within the Politburo's Standing Committee after 1958, Mao found himself increasingly cut off from the operational machinery of the Party, and saw his general policy directives distorted

---

[120] These measures were seen as necessary for preventing a "revisionist" usurpation of Party leadership such as had occurred, they said, in the case of Khrushchev's leadership of the Communist Party in the Soviet Union.

[121] The Editorial Departments of the *People's Daily* and *Red Flag*, "On Krushchev's Phony Communism and Its Historial Lessons," July 14, 1964, trans. in *CB*, No. 737 (July 17, 1964).

in application.[122] This loss of influence over the policy implementation process must have enraged Mao,[123] and presented him not only with a threat to the implementation of his personal will, but also with a situation in which he saw the Party apparatus as increasingly bureaucratized and self-serving, full of "careerists and conspirators like Khrushchev." In a sense he must have seen the Party and governmental system turning into just the type of state apparatus that he had spent a lifetime working to destroy in the struggle for power with the Nationalists.

What is more, Mao evidently saw the cooperative-collectivist style of leadership, with openness of communication not only "vertically" between the different levels of the political system but more significantly in relations among his closest associates in the Party's leading bodies,[124] giving way to self-serving "revisionism"—cliquishness and the desire to protect personal bases of power in various governmental organizations.[125] This seems to be part of the burden of his remarks that "revolutionary successors" must be capable of "uniting with those who disagree and even with those who formerly opposed them and have since been proved wrong," and his warning that "careerists and conspirators like Khrushchev" must be prevented from "usurping the leadership of the Party and government at any level."

[122] See these complaints in a speech attributed to Mao translated in *Current Scene* (Hong Kong), V, No. 9 (May 31, 1967), 6.

I would assume that Red Guard assertions that Mao was removed from the office of state chairman in December, 1958, are not accurate, but represent subsequent efforts by his supporters to undermine the position of his opponents. See a report of these charges in the *New York Times,* January 6, 1967, p. 1.

[123] A Red Guard publication reported that Mao complained at a Central Committee meeting of October, 1966, that Liu Shao-ch'i and Teng Hsiao-p'ing had treated him "as if I were their dead parent at a funeral." Cited in *China Topics* (London), No. 421 (March 10, 1967), pp. 1, 8.

[124] Mao's frustration at the distortion of "vertical" communication flows within the political system, first revealed in the *Kung-tso T'ung-hsün,* has been discussed in my article, "Communication Patterns and the Chinese Revolution," pp. 108–9; and in Neuhauser, "Chinese Communist Party in the 1960's," p. 22 and *passim.*

More recent attacks on P'eng Teh-huai have asserted that he "either refused to transmit the directives of the Party Central Committee and Chairman Mao or distorted and emasculated them or obeyed them publicly while disobeying them in secret." He is also said to have "maintained illicit connections" with Soviet leaders: "In 1955, 1957, and 1959, taking advantage of his many trips abroad, P'eng Teh-huai made secret deals with Khrushchev." ("Principal Crimes of P'eng Teh-huai, Big Ambitionist and Schemer," Canton *Ching-kang-shan* and *Kuang-tung Wen-i Chan-pao* [Chingkang Mountains, and Kwang-tung Literary and Art Combat Bulletin], September 5, 1967, trans. in *SCMP,* No. 4047 [October 25, 1967], pp. 5, 8.)

[125] See Neuhauser, "Chinese Communist Party in the 1960's," pp. 17–18 and *passim* for a discussion of Party cadre efforts to prevent "rectification" or supervision by mass organizations during the early 1960's.

A more specific but conjectural interpretation of these last two intriguing phrases may be advanced in the light of evidence made public as a result of the Cultural Revolution struggle. Open attacks on Liu Shao-ch'i in the spring of 1967 assert that in 1962 he defended P'eng Teh-huai for his criticisms of the Great Leap Forward at the 1959 Lushan Central Committee Plenum. Liu is also said to have "openly tried to reverse the verdict on P'eng Teh-huai at the enlarged Work Conference of the Party's Central Committee held in January 1962," and to have encouraged P'eng to write a defense of his own position which was circulated just before the Tenth Plenum in the fall of that year.[126] If these charges contain an element of fact, they suggest that Liu challenged Mao's authority during 1962—or at least that Mao construed Liu's actions as a direct attack on him. And while the Tenth Plenum of September, 1962, reaffirmed the leading role of the "thought of Mao Tse-tung" and attacked "modern revisionism," Liu evidently had sufficient power, unlike the hapless P'eng, to defend himself against an immediate Maoist counterattack.

It may not have been until 1964 that Mao felt he had sufficient backing to counterchallenge Liu successfully, and this he may have done indirectly or "esoterically" in the context of the movement for "cultivating revolutionary successors" launched in the summer of that year—with Liu, at that time still designated as *the* successor to Mao's leadership position, being attacked by implication.[127]

In the 1964 article from which we have been quoting, Mao seems to offer what is almost a *mea culpa* for his past policy misjudgments, but in the context of an attack on Liu for his unwillingness to "unite" or cooperate with him, and for his "factional" criticism at the Tenth Plenum: ". . . [revolutionary successors, that is, Liu] must also be good at uniting with those who disagree and even with those who formerly opposed them and have since been proved wrong [that is, Mao], . . . They must not be despotic like Khrushchev and violate the Party's centralism, make surprise attacks on comrades [that is, Mao] or act arbitrarily and dictatorially."

---

[126] See the *Red Flag* editorial, "From the Defeat of P'eng Teh-huai to the Bankruptcy of China's Khrushchev," trans. in *Peking Review,* No. 34 (August 18, 1967), pp. 18–20, 35.

[127] The Baum and Teiwes study, *Ssu-Ch'ing,* pp. 26–46, strongly suggests that by mid-1964 Mao's counterchallenge was being mounted on a broad front: policy for the "Socialist Education Campaign" was adjusted in a more radical direction; the army was put forward as the model political organization to be emulated in the "Learn from the PLA" campaign (thus indirectly slighting the Party); and extensive efforts were made to promote the study of "Chairman Mao's Thought."

Inasmuch as Liu is now referred to in the public mainland press as "China's Khrushchev," it seems not unlikely that it is he whom Mao had in mind in 1964 when he asserted that revolutionary successors "must especially watch out for careerists and conspirators *like Khrushchev* and prevent such bad elements from usurping the leadership of the Party and government *at any level*" (that is, even in the top leadership).[128]

If these tentative interpretations are correct,[129] it seems likely that by signaling, in 1964, that he was dissatisfied with Liu's status as his successor, Mao may have stimulated a premature succession struggle in which various leaders began to vie among themselves for Mao's blessing as *the* revolutionary successor.[130] Whether Mao did this delib-

---

[128] By early 1965 Mao apparently was even more explicit in identifying the focus of his displeasure when it was noted, in the "Twenty-three Articles" of the socialist education campaign, that "there are some people . . . even in the work of . . . Central Committee departments, who oppose socialism." See *ibid.,* p. 37.

Since this analysis was first written in the spring of 1967, additional material has been published on the mainland which seems to confirm the interpretation we have given to these documents of 1964 and 1965. A *Red Flag* editorial of August, 1967, notes:

"The document *Some Current Problems Raised in the Socialist Education Movement in the Rural Areas,* referred to as the 23-article document, worked out under the personal guidance of Chairman Mao in January 1965, put it clearly for the first time: 'The main target of the present movement is those persons within the Party who are in authority and are taking the capitalist road.' China's Khrushchov [that is, Liu Shao-ch'i] is the one in the highest position among the persons mentioned here." ("Completely Smash the Bourgeois Headquarters," trans. in *Peking Review,* No. 33 [August 11, 1967], p. 7.)

[129] The major qualification to this interpretation centers about the subsequent "responsibility" given by Mao to P'eng Chen and Liu Shao-ch'i to initiate the Cultural Revolution. If Mao was at odds with these men, why did he "rely" on them to implement his policies? Unfortunately, we know so little about decision-making processes at the top of the Chinese political system, or of the actual balance of forces that may have existed among the top leaders, that we can do no more than to speculate: Did Mao attempt to "test" or "entrap" these men? Did he seek to play one off against the others, and one by one remove them from power? Was he only *primus inter pares,* finding it necessary to compromise, finally turning to the PLA for support when other methods had failed? Or was there a more complex process of interaction in which Mao's efforts to restructure power relations in the Party, army, and government provoked resistance and "coup" attempts against his leadership faction? Such questions remain to be clarified.

[130] In several public statements during late 1964, Mao disclosed that death and succession were very much on his mind. See Edgar Snow's interview with Mao, *New Republic* (February 27, 1965), pp. 17–23.

The succession issue, it seems to this writer, provides the most convincing explanation for the largely unanticipated fragmentation of the Long March generation of Party leaders, and for the curious discrepancy between the virulent attacks made on various "revisionist" leaders and the often absurd and abstract errors with which they have been charged. If grounds other than a personal power struggle existed for attack, would they not be used to mobilize support?

As we suggested in Part I, on p. 308 above, the authority system which traditionally characterized the Chinese polity has historically proved itself to be vulnerable to the

erately as a way of breaking down his opposition, or as a strategy for entrapping his rivals by making them expose their ambitiousness prematurely, is something about which we can only speculate.

In addition, we can only infer to what degree it was Mao's own obduracy in continuing to insist on policies which had proven unworkable in practice, or his overweening belief that only his "thought" could guide China into the modern world, which provoked the opposition of long-time comrades.[131]

While it may be some time before we know with greater certainty the reality which lies behind these documentary materials, they do make it clear that cooperative relations among China's leaders were seriously compromised by late 1964. The main purpose of this interpretive exercise has been to detail the extent to which the Maoist *image* of a new style of leadership—of unity, cooperation, and openness in communication both within the Party and between mass and elite, of critical checks on lower level cadres wielding Party authority, in short, the set of leadership concepts which we explored in Part II—gradually fell by the wayside during the 1960's. What is more, serious factionalism, seen earlier in the purgings of Kao Kang and P'eng Teh-huai, once again threatened Party unity, as is now revealed in the attacks on P'eng Chen for having created an "independent kingdom" in the Peking Party committee.

As well, Mao evidently felt that his "revolutionary" goals were being threatened by a Party and governmental system increasingly resorting to what he interpreted as "traditional" misuses of authority. This would seem to be the burden of continuing attacks on Liu Shao-ch'i for having propagated a doctrine of "slavish obedience" to Party authority, and for seeking to train cadres to be "docile tools" of the Party.[132] Such phrases certainly echo Mao's aversion to the dependency orientation toward authority which we explored above; and they may be additional indication of Mao's rage at those who sought to put the Party above his own authority.

Liu is also accused of wanting to play down the promotion of "class

---

matter of succession or transfer of power. It would seem that the Cultural Revolution has once again exposed this vulnerability, and the endurance of traditional political attitudes and behavior.

[131] The role that the propagation of "the thought of Mao Tse-tung" has played as an issue in the conflict between Mao and Liu is analyzed in an interesting article by Cheng Chu-yuan, "The Root of China's Cultural Revolution: The Feud Between Mao Tse-tung and Liu Shao-ch'i," *Orbis,* XI, No. 4 (Winter, 1968), 1160–78.

[132] See, for example, "Growing Mass Movement to Criticize and Repudiate the Book on 'Self-Cultivation' of Communists," *Peking Review,* No. 17 (April 21, 1967), pp. 14–15.

struggle," the criticism and confrontation of the enemies of change within China.[133] Mao apparently feared that his efforts to make mediated conflict and criticism an integral part of China's new political order were threatened by those men in power who, in his opinion, were still burdened with the "four olds" of the traditional culture. He saw their influence leading in time to a "restoration of capitalism," that is, a return to government by a narrow and privileged elite such as had characterized China at an earlier stage of her social development.

In any event, Mao and certain close supporters responded to what they saw as a challenge to their influence and style of leadership by turning for mass support to the first generation fully educated under China's new socialist order.[134] Mao's massive mobilization of the youth of the country into the Red Guard organizations during the summer and fall of 1966 has some of the quality of a reaching out for supporters wherever he could find them, as well as an effort to deny his opponents a source of organizational manpower; but it also seems to be a form of political combat in continuity with what we have detailed earlier as Mao's style of political action: the belief that change is most effectively promoted through active participation and "struggle," and the tendency to check those with operational political power by subjecting them to criticism from below.[135] And, as appears with such clarity in 1967, Mao as early as the summer of 1964 publicized his intention to rebuild the revolutionary vitality of the Chinese Communist Party through renewed storms of mass struggle which would mobilize a new generation of "activist" cadres: "Successors to [lead the] revolutionary cause of the proletariat come forward in mass struggles and are tempered in the great storms of revolution. It is essential to test and know cadres and choose and train successors in the long course of mass struggle."[136]

From a psychological perspective the Cultural Revolution has the

---

[133] See "Betrayal of Proletarian Dictatorship Is Essential Element in the Book on 'Self-Cultivation,'" by the editorial departments of *Red Flag* and *People's Daily,* trans. in *Peking Review,* No. 20 (May 12, 1967), pp. 7–11.

[134] These young people were mobilized by Mao's supporters in the one organization he evidently felt reliable, the People's Liberation Army. It should be noted, however, that the precise relationship between Mao and the army leadership, and Lin Piao in particular, remains one of the most obscure aspects of the Cultural Revolution.

[135] The similarity between Mao's use of the Red Guards to criticize Party cadres "from below," and earlier Maoist forms of political control such as the "Congresses of Poor and Lower-middle Peasants" mentioned above has also been noted and discussed by Philip Bridgham in "Mao's 'Cultural Revolution': Origin and Development," *China Quarterly,* No. 29 (January–March, 1967), pp. 10–11.

[136] "On Khrushchev's Phony Communism . . ." in *CB,* No. 737 (July 17, 1964).

eerie quality of a psychological recapitulation of Mao's entire political career, for in mobilizing China's youth to attack the Party structure itself, and in telling them that the essence of Marxism is the notion that "to rebel is justified," Mao seems to be reliving vicariously, in the struggles of the younger generation, his own youthful rebellion against authority. What satisfaction (or sadness?) comes in seeing them attack the political structure of his own creation, an organization which apparently had come to represent for him all of the outrageous misuses of authority and power which he had spent a lifetime opposing in struggle?

There is, as well, a broader sense in which the Cultural Revolution recapitulates Mao's career: by re-exposing the fundamental political problems which have marked his rise to power. This is most obviously indicated by the republication of a whole series of his early articles dealing with the organizational and ideological "deviations" which had hampered the growth of the Communist Party.[137]

From the point of view of our focus on the problem of political integration, the Cultural Revolution has clearly revealed the shallowness of change, relative to Mao's revolutionary objectives, that in fact has occurred in China since 1949. Two problems stand out in particular: the inability of the younger generation to keep political conflict within the "principled" bounds of national policy objectives—to prevent the Cultural Revolution from degenerating into *luan;* and their continuing inability to prevent lateral social fragmentation by maintaining cooperative relationships among their peers.

One of the fundamental questions concerning interpretations of the Cultural Revolution is the degree to which it is a personalized struggle for power, or a conflict over policy and principle. While a mixture of both factors probably underlies the turmoil, it is evident from the documentary material available that Mao has sought to define limits to the conflict within the context of an attempt to "prevent a restoration of capitalism," that is, to forestall the implementation of certain policies or the re-emergence of a style of political leadership which would lead to the re-establishment of a more "traditional" political order. The

---

[137] Mao's 1929 article, "On Correcting Mistaken Ideas in the Party," was republished in February, 1967; his "Talks at the Yenan Forum on Literature and the Arts" (1942), was republished in May; a series of four other articles from the past three decades dealing with policy toward the arts was republished in late May; and the notable 1957 speech, "On the Correct Handling of Contradictions among the People," was republished in June, 1967. The *"san-lao,"* "Serve the People" (1944), "In Memory of Norman Bethune" (1939), and "The Foolish Old Man Who Removed the Mountains" (1945) have been given particularly wide recirculation.

struggle of the Red Guards, in conception at least, is an ideological confrontation, or as the oft-repeated slogan goes, *"yao yung wen-tou, pu-yung wu-tou"* (we must use verbal struggle, not armed struggle).

The mass media have consistently revealed, however, that efforts to carry out the conflict within the bounds of political principle have from the start foundered on two rocks: the tendency of the Revolutionary Rebels to be indiscriminate (*luan*) in their attacks on authority;[138] and the (successful) efforts of Mao's opponents to defend themselves by forcing the conflict out of the realm of "principle" and into the arena of violence. Newspaper articles complain that those "taking the capitalist road" incite the masses to struggle among themselves, or provoke them into "directing the spearpoint of the struggle" against the PLA.

The Cultural Revolution has re-exposed the tendency of the society to fragment into self-serving cliques focused around individual authorities, and even the more anarchic tendency to reject the discipline of any authority whatsoever.[139] The response to this political fragmentation—to "bourgeois" manifestations of "individualism," "sectarianism," "particularism," "small group mentality," "departmentalism," "ultra-democracy," "liberalism," "reputationism" (*feng-t'ou-chu-yi*), "mountain strongholdism" (*shan-t'ou-chu-yi*)—has been an all too familiar cry: "Down with 'selfishness,' establish the collective (*p'o-szu, li-kung*), and establish a great proletarian unity through unending criticism–self-criticism."[140] The plea is for a resolution of disputes among the fragmented "revolutionaries" through Mao's formula of

---

[138] A *People's Daily* of early February, 1967, states with concern: "It is completely wrong to regard all persons in authority as untrustworthy and overthrow all of them indiscriminately. This idea of opposing, excluding and overthrowing all indiscriminately and its implementation run completely counter to Marxism-Leninism, Mao Tse-tung's Thought." *People's Daily* editorial, "A Good Example in Struggle by Proletarian Revolutionaries to Seize Power," February 10, 1967, trans. in *Peking Review*, No. 8 (February 17, 1967), p. 19.

And Chiang Ch'ing appealed in April of 1967:

There is no contradiction in the struggle, criticism, and repudiation [carried out by the newly formed Peking City revolutionary committee], or in its work of criticizing the biggest authority in the Party taking the capitalist road [Liu Shao-ch'i]; this can be done with unity . . . But in doing this you must use your brains, think things through well. You must study well the works of Chairman Mao and thoroughly carry out the work of investigation and research. You must keep cool (*yao yung leng-ching*), and be able to sit down and consult about things, and not continually be squabbling, or even worse get up and start fighting among yourselves. (*People's Daily*, April 21, 1967, p. 2).

[139] See, for example, the *People's Daily* editorial, "Down with Anarchism," April 26, 1967.

[140] See, for example, the article by the Third Headquarters of the Capital Red Guards, "Down with 'Selfishness,' Promote a Great Alliance of the Revolutionary Rebel Groups," *People's Daily*, January 31, 1967, p. 3.

"unity–criticism–unity"; otherwise the future of the Cultural Revolution could only be the fighting of "civil war" (*ta nei-chan*) and "armed struggle" (*wu-tou*).[141]

The outcome of the present political disintegration and conflict on the mainland is obviously not something in the realm of predictable human events; but in terms of our analytical focus on the problem of the reintegration of the Chinese polity it seems clear that we are now witnessing a return to more traditional forms of political control: the repersonalization of a guiding authority ("defend Chairman Mao"); the increased use of organizational measures to control individual behavior ("support the army"); and the active promotion of "educational" procedures so as to re-establish political discipline ("study the thought of Chairman Mao"). The alternatives to the use of such measures seem limited, for the "four olds" of China's traditional customs and habits, culture and social thought continue to exercise their influence. Indeed, Defense Minister Lin Piao could even spell out one fearful prospect in symbols that must evoke the image of the political fragmentation which characterized the warlordism of the 1920's:

Our country is a great land of 700 million people; and the entire country must have unified thinking. If we unite on the basis of the thought of Mao Tse-tung, then we can have united action. But if a nation of 700 million people does not have unified thinking then it will be just like a sheet of scattered sand.[142]

Only time will tell if the PLA, or some coalition of political forces, has both the sense of internal unity and the capacity to coerce into being and construct a new national political order. At various times during the evolution of the Cultural Revolution, the Maoists have sought to reassert their authority through new structures of political control, most notably the Paris Commune form of mass based government which was attempted in Shanghai in early 1967, and the subsequent "triple alliance" (*san chieh-ho*) of loyal military and cadre leaders in combination with "revolutionary" mass organizations. More recently the "revolutionary committee" has been put forward as the appropriate combination of military, "liberated" cadre, and mass power which will give life to Mao's dream of a truly participant and well-integrated polity:

---

[141] See the *People's Daily* editorial, "Immediately Restrain Armed Struggle," May 22 1967.

[142] *Red Flag* editorial, "Victoriously Advance on the Road of Mao Tse-tung's Thought," No. 11 (1966), p. 21.

This "three-in-one" organ of power enables our proletarian political power to strike deep roots among the masses. . . . Direct participation by the revolutionary masses in the running of the country and the enforcement of revolutionary supervision from below over the organs of political power at various levels plays a very important role in ensuring that our leading groups at all levels always adhere to the mass line, maintain the closest relations with the masses, represent their interests at all times, and serve the people heart and soul.[143]

Does the failure of the Maoists to mention the Communist Party in their scheme for restoring order to Chinese society mean that the leader will now attempt to exert his influence directly without an intervening—and always corruptible—party organization? Or does the Party remain an organization capable of challenging the influence of the Maoists? These are questions we can only keep in mind during the coming months as the Chinese seek to re-establish for themselves a political order which will give a renewed image of unity to their increasingly disintegrated society.

[143] Editorial of *People's Daily, Red Flag,* and *Liberation Army Daily,* "Revolutionary Committees are Fine," March 30, 1968, trans. in *Peking Review,* No. 14 (April 5, 1968), p. 6.

APPENDIX A

ATTITUDE SURVEY STATEMENTS AND THEMATIC APPERCEPTION TEST
(TAT) PICTURES

A SURVEY OF PEOPLE'S OUTLOOK ON CONTEMPORARY LIFE*

Introduction

During the past several decades all our lives have changed very much. Some changes are for the better; some are not so good. Some people approve of recent developments; some object to various aspects of life today.

We are interested in your point of view concerning various aspects of contemporary life. This will give us a better understanding of those recent developments which people in general think are good, as well as those which perhaps are not so popular.

We will appreciate your help and cooperation in this survey of popular opinion. It should be emphasized that in asking for your point of view there are no "right" or "wrong" answers. The best answer is your personal opinion. You can be sure that, whatever your own opinion, some people may disagree, and others are sure to agree with you.

In this survey we have tried to include many aspects of contemporary life as well as various different points of view. You will probably find yourself agreeing strongly with some statements, disagreeing with others, and perhaps agreeing only slightly with still others.

If you are willing to help us in this survey, please answer the questions as follows:

1. Read each statement carefully, and mark it according to your first reaction. It isn't necessary to consider any one statement too long; each one should take you about a minute. Or in other words, to complete the entire survey should take you not much more than 30 minutes.
2. Answer every question.
3. Try your best to give your true and accurate point of view.
4. Respond to the statements as follows. If you:

Strongly agree, mark +3   Strongly disagree, mark −3
Agree somewhat, mark +2   Disagree somewhat, mark −2
Agree a little, mark +1   Disagree a little, mark −1

For example, if you strongly disagree with the statement, "The style of the most recently constructed buildings in the city is ugly," mark in the answer box −3 . If you slightly agree with the statement, mark +1; if you agree, but not strongly, mark +2; etc.

This survey, like any study of popular opinion, works just like an election: your answers are private, and you need not write down your name.

1. It is basically a good thing that young people can have more fun these days, such as by going out dancing or walking hand in hand in the park. ☐

2. The nation naturally has its importance; but family life is more

* Translation.

352

important. ▢

3. Schools today put too much emphasis on mathematics, physics, and chemistry, and not enough on such worthwhile subjects as classical literature and calligraphy. ▢

4. In the long run it is a good thing that a young man select for himself his own career. ▢

5. A large part of the crime and immorality around here these days is due to so many strangers and travelers from abroad. ▢

6. Although laws and political programs have their place, what our country needs even more is a few courageous, firm, and dedicated leaders in whom the people can put their trust. ▢

7. Although many people think that fortunetelling is nonsense, in the future it just may be proved that it really can explain many things. ▢

8. It is an unfortunate thing that today there are many young women who prefer having a career to remaining at home and having a simple, happy family life. ▢

9. Although the theories of Confucius and Mencius in the past had their value, their works cannot explain the many problems of interpersonal relations in society today. ▢

10. Just as foreigners have come to appreciate many Chinese things, we also ought to adopt various good customs and habits of foreign countries. ▢

11. Obedience and respect for their elders are the most important virtues children should develop. ▢

12. Nowadays a young man can make a valuable and interesting career for himself in commerce. ▢

13. It is more important to prove you are right in a discussion than to take an attitude of "why bother" or "forget it" just for the sake of friendliness or out of a desire not to hurt the other person's feelings. ▢

14. There are few things more enjoyable for entertainment than China's traditional songs and regional operas. ▢

15. It is better, in these modern times, if parents are not so strict in expecting their children to do things just the way they do them. ▢

16. If a neighbor is making a public nuisance of himself, it is better just to try to ignore him or avoid the trouble of involvement than to attempt to correct the situation. ▢

17. If China would place greater emphasis on putting into practice her time-tested customs, habits, and social virtues, then many problems of contemporary society could be solved. ▢

18. Although criticizing the thoughts and suggestions of our superiors is useful for improving our work, it can lead to much trouble, and hence is best avoided. ▢

19. Although Chinese history possibly can provide some good experience,

there are many important things we need to learn from modern economics, science, and social research. ☐

20. While it might not be bad for a son to live with his parents after marriage, it is basically better for a young couple to set up their own household. ☐

21. If there were not so many foreigners attempting to help other people deal with their own problems, then the world would be a much more peaceful place. ☐

22. In contemporary society, the professions of a scientist or engineer are particularly interesting and valuable. ☐

23. It is essential for effectiveness in study or work that our teachers or superiors give us detailed explanations and directives. ☐

24. For understanding different social customs and ways of interpersonal relations, as well as various foreign things, foreign movies are worthwhile to see. ☐

25. Human nature being what it is, unfortunately there will probably always be interpersonal disputes, conflicts, or war. ☐

26. History will probably prove that the contribution of the scholar or artist has been more important for society than that of the scientist or manufacturer. ☐

27. It is annoying to hear people always stressing the virtues of patience, compromise, and restraint. We should be bold enough to work for great change and seek to improve things now, even though some people may be opposed. ☐

28. If someone is lying hurt in the street, it is best not to rush right up and help, and thus avoid bringing on a lot of trouble, as someone whose proper job it is will always come along quickly to take charge. ☐

29. It is an unfortunate thing that during one's life it is so difficult to find true friends with whom one can share the thoughts and feelings deep in one's heart. ☐

30. Although sciences like chemistry, physics, and medicine have helped in the advancement of mankind, there are many important things which can never be understood by human intelligence. ☐

31. When the national situation gets a bit difficult, it is only natural and proper that people be expected to make a greater contribution, such as by extending the time of military service, controlling consumption, or directing people in their work and study, etc. ☐

32. If two people really love each other but both their parents object, it is better for their long-run happiness that they not marry. ☐

THEMATIC APPERCEPTION TEST (TAT) PICTURES*

* The actual test pictures are approximately eight by ten inches in size, and mounted on individual nine by twelve inch white cards. These picture cards are handed to the interviewee one by one in a regular sequence during the administration of the test.

I

II

III

IV

V

VI

VII

VIII

IX

APPENDIX B

A Representative Interpretation of TAT Card IV*

This [older] person is rather experienced in social matters; an understanding person. This other fellow is relatively young and inexperienced. They have some kind of a relationship. [What kind?] Like commercial people, but yet not like that; like landlords, but yet not. In any case, rather low level in society.

The older man is telling the younger to do something. [What kind of a thing?] Not too enlightened a thing. [Why?] You can tell just from their appearances. The younger fellow is fearful; he is unwilling to do it. [What kind of a thing might it be?] Just not proper. That could include many things [laughs].

[What does the older man feel about the younger?] He is just telling him to do the job and not to worry about it as the responsibility is all on his shoulders. [How does the younger feel about the older?] He is afraid; he doesn't dare do the thing.

[What is the result of this situation?] He goes and does it. [Does he succeed?] From his expression he does it and fails, because he is afraid. [Afterward what is the relationship between the two men?] The older one feels the younger is of no use. [What about the younger?] He thought it could not be avoided, doing that thing, so he did it. [How does he feel toward the elder man?] Nothing in particular; he just had to do the thing. [Then what is their relationship?] The younger man is arrested. [By whom?] The police, another organization, or intelligence group. Then the older man runs away. The younger is very straightforward in telling [his new captors] about the thing.

* The respondent was a twenty-eight-year-old worker in an electrical factory from Kwangtung Province.

APPENDIX C

TABLE 45

COMPARATIVE "NEED AFFILIATION" AND "NEED POWER" DATA, BASED ON
THE ANALYSIS OF THEMATIC CONTENT OF PRIMARY SCHOOL
EDUCATIONAL MATERIALS

Area	"Need Affiliation"*	"Need Power"*
"Republican" China, 1920's†‡	−2.02§	+1.53§
Communist China, 1950's‡‖	−0.55	+3.27
Nationalists, Taiwan, 1950's‡‖	−1.91	+0.57
United States, 1920's#†	+0.91	−0.39
United States, 1950's#‖	+0.42	+0.29

* A full description of these content analysis categories will be found in John W. Atkinson (ed.), *Motives in Fantasy, Action, and Society* (Princeton, N.J.: D. Van Nostrand, 1958).

† Standard scores for the 1920's series are computed from a total sample of twenty-six countries.

‡ Data from David C. McClelland, "Motivational Patterns in Southeast Asia, With Special Reference to the Chinese Case," *Journal of Social Issues,* XIX, No. 1 (1963), 12.

§ These figures are "standard scores," designed to indicate the *relative* position of the measurement for the given subsample when compared to a larger number of cases. It is basically a "standard deviation" figure, which means that a "standard score" of 0 for a subsample indicates that its absolute score is equal to the mean (average) for the entire sample. A standard score of +1 would be *higher* than about 85 per cent of the rest of the sample; a standard score of −2 would be *lower* than about 98 per cent of the sample; a standard score of +0.5 would be higher than about 70 per cent of the sample, and so forth.

‖ Standard scores for the 1950's series are computed from a total sample of forty-three countries.

Data from McClelland, *The Achieving Society*, pp. 461–62.

APPENDIX D

A Representative Interpretation of TAT Card I*

These five people are holding a meeting to discuss something. This fellow on the side disagrees with the proposal supported by most of the others, and so he is unhappy. He has stood up and is preparing to leave the group, or is thinking of opposing them. He is not the leader of the group. Probably he just has his own proposal.

[What kind of an affair might they be discussing?] This is difficult to say. Probably it concerns the progress of their work.

[How do these people in the group feel?] Because of the fellow on the side getting up to leave, they have been provoked into feeling tense. Consequently they have put their heads together to discuss the situation and there are many opinions: some are saying let the fellow go and be done with it; some think that his opinion is not bad and should be reconsidered.

[What is the result likely to be?] Right now they are energetically discussing the situation. I can't really discern what the situation might be. [But perhaps what might be the most likely outcome?] They are just divided against each other (*chüeh lieh pien yüan*), but there is no outcome as yet.

[How does the fellow on the side feel about the others?] He feels that their opinions are nonsense. He wants to support his own proposal but the others won't listen to him. Hence he is unhappy. He is pacing up and down, considering whether to participate in the discussion or to leave the group.

[What is the outcome?] This fellow is very unhappy; and so he withdraws from the group—indicates his disapproval and goes.

[In the future what relationship do these people have with the fellow who departed?] They have no mutual concern: "You take care of your's, and I'll take care of mine."

* The respondent was a sixty-eight-year-old former Nationalist governmental employee from Fukien Province.

PART IV

Rural Control and Mobilization

THOMAS P. BERNSTEIN

Cadre and Peasant Behavior Under Conditions of Insecurity and Deprivation: The Grain Supply Crisis of the Spring of 1955

INTRODUCTION

During the socialist transformation of agriculture in China, control over many aspects of the peasants' economic life was transferred from the peasant household to the political system. In the case under consideration here, the state in November of 1953 imposed a monopoly on trade in grain.[1] Under a new system of unified purchasing and marketing,[2] the state told a peasant how much of his surplus the state would buy and at what price. If he did not produce enough grain to cover his own needs, it was now the state that determined how much he needed and how much he would be entitled to buy. A peasant was no longer allowed to operate as an individual entrepreneur, seeking maximum advantage for himself; he was now subject to and dependent upon a new and complex state mechanism. Naturally this was a radical change in the peasant's way of life.

Previously the peasant had been dependent on various forces, such as the market. And, as the Chinese Communist Party (CCP) never

[1] See "GAC Order on Enforcement of Planned Purchase and Planned Supply," promulgated November 19, 1953, published by NCNA, Peking, February 28, 1954, trans. in *SCMP*, No. 759 (March 4, 1954).

[2] Henceforth abbreviated as UPM, UP to mean "unified purchasing" and UM to mean "unified marketing." The Chinese term *t'ung-kou, t'ung-hsiao* is also sometimes translated as "unified purchase and supply."

tired of pointing out, those peasants—the vast majority, according to the CCP—who were unable to compete effectively in the market were subjected to cruel exploitation while a few peasants got rich. From the viewpoint of a particular peasant, however, the old system, though risky, had the virtue of familiarity, and it contained the hope that while others lost, he might gain. This "small-producer mentality," as the Party called it, was now to be traded for the socialist mentality. Peasants were asked to put their trust and confidence in the new state-run mechanism, to stake their livelihood on it, and not to try to evade the restrictions which it imposed upon them.

The CCP acknowledged that the restrictions of the UPM system would be regarded by peasants as an "inconvenience": "The peasants are individual small producers and for thousands of years they have cultivated the habit of only paying rent and paying taxes and of at least formally disposing of their surplus grain freely."[3]

Unified purchasing and marketing was a deprivation first and foremost for those peasants who produced a surplus. The CCP insisted that the prices paid by the state were in fact fair and reasonable. But there is little doubt that peasants could have obtained a higher price on a free grain market, if only because grain prices would probably have risen as the demand for grain increased with urban growth and industrialization.[4] One of the reasons for the imposition of the state monopoly had been that in 1953 peasants were not selling enough to the state at the official price. In one area, for example, private merchants reportedly paid peasants 40 per cent more than the state.[5] Under the old system, moreover, peasants able to do so could take advantage of seasonal fluctuations in price and hold their stock until prices rose in the spring. Now this possible source of profit was eliminated.

UPM was also a source of deprivation for peasants generally, since it now became possible for the CCP to change long-established patterns and habits. State control enabled the state to begin to alter peasant consumption patterns, for example, by making them substitute an unpopular type of food for a popular one, such as sweet potatoes for rice. When the state rather than a private merchant paid peasants for their produce, the state could withhold part of the payments and bank

[3] Ch'en Yün, "On the Question of the Unified Purchase and Distribution of Grain," speech to the National People's Congress (henceforth NPC), July 22, 1955, in CB, No. 339 (July 27, 1955).

[4] Dwight H. Perkins, *Market Control and Planning in Communist China* (Cambridge, Mass.: Harvard University Press, 1966), pp. 49–50.

[5] *JMJP* editorial, March 1, 1954, by NCNA, Peking, in *SCMP*, No. 759 (March 4, 1954).

them, instead of allowing peasants to use the money as they saw fit.[6] The subordination of the peasants to state goals and plans thus undoubtedly constituted a real deprivation for the peasants.

At the same time, the extent of peasant deprivation in having to sell grain to the state should not be exaggerated. The severity of the procurement program was limited by the fact that state policy aimed both at extraction of grain and at development of agricultural production. China's goal of industrialization required a large and growing agricultural surplus; yet the fundamental problem for China has always been to create a surplus large enough to finance full-scale industrialization in the first place.[7] The CCP, at least during the years of the first five-year plan (1953–57), was conscious of the need to keep peasant alienation within bounds. It was afraid of harming the peasants' "enthusiasm for production" (*sheng-ch'an chi-chi hsing*) and of allowing peasant motivation to deteriorate to the point of passive or active resistance.

The goal of fulfilling annual extraction quotas necessarily took priority over the long-run target of development, however, and at times the regime approached the boundaries of what it had itself established as permissible, and occasionally exceeded these boundaries. The balance between the two conflicting goals—maximizing extraction and gaining peasant cooperation for development—was further upset in favor of the former by unstable agricultural output and by errors and excesses in policy implementation. But the developmental goal did impose a restraint. When, as in 1954–55, extraction had been carried to excess, the Chinese leaders moderated the procurement program in the following year (see below). The same point emerges in comparative perspective. In the Soviet Union, Stalin assumed in the late 1920's that a huge surplus existed in the countryside. This assumption resulted in the absolute priority of extraction over development, and at times the Stalin regime was prepared to reduce the village to famine in order to extract the maximum output (for instance in 1932 and 1947).[8]

---

[6] *JMJP,* March 3, 1955, in *SCMP,* No. 1004 (March 10, 1955).

[7] K. C. Yeh, "Soviet and Communist Chinese Industrialization Strategies," in Donald W. Treadgold (ed.), *Soviet and Chinese Communism: Similarities and Differences* (Seattle: University of Washington Press, 1967), p. 350.

[8] On the Soviet case, see Jerzy F. Karcz, "Thoughts on the Grain Problem," *Soviet Studies,* XVIII, No. 4 (April, 1967), 399–434. On famine in the early 1930's, see Dana G. Dalrymple, "The Soviet Famine of 1932–1934," *Soviet Studies,* XV, No. 3 (January, 1964), 250–84. For a reference to starvation in 1947 on account of state purchase of grain, see Khrushchev's speech to the Central Committee, *Pravda,* December 10, 1963, in *Current Digest of the Soviet Press,* XV, No. 48 (December 25, 1963). Differences in Soviet

For its part, the CCP granted that UPM was clearly a deprivation for class enemies—rich peasants and speculating merchants[9]—and that it was "inconvenient" for some or all peasants, but the Party stoutly maintained that the policy was beneficial in terms of both the long-run and the short-run interests of the peasants. In explaining UPM (and socialist transformation generally), the CCP used universalistic and particularistic arguments. The former were arguments that went beyond the peasant's horizon and his perception of his immediate interests. The CCP presented the peasants with a simple model of industrialization, which it said would ultimately benefit the peasants by lifting them out of their state of poverty. In order to bring this blissful future about, peasants should support their (then) "elder brother," the working class, by selling grain at state prices. The CCP told them that a period of "hard struggle" in support of industrialization would enable industry to supply them with machines, tractors, and chemical fertilizer, and would therefore ultimately enrich them.[10] In addition to outlining a simple picture of industrialization and the peasants' supporting role, universalistic propaganda stressed patriotism, support for the People's Liberation Army (PLA), and the liberation of Taiwan.[11] Propaganda was also designed to expand the mental horizons of peasants beyond their own locality by getting them to identify with peasants in other parts of the country: "Since the country is a big family in which all the peasants are brothers and sisters, they who reap a bumper harvest have of course the obligation to sell more grain to the government in order to make up the shortage from famine areas."[12]

Propagandists found it easier to make a hit with the peasants when they reshaped universalistic arguments by concentrating on more immediate benefits.[13] Particularistic arguments stressing the immediate

and Chinese policies toward the peasants, particularly with regard to grain procurements, are analyzed in my dissertation on Soviet and Chinese collectivization of agriculture.

[9] Under UPM, grain merchants were subject to state control; those who evaded controls were regarded as class enemies subject to punishment. Rich peasants were class enemies because they "exploited" long-term hired laborers, and in this regard they differed from middle peasants who were able to farm successfully on their own resources, and even more so from poor peasants, who were unable to farm successfully on their own and hence were the CCP's base for socialist transformation.

[10] *JMJP* editorial, November 21, 1954.

[11] For one example of this propaganda appeal, see *NFJP*, November 20, 1954, in *SCMP*, No. 971 (January 19, 1955), supplement.

[12] *Kuang-hsi Jih-pao*, March 18, 1955, in URS, I (September 22, 1955).

[13] *JMJP* editorial, November 21, 1954, criticized excessive stress on light industry and immediate benefits in the propaganda on industrialization that was directed at the peasants. See also *"Shan-hsi Jih-pao* Initiates Debate on Mistaken Conception of According Priority Development to Light Industry," *Hsüeh-hsi* (Study), No. 1 (January 2, 1955), in *SCMP*, No. 1000 (March 4, 1955).

benefits of UPM held that surplus-producing peasants would no longer be fleeced by profiteering merchants. Instead they would now receive a fair and reasonable state price, and it would no longer be true to say that a bumper harvest leads to financial loss. Grain-short peasants would no longer have to borrow in the spring at usurious rates in order to be able to meet their requirements until the next harvest.[14]

Even more importantly, UPM was presented as a form of insurance. Government control over grain would enable the state to protect peasants from natural disasters. The state would supply disaster-stricken areas with the necessary grain, while prices, in contrast with pre-Communist times, would remain stable. By placing their trust in the government, therefore, peasants would no longer face the specter of starvation. The regime's propaganda cited many concrete examples, such as the following. The crops in Shih-shan *hsiang* in Wu-ch'en *hsien*, Hupeh, were largely ruined by floods in 1954.[15] In the preceding five years the *hsiang* had marketed a total of 370,000 catties of grain, but during the one disaster year 1954–55 the state supplied the *hsiang* with a total of 1.1 million catties (1 catty = 1.1 pounds). This showed that if the villagers had depended on their efforts alone, they would have starved even had they saved all the grain that was sold. "This truth must be repeatedly and fully explained to every household in the rural areas,"[16] or as one peasant reportedly said: "Chairman Mao is dearer to us than our own mother. As soon as he hears that we are famine stricken, he brings us food from several thousand li away. Had it not been for the food brought us by the government, we wonder how many of us would have starved to death, as in the days before the liberation."[17]

Some of these arguments undoubtedly had merit, and the CCP felt confident that it could persuade many or most peasants to accept the new system. This it attempted to do in the massive 1953–54 propaganda campaign on the "general line" of the transition to socialism, and more or less intensively thereafter as well. Because of the deprivational aspects of UPM and because of the peasants' "spontaneous tendency toward capitalism" (which meant that left to themselves, many peasants would not have accepted UPM), the mobilization effort

[14] See, for example, *JMJP* editorial, January 5, 1955, in *SCMP*, No. 727 (January 14, 1954), and *JMJP* editorial, March 1, 1954.

[15] The *hsiang* was the lowest administrative level in the rural areas; in the early 1950's a *hsiang* consisted of perhaps four or five natural villages, or *ts'un*. A *hsien* is a county.

[16] *JMJP* editorial, June 26, 1955, in *SCMP*, No. 1083 (July 7, 1955).

[17] *JMJP* article, March 1, 1954, in *SCMP*, No. 768 (March 17, 1954).

to secure compliance with UPM did not rely on persuasion alone. Coercion was explicitly aimed at class enemies—particularly at rich peasants and merchants—who were presumed to be violators of the new policy.[18] This coercion served as a form of pressure on the surplus-producing middle peasants, who were most likely to resent having to sell to the state at fixed prices. They were the prime targets of "patient education," which could legitimately be carried to this point: ". . . in the case of some individual middle peasants whose spontaneous tendencies are particularly marked, appropriate criticisms may be made against them by the masses at their sessions of self-criticism, but struggles in any form must be avoided."[19]

Mobilization for the purpose of implementing UPM may thus be regarded as a procedure for making peasants do something that was contrary to their spontaneous inclinations. It consisted of a three-pronged effort: eliciting mass support, applying pressure, and employing coercion. These three aspects of mobilization tended very broadly to correspond to the threefold division of the village into poor, middle, and rich peasants; poor peasants, who had least to lose and most to gain from UPM, were the group most likely to support the policy. Mobilization did not seek simply to secure obedience to directives handed down from above; a central aspect of mobilization was the attempt to involve as many peasants as possible in the process of implementation. The most important participants in the mobilization effort were village level cadres. These village leaders maintained organizational links to the ordinary peasants. At least in theory, they were able to activate these links for the purpose of gaining participation by peasants in the various aspects of policy execution. They were to conduct lengthy educational discussions to familiarize peasants with the policy, and to seek participation of peasants in the allocation of sales quotas to particular households. A major goal of mass participation was to enhance the acceptability of UPM by reducing as far as possible the peasants' fear that they would be subjected to an arbitrary and unfairly enforced measure.

How fairly and correctly the UPM policy was carried out was therefore a most important determinant of the extent to which the peasants' feeling of deprivation went beyond the unavoidable minimum. Any mobilization drive can easily get out of hand, for example, by exceeding the delicate limits to the degree of pressure aimed at such

[18] For one of many articles on "unscrupulous merchants" and rich peasants, see *CFJP* July 14, 1954, in *SCMP,* No. 892 (September 21, 1954), supplement.

[19] *NFJP*, November 20, 1954.

groups as the middle peasants. Much depends on the concrete application of the rules, and by this criterion UPM was not overly successful in its first two years. This lack of success was in part due to inexperience in coping with the enormous administrative problems of applying UPM. As an editorial put it, rather plaintively: "It is . . . a most complex and difficult task to investigate thoroughly the food production, consumption, and stocks of surplus food of more than one hundred million agricultural households in the country."[20] However, it was also due to the regime's determination not to let such troubles as natural calamities slow down industrial construction by reducing the quantity of food bought from the peasants. These two factors caused the feeling of insecurity among the peasants that underlay the supply crisis of the spring of 1955. Before describing peasant and cadre behavior in that period, therefore, we must outline the application of UPM in 1954–55.

The Supply Crisis in the Spring of 1955 and Its Origins

In the spring of 1955 the peasants were "abnormally nervous."[21] Many of them claimed that they did not have enough to eat, and they clamored for grain (*chiao-han liang-shih*). As anxiety spread among the peasants, a "tense situation"[22] arose in many villages. Because cadres frequently gave in to peasant demands, there was an unexpected rise in state grain sales to peasants. This result so alarmed the nation's leadership that in May, 1955, a campaign was launched to mobilize the peasants to reduce grain consumption.

As reported by Ch'en Yün, a Politburo member who specialized in economic matters, grain sales to peasants actually began to rise above plan in September, 1954, reaching a peak in the spring of 1955 when the following amounts were sold to the peasants:[23]

March, 1955:	9.3 billion catties
April, 1955:	9.6 billion catties
May, 1955:	8.4 billion catties
June, 1955:	6.4 billion catties

While Ch'en did not reveal by how much these quantities exceeded the state supply plan, he did say that normally the largest quantity is sold in May; this year it was in March and April. He reported that in the

---

[20] *JMJP* editorial, June 26, 1955.

[21] NCNA, Peking, April 30, 1955, in *SCMP*, No. 1041 (May 5, 1955).

[22] The term "tense situation" or, better, "man-made tension" (*jen-wei ti chin-chang*) was widely used. See, for example, *JMJP* editorial, April 24, 1955.

[23] Ch'en, "On the Question of the Unified Purchase and Distribution of Grain."

grain year from July, 1954, to June, 1955, 36 billion catties of un-husked (marketable) grain was sold to the peasants, enough to supply 300 million persons at one catty per day for four months.[24] This was clearly in excess of need, he argued, for out of 500 million individual peasants, the state was supposed to provide grain for only about 140 million:[25]

30–40 million individual peasants who grew industrial crops
40 million individual peasants in disaster-stricken areas
50 million individual peasants who were normally grain short
12 million individual peasants engaged in pastoral, fishing, or forestry activities

132–142 million total

According to state estimates, many of these grain-short peasants did not require grain for the entire year, but typically only for the three to five months immediately preceding the summer harvest.[26]

The official analysis of the grain-supply crisis claimed that the biggest problem was excess supply to peasants not really in need of grain, but also conceded that in a minority of cases the peasants did not in fact have enough to eat: "Some of the farm households which should have been given a supply of grain were not so supplied whereas a more prevalent phenomenon was found in which those who should not have been supplied were nevertheless supplied and those who should have been supplied less were instead supplied more."[27] Ch'en complained that in some provinces enough grain was sold to peasants to feed 70–80 per cent of the entire population at the rate of one catty per day (although he failed to specify how long this went on). In some

[24] Ch'en Yün said four hundred days as his statement was translated by CB, ibid.; the Chinese original, as printed in TKP, July 22, 1955, reported that Ch'en said four months. (All references to Ta Kung Pao are to the Tientsin edition.)

[25] Ibid.

[26] The source for the statement that supply needs ranged from three to five months is Li Ssu-heng, "What Are the Problems in Food Supply to Rural Villages," Shih-shih Shou-ts'e (Current Affairs Handbook), No. 9 (May 10, 1955), in SCMP, No. 1071 (June 17, 1955), supplement. Ch'en Yün also noted that there were about one hundred million individuals who sold some grain in the autumn and bought back an equivalent amount in the spring, either in order to obtain cash in the fall or to buy a different variety of grain. For those peasants who were severely struck by natural disaster, supply apparently was more in the nature of a relief operation, and grain was given out either as a loan or as an outright grant. As far as one can tell, however, the disaster supplies were included in the total supply quantity. For a report on 1954–55 operations in disaster areas, see the speech by Hsieh Chüeh-tsai, the Minister of Internal Affairs, to the NPC, July 25, 1955, in CB, No. 357 (September 15, 1955).

[27] P'an Ching-yüan, "Two Years of Planned Purchase and Planned Supply of Grain," Hsin Chien She (New Construction), No. 9 (September, 1955), in ECMM, No. 9 (October 11, 1955).

hsien, he said, 95 per cent of the population was reportedly supplied. Other accounts echoed these claims of unnecessary supply. In Shansi the plan had called for supplying grain to 10 per cent of the agricultural population; in March, 24.2 per cent was supplied at the rate of thirty catties per capita per month. In the same province, 10 per cent of the grain-supply tickets were issued to households not needing them; in some *hsien,* this percentage rose to 38.[28]

In order to provide a perspective on the grain situation in 1954–55, Table 46 compares output, purchase, and supply for three years:

TABLE 46

THE ALLOCATION OF CHINA'S GRAIN OUTPUT, 1954–57*

	1954–55	1955–56	1956–57
1. Total output (billion catties)	339	367.9	385.5
2. UP (billion catties)	107.8	104.1	99.4
3. Percentage of total output bought by the state	31.8%	28.3%	25.8%
4. UM to rural areas (billion catties)	49.4	40.5	49
5. UM to rural areas as percentage of total UP	45.9%	38.9%	49.3%
6. Total grain taken out of rural areas (billion catties)	58.4	63.6	50.4
7. Total grain taken out of rural areas as percentage of total output	17.2%	17.3%	13.1%
8. Quantity of grain in rural areas, including state supply (billion catties)	280.6	304.3	335.1
9. Per capita supply of grain (catties)	549	577	622

* Chou Po-p'ing, "The Policy of Unified Purchase and Sale of Grain Shall Not Be Frustrated," *Liang-shih,* No. 7 (July, 1957), in *ECMM*, No. 101 (September 9, 1957). Lines 3 and 8 have been calculated from Chou's figures.
There are some obvious problems with this table. Ch'en Yün reported total state supply to the peasants as 36 billion catties of marketable or unhusked grain. Chou's figures apparently refer to husked or primary grain, and converting Ch'en's figure yields approximately 41.7 billion catties, which is still much below Chou's supply figure. Ch'en also put the percentage of grain taken out of rural areas at 18, while claiming that the peasants had a per capita supply of 280 kilograms, which comes to 560 catties. If one divides the 280.6 billion catties left in the villages according to Chou by 500 million peasants, a per capita supply of 561 results. And, finally, a Japanese economist reports a total supply figure for the rural areas of 46.36 billion catties, apparently from *T'ung-chi Kung-tso,* No. 19 (1957); see Reijitsu Kojima, "Grain Acquisition and Supply in China," in E. Stuart Kirby (ed.), *Contemporary China; Economic and Social Studies, Documents, Chronology, Bibliography.* Vol. V, *1961–1962* (Hong Kong: Hong Kong University Press, 1963).

[28] The source for the information on excess supply in Shansi is "Pu-chih hsia-cheng ho hsia-chi liang-shih kou-hsiao kung-tso" (Arrange the Work of Summer Taxation and Summer Purchase and Supply), *Shan-hsi Jih-pao,* May 19, 1955. The source for the figure 38 per cent is "Wo sheng cheng-tun liang-shih t'ung-hsiao kung-tso" (Our Province Is Reorganizing Grain Supply), *ibid.,* May 5, 1955. For reports from elsewhere, e.g., Kwangtung, see *TKP,* editorial, March 31, 1955, and *JMJP* editorial, April 24, 1955. Titles of newspaper articles are given only when a single issue contains more than one article cited in this paper.

The table shows that, in comparison with the other two grain years, in 1954–55 the state bought the largest percentage of output and left the smallest amount of grain in the village, so that per capita supply in 1954–55 was the lowest of the three years. Still, according to the minimum consumption standard of one catty of grain per person per day (used in determining state supply), 549 catties for one year would appear to be adequate. But this table also shows that an unusually high level of purchase was accompanied by an unusually high level of marketing. Supply to the peasants, however, takes place in the spring, at the time of actual need. In the interval between autumn and spring, many peasants from whom the state had purchased large amounts, or who were grain short to begin with, became more and more anxious over whether they would be supplied in time. This anxiety provided the point of departure for the spring supply crisis.

Why the high level of purchase? In 1954 floods ravaged the lower Yangtze Valley. Not only were the harvests in some large areas ruined or reduced, but the demands on state supply (or rather relief) increased greatly. In order to meet these demands while at the same time not cutting down on the industrialization program, the state decided to "buy a little more" from areas that had not suffered from calamities, and particularly from those that had reaped a bumper harvest. As Ch'en Yün put it,

. . . there was an overestimation of the grain production of a very small portion of the bumper harvest areas, and so larger purchases were made in those areas, with the result that the food of the peasants in these villages and the fodder for the livestock retained became a little less; this led to a reduction of livestock in the areas and the development of a temporary tense situation. This was not correct and must be rectified.[29]

One should keep in mind the official explanation that except for these few areas UP had on the whole been fair and reasonable, since it played an important role in cadre and peasant mobilization in May, 1955, when the regime sought to restore confidence and to cut down on grain consumption. Nonetheless, it is likely that state purchases in 1954 were excessive in more than just a few areas. One source in 1957 stated that the state bought "an excessive quantity of 7 billion catties of grain" in 1954–55.[30] In 1954, moreover, national editorial directives

[29] Ch'en, "Unified Purchase and Distribution of Grain."

[30] Chang Chien, "The Important Significance of Restricting Sales in the Unified Purchase and Unified Sales of Grain," *Liang-shih* (Grain), No. 8 (August 25, 1957), in *ECMM*, No. 107 (November 12, 1957).

called for "buying a little more," collecting "a little more tax," and "buying as much as possible"; emphasis was placed on the purchase of the entire surplus[31] (in contrast to 80–90 per cent of surplus under the "three-fixed" [*san-ting*] directive of 1955; see below).

These directives indicate the tremendous pressure put on cadres to come up with outstanding results in the purchase campaign. They were "armed" ideologically to give first place to the state's interests, while criticism was made of any "onesided peasant viewpoints."[32] Optimistic and confident appraisals of the purchase campaign indicate that the peasants were put under extraordinary pressures to sell, with quotas in nondisaster areas apparently being fixed on the assumption that everybody's output had increased: "Very many peasants said: 'It is only because of the state's assistance that our grain output rises year by year; from now on we will get even more assistance, and so we must first of all support industrial construction, sell more surplus grain to the state and advance the transition to socialism.' "[33] When the press quotes peasants as voicing such universalistic sentiments, it usually means that the balance between peasant interests and state interests has swung far in favor of the latter. The same article reported that even households that had been grain short in the previous purchase season were now selling to the state, and that some areas were overfulfilling both purchase and tax quotas.

Because of the pressure put on cadres, those aspects of the process of mobilization that were designed to maximize support and minimize grievances were neglected in the purchasing campaign of 1954. Instead, the UP campaign was characterized, at least in some and probably in many areas, by "commandism": "The main problem in this work was that in the course of unified grain purchasing, some local authorities failed fully to investigate and understand the grain situation and to adopt methods to pursue the mass line, thus giving rise to commandism and to the practice of lowering consumption quotas. . . ."[34] Mobilization in theory required lengthy propaganda on

[31] See *JMJP* editorial, June 19, 1954, in *SCMP*, No. 835 (June 24, 1954); *JMJP* editorial, October 6, 1954, in *SCMP*, No. 919 (October 30–November 1, 1954); *JMJP* editorial, November 17, 1954, in *SCMP*, No. 935 (November 25–26), 1954. In 1957 it was reported that if the tax collected from peasants were put at 100 for 1952, it would have stood at 90.46 in 1953, at 97.93 in 1954–55, and at 94.84 in 1956, thus indicating that in tax work, also, a peak of extraction was reached in the period under consideration. See Chang Hao-jen, "Is the Peasants' Burden Too Heavy?" *Hsüeh-hsi*, No. 18 (August 8, 1957), in *ECMM*, No. 104 (October 22, 1957).

[32] *NFJP*, November 20, 1954.

[33] *Shan-hsi Jih-pao*, January 1, 1955.

[34] *Ho-pei Jih-pao*, February 2, 1955, in *SCMP*, No. 1056 (May 26, 1955), supplement.

the "good points" of selling to the state. But these explanations were not made, and this fact reportedly left both grain-short and grain-surplus households worried and insecure.[35] UP also required a complex and lengthy process of fact-finding aimed at carefully separating grain-short from self-sufficient and from grain-surplus households (with purchase then being made only from the latter). These distinctions were extremely difficult to make, and working them out would have required the participation of many peasants. This was not done; instead, in 1954 quotas were in many cases levied arbitrarily. One household would find itself overassessed and would have to sell part of its ration allotment (*k'ou-liang*), while another's surplus might be tapped only partially or not at all. An investigation of three hundred *hsiang* in Shansi showed that 4 per cent of households should have been classified as surplus holders but were not, while 3 per cent should have been classified as grain short but were not.[36] These percentages may seem rather low, but in particular areas or villages the errors were undoubtedly much greater.[37] However large the misclassifications and the excess purchases, they caused a good deal of dissatisfaction, fear, and anxiety.

The provincial and national measures that were subsequently adopted recognized this fact. In Shansi, for example, soon after the UP campaign had been completed a drive was launched to return excess purchases to the peasants (*t'ui-pu*), but according to reports in May the drive was not handled well and did not prevent supply crises.[38] More importantly, in March, 1955, the government promulgated the "three-fixed" (*san-ting*) directive, according to which each *hsiang*'s output, purchase, and sales quotas were to be established and made known before spring planting in 1955. State purchase quotas were made known in advance in order to assure peasants that if they produced more, the state would not buy more from them, as had happened in 1954. The very important exception to this was that 40 per cent of any additional surplus could be bought in bumper-harvest areas. This policy was admittedly promulgated to boost peasant morale. In the summer and autumn of 1955 *san-ting* was extended from the *hsiang* to

[35] *TKP* editorial, March 9, 1955.

[36] "Speech by T'ao Lu-chia," Secretary of the Shansi Provincial Party Committee, to the NPC, July 26, 1955, in *CB*, No. 356 (September 13, 1955). See also the original in *Shan-hsi Jih-pao*, July 29, 1955.

[37] *TKP*, editorial, March 9, 1955; "Pu-chih hsia-cheng," *Shan-hsi Jih-pao*, May 19, 1955, also referred to purchases of peasants' rations, seed, and feed grain.

[38] *Shan-hsi Jih-pao*, May 19, 1955.

each household. The peasants were told that the state would buy only 80–90 per cent of their normal surplus, and that quotas would not be changed for three years. *San-ting* was thus designed to give the peasants a feeling of security concerning the state's claims on them.[39]

If the UP drive of 1954 had left many peasants upset, the handling of supply (unified marketing, or UM) in the first few months of 1955 did not exactly restore their confidence. In large part this reaction resulted from the low priority of UM. As Ch'en Yün pointed out, from November, 1953—when UPM was put into effect—to April, 1955, the leadership had been concerned primarily with state purchases. This emphasis was natural enough, since the main purpose of the system initially had been to assure supply to the state. But from the peasants' viewpoint this meant that they could not depend on what the state had promised—namely, prompt supply at the time of need. In 1954 purchases were made in Kwangtung, Kwangsi, and southern Hunan on the assumption that these areas would reap an adequate sweet potato crop. Frost ruined this crop in January, 1955, however, and in the first weeks of May, because the leaders underestimated the extent of the calamities, "for a time" supply was "insufficient."[40]

Each administrative level down to the *hsiang* was supposed to draw up a grain-marketing plan at the time when state purchases were made. The plan was to include estimates of the quantities of grain needed by grain-short households, and also a schedule of deliveries. Actual supply was to be made only at the time of need, in order to forestall waste, but in the meantime peasants were supposed to receive grain-supply tickets or at least be told how much they would be allowed to buy. According to one report on Shansi, the grain-market plan and the issuing of the tickets took place under the same "socialist" pressure as purchasing; the emphasis was on "greatly reducing" the number of households asking for state supply.[41] There were long delays elsewhere in the issuing of the grain tickets. In Han-chung special district, Shensi, for example, UP was completed by the end of December, but the district did not get around to dealing with state supply until

[39] For the March directives on *san-ting,* see "State Council Decision on Spring Plowing and Production," adopted March 3, 1955, published by NCNA, Peking, March 9, 1955, in *CB,* No. 318 (March 15, 1955). See also *TKP* editorial, March 9, 1955, and *JMJP* editorial, March 9, 1955, in URS, I (September 23, 1955). In August, "Provisional Measures for Unified Purchase and Unified Sale of Grain in Rural Areas" were promulgated; NCNA, Peking, August 25, 1955, in *CB,* No. 354 (September 7, 1955).

[40] Ch'en, "Unified Purchase and Distribution of Grain."

[41] *Shan-hsi Jih-pao,* January 1, 1955.

February. Purchase tickets had not been issued to peasants in 30 per cent of the *hsiang* as late as April 15, presumably well into the time when grain stocks of partially grain-short households were becoming exhausted.[42] Similar delays in supply were also reported in other provinces.[43]

Not only was state supply overshadowed in importance and priority by state purchase, it was also eclipsed by other pressing tasks in which rural leadership was engaged. Until a Central Committee and State Council directive made supply work into a top priority item at the end of April, 1955 (see below), rural leaders were engaged in cooperativization, the rectification of abuses from cooperativization, spring planting, *san-ting* work, and a variety of other matters. Not only did supply work have a low priority, but also policy on the matter was not very clear, and hence when peasants began demanding grain, all sorts of errors were made. According to the regime, as we have seen, the main error was excessive liberality, but in some cases the opposite error was also committed. Let us now look at peasant behavior and at the reaction of local cadres.

Peasant Behavior During the Supply Crisis

Fear and panic spread through many villages in the spring of 1955. Peasants asked cadres to give them supply tickets; they complained bitterly of hunger and even of impending starvation. One peasant, later exposed as an owner of adequate grain stocks, reportedly complained: "During last autumn's purchase they cleaned us out; now there's nothing to eat."[44] In the same *ts'un* in which this complaint was made, thirty to forty people would seek out cadres every day to request grain tickets. One peasant would ask for three hundred catties of grain, another for five hundred. If cadres did not grant the request, they would cry or scold the cadres (*yu k'u yu ma*); some would even "intimidate" them. Sometimes entire *ts'un* would claim to be grain short; in other cases a large proportion of the population of a *hsiang* or even of a *hsien* would ask for grain.[45] Elsewhere disturbances broke

---

[42] *Shen-hsi Jih-pao,* May 5, 1955.

[43] *Ho-pei Jih-pao,* February 2, 1955.

[44] *Shan-hsi Jih-pao,* May 3, 1955.

[45] See *TKP* editorial, April 23, 1955; *TKP* editorial, April 30, 1955, in *SCMP,* No. 1041 (May 5, 1955); *JMJP* editorial, April 24, 1955; for generalizations about peasant grain demands. For a report on a *ts'un,* all of whose households, including cadres and Party members, claimed grain shortage, see "Pu shih kou ti to, yeh pu shih kung to hsiao" (Neither Was Too Much Bought nor Too Little Supplied"), *Shan-hsi Jih-pao,* May 19, 1955.

out, or peasants fled to the cities in the expectation that food was to be had there.[46]

A particular case may serve to illustrate the issues as the Chinese regime saw them. In 1954 the harvest in T'an-chen *hsiang,* Ling-shih *hsien,* Shansi, had been allocated as follows:[47]

Tax:	213,823 catties or	13.94% of the harvest
UP:	468,374 catties or	30.53% of the harvest
Seed:	19,083 catties or	1.24% of the harvest
Fodder:	97,877 catties or	6.39% of the harvest
Rations:	734,421 catties or	47.90% of the harvest
Harvest:	1,533,578 catties or	100.00% of the harvest

According to these data, each member of the *hsiang*'s 460 peasant households, a total of 1,697 persons, had available to him an average of 433 catties of grain, which exceeded the minimum per capita ration of 360 catties. Yet 177 households (39 per cent) claimed to be grain short, and most of them asked for over 200 catties. Investigation revealed that of the 177 households only 82 (46.3 per cent) really lacked grain, while the remaining 95 (53.7 per cent) had made false claims. Of the 82 grain-short households, 63 had been victims of excess purchase and taxation in the 1954 UP campaign; the other 19 households were not able to produce enough to meet their own requirements because of inadequate land or manpower.

The fact that genuinely grain-short households should have asked for state supply is not surprising. The main analytical interest is in those peasants who should not, according to the regime, have complained at all. But even among the genuinely grain short, there were some whose motives illustrate the peasants' fear that they could not depend on the state. These peasants still had some grain stock on hand, but it would be consumed before long. For fear that the state reserves would soon be exhausted, they put in their requests ahead of time. The story of T'an-chen *hsiang* attributed these peasants' attitude to gullibility in believing rumors spread by counterrevolutionaries and bad elements—an issue to which we shall return. Fear that state reserves would not last was apparently quite widespread, and thus when one peasant saw his neighbor ask for grain, he hurried to do the same.[48]

[46] For mention of disturbances and riots, see below; for mention of peasants' going to the cities, see *Shan-hsi Jih-pao* editorial, May 5, 1955, and "Pu shih kou te to," *ibid.,* May 19, 1955.

[47] *Ibid.,* July 19, 1955. The story said that the harvest was 1,532,986 catties, which is 592 catties less than the total indicated here.

[48] *Ibid.* For a generalization of this kind of behavior, see *TKP* editorial, April 30, 1955.

Why did peasants who reportedly had adequate stocks claim to have exhausted them? According to the story on T'an-chen *hsiang,* these peasants looked upon lax control over state supply as an opportunity to hoard and to accumulate a reserve against future emergencies. They too did not trust CCP assurances that the UPM system would protect them against future harvest failures.[49] Other surplus households were anxious to be classified as grain short in the hope of evading future state purchases, which they feared would be even larger than those in 1954. One peasant in T'an-chen *hsiang* was quoted as saying, "Just recognize us as a grainshort household . . . you don't actually have to sell us any grain." Other peasants were afraid of "disclosing wealth" by not claiming grain shortage. They ware afraid that if cadres found out that they still had grain reserves, they would be asked to make another sale to the state or to peasants at the state-run grain markets. What was more, they feared criticism for having concealed true output during the 1954 purchase campaign, and possibly even more serious punishment.[50] One other implication behind these attitudes is not hard to discern: on the one hand the CCP told peasants that producing a surplus and selling it to the state was "glorious," but on the other hand, most surplus producers were at least middle peasants and maybe even rich peasants (class enemies). At a time when peasant class status was in a state of flux, producing a surplus raised issues of political status and even of security. This issue may have prompted some peasants to take evasive action. Finally, and very generally, peasants simply behaved in their time-honored, self-interested, "petty-bourgeois" way and not in accordance with Communist ethics: " 'Let us first consume the food of the state and then come to our own' " . . . " 'let us buy more food from the state, store it up, and it will prove very convenient.' "[51]

Rumor played a very important role in communicating anxiety and prompting peasants to ask for state supply even when they did not really need it. Rumors that state grain reserves would soon be exhausted apparently spread rapidly and were widely believed. In one case from Kiangsu Province, a peasant's wife who heard one such rumor promptly went to Shanghai to live off relatives while concealing the rice her family still had.[52] This case illustrates the efficacy of

---

[49] *TKP* editorial, April 30, 1955.

[50] For one example of this fear, see "Tsu-chih shih-ch'ang chin-hsing t'iao-chi" (Organize Markets for the Purpose of [Grain] Regulation), *Shan-hsi Jih-pao,* May 7, 1955.

[51] *JMJP* editorial, June 26, 1955.

[52] *Hsin-hua Jih-pao* (New China Daily), Nanking, May 29, 1955.

rumor, particularly in the case of those who were least well socialized into the Communist system.

Almost invariably the CCP charged that rumors originated with those individuals in the villages who were regarded by the regime as class enemies, such as individuals classified during or after land reform as "counterrevolutionaries," "bad elements" (petty criminals), "rich peasants," or "landlords." The CCP took care to differentiate between these enemies and the "backward masses" who were influenced by them.[53] Rumor mongering was a prominent offense attributed to class enemies. In the case of UPM, the press asserted that class enemies opposed it because it was part of socialist transformation generally or because it was specifically disadvantageous to them, as was true in the case of rich peasants. (According to one account, ordinary peasants were to sell 70–90 per cent of their surplus but rich peasants 95 per cent.[54]) Sabotage of UM was reportedly carried out by taking advantage of defects in the implementation of the system and by utilizing the peasants' traditional outlook. Class enemies thus sowed rumors that slandered and distorted policy and that sought to undermine peasant confidence in the government and to drive a wedge between government and people. A bad element in Anhwei, for example, aroused the masses with the rumor that whoever did not ask for state supply was thereby indicating that he still had surplus grain and hence had concealed it in 1954. This kind of talk fanned the fears previously mentioned. In a Honan village a rich peasant goaded nine households to quarrel with the *hsiang* government over supply.[55] In a Shansi village a reactionary landlord intimidated cadres, spread rumors, incited a crowd to disturb the peace by brawling with the staff of a local granary, and attempted to start a riot.[56] In another case an "unlawful element" in a Kwangtung village persuaded fifty peasants to "abandon production" and go to the *ch'ü* government (the subdistrict superior to the *hsiang* and subordinate to the *hsien*) and ask for grain, thereby creating a tense atmosphere.[57]

Besides speading rumors and inciting peasants, class enemies were charged with intentionally undermining UPM by having concealed

---

[53] *TKP*, May 11, 1955, in *SCMP*, No. 1040 (May 18, 1955).

[54] "Pu chih hsia-cheng," *Shan-hsi Jih-pao*, May 19, 1955. For an important editorial on sabotage of grain marketing, see *TKP* editorial, May 18, 1955, in *SCMP*, No. 1056 (May 26, 1955).

[55] *TKP* editorial, May 18, 1955.

[56] *Shan-hsi Jih-pao*, May 21, 1955.

[57] *Vüeh-tung Nung-min Pao* (East Kwangtung Peasant Newspaper), June 3, 1955.

their own surpluses in 1954 and by faking shortages in the spring.[58] In general, class-enemy activity was regarded as one of the "important causes" of the grain crisis. In Haimen *hsien,* Kiangsu, for example, a grain crisis erupted in 81 out of the 146 *hsiang;* in 18 of these, "bad elements" were said to have undermined UPM.[59] As a report from Szechwan put it, "This can be said: where grain shortage was serious, there the sabotaging activities of the class enemy were the most rampant."[60]

How can this aspect of the grain crisis be evaluated? The presence of class enemies is not really necessary to account for peasant behavior. In the prevailing atmosphere of uncertainty and anxiety, rumors undoubtedly circulated even without the help of class enemies. Hence one might conclude that the regime used this issue as a way of finding scapegoats and as an indirect means of putting pressure on the peasants. It is also improbable that in villages in which Communist political controls were strong, known class enemies, such as former landlords —who were the most obvious targets for repression and struggle— would have drawn attention to themselves by "sabotaging" UPM. In the years after land reform, however, political controls appear to have eroded to some degree as vigilance was relaxed.[61] In some villages land reform itself was not carried out too well, while in others control was later "usurped" by class enemies. A national appraisal in October, 1955, said that "feudal forces" were still in control of 5 per cent of *hsiang-ts'un,* while a report from a Hunan special district consisting of 13 *hsien* stated that "democratic reforms" were carried out in 1955–56 in 78 out of a total of 762 *hsiang.*[62] These percentages may give some indication of the degree to which political control was an issue in Chinese villages in 1955.[63] It may plausibly be concluded that in those

[58] For instances of this sort, see *Szu-ch'uan Jih-pao,* April 30, 1955, *Shan-hsi Jih-pao,* May 25, 1955, and *Hsin-hua Jih-pao,* Nanking, June 2, 1955.

[59] *TKP* editorial, May 18, 1955.

[60] "Speech by Deputy Liu Wen-hui," July 28, 1955, to the NPC, in *CB,* No. 349 (August 25, 1955).

[61] Periodic newspaper editorials criticized local cadres for having become careless about the threat of class enemies. For one example, see *JMJP* editorial, April 28, 1954, in *SCMP,* No. 805 (May 11, 1954).

[62] See *Decisions on Agricultural Co-operation* (Peking: Foreign Languages Press, 1956), p. 29, and *Ch'en-chou Ch'ün-chung Pao* (Ch'en-chou Masses Newspaper), Hunan, May 10, 1956.

[63] These data would seem to indicate that the problem of political control was less severe than some scholars have believed it to be. In his *Ideology and Organization in Communist China* (Berkeley and Los Angeles: University of California Press, 1966), Franz Schurmann writes of the 1955 period that "power had to be seized from the traditional village leadership" (p. 446). The kind of power struggle implied in this quotation seems to have taken place only in a small minority of villages.

villages where members of the pre-Communist rural elite (landlords, for example) or a newly risen elite, such as rich peasants, retained or gained influence among the peasants, the grain crisis was at least in part caused by them, particularly when such enemies occupied formal leadership positions.

LEADERSHIP AND THE SUPPLY CRISIS

In the preceding section we discussed the reaction of "the masses." The fact that they did not behave in accordance with Communist norms was not perhaps very surprising even to the CCP, for the masses by definition are easily misled, particularly when policy is poorly implemented, and by themselves the masses cannot recognize their "true" interests. But what about the leadership? In a situation such as the supply crisis, the task of leadership—from the Communist point of view—was that it should not merely aggregate, give shape to, and champion the mass demands (in this case, for more grain). Doing so would be committing the deviation of "tailism." Instead, leaders were expected to analyze the situation in a village in the light of CCP policy and goals, "seek [Communist] truth through facts," find out whether the mass demands were justified, and mobilize the masses to understand and abide by policy, ending any unjustified clamor for grain. During the supply crisis, however, many cadres behaved quite differently. Let us first look at the behavior of basic level (*hsiang* and *ts'un*) cadres and then at the behavior of *hsien* level cadres.

National evaluations took a rather critical view of cadre behavior, as these quotations indicate:

These very serious problems that have arisen in the grain supply are completely inseparable from weaknesses in the work of certain basic-level cadres.[64]

. . . Many of our basic-level cadres blindly echo the cry [of the masses for grain] without analyzing the situation and let planned marketing take [its] own course.[65]

To refrain from investigation and analysis . . . to take up immediately what one hears from other people . . . on the food problem and thereby create an alarming atmosphere betrays an attitude of irresponsibility which easily causes damage.[66]

Basic level cadre behavior fell into several categories. At one extreme, a "very small number"[67] were guilty of favoritism and other malpractices (*hsün-ssu wu-pi*). They gave grain tickets to relatives

[64] *JMJP* editorial, April 24, 1955.
[65] NCNA, Peking, April 30, 1955, in *SCMP*, No. 1041 (May 5, 1955).
[66] *JMJP* editorial, June 26, 1955.
[67] *Ibid.*, April 24, 1955.

and friends, forged or altered tickets, and reported themselves as grain short even though they were not. Hence they lost their crucial model function vis-à-vis the masses (the *tai-t'ou* role). Instead of setting an example and stimulating the peasants to abide by state policy, they in effect encouraged the peasants to imitate their wrongdoing. The press criticized cadres for falsifying grain holdings, for taking more than their share (*mao-ling*), and for other corrupt practices.[68] The simple act of incorrectly reporting one's own holdings was perhaps most common: ". . . Among our rural CCP members there are even branch committee members who falsely reported shortage of grain . . . or who reported severe shortage even though they needed only a little and who thus fell among the 'ideologically grain-short households.' "[69]

Political vulnerability played a role in motivating cadres to report themselves as grain short. After land reform quite a few cadres became middle peasants, including some who rose to well-off middle peasant status, while a few even became rich peasants. Analyses of attitudes of rural Party members indicated that some who belonged to these class categories had become property conscious to the point of "dissatisfaction" with UPM and with socialist transformation generally.[70] Most of them, however, must have felt themselves to be in a precarious position—and possibly subject to purge. In 1955 the CCP increasingly emphasized "reliance" on still poor peasants and recruitment of new cadres from the lowest social stratum. Middle peasant Party members and cadres probably became anxious to improve their class status; one way of doing so was to claim shortage of grain. One article described a member of a *hsiang* Party branch committee who still owned one hundred catties and was afraid of being regarded as well-off. Hence he asked for thirty catties of state supply: enough, presumably, to put him on the safe side of the political ledger.[71]

"Selfish" or corrupt cadre behavior involved a variety of village institutions. Newspaper reports charged some staffs of the village supply and marketing cooperatives with misappropriation and misuse of grain.[72] An interesting and widely publicized case was that of the manager of a producers' cooperative—concurrently a Party branch official—who succeeded in obtaining an unnecessarily large grain allo-

---

[68] *Ibid.* See also *TKP* editorial, March 31, 1955, and *Shan-hsi Jih-pao* editorial, May 5, 1955.

[69] *Shan-hsi Jih-pao,* April 10, 1955.

[70] For a very interesting article on this issue, see *ibid.,* July 21, 1955.

[71] *Ibid.,* April 10, 1955.

[72] *Ibid.,* June 13, 1955, and July 6, 1955.

cation for his cooperative by nearly doubling the feed requirements for its livestock. The exposé stated that this cadre had a "localist" and "special privilege" mentality and then generalized the case by pointing out that "almost all" cooperatives had tried to deceive the state (although it was unclear whether the newspaper was referring to the cooperatives in this one Shansi *hsien* or to cooperatives generally).[73]

Corruption and malpractices were most severe in those cases, already mentioned in the preceding section, where village institutions such as *hsiang* governments, Party branches, or cooperatives were under class-enemy control or where cadres had been "bought" by class enemies. A speech to the 1955 session of the National People's Congress, for example, described a *ts'un* in Szechwan which required 15,990 catties of state supply but got 71,000 because of the machinations of a counterrevolutionary who had used small favors to "win over" the village head, the chief of the militia unit, and members of a production committee. This culprit "intimidated" a hundred people and got them to surround the *hsiang* government building and to demand state supply.[74]

Another case was that of a Party member in Kiangsu *ts'un*, a poor peasant and concurrently a militia squad leader, who had allowed a rich peasant to lend him money. Because of this relationship, the rich peasant was able to evade state purchase and to obtain grain-supply tickets fraudulently. This so influenced the peasants in the village that a tense supply situation arose. The Party member's misbehavior was discovered; he made an agonizing reappraisal, criticized himself, and was put on probation for a year.[75] Cases of wealthier peasants' corrupting poor cadres probably were not isolated, although the over-all frequency of class-enemy activity should not be overstated. Not many reports showed a frequency comparable to the one reported for Hsin-fan *hsien*, Szechwan, where in 1954 the enemy was said to have corrupted 171 *hsiang* and *ts'un* cadres on the issue of UPM, including members of the Party and Youth League.[76] Even this large number needs to be put in perspective, since there are several thousand basic level cadres in a *hsien*.

According to the press, however, the main cause of basic level cadre

[73] The *hsien* was Ting-hsiang *hsien*, concerning which *Shan-hsi Jih-pao* published a major exposé to which I shall refer on several occasions. See "Yu pei-tung chuan-hsiang chu-tung" (Turn from a Passive to an Active State), *ibid.*, May 25, 1955.

[74] "Speech by Deputy Liu Wen-hui."

[75] *Hsin-hua Jih-pao*, Nanking, September 18, 1955.

[76] "Speech by Deputy Liu Wen-hui."

deviations was not corruption or "selfishness," but poor implementation of policy. The main charge was that cadres had misunderstood policy and had failed to tackle the supply issue; they were criticized for not having mobilized the masses to separate valid from false claims. Instead, cadres accepted the claims of all comers. Fearing "to offend anyone,"[77] cadres distributed supply tickets on an egalitarian basis, or simply wrote out tickets to the amount requested by given households. Egalitarian supply left the genuinely grain-short peasants dissatisfied, since they got less than the amount they needed.[78] Egalitarian or lax distribution of supply tickets resulted in the rapid exhaustion of supply quotas. When the cadres of a *ts'un* asked their superiors to increase the quota, the next higher level (the *hsiang* or *ch'ü*) sometimes responded by stopping all supply and refusing to honor tickets already issued. The press noted that this made those who did not have enough to eat "very dissatisfied."[79] Stoppage of all grain sales widened the circle of peasant anixety, since there was an additional group of peasants—estimated at one-fifth of the peasant population—who were not considered grain short but who sold some grain in the autumn and expected to buy back an equivalent amount in the spring. "Revolving grain stocks" had been kept on hand for them. Refusal to sell from these stocks now caused additional deprivation.[80] Elsewhere cadres "didn't dare" announce to the masses what the original supply quota had been,[81] while in "some localities mistaken practices such as blindly carrying out all-round readjustment . . . indiscriminately cutting down supply plans and universally withdrawing all grain purchasing certificates or issuing additional ones have given rise to a new state of confusion."[82]

Aside from the light that the supply crisis sheds on the level of cadre competence—especially on their ability to analyze a situation according to Communist standards—a major point of interest is the susceptibility of cadres to pressure from the peasants. They were "deceived"

[77] *JMJP* editorial, May 10, 1955, in *SCMP,* No. 1050 (May 18, 1955).

[78] In one case of egalitarian distribution, each recipient in a *ts'un* got eighteen catties of grain per month; "Pu shih kou ti to," *Shan-hsi Jih-pao,* May 19, 1955.

[79] *TKP* editorial, April 23, 1955.

[80] For mention of this additional fifth of the peasants, who buy and sell grain, see Ch'en, "Unified Purchase and Distribution of Grain," and Chou Po-p'ing, "The Policy of Unified Purchase and Sale of Grain Shall Not Be Frustrated," *Liang-shih,* No. 7 (July, 1957), in *ECMM,* No. 101 (September 9, 1957). For material on the mishandling of the revolving grain stocks, see *TKP* editorial, March 31, 1955, and *JMJP* editorial, June 26, 1955.

[81] For one example of this, see "Tsai kuo-chia k'ung-chih chih-piao nei ho-li kung-ying" (Reasonably Supply [Grain] Within the State's Control Norms), *Shan-hsi Jih-pao,* May 7, 1955.

[82] *NFJP,* April 17, 1955, in *SCMP,* No. 1056 (May 26, 1955).

by the mass clamor for grain, and they agreed with the masses that "too much" had been bought in 1954 and "too little was being supplied."[83] Moreover, "lacking plans and for fear of being stuck with inadequate sales quotas, some *hsien, ch'ü, hsiang,* and *ts'un* cadres [were] only concerned with requesting grain supplies from superior levels without analyzing supply and sale of grain in rural districts."[84] Quite a few articles described how cadres would "stretch out their hands" (*shen-shou*) and in effect lobby a higher level for more grain. One *ts'un* cadre reportedly drew up a supply plan for twenty-eight households in his village and threatened to resign unless it was met; it was only after "education" by his *hsiang* branch that he admitted that no one actually needed the grain.[85]

Although it would be difficult to document this, it is likely that pressure from friends and relatives was greatest in the case of *ts'un* cadres, since they were in constant and close contact with ordinary peasants and hence were presumably most susceptible to the pull of particularistic relationships. Nor were basic level *hsiang* cadres immune to such pressures, since they too were locally recruited cadres who shared membership in a *ts'un* (one of the component villages that made up the *hsiang*).[86] The quotation cited above also describes cadres at the *ch'ü* and *hsien* levels as championing peasant interests. In their case it may be surmised that it was not so much pressure from friends and relatives that made them "stretch out their hands" as it was a more general fear of losing authority in the eyes of the peasants. In its appeals to the peasants, the CCP claimed that it had brought a new form of rule to China, one characterized by genuine concern for popular welfare, and one that contrasted sharply with the callous attitude of previous regimes. In the spring of 1955, however, peasants on a wide scale complained of hunger for the first time. Quite possibly, even leading cadres at the *hsien* level may have panicked for fear of losing face with the peasants.

Whatever the validity of this interpretation, the press did cite a specific instance of a *hsien* Party committee that "lost its head" and in

---

[83] *Yüeh-tung Nung-min Pao,* June 6, 1955, and *Shan-hsi Jih-pao* editorial, May 20, 1955.

[84] NCNA, Paoting, May 2, 1955, in *SCMP,* No. 1043 (May 7–9, 1955).

[85] NCNA, Nanking, May 2, 1955, in *SCMP,* No. 1043 (May 7–9, 1955).

[86] "Pu shih kou ti to," *Shan-hsi Jih-pao,* May 19, 1955, said that "Many *hsiang* and *ts'un* cadres were deceived by the people shouting 'grain shortage.' . . ." The same article described a *ts'un* in which all peasants, all Party members, and all cadres claimed to be short of grain. For another case of cadre identification with peasants, in a Hopei village, see *JMJP,* July 2, 1955.

effect abandoned Communist principles of leadership. The Ting-hsiang *hsien* committtee, Shansi, surrendered to the defeatist notion that UP had been excessive and that the peasants were entitled to more grain. In the view of the national and provincial press, however, these peasant demands were unfounded. The Ting-hsiang *hsien* Party committee had not grasped the "central link" in handling supply (political work), had not investigated conditions, and had failed to uncover and correct rightist thinking. Hence "very many" *hsiang* chiefs, Party branch secretaries, cooperative chairmen, and peasants asked the *hsien* committee for more grain. Instead of sticking to the planned total of 4.8 million catties, cadres issued supply tickets amounting to 8.29 million catties. The *hsien* committee entertained the "illusion" of asking its superior, the Hsin-hsien special district committee, to allocate the difference, and it was only when the special district committee sent "assistance" that the Ting-hsiang *hsien* committee began to rectify its errors.[87]

Another *hsien* committee, that of P'ing-yao, Shansi, committed two different errors under the impact of the supply crisis. This committee panicked and issued a directive in late April allowing and encouraging free trade and unrestricted borrowing and lending of grain. Within a few days grain prices rose, leading to "speculation" and "exploitation." P'ing-yao's superior committee uncovered this violation of state policy and ordered it revoked immediately, but not before "serious political damage" had been done. Simultaneously the committee adopted the adventurist policy of encouraging search for and seizure of hidden grain reserves. In three days in one village, 2,506 catties of grain were seized forcibly from 37 middle peasants, undermining the unity of the peasants and causing "great damage" to the influence of the Party among the masses. This error too was uncovered by P'ing-yao's superior committee.[88]

In concluding these two sections on peasant pressure and leadership deviations, it must be noted that many questions remain unanswered —and may be unanswerable, given the nature of the newspaper reports. For example, one would like to know why a supply crisis occurred in X *hsien* but not in Y *hsien*. In Shansi a "tense situation"

---

[87] "Yu pei-tung chuan-hsiang chu-tung," *Shan-hsi Jih-pao*, May 25, 1955. See also the editorial in the same issue: "Chieh-shou Ting-hsiang hsien tsai liang-shih t'ung-hsiao kung-tso chung ti chiao-hsün" (Learn the Lesson of Ting-hsiang *hsien* in Grain-Supply Work). The case was given national prominence in a *JMJP* editorial, June 26, 1955.

[88] *Shan-hsi Jih-pao*, May 20, 1955, and June 18, 1955.

erupted in all but twenty *hsien*,[89] but apparently no comparative material was published on these *hsien*. Moreover, *Shan-hsi Jih-pao* reported only on less than half of the *hsien* in which grain crises did occur (twenty-nine out of seventy-two, by one rough count). The amount of information released about each *hsien* was usually fragmentary, frequently dealing with only one *hsiang* or even *ts'un*. Hence, many variables that may have influenced peasant and cadre behavior remain obscure, as, for example, differences in organizational strength and social structure.

On one issue, however, a generalization may be advanced: in Shansi, grain crises occurred both in *hsien* that had been part of the wartime anti-Japanese bases and in *hsien* liberated only after World War II. The former included *hsien* in Ch'ang-chih special district in southeast Shansi and Wu-t'ai *hsien* in the northeast, both of which areas were part of wartime border governments.[90] One might have expected that in such areas both peasants and cadres would have behaved more in accordance with CCP principles than in other areas. These cases, incompletely described as they are, seem nonetheless to suggest that the wartime relations between CCP and peasants may not necessarily be relevant for an understanding of CCP-peasant relations in the post-1949 period, and that there may not necessarily have been anything lasting about these relationships. The distinction between the anti-imperialist, antifeudal, New Democratic revolution and the socialist revolution may thus be of greater importance than is sometimes realized. The issue is too complex to be fully analyzed here. Greater rural organizational strength in the old liberated areas facilitated socialist transformation, for example, as is indicated by statistics on the rate of cooperativization. On the other hand, because of the long time interval between land reform and socialist transformation, the old areas had to cope with a more serious problem of cadre class mobility to middle peasant and rich peasant status, which complicated the tasks of building socialism.[91] One may tentatively conclude that having been

[89] "Speech by T'ao Lu-chia."

[90] For a report on Ch'ang-chih special district, see *Shan-hsi Jih-pao*, April 30, 1955; for an article on Wu-t'ai *hsien*, "Wu-t'ai hsien ti liang-shih t'ung-hsiao kung-tso" (Grain-Supply Work in Wu-t'ai *hsien*), *ibid.*, May 14, 1955. In Wu-t'ai *hsien*, 80 per cent of surplus households asked for supply and 40 per cent of all households were supplied. For a map of base areas, see Wang Chien-min, *Chung-kuo Kung-ch'an tang shih-kao* (Historical Materials of the Chinese Communist Party) (Taipei, 1965), III, 330.

[91] On class problems of rural Party members, particularly in old areas, see *Shan-hsi Jih-pao*, July 21, 1955. Recently Liu Shao-ch'i was criticized for having condoned the existence of rich peasant Party members in the Northeast; see *Peking Review*, No. 28 July 7, 1967).

part of a wartime base did not imply peasant or leadership behavior in accordance with CCP norms in the post-1949 period.

MOBILIZING THE VILLAGE TO REORGANIZE AND REDUCE SUPPLY

On April 28, 1955, the Central Committee and the State Council issued a joint directive that made grain supply a top-priority item in rural work and addressed itself clearly and unambiguously to what the regime considered to be the main problem—excess supply.[92] The directive asserted that grain sales were largest in those places where the peasant outcry was loudest, that this was "extremely abnormal," that the trend had to be "reversed instantly without any hesitation," and that sales could and should be reduced by 20, 30, or even 50 per cent, still meeting the needs of genuinely grain-short peasants. It ordered government and Party organizations in areas where grain sales exceeded quotas to mobilize themselves "forthwith" and to send cadres to the villages. These cadres were to announce to the peasants the state sales quota for each *hsiang,* and to explain that the quotas should not and could not be increased and that they were in fact adequate, provided only needy peasants were supplied. Each request for supply was to be considered separately, and unjustified ones were to be "resolutely" slashed. "Patient" criticism was to be aimed at peasants who had asked for unnecessary supply, while those who had already bought but not yet consumed excess grain were to be "educated" and "persuaded" to return the unneeded portion.

The directive of April 28 also warned against abusing surplus-holding middle peasants:

. . . We should not permit mobilization of the peasants to go so far as to ask surplus grain owners to offer part of the surplus grain originally in their possession. For that could easily lead to a squeeze on the middle peasants, thereby giving rise to chaos in the rural areas, hindering spring plowing and production and offsetting the positive significance of the '3-fixed' measure. It would be unfavorable to the solidarity of the peasants and incompatible with the state policy on the middle peasants.

The reason for this strong warning against anti-middle peasant practices was that in April, 1955, much of rural policy had been aimed at rectifying abuses of middle peasant interests committed during the cooperativization campaign of the preceding winter.[93] As the quotation

[92] "State Council and CCP Central Committee Directive on Intensified Reorganization of Planned Marketing of Grain," NCNA, Peking, April 28, 1955, in *SCMP,* No. 1041 (May 5, 1955).

[93] See "State Council Decision on Spring Plowing and Production," NCNA, Peking, March 9, 1955, in *CB,* No. 318 (March 15, 1955).

suggests, the main purpose of *san-ting* was to reassure middle peasants, and an abusive drive to reorganize supply would have threatened to undo what *san-ting* was trying to accomplish. The point was not lost on some cadres, who did not quite understand how they could reconcile supply reorganization with persuasive *san-ting* propaganda.[94] The problem was that although state supply was not to be increased, grain-short peasants had to be fed; grain had to come from somewhere, and one source apparently was hidden grain reserves. Nonetheless it is important to note that the mobilization effort that was called for was characterized by its careful limitation of the degree of pressure that could be brought to bear on the middle peasants.

Mobilization of the masses—previously defined as an effort to make peasants do what they normally would not do (in this case reduce their claims on state supply)—presupposed mobilization of leadership. This required unifying their attitudes, thoroughly familiarizing them with the policy they were to implement, and persuading them of the merits of that policy. Mobilization of leadership began at the level of "responsible leadership," the *hsien*. In those *hsien* where the leadership had committed serious errors, special emphasis was placed on this initial step in the process of mobilization.[95]

When mobilization was extended to basic level leaders, the two most common techniques were to hold a *hsien* level meeting and to send a work team composed of *hsien* cadres to the village. Holding a meeting at the *hsien* had the advantage of physically removing basic level leaders from their native villages and hence from the pressure of their friends and relatives. If one visualizes basic level leaders as exposed on the one hand to pressure from the peasants and on the other hand to pressure from their organizational superiors, then the *hsien* meeting was an opportunity to expose village leaders to universalistic principles at a time when the impact of particularistic realities was reduced. The purpose of such a meeting was to make village cadres believe that the UPM policy as a whole was a very good thing but that it had been misapplied in specific instances—thereby restoring their faith in the CCP. Inasmuch as particularistic influences on them could not be eliminated, however, it seems reasonable to assume that basic level cadres would not have swallowed this explanation and acted on it unless at least to some extent they accepted the view that the policy as a whole had merit. It does not seem likely that village cadres would

[94] *JMJP* editorial, May 10, 1955.
[95] "Yu pei-tung chuan-hsiang chu-tung," *Shan-hsi Jih-pao*, May 25, 1955.

have cooperated with any degree of zeal if UPM and supply reorganization had appeared to them as a total and unmitigated deprivation.

An example of such a meeting was a two-day meeting for twenty-six hundred *hsiang* Party members, leaders of the Youth League, and activists, held by the Ting-hsiang *hsien* committee. The conference exposed irrational supply practices and hammered home the message that the crisis was due to mishandling of the quotas rather than to inadequate quotas. Cadre deviations were criticized sternly, which served to remind cadres that they were subject to disciplinary sanctions. An example was made of the cooperative manager previously cited, who had misappropriated feed grain; for this and other offenses he was expelled from the Party. The behavior of such culprits was contrasted with that of a model Party member who had successfully coped with the supply situation in his village. *Hsien* level meetings of this type also had the advantage of bringing together leaders from different villages and stimulating a sense of competition among them, which increased their zeal to do well.

When a work team went to a *hsiang* (or sometimes directly to a *ts'un*), it would follow a procedure that varied locally only in detail. The procedure began with the mobilization of the village leadership.[96] The team would convene a Party branch conference (or some other meeting that included most of the village elite) for the purpose of studying the nation's grain policy, ascertaining and rectifying the attitudes of Party members, and analyzing the grain situation in the village. The first goal of the meeting was for every participant to gain a "correct" understanding of the supply crisis, so that everyone's state of mind would be changed from a passive and pessimistic to an active and optimistic state. Next came sessions of criticism and self-criticism, in which each local Party member would report on how he had behaved during the crisis. Those who had joined in with grain-short claims now confessed their error: ". . . I had enough [grain] to last till June, but when spring came, I too shouted 'grain-shortage,' being afraid that [state] supply would run out . . . I reported shortage early, influencing several households to do the same. This was wrong."[97] Cadres who had violated CCP norms felt threatened by disciplinary sanctions and

[96] This summary of work procedure is an amalgam from various articles, including *JMJP* editorial, April 24, 1955; *Shan-hsi Jih-pao*, April 10, 1955, in which an early instance of supply reorganization is described as having been undertaken by a work team; "Wo sheng cheng-tun liang-shih t'ung-hsiao kung-tso" (The Work of Reorganizing Grain Supply in Our Province), *ibid.*, May 5, 1955.

[97] "Ts'ung san wan liu ch'ien chin tao pa ch'ien wu pai chin" (From 36,000 Catties to 8,500 Catties), *Shan-hsi Jih-pao*, May 14, 1955.

no doubt redoubled their efforts to cooperate in the drive to reorganize supply.

Policy study and criticism sessions served to reassert the ties of village leaders to the system as a whole. The members of the work team, with whom the village leaders shared Party or other organizational membership, were now in a position to ask the village cadres to analyze specific supply conditions in the village. This sequence in the mobilization of local leaders made it possible for the outsiders, the work team, to use the village elite for the purpose of obtaining crucial information about the village, such as data on the grain holdings of particular households. This illustrates the importance of village level leadership; even though many village level leaders deviated during the supply crisis, they were indispensable during the movement to rectify the crisis. The alternative would have been to undertake a much lengthier and more complex effort by outside work teams to gain access directly to the peasants, a process that would have been analogous to land reform when Communist-oriented village leaders had not yet been recruited.

Following the mobilization of village leaders (a process that usually also included mobilization of secondary organized groups, such as the Youth League, the women's group, and activists' groups),[98] work team and village cadres turned their attention to the masses. Mobilization of the masses required first and foremost intense propaganda. Peasants were told of the advantages and benefits of the UPM policy both to the state and to themselves, and it was explained that the crisis was due to local errors, not to the policy as such. Propaganda also emphasized the glories of economizing in the consumption of grain, and it spread the message that if everyone abided by and trusted in state plans, the needs of the genuinely grain short would be met. The propaganda emphasized the virtues of self-reliance; it was not a good thing to keep asking the state for handouts. Just because the peasants now had a government that would let no one starve to death did not mean that they should develop a dependent mentality with regard to it.[99]

Following the announcement of the state's supply quota for the locality in question, meetings would be held to evaluate each request. Local cadres took the lead, bringing into play their *tai-t'ou* role of setting an example of correct conduct while also providing cues for everyone. Party members and other cadres who had erred in reporting

[98] *Ibid.*, May 3, 1955, and *Chiang-su Jih-pao*, May 6, 1955.
[99] *Yüeh-tung Nung-min Pao*, May 5, 1955.

false shortage made public self-criticisms. Meetings were called for all those who had reported themselves as grain short. Some of those who had requested supply did not show up in view of the changed political atmosphere; in one case only sixty out of ninety-nine households attended.[100]

In evaluating supply requests, cadres were able to utilize the cleavage between the genuinely grain short (usually poor peasants) and those who had falsely claimed shortage (usually middle peasants). When the number of supply requests escalated, as we have seen, cadres either distributed tickets equally or stopped supply altogether. In either case, the really grain short had cause for complaint. Households in this category were apparently used to expose the unnecessary claims advanced by their competitors. Thus self-evaluation (*tzu-pao*) was followed by public and critical scrutiny of those present. Under this kind of pressure, peasants hastened to reduce or even to withdraw their claims. In one village in Shansi, participants at such a meeting were both "startled" and "respectful" when a middle peasant, who previously had complained loudly, rose to speak:

I have something to say. My family has enough to eat. We don't really need supply from the state. Formerly my thinking was muddled; I have come to recognize my error through the cadres' explanation and education. Now I want to return 37 catties of rice to the state and help really grain-short households to solve their difficulties, so that all of us can work in peace.[101]

Once the requests had been publicly scrutinized, they were examined by the *hsiang* people's councils, which then announced the names of the grain-short households and the amounts to which they were entitled.[102] Judging by press reports, many peasants withdrew or reduced their requests, while others returned grain. But supply was by no means eliminated altogether. In Sung-tien *hsiang*, Wen-hsi *hsien*, Shansi, for example, 171 households returned 22,400 catties, while 90 households in the *hsiang* received 16,186 catties.[103] Another report from T'ai-ku *hsien*, Shansi, where supply conditions had been "unusually confused" and where the *hsien* committee had "blindly" given in to the masses, indicated that 23 *hsiang* returned 220,000 catties; 9 did not require additional state supply because they adjusted needs within the villages by means of lending and borrowing of grain; while 16 *hsiang* still

---

[100] "Yu pei-tung chuan-hsiang chu-tung," *Shan-hsi Jih-pao*, May 25, 1955.

[101] "T'ui-liang" (Returning Grain), *ibid.*, May 19, 1955.

[102] "Tsai kuo-chia k'ung-chih chih-piao nei ho-li kung-ying," *ibid.*, May 7, 1955.

[103] "Cheng-tun liang-shih t'ung-hsiao kung-tso ti cheng-kuo" (The Fruits of the Work of Reorganizing Grain Supply), *ibid.*, May 7, 1955.

needed some state supply.[104] In Soochow special district, Kiangsu, supply was reduced by 20–30 per cent in "most" of 1,100 *hsiang* where supply reorganization had been "basically concluded." In some *hsiang* supply was reduced by 70 per cent. The same article also referred to 125 *hsiang* in which "proper" increases in state supply were made.[105] In all of Shansi, grain-short households were cut by 20 per cent and the total amount supplied by 23 per cent.[106]

The threat of coercion was an important element in securing peasant compliance with the mobilization to reorganize supply. (In the case of cadres, we have already mentioned the tightening of organizational discipline and the expulsion of a Party member; in some cases supply reorganization was accompanied by the rectification of village branches.[107]) The threat of coercion consisted of the publicity given to the arrests and sentencing of class enemies who had allegedly undermined grain supply. I have found no cases of struggle meetings in the villages; such practices may not have been in fashion at a time when Soviet legal practices were being emulated. The publicity of a court sentence meted out for spreading a rumor or wrecking supply, however, was undoubtedly an indirect but potent reminder of the potential consequences of noncompliance. Probably it was most effective with regard to those peasants, such as well-off middle peasants, whose own class status put them in an ambiguous position. A nationwide campaign against concealed counterrevolutionaries gained in intensity during the summer of 1955, and it was an important underpinning not only for the supply reorganization but also for other rural policies, such as the "upsurge" in cooperativization that got under way in the autumn.[108]

It may be that this undercurrent in the campaign was a factor prompting peasants not only to return grain which, according to the regime, they were not entitled to but also to "help really grain-short households" (as the peasant quoted on page 394 put it). Before the reorganization movement got under way, a good deal of publicity had been given to the utilization of peasant holdings of grain. In order to reduce the strain on state reserves, cadres encouraged peasants to sell or exchange grain at local, state-operated primary grain markets, or to lend to needy households at no interest until the next harvest. This

---

[104] "T'ai-ku hsien chi-chi cheng-tun nung-ts'un liang-shih t'ung-hsiao kung-tso" (T'ai-ku *hsien* Is Enthusiastically Reorganizing Rural Grain Supply), *ibid.*, May 5, 1955.

[105] NCNA, Nanking, May 3, 1955, in *SCMP*, No. 1045 (May 11, 1955).

[106] "Speech by T'ao Lu-chia."

[107] "Yu pei-tung chuan-hsiang chu-tung," *Shan-hsi Jih-pao*, May 25, 1955.

[108] For particular instances, see *ibid.*, May 21, 1955; *Hsin-hua Jih-pao*, Nanking, June 2, 1955; and *Yüeh-tung Nung-min Pao*, June 3, 1955.

process, called the "balancing" or "regulating" of grain requirements within a village (*t'iao-chi*), was publicized as a way of coping with the supply crisis.[109] As we have seen, however, the Central Committee–State Council directive of April 28 warned in strong terms against compelling middle peasants to sell additional grain, a warning that was reiterated in a *People's Daily* editorial on May 10.[110] In some villages, nonetheless, cadres continued to mobilize peasants to sell grain. In one Shansi *hsiang,* for example, a work team reportedly dispelled the peasants' fears of "disclosing their wealth," and persuaded seventy households to market ten thousand catties of grain.[111] Although it is difficult to say how widespread selling and lending of peasant grain was during the reorganization drive, the practice may illustrate the efficacy of the coercive pressures unleashed in the villages.

A national appraisal of the movement to reorganize supply said that great achievements were scored.[112] Nonetheless, as is generally the case in rural mobilization movements, deviations from the national model occurred in a sizable proportion of villages. In Shansi, for example, supply reorganization was not well carried out in 30 per cent of *hsiang.*[113] These deviations included a wide range of shortcomings; among them were continued liberality in supplying grain and continued "unreasonable" attitudes and practices. The report on Shansi did not single out the most characteristic deviation of any effort at peasant mobilization—namely, overdoing it. When a movement is launched, cadres are put under great pressure to come up with results, and hence they are prone to adopt "hasty" (*chi-tsao*) or impatient methods. They employ direct forms of coercion (*ch'iang-p'o ming-ling*) that go beyond the coercive pressure on peasants which is a normal aspect of mobilization. Such direct forms of coercion exceed the permissible, and are condemned by the regime. In the May drive the press referred to instances in which all supply tickets were arbitrarily revoked and supply quotas were summarily reduced.[114] In such cases major elements

---

[109] *TKP,* March 29, 1955; and "Tsu-chih shih-ch'ang, chin-hsing t'iao-chi" (Organize Markets for the Purpose of Regulating [Grain]), *Shan-hsi Jih-pao,* May 7, 1955. The latter article describes a market organized in late March, which may have been successful because cadres allowed prices to rise 3 to 4 per cent above state levels.

[110] *JMJP* editorial, May 10, 1955.

[111] "Yu ling-tao ti fa-tung ch'ün-chung hu-t'ung yu-wu" (Use Leadership to Mobilize the Masses to Exchange [Grain] Among Themselves), *Shan-hsi Jih-pao,* May 7, 1955.

[112] *JMJP* editorial, June 26, 1955.

[113] *Shan-hsi Jih-pao* editorial, July 28, 1955.

[114] *Ibid.,* May 20, 1955; also "Yu pei-tung chuan-hsiang chu-tung," *ibid.,* May 25, 1955.

in mobilization drives—propaganda and education, patient rectification of attitudes, and mass participation—were missing. The result of such methods was that the masses remained "disturbed" (*pu an-ting*) and hence were not willing to do their best in production. On balance it seems that such cases of outright coercion were in the minority. It also seems clear, however, that among the three possible approaches to the peasants—eliciting mass support, applying pressure, and employing coercion—the middle one, pressure, was the dominant approach necessary in mobilizing to reorganize rural marketing. Given the goal of the reorganization—namely, the reduction of supply—this conclusion is not very surprising.

Conclusions

This case study illustrates the enormous complexities and problems involved in the process of implementing the policies of socialist transformation. Crises sometimes arose simply because rural leaders were overburdened by the multiplicity of policies they were supposed to introduce. Thus one cause of the supply crisis was the low priority of supply as compared with other tasks, such as the concurrent campaign to set up agricultural producers' cooperatives. Socialist transformation consisted of innovations that placed a greater burden on leadership than do the changes that are associated with guided modernization in non-Communist countries. In both cases the scope and role of politics increase, but in the Chinese Communist case it increased far more, because matters that elsewhere are left under private jurisdiction were brought under political control and responsibility. It is therefore not very surprising that inefficiencies and periodic breakdowns should have occurred.

Implementation of UPM involved complex interactions between leaders at the higher policy-making levels, leaders in the villages, and the peasants. The attitudes and interests of these groups of participants were not always the same, and the control exerted by the national policy makers over what was going on in the villages was by no means total. Campaigns of mobilization were a major tool used by the national leaders for the quick and effective execution of a policy such as the grain monopoly. Part of the campaign consisted of unleashing intensive pressures on the lower levels of the Party and government hierarchy; these pressures were designed to produce a common understanding of the goal and priority assigned to the campaign. In the UPM case these pressures were effective in securing performance by the leadership hierarchy. The campaign approach to implementation was costly, however, in that it led to excess, first in the autumn of 1954 and again (although to a far smaller degree) in May, 1955. The excess occurred because the pressures for results gained such momentum that overfulfillment of the goal became a vital concern of the lower level leaders. One way of mitigating this tendency was for the regime to include careful restraints in the directives it issued to launch the campaign; this may have been a factor accounting for the relatively low degree of excess in May, 1955. But the tendency to excess can be found in most campaigns of mobilization, as, for example, in collectivization movements.

Village cadres played a central role in the process of implementation. The higher level leaders worked through them, and their availability made it possible for the national leaders to gain access to the peasants for the purpose of introducing change. Through them the regime was able to mobilize the peasants to comply with a policy, and to involve peasants in policy implementation by getting them to participate in village meetings and other organizational activities. In comparison with other developing countries that seek to mobilize peasants, a distinctive feature of the Chinese political system has been the capacity of its national leaders to carry out far-reaching innovations by using village leaders. Yet the position of these village cadres is a difficult one, since they are exposed to conflicting pressures from the regime and from the peasants. When the 1954 UPM campaign was launched, village cadres were pressured into responding quite exclusively to regime goals; but peasant pressures re-emerged after the campaign and strongly influenced cadre behavior in the first three months of 1955. These peasant pressures became so powerful that the regime was compelled to react to them.

The grain crisis indicates that the village cadres are an important asset to the Chinese political system. To make full use of this asset, however, places some broad limitations on the kinds of policies that the national leadership can adopt. While the UPM campaign demonstrated the regime's effectiveness in gaining the cooperation of village cadres in the execution of a policy which many peasants perceived as being detrimental to their interests, it seems unlikely that cadres would blindly carry out any and all of the regime's policies, no matter how disadvantageous to the peasants. It would be very difficult to predict at what point village cadres would side with and even lead the peasants in resisting the regime. But if in policy making regime interests should come to prevail completely over peasant interests, a different form of leadership, such as reliance on bureaucratic and predominantly coercive controls wielded by outsiders, would probably become necessary. This form of leadership, in fact, was characteristic of Stalinist Russia. It did not eliminate peasant pressures, but it made them less effective, and it achieved the Stalinist goal of extracting a large marketable surplus, although at the price of long-term agricultural stagnation.

The grain crisis indicates also that rural mobilization did not depend on the ordinary peasants' lasting and wholehearted commitment to the Communist cause. Peasants clearly were unhappy with the regime during the crisis. Their behavior revealed commitment largely to their own interests. When these interests were threatened, the peasants became active on their own, and at least some of them sought to profit when the opportunity arose. Yet this did not prevent a reasonably successful mobilization effort for the reorganization of supply. Peasant alienation in the early spring of 1955 was also no obstacle to the vastly greater mobilization for all-out collectivization in 1955–56. Provided that the Chinese leaders do not push peasant interests aside completely, it seems likely that they will continue to be able to introduce change in the village by means of mass mobilization.

R. J. BIRRELL

The Centralized Control of the Communes in the Post-"Great Leap" Period

INTRODUCTION

The object of this study is to describe and give at least a partial explanation of certain aspects of the controls employed by the Chinese Communist Party (CCP) to influence the operation of China's agricultural collectives, or communes, as they have been termed since 1958.

Briefly, the argument will be as follows. There are a limited number of means by which an agent can influence the behavior of a subject. Following Amitai Etzioni's classification, we can identify three general types of controls: remunerative, normative, and coercive.[1] Remunerative control is the manipulation of material rewards, to which a subject voluntarily responds because he considers the inputs of effort and other valued resources required to be worth the value of the material rewards. Normative control is behavior induced by the subject's belief in, and commitment to, a set of attitudes. Coercive control is, residually, behavior induced by sanctions which are neither remunerative nor normative; it includes the use of force or threats of force, fines, and other similar deprivations.

Between 1959 and 1962 the CCP made a serious attempt to restructure the communes, with the objective of establishing an effective system of remunerative controls and at the same time decentralizing their administration. This effort, however, was, and has continued to

---

[1] Amitai Etzioni, *A Comparative Analysis of Complex Organizations* (New York: The Free Press of Glencoe, 1961), p. 51.

400

be, deficient in the sense that it has failed to motivate the commune members to behave in ways consistent with the CCP's ends. In order to identify these deficiencies, I will analyze the remunerative control system in detail below. Assuming for the moment that such deficiencies exist, the next question is what their implications are for the efforts of the CCP to influence agricultural operations. I will argue that one of the CCP's responses has been to make extensive use of agencies outside or above the basic production units (in the period in question, the production teams and the individual peasants) to influence behavior within these units, thus substantially nullifying its efforts to decentralize their administration. Along with this development there has been an increasing use of normative and coercive controls since 1962. However, the focus here will be primarily on the involvement of state agencies in the commune's activities (referred to for convenience as centralization of control).[2]

I will describe some aspects of the centralized control system, and seek to establish the linkages between this system and the hypothesized deficiencies in the remunerative control apparatus. The theory to be discussed certainly does not provide a complete explanation of the phenomenon of centralization in the organizational structure of the communes, though I believe it to be a major determinant. There have been other important factors, some of which will be briefly identified below.

The term "centralization" already carries some complicating definitional baggage in the secondary literature. Franz Schurmann, for example, distinguishes between decentralization carried to the level of the production units themselves, as against decentralization carried only to some intermediary level, such as the province.[3] "Centralization" will be used here to refer to a situation where most major decisions regarding the production and distribution of agricultural commodities are placed in the hands of CCP agencies outside or above the basic level production units. I will, however, be mindful that the actual level at which decisions are made is important in relation to the impact of centralization on such matters as the degree of concern the decision makers show for local conditions in innovative activities, and their ability to take account of changing local conditions in pro-

---

[2] I have discussed elsewhere the degree of use of normative and coercive controls. R. J. Birrell, "The Structure of the Chinese Collectives" (Ph.D. dissertation, Princeton University, 1969), chap. viii.

[3] Franz Schurmann, *Ideology and Organization in Communist China* (Berkeley and Los Angeles: University of California Press, 1966), p. 175.

duction decisions; thus I will try to locate the decision-making agency and the level at which it operates when I describe the phenomenon of centralization.

REASONS FOR STUDYING CENTRALIZATION

Before beginning the analysis, I should justify my emphasis on centralization. There is still an issue as to whether one can validly describe the control of agriculture in the mid-1960's as highly centralized. Some ground for debate exists, because the reforms of 1959–62, including the reduction in the size of the basic production and accounting unit to the team level (twenty to thirty households), the restoration of the private plots, and the reopening of the free markets, all might suggest that the present administrative system is relatively decentralized.

Before getting into this issue let me first indicate that when I make comparative statements as to the degree of centralization in the administrative structure of the communes, I am using as the comparative base line the administrative model the CCP itself propagated during the 1959–62 period. For during this period the CCP made an explicit effort to reform the structure of the communes, one of the major objectives being to increase the decision-making autonomy of the basic production units (the brigades and, later, the teams). Those responsible for policy concerning the communes at this time seem to have been fully aware that during the Great Leap Forward the extreme dominance of commune level cadres over decision making vis-à-vis agricultural activities had deleterious effects on the production performance of the communes. They also seem to have been aware that the problem was not merely that cadres at the commune level, running units with thousands of households, had difficulty taking account of local conditions in making decisions; there was also the fact that in the politically charged atmosphere of the early commune movement, these cadres were extremely sensitive to orders or even suggestions from higher levels as to production plans and innovations, and tended to act on these without much consideration of conditions within their localities. Thus, in the light of the CCP's recognition of these circumstances, and its reform goals in this respect, I am interested first in whether the CCP has actually carried out such reforms.

The empirical issue has been confused somewhat by the fact that the reforms of 1959–62 were accompanied by much public rhetoric (which still continues) as to the importance of local autonomy in agriculture.

Thus, one must be careful to avoid confusing the ideal models so frequently enunciated at this time with the actuality of commune administration. Certainly the fact that by 1962 the team was the production and accounting unit does not in itself guarantee local decision-making autonomy. It first has to be established that the team cadres and members are not simply doing what higher level cadres tell them to do. However, the CCP was anxious to restore the peasants' morale and to make a serious effort to implement its reforms between 1960 and 1962. So there is something to the arguments of John Lewis[4] and James Townsend[5] that during this period the basic production units were permitted a good deal of autonomy. However, since 1962, as will be indicated below, whatever autonomy was allowed has been decreased.

But a more important reason for my interest in centralization is that it has some significant theoretical implications for our interpretations of Chinese Communist society. For the actual centralization of the control structure as I will describe it below is in striking contrast both to the administrative model indicated above, and to the more general nature of the CCP's ideology as it relates to control. Thus, in its leadership theory, the CCP has consistently advocated some variant of democratic centralism as an ideal pattern. The masses are supposed to be involved in the process of decision making, and only then to be made to follow these decisions with discipline. This ideal, of course, is the essence of the "mass line" which has been at the center of the ideological pronouncements of the CCP in the 1960's.[6] The thesis that emerges from this study is that, the CCP's no doubt genuine commitment to this administrative ideology notwithstanding, control problems have prohibited the implementation of a system embodying it without prejudicing other more crucial goals (notably production and taxation objectives). That is, to allow the level of decentralization suggested by the ideology would be to put power into the hands of local cadres and members whose interests are such that they tend to use such power for ends contrary to the CCP's. We can observe the problems which arose in the course of the CCP's efforts to carry out the 1959–62 reforms,

---

[4] John W. Lewis, *Leadership in Communist China* (Ithaca, N.Y.: Cornell University Press, 1963), pp. 232–42. Chap. vii of this book also provides the most systematic account of the CCP's administrative model as far as its decentralization goals at this time are concerned.

[5] James Townsend, *Political Participation in Communist China* (Berkeley and Los Angeles: University of California Press, 1967), p. 170.

[6] Lewis, *Leadership in Communist China,* chap. iii.

and by noting the responses to these problems get a clearer idea of the factors influencing the CCP and its lower level cadres responsible for making and implementing decisions vis-à-vis the communes.

Since the administrative system I will describe below does not even remotely approach the model articulated for the reforms after the Great Leap Forward, it is obvious that one has to look elsewhere for factors to explain developments in the administration of the communes. The following discussion will, I think, indicate that the CCP's problems have been largely caused by pressures to plug up the gaps in its control apparatus (primarily resulting from deficiencies in its remunerative control system). For, in essence, the CCP had hoped that by reforming the remunerative control system, as it had after the Great Leap Forward, it could entrust the commune members with considerable decision-making autonomy, since the reformed system was expected to motivate them toward ends consistent with the CCP's. But in fact the Party has had to order greater intervention from outside the production units either to forestall or to correct shortcomings in performance. I will make no attempt here, however, to answer the larger question as to why the CCP insists on pursuing taxation and production goals which, I will suggest below, tend to undermine its remunerative control system.

Another reason for my interest in the centralization of rural administration in China is its consequences for agricultural development. The CCP's concern about this matter has been consistent with experience in a number of other Asian countries. Thus, numerous studies have documented the dysfunctions of the operation of the also relatively centralized agricultural extension or development administrations in India,[7] Pakistan,[8] Burma,[9] and Thailand.[10] These studies corroborate what appears to be the case in China, namely, that a centralized administrative system usually has as its corollary a limited degree of involvement on the part of the cultivators in the activities directed by the administration. This in turn usually seems to inhibit the effectiveness of the measures in question. The Indian government, for example, has been sufficiently concerned about the inability of its community

[7] Henry C. Hart, *The Village and Developmental Administration* (Bloomington, Ind.: Comparative Administration Group, Occasional Papers, 1967).

[8] Inayatullah and Q. Shafi, *Dynamics of Development in a Pakistani Village* (Peshawar: Pakistan Academy for Rural Development, n.d.), pp. 50–57.

[9] Manning Nash, *The Golden Road to Modernity* (New York: Wiley, 1965), chap. vi.

[10] Nicholas Luykx, "Rural Government in the Strategy of Agricultural Development," in J. D. Montgomery and W. J. Siffin (ed.), *Approaches to Development* (New York: McGraw-Hill, 1966), chap. v.

development program to discover and help solve effectively the peasant's "felt needs" that it has in the 1960's sought to increase peasant involvement in the development program by fostering a system of local councils (Panchayats) which are to help in its administration.[11] I do not intend here to go into the question of the significance of the role of centralization in the relative success of the various rural development programs in Asia. I merely wish to note the importance of the subject, not merely for the political development of China, but also for its agricultural development.

In developing the argument, I will first analyze the remunerative control system as it was set up by 1962, then discuss the relationships between this system and the centralized administrative structures which seem to characterize the control of the communes in the mid-1960's.

THE REMUNERATIVE CONTROL SYSTEM

By 1959 the CCP was ready to make some substantial reforms in the structure of the communes. One of the most important of these reforms involved, as noted above, a return to the use of remunerative controls, these controls having been largely abandoned in the early stages of the Great Leap Forward. Of course, the limitations of the remunerative control system at that time do not entirely explain the agricultural disasters between 1959 and 1961. However, one of the techniques the CCP used to revive production was to place renewed emphasis on remunerative controls.

There is no need to detail the organizational changes made between 1959 and 1962; these have already been documented elsewhere.[12] Essentially they involved the reduction of the size of the production and accounting unit from the commune to the team level (twenty to thirty households), and a decision that members should be rewarded for their

---

[11] Hart, *Village and Developmental Administration.*

[12] For example see P. P. Jones and T. T. Poleman, "Communes and the Agricultural Crisis in Communist China," *Food Research Institute Studies* (Stanford), III (February, 1962), 5–19; and T. A. Hsia, *The Commune in Retreat as Evidenced in Terminology and Semantics* (Berkeley: Center for Chinese Studies, Institute of International Studies, University of California, 1966).

The most important Chinese documents itemizing the reforms (including the remunerative controls and the decision to decentralize the administration of agriculture) are the unpublished "12 Articles" (promulgated November, 1960) and the "60 Articles" (May, 1961), copies of which can be found in the Hoover Library at Stanford University. Though to my knowledge these documents were never published in the Chinese press, their contents were paraphrased many times in the press during 1960–62. I have also dealt with these decisions in some detail in "Structure of Chinese Collectives," chap. vii.

work according to the contribution of that work to the over-all profit-
ability of the team.

I will confine myself to an analysis of the system installed by 1962,
by which time most of the communes had made an attempt to implement the reforms in question. In emphasizing the system's limitations,
I do not intend to imply that it has been completely ineffective; on the
contrary, it has clearly helped to promote the recovery of agricultural
production since 1961. However, from the CCP's point of view, the
behavior resulting from this system still leaves much to be desired.

The CCP has tried to relate the commune member's interest in
increasing his cash and grain receipts to its own interest in increasing
agricultural production and taxation, by allocating rewards to the
members in terms of the amount and quality of their efforts in the
commune. I will attempt to assess the effectiveness of the system by
establishing whether the members' and the CCP's interests do in fact
harmonize in regard to three key aspects: (a) the calculation of
the amount and quality of work done by the member; (b) the method
by which this calculation is converted into a share of the total income
to be distributed to the members; and (c) the method by which the
income of the commune is apportioned for consumption, taxation, and
investment.

Underlying the analysis is the assumption that commune members
are concerned to maximize the return from their inputs into the commune. That is, they try to maximize the difference between the rewards
they receive from the commune, and the costs to them of these inputs.
Clearly, this is a complex calculation influenced by a variety of factors,
social as well as economic. An attempt will be made to take account of
the most important of these variables, though I must admit that the
complexity of the problem, and sometimes the paucity of information,
does make some of my conclusions rather speculative.

THE CALCULATION OF THE AMOUNT
AND QUALITY OF THE MEMBERS' INPUTS

Calculation of the amount and quality of commune members' inputs
is a complex task, and one that for good reason has severely taxed the
energies of the local cadres (this term refers to the team cadres).
First of all, to avoid reducing the member's interest in a particular job,
the points allocated for each job have to be rationally and fairly
assigned. That is, there must be no work quotas set in such a way that
a member feels that he is doing heavier or more skilled work than

someone else in his team yet is not getting recognition for this in terms of the number of points allocated on completion of the quota.

When a member feels that there is some injustice in work-point calculation, the evidence suggests that he will tend to reduce his work input if he can get away with it. For example, in a unit where a small number of points was allocated to a weeding job, one member commented, "No matter whether the weeds are dense or thin, work points are awarded just the same. You give me 7½ points for weeding one mou (roughly one sixth of an acre), I just do work worth 7½ points."[13] Similarly, surveys of the quality of work done in the training and care of draft animals indicated that one of the major causes for the poor work discovered was the low number of points allocated to animal tenders. In one *hsien* (county) it was shown that the reason why animals were being used inefficiently was that too few work points could be gained by training younger animals or using older ones.[14] To repeat, this argument only applies if the peasant can reduce his work input to the level he feels is reasonable in terms of the points assigned to the job without being penalized by having points deducted for inadequate work.[15] (Assuming that he needs as many points as he can get—an assumption which we will argue below is not always a valid one.)

To avoid these problems the local cadres have to devote considerable energy to the business of establishing reasonable piece rates; then they must find some way of checking the work of the members so that they cannot "get away with" reducing their work inputs. The latter is particularly important, because members may have other reasons for wanting to "get away with" working at standards lower than those provided for in the piece-rate quotas—including laziness, general dissatisfaction with their lot as commune members, or a desire to use their inputs for their private activities. I will discuss these two problems, and in passing note the significance of the local cadre's contribution in making this aspect of the system work. This point is relevant to a later part of the argument, when the CCP's problems in motivating the local cadres are discussed. Because the role of local cadres in the system is significant, if they cannot be relied upon to perform it properly, outside interference may be necessary.

[13] *Pao-an Bulletin,* No. 61 (September 27, 1961), in URS, XXVII, No. 7 (April 24, 1962).

[14] Cited in *China News Analysis,* Hong Kong, No. 379 (July 7, 1961), p. 3.

[15] For an account of a cadre apparently dealing successfully with these problems, see *JMJP,* July 22, 1964, in *SCMP,* No. 3283 (August, 1964), p. 10.

The setting of piece rates is difficult because of the variety of tasks to be performed on the commune. It is far easier for manufacturing industries to set up standards for the various jobs to be performed, because the production process usually involves fewer operations and the same individuals can be kept at the same job over extended periods of time. In the communes, members have to move from job to job according to the season and in response to the inevitable crises brought on by the weather or other natural causes. Under these conditions, the task of preparing quotas for the jobs, and adjusting them according to changing work conditions, is enormous. The number of such quotas in a production unit may run as high as thirteen hundred.[16] Some jobs are of such short duration that it is useless to establish a quota at all. Others, such as harvesting, may be better facilitated by a work group, in some cases by a team of four.[17] As an illustration of the complexity of the effort needed to establish a set of reasonable quotas, consider the following account of the calculations made by one unit in regard to ploughing. "Differences in crops, in the size of fields, in their distance from the village, in the quality of farm tools, in the quality of draught animals, in hardness of the soil, in depth of ploughing required, in the four seasons, in turning and harrowing the earth,"[18] and so on, all had to be taken into account if the quota were to be accurately and fairly established.

Probably of greater significance in terms of the effective operation of the system, however, has been the second of the two problems indicated above, that is, actually measuring the member's work performance. Again, by comparison with the problem in manufacturing industries, the difficulties of checking performances are of greater magnitude in agriculture. In industry, a workman usually produces or processes units that can be easily counted and checked for quality. But the commune members, in performing their tasks, are often widely distributed geographically, making it physically difficult to check their work.[19] There is also likely to be frequent movement from job to job. Moreover, it may be difficult to check their work even if distance is not

---

[16] "An Investigation of the Building of Socialist New Rural Areas," *Economic Research*, No. 2 (February, 1966), in *SCMM*, No. 527 (June, 1966).

[17] A. Nathan, "China's Work Point System," *Current Scene* (Hong Kong), II, No. 31 (April 15, 1964), 1–14.

[18] "A Vivid Lesson in Bringing Politics to the Fore," *JMJP*, March 22, 1966, in *SCMP*, No. 3675 (April, 1966), p. 13.

[19] *Ibid.*, p. 11.

a problem. Often the quality of the work can be assessed only at the end of the agricultural season, by which time so many factors have influenced the results that it may be impossible to attach blame to any one individual.

The CCP has tried to solve these problems by urging cadres to go into the field systematically to inspect work in progress, and by attempting to get the members themselves to report on the work done by others. But in practice, neither the local cadres nor the members have been diligent in performing these tasks.

As for the local cadres, apart from the physical difficulties involved, they appear to be reluctant to search out and penalize members whose performance is inadequate. As I will argue below, the local cadres are dependent on a certain amount of genuine cooperation from the members, and in order not to antagonize them, the cadres will often avoid checking thoroughly or assessing penalties.[20] The members appear to be even more reluctant to point up deficiencies in each other's work, mainly because they are anxious to avoid the bickering, hurt feelings, and problems of face[21] which arise from such criticism. This is hardly surprising when we remember that team assignments are permanent, and members must constantly interact with each other because of their work relations and common residence in the village. Thus, as one report put it, the members have to be "coached" intensively before they will cooperate in checking each other's work, since they are inclined to emphasize that "we are all of one family now, and in the future want to live together."[22]

These measurement problems have at least two implications for my argument. First, they emphasize the importance of the local cadre's part in the operation. If these cadres are not active in managing the system, work performance will be measured imperfectly, and of course the members will have less incentive to complete their quotas. A second implication is that when the measurement system is imperfect, it allows those members who are not motivated to do their job as required a greater chance to avoid detection. Some of these motivational problems

[20] For example, see *Pao-an Bulletin,* No. 64 (October 6, 1961), in URS, XXVII, No. 8 (April 27, 1962), 134.

[21] Nathan, "China's Work Point System," p. 4. These problems were also found in the pre-"Great Leap" period. For example, see *JMJP,* October 12, 1957, p. 2. The CCP has tried to handle this problem in part by indoctrinating members as to the immorality of group solidarity, e.g., see *CKCNP,* December 17, 1966. An article entitled "The Error of Amicability" in *JPRS,* No. 29480 (April 7, 1965), p. 71.

[22] *JMJP,* October 12, 1957, p. 2.

will be discussed in the course of the analysis of other aspects of the remunerative control system.

THE CALCULATION OF THE MEMBER'S SHARE OF THE COMMUNE'S INCOME

Even if piece rates are set accurately, it may still be in the member's interests, in order to maximize the return from his work, to minimize the effort devoted to collective work. The CCP has tried to counteract this tendency by relating the member's income directly to the income of the team, a reform that was instituted in two steps: first by directing in late 1959 that the brigade rather than the commune constitute the basic unit of ownership and accounting, and then by establishing in early 1962 the team as the basic unit. Thus, a peasant's income is made to vary directly with the profit of the team. His share is based on the number of work points he earns as a percentage of the total number of work points accumulated in his basic unit. The CCP is aware, of course, that the smaller the size of the production and accounting unit, the closer will be the connection the member perceives between his income and the profit of his team.

However, while these reforms have done much to facilitate the relationship sought, even at this level there are many circumstances in which it is in the member's interests to devote himself primarily to accumulating his own work points without devoting his main attention to the over-all performance of his team. In particular, members may neglect the quality of their work simply in order to complete a quota —such as so many fields ploughed or fertilized in a day. Or, in completing a quota a member may fail to perform other tasks important for the productive level of the team. These situations often arise because of the difficulties of checking work, and the complications of assigning work on the piece-rate system—taking account of such emergencies as dikes breaking, cattle straying onto the fields, and so on. A member knows that any reduction in the team's production that results from his work or negligence will have to be shared by all the other members of the team. Only if the loss occasioned by his failures is particularly large and obvious would his income level be threatened. (This assumes, of course, that he can in many such situations "get away with" doing poor work.)

The degree to which members may be motivated to maximize their work points at the expense of the quality of their work depends on a number of factors, including how successfully the regime has inculcated a sense of commitment to the collective, and the regime's success in this regard depends in part on the members' sense of the fairness of the actual rewards they receive for their work.

I will argue shortly that there is evidence to suggest that many commune members appear to be dissatisfied with their rewards, and I have argued elsewhere that there is reason to believe that the regime has not been successful in producing this commitment to the collective.[23] Rather, commune members seem to be primarily concerned with getting the most they can out of the collective.

Motivating commune members to concern themselves with the collective's performance under the present type of remunerative control system has thus been a serious problem for the CCP. Consequently, in the aftermath of the Great Leap Forward, *hsien* and commune authorities sometimes found it expedient to contract agricultural work to individual households. Thus, in Pao-an *hsien* (Kwangtung) in 1961 the Party Committee decided to contract the growing of third-grade paddy (low-grade rice) to the small group (*ad hoc* units under the team) and household level, the decision being implemented by work teams sent to the localities by the *hsien* committee, with the apparent ready agreement of the brigade and team cadres.[24] During that period this practice seems to have been fairly widespread; sometimes it was directed by cadres desperate to do something about the food crisis, as in Pao-an, but sometimes it was done without any Party authorization at all.[25]

Since 1962, however, such practices have been curtailed. But there have been many reports of members ignoring the collective's interests in pursuit of their own. To cite an illustrative though perhaps extreme example, it was said that when the piece-rate system was used in the Ta Chai Brigade (now a national model), "it was every man for himself."[26] People would simply fulfill their quotas and do no more. "Those whose job it was to hoe land would not get rid of the weeds at the side, while those who were to trim the sides would not pick up

[23] Birrell, "Structure of the Chinese Collectives," chap. v.

[24] *Pao-an Bulletin,* No. 59 (September 23, 1961), in URS, XXVII, No. 7 (April 24, 1962), 112–13.

[25] For example, see the Lien-chiang Documents, especially the report of Wang Hung Chih, "Further Consolidate the Collective Economy and Develop Agricultural Production."

[26] "A Vivid Lesson in Bringing Politics to the Fore," p. 14.

stones in the earth. If you asked one of them why he did not remove the rock which he could see, he would tell you that there were no work points for removing rocks."[27]

Cases of members doing poor quality work,[28] showing little concern for the treatment of the collective's land, animals, and tools,[29] or for the collective's performance generally, are reported often enough to indicate that the remunerative control system has been seriously deficient in this regard. In fact, as I have tried to show elsewhere, one of the major factors stimulating the beginning of the socialist education campaign at the end of 1962 was the CCP's growing awareness of this situation.[30]

One way of dealing with these problems, of course, would be to reduce still further the size of the basic accounting unit to the small group or household level (as was done in some areas, as indicated above). However, for a variety of reasons the CCP has resisted such suggestions.

THE VALUE OF THE REWARDS RECEIVED FROM THE COLLECTIVE

In the last analysis, even a perfectly organized piece-rate system, with distribution based on a smaller unit even than the team, would still be ineffectual, as long as the absolute size of the rewards received was unsatisfactory to the commune members. It is difficult, of course, to be sure about what standards the members use to evaluate the adequacy of their income. My analysis, tentative as it is, does suggest that this income generally falls well short of what most commune members think they ought to receive in relation to the inputs they are required to make in their work on the collective.

Before discussing how commune members make this calculation, we should note that the distribution system the CCP has implemented has in practice not been applied as formally prescribed. In theory, the

---

[27] *Ibid.*

[28] For example, "Slackness Should Be Thoroughly Overcome," *NFJP*, February 20, 1963, in *SCMP*, No. 2945 (March, 1963). This concerns a case where the members ignored the preparations for spring ploughing. The writer indicates that "As far as I know, a similar situation also exists in other places."

Also, "The Secretary of Hsiao Chiang Commune Party Committee Penetrates Deep," *JMJP*, July 10, 1963, in *SCMP*, No. 3028 (July, 1963). Here the cadre found members showing "a state of indifference toward insect pests."

[29] For example, "How Can Production Teams Establish and Perfect Operation Groups," *NFJP*, April 9, 1963, in *SCMP*, No. 2977 (May, 1963). Here the problem was that they had found "no way to encourage the Commune Members to carry out processing and top dressing better."

[30] Birrell, "Structure of the Chinese Collectives," chap. vii.

grain and cash distribution to members should be based on a calculation made once or twice annually, when the accumulated work points
are calculated and matched (according to the principles described
above) to the grain and cash available for distribution. That is, after
taxation, investment, seed, welfare, and other claims on the team's
total income are satisfied, the net profit should be distributed to members on the basis of the number of points each has earned. In practice,
however, the principle of more pay for more work is significantly
violated because of the nature of the rationing system. The teams, for
example, provide allowances to households which are short of able-bodied workers.[31] More significantly, they also distribute grain and usually
cash in advance, during the course of the year, according to how much
is available from the previous harvest. The size of the ration distributed seems in many instances to be based not only on the work-point
totals accumulated by members, but also "according to the actual
needs of an individual in order to insure the basic needs of every
commune member."[32] When the time for the autumn distribution ar-
rives, sometimes the team does not have sufficient resources to allocate
extra cash or grain to those members who have accumulated higher
than average work-point totals.

Though the evidence on this matter is fragmentary, I am inclined to
think that this is a common problem. There are reports which explicitly and concretely describe such circumstances.[33] Moreover, it seems
likely that the procedures followed in allocating grain, and the pressures exerted by the CCP to get the teams to invest or sell to the state
any grain held in excess of the ration needs of the team members, often
produce such a situation. Also, the CCP appears anxious to prevent
members from obtaining large personal stores of grain[34] (in part to

[31]"Youths in Ts'ao Chia Yuan Production Team Regularly Educated in Village and
Family Histories," *JMJP,* June 22, 1963, *SCMP,* No. 3022 (July, 1963). Here the making
of these allowances was accompanied by a campaign amongst better-off households to
make them recognize their duty to provide for poorer members of the commune.

[32] "A Preliminary Discussion of the Question of Implementation of the Principle of Pay
According to Work," *TKP,* June 9, 1961, in *SCMP,* No. 2533 (July, 1961), p. 8. All
citations to *Ta Kung Pao* are to the Peking edition.

[33] For example, "The Grain Supply Is Very Good," *Li-lun Hsüeh-hsi* (Theoretical
Study), No. 18 (December 1, 1959), in *ECMM,* No. 202 (February 29, 1960). This article
gives a detailed account of how and why high work-point scorers received less than their
due prior to the commune movement, when the method of distribution employed was
similar to that in the post-"Leap" period.

Also see "Persistently Hold Examination and Rating, Firmly Carry Out the Party's
Policies," *NFJP,* August 5, 1962, in *SCMP,* No. 2806 (August, 1962).

[34] "Set Up Collective Grain Reserves of Production Teams," *TKP* editorial, October 26,
1964, in *SCMP,* No. 3335 (November, 1964), p. 4.

prevent them from increasing their independence from the collective). Furthermore, it can be politically dangerous for a member to accumulate more income and property than other members of his team. Thus, there are fundamental weaknesses in the remunerative control system: although everyone can feel assured of a minimum income, at the same time commune members are uncertain as to whether they will receive increased income for increased work on the collective; and consequently the incentives to accumulate work points are limited.

Undoubtedly some effort has been made to give more income to those who work more. But even when this principle has been successfully applied, the limits to the total income which a member can earn have tended to reduce the member's motivation to work voluntarily and actively on the collective. When comparing their actual income with what they think they ought to receive from their inputs, many members undoubtedly feel deprived. Equally important, in terms of a strict calculation of the opportunity costs of their inputs (that is, the return they could get from an alternative use of these inputs), they clearly feel that often it would be better to apply one's time and effort to individual rather than collective effort.

The Fairness of the Distribution. There is a variety of standards which a commune member may take into account in assessing the fairness of his income. Three appear to be dominant: (a) his comparison of his own income as a peasant with that of other social groups, particularly the urban workers; (b) the comparison of actual income with what he considers necessary for a reasonable standard of living; and (c) his judgment as to his rightful personal share of any increases in production achieved by his team. In each case it seems likely that the actual income distribution often makes many members feel that the distribution is unfair.

This is caused to a large extent, of course, by the fact that agricultural productivity has been relatively low, but the regime's taxation and investment policies are major factors too. Through direct taxation, compulsory procurement, and pressures to maximize local investment, the regime has consistently aimed at limiting the level of consumption in rural production units.[35] Sometimes it has imposed this policy at the expense of even minimal rations for the members.[36] Often the pressures

---

[35] For an example of the frequently stated principle that when more is produced, more should be procured, see, "Some Problems of Procurement of Agricultural Products," *JMJP*, October 25, 1961, in *JPRS*, No. 11969 (January 15, 1962), p. 10.

[36] John C. Pelzel, "Production Brigade and Team Management" (paper for the Columbia University Seminar on Modern East Asia: China; February 16, 1966), p. 4.

to meet procurement quotas persist regardless of the actual production figures, so that when production falls or the original procurement targets are set too high, the commune members are likely to suffer the consequences. For example, in one of the brigades in Pao-an *hsien* in 1961, the output of late paddy was estimated at 139,800 catties. A *hsien* work team investigating the area indicated that 80,880 catties were to go to the state, and thus after seed and fodder reserves had been set aside, only 34,920 catties were to be left for distribution to the members. This represented a very low prospective monthly ration of 29 catties per head for the following year.[37] The work team did help the brigade to improve its production, but there was no suggestion that procurement levels would be lowered.[38]

When production increases, as has been the case since 1961, the tendency has been to raise procurement levels.[39] Since 1961 the press has been full of accounts of brigades and teams which have been pressured to overfulfill their procurement quotas by selling their "surplus grain" to the state.[40] To prevent the "squandering" of surplus grain on consumption, moreover, the CCP's practice of having the local grain authorities store it on behalf of the teams has become increasingly prevalent.[41]

The level of income actually allocated to commune members is also influenced by the regime's investment policies. Increases in a team's income are likely to be accompanied by pressures from cadres at the *hsien,* commune, and brigade levels to devote much of the income to investment in items such as animals, farm implements, or chemical fertilizer. As John Pelzel remarks in reference to the brigades in Kwangtung which he studied, "The policy of withholding earned income from private use, and its conversion to collective investment capital, is firmly pursued and apparently well understood (whether

[37] K. C. Yeh, "Soviet and Communist Chinese Industrialization Strategies," in Donald W. Treadgold (ed.), *Soviet and Chinese Communism: Similarities and Differences* (Seattle: University of Washington Press, 1967), indicates (p. 346) that the traditional standard for grain consumption per year was around five hundred catties of unhusked grain.

[38] *Pao-an Bulletin,* No. 58 (September 22, 1961), in URS, XXVIII, No. 6 (July 20, 1962), 96–97.

[39] For one estimate of the increased procurement following the relatively good harvest in 1964, see Alexandra Close, "Correcting the Cadres," *Far Eastern Economic Review,* February 18, 1965, p. 289. She claims there was a 10 per cent increase in procurement levels in 1964. See also *TKP,* October 20, 1964, p. 2.

[40] For example, *TKP,* December 7, 1964, p. 1.

[41] "Food Department Stores Reserve Grain on Behalf of Production Teams," *ibid.,* October 27, 1964, in *SCMP,* No. 3335 (November, 1964).

approved or not) locally."[42] The regime's price policy also influences income. Prices for grain procured by the state appear to be far below the free market price,[43] and certainly are less than grain is actually worth to individual commune members, to judge from their resistance to the overfulfillment of procurement quotas (a point I will take up again below).

Thus, there is considerable evidence of member dissatisfaction along the lines suggested above. The regime has faced the constant problem of antagonism to the outflow of grain and cash from the countryside to the cities, to support the urban workers.[44] A striking statement of these grievances contained in a Red Guard poster may be illustrative. The grievances included the claim that "Workers in state enterprises are paid several tens of yuan [according to the regime's official exchange rates a yuan is worth 38 cents] or several hundreds [of yuan]. We peasants are paid only ten, twenty, or thirty yuan a year." The poster further commented that "Many workers in the towns live in blocks of flats. We live in [thatched huts?] which are often in a state of collapse, and we are exposed to wind and rain. Just what attitude do the dogs of officials responsible in the towns have toward the peasants?"[45]

As to the standard of living, the available data suggest that the average annual per capita grain supply available to commune members between 1955 and 1957[46] was larger than that available in the mid-1960's,[47] even though by the mid-1960's it was not as low as in the 1959–61 crisis period. The seriousness of this situation, as it affects peasants' morale, derives not only from the likelihood that in absolute terms their income has declined, but also from the fact that since 1955 they have been repeatedly promised large increases in income. One of the responses to this situation, and to the apparently meager cash

[42] Pelzel, "Production Brigade," p. 10.

[43] Three to four times lower in the area Barnett studied; see A. Doak Barnett (with a contribution by Ezra Vogel), *Cadres, Bureaucracy, and Political Power in Communist China* (New York: Columbia University Press, 1967), p. 376.

[44] Prior to the Great Leap as well as after it, e.g., "Rural Cadres Debate on the Different Living Standards for Workers and Peasants," *JMJP*, October 28, 1957, in *SCMP*, No. 1649 (November, 1957), p. 1.

[45] Red Guard poster, Shanghai, January 14, 1967.

[46] "The Policy of Unified Purchase and Sale of Grain Shall Not Be Frustrated," *Liang-shih* (Grain), No. 7 (July, 1957), in *ECMM*, No. 101 (September 9, 1957). Figures for these years are presented in Thomas P. Bernstein, "Chinese Cadre and Peasant Behavior," p. 373, above.

[47] For example, Pelzel, "Production Brigade," indicates that the rice ration was thirty catties a month in the area he studied. See also "In a Production Team," *Peking Review*, No. 13 (March 25, 1966), p. 16. Here the grain ration for the year seems to be three hundred catties per person.

distribution, has been the development of the attitude that one works for the collective simply to fulfill state obligations rather than in pursuit of individual material rewards—thus the oft quoted and criticized comments of members that one must "rely on the collective for food, on the individual for money to spend, and on speculation to get rich,"[48] or that "We rely on the collective in fulfilling state tasks, but must rely on ourselves in earning money for our own use."[49] Such attitudes appear to have inhibited the development of the kind of loyalty and commitment to the collective which the regime has sought.

In regard to the third of the comparative standards which commune members appear to use in judging the fairness of their income, many peasants seem to be resentful about the size of their individual share in any increases in their team's production. Numerous examples of this can be cited. For example, "some" members of a team in Hunan, when they met with pressure for the overfulfillment of their procurement quota, reportedly felt that, "Now that we have produced more this year, we should eat more. Otherwise a bumper harvest doesn't make much difference."[50] And at a meeting held to convince members of a Kwangtung brigade of the correctness of the procurement policies, a woman member reportedly asserted that "To sell more and to have less to eat ourselves; what rot that this policy is good."[51]

Opportunity Costs. A number of aspects of the opportunity cost structure in which commune members operate affect their attitudes. Here I will focus attention on two of the most significant of these: the opportunity costs of the time, energy, and resources (such as household manure) which they must devote to the collective, and the opportunity costs of grain and other commodities sold outside the collective.

When a member devotes his time and effort to the collective, he is likely to make a more or less explicit calculation as to the return he will get from this input and to compare this with the return he could get from some alternative use of it. If the opportunity cost is higher than the return for work done on the collective, then the member (assuming he is interested in maximizing his return) will be motivated to limit or withdraw the inputs in question and apply them in a more profitable direction. Although there are many factors involved, it seems clear that

[48] "A Talk on Understanding the Middle Peasant Problem," *NFJP*, March 23, 1963, in *SCMP*, No. 2975 (May, 1963).

[49] "Poor and Lower Middle Peasants Are the Backbone of a Production Team," *ibid.*

[50] "See More Surplus Grain and Have Proper Grain Reserves," *JMJP*, November 22, 1964, in *SCMP*, No. 3354 (December, 1964).

[51] "Uncle Hsiang," *NFJP*, October 30, 1963, in URS, XXXIV, No. 4 (January 14, 1964), 52.

the alacrity with which commune members (when they have had the opportunity) have devoted their resources to their own private plots and private sidelines,[52] and to full- or part-time commercial activities outside the commune,[53] can largely be explained by the fact that they can earn a higher return from these activities than from work for the commune.

In regard to the sale of commodities produced either by the team or by the individual members, the members are likely to make some calculations as to whether these commodities, if retained, are worth more to them (for example, as consumption items) than the cash they can receive from their sale. In a free market system, of course, prices would tend to rise if enough peasants decided that, at the current price, they would prefer to consume or store more grain themselves rather than sell it. However, prices in Communist China, as suggested above, are only marginally determined by market forces, since the state monopolizes marketing for all important agricultural commodities. In fact, prices tend to be lower than a free market would support. This situation, plus the circumstance that individual commune members have little control over the volume of commodities they sell to the state, generates pressures from the members for the team to produce commodities not subject to the procurement system, or it impels them to try to avoid the procurement system and sell on the free market whenever possible. (When we examine the activities of the supply and marketing cooperatives, we will see that one of their major concerns is to stop illicit trading in commodities which are supposed to be sold to the state.)

All of the deficiencies in the remunerative control system that I have so far noted have implications for the regime's administrative policies, which I will now try to analyze.

IMPLICATIONS OF THE DEFICIENCIES IN THE REMUNERATIVE CONTROL SYSTEM

I have attempted to show that deficiencies in both the calculation of work inputs and the calculation of commune members' shares of the

---

[52] Thus the response of the members to the contracting of crops down to the household level described above. Getting members to give up their farmyard manure has also been a serious problem. For example, *Pao-an Bulletin,* No. 61 (October 6, 1961), in URS, XXVII, No. 7 (April 24, 1962), 138.

[53] This was a particularly serious problem between 1960 and 1962, when the free market was first reopened. However, there are still many references to members moving into commerce when they have the chance. For example, "It Is Not Correct to Say 'We Must Rely on Our Own Effort for Spending Money,'" *JMJP,* November 20, 1964, in *SCMP,* No. 3354 (December, 1964), pp. 6–7.

team's income have tended to weaken members' incentives to apply themselves diligently to collective work, and that the operation of the rationing system also has contributed to this tendency. In addition, I have tried to show that the members' sense of injustice at their income levels, and dissatisfaction with their share of any increments in production increases, have worked in the same direction.

As a result, many commune members appear to have relatively little sense of obligation toward the collective. If there were a more equitable distribution system (as members perceive it), the regime would be in a better position to inculcate attitudes based on the idea of "a fair day's work for a fair day's pay," and consequently would have found it easier to promote a more generalized loyalty to the collective. However, as suggested before, the prevailing attitude of many members toward the communes appears to be highly manipulative, and they seem to be interested mainly in doing the best they can for themselves in a difficult situation. A number of other factors have influenced this development, not the least being the increasing application of coercive controls subsequent to the 1960–62 period of "liberalization" (a development which we will not be able to pursue in detail in this paper). And because of the nature of the opportunity cost structure, even when the CCP has been able to prevent members from employing their resources in individualistic and more profitable ways, the fact that the peasants know that in many instances they could do better individually helps to increase their disenchantment with the communes.

The manipulative orientation of the peasants is particularly dangerous from the regime's point of view because, as we noted above, the reporting and checking system has sufficient limitations that members can often "get away with" behavior prejudicial to the regime's goals. Thus, we find many reports during the 1960's of the CCP's efforts to combat the commune members' lack of initiative and enthusiasm, their tendency to do poor work, and other shortcomings.[54]

As one might expect, in the light of the opportunity cost structure,

[54] See notes 28 and 29 above. This assertion is based on the frequency of reports such as the above and the following, e.g., "With Its Leader Playing an Exemplary Role," *JMJP,* September 24, 1963, in *SCMP,* No. 3080 (October, 1963). Here two local peasants discussing the good performance of one team tell the *JMJP* correspondent that "land in the [exemplary Team] was unlike that in other Teams in that it had been ploughed with great care." "Quality of Farm Work Depends on Ideological-Political Work," *JMJP* editorial, July 12, 1964, in *SCMP,* No. 3271 (August, 1964). This editorial, like many others, may be interpreted as expressing dissatisfaction with the members' work on the collective. Thus it contains such statements as, "Whether we should strive for quantity while maintaining a standard of quality, or strive for work points, disregarding quality, is a struggle between socialist responsibility and capitalist selfishness."

there is considerable evidence of the members' efforts to employ their labor and resources outside the collective. Thus, the regime has found it necessary to fight a constant battle (to be described later) to prevent members from utilizing too much of their time, energy, and other inputs on their private plots and private sideline activities.[55] Another battle has been fought to stop members from engaging in part- or full-time trading activities outside the teams.[56] (The problem sometimes has been one of stopping the local cadres, and even higher level cadres, from allowing members to behave in these ways.[57]) The regime has also had to combat the pressures which peasants have put on the local cadres to plan the commune's production so as to emphasize production of commodities which will yield the team the greatest income and security, even if this means producing less of those crops which the regime's policy stresses. For example, there has been considerable peasant resistance to the regime's recent program to increase cotton acreage, apparently because commune members value secure stocks of grain more than uncertain returns from cotton sales.[58] To maximize the commune's income, members have urged the local cadres to understate the harvest,[59] to leave a portion of the crops on the stalk for members to harvest privately,[60] to allow privately owned animals to feed on the collective's crops, or to distribute more grain and cash than the regime considers appropriate.[61] Sometimes, of course, the members simply take matters into their own hands, bypassing the local cadres. And sometimes the local cadres indulge in these deviations on their own initiative. In any case, the result has been disturbing to the regime, which has felt it necessary to take preventive action.

[55] See note 45 above. One of the explicit objectives of the movement in the mid-sixties to increase the control of the collective over sideline activity has been to curb the practice of members working at their private activities at the expense of the collective. For example, see *NFJP*, October 9, 1964, editorial, "Multiple Undertaking Develops in a Certain Production Team in Kwangtung," in *SCMP*, No. 3345 (November, 1964).

[56] For example, "Real Achievement in Flexibility Without Confusion, and Control Without Rigidity: The Experience of An Liu Market, Wu Hua County in Controlling Trade Fairs," *NFJP*, April 26, 1963, in URS, XXXII, No. 21 (September 10, 1963).

[57] For example, *JMJP*, April 9, 1966, p. 2. Here the problem was that local cadres were giving members too many holidays to perform their private work.

[58] For example, "In a Production Team," p. 15.

[59] Reports of this nature were particularly frequent in 1957. E.g., *Hsin Hu-nan Pao*, July 21, 1957, and *Shan-hsi Jih-pao*, August 14, 1957.

[60] For example, *NFJP*, January 7, 1957.

[61] On the distribution of grain, see "Set Right the Relationship Between the State, the Collective and the Individual . . . ," *TKP*, December 7, 1964, in *SCMP*, No. 3366 (December, 1964), p. 7. For an example of how these pressures relate to cotton, see "Three Not to Retain in the Delivery and Selling of Cotton," *TKP*, November 21, 1964, in URS, XXXVII, No. 22 (December 15, 1964).

The list of shortcomings and deviations that I have discussed appears formidable indeed. I will grant that by emphasizing the weaknesses of the system, I may be picturing more serious disorganization within the communes than actually exists. No doubt in many areas peasant pressures have been successfully contained and the problems I have discussed kept under control. Nevertheless, though it is extremely difficult to generalize accurately as to the extent of the existing problems and shortcomings, what does seem clear is that they have been sufficiently widespread to provoke a set of curative and preventive responses from the CCP.

A variety of measures has been adopted. For example, greater pressure has been put on the local cadres to make more intensive efforts to operate the remunerative control system properly. As we have pointed out, how well the system operates and how effectively pressures from the members to deviate from the regime's policies can be resisted depends greatly on the local cadres' activism. On balance, however, it seems clear that the local cadres' work performance and ability to resist peasant pressures have been less than satisfactory from the regime's perspective. As a result, the CCP has been unwilling to trust them to carry out its policies autonomously and has felt it necessary to increase the extent of outside intervention into the affairs of the teams.

THE PROBLEMS OF CONTROLLING THE LOCAL CADRES

The local cadres are caught in a classic situation of conflicting expectations, that is, from higher level cadres (and ultimately the top leaders of the regime) and from the commune members under them. Both have the capacity to reward and punish the local cadres. However, the balance of pressures on the local cadres is such that the regime cannot wholly rely on them to carry out its directives.

There are serious limitations to the attractiveness of their position. Though the regime could make it possible for the local cadres to receive substantially higher incomes than ordinary commune members, it has been reluctant to do this because of its concern that significant class distinctions might emerge between members and cadres, which would be damaging to the members' morale. The regime has thus insisted that the local cadres (usually including the brigade cadres) derive their income primarily from work points earned through manual labor, with only a small supplement being received for their administrative work. Consequently, most local cadres have little to look forward to in terms of material rewards (unless they use their position to increase their income illegally). Since 1960, because the regime has stressed the need to strengthen leadership at the brigade and team levels, there has, furthermore, been little hope of moving up to higher positions.

The local cadres can, however, expect with some certainty—to judge from their experience since 1955—strong pressure from the regime to work harder, and they are liable to rather severe sanctions when the results of their work are not satisfactory (as is frequently the case, in view of the expectations of the regime and the control system within which the cadres must work). These conditions, plus the sanctions the commune members can apply to them when they try to implement policies displeasing to the members, make the local cadre's lot a particularly unhappy one. Their situation is neatly summed up by the complaint of one team leader who saw himself caught in the middle and felt that he "pleased nobody."[62] These facts help to explain both the difficulties which the regime has had in recruiting and keeping local cadres on the job[63] and the frequent complaints made by cadres themselves about the arduousness of their work and the inadequacy of the rewards they receive.[64]

This set of circumstances has clearly affected the enthusiasm and activism of local cadres. It may also have made the regime's sanctions seem less threatening to them. Though politically their position may be difficult, in financial terms they suffer no great loss if they lose their cadre position, so that they might well ask themselves why they should slavishly devote their energies to implementing the regime's policies, especially when they may antagonize many commune members. This attitude is illustrated by a case involving new cadres in one of the Pao-an brigades. After indicating that they expected to be the targets of periodic "rectification," they are quoted as saying, "Be it good or bad, we have four months to go; why should we make others hate us."[65]

The members of communes also have some ability to control or

[62] "Not to Be a Good Cadre Is the Greatest Loss One Can Suffer," NFJP, April 26, 1966, in SCMP, No. 3698 (May, 1966), p. 11.

[63] For example, "Further Launch a Large Scale Production Increase, Economy, and Socialist Education Movement," Lien-chiang Documents, February 9, 1963. This report indicates that before the campaign there were some 172 brigade cadres and 1,016 team cadres who said they did not want to be cadres.

[64] "Cadres of Lung-Mei Brigade Chao-an Hsien Discuss the Relationship Between Politics and Production," Yang-ch'eng Wan-pao (Canton Evening Paper), February 18, 1966, in SCMP, No. 3648 (March, 1966). A cadre here is quoted as saying that he "always thought it a personal loss to serve as a cadre."

[65] "Conditions and Problems of Late Crop Production," Pao-an Bulletin, No. 59 (September 23, 1961), in URS, XXVII, No. 7 (April 24, 1962), 119.

influence the local cadres, even though their position is a relatively deprived one. The major measure of a cadre's success is the production and sales performance of his unit, but to attain this success he must depend to some extent on the cooperation of the members, since the tasks to be performed on the commune are sufficiently complex, unpredictable, and difficult to check that at least a degree of initiative and cooperation from the members is essential. Should they refuse to cooperate, as they appear to have done at times (as when confronted with some of the demands of the Great Leap Forward[66]), the results can certainly embarrass the local cadres,[67] and ultimately the regime. The members can also influence the cadres by threatening to expose them during "rectification" campaigns. Though this can be a dangerous practice, given the possibility of "revenge," it is something that the local cadres cannot ignore. The members can also make life difficult for the cadres by criticizing them privately, perhaps thereby undermining their authority, or at times by actually ostracizing them. Since most cadres at the brigade and team levels have lived in their localities for years and usually have long-standing neighborhood, friendship, and often kinship ties with the members, this can be a serious matter. (I have already indicated one manifestation of the strength of these ties in reference to the local cadres' reluctance to penalize inadequate work.)

It should be noted here that, paradoxically, collectivization in many ways may have promoted the strength of local solidarity, particularly at the team level. In some respects, individual farmers now have greater economic incentives for local cooperation than before, and they also interact together as a unit far more than they did prior to collectivization, when most activities occurred in the context of the family. Many of the previous causes of local dissension, such as interfamily conflicts over water rights and competition for land, have been removed. The abolition of tenancy has also removed one of the chief sources of intravillage stratification cleavages. (This, of course, is not to say that no cleavages exist within the teams—the regime, in fact, has done its best to create a division between "bad elements" and other members, and certainly a cleavage exists between the cadres and the members.)

[66] For one account of this response during the Great Leap, see Isobel and David Crook, *The First Years of Yangyi Commune* (London: Routledge and Kegan Paul, 1966), p. 121.

[67] "Further Consolidate the Collective Economy and Develop Agricultural Production," Lien-chiang Documents, p. 27. A case is cited where members threatened a cadre by reminding him that "It is the cadres who will be held responsible for losses in production."

In general, knowledge of the influence which commune members can bring to bear on them, plus the sense of solidarity linking team members and cadres, appear to make the local cadres reluctant to implement policies which conflict with the members' interests. Thus, complaints that cadres "try every possible means to look after the interests of the peasants, and those of their own locality, but not the interests of the state and of the whole" have been common, especially in the early 1960's when the CCP was discovering some of the weaknesses of the remunerative control system.[68]

There are also other factors which lead cadres to identify with commune members. Since they are paid on a similar basis as the members, they too have a stake both in increasing the collective's income and in expanding the percentage of income distributed for consumption. Like the members, they need to supplement their income through private activities and are therefore anxious to devote as much of their resources as possible to these activities.[69] For their own protection, cadres are sometimes impelled to send false reports to higher authorities.[70] It is often in their interests to keep secret grain reserves, in order to handle sudden demands for more grain either by the regime or by commune members, or to prevent the higher authorities from knowing the real output potential of their unit (for example, to forestall increases in state procurement targets).[71]

As noted earlier, one of the measures the regime has adopted to handle the deficiencies in the existing system, and to combat the resultant pressures from commune members, has been to put increasing pressure on the local cadres to work more actively to carry out the regime's policies. They have tried to recruit the most important local cadres (especially the team leaders) into the Party or Youth League, thus subjecting them to the discipline these organizations can exert. More recently they have fostered poor and lower middle peasants' associations, which are supposed to act as watchdogs to insure that

[68] "Strengthen Attention to the State, Assign Purchasing Tasks Definitely," *NFJP* editorial, March 2, 1963, in *SCMP*, No. 2949 (March, 1963), p. 3.

[69] Thus one of the local cadres' complaints as to the onerousness of the cadre's life is that he often does not have enough time to devote to his private plot. See "To Be a Cadre in My Opinion Is to Suffer a Loss," in *SCMP*, No. 3698 (May, 1966), p. 13.

[70] On the tendency for local cadres to give dishonest reports see, "Exaggeration and Dishonesty Must Be Eliminated when They Emerge," *NFJP*, March 20, 1963, in *SCMP*, No. 2960 (April, 1963).

[71] For analysis of why local cadres try to keep extra grain stocks, see "Tsengch'eng Resolutely Reduces Additional Transferable Grain," *JMJP*, May 31, 1962, in URS, XXVIII, No. 6 (July 20, 1962).

there are no deviations from the regime's policies on the part of either the local cadres or ordinary commune members.

These measures do not, however, have much influence on the economic calculations of commune members, though they do increase normative and coercive sanctions. Moreover, to judge from the continued incidence of troublesome deviations, such measures do not appear to be very successful in motivating the local cadres to increase their activism, or to resist pressures from commune members. To deal with the situation, therefore, the regime has been impelled to move toward greater centralization of the control structure.

THE CENTRALIZATION OF CONTROL OVER THE COLLECTIVES

In examining the control structure, the pattern of relations between the team and its members and state agencies outside or above it deserves special attention.

The centralized nature of the control system does not, of course, derive entirely from deficiencies in the remunerative control structures which I have described. In terms of the wide sweep of CCP policies, including its goals of restructuring Chinese society according to an over-all Marxist blueprint, political control of events at the village level, and even at the level of the individual peasant, has always been a fundamental requirement. The extension of the Party organization down to the village level by the mid-1950's was designed to establish such control. Moreover, because many of the CCP's goals for rural China remain unfulfilled, the regime still resists any policy changes (such as the widening of the free markets or a decrease in the size of the basic accounting units) which might imply a loosening of political control.

Certain aspects of the regime's leadership theory, most specifically the "mass line" doctrine, emphasize the importance of thorough knowledge of, and reporting upward about, the situation at the local level.[72] In practice, this too has often reinforced tendencies toward centralization; the information derived from the villages can be used to reduce local autonomy (even though another aspect of the "mass line" emphasizes local political participation).

Recently, the regime has also put high priority on the need to bring about a technological revolution in Chinese agriculture. Agricultural programs in the 1950's were largely aimed at intensification of traditional approaches (such as building irrigation works with mobilized

[72] Lewis, *Leadership in Communist China,* chap. iii.

labor). However, recently more emphasis has been placed on modern factors, including improved seeds, chemical fertilizer, and insecticides. (Since 1963 one campaign has pushed for "scientific experiment" in agriculture.) This requires much more intervention from outside the team, both to transmit new knowledge and to gain the cooperation of farmers who know little or nothing about modern agriculture.

It should also be noted that centralization of the control system did not by any means begin in the 1960's. There were similar tendencies in the 1950's, and even during the Great Leap Forward, though, as indicated above, the communes during the Great Leap Forward probably had more autonomy than did the collectives in the earlier period. What I am concerned with here, however, is to analyze to what extent the CCP was able to carry out the decentralization reforms which in theory it favored in the period after the Great Leap Forward. The evidence suggests that the results were limited, and in practice the deficiencies of the remunerative control system compelled the regime to move away from the administrative ideals propagated in the 1959–62 period.

Earlier I argued that if the regime wishes to insure achievement of its production and taxation goals, it cannot rely solely on the teams to carry out these policies autonomously. What have the regime's responses to this situation been? The evidence suggests that in order to obtain compliance and ensure implementation of its policies, it has been compelled to use agencies outside the team to intervene in most phases of the production and distribution process. This intervention has involved setting targets for production, efforts to improve the reporting and inspection of the production process (with special attention to harvest reports), and directives specifying how the produce should be distributed. It has also involved an effort to decrease the opportunities for the teams and their members to operate outside the state-controlled commercial institutions. I will trace each of these developments below.

I would suggest that this was the only response the regime could make, given its over-all production and taxation goals and its determination to continue with collectivized agriculture. To apply any sort of sanctions against those teams which do not conform with the regime's policies or live up to its expectations, the regime must first define clear criteria against which to judge the performance of the teams, and it must have continual detailed information as to performance so that it can deal promptly with shortcomings, deviations, and nonconformity (before too much damage is done). Unfortunately, space prohibits extended consideration of the complex blend of remunerative, normative, and coercive controls applied to cadres and commune members in units whose performance is found to be unsatisfactory, but I will describe below various ways in which external agencies intervene in team activities to ensure centralized direction.

THE SETTING OF PRODUCTION TARGETS

I indicated previously that state procurement prices are only to a limited extent influenced by market pressures. The regime has therefore had to involve itself directly in the process of planning production activities, because the production teams, if left to themselves, would not necessarily produce the commodities that the state feels it essential to procure. In the words of one Communist writer, the concern of communes is to "produce whatever things that could yield them a good profit."[73] Earlier, I cited cases of teams anxious to grow grain rather than an industrial crop like cotton. The teams often wish, also, to produce commodities they can sell profitably on the local free market, rather than meet the state's demands for grain or cotton.[74] It should be noted here that in one sense the restoration of the free markets in the 1960's has been a great source of trouble to the regime precisely because it has provided an alternative and potentially more profitable sales outlet to the teams and their members. The attempts to curtail the operation of the free markets (to be examined below) can be partly understood in this context.

Control over the setting of production targets is also important to the regime, because it provides an indispensable basis for evaluating production performance. Aside from its concern that the teams may not want to produce the commodities sought, the regime has also found it necessary to control the target-setting process because it wants production targets to reflect truly the potential of the team, whereas the local cadres are often interested in keeping these targets low so as to free themselves from increased pressures for performance or to prevent increases in procurement demands. Ideally the regime's interests would be best served by a cost accounting system whereby all the factors influencing production and profit potential could be accurately calculated and then measured later against actual performance.

[73] "A Talk on Understanding the Middle Peasant Problem," p. 3.

[74] For example, "Agriculture and Sideline Production Must Not Be Displaced," *NFJP*, March 2, 1963, in *SCMP*, No. 2966 (April, 1963).

Though such a system has been mooted by Communist economists,[75] its complexity has so far prevented a serious effort to install anything but a crude approximation to it.

The regime has attempted to handle the production planning problem by putting much of the authority for decision making in the hands of cadres above the team level. This is not entirely a development of the 1960's. On the contrary, at no time since 1955 have the basic production units (except perhaps for a brief period in 1958–59) had much genuine autonomy in this process. The CCP apparently would have liked to have given increased autonomy to the brigades and teams after the Great Leap Forward, and did make some effort at that time to do so, but for the reasons I have discussed this has not proved, in practice, to be feasible. In fact, while there have been ideological pronouncements and even explicit directives favoring decentralization, administrative developments have moved precisely in the opposite direction.

What we find, then, is that in the mid-1960's targets for production levels and procurement (usually in the form of "contracts" with the grain or other government commodity departments) are filtered down through the various levels of the system, the provinces being allocated targets which are then successively handed down through the special district, *hsien,* commune, and brigade levels.[76] In this process cadres are exhorted to investigate the production potentials of the teams; however, what generally seems to happen in practice is that each level in the administrative hierarchy merely assigns as fairly as possible the targets handed down by its superiors. The original targets are not built up from initial estimates of performance capabilities assessed by the teams themselves, partly because of the administrative difficulties involved, and partly because the teams cannot be trusted to set realistic performance targets.

Most of the regime's attention has been given to so-called first- and second-category goods, that is, goods over which the state claims a marketing monopoly, including grain and cotton. But since 1961 increased attention has been given to the control of third-category goods (goods which the state does not claim a monopoly over—such as

---

[75] "Investigation of the Costs of Agricultural Commodities and an Inquiry into the Problem of Methods of Computation," *Economic Research,* No. 8 (August 17, 1961), in *JPRS,* No. 16093 (November 8, 1962).

[76] The process is outlined in detail in two articles in the *Peking Review:* "Brigades and Teams," No. 12 (March 18, 1966), 8, and "In a Production Team," p. 15.

handicrafts and various fruits and vegetables). Here, too, the state has been unwilling to use market prices to determine production. Thus, the same problems have arisen, as indicated by the fact that the regime has found it necessary to devise some other way of insuring needed supplies. Accordingly, outside agencies have been given the authority to set production targets. While this does not yet apply generally to third-category goods,[77] the regime has recently put great pressure on the supply and marketing cooperatives (hereafter SMC's) to sign contracts with the teams, and sometimes with individual members, to sell the desired items at state prices. The SMC personnel are expected to make detailed studies of the teams' potentials for production of third-category goods, to set targets for them, and to sign contracts for their purchase later in the season.[78]

Another significant development has been the recent effort to transfer the production of third-category goods into the hands of the collective. The original commune reforms in 1960–62 had given individual members control over most of these goods. But although this reform helped to promote production of goods involved, it made state control over production decisions more difficult. Thus, one of the objectives of the campaign to increase collective control over sideline activity has been to make it easier for production plans to be controlled, and for SMC's to contract for these goods.[79] Outside control of the production plans for third-category goods has also been stimulated by the desire to prevent members from devoting too much of their time to them, at the expense of commune production of first- and second-category goods. This point will be taken up again when I discuss the free market.

THE PRODUCTION PROCESS

Relatively little attention has been paid in the secondary literature to the level of outside involvement in the actual production process. However, upon examination this involvement appears to be quite ex-

[77] "Handle Correctly Various Relations in Sideline Production," *TKP*, June 2, 1965, in URS, XXXIX, No. 26 (June 29, 1965), 373–75.

[78] For an extreme example of the research, see Supply and Marketing Department of Ch'i Hsia Ying, Tso Chih *hsien*, "Inner Mongolia Realistically Distributes Quotas of Fresh Eggs to Be Purchased by the State," *TKP*, April 18, 1961, in *SCMP*, No. 2496 (May, 1961).

I have found G. William Skinner, "Marketing and Social Structure in Rural China," Part 3, *Journal of Asian Studies*, XXIV, No. 3 (May, 1965), and Richard M. Pfeffer, "Contracts in China Revisited," *China Quarterly*, No. 28 (October–December, 1966), extremely helpful in trying to understand rural trade and the functions of the SMC's.

[79] For example, *TKP*, October 28, 1964, p. 2.

tensive when compared with the ideals concerning the decentralization of the production process articulated during the 1960's. The following survey indicates that although the size of the basic production unit was reduced strikingly between 1959 and 1962, this has not meant that the local cadres and commune members have been given much autonomy in the decision-making process concerning production activities, at least as regards such key questions as when sowing is to begin, how much fertilizer is to be used, how many crops are to be planted, and so on.

The regime itself has put pressure on the lower level cadres to involve themselves in the production activities of the teams, despite its propaganda concerning the importance of decentralization. This action is the result of the official concern that the teams, if left to themselves, may not perform as the regime would like to see them perform.[80] Thus, there have been repeated warnings to cadres that if they do not follow events closely, "Many important farming opportunities will slip by."[81]

However, cadres at intermediary levels in the control system have their own reasons for getting involved in the local production process, and often they seem to have taken the initiative in setting up regulations as to how productive activities should be performed. Confronted with evidence of the unreliable performance of many teams (which has been related to the limitations of the remunerative control system), or fearful of poor performance, they have sought to ensure good performance by stipulating in advance the tasks, and completion dates for these tasks, necessary for the teams under their jurisdiction. They have been motivated to do this, in part at least, because their positions in the Party bureaucracy depend to some extent on their success in carrying out their assigned production and procurement tasks.

The following two examples taken from reports in 1962 illustrate this process. They are indicative, I think, of the fact that cadres responsible for the teams' activities at this time were aware that they could not sit back and let the teams act autonomously in managing their production activities, as the regime had originally thought would be possible when the decentralization reforms were promulgated. After receiving evidence that local teams were not meeting their procurement quotas, the *hsien* Party secretary in Lienchiang *hsien* (Fukien) insisted

[80] For example, "Examine the Preparation of Seeds," *JMJP,* February 24, 1963, in *SCMP,* No. 2944 (March, 1963). Here the problem was that five teams had let their seed go rotten. See also notes 28, 29, and 54, above.

[81] "Seize the Initiative in Farm Production in the Production Struggle," *JMJP* editorial, February 20, 1965, in *JPRS,* No. 29101 (March 12, 1965).

that, "Hereafter, the lower echelons cannot keep their thought from the upper echelons. Instead there must be mutual reporting between them, instructions must be requested prior to the disposition of any problem, and a report must be made after the matter is settled. Independent kingdoms cannot be tolerated."[82] In a similar case, where a special district committee discovered evidence of lax winter farming preparations, the response was to issue a bulletin stipulating what the local teams' tasks were, and how and when they should be performed, to fix attendance quotas to insure the appropriate labor supply, and finally "to make investigation once every few days and appraisal-comparison every eight to ten days."[83]

In the mid-1960's the regime has made a greater effort to stimulate the introduction of new techniques, new types of seed, and so on, which has necessitated more work on the part of lower level cadres to provide the technical information and direction necessary for the production process. However, the main problem in the 1960's for the regime and the cadres responsible for production has been to get the teams to make effective use of traditional farming techniques, including already well-known means of improving production, such as the expansion of the irrigation system and the more intensive use of organic fertilizer. Thus, as will be indicated below, in their scheduling, reporting, and inspection activities, cadres above the team level have been primarily concerned with what would normally be routine farming processes, which the members could carry out quite well on their own initiative if they so desired.

Schedules. The authorities responsible for insuring production performance have attempted to prevent management errors, or perhaps negligence, by setting up schedules for production activities and targets for the level of performance of basic units during the production cycle. Thus, we find targets for the amount of manure for spring planting and the time by which it should be prepared,[84] targets for acreage and the time by which spring planting should be completed,[85] and so on. One could detail these schedules endlessly; in fact, it seems that the teams are deluged with directives of this nature throughout the season. As

---

[82] "Further Consolidate the Collective Economy," Lien-chiang Documents.

[83] "Winter Production Begins Steadily in Shao Kuan Special District," *NFJP,* December 26, 1962, in URS, XXX, No. 19 (March 5, 1963), 321.

[84] "Rural Areas of Three Northeastern Provinces Firmly Grasp the Winter Season to Launch Activities of Accumulating and Delivering Manure," NCNA, Peking, January 3, 1963, in URS, XXXII, No. 10 (August 2, 1963).

[85] "Seize the Initiative in Farm Production in the Production Struggle."

one brigade cadre put it, "A thousand and one jobs are handed down by the upper levels to the lower levels."[86]

Reports. Impressive energy has been devoted to the task of discovering how effectively the teams are performing their allotted targets. Reporting systems have been established to enable the local cadres—via statistical reports, telephone reports, or conferences at brigade, commune, or higher levels—to reveal the performance of their units. Much of the responsibility for this activity seems to have been lodged in the hands of the brigade cadres. They are uniquely situated to handle such tasks because they no longer have responsibility for directing day-to-day agricultural operations, as they did in the early days of the commune movement, but are now specifically entrusted with general supervisory and inspection tasks.

Reports are required regularly from local cadres on all the major agricultural operations. They must include information on activities such as seed soaking, sowing, and manure collection.[87] Some indication of their extent may be taken from cadre complaints about the amount of work this reporting causes them. According to one brigade cadre, "Every three days there are large and small meetings, telephone meetings, and *hsien* and commune cadres sent down to take time with reports they have to prepare."[88] At crucial times like the harvesting period, reports have sometimes been required on a daily basis.[89] In some places local cadres have had to send a report to the *hsien* every three days.[90] In one account of the system, it was indicated that after examination of the problems caused by the volume of these reports, the brigade was "only" required to submit a progress report once every ten to fifteen days.[91] Presumably, these reports yield the voluminous statistics, periodically quoted in the press during the agricultural season, on the progress of farming operations.

Inspections. The regime has not confined itself to the gathering of

[86] "Participation in Labor Becomes the Rule Among Cadres in Hsi-Yang," *JMJP*, June 21, 1963, in *SCMP*, No. 3006 (June, 1963), p. 7.

[87] "Bring Politics to the Fore, Put the Thought of Mao Tse-tung in Command of Everything," *Red Flag*, No. 5 (April 5, 1966). This is a good example of a number of articles at this time criticizing *hsien* officials for their preoccupation with matters like "figures pertaining to what progress has been made in production and how much manure is accumulated."

[88] "Participation in Labor," p. 7.

[89] "Where Lie the Contradictions," *JMJP*, July 1, 1963, in *SCMP*, No. 3028 (July, 1963), p. 3.

[90] "How Can We Do Well in Both Administrative Work and Labor," *JMJP*, August 18, 1963, in *SCMP*, No. 3060 (September, 1963), p. 6.

[91] "Where Lie the Contradictions," p. 3.

reports from the teams. As we might expect from our earlier discussion of the competing pressures on the local cadres, the regime has not been able to have unlimited faith in the accuracy of the reports it receives from the lower levels. As I indicated earlier, the team cadres have been, in some situations, under considerable pressure to prevent the regime from gaining accurate knowledge of conditions in the team. They (and to some extent the brigade, commune, and even *hsien* cadres as well) have also been reluctant to expose their own leadership shortcomings —for example, revealing failure to meet their targets—because this would in all probability lead to their being subjected to criticism, or worse punishment, from higher level cadres sent down to deal with the situation. As a *hsien* Party secretary notes, one needs personal experience before one can evaluate reports. Many of them are "not first hand data," and "many of the things in them are hearsay."[92]

Consequently, the regime, and the cadres who must deal with subordinates whose performance they cannot be sure of, have tried to organize a massive inspection system, actually sending cadres from the province to the brigade level to the production units to check personally on the progress of farming operations. The intensity and scope of this system has increased during the 1960's as cadres at various administrative levels have either realized themselves, or have been ordered to concern themselves with the fact, that they could not rely solely on the 1959–62 reforms in the remunerative control system to motivate cadres and commune members beneath them to carry out their tasks satisfactorily.

One specific manifestation of the regime's concern was the initiation of the *ssu-ch'ing* "four clearances" campaign during 1963, when cadres at all levels were involved in checking various aspects of the teams' operations, including the contents of their storehouses. A rather bizarre indication of this concern was revealed recently when it was reported that Liu Shao-ch'i, apparently unable to trust anyone to supply a realistic picture of conditions in the communes, sent his wife in disguise to an area in Hopei to do a special study.[93]

[92] "The Key Is Revolutionization of Thought," *JMJP,* August 26, 1964, in *SCMP,* No. 3300 (September, 1964), p. 3.

[93] "Exposing a Big Scheme for Restoring Capitalism," *Peking Review,* No. 38 (September 15, 1967), pp. 23–24. The extent of the CCP's concern about these matters is revealed in an important resolution of the Central Committee of the CCP on May 30, 1963, known as the "First Ten Points," especially Point VIII, which discusses the need for the "Four Clearances" movement. See "Draft Resolution of the Central Committee of the Chinese Communist Party on Some Problems in Current Rural Work, May 30, 1963," in Richard Baum and Frederick C. Teiwes, *Ssu-ch'ing: The Socialist Education Movement of*

In the 1960's great emphasis has been placed on the need for higher
level cadres to get out of their offices, avoid dependence solely on
reports, and instead go down to the production units to find out what
"the actual situation of the production struggle is."[94] Or, in the words
of one editorial, it is necessary to listen to reports from lower levels,
but it is even more important that "one should personally go down to
make investigation." By so doing, "It is possible to find out the actual
conditions and timely discover and solve the problem."[95] Reports are
often cited of discoveries of negligence or inefficiency as a result of
such inspections,[96] implying, of course, that the teams cannot be
trusted to do the job without higher level supervision.

This inspection work has taken a number of forms. The most direct
has been that of dispatching cadres with explicit orders to check the
performance of the brigades and teams at crucial periods throughout
the season. According to one report, "After a work assignment is
transferred, the *hsien* sees to it that leading cadres are sent to the spot
to investigate and find out the progress."[97] In many areas the inspection process has been systematized since 1960 by scheduling cadres at
the *hsien*, commune, and brigade levels to spend several days each
week at the brigade and team levels (following the so-called two–five,
three–seven systems, that is, spending two or three days in the office,
followed by five to seven days in the production units).[98] Though
inspecting the performance of local units is only one of the cadres'
functions in this system, press discussions make it clear that this is an
important task.[99]

Inspections are made of all major activities, such as spring plant-

1962–1966 (Berkeley: Center for Chinese Studies, University of California, China Research Monograph No. 2, 1968), pp. 58–71.

[94] "Steadfastly Uphold the System of Participation in Collective Productive Labor by
Cadres," *JMJP*, January 16, 1965, in *SCMP*, No. 3387 (January, 1965), p. 6.

[95] Hunan People's Broadcasting Station, monitored by URI, April 12, 1963, an editorial
"To Take Shock Action in the Accumulation of Manure," in URS, XXXII, No. 10
(August 2, 1963), 190.

[96] For example, "Exaggeration and Dishonesty Must Be Eliminated when They
Emerge," *NFJP*, March 20, 1963, in *SCMP*, No. 2960 (April, 1963). Also "Moving the
Organ and the Cadres to the Village to Further the Half-Day Work, Half-Day Labor
Program," *JMJP*, December 12, 1964, in *JPRS*, No. 28766 (February 16, 1965). Here the
cadres discovered that their irrigation program had produced a stagnant water problem.

[97] "Leadership Cadres of Ting Hsien Persist in Carrying Out the Method of Investigation by Staying on the Spot," *JMJP*, August 20, 1963, in *SCMP*, No. 3060 (September,
1963), p. 9.

[98] Lewis, *Leadership in Communist China*, pp. 230–32.

[99] For example, *JMJP*, June 15, 1960, p. 1.

ing,[100] summer hoeing,[101] and of course harvesting, as I will indicate below. Typically, reports of inspection activities cite enormous figures for the number of cadres involved. Thus, in the course of spring sowing in Hunan in 1965, some seventeen thousand cadres from the province, special district, and *hsien* levels alone are said to have been sent down to penetrate the production teams.[102] The scope of the activity is suggested in an article describing the functions of commune cadres in inspection, which reports that "Such supervision and help continues throughout the year from sowing . . . to the distribution of income at the year's end."[103]

Some attention has been given in the secondary literature to another technique of inspection, that is, the so-called *hsia-fang* campaigns.[104] These campaigns were particularly important in the immediate post-Great Leap Forward period, when the regime was anxious to strengthen leadership at the brigade and team levels. However, in various forms they have been maintained throughout the period in question. They have involved the dispatching of cadres down to the lower administrative levels for extended periods of time, frequently with orders to live and work with the commune members. The movement has been accompanied by much Communist rhetoric concerning the need to improve the working style, class consciousness, and general ideological level of the cadres involved, so much so that the implications of the movement for inspection may not be immediately clear.

Nevertheless, a rather obvious by-product of these campaigns has been an increase in the available channels and sources of information concerning performance at the team or brigade level. The regime has made it quite clear that cadres sent down are to devote part of their time to investigating the implementation of the regime's policies.[105] Cadres are reminded that they are not sent down "merely as an addition of one manpower unit to the production team," but that "Participation of Cadres in production aims at supervising production

[100] For example, "Spring Plowing Organized in Many Provinces with Great Political Exuberance," *JMJP*, March 3, 1965, in *JPRS*, No. 29397 (April 2, 1965).

[101] "Emphasize Politics in Consummating Summer Hoeing," *Hei-lung-chiang Jih-pao,* Harbin, May 25, 1965, in *JPRS*, No. 34991 (April 11, 1966).

[102] "Hunan Further Strengthens Leadership of Spring Sowing," *JMJP*, March 10, 1965, in *JPRS,* No. 29478 (April 7, 1965).

[103] "In Yantan People's Commune," *Peking Review,* Nos. 10–15 (March 4, 11, 18, 25, April 1, 8, 1966), in *SCMM,* No. 524 (May, 1966), p. 14.

[104] Lewis, *Leadership in Communist China,* pp. 220–30.

[105] For example, see "Without Squatting at a Point One Cannot Direct over the Whole Surface," *JMJP,* August 26, 1964, in *SCMP,* No. 3300 (September, 1964).

more fruitfully."[106] The regime has been particularly insistent that the brigade cadres devote much of their time to manual labor in the teams; it was believed that by actually involving themselves in the production process, the cadres would have a better chance of finding out the real situation in the teams. As with the regular inspection activity, the implication, sometimes openly admitted, is that unless they do get down to the operational level, inefficiencies, mistakes, and so on will occur.[107]

Cadres involved in *hsia-fang* campaigns have not been assigned randomly. They have been sent to areas where performance has been suspect or where deficiencies have already been discovered through the regular reporting and inspection system.[108] Their task has been to strengthen local leadership and deal with existing problems. In reference to our theme of centralization, however, the extensive reliance the regime has placed on this technique gives some indication of how dependent it has become on using direct intervention from outside to influence the teams' behavior.

A final inspection practice worth noting is the recent stress on emulation campaigns. By making comparisons among teams, using as models the performance of the more efficient basic production units, or even the experimental or model plots run by higher level cadres, any weaknesses in the operation of particular units may be more easily brought to light. Though this movement does not appear to be fully systematized as yet, it is recognized as an important leadership method.[109]

THE COLLECTION AND DISTRIBUTION OF THE HARVEST

The intervention of agencies outside the teams has been particularly intensive and important in regard to the collection and distribution of the harvest. The reasons appear to be clear enough, for as my analysis of the remunerative control system indicated, the commune members, and to some extent the local cadres, have an interest in limiting the

[106] "New Development in Participation by Cadres in Production and Supervision of Production," *JMJP*, July 30, 1960, in *SCMP*, No. 2317 (August, 1960), p. 10.

[107] For example, "Over 5000 Cadres Dedicate Themselves to Production Deep in the Countryside, Bringing About a Rapid Change over the Production Features of Chao Ch'ing Administrative District," *NFJP*, February 14, 1963, in *SCMP*, No. 2936 (March, 1963). Here they discovered that among other things, "The attendance rates in many areas reached only around 70% of the total laborers."

[108] For example, "30,000 Cadres from Various Levels in Kwangtung to Help Strengthen Leadership over Spring Ploughing in Rural Areas," NCNA, Canton, February 22, 1963, in *SCMP*, No. 2929 (March, 1963).

[109] "Without Squatting at a Point," p. 7.

outflow of grain and other commodities to amounts below those sought by the regime. Moreover, since the reopening of rural free markets in 1959–60, the teams and commune members have had some opportunity to sell items at prices which are higher than those they can get from the state procurement authorities. The vigor of the free market (and sometimes the black market) has been promoted by the possibilities it provides for former private traders and merchants, and often for the commune members themselves, to earn greater incomes from trading than from full-time work on collective activities. Repeated references to this subject indicate that the regime is seriously concerned about the proliferation of "speculative" merchants[110] and the possibility that the teams will evade their procurement responsibilities if they have the opportunity to sell their produce to such individuals.[111]

All this poses a major problem to the regime, which has a continuing interest in controlling the distribution of commodities, and since the beginning of the sixties it has responded by attempting (with incomplete success as yet) to control these "deviant" tendencies, most often by instructing the local Party committees or the SMC's to regulate the private activities of the members and the free market traders.

In attempting to insure proper harvesting (insuring that grain and other crops actually get into the collective's hands) and to assure that the state procurement quotas are met, the regime has made special efforts to dispatch cadres from the Party, government, and purchasing organizations to supervise the operation.[112] As one *People's Daily* editorial notes, given the facts that "at present China's agricultural production level is comparatively low," and that there is a "struggle between the Socialist and Capitalist road," which is "bound to be reflected in our work of purchasing farm products, . . . Party committees have always listed purchasing work as one of the central tasks of autumn and winter."[113]

Typically, reports on the harvest indicate that cadres from all levels

[110] For example, "Some Problems of Procurement of Agricultural Products," *JMJP*, October 26, 1961, in *JPRS*, No. 11969 (January 15, 1962), and, "How Supply and Marketing Coops Expand Their Business," *JMJP*, December 20, 1962, in *JPRS*, No. 18240 (March 20, 1962).

[111] "Grasp the Opportunity and Strengthen Leadership to Speed Up Fulfillment of Procurement Plans for Farm Produce," *JMJP* editorial, November 24, 1964, in *JPRS*, No. 28543 (January 29, 1965). The editorial notes that "speculators always try their very best to sabotage the policy of planned purchase and to seize the sources of farm products."

[112] For example, *JMJP*, July 1, 1963, p. 1, and July 3, 1963. Here some sixty-five hundred *hsien* and commune cadres in eight *hsien* are reported to have led the harvest.

[113] "Fully Recognize the Current Favorable Situation," *JMJP* editorial, September 21, 1964, in *SCMP*, No. 3308 (September, 1964).

up to the province are mobilized to go down to the teams to insure adequate performance. For example, in three special districts in Hopei it was reported that some seven thousand cadres from the communes, *hsien,* and special districts were mobilized to participate in the 1963 wheat harvest.[114] Ideally, the regime would no doubt like to improve the control of procurement operations everywhere to the point reached by the grain authorities in Hupeh, who "stationed staff members in production brigades at night, conducted quality inspection early in the morning and late at night, and returned to their own premises during the day to check agricultural products into storage."[115] Despite such efforts, the regime is still troubled by the problem of ascertaining grain output levels in the teams. Thus, the "four clearances" campaign was launched, with one of its objectives being, as noted above, the clearing or checking of local grain storehouses.[116] This campaign, incidentally, was directed by work teams from outside the local communes' teams.

In order to prevent unauthorized sales of commodities classified as first- or second-category goods, the regime has tried to restrict the operation of the free market and of private trading generally. Apart from ordering the local Party authorities to concern themselves with this problem, the regime has sought to strengthen the involvement of the SMC's in rural trade, both in limiting the extent of the free market and in directly participating in trading transactions. As we indicated above, local autonomy in the production and sale of third-category goods is threatening to the regime, because it gives the teams and their members opportunities to concentrate on products which are more profitable than those classified as first- and second-category goods. It also stimulates the free market, thereby increasing the possibility of engaging in illicit business in first- and second-category goods at the expense of procurement targets.

Particularly since 1963, the SMC's have been used to curb such practices, first of all by concluding contracts with the teams or their members for the purchase of third-category goods at state prices. This policy, apart from insuring needed supplies, decreases the opportunity for the teams to produce goods more profitable than those in the first and second categories, because the regime tries to keep prices low in these contracts, and, of course, because it leaves little scope for the

---

[114] *JMJP,* July 1, 1963, p. 1.

[115] "Hopei Party and Government Authorities Take Steps to Accelerate Farm Products Purchasing," *TKP,* November 18, 1964, in *JPRS,* No. 28891 (February 25, 1965).

[116] For example, see "Clearing the Work Points and Clearing the Thoughts," *NFJP* editorial, December 26, 1964, in URS, XXXVIII, No. 5 (January 15, 1965), 69.

production of other third-category goods not contracted for by the SMC's. The policy also has the effect of reducing the volume of commodities available for sale to private merchants. Thus, one of its objectives has been to "strengthen the struggle against speculative merchants."[117]

A second technique employed to control the free market, also used increasingly since the beginning of 1963, has been to direct the SMC's to organize and run fairs themselves, and to expand their purchasing staff, often by recruiting former peddlers and merchants.[118] This helps the regime to control the activity of the free market, and in particular to control prices.[119] As I have suggested, the concern with prices of third-category goods seems to derive in part from the fear that they will compete with first- and second-category goods for the attention of teams and their members. Full control of the free market is far from established, but at least until 1966 the trend has been for the regime to promote the increased involvement of its agencies in all aspects of local commerce in an attempt to achieve such control.

THE DISTRIBUTION OF INCOME

There is also some evidence of centralized control in the way teams employ the resources that are left for them after the harvest and procurement process is complete. I indicated above that procurement targets are derived primarily from decisions made above the team level, and the teams normally sign "contracts" for the sale of procurement items. In addition, further demands are often made on them, if they have a bumper year or if the regime decides that some special taxes are necessary. The need to try to overfulfill procurement quotas is frequently discussed in the press, and it is made clear that commune members are expected to conform to the regime's demands, even if they have objections. Commune members often do object, because the prices paid by the state tend to be less than the value of the commodities in question to the members themselves. This is particularly the case with

---

[117] "On the Nature and Effect of the Rural Supply and Sales Cooperatives," *TKP*, October 6, 1961, in *JPRS*, No. 11768 (January 4, 1962).

[118] See Skinner, "Marketing and Social Structure," p. 381, and Pfeffer, "Contracts in China," pp. 119–25.

[119] "The Law of Value and Our Pricing Policy," *Red Flag*, No. 7–8 (April 10, 1963), in *SCMM*, No. 364 (May 13, 1963). This describes general price policy. "How Supply and Marketing Coops Expand Their Business," *JMJP*, December 20, 1962, in *JPRS*, No. 18240 (March 20, 1963). This article reports that in expanding their business the SMC's have as an important task the "suppression of community prices and eliminating speculation and hoarding."

grain, since "overfulfillment" sometimes means that their ration will have to be reduced from the level at which it otherwise could have been set.

Similarly, because of the low returns the members receive from any increments in production, it is not surprising that sometimes they do not want to increase investment in the commune at the expense of immediate consumption needs. Since increases in production often tend to be followed by increases in procurement or local investment, the individual member is not likely to see his short-term interests as being served by investment in the commune. As a result, the regime has often found it necessary to intervene in order to influence the decisions on how the teams will use their funds, especially to insure that there is local financing of projects like hydraulic works and purchases of chemical fertilizer aimed at developing agriculture. Thus, it was discovered in the early 1960's, when the brigades and teams were given some decision-making autonomy in these matters, that teams tended to distribute their income "without regard for appropriate accumulation."[120] Or, as a *People's Daily* reporter discovered after talking to the members of one brigade, "Some of them held that after a year's hard work . . . they should be given more money and that every thing they produced in that year . . . should be distributed."[121] At such times some local cadres apparently tended to interpret the "mass line" as requiring them to respond to members' demands. As one report indignantly notes, some local cadres have bowed to the "members' view of their interests." For example, "Some even held that letting the masses have several lavish dinners was in the interests of the masses themselves and that this could be regarded as a mass viewpoint."[122]

The regime has attempted to handle this widespread problem by instructing the cadres at the *hsien,* commune, and brigade levels to mobilize commune members to support proposals for local investment. This, of course, limits the team's ability to reach independent decisions on such matters. Cadres are also expected to insure that the teams do not use their funds for such purposes as unnecessary building or festive occasions.[123] Other agencies involved in the use of local funds, including the state bank and the SMC's (which may make loans or give advances

[120] "Production Teams That Have Increased Their Output Should Not Distribute and Consume All Their Output," *NFJP,* August 21, 1962, in *SCMP,* No. 2814 (September, 1962).

[121] *JMJP,* February 5, 1963.

[122] "Production Teams."

[123] For example, *JMJP,* June 21, 1964.

on future sales), are expected to see that the teams make appropriate use of these funds. Though it is hard to tell just how thoroughly these agencies are involved in the affairs of the teams, there does seem to be a consistent trend in the direction of more outside control.

Since 1964 a movement has also been initiated to help insure that the teams do not distribute grain "excessively," and this has involved the establishment of centralized grain storage centers to which the teams must send their "surplus" grain.[124] Even though it is unlikely that this movement has yet been implemented throughout the country, one of its aims has been to prevent "excessive amounts of grain being distributed to the commune members,"[125] and it is therefore another example of how the regime has tried to control the activities of the teams.

CONCLUSION

In this discussion I have concentrated primarily on relations between the regime and the teams. However, one could analyze the implications of weaknesses in the remunerative control system established between 1959 and 1962 from the standpoint of relationships between the local cadres and commune members. In order to prevent members from allocating too much of their time and resources to their private plots, or to other private activities, the teams generally establish quotas for the time the members must work on the commune, for the amount of household fertilizer they must contribute to the commune, and so on. I have not dealt with this, or with the question of what kinds of sanctions the cadres apply to the team members when they discover shortcomings or deviant activity.

I have argued earlier that the regime has tried to supplement remunerative sanctions with a blend of normative and coercive sanctions, and that, in practice, these usually turn out to be more coercive than normative.[126] The renumerative control system as established by 1962 has in theory continued to remain in force, but there have been no major reforms since 1962 adequate to deal with the basic problems I identified in the first part of this discussion.

What I hope has been demonstrated here is that there has been an important relationship between control problems and the degree of centralization of the commune administration. The administrative structures and practices which I have described in the second part of

[124] "Set Up Collective Grain Reserves of Production Teams," *TKP* editorial, October 26, 1964, in *SCMP*, No. 3335 (November, 1964).

[125] *Ibid.*, p. 4.

[126] See Birrell, "Structure of the Chinese Collectives," chap. viii.

my analysis are in sharp contrast, in many respects, to the explicit
intentions proclaimed by the regime when it initiated its decentralization reforms between 1959 and 1962, and they have continued to be
inconsistent in important respects with the leadership ideology articulated throughout the 1960's.

I have argued that the major reason for this state of affairs is that
the regime has been unable to attain its production and taxation ends
without resorting to such a system, since the resources allocated to
reward the peasants, and the attendant distribution system, have not
been adequate to achieve all of the regime's goals. This does not mean
that the 1959–62 reforms achieved no favorable results, but it does
mean that they did not achieve results which could satisfy the regime.
It would be wrong to conclude that no decentralization at all was
accomplished by the 1959–62 reforms as compared with the commune
system of 1958–59; in fact, some aspects of the decentralization still
persist. The teams are still free from the relatively unlimited manipulation and mobilization efforts employed by commune level cadres during
the Great Leap Forward. However, I do argue that my analysis of the
relationships between the regime's agents and the teams indicates that
the reduction in the size of the production and accounting unit and
other reforms during the 1959–62 period have not resulted, in practice,
in much decision-making autonomy at the team level, certainly far less
than the ideological pronouncements and original objectives of the
reforms would suggest.

Some might argue that in trying to trace the above relationships and
then to generalize for all of Chinese agriculture, I have focused too
much on what might be called the "hypothetical backward village,"[127]
and thus perhaps have given a misleadingly critical view of the Chinese
communes. Though I believe that the practices and behavior I have
described are representative of communes throughout China, it is true
that of the thousands of reports in the Chinese press on the subject, I
have chosen to emphasize those indicating difficulties with the system,
rather than those which describe it as working to perfection (though
even the latter are frequently presented as ideals rather than as realistic descriptions). However, even if only a minority of the teams in
China manifest behavior of the sort I have described, there are reasons
to believe that the administrative response may be similar to what it
would be if the majority behaved in this way. In deciding on policy at

[127] Comments by James R. Townsend at the Conference on the Microsocietal Study of
the Chinese Political System, August 29-September 1, 1967.

the center, or at levels such as the *hsien,* cadres often tend to adopt generalized news about existing problems and the required responses. This tendency may have several causes: a concern that apparently satisfactory teams may in fact be behaving improperly; or a fear that they will behave improperly in the future if the shortcomings of unsatisfactory teams are not corrected; or the fact that it is difficult to establish special systems of reports, inspections, production planning, and so on only in selected areas where the problems are most evident.

In conclusion I might note that, although my analysis suggests that control problems have been a more important determinant of administrative behavior affecting the communes than ideology, events in China since the start of the Cultural Revolution also suggest that important tensions have been generated within the system as a result of the incongruencies between the prevailing ideology and the reality of commune administration. Mao Tse-tung's criticism of the Party apparatus as it has functioned in relation to the communes has some basis. The proliferation of the essentially bureaucratic control techniques described above has made it difficult for the Party to engage in the kind of decentralized mobilization techniques which Mao has demanded in the name of his "mass line" ideology. Drastic reform of the whole administrative structure in China may indeed be the only way to try to attain Mao's ends, for, as my study has shown, propaganda from the center in itself will not alter the actual style of local leadership exercised in solving control problems in the communes. My analysis would also suggest, however, that unless fundamental changes in the regime's allocation of resources to rural areas are adopted, no amount of administrative reorganization is likely to make possible the kind of mobilization of peasants which Mao has sought to achieve.

PART V

*Policies Toward Youth,
the Bourgeoisie, and the Workers*

JAMES R. TOWNSEND

Revolutionizing Chinese Youth: A Study of Chung-kuo Ch'ing-nien

The Cultural Revolution, which began in late 1965 and was still in progress in the fall of 1967, has dramatized one of the most important problems in Communist China—the socialization of youth into a Communist political culture. Much of the drama lies in a seeming contradiction in the role of youth in this campaign. On the one hand, young people were the most active and fanatical supporters of Mao Tse-tung's attempt to eradicate what he regarded as non-socialist influences in Chinese society. The Red Guards, as these young activists were known, displayed an ideological intensity which suggested that nearly two decades of Chinese Communist Party (CCP) rule had indeed "revolutionized" their generation of Chinese. On the other hand, among the major casualties of the Cultural Revolution were the Communist Youth League (CYL—sometimes known as the Young Communist League) and its leading publications, *Chung-kuo Ch'ing-nien* (Chinese Youth) and *Chung-kuo Ch'ing-nien Pao* (Chinese Youth Journal), as well as much of the formal educational structure. This evidence suggests the contrary conclusion that the youth movement, at least in its organizational aspects, was actually one of the "revisionist" targets of Mao's attack.

While the contradiction suggested above remains obscure in many details, its general development emerges clearly from analysis of the CCP's message to youth over the years between 1949 and 1965. The primary theme of this message was the Party's insistence that youth must "revolutionize" themselves, that each of them must undergo a personal transformation leading toward a permanent inner commit-

447

ment to "revolutionary" goals and behavior. The tension, or contradiction, in the message emerged with a growing realization on the part of the leadership that the desired revolutionary transformation does not follow automatically from the creation of socialist institutions. Hence, the message was intensified after 1956–58, the period in which early Communist optimism about the ease of socialist transformation yielded to a more pessimistic view that special efforts were necessary to "implant the red flag" of socialist thought in the minds of youth. Intensification of the message had its impact, as the Cultural Revolution shows, but equally significant is the other perspective, also illustrated in the recent campaign, which underscores the resistance and shortcomings that made this intensification necessary.

Chung-kuo Ch'ing-nien, the official semimonthly (twenty-four issues per year) magazine of the CYL Central Committee, is a useful source for exploring some of the dimensions of this problem. As an organ of the Party's youth auxiliary, and as one of the most widely circulated periodicals in China, it carried much of the responsibility for the explanation and dissemination of the CCP's message to youth in the period under discussion.[1] The magazine has a long history, tracing its origins back to 1923. After many suspensions and changes of name in the pre-1949 period, it emerged with its contemporary name and form in December, 1948. When the New Democratic Youth League (NDYL —the name of the league until 1957, when it became known as the Communist Youth League) was established by the Party early in 1949, *Chung-kuo Ch'ing-nien* became its official organ. The creation of *Chung-kuo Ch'ing-nien Pao* as the NDYL Central Committee's newspaper in April, 1951, ended the magazine's monopoly of official coverage of league affairs, but it remained one of the more important political publications of mainland China. In addition to "guiding Youth League Work" and "organizing youth for study," *Chung-kuo Ch'ing-nien* held a special responsibility for reaching "youth and youth cadres of a middle cultural level," that is, those young people who had reached at least a middle school level of education and thereby formed part of the intellectual elite of China. In keeping with this relatively well-educated readership, the magazine was also expected to give special emphasis to discussion of theoretical and ideological questions.[2]

---

[1] For a fuller discussion of *Chung-kuo Ch'ing-nien*'s organization and role, see James R. Townsend, *The Revolutionization of Chinese Youth: A Study of Chung-kuo Ch'ing-nien* (Berkeley: Center for Chinese Studies, University of California, China Research Monograph No. 1, 1967), pp. 14–36. The present paper is a revised portion of this monograph.

[2] *Ibid.*, pp. 14–15, 25–29.

Despite its special concern for a more literate audience, *Chung-kuo Ch'ing-nien* remained one of the leading mass media in China until its suspension in August, 1966. That fact does not in any way lessen its subordination to official doctrine and controls from above; the magazine was an arm of the League Central Committee and the Propaganda Department of the CCP, with a primary duty of publishing only those materials which these controlling agencies wished disseminated. As a mass medium, however, its contents were not only open to all who could read but were designed for oral transmission to an even wider audience by literate cadres and activists. Thus, the magazine tried to present in a clear and readable way the information, concerns, and values which the Party wanted young people to receive and absorb. It reflected faithfully the leadership's view of the prevailing political situation among youth, and how and why this situation ought to change.

It would be a mistake to assume that *Chung-kuo Ch'ing-nien's* mission was only political indoctrination in a narrow sense. When the CCP speaks of socialist construction, it has in mind a transformation which affects all aspects of social behavior. Moreover, Chinese youth constitute a vast and diverse segment of Chinese society. In 1965, upwards of 60 per cent of the Chinese population was under twenty-five years of age; and the CYL, nominally an elite group for those in the fifteen to twenty-five age bracket, had around twenty-five million members in the early 1960's. Given the scale of this transformation and audience, the contents of *Chung-kuo Ch'ing-nien* necessarily touch on a great many subjects. The magazine might be studied for what it reveals about a variety of policy issues in China or, even more profitably, for its treatment of general problems of value change in modernizing society. The analysis that follows will note some such points, but space prohibits thorough discussion of them. Our objective is to identify major themes, with particular reference to the development of one of them—the demand that Chinese youth "revolutionize" themselves.

The contents of five different periods in *Chung-kuo Ch'ing-nien's* post-1949 history serve as the principal basis for this study. These periods are the first six months (January through June—twelve issues) of 1951, 1956, 1959, 1962, and 1965. The choice of dates is arbitrary, the main purpose being to select periods which represent different moods in Chinese politics without being totally dominated by one particular campaign. The content analysis employed is qualitative rather than quantitative. Articles have been classified and counted in some cases, but the classification is generally too imprecise to justify presentation of results in numerical form. Therefore, the analysis relies mainly on important articles, editorials, and debates over letters from readers to support conclusions about the general weighting of contents in different periods. Following a review of each of the periods studied, we shall examine general trends and variations down to 1965, and try to assess their relevance to the Cultural Revolution.

1951

In the first six months of 1951, as in every other period studied, most of the contents of *Chung-kuo Ch'ing-nien* consisted of articles dealing explicitly with current youth work. Such articles fall into three general types: current policy—description of current policy and discussions of how and why to implement it; organizational—discussion of organizational and administrative problems in youth work; and ideological—discussion of both abstract theory and the proper approach to "study" and "work style." In 1951 there were several articles of each type in every issue, with the organizational and ideological types being most numerous. Long articles and editorials were relatively scarce, the preferred format being a short article of one or two pages or a brief comment or vignette less than a page in length. Most materials on current youth work were simple, serious, and humorless; they made their point in an obvious way, with a great deal of repetition in both style and substance. All of these traits are generally characteristic of *Chung-kuo Ch'ing-nien* and need not be noted again.

The most striking feature of the 1951 period was the dominance of a single central theme: the integration of Chinese nationalism and commitment to socialism. This theme was developed most fully through propaganda on the "resist America and aid Korea" campaign, which the magazine emphasized more than any other current movement, and a number of articles discussing patriotism and patriotic education; materials on Chinese history, anti-American and anti-imperialist propaganda, and articles dealing with the international "peace" movement also contributed to the discussion. Five of the twelve issues focused on topics related to this theme, and its presence was evident in every issue. It is not surprising that the Korean War should produce appeals to patriotism and ample material for propagandizing the spirit of collective sacrifice. What is significant in this message is the insistence that patriotism as such—love for one's country and willingness to sacrifice for it—can be, and must be, combined with support for the socialist (that is, Communist) system.[3] Respect for China and the glory of its past is good; it is in fact insufficiently developed due to "imperialist suppression," and must be deliberately encouraged. At the same time, it must be raised to a new level by the addition of commitment to the socialist future in both the national and international realms.

The other major movements in progress in 1951—the campaign to suppress counterrevolutionaries, and land reform—received much less attention in the youth magazine. Articles on land reform were, for the most part, routinely descriptive, perhaps indicating a realistic awareness that most readers were not deeply involved in that campaign. Suppression of counterrevolutionaries was a more prominent subject, but the emphasis was mainly on encouraging a resolute rejection of one's friends and relatives who were so classified. The fact that the "new patriotism" issue was elevated above these two campaigns suggests that the leadership was not particularly worried about youth support for its basic policies. What it was concerned about was whether this support came solely from the proven appeal of nationalism—a willingness on the part of youth to support any progressive government actively committed to national regeneration—or whether it was also to come from a real acceptance of the socialist future. The assertion that it must come from both was the primary message of the period.

Chung-kuo Ch'ing-nien's handling of youth problems in 1951 leaves a mixed impression. On the one hand, the magazine responded forthrightly to a number of rather technical organizational problems. Questions relating to league admissions, transfer of membership from one branch to another, when to invoke league punishment against members and how severe it should be, and how to handle Party members within the league who were not performing their duties—to cite a few examples—were published and answered in a concrete and reasonable way. These were no doubt very real problems to local league cadres, and the magazine performed a useful service in responding to them. On the other hand, *Chung-kuo Ch'ing-nien*'s treatment of more abstract and personal questions was not very illuminating. The best example was a series of letters on the subject of how a league member could maintain contact with the masses. The exchange began with a letter (No. 56 [January 13], p. 46) to this effect and an editorial comment that the issue was important and should be discussed. The debate dragged on,

[3] For important examples of this theme, see No. 56 (January 13, 1951), pp. 10–16; No. 58 (February 15, 1951), pp. 15–19; No. 65 (May 19, 1951), pp. 4–5, 14.

some readers saying that they found it difficult to keep in touch with the masses, others saying that a league member must do so because the masses are the "movers of history." When the topic was concluded with an article on June 2 (No. 66, pp. 8–10), the genuineness of the problem and the doctrinal reasons for overcoming it were clear, yet little had been said about concrete personal motives and responses. The implication was that the principle was the important thing; once it was truly accepted, correct action would follow automatically.

A similar conception apparently affected the choice of "models and heroes" in this period. There was no shortage of biographical materials, but they had little direct relevance to the life situation of most Chinese youth. Articles on the past activities of Jen Pi-shih, a long-time leader of the league who had died in October, 1950, and Mao Tse-tung appeared at the rate of about one per issue, and there was a five-part series on the life of Friedrich Engels. Lesser figures selected for emulation and honor were mostly "martyrs" who had sacrificed their lives in the Korean War, the war against Japan, or earlier revolutionary action. The choice of such illustrious and heroic models is understandable, and may well have had some effect in establishing the ideal of revolutionary accomplishment and sacrifice. It was nonetheless a romantic choice which provided little practical guidance for most of the magazine's readers.

The general tone of *Chung-kuo Ch'ing-nien* in 1951 was, therefore, one of national mobilization and sacrifice, approached with an optimistic and romantic spirit. There was great hostility toward China's domestic and foreign enemies and little room for individual expression of criticism. In fact, there was virtually no significant criticism in 1951, except for occasional attacks on individual cadres who had abused their authority (particularly with reference to the marriage law); the only statements about individualism were reminders that collective interests must take precedence. Nonetheless, the magazine's approach to these issues was not at all repressive. The basic assumption was the optimistic one that China's real enemies were few and that the need for their defeat would be obvious to all patriotic Chinese; almost everyone, including those who came from a reactionary class origin, would join in the national effort and would eventually accept the socialist system. Statements about admission to the league and the conduct of patriotic education made it clear that a youth who came from a reactionary class, or was not yet fully committed to socialism, was not to be treated as an enemy. So long as he separated himself sharply from the real enemies, he was to be tolerated and encouraged; he was one of the "people" and would respond to education. There was little recognition of the possibility that "education" might not overcome all personal conflicts with the political system. The problem as perceived in 1951 was that many youth wanted to work for socialist construction but did not yet understand fully what was required of them. Once they grasped the principles and consciously accepted them—and the Party was confident that they would do so—they would fulfill their revolutionary potential.

1956

The 1956 contents of *Chung-kuo Ch'ing-nien* are more interesting and provocative than those of any other period studied. They are also the most diffuse and difficult to summarize. One could say that 1956 was a period of "liberalization," but that sheds little light on the substance of the issues that appeared in the magazine at this time. We shall discuss here five points which, taken as a whole, give a general image of the period, even though none of them actually dominated it.

First, in 1956 the magazine reduced its preoccupation with current youth work and tasks. This general category necessarily remained large, but there were fewer articles dealing with current policy and organizational problems, while those dealing with ideological problems were less abstract. The trend was toward a more realistic recognition of and confrontation with the everyday problems of youth. One sign of this was a change in the treatment of models. There were no biographical series on leading Chinese Communists and no real efforts to publicize heroic or romantic martyrs. Models presented were, for the most part, ordinary people or cadres engaged in ordinary tasks. Another sign of the shift was an increase in the space devoted to readers' letters and discussions of them. In fact, debates centered on letters became the magazine's most prominent method for trying to come to grips with some of the real conflicts that Chinese youth were facing.

A discussion of whether youth could be excused for being discontented with rural work is an excellent example, partly because it was the main such exchange in 1956 and partly because it contrasts with the 1951 debate (discussed above) on a related issue. The debate began with a letter from one Li Nan-feng and an editorial appeal for reader response (No. 1 [January 1], pp. 16–18). Li stated that many youth were dissatisfied with work in rural towns and villages; more provocatively, he added that this was not a problem of "standpoint" or "philosophy of life" (the standard doctrinal answer to such complaints), but simply an "objective" evaluation of their circumstances. He then cited a number of reasons for what he obviously regarded as justifiable discontent, among them the following: youth coming from cities, where the standard of living is improving rapidly, have a right to expect improvements in village life as well, since the aim of communism is a better life for all; many youth in the countryside are living away from their homes and customary conditions, which most rural cadres are not, and so must be excused for homesickness; village life is in fact unhygienic and urban youth are right in calling attention to it and demanding rapid change; rural cadres are frequently not sufficiently advanced and do not provide good education for those beneath them, hence, it is difficult for youth to improve themselves in rural work; the government has not done enough for the villages in providing improvements in transportation and communications, but rather seems to have devoted most of its attention to improvements in the cities; most youth going to the countryside are males and cannot find wives there.

Publication of reader response began two issues later. The editors stated that they were receiving over two hundred letters a day on the subject, the "great majority" disagreeing with Li; they announced that they would print only letters of disagreement, since Li's point of view had already been expressed. The letters published, although critical of Li's conclusions, did not deny that many of the conditions he described existed. Generally, they emphasized the necessity for some personal sacrifice, and argued that improvements in rural life would result from urban youth's work in the countryside but could not realistically be a precondition for it. The debate concluded, after a reported eight thousand letters had been received, with an article of April 16 (No. 8, pp. 2–7). The article was predictably an uncompromising refutation of Li's argument, stressing the need for struggling against obstacles and having faith in the revolutionary future. Still, it maintained the realistic tone of the exchange by observing that the villages were indeed backward and would remain so until the growth of industry and culture in the cities laid the foundation for their modernization. Chinese cities are backward, too, said the author, and they must retain priority in development for some time to come; to talk of urban-rural equality now is foolish. While this conclusion may not have persuaded Li Nan-feng and his supporters (and we must remember that he did receive support, though it was not published), he had obviously touched off a serious public discussion, and received a serious answer, on a question of immediate importance to Chinese youth. There were many other discussions, such as whether one ought to follow a cadre's order when convinced it was unsound (conclusion: obey the order but petition for reconsideration), and how children of bourgeois families would be affected by socialist reform (conclusion: their standard of living will be lowered but their political status will be improved by removal of the class stigma), which reflected an equally deliberate appraisal of genuine conflicts arising in Chinese society.

Second, the 1956 period included a large number of articles on the question of individualism and individual interests. As the Li Nan-feng debate demonstrated, the supremacy of collective interests remained official doctrine. Other articles made the same point, notably one on the new selective military service system (No. 1 [January 1], pp. 12–13, 31), which criticized those youth who were not eager to serve or who liked service for "selfish" reasons, such as a desire for a good life or personal honor. However, while *Chung-kuo Ch'ing-nien* continued to stress the principle of personal sacrifice for the national cause, it also tacitly recognized (as indeed the article on military service had) the existence of substantial misgivings about or violation of this principle. The majority of articles on this subject clustered around the question of whether it was a sign of "individualism" or "individual heroism"— pejorative terms which had been freely applied—for one to pursue private hobbies and interests in his spare time, to devote himself to study in an effort to advance his position, or to express his own views in study and discussion. These questions were usually raised by readers who had been criticized for their extracurricular activities and who felt that cadres were discouraging their hopes for further study and advancement. It is significant that these readers defended themselves publicly and even more significant that the magazine was cautiously receptive to their complaints. The editors' response was that one should never strive for advancement purely for personal reasons and that, from a realistic point of view, one ought not to undertake too many activities or set his sights too high. At the same time, they agreed that cadres should not discourage private interests or hopes for advancement by applying the "individualist" label; they pointed out that personal advancement was actually consistent with collective interests in view of current national needs.

Third, there was a marked increase in receptiveness to individual expression. The obstacles to courtship and marriage created by overzealous cadres and rural assignments were considered openly and at times sympathetically. Letters about personal dress established the rule that thrift was a virtue but that individual choice should prevail; colorful dress was not in itself a symbol of "bourgeois" life. The volume of short stories, songs, and poems published in the magazine increased significantly. While emphasizing that art and literature should serve socialism, articles encouraged youth to become artists and writers and to improve their technical skills in these fields.

Fourth, 1956 brought a "march to science" campaign which had a major impact on the contents of *Chung-kuo Ch'ing-nien*. Articles praising science and the pursuit of knowledge appeared in almost every issue. Much of the material devoted to "study," which in other periods normally meant political study and self-cultivation, took on more academic overtones. The value of learning from "old professors" (that is, bourgeois intellectuals) was recognized. An editorial on May 1 (No. 9, pp. 4–5) put weight behind the campaign by observing that students had a "burden of excessive social work" which was hindering their studies and the march to science. Schools are a place for developing cadres, science, and culture, said the editors; "free" the students and let them study.

Even more striking was an article by Hsiao Wen-hui (No. 5 [March 1], pp. 24–25), which put the matter squarely on the line. First, Hsiao said that some believe that those who attend meetings and speak regularly in political discussion are participating in politics, while those who do not are "escaping politics." He stated flatly that this is not true, because those who concentrate on their own work are, by marching to science, fulfilling a primary requirement of socialist construction. Next, he observed that many cadres believe it is permissible for nonactivists to concentrate on academic work but that Party and league members must attend to political work. This is not true either, he said, since Party and league members are the cream of Chinese youth and must contribute their best; if they have a "non-political profession," then they should give it primary attention and reduce their political work. In reality, said Hsiao, it is those who deny these facts who are "escaping politics"; they are old cadres, educated before liberation and recruited during the early campaigns, who do not understand that the political situation has changed and, with it, the primary tasks of youth. In the future, some will still specialize in political work because it is a job that has to be done. Others will do some political work in their spare time. But concentrating on study and the development of science is also a primary demand of the present political situation. Hsiao's views did not represent official policy, of course, but they were not refuted, and they were repeated, in less forthright terms, in other articles and letters.

Finally, as the preceding discussion suggests, *Chung-kuo Ch'ing-nien* carried in 1956 a substantial volume of significant criticism. This criticism was not as sweeping as that which emerged in the Hundred Flowers campaign a year later; that is, it did not attack the existing system as such, either as inherently unsatisfactory or as a perversion of a "true" socialist system. It did, however, go considerably beyond *pro forma* comments that things have been well done but can still be improved or attacks on individual cadres who had, in presumably exceptional cases, committed errors. Cadres were the main objects of criticism in 1956, but the criticism was frequently cast in general terms suggesting that the error was due to a flaw in the system rather than individual deviation. In addition to charges of suppression of individual initiative, referred to above, there were complaints about bureaucratic behavior, about the use of cadre status for personal gain and advantage, about excessive cadre demands for criticism of oneself or one's colleagues which simply led to fabrications and personal conflicts, and about cadres' lack of interest in youth problems and suggestions. The magazine treated these complaints sympathetically and at times carried cartoons lampooning the behavior in question.

There is no reason to believe that *Chung-kuo Ch'ing-nien*'s 1956 editorial policy was out of step with official policy. The magazine continued to give full support and coverage to the major policies of the period, such as the collectivization of agriculture. When necessary, as in the Li Nan-feng debate, it tried to refute views which were seen as seriously opposed to orthodox policy or values. The new tone of *Chung-kuo Ch'ing-nien* was, therefore, a reflection of a shift in mood at higher levels, a shift which permitted the mass media to become, temporarily, much more responsive to the needs and questions of readers. This mood was still optimistic about the basic revolutionary tendency of youth; otherwise it could not have tolerated such open discussion of dissatisfaction. However, its main feature was a realistic understanding that youth were not to be revolutionized by a romantic gloss which ignored or painted over their misgivings. The mood of 1956 ended a year later when expression of discontent surpassed what the

Party regarded as tolerable limits. But this brief period of more open political communication had shown that the socialization of youth into a revolutionary political culture was far from complete.

1959

The most prominent feature of the 1959 period was a revival of emphasis on current youth work and tasks. However, in contrast to 1951 and 1956, the organizational type of article received very little attention. In place of discussion of league organizational and administrative problems was an overwhelming volume of material on current policies and abstract ideology. Articles on the people's communes and the Great Leap Forward were published in every issue, and these policies were actually the subject of many more general discussions of youth work. The ideological emphasis appeared most strikingly in a fourteen-part series of "Lectures on Socialism and Communism," prepared by the CYL Propaganda Department, which occupied a total of thirty-four pages—roughly the equivalent of one complete issue of the magazine. This lecture series was distinct from another large group of articles on formal Communist theory.

The relative decline of the league organizational focus did not signify less guidance from authoritative sources. On the contrary, the weight of higher authority was very evident in *Chung-kuo Ch'ing-nien* in 1959. The CYL Propaganda Department contributed several articles in addition to its lecture series. Prominent national figures, such as Ch'en Yi, T'ao Chu, Hu K'o-shih, Teng Tzu-hui, Hsü T'e-li, and Li Ta, wrote pieces for the magazine. Moreover, there were again, as in 1951, a number of articles about Party leaders, including six on Mao, four on Liu Shao-ch'i, and three on Chou En-lai.

The expression of dissatisfaction that had flourished in 1956 predictably disappeared, to be succeeded by a euphoric affirmation of China's progress in socialist construction. The only criticism that appeared was a general chiding of those who were not "leaping forward" fast enough or who expressed "conservative" doubts about China's ability to overcome all obstacles by human effort. The latter issue furnished the substance of the major letter exchanges of the period. Readers who confessed to discouragement about their positions or abilities, or who raised questions about the value of heroic sacrifice, were deluged with exhortations to continue their struggle, have faith in the future, and forget their personal ambitions and interests. Actually, these debates were not entirely one-sided, for the editors did give some space to counterarguments. Although the official response was evident from the first, it is significant that an attempt was made to maintain some lines of communication. *Chung-kuo Ch'ing-nien* was not open in 1959 to criticism of Party policies, but it was interested in discussing some of the personal problems that these policies created.

The blatant romanticism and optimism of 1959 is on the surface reminiscent of 1951, but the similarity is misleading. In retrospect, it is clear that much of the exuberance of 1959 was not only false confidence, but even falsified confidence. Even without retrospect, one can see crucial differences in the tone of the 1959 and 1951 contents of the magazine. One of these is the overpowering presence and dominance of the Party in the later period. In 1951, there was some sense of distinction and even autonomy about the youth movement. The league was, to be sure, a CCP auxiliary, obligated to assist the Party in its work, but at the same time it had an organizational life of its own which reflected the distinctive problems of young people who were not yet assuming full adult roles in society; with this distinction went a greater tolerance for the gradual development of socialist consciousness among youth. By 1959, however, the Party had increased greatly its leadership over the youth movement in an effort to bring youth directly and totally into the struggle for socialist construction. The Party's tasks were far too urgent to permit youth to stand aside; they were to take part in productive labor and the war against nature, reform their thoughts immediately, and take the lead in nationwide socialist education.

Another significant difference of 1959 was the appearance of signs of uneasiness about the revolutionary qualities of Chinese youth, although the general theme of reliance on their basic progressiveness remained. A long summary of Mao's ideas on this subject, prepared by the editors of *Chung-kuo Ch'ing-nien* and published on May 1 (No. 9, pp. 2–9), demonstrated the new tone. In statements made during 1957, Mao made reference to three points which foreshadowed the Party's increasing anxiety about the revolutionization of youth. First, he stated that the real socialist revolution was not simply change in the system of ownership of means of production, which had already taken place, but political and ideological change in man; this implied that the most difficult tasks of the revolutionary period still lay ahead. Second, Mao observed that political and ideological work among youth was in some cases weak; it must be improved so that all youth would attain a correct political standpoint. Finally, he pointed out that some youth lacked social experience and held illusions about an easy life under socialism in which there would be no further need for struggle. These ideas, which may not have received much attention when first expressed, were selected by the editors in 1959 for inclusion among Mao's most important statements about Chinese youth. Moreover, they appeared over and over again in those articles which discussed current ideological work among youth. The romanticism of 1959 tended to obscure the long-range implications of this new attitude toward youth. In fact, the CCP had already ceased to take for granted the revolutionary qualities of youth and had begun a deliberate effort to revolutionize them by a combination of ideological indoctrination and immersion in "revolutionary" struggle.

1962

For *Chung-kuo Ch'ing-nien,* as for China generally, 1962 was a period of difficulty and uncertainty. Both the economic strain and the crisis of confidence which accompanied it were evident in the magazine. The economic setback that followed the Great Leap Forward was probably responsible for a sharp reduction in the size of the magazine. From an average size of about forty pages per issue in earlier periods, it was cut to about twenty-five pages per issue; moreover, there were only ten issues in the first six months of 1962, as numbers were combined on two occasions. A total absence of editorials or reproduction of higher directives presumably reflected uncertainty at higher levels. There was also a noticeable decline in the quality of the section of letters from readers; the period failed to produce a single sustained readers' debate, and many potentially fruitful questions raised in letters were left dangling without much response.

Despite evidence of political and economic restraints on its contents, *Chung-kuo Ch'ing-nien* continued to transmit the Party's current concerns about the youth movement. Although authoritative clues from editorials and centrally directed campaigns were absent, the weighting of contents outlined three major themes. One of these was a drive to educate youth in "lofty Communist morality." There was nothing novel about the virtues that this drive extolled. Diligence, thrift, social discipline, and dedicated service to society were the main ingredients —all by this time familiar appeals to Chinese youth. However, in the past the CCP had not stressed so explicitly the moral basis of these virtues, but had emphasized their instrumental value. For example, thrift was a virtue in the Korean War to save money for the war effort, serving the collective interests was in the long run the rational way to advance individual interests, hard work for a few years in the Great Leap would produce a beautiful society in the future, and so forth. These instrumentalist arguments were still used in 1962, and it is obvious that hard times and a threatened breakdown of public order gave the virtues mentioned a very practical justification. Nevertheless, the Party chose in 1962 to define these virtues in moral terms, thereby giving them a universal and permanent value that transcended the current situation. Puritanical and selfless struggle was to be part of every youth's basic character, now and in the future, not just a way out of the "three bad years."

A closely related theme was "cultivation of revolutionary successors." Although that specific slogan was not widely used in 1962 (it was to be most prominent in 1964), the arguments and concerns connected with it were very much in evidence, particularly in discussions of Communist morality.[4] Simply put, the argument stated: first, no one develops Communist morality or revolutionary spirit naturally, not even those who are raised in socialist society or are children of cadres and other "revolutionary" class families; second, the creation of a Communist society will take several generations and will, therefore, fail unless deliberate efforts are made to pass on the revolutionary spirit to each succeeding generation. The reasoning behind these assertions need not concern us here. Developments from 1957 through 1961 certainly offered empirical evidence for both of them; doctrinal explanations cited the influence of bourgeois family backgrounds and "thousands of years of feudalism," plus a dangerous tendency for some cadres and their families to succumb to "bureaucratism," desire for special privilege, and so forth. Whatever the explanation, by 1962 there had been a significant intensification of the CCP's message that youth must revolutionize themselves. In 1959, the uneasiness about this question had appeared mainly in discussions on the theoretical plane. Three years later, it had become a demand for Communist education in the family, in the school, and in society at large; youth must be trained to think and live according to Communist morality and a revolutionary spirit.

The third theme which received considerable attention in 1962 was that cadres must renew their efforts to get close to the masses, the specific reference naturally being to league cadres and others with close

[4] The most authoritative treatment of this subject was an article by Hu K'o-shih in No. 6 (March 16, 1962), pp. 2–5. Other good examples are found in Nos. 3–4 (February 5, 1962), pp. 24–26, and Nos. 9–10 (May 7, 1962), pp. 13–15, 22.

youth contacts. This was not an extension of the 1959 "mass line" euphoria, which had extolled the limitless power and creativity of mass action. It was instead a reassertion of the more sober aspect of the "mass line," which holds that the people must always be consulted to develop popular support by persuasion and to check against bureaucratic errors. Thus, the "mass line" literature of 1962 had a basically critical attitude toward cadres in the youth movement. The point raised most frequently was that cadres must not regard themselves as "something special," must not avoid contact with the masses outside their official routine; rather they must extend themselves to make friends with noncadres in order to understand popular problems and needs. Another common point was that cadres must listen to all opinions, however diverse and from whatever source. Though it would be a slow and possibly painful method for cadres, they must stick to it with confidence that it is the best way to resolve problems and educate all concerned.

An interesting feature of these three themes is that each had both an idealistic and realistic side. That is, although each set a high ideal standard—for Communist morality, perpetuation of the revolutionary spirit, or cadre-mass relations—each also expressed a very somber awareness of the current gap between ideal and reality. The ideal suggested a world of revolutionary struggle and sharp class consciousness, whereas the real world of early 1962, as presented in *Chung-kuo Ch'ing-nien,* was relatively free of either revolution or class struggle. To be sure, doctrinal statements attributed the deficiencies of 1962 to bourgeois, feudal, and revisionist influences, but doctrine was silent on precisely where these influences were to be found in China and how they were to be struggled against. By explicit admission, class origin and family background were no guarantee of immunity to reactionary influences. The suspect groups of 1959 (intellectuals, specialists, and children of bourgeois families) not only escaped consistent criticism in 1962 but were accorded a certain amount of recognition for their useful services.

In short, Chinese youth were given a clear message to revolutionize themselves through study, struggle, and self-cultivation. They received, too, a list of the virtues they were to develop and the evils they were to oppose. But the revolutionary struggles in which they were to steel themselves were nonexistent, and the evils were pervasive phenomena scattered throughout society without connection to specific classes or social strata. During the Great Leap, revolutionary spirit could be cultivated and used in a struggle against nature and all manifestations of conservative thought. By 1962, however, nature had proved unconquerable, and some of the "conservative" notions of 1959 had acquired official sanction. Beneath the propaganda appeals of 1962 lay the contradiction of how youth were to revolutionize themselves in a nonrevolutionary situation.

1965

Chung-kuo Ch'ing-nien's most obvious characteristic in 1965 was the revival of its role as a vigorous propaganda organ. It returned to publication of twelve separate issues for the six-month period and increased its size to about thirty to thirty-five pages per issue, still less than in the 1950's but substantially more than in 1962. More significantly, the editorial department of the magazine came out into the open again. Thirteen full-length (two to three pages) editorials, one short editorial, and two long articles by the editorial department were published in the period. Finally, the magazine restored its coverage of league organizational problems to a level roughly comparable to 1951 and 1956. It not only printed a large volume of material dealing explicitly with league work, but drew heavily on middle-ranking league officials (provincial and municipal league committees and committee members) for reports and articles.

The clarity and focus of propaganda campaigns that had been absent in 1962 were also restored. The Tenth Plenum of the CCP Central Committee in September, 1962, had promised renewed efforts to promote class struggle and socialist education, and by 1965 these efforts had materialized in three main themes which dominated the pages of *Chung-kuo Ch'ing-nien*. One of these was glorification of the thought of Mao Tse-tung, stressing its usefulness in solving problems of any nature and its importance as the guide for all revolutionary action. Another was "serving the poor and lower-middle peasants," a theme which extolled the revolutionary class character of these groups and the ideological value of maintaining close contact with them. For intellectual youth, "serving the peasants" meant respecting them as people, demonstrating personal concern for their problems, and assisting them in education and the acquisition of modern knowledge. The third theme was glorification of physical labor in rural and mountain areas, and its slogan was, "One must revolutionize through labor" (*ko-ming-hua chiu tei lao-tung-hua*). Hard labor in the mountains and villages was not only an essential task of economic construction, but was also, for intellectual youth, the only way to acquire the "redness" of proletarian experience to go with their "expertness."

Chung-kuo Ch'ing-nien handled these themes seriously. It gave them heavier editorial emphasis than it had given to the major issues of any other period studied. It provided model reports on how they were implemented at the local level and published large numbers of letters bearing individual testimony and experience. It acknowledged no exceptions to or compromise with the general principles of accepting Mao's thought, serving the peasants, and universal participation in physical labor. It wove them together into a model image of a militant, active, class-conscious youth who was trained simultaneously in modern knowledge and physical labor, who despised all forms of privilege, personal ambition, and soft living, and who was prepared to study and follow without question the teachings of Mao Tse-tung. This militant message was amplified by other materials, such as a continuation of the "learn from Lei Feng" campaign, a great deal of "support Vietnam–oppose American imperialism" propaganda, and much discussion about strengthening the militia and its military training. Thus, the specification of where and how to struggle, which had been missing in 1962, was now supplied, at least at the propaganda level. Whether there were real social conditions for a renewal of class conflict and revolutionary struggle in China is, of course, a different question.

The militancy of *Chung-kuo Ch'ing-nien* in 1965 is particularly significant in light of the magazine's suspension in August, 1966. If it was actually following the Maoist line so faithfully, why should it have been a casualty of the Cultural Revolution? Was there any evidence in 1965 of tendencies which would have proved politically embarrassing a year later? A search for these tendencies does not lead to conclusive answers to the questions, but a few points deserve mention.

First, *Chung-kuo Ch'ing-nien*'s position on the development of revolutionary spirit within the educational system, a question in which it naturally had a deep interest, was "correct" but nonetheless cautious. It supported fully the proposition that all students and intellectuals should be both red and expert, that all those primarily engaged in intellectual work should also engage in physical labor and political activities. It supported, too, the imposition of political qualifications in admission to higher schools and the absolute priority of state needs in deciding postgraduation assignments. Significantly, however, it gave no indication of a desire for major changes in the existing system, a demand which was to become one of the key issues in the Cultural

Revolution. The magazine's position, despite the revolutionary phrase-ology, was essentially support for the *status quo*—an educational system which provided institutionalized channels for political activity and periodic physical labor, but which did not allow these activities to disrupt the academic process. This position was quite evident in an editorial of April 16 (No. 8, pp. 12–13) which praised the revolution-ary campaigns but then added that schools were, after all, a place for study. Students should not neglect their studies, take examinations lightly, or disparage the idea of academic training, said the editors, noting that the emphasis on physical labor and rural service sometimes had this effect; nor should political activities ever become so frequent or demanding that they interfered with study time, rest periods, or the normal operation of the schools. The editors obviously could not have approved the storms that erupted in the schools in June, 1966, and brought formal education in China to a complete halt.

Second, the magazine's policy on league admissions was contrary to the spirit of the Cultural Revolution and the Red Guards on one important point—the attitude toward children from bourgeois, land-lord, and rich peasant families. *Chung-kuo Ch'ing-nien* gave full support to the CYL Central Committee in its insistence that such youth should be admitted, irrespective of their family history and even of their own previous mistakes, if they gave assurance that they were now committed to socialism. The magazine published many letters on this question throughout the first six months of 1965, always stating the policy clearly. There is no doubt that the league's position here could have been interpreted later as "soft" on class struggle.

Finally, the magazine published one article (No. 4 [February 16], pp. 5–7) by the Construction Department of the Peking Municipal Committee of the CYL. As we shall note later, this committee was the most prominent league organization to be denounced and purged dur-ing the Cultural Revolution. Among the sins ascribed to it was praising "model" branches which did not give sufficient weight to the thought of Mao Tse-tung. The *Chung-kuo Ch'ing-nien* article is a case in point, although it was not the incident held up for criticism later. The main virtue of the league branch praised in this article was that it had overcome existing hostility toward young workers from reactionary families; little emphasis was given to Mao's thought in the article, although there were a few unimportant citations. The magazine also published articles on model branches which did indeed emphasize Mao's thought and were to receive the stamp of approval in the

Cultural Revolution. However, it is possible that even a single error, such as publishing a tainted article from the Peking CYL Committee, could have hurt the magazine.

There were, then, a few important points on which *Chung-kuo Ch'ing-nien* deviated from its Maoist militancy in the first six months of 1965. In none of these cases, however, is there strong evidence to show that the magazine was engaged in deliberate opposition to established practice of that period; it was simply taking its cue from the CYL Central Committee and the mainstream of official propaganda on certain problems of particular concern to youth. Its deviations from Maoism were not, in 1965, deviations from the policies of its guiding organizations. They were, rather, signs of a significant but subdued contradiction that had developed in the Party's message to youth. The essence of this contradiction lay in the simultaneous attempt to propagate the revolutionary Maoist vision and yet somehow restrain the most disruptive consequences of a literal implementation of it.

The Revolutionary Message

The primary function of the mass media in China is the broadly educational one of communicating officially approved messages and material to develop among the people the values and behavior desired by the regime. The mass media also transmit "objective" information and encourage the growth of two-way communications between officials and the public, but their performance of these functions is always subordinate to, and heavily penetrated by, the educational one. Our survey of the contents of *Chung-kuo Ch'ing-nien* in selected periods has illustrated this point. The magazine has grappled sporadically with problems as perceived by youth themselves and has carried a certain amount of basic news and information of interest to its readership. It has tried most consistently and thoroughly, however, to define and structure the role which the CCP wishes youth to assume in Chinese society.

For *Chung-kuo Ch'ing-nien,* the central issue over the years between 1951 and 1965 was how long the "revolutionary" period was to endure and what demands it was to make on Chinese youth. A basic shift in elite expectations on this issue occurred, in approximate terms, in 1956–58. The "approximate" qualification is necessary since the data analyzed here do not permit precise dating of policy changes or any conclusions about the development of new attitudes among specific groupings within the Chinese leadership. The shift probably took place over a long period of time and had quite different degrees and timing of acceptance among different sections of the leadership. However, the main components of the shift can be described.

Before 1956–58, the CCP anticipated a relatively short and sharp conflict with its class enemies, to be followed by socialist construction perceived largely in institutional terms. The Party demanded ideological reform among the people but assumed it would develop in a relatively harmonious way, through peaceful persuasion and education, in step with institutional changes. Revolution and class struggle were very real, but their targets were mainly clear-cut enemies who were opposed to socialism or could, by class analysis, be presumed to be opposed; the main exception was a small group of Western-trained intellectuals who were counted among the "people" because of their support for the Party but who also faced intensive ideological remolding because of their heavy exposure to bourgeois influences. The Party appeared confident that socialist construction would take place in a context of basic national unity once the obvious enemies were destroyed.

Chung-kuo Ch'ing-nien's effort in 1951 to make an explicit connection between patriotism and socialism, suggesting that the former was an appropriate point of departure for the creation of socialist consciousness, illustrated these early hopes for broad national unity in the march toward socialism. Significantly, this theme was not continued; there was not a single discussion of the ideological implications of nationalism in any of the later periods studied. Although the CCP continued to capitalize on patriotic feelings, particularly in times of crisis, it did so without suggesting that nationalistic unity was the foundation of the Chinese state. The growing belief among the leadership that revolutionary action and class struggle must continue meant that conflict rather than unity, and class rather than nation, were the defining characteristics of Communist China for some time to come.[5]

The shift to which we are referring was, therefore, in simplest terms, a new expectation that the revolutionary period would last indefinitely, with all the struggle, conflict, and sacrifice that revolution demands. It included at least two steps, both very evident in *Chung-kuo Ch'ing-nien*. The first was a realization that the Chinese "people" would not develop socialist consciousness quickly or easily, even when the institutional establishment of socialism was complete. On the assumption that

---

[5] See the discussion in Franz Schurmann, *Ideology and Organization in Communist China* (Berkeley and Los Angeles: University of California Press, 1966), pp. 115–18.

the revolutionary period was ending and that the universal growth of socialist consciousness had begun, the CCP began in 1956 to relax its controls over communications, to permit a fuller expression of opinions, problems, and criticisms. This trend was not simply an imitation of Khrushchev's de-Stalinization in the Soviet Union nor a product of the Hundred Flowers slogans, for it antedated both. The relaxation reached its peak in the spring of 1957, but it had then been in progress for over a year. The point is that the "liberalization" of 1956–57 was the beginning of a long-term trend which was consistent with the Party's early optimism about the rapid conclusion of the revolutionary period. The trend was reversed, of course, in June, 1957, but it was reversed only with what must have been a profound sense of disillusionment with the meager results of the Party's efforts in the ideological field.

The first step, then, was an insistence that the real revolutionary task was the ideological struggle to create socialist man, a struggle which institutional reform had manifestly not resolved. Briefly, in the early part of the Great Leap Forward, the leadership still seemed to believe that this task, difficult as it was, could nonetheless be accomplished in one generation by prodigious efforts to indoctrinate and mobilize the population. The second step, which completed the shift, was the realization that several generations of struggle would be necessary to carry out the revolution. Some signs of this belief were evident in *Chung-kuo Ch'ing-nien* in 1959; by 1962, after the failure of the Great Leap and the emergence of Soviet "revisionism," it was a dominant theme.

The change in Party expectations about the revolution had a profound impact on the Chinese youth movement. Up through 1956, the political role of Chinese youth was not a salient national issue. The regime was preoccupied with the destruction of the old system and a series of campaigns against what it regarded as its primary enemies. It largely took for granted youth support in these struggles, provided only that youth study and organize under proper leadership. As a result, the youth movement had a certain degree of autonomy. Although it was exposed to, and expected to respond to, national issues in a prescribed way, the league and its publications were also free to devote a good deal of attention to problems of concern to youth and the league but not directly relevant to national politics. By 1959, the combination of anxiety about youth shortcomings and hope that they would nonetheless lead the revolutionary effort had made the youth movement as such a macropolitical issue. Literally everything that transpired within it was either a response to initiative from higher authorities or else was vulnerable to doctrinal evaluation and interpretation in terms of central policy demands.

The way in which *Chung-kuo Ch'ing-nien* transmitted to its readers the substance of the CCP's growing concern about their revolutionary quality has already been described. Equally instructive is the effect which this concern had on the magazine's performance of its multiple roles. Our study of the magazine suggests that it has formal responsibility for filling three main roles: Party propaganda journal; "house organ" for the Youth League; and general youth magazine. Obviously *Chung-kuo Ch'ing-nien* has been most consistently a Party propaganda journal—the role which has been the easiest and safest to fill and which has corresponded most closely to its public image. In two of the periods studied—1959 and 1962—it was almost wholly devoted to exposition of the official Party line. Nevertheless, it has at times tried to meet the demands of its other roles, and its success or failure in doing so is relevant to this analysis.

In 1951 and even more in 1956, *Chung-kuo Ch'ing-nien* was in part a general youth magazine. There were in the former period a significant number of articles on Chinese history, different regions and resources of China, and various aspects of life in the Soviet Union, which presented informative general knowledge even though their contents supported current propaganda themes. The editorial tone of the magazine was light relative to later years. Editorials were very short, and the editors engaged in both self-criticism and informal commentary in which they wrote freely about complaints received and how they were responding to them. The magazine did not, in fact, probe personal problems very deeply, but it gave the impression of being genuinely open to its readers' interests and questions.

It was in 1956 that *Chung-kuo Ch'ing-nien* achieved its best balance among its assigned roles, devoting almost equal attention to official propaganda, general youth problems, and league problems. Although articles on the Soviet Union were already tapering off (there were in 1956 about one-third the number of such articles in 1951; in 1959 there were only five, in 1962 none, and in 1965 only critical references), there was a wide scattering of information on other countries, including non-Communist ones. The volume of poetry, fiction, and song was at its peak in 1956, as was the amount of critical and penetrating discussion of youth problems. Perhaps the most striking

sign of the magazine's service to its youthful readership was its coverage of educational and academic subjects. This emphasis was due in
part to the "march to science" materials, representing an official campaign, but there were also descriptive discussions of scientific and
technical subjects for their own sake. Nineteen fifty-six was the only
year studied of which this can be said. In other periods, articles on
science and technology were either doctrinally oriented (for example,
on the "red and expert" problem or general praise of modernity and
scientism in a socialist society) or else were confined to a few prominent examples of applied science (most commonly, personal health and
hygiene, agricultural technology, and public sanitation). It is conceiva-
ble that in 1956 a Chinese student might have read *Chung-kuo Ch'ing-
nien* for *pleasure*—a most unlikely event at any other time. In any
case, the general interest content of the magazine fell off sharply in
1959, 1962, and 1965. One could find at most only a handful of articles
in any of these periods which offered general information on subjects
other than Party doctrine and policy, and league affairs.

   Chung-kuo Ch'ing-nien's performance as an official organ for the
league followed a similar pattern. It filled this role best in 1951 and
1956, and then tended to play it down in 1959 and 1962; however, in
contrast to the general youth magazine role, the league role was very
prominent again in 1965. One measure of this pattern is the volume of
editorials and documents on league affairs, which declined steadily
from 1951 through 1962. There were fourteen editorials in 1951, six in
1956, one in 1959, and none in 1962; similarly, several League Central
Committee directives were printed in 1951, a few in 1956, and none in
1959 or 1962, although the CYL Propaganda Department contributed
a large volume of doctrinal argument in 1959. Routine documentation
is not in itself a particularly good measure, of course, since *Chung-kuo
Ch'ing-nien Pao* assumed major responsibility for this after 1951. On
the other hand, *Chung-kuo Ch'ing-nien*'s general treatment of league
affairs and organizational problems, in the form of articles and reader-
editor exchanges, followed closely the editorial and documentation
pattern. The pattern held in the revival of 1965 as well, for the sixteen
editorials and editorial articles that appeared in that period were
accompanied by numerous reports on CYL affairs from various league
committees. Actually, the 1965 volume of editorials and high level
league reports exceeded that of 1951, since the editorials and directives
printed in the earlier year were normally very short.

   From these comments, it appears that *Chung-kuo Ch'ing-nien*'s

changing performance of its roles reflected the CCP's post-1956 eleva-
tion of youth problems to the national policy level. Although the
magazine was never formally relieved of its other duties, it became in
practice a mouthpiece of the CCP's propaganda network. It would be a
mistake, however, to read into this development any conclusions about
inevitable or irreversible tendencies toward the stifling of communications media in China. While the function of the communications system plainly makes it susceptible to rigid content control from above
and to lack of responsiveness to lower levels, this fact did not prevent
Chung-kuo Ch'ing-nien from filling a more open, varied, and responsive role at certain times. It, or its successor, could presumably do so
again if the Party's obsessive concern about revolutionizing youth were
to slacken.

The power and intensity of *Chung-kuo Ch'ing-nien*'s message in the
post-1956 years must have had some effect on Chinese youth. There is
no way for an outsider to measure this effect, but some of the relevant
factors are evident. On the negative side, there is the twin problem of
disbelief and loss of interest that heavy-handed propaganda always
risks. If a reader's image of reality does not support what he reads, he
may cease to believe what he sees in a journal like *Chung-kuo Ch'ing-
nien;* or, even if he believes, he may simply cease to take seriously
what is presented in such monotonous and doctrinal terms. Even more
powerful resistance may come from perceived conflicts between official
line and a reader's personal interests and values. The whole point of
the campaign to revolutionize youth is an open acknowledgement of
the presence of such factors.

On the positive side are equally significant points, however. Though
the intensity and totality of the message is relatively new, the language
and symbols are not. The "goodness" of revolution, struggle, and
sacrifice, and the "badness" of personal interests, soft living, and
bourgeois influences, are well-established stereotypes in Communist
China. One cannot dismiss as meaningless appeals to symbols which
have been defined so clearly, even when the appeals may be repetitive
and obscure from an objective point of view. Moreover, the appeals are
directed at youth, presented in idealistic terms, and graced by the
personal blessing of a man with awesome national prestige. While these
conditions cannot guarantee universal youth responsiveness, they suggest that those at the most impressionable ages are the most likely to
respond with unreserved energy. Finally, there is the over-all impact of
the communications system which has, since the Great Leap, steadily

focused ever sharper attention on the fundamental issue of how to keep China "red." As information on other subjects and issues has decreased, both the relative and the absolute salience of this issue have been raised. There is no point in speculating on how youth might respond if they had a more varied flow of information. The fact is that youth in China have been deprived of much information not only about the outside but even about their own country. Their attention has increasingly been directed toward domestic issues, presented in crisis terms but with only a minimum of hard information to back up moralistic and doctrinal exhortations. In such circumstances, youth may well respond positively and genuinely, and even emotionally, to issues which in other times and places would have little appeal. It is true that *Chung-kuo Ch'ing-nien* tells us only the message and not how it is received. But there is good reason to believe that the message has had a significant influence on the values and behavior of many Chinese youth.

In assessing the impact of the drive to revolutionize youth, the 1965 revival of *Chung-kuo Ch'ing-nien*'s editorial assertiveness and emphasis on league affairs commands special attention. From one point of view, it is evidence of the magazine's ability to alter its style in the midst of a long-term trend toward more rigid and uniform control of communications; as such, it supports the earlier suggestion that the reduction of *Chung-kuo Ch'ing-nien* to a Party propaganda organ was not irreversible. More significantly, however, it raises the question of why the magazine should have moved in this direction. The move was plainly not a return to the more open stance of 1956 or even 1951, since the heavy-handed doctrinal approach of later years was retained and even heightened. Nor was the move part of a direct "opposition" to the then current line, for *Chung-kuo Ch'ing-nien* remained energetically articulate in its support for the campaigns of that time. The evidence suggests that the magazine's 1965 performance was a function of new assertiveness from the CYL leadership, passed on to the magazine with the approval of the Party Propaganda Department. Moreover, events since the spring of 1965 indicate that the league's aggressiveness in 1965 was not a chance phenomenon but rather was directly related to the general conflict that erupted in the Cultural Revolution.

THE CULTURAL REVOLUTION

Although space prohibits real discussion of the Cultural Revolution here, reference to some of its features is essential to an understanding of the CYL's role in it. The movement began in the fall of 1965, following a special meeting of the CCP Central Committee in which Mao Tse-tung apparently declared his intention to push the campaign against bourgeois and revisionist influences to a new peak. In a sense, this campaign had actually been in progress since the latter part of 1962, operating under various names and from time to time shifting its focus of attack. On the propaganda level, it had been pushed vigorously. Mao believed, however, that it had not been pushed hard enough in practice, and that both domestic and international threats to his vision of China's future were greater than ever before. The first step was an attack on a small group of men in the cultural and educational field. The "bourgeois" ideas and "anti-Party" activities of these men soon became symbols which had to be rejected decisively by all who were to stand on the Maoist side. The struggle intensified in the spring of 1966. By June, several important figures and groups had been identified—allegedly by their failure to support the campaign against the bourgeois "black gang"—as reactionary opponents of Mao's brand of socialism. Among the major groups criticized, all of them partially reorganized, were: the CCP Peking Municipal Committee, headed by P'eng Chen; the CCP Propaganda Department and several leading figures in cultural and educational circles; and the Peking Municipal Committee of the CYL.

It is difficult to imagine a grouping more closely associated with *Chung-kuo Ch'ing-nien* or, in view of the seriousness of the charges, more likely to compromise it. After these accusations and purges, the magazine could not have avoided some self-criticism and explicit repudiation of what had been its leading organizations. Among *Chung-kuo Ch'ing-nien*'s direct superiors, only the CYL Central Committee remained untarnished, and for a few more weeks it appeared that the league might weather the storm. Criticism of the CYL Peking Committee carefully absolved the League Central Committee by listing among the Peking Committee's crimes several instances of violation or disregard of directives from the League Central Committee. The first meeting of the new, reorganized CYL Peking Committee (July 3–11) was called under the "direct leadership of the CCP Peking Municipal Committee [also now reorganized] and the CYL Central Committee," and included Hu K'o-shih of the League Central Committee as a main spokesman. All was not well with the league, however. First Secretary Hu Yao-pang had disappeared from the news early in the year. At the July 3–11 meeting, there were references to a need for "reorganization" of the league to bring out its "militant core." Nevertheless, whatever its shortcomings, the CYL continued to speak of its present and future tasks as though it had no doubts about its survival, and on July 25 *Chung-kuo Ch'ing-nien Pao* announced that it would soon increase publication from three to six times a week.[6]

The critical break came with the Eleventh Plenum of the CCP Central Committee, held in Peking August 1–12, 1966. The Plenum released two major documents, neither of which made any reference to the CYL, although both paid tribute to the importance of "revolutionary" youth. On August 18 came the first massive Red Guard rally in Peking; thereafter, the league simply disappeared, while Red Guard units became the dominant and approved form of youth organization. *Chung-kuo Ch'ing-nien* had published on schedule on August 1, but its next issue of August 15 never appeared; *Chung-kuo Ch'ing-nien Pao* published its last issue on August 19. The significance of the Eleventh Plenum emerged gradually during subsequent months. During June and July, Mao and his "close comrade in arms," Lin Piao, had tried to extend the Cultural Revolution into a mass movement which would search out all traces of bourgeois "cultural" influence. The universities became the main arena of struggle and were thoroughly disrupted, but many high level cadres tried to check the scope and intensity of the campaign. The Mao–Lin group responded to this resistance at the Eleventh Plenum by citing as the "main targets" of the movement "those within the Party who are in authority and are taking the capitalist road." These authorities included a large number of top Party officials, headed by Liu Shao-ch'i and Teng Hsiao-p'ing. Thus, with the Eleventh Plenum, the Cultural Revolution turned into a bitter struggle for power between the Mao–Lin group and much of the established leadership of the state and Party bureaucracy. The league and its publications were among the first victims of this new phase, not because they had overtly opposed Mao, but because their past policy and organizational associations with the Liu–Teng group made them suspect institutions.

These events seem to confirm the hypothesis that the drive to revolutionize Chinese youth has had contradictory implications and results. As noted, the contradiction appeared indirectly in the pages of *Chung-kuo Ch'ing-nien,* but it had a direct and ultimately disastrous impact

[6] *CKCNP,* June 23, July 26, 1966, *SCMP,* Nos. 3735 (July 11, 1966) and 3756 (August 9, 1966).

on the Youth League. For if the revolutionization of youth was to have concrete meaning, it would have to realize that meaning through the elite organization which held a virtual monopoly on the political activity, recruitment, and advancement of young people. The intensification of revolutionary propaganda posed no exceptional difficulties for *Chung-kuo Ch'ing-nien;* the printed page is easily changed to meet the demands of the times. An organization cannot transform itself so easily. Increasingly after 1958, the CYL found itself propagating standards which it did not meet as an organization; increasingly, too, league members and units were offered as examples of the bureaucratization and incipient revisionism that the revolutionary message was to overcome.

By 1965, the CYL was trapped. Unless it changed rapidly and radically, it could no longer claim to be the vanguard of a new generation of revolutionary youth. On the other hand, if it truly set out to implement the Maoist line, it would in effect be directing a revolution against itself as an institution. The league's assertiveness in 1965 must be seen in this light, as an attempt to revitalize itself without destroying its leadership and without sacrificing some of the more moderate policies it had supported in previous years. As the major thrust in this attempt, the CYL carried out a large-scale recruitment campaign in 1965, designed to bring in new and younger members and to restore its effectiveness as the leading youth organization in China.[7] The campaign proved to be a case of too little and too late, however. When Mao decided to go ahead with a fight to the finish against his opponents, he apparently suspended the league and appealed directly for support from the new generation of youth.

Initially, the Red Guards probably fulfilled Mao's hopes and expectations. It is possible, too, that the Maoists are right in claiming that the struggles of the Cultural Revolution have produced large numbers of youth who have now been truly "revolutionized" by their participation in it.[8] But as the Cultural Revolution continues without a decisive victory for the Maoists, it becomes more evident that the significance

---

[7] The recruitment campaign and other issues mentioned here are discussed more fully in John Israel, "The Red Guards in Historical Perspective: Continuity and Change in the Chinese Youth Movement," *China Quarterly,* No. 30 (April–June, 1967), pp. 1–32; and Townsend, *Revolutionization of Chinese Youth,* pp. 62–67.

[8] See, for example, Lin Chieh, "Courageously Forging Ahead in the Teeth of Great Storms of Class Struggle," *Hung Ch'i* (Red Flag), No. 5 (March 30, 1967), *SCMM,* No. 571 (April 10, 1967).

of the revolutionary message lies as much in the extent of resistance that made it necessary as in the results it has achieved. Moreover, the fact that the message contributed to the downfall of the very institutions that had propagated it suggests that its long-range results will not be easy for the Maoists to anticipate or control.

JOHN GARDNER

The Wu-fan *Campaign in Shanghai: A Study in the Consolidation of Urban Control*

The implementation of policy by means of mass mobilization is one of the most distinctive features of the Chinese Communist political process. Since 1949 the Chinese masses have participated in over one hundred mass movements, all of which, to some degree, have been designed to assist the revolutionization of society.[1] The official attitude toward the use of this technique has been succinctly expounded by Chou En-lai, who noted in 1959 that: "The Party has always paid attention to combining its leadership with broad mass movements, guiding the masses to raise the level of their revolutionary consciousness constantly, and to organize their own strength to emancipate themselves step by step, instead of imposing revolution on the masses or bestowing victory on the masses as a favor."[2] It is, of course, necessary to mention that not all campaigns have been supported by all members of the leadership; indeed, some senior Party members have questioned the validity of such processes in certain circumstances.[3] Nevertheless, from 1949 up to the present, the mass campaign has been

[1] For a recent general outline of the nature and functions of mass campaigns see F. T. C. Yu, "Campaigns, Communications, and Development in Communist China," in Daniel Lerner and Wilbur Schramm (ed.), *Communication and Change in Developing Countries* (Honolulu: East-West Center Press, 1967), pp. 195–215. Professor Yu lists eighty-one "generally known" mass movements for the 1949–59 period.

[2] Chou En-lai, "A Great Decade," in *Ten Great Years,* comp. by State Statistical Bureau (Peking: Foreign Languages Press, 1960), p. 57.

[3] K'o Ch'ing-shih, "Mass Movements on the Industrial Front," in *ibid.,* pp. 191–92.

an essential and important component of the leadership's political style.

It is the purpose of this study to examine one of the major mass campaigns of the consolidation period (1949–52), a campaign through which the new elite, created largely in the rural hinterland, attempted to extend its authority to an alien environment previously controlled by its rivals. The *wu-fan* (five anti) campaign, which is discussed below, was implemented throughout urban China in the first half of 1952. It was directed against industrialists and businessmen who, it was alleged, were guilty of breaking the law by speading "five poisons": bribery, tax evasion, theft of state property, cheating on government contracts, and stealing state economic information.[4]

This study will analyze the dynamics of the *wu-fan* campaign in Shanghai. Limitation of the study to one city reflects both the importance of China's major urban center and also the need to keep the paper as "microsocietal" as possible. However, more general and comparative data have been included where they were felt to be appropriate, particularly in those sections dealing with the leadership's urban policies, the position of the bourgeoisie after the campaign, and the interpretations of the campaign which have been made by the leadership over the past fifteen years.[5] Only those aspects of the campaign which may be properly termed "political" have been considered. Clearly, in studies of Communist China any distinction between what is "political" and what is "economic" tends to be nebulous. Nevertheless, economic factors are discussed only insofar as they have "political" significance. For example, the growth of "state capitalism" after the campaign is dealt with in the last section of the study, as it was of the utmost importance in the leadership's attempt to exercise and increase the degree of control over the bourgeoisie, but the impact of the *wu-fan* campaign on industrial production, while important, is not included, as it is a subject more properly left to the economist.

The argument advanced in this study may be summarized as follows. In 1949 the Chinese Communist leadership was faced with great prob-

---

[4] The crimes allegedly committed by the bourgeoisie were so numerous and complex that there is little point in attempting to list them in detail. The finest account of the dubious business practices which were widespread in Shanghai is to be found in a novel. See Chou Erh-fu, *Morning in Shanghai,* trans. by A. C. Barnes (Peking: Foreign Languages Press, 1962), Vol. I.

[5] The *san-fan* campaign, which overlapped with and was closely related to the *wu-fan,* has also been left out of this paper as it was directed *primarily* against Party and government cadres. This paper is concerned only with the bourgeoisie.

lems: the assumption of national power was accompanied by the need to work from urban centers, which were the object of Communist suspicion and in which the Communist Party lacked mass support. The Party was forced to rely heavily on the skills of industrialists and businessmen who, very often, occupied a dominant position in the urban areas, and in order to win their support the Party made a number of very moderate policy statements in 1949.

Such statements appear to have caused many "capitalists" to assume that they would not be subjected, at least for the forseeable future, to strict controls; consequently, they persisted in a variety of corrupt business practices which frequently involved the connivance of Party and government cadres who succumbed willingly to the "sugar-coated bullets" of the bourgeoisie. The leadership, fearing that revolutionary "purity" in the ranks was in danger, purged the Party and bureaucracy of "corrupt elements," and, in order to deal with this problem "at source," as it were, initiated a mass campaign directed against the bourgeoisie, the class allegedly responsible for all the corruption to be found. This study examines the methods used by the leadership in the case of Shanghai and reveals how the leadership was extremely successful in weakening bourgeois power and status by means of this campaign. In conclusion, it is noted that while the leadership appears to have been highly successful in controlling the bourgeoisie since 1952, it has not apparently been able to eliminate corruption entirely within the ranks of the Party.

THE PROBLEM OF URBAN CHINA

The rapid extension of Chinese Communist power to encompass urban China during 1948–49 gave rise to many problems for the new elite. The basic difficulty was that of handling what *The Times* described as "administrative indigestion." The Chinese Communist Party had developed a high degree of organizational skill in an agrarian environment, and by 1949 it appears to have enjoyed considerable legitimate support in rural China, but it remained to be seen whether it could handle the task of controlling the relatively sophisticated and functionally diffuse urban sector of society. As will be shown later, the Party leadership included a number of men who had considerable experience of the urban areas, and a reference in *The Times* to the "ex-troglodytes of Yenan" was somewhat unjustified.

Nevertheless, a valid point was made when that paper informed its readers that:

A well-disciplined but relatively small field force of outlaws has in a matter of months made itself master of all Manchuria and most of North China from the Great Wall to the Yangtze. Three quarters of the railways, three quarters of the heavy industries, and the most important coal and iron mines in China are in the "liberated areas": ports, factories, banks, universities, newspapers, as well as various small scale but potentially conspicuous foreign communities all add to the responsibilities of the new regime.[6]

The problem, then, was an acute shortage of manpower of the type which was required to fill numerous and complex roles in urban China. At that time the Chinese Communist Party was weak in numbers, quality, and urban skills. Although a policy of rapid recruitment had been followed since 1945, there were only 4,488,080 Party members in October, 1949.[7] Moreover, as was rapidly to become apparent, among the 3,276,000 recruited during that period, there were many who, from the leadership's point of view, were of low ideological "consciousness," as they had not undergone adequate political education.[8] It was also evident that young peasants, recruited as soldiers, were lacking in the skills required to fill numerous positions of responsibility in the cities.

The leadership's view of the urban areas mirrored two attitudes which are to be found in most underdeveloped countries. One sociologist has rightly noted that "Almost all countries outside of Western Europe and possibly the United States experience the cultural tension between metropolis and province."[9] Given the importance of the rural areas in the history of the Chinese Communist Party, it is scarcely surprising that the leadership viewed the cities with some hostility and suspicion. This animosity toward them was further strengthened by the Party's "anti-imperialist" outlook, an outlook based not only on Marxist-Leninist ideology but also on the unhappy experiences of China since the Opium War.

H. Arthur Steiner, one of the earliest writers on the Party's urban policy, has pointed out that, "One observes a persistent reflection in the literature of Chinese Communism of a peasant-inspired and Puritanical distrust of the cities." He went on to quote an editorial distributed by the New China News Agency in January, 1948, which had explained that, because urban life had been "infected" by the "vicious

[6] *The Times* (London), April 22, 1949.

[7] *Shih-shih Shou-ts'e* (Current Affairs Handbook), No. 18 (1956), as quoted in Franz Schurmann, *Ideology and Organization in Communist China* (Berkeley and Los Angeles, University of California Press, 1966), p. 129.

[8] *CFJP*, November 11, 1951.

[9] E. A. Shils, *Political Development in the New State* (The Hague: Mouton, 1962), p. 11.

and lavish" influence of imperialism, "unless steps are taken, both in ideas and organization, to overcome the lavishness and discrepancy of living, particularly in cities, all the advantages of the cities will be cancelled." It was felt that the great cities were alien and could not be trusted. For a long period they had been subverted by foreign concessions, treaty ports, and extraterritoriality, and, therefore, had to "be truly Sinified."[10]

The Party was particularly wary of Shanghai, the largest and most alien city in China. In many respects a foreign creation, Shanghai had been a principal center for European and Japanese "imperialists." Furthermore, it can hardly be argued that this "imperialism" was a matter of the distant past. To cite but one example of the extent of foreign influence in Shanghai, it is worthy of note that in 1934–35, 57,607 of its inhabitants were foreigners.[11] Constituting 6.4 per cent of the population at that time, foreigners had played a leading role in the city's political and economic life. In addition, as Communist sources never tired of emphasizing, Shanghai had been a major base of the Kuomintang.

P'an Han-nien, who was appointed deputy mayor after the takeover, made clear the city's significance in a speech to "people of all circles" on the first anniversary of Shanghai's "liberation."[12] "Shanghai," he remarked, "is China's largest city with a population of over five million, and is the heart of China's economy. In the past hundred years the imperialists made it their formidable fortress for invading and enslaving China, and it was, moreover, the heart of the Kuomintang reactionary clique which oppressed the Chinese people for more than twenty years." Its "liberation" was of the utmost importance, for it "proclaimed the destruction of imperialism's attempt to invade China," and it marked the end of Kuomintang rule. "This," said P'an, "was not only a victory for the people of Shanghai and the people of the whole country, but was a victory for the people of the whole world."

In like manner, Madame Soong Ch'ing-ling wrote of her city's "liberation" that:

We have become a symbol of the struggle against the dead weight of imperialism and cynicism of bureaucratic capitalist speculation. These blights have ridden the

[10] H. Arthur Steiner, "Communist Chinese Urban Policy," *American Political Science Review,* XLIV, No. 1 (March, 1950), 62.

[11] Olga Lang, *Chinese Family and Society* (New Haven, Conn.: Yale University Press, 1946), p. 80.

[12] Chieh-fang Jih-pao She, *Shang-hai Chieh-fang I-nien* (One Year of Liberated Shanghai) (Shanghai: Chieh-fang Jih-pao She, 1950), p. 1.

backs of our workers almost from the very first day of Shanghai's existence. The rest of the country knows how deeply embedded is the rot of these blights. Therefore they encourage us as we struggle to make this a people's city, to make its factories and mills work for our country.[13]

Such comments on the historical development of Shanghai and its foreign characteristics can be found in virtually every speech and article dealing with the problems of the city. Even after "liberation" it was felt that Shanghai's economic life was still dominated too much by the world outside. It was a "very good example of a semi-colonial city" in that it relied on foreign supply for a large part of its industrial raw materials, and its industrial goods did not go to the villages.[14] One is reminded of Frantz Fanon's judgment of another "foreign enclave," which he described as "a well-fed town, an easy-going town, its belly is always full of good things. The settlers' town is a town of white people, of foreigners."[15] Although the foreigners had gone, they had left a "contaminated" Chinese bourgeoisie behind, and this class possessed great power in Shanghai. The leadership's suspicions were justified, because it lacked the support necessary to gain immediate control over the industrialists and businessmen of the city.

Consider, for example, certain socioeconomic conditions which prevailed in Shanghai at the time of its "liberation." These indicate that factors were present which militated against the possibility of developing immediate and extensive working class support for radical policies directed against the bourgeoisie.

It may be noted that the city's working class was very different from the classic type which provides ideal material for mobilization by extremist elites, as its members were, by and large, not "atomized" or alienated from the environment in which they labored. Rapid economic development was no new phenomenon in Shanghai, and there had been extensive industrialization since the First World War. Because of this, it seems that for many workers the discontinuities which accompany the initial industrialization experience were a thing of the past.

The growth of an indigenous working class with urban affiliations can be traced to the 1930's. In 1935, 65 of China's 141 cotton mills were located in Shanghai, as were a large number of the other industrial plants of the country. By the early 1930's, half of China's

---

[13] Soong Ching Ling (*sic*), "Shanghai's New Day Has Dawned," in *The Struggle for New China*, English trans. (Peking: Foreign Languages Press, 1963), p. 246.

[14] *CFJP*, December 15, 1951.

[15] Frantz Fanon, *The Wretched of the Earth* (Harmondsworth, Eng.: Penguin, 1967), p. 30.

industrial workers were in that city. Most of these workers, of course, came from the countryside. Even then, however, one survey, based admittedly on a very small sample, noted that it "was not without significance that there were already a group of workers of the second generation, this category being rather considerable among the skilled workers."[16] Moreover, a trend had begun for workers, particularly those in industrial as opposed to traditional occupations, to bring their families with them to Shanghai. Thus, by 1949 there was nothing alien about the urban environment for many of Shanghai's workers.[17]

A further disincentive to the development of deep feelings of grievance among the labor force was the diversification of industry and commerce. Nationalist statistics for the first half of 1949 showed that there were 110,000 firms in the city, embracing 238 trades. The vast majority of these firms (93,064) were commercial. At this time Shanghai had a labor force of just over 1,000,000, of whom 300,000 were classified as "shop workers" (*tien-yüan*), 63,000 of them being employed in restaurants, bathhouses, hotels, coffee shops, and hairdressing establishments.[18]

Despite the presence of large factories, many of Shanghai's workers were employed in small firms. Writing of the 1930's, one observer commented that "The modern factories did not destroy the old Chinese handicrafts, and the side streets . . . were full of small workshops of the traditional type, sometimes utilizing a few modern techniques."[19] The pattern of small-scale industrial and commercial organization persisted in Shanghai, and throughout urban China, up to and after 1949. Indeed, one economist has claimed that the "greatest single factor militating against highly centralized planning in China is the existence of large numbers of small-scale industrial enterprises using widely varying, often primitive techniques," and that "the Communists have struggled with the problems of controlling these small-scale firms almost from the beginning of their attainment of power in 1949."[20]

Such firms presented great political problems as well as economic ones. Among the many conditions which can assist the development of

[16] Lang, *Chinese Family and Society*, pp. 80, 86, 87.

[17] Since 1949 it has become increasingly apparent that urban China exerts a strong appeal to rural dwellers. The Party has, on occasions, attempted to prevent rural immigration to the cities. Similarly the regime has encountered great difficulties in attempting to "persuade" urban Chinese to go to the rural areas.

[18] *Shang-hai Chieh-fang I-nien*, p. 47.

[19] Lang, *Chinese Family and Society*, p. 80.

[20] Dwight H. Perkins, "Incentives and Profits in Chinese Industry," Current Scene, IV, No. 10 (May 15, 1966), 3.

strong antagonisms between employer and employed, three of the most important are the single-industry environment, the large and impersonal work unit, and the absentee proprietor. In Shanghai the first of these elements was obviously not present, and for many employees the other two were missing also.

The evidence of numerous cases which arose during the *wu-fan* campaign indicates that in Shanghai, in small firms particularly, the workers often had extremely close relations with their employers. This is not to argue that the capitalists of Shanghai were paragons of virtue in relations with their employees, but merely to point out that simple class hatreds were not so markedly pronounced as the leadership of the Chinese Communist Party might have wished.

At all levels of the economic ladder there were strong personal ties which alleviated to some degree those tensions which invariably arise when relations between employers and employed are based purely on monetary considerations. In view of the role of the extended family system in China, it is scarcely surprising that one finds numerous cases of employers whose relatives worked for them. For example, in the metal shops of Laocha *ch'ü* (district), the fact that "many people were related to capitalists and others had enjoyed amicable relations with them for a long period" constituted a "mental block" to the campaign's development there.[21]

In the Chung Nan Rubber Company, there were some workers "who were capitalists' relatives, and some who were natives of the same area (*t'ung-hsiang*)."[22] It is not possible to estimate the extent of such relationships with any degree of accuracy. However, reports on the difficulty of persuading the workers to denounce their employers, which appeared frequently in the early stages of the *wu-fan* campaign, suggest that such a pattern was widespread.

The presence of so many small firms meant that the workers were widely scattered geographically, a situation which aggravated the difficulties of mobilization. The leadership complained that "because the shop workers were comparatively scattered, very many people failed to break away from their attitude of having affection for capitalists."[23] The job of penetrating to the lower levels was fraught with difficulties, and a claim that 816,000 of Shanghai's 1,017,057 workers had been unionized by April, 1950, must be treated with suspicion.[24] Even if this

---

[21] *CFJP*, February 8, 1952.
[22] *Ibid.*, May 21, 1952.
[23] *Ibid.*, February 7, 1952.
[24] *Shang-hai Chieh-fang I-nien*, pp. 80–81.

figure is correct, there is no reason to assume that union organizations were always effective, nor that they were under strict control. Large numbers of competent and loyal union cadres could not be created overnight, and, as will be discussed later, in some places the unions were under the control of "agents of the bourgeoisie," and were manipulated in the interests of the employers.

A further point which must have hindered the development of strong class hatreds was that some capitalists were in the habit of "doing small favors for shop workers, workers, and clerks, such as letting them become shareholders, paying extra allowances, and sharing profits." Such capitalists, it was alleged, did this in order to "facilitate their unlawful acts." Recent evidence supports the view that this type of behavior was important in lessening the workers' sense of grievance.

One capitalist, supposedly associated with Liu Shao-ch'i in 1949, was Sung Fei-ch'ing, general manager of the Tung Ya Woolen Textile Factory in Tientsin. It is alleged that Sung "tried to cover up brutal exploitation of the workers by the bourgeoisie" by "the treacherous means of issuing 'shares' to workers." Liu Shao-ch'i, it is claimed, approved of the cooperative nature of this venture, and this has been held up as "proof" that he "wrote off class struggle and class contradiction" and "covered up the substance of exploitation of the working class by the bourgeoisie."[25] Whatever the veracity of this charge, it is of the greatest significance that it should have been made. It indicates that many workers may have had sound economic reasons for wishing to refrain from "struggle" with the bourgeoisie.[26]

Thus, the urban working class, which one would naturally assume to be the "backbone" of Party work in the cities, was not entirely amenable to Party control. Many workers were linked to their employers by personal ties, relationships based on familiarity, regional affiliations, and kinship. It would, of course, be naïve to imagine that conflict did not exist; the conditions of many workers were deplorable. However, for a substantial number, the situation was ameliorated by the factors outlined above.

The position of the bourgeoisie, in contrast to that of the Chinese Communist Party, was relatively strong, not only in Shanghai but

[25] "A History of Opposing the Party, Socialism, and the Thought of Mao Tse-tung," in *8.13 Hung Wei Ping* (August 13 Red Guard), No. 68 (May 13, 1967). This extremely long article is the most detailed account of Liu's activities in Tientsin from 1949 onward. It has been translated in *SCMM*, No. 585 (July 24, 1967), No. 587 (August 8, 1967), and No. 588 (August 14, 1967). This reference is to *SCMM*, No. 585, pp. 28–29.

[26] It is interesting to note in this context that Liu Shao-ch'i has recently been accused of diverting the workers from political activities into "economism."

throughout urban China. The class possessed commercial and industrial skills which were essential to the needs of the new regime. The
restoration and development of production in pursuit of China's goal of
"wealth and power" (*fu-ch'iang*) necessitated the utilization of such
rare talents. Moreover, members of the bourgeoisie were wealthy, and
were accorded considerable status by their workers. The bourgeoisie,
because of its strength, skill, and status, constituted something of a
pressure group on behalf of moderation, and might well be regarded as
a "proto-opposition."

THE PARTY AND THE BOURGEOISIE[27]

In the spring and summer of 1949, there was extensive discussion of
urban policy within the Chinese Communist Party leadership. A major
subject in the debate on the cities was the question of what political
and economic roles were to be accorded to the bourgeoisie. Mao himself was prepared to accommodate many bourgeois interests *under
certain specified conditions*. Evidence which has become available in
the course of the Great Proletarian Cultural Revolution shows that
some Party leaders were prepared to go further than Mao was.

In March, 1949, the Seventh Central Committee of the Party held
its Second Plenary Session in a village in Hopei. In his *Report* to this
meeting, Mao outlined the role he was prepared to allocate to the
urban bourgeoisie. In a discussion on economic policy, he explained
that:

China's private capitalist industry . . . is a force which must not be ignored.
Because they have been oppressed or hemmed in by imperialism, feudalism, and
bureaucratic-capitalism, the national bourgeoisie of China and its representatives
have often taken part in the people's democratic revolutionary struggles or maintained a neutral stand. For this reason and because China's economy is still
backward, *there will be a need for a fairly long period after the victory of the
revolution, to make use of the positive qualities of urban . . . capitalism as far as
possible, in the interests of developing the national economy. In this period, all
capitalist elements in cities . . . which are not harmful but beneficial to the national
economy should be allowed to exist and expand. This is not only unavoidable but
also economically necessary.*

Naturally, Mao argued that capitalism would have to be controlled and
would not be "unrestricted and uncurbed as in the capitalist countries." However, such control was not to be too severe:

[27] In this paper the term "bourgeoisie" is used to cover those members of the "petty"
and "national" bourgeoisie who were engaged in industrial and commercial occupations. It
does not include "bourgeois intellectuals."

It is necessary and useful for us to apply Sun Yat-sen's slogan of "regulation of capital." However, in the interest of the whole national economy and in the present and future interest of the working class and all the laboring people, *we must not restrict the private capitalist economy too much or too rigidly, but must leave room for it to exist and develop within the framework of the economic policy and planning of the people's republic.* The policy of restricting private capitalism is bound to meet with resistance in varying degrees and forms from the bourgeoisie, especially from the big owners of private enterprises, that is, from the big capitalists. Restriction versus opposition to restriction will be the main form of class struggle in the new-democratic state. It is entirely wrong to think that we can discard the slogan "regulation of capital"; that is a Right opportunist view. *But the opposite view, which advocates too much or too rigid restriction of private capital or holds that we can simply eliminate private capital very quickly, is also entirely wrong;* this is a "Left" opportunist view.[28]

Mao expanded these views in another extremely important statement three months later. In this, he acknowledged that the Party was weak in connection with the needs of national economic work, and gave the bourgeoisie further grounds for optimism. He noted that:

The serious task of economic construction lies before us. We shall soon put aside some of the things we know well and be compelled to do things we don't know well. This means difficulties. The imperialists reckon that we will not be able to manage our economy; they are standing by and looking on, awaiting our failure.

We must overcome difficulties, we must learn what we do not know. *We must learn to do economic work from all who know how, no matter who they are. We must esteem them as teachers, learning from them respectfully and conscientiously.*[29]

Whatever anxieties troubled the bourgeoisie as the Nationalists beat an ignominious retreat must have been, to a considerable extent, alleviated by such pronouncements. Only the "bureaucratic capitalists" were to suffer immediate expropriation. Party policy at the time of "liberation" was supposedly aimed at regulating capitalism and not at destroying it. It is true that Mao spoke of the "reform" of the bourgeoisie. The industrial and commercial class was, in Mao's eyes, guilty of "exploitation," and also of "liberalism." "Bourgeois ideology" was characterized by the pursuit of selfish interests at the expense of the public good. Nevertheless, Mao talked of "education," and there appeared to be no urgency about this. Mao explained that many of the bourgeoisie could receive a good deal of suitable education at the time

[28] Mao Tse-tung, "Report to the Second Plenary Session of the Seventh Central Committee of the Chinese Communist Party" (March, 1949), in *Selected Works* (Peking: Foreign Languages Press, 1964), IV, 367–68 (henceforth cited as *SW*) (emphasis added).

[29] Mao Tse-tung, "On the People's Democratic Dictatorship" (June, 1949), in *SW*, IV, 422–23 (emphasis added).

of "liberation," but he also mentioned that the capitalists would be "remolded" a step further when the time came to realize socialism and nationalize private enterprises. As Mao had promised that capitalism would be permitted to exist "for a fairly long period" after 1949, it seemed that he was prepared to follow a reasonably gradualist approach in reforming the bourgeoisie.

There was, of course, considerable ambiguity in Mao's statements. In his *Report*, he had mentioned that, following the nationwide victory and the solution of the land problem, the basic internal contradiction would be that between the working class and the bourgeoisie. Moreover, while members of the bourgeoisie were to be counted among "the people," they were to have a somewhat lower status than other groups. For the "people's democratic dictatorship" was to be "based on the alliance of the working class, the peasantry, and the urban petty bourgeoisie, and mainly on the alliance of workers and peasants." Yet Mao also said:

We must regard the majority of non-Party democrats as we do our own cadres, consult with them sincerely, and frankly to solve those problems that call for consultation and solution, *give them work, entrust them with the responsibility and authority that should go with their posts and help them do their work well.* Proceeding from the desire to unite with them, we should carry out serious and appropriate criticism or struggle against their errors and shortcomings, in order to attain the object of unity. It would be wrong to adopt an accommodating attitude towards their errors or shortcomings. It would also be wrong to adopt a closed door or perfunctory attitude towards them.[30]

The two statements discussed above formed the basis for similar statements in the Common Program. This document, promulgated in September, 1949, embodied the constitutional principles on which the People's Republic was, supposedly, to be run until the establishment of a formal Constitution (one was adopted in 1954). It was stated therein that "economic interests and private property of workers, peasants, petty bourgeoisie and the national bourgeoisie" would be protected, and that economic construction would be based on the policy of "taking into account both public and private interests, of benefiting both labor and capital." The government was to encourage the "active operation of all private enterprises beneficial to the national welfare and the people's livelihood" and would assist in their development. It was stated that private industry would be "encouraged" to develop in the direction of state capitalism, but this need not be interpreted as auto-

[30] Mao, "Report," in *SW,* IV, 373 (emphasis added).

matically disadvantageous for private firms, because the state would place processing orders with them.

Thus the bourgeoisie was assured of a "glorious future" in the People's Republic of China. Although the state-owned sector of the economy was to be most important, a "mixed economy" was to be permitted. There was to be no immediate confiscation of private enterprises, and the industrial and commercial classes could look forward to the enjoyment of their assets for a reasonably long period. Also, they were assured, so it seemed, of access to positions of influence in the political and economic structures of the new regime. All this depended, however, on one extremely important condition. They were to behave in a way "beneficial" to the regime and people. Mao took this point very seriously; it is doubtful if its significance was apparent to the bourgeoisie. Even if there were capitalists who did fully appreciate the nature of Mao's offer, the statements of other Party leaders may well have helped to dispel their anxiety.

In the Great Proletarian Cultural Revolution, Liu Shao-ch'i has been labeled as the man behind virtually every "anti-Maoist" opinion and policy to have appeared in China since, and in some instances, before, 1949. Some of these charges relate to statements he is alleged to have made in Tientsin after the Communist takeover in that city. One must exercise considerable caution in evaluating such accusations. However, in this particular case there is some circumstantial evidence which tends to corroborate the view that Liu attempted to pursue an extremely moderate policy toward the bourgeoisie.

In his *Report* of March 5, 1949, Mao had condemned "muddle headed comrades" who thought that in the cities the Party should rely on the bourgeoisie, and concentrate on developing private enterprise rather than state enterprise. Such opinions were, he said, "Right opportunist." Thus, a "moderate" faction undoubtedly existed in the Party at that time, and its views are probably well represented by those attributed to Liu. Moreover, it seems quite possible that Liu was a "Right opportunist" at this time. As a senior Party leader with extensive urban experience, Liu was far more likely to have had a sensitive appreciation of work in the cities than Mao. He must have been particularly well aware of the problems of labor organization, and of the needs of industry and commerce. He must also have known the power and status of the urban bourgeoisie. Many of the remarks that have been attributed to him are very similar to the statements made by Mao at the time, and can be distinguished only by slight changes in emphasis. They do not constitute "irrefutable proof" of Liu's desire to establish a "bourgeois dictatorship," but they apparently do reflect the opinions of a section of the leadership which was prepared to compromise with certain political and ideological goals in order to lay the basis for the rapid restoration and development of the economy.[31]

Consider, therefore, the statements *allegedly* made by Liu in the spring of 1949. The circumstances surrounding the "Tientsin Talks" indicate clearly the need to restore the confidence of the capitalists in that city. Following the fall of Tientsin, it appears that some capitalists withdrew their capital and closed their factories. Huang K'och'eng, chairman of the Tientsin Military Control Committee, asked Liu to "mediate." Liu visited the city for three weeks in April and May, where he addressed several meetings of industrialists and businessmen, and had "confidential talks" with some capitalists. In his talks, reports, and directives on work in Tientsin, he made a number of statements on the position of the various urban groups, and on the roles they should play under the new regime.

Liu argued that the capitalists knew more about production in the cities than either the Party or the workers, that they held a very important position in urban production, and that it was necessary to cooperate with them. While noting that the state depended on the workers and office employees, Liu pointed out that "it depends particularly on the factory manager, the engineer, and the technician."

He claimed that, in the period following "liberation," capitalist exploitation was beneficial and should be encouraged. This startling opinion, however, was justified on two grounds. Liu explained that if the capitalists were able to increase their profits, they would set up more factories and so provide increased employment opportunities for the workers. He noted that, "As soon as operations begin, the workers will have rice to eat and money to earn. Though they are exploited they will feel better than if they are unemployed and not exploited." Secondly, as Liu told the capitalists, increased production would lead to an increase in the revenue the government would collect through taxation; "then, it is the state which is exploiting you."[32]

Liu did not ignore the question of "struggle" in his talks, but his discussion of the problem hardly stressed its importance, as is evident from the following remarks:

---

[31] For a fairly comprehensive list of Liu's "crimes" in general, see the eight articles translated in CB, No. 836 (September 25, 1967).

[32] *SCMM,* No. 587 (August 8, 1967), p. 28; No. 585 (July 24, 1967), p. 30.

. . . we both unite and struggle with the bourgeoisie. But which is the point of emphasis? Confining ourselves to the present, the point of emphasis should be unity. Will this change in the future? Probably. But *the period when the point of emphasis is unity is going to be rather long. Today, the point of emphasis is unity, especially economic unity.* . . . Concerning the question of workers, political questions, and theoretically and ideologically, we have disputes with them. It must be made clear as to where we may cooperate with them and where we should restrict such cooperation.

Comrades in Tientsin seem unwittingly to regard the free bourgeoisie as the object of struggle. This is wrong. The objects of our struggle are imperialists, the bureaucratic bourgeoisie, and the feudal class. Comrades have raised their fists of struggle. But they don't seem to see imperialists, the bureaucratic bourgeoisie, and the feudal class. They regard friends as enemies, and fail to strike at those they should strike at.[33]

Mao and Liu appear to have agreed that the major enemy in 1949 was represented by "imperialism, the bureaucratic capitalists, and feudalism." Whereas Mao, however, had prophesied that "restriction versus opposition to restriction" would be the main form of class struggle in the new democratic state, Liu emphasized unity, "especially economic unity." This, he said, was to be the point of emphasis for a "rather long" period, although it would *"probably"* change.

Liu apparently wanted to control "Leftist tendencies" among Party cadres and workers. He acknowledged that in the past the workers had suffered at the hands of their employers. But, he pointed out, they were not to seek purely one-sided benefits. He criticized workers who were bad timekeepers, who did not work hard, and who made excessive wage demands. Such behavior, he warned, could force capitalists to close down and put their employees out of work. Workers were to put up with "temporary suffering" and were not to struggle too much with the bourgeoisie. He is reported to have stated specifically that workers were not permitted to change capitalist enterprises into cooperatives, and he warned that those who had the "destructive instincts of the hooligan proletariat" and wanted to bring about the collapse of the factories would be stopped by force.

In order to "make capitalists feel at ease," Liu instructed trade union cadres to try to persuade the workers to cooperate. He also proposed that members of the democratic parties representing the bourgeoisie should be permitted to join unions, and should be eligible for election to posts within them.[34]

[33] *Ibid.,* No. 585 (July 24, 1967), p. 29 (emphasis added).
[34] "Leader of the Workers' Movement or No. 1 Scab?" *JMJP* editorial (undated) in *Peking Review,* No. 50 (1967), p. 30.

Thus Liu appears to have given considerable attention to the problems of the urban areas. In his desire to calm the fears of certain capitalists, he seems to have been anxious to control the sans-culottes within the ranks of the Party and the labor force. Mao's statements, though cautious and conditional, were reasonably moderate. It may be argued that, when taken in conjunction with those attributed to Liu Shao-ch'i, such declarations of intent must have encouraged industrial and commercial groups to believe that they were not to be subject to either immediate or severe discipline at the hands of the Party. The exigencies of the situation caused Party leaders to give a minor role to such questions as the existence of "contradictions," the place of "struggle," and the need to "reform" the bourgeoisie. As a result, it seems likely that many capitalists took Party statements as evidence of the Party's admission of weakness vis-à-vis the urban areas. By so doing, they underestimated both the organizational skills and ruthlessness of the leadership of the Chinese Communist Party. The belief that the new regime would be neither willing nor able to exercise strict control over the bourgeoisie must have encouraged many industrialists and businessmen to continue to behave as they had done under the Nationalists, and to indulge in various corrupt practices which were an accepted part of urban life before the Communist takeover. There may well be considerable validity in the recent comment that, following Liu's talks in Tientsin, many law-breaking capitalists cast away their worries and felt as great a satisfaction as if they had been given a "shot in the arm."[35]

THE GROWTH OF CORRUPTION

On entering Shanghai in May, 1949, the Communists behaved with the same propriety as they had in other urban areas. They did, however, confiscate immediately those firms which were run by "bureaucratic-capitalists" and which, "through their monopolistic practices undoubtedly hampered the trade of the city."[36] For most industrialists and businessmen the takeover brought benefits. Although many firms of a speculative nature were forced out of business by price controls, the restoration of peaceful conditions resulted in increased production and, it was claimed, the growth of new markets in the hinterland.

In Shanghai, and throughout urban China, senior Party members were placed in key positions. However, the general lack of manpower

[35] *JMJP*, April 15, 1967, in *Peking Review*, No. 17 (1967), p. 10.
[36] *The Times* (Shanghai Correspondent), June 24, 1949.

at the lower levels necessitated continuing recruitment of new members into the Party, and also reliance on those who had served the Nationalists. Ch'en I, the mayor of Shanghai, claimed that over 95 per cent of the former Kuomintang personnel had stayed at their posts after the Communists entered the city.[37] Hence, in Shanghai, as in the other urban areas, veteran and new Party cadres were put to work alongside ex-Nationalist officials in an environment in which the bourgeoisie retained a dominant position. One result of this was corruption.

Following the victory of the Communist forces and the establishment of the People's Republic in October, 1949, many Party members became complacent and adopted the attitude of "eat well, sleep well, the job is finished."[38] Some of them went even further and began to exploit their official positions for personal gain. This phenomenon was not confined to new Party members; many veterans too were willing to enrich themselves by engaging in a wide variety of corrupt practices, which included the acceptance of bribes, the use of public funds for private business ventures, and the sale of public property to private individuals.

Such behavior was possible because of the general atmosphere of permissiveness which was prevalent in urban China at the time of the takeover. In the cities, and especially in Shanghai, standards of probity, as conceived by either Western or Communist observers, had been notoriously low. In part this moral deficiency had arisen because of the appalling ethics which had developed in Chinese society under the rule of the Nationalists, and it had been exacerbated by the concentration of political, social, and economic power in the hands of the groups which dominated the Republican period. Given the difficulty of survival in an environment dislocated by strife for half a century, it is not surprising that many urban dwellers had fallen into the habits of improper dealings which characterized so many of their superiors.

However, much of what the Party leadership considered corrupt had older origins. While acknowledging the onus which must be placed on the so-called "bureaucratic-compradore-capitalist mentality," we must look also at certain elements which went deep into the Chinese tradition. There was a prevalent view that an official of any level would use his office to supplement his meager salary. Added to this was the attitude, common to all societies which have strong kinship patterns,

---

[37] Quoted in Steiner, "Communist Chinese Urban Policy," p. 59.
[38] The phrase was used by Po I-po in a major statement on the need for the *san-fan* campaign. *JMJP,* January 10, 1952.

that a man fortunate enough to achieve prominence either in business or public life, would use his influence for the benefit of his kinsmen, friends, and people from his own region. The strength of such beliefs is well attested by the poignant comment of one official in the 1930's: "When I was poor I lost all my relatives and friends. When I became rich and prominent I discovered that I had scores of relatives though many of them were not within the five grades of relationship."[39]

The problem of corruption in Shanghai and other urban areas where Party cadres were working in close proximity to "bourgeois elements" was, therefore, extremely serious. To combat it the leadership organized a purge of "corrupt elements" within the Party, the bureaucracy, and in the state-operated enterprises (many of which had originally been the property of "bureaucratic-capitalists" prior to 1949). This *san-fan* (three anti) campaign—directed against corruption, waste, and bureaucracy—was launched by Kao Kang, the Party leader who controlled Manchuria, on August 31, 1951. After a "trial run" there, it spread to the rest of China in the fall of that year, and by December was being actively implemented in Shanghai.[40]

The point may be made here that there appears to have been unanimity in the highest echelons of the Party leadership concerning the need to take strict measures to stamp out corruption. Even Liu Shaoch'i, who is alleged to have argued in Tientsin that Party veterans should be given a better standard of living after the takeover of the cities, had at that time specifically forbidden them to engage in corrupt or speculative activities. Despite his "Right opportunist" views, it does not appear that he was willing to tolerate such phenomena. According to one Japanese report of his "third self-confession" of August 2, 1967, Liu has claimed that he pushed forward the *san-fan wu-fan* campaigns, and there is no reason to doubt this.[41]

The anxiety of the leadership was quite justified. Although reference was made only to "a few weak-willed cadres," who were allegedly not typical of the Party as a whole, failure to take ruthless action would have caused the disease to spread to the most upright and experienced, for a decline in standards is a feature of all revolutionary movements, and in this particular case, at least, history was on Mao's side. The dangers facing reformers operating in an environment where they constitute but a small minority has been well described by two writers

[39] Lang, *Chinese Family and Society,* p. 167.
[40] *CFJP,* December 31, 1951.
[41] *Mainichi* (The Daily), August 3, 1967, in American Consulate General (Tokyo), *Daily Summary of the Japanese Press,* August 4, 1967.

who have studied this phenomenon in underdeveloped countries, and who have identified one aspect of the problem thus:

Those who have tried to live as moral men in an amoral society have generally given way sooner or later under agonizing pressures; the pressure of legitimate ambition which can only be achieved by illegitimate means; the pressure from families insatiable for help; the slow, insidious pressures of a society in which material success is adulated, and where, moreover, material failure is ruthlessly mocked; the pressure of increasing defeatism, on realizing that public opinion stigmatizes the transgressor so lightly, and that so little seems to be gained from trying to swim against the tide.[42]

Therefore, it was necessary to do more than purge the ranks. In order to make corruption a sin and not just a crime, to inculcate new values and destroy old ones, the leadership decided to attack the bourgeoisie, for that class was regarded as the source of the antisocial and decadent attitudes of urban China. Moreover if recent reports are to be believed, some industrialists and businessmen, in Shanghai at least, were saying, "state enterprises are not qualified to lead private enterprises because the two are on an equal footing,"[43] and thereby claiming more influence than the leadership was prepared to give them.

Hence the *wu-fan* campaign was launched against those who were spreading the "five poisons." It is impossible, of course, to know how many of the many thousands who confessed were really guilty of corruption; A. Doak Barnett in his account of the *wu-fan* campaign has pointed out that the leadership regarded "large profits" as "illegal," as they involved "stealing from the people."[44] What matters is that they were accused of corruption, and the campaign to check and "purify" them successfully weakened bourgeois power, as this study of Shanghai will show.

The Dynamics of the Wu-fan Campaign in Shanghai

In any mass campaign the principal actors are "the masses," although, of course, they perform their roles under the careful guidance of the elite. To evaluate the *wu-fan* campaign, it is necessary to consider briefly the leadership's attempts to politicize the masses in Shanghai up to the end of 1951.

---

[42] R. Wraith and E. Simpkins, *Corruption in Developing Countries* (London: Allen and Unwin, 1964), p. 11.

[43] "The Defender of Capitalist Economy," *Kuang-ming Jih-pao* (Bright Daily), July 21, 1967, in *CB,* No. 836, p. 32.

[44] A. Doak Barnett, *Communist China: The Early Years, 1949–1955* (London: Pall Mall Press, 1964), p. 150.

After entering the city in May, 1949, the leadership had carried out some policies which introduced the masses to actions of a political nature. A wide range of deliberative organizations were created for the purpose of familiarizing them with the regime's policies. These gave the masses some opportunity to acquire basic political knowledge and low level training in citizenship. Apart from the consultative committees established at all levels, many people had gained direct experience from participating in the street and lane residents' committees. By December, 1951, there were 2,083 of these committees with a membership of 24,862, representing 239,000 of Shanghai's working class residents.[45] These committees had already played a part in two great movements—the campaign to resist America and aid Korea and the campaign to suppress counterrevolutionaries, which had taken place in 1951, and which provided opportunities for political involvement of a mass nature. However, they do not appear to have played a significant part in the *wu-fan* campaign.

The campaign to suppress counterrevolutionaries was important in that it introduced the populace to the processes of institutionalized violence, both physical and mental, which are essential components of the political style of the regime. In some of its aspects this campaign was a harbinger of the *san-fan* and *wu-fan* campaigns, as it depended to an extent on processes which weakened primary allegiances and introduced the urban population to ferocious "struggle." Over two thousand committees for the suppression of alleged enemies of the state were set up in Shanghai, and three thousand accusation meetings were held. Committee members helped the leadership to collect material on forty thousand cases, and the regime claimed that the masses' opinions, as revealed at public trials, were followed "for the most part" when meting out punishment. This campaign undoubtedly had some effect on raising political consciousness. P'an Han-nien, the deputy mayor of Shanghai at that time, claimed that even old people and peasant women, who had never had any interest in world affairs, had participated.[46]

The Party had also carried out a certain amount of work with two groups whose role was to be emphasized in the *wu-fan* campaign. The first of these was youth. The Party had paid particular attention to this section of the community, not only because of the propensity of the young to seek causes which enable them to destroy the institu-

---

[45] *CFJP*, December 15, 1951.
[46] *Ibid.*

tions of their elders, but because the young of all classes in Shanghai "had little experience of constructing the new society and using their own power," as a result of the previous history of the city. Therefore, an energetic attempt had been made to set up branches of the New Democratic Youth League (later renamed the Communist Youth League) in Shanghai. Within one year of "liberation" a network of 1,901 branches with a membership of over 60,000 had been established. Of these branches 258 were in factories and enterprises, and great success appears to have been achieved in schools, 76.2 per cent of which were reported to have set up branches by this time.[47]

Organization had also been extended to a considerable number of shopworkers who had been given training in tax collection work. P'an Han-nien boasted that, in the first nine months of 1951, the government's tax collection work had brought in more revenue than had been expected. He attributed this to the patriotism of the industrial and commercial world in responding to the "resist America and aid Korea" campaign. This movement had made the early or prompt payment of taxes an important element in the so-called "patriotic pacts" promoted at the time. However, a more plausible explanation may well have been the pressure exerted on the business community by the Shop Workers' Trade Union. In June, 1951, this union established organizations at all levels to help with tax collection work and recruited 20,000 cadres for this purpose. From July to November, shopworkers and employees uncovered many cases of tax evasion by employers and mobilized many employers to confess, make up their taxes, and make inventories of their merchandise. Partly because of their militant efforts, 10,805 firms had to pay considerable amounts in back taxes and fines. During this time the municipal committee of the Shop Workers' Trade Union set up classes in all districts to provide regular instruction in tax collection work. By December, 1951, some 6,000 shop workers were receiving such training.[48] No evidence on their activities in the *wu-fan* campaign has been found, but it is safe to assume that they were given "core cadre" roles in the movement.

While the activities mentioned above were important in creating a certain degree of political and organizational experience on which to base the *wu-fan* campaign, they should not be overemphasized. At the end of 1951, P'an Han-nien commented that relations between the government and the people, particularly those of the laboring classes,

[47] *Shang-hai Chieh-fang I-nien,* p. 87.
[48] *CFJP,* December 23, 1951.

were insufficiently developed, and that "various kinds of planning have been deficient because we have not tried to get the masses to participate and discuss."[49] He also admitted that some residents' committees had become unpopular because of their arrogance, and that some cadres had "left the masses."

The urban population was still for the most part uneducated as to what political functions they were to be assigned; this was particularly true of the workers, whose organization was to be one of the major elements active in the *wu-fan* campaign. For many persons, participating in mass activities must have been limited to public health campaigns and air raid precautions. Even the campaign to suppress counterrevolutionaries must be regarded as being in a different category from what was to come in 1952. It was a campaign waged entirely outside the united front, as its targets were "enemies of the people," many of whom were widely unpopular. While it must have been comparatively easy to create feelings of hatred toward many Kuomintang agents (and it must be remembered that the targets included anti-Communist guerrillas) in a period when there seemed to be the possibility of an American invasion, it was much more difficult to mobilize the population of Shanghai against its leading social group, the industrialists and businessmen. In initiating this campaign, the leadership still faced the task of creating a powerful political machine, so that the campaign could really be effective.

One of the major political problems facing the leadership was that of creating an effective propaganda network. Participation in the mass campaigns of 1950 and 1951, although of some value, had only begun to reach and affect the nonpolitical populace. Knowledge of the goals of the elite existed at a superficial level, but most of the city's inhabitants could have had little real understanding of the leadership's policies or the role they were supposed to play in implementing them.

This lack was in part due to the esoteric language used by the leadership, as was evident from descriptions of workers desperately trying to make sense of the unfamiliar vocabulary in the discussions which accompanied the meetings of "newspaper reading teams." While more educated than the rural population, the citizens of Shanghai were still of a relatively low "cultural level," as may be seen by a summary of educational statistics compiled by the Cultural Department of the Shanghai Federation of Trade Unions in 1950. These covered all employees in the city and tend to give a somewhat favorable picture of

[49] *Ibid.*, December 15, 1951.

the educational standards of the masses. They revealed that only 1.1 per cent had been educated at universities or had received other specialist training; 9.9 per cent had been to middle school; 34.5 per cent had attended elementary school; 46 per cent were illiterate; and 8.5 per cent could read but had not been to school.[50] Clearly, such widespread illiteracy must have prevented many workers from reading the Party's newspapers and pamphlets, even had they wished to do so. Hence, the ability to rely on the written word was, to say the least, limited.

The difficulty of transmitting information received a great deal of coverage in the Shanghai press from the middle of December, 1951. The deficiencies noted in these articles were not viewed solely as a hinderance to the development of the mass campaigns of the time, but rather as part of the wider problem of communication as such. Nevertheless, solving this problem was obviously significant to the *wu-fan* movement. A number of articles, moreover, stressed the necessity of relating the work of strengthening the Party's propaganda network to the tasks of the campaign, and pointed out that the propagandists were to play a vital role in transmitting information about the movement to all sections of the city's population.

From these articles it is apparent that the municipal propaganda network was neither universal nor experienced. The Party Central Committee had issued a directive on January 1, 1951, instructing all Party organizations to set up "propaganda networks." In Shanghai, 72 per cent of Party branches in factories had established such networks by October, 1951, but only 48 per cent of branches in organs, schools, and enterprises had done so. By the end of December, 1951, networks had been established by only 66 per cent of all Party branches in Shanghai. In fact, the Party's performance compared unfavorably with that of the Youth League. The league had the responsibility of setting up networks in places where it had its own basic level organizations, but where Party branches had not been established. Of such places 70 per cent had set up networks.[51]

Not only were the propagandists distributed unevenly, but they were also numerically weak, with only 15,311 members in the entire city. If the population of Shanghai in 1951 is taken as 5,000,000 (it was officially stated to be "over" this figure), this gives at best a ratio of one propagandist to 326 people. This appears to have been near the

---

[50] *Shang-hai Chieh-fang I-nien,* p. 79.
[51] *CFJP,* December 12, 25, 1951.

national average, as official sources claimed that there were 1,550,000. propagandists in China by October, 1951. However, it was considerably less than that of some rural areas in the East China region, the best of which, like Fushan *hsien* (county) in Shantung, had a ratio of one propagandist to 40 people.[52]

In addition, the quality of the propagandists was not particularly high. Only 32 per cent were Party members, and 40 per cent came from the Youth League, while the remaining 28 per cent had been recruited from the masses. One particular stumbling block to the effectiveness of the propagandists may well have been the fact that they shared the high degree of illiteracy common to the general population. No direct figure has been found for Shanghai, but the Party East China Bureau's Propaganda Department reported that only half of their 650,000 propagandists had been to elementary school "or higher" schools, while half were illiterate or semiliterate.[53] Despite the higher cultural levels of the towns, in view of the rather loose definitions of literacy used by the leadership, it seems that many of Shanghai's propagandists could not read. The Party was, therefore, attempting to transmit information through a core of "specialists" which included many who themselves had difficulty in reading and understanding the official pronouncements.

The newspapers contained numerous references to the prevalence of "formalism" in the propaganda network, evidence of the fact that although recruitment had been carried out in accordance with the Central Committee's instructions, those taken into the ranks had received little training. The ineffectiveness of some propagandists is shown by a statement of the Shanghai Party Committee's Propaganda Department that (of a sample of 7,234 propagandists), only "55% were acting comparatively positively and could usually be effective."[54] The East China Bureau admitted that many propagandists had failed to be effective because they had not been recruited with care, they had not been given education after recruitment, and "leadership had been laid aside." As a consequence, it is not surprising that the leadership complained that "erroneous ideas" persisted among the masses.

To solve these problems, the leadership emphasized several measures which had been introduced earlier and were now to be made universal. These were embodied in the "Party Responsibility System,"

---

[52] *Ibid.*, December 19, 23, 25, 1951.
[53] *Ibid.*, December 12, 19, 1951.
[54] *Ibid.*, December 12, 1951.

which was introduced in all Party committees and branches at the end of 1951. In essence this system required that all Party committees should pay more attention to the management of the propaganda network, and spend more time in regular discussion and summarizing of its activities. For purposes of liaison, municipal and *ch'ü* Party committees were to call frequent meetings of propagandists, and also of branch secretaries, so as to keep the propagandists in close touch with Party policy. Some *ch'ü* had already carried out such work and were praised for this, as in the case of Chiangning *ch'ü,* where eighteen meetings of branch secretaries and thirteen conferences of the *ch'ü* propagandists had been held during the fall. At meetings of this sort, the Party leadership insisted, reports on the current situation should be given by the Party committee secretaries or by the chiefs of propaganda departments.[55]

Party committees were also instructed to give more attention to the "nurturing" and training of propagandists, and this was to consist of both political education and training in "professional" techniques. Such instruction could be given either by special "propaganda training squads" or by admitting propagandists to the night schools run by the Party and to lectures given by Party branches. "Material" for propagandists was made the responsibility of the *ch'ü* committees, which were to issue propaganda handbooks, current affairs guides, and specially duplicated sheets of propaganda themes, as well as volumes of study documents. Documentary assistance was not always effective, however, and it was felt "by all *ch'ü* committees that these articles were often inappropriate for the propagandists' level."[56] This, presumably, was a reflection of many propagandists' inability to cope with the written word.

As a result of the introduction of the "Party Responsibility System," the propagandists were reformed to some extent and were made a more effective force with which to wage the *wu-fan* campaign, in which they "enhanced their role still further." While most propagandists were relatively inexperienced, mention may be made of the propaganda elite, the "reporters," of whom there were 256 by the end of December, 1951. These were mainly members of Party committees who confined their activities to addressing large gatherings, usually on specific occasions such as the Chinese New Year celebrations. They were generally responsible for "making the masses understand completely the political

[55] *Ibid.*
[56] *Ibid.*

opinions of the Party in a specific period, and for leading the propagandists to carry out their work."[57]

Propaganda tasks were not confined to propagandists alone but were the duty of all, especially senior cadres in all organs, who were instructed to take an active part in working out ideas for propaganda articles, and to organize and lead all cadres to read and study the relevant documents.[58] As will be discussed later, propaganda was also carried on extensively by all mass organizations, especially trade unions.

Pre-eminent among the features which characterized the style of propaganda during the *wu-fan* campaign was the stress placed on simple methods of work and personal contact. Individual propagandists were encouraged to confine their activities to a small number of people. In this way they could come to know them well, gain their confidence, and acquire understanding of their particular ideological problems. Together with this insistence on the development of face-to-face relationships between the propagandists and the masses, emphasis was placed on specialization in the choice of propaganda tools. Propagandists were to confine their activities to developing expertise in one medium, such as "blackboard newspapers" or directing a newspaper reading team. Generally speaking, the masses received most of their instruction by means of examples which were within the compass of their own experience.

Having laid the basis for the development of effective communication between the elite and the masses, the Party established a leadership organization for the *wu-fan* campaign on December 27, 1951. This was the Shanghai Increase Production and Practice Economy (IPPE) Committee; it had the specific function of controlling the processes of propaganda and inspection, and the handling of cases.[59] It is useful to

[57] *Ibid.,* December 12, 25, 1951.

[58] *Ibid.,* December 30, 1951.

[59] The biographical data for this section of the paper are taken from: Kasumigaseki-kai, *Gendai Chugoku Jimmei Jiten* (Biographical Dictionary of Contemporary China) (Tokyo: Konan Shoin, 1966); *Who's Who in Communist China* (Hong Kong: Union Research Institute, 1966); occasional references in Hua Ming, *San-fan Wu-fan ti P'ou-shih* (Analysis of the San-fan Wu-fan Campaigns) (Hong Kong: Yu-lien Ch'u-pan She, 1952); and *CFJP.* In addition, D. W. Klein of Columbia University very kindly permitted me to use his biographical files on the leadership. I am particularly indebted to him for providing me with biographies he has prepared on six members of the committee. However, these sources do not provide full details of all members of the committee. Some members are not mentioned at all, and in other cases there is no information on activities prior to 1949. Nevertheless, where data are available (as in the case of those members mentioned in this paper), they are consistent in indicating that the committee members were often men who had experience in dealing with urban problems.

examine the membership of this body, which had P'an Han-nien as director and Sheng P'i-hua and Liu Ch'ang-sheng as deputy directors (plus forty-six members).[60]

An analysis of the limited biographical data available on some of these men reveals certain features of interest and importance. It may be noted that many of them appear to have had considerable knowledge of the Shanghai area. Of the seventeen whose place of birth is known, fifteen were natives of East China, including seven from Chekiang and four from Kiangsu. At least eleven committee members had worked in Shanghai for long periods before 1949, as students, teachers, businessmen, and underground workers for the Party.

This last-named group is particularly significant. The saga of the Long March and Yenan communism has tended to obscure the existence of the Communist movement in urban China. Although the overwhelming majority of Party members at the time of the takeover were of peasant background, devoid of urban skills, there was a small group of Party leaders who had worked in the cities. Some of these men were on the IPPE Committee. Liu Ch'ang-sheng, for example, had joined the Party in 1928. In 1937 he was sent to Shanghai; he spent the period from 1937 to 1945 working in the Party underground in that city, and he also worked in districts nearby which were under the control of the Communist New Fourth Army. After the war he worked as an official on the Shanghai Party Committee and was a labor organizer.

Liu Hsiao, a Hunanese, had worked in Shanghai as early as 1927, when he helped to organize the Communist-led opposition to the warlord control of the city. He had then worked as a Party operative among the salt workers outside of Shanghai, and had been imprisoned twice for his activities. He took part in the Long March, but after the outbreak of the Sino-Japanese War, he returned to Kiangsu and worked in the Party underground. By 1942 he was secretary of the Kiangsu Provincial Party Committee. He operated in Shanghai after the war and was serving as the secretary of the Shanghai Party Committee by 1947.

[60] The members were: Chang Ti-hsiang, Chao Hsien, Chao P'u-ch'u, Chao Tsu-K'ang, Ch'en Jen-ping, Ch'en Yü-sun, Chiang Yung, Chin Chung-hua, Ching Shu-p'ing, Chu Chün-hsiu, Chu Ju-yen, Fang Hsing, Han Hsi-ya, Han Hsüeh-chang, Hsia Yen, Hsü xxx xxx [text illegible], Hsü Ti-hsin, Hu Chüeh-wen, Hu Ju-ting, Jung I-jen, Ku Chün, Lin Li, Li Yü, Liu Hsiao, Lu Kuang, Lü Chen-chung, Ma Hsiao-ti, P'eng Wen-ying, Shen Chih-yüan, Shen Han, Shen Yin-mo, Sheng K'ang-nien, Tai Pai-tao, T'ang Kuei-fen, Ts'ao Man-chih, Wang Hsing-yao, Wang Liang, Wang Yao-shan, Wang Yü-hsien, Wu Chen-shan, Wu Hsüeh-chou, Wu Juo-an, Yang Kuang-ch'ih, Yang Yen-hsiu, Yeh Chin-ming, Yen O-sheng. *CFJP,* December 29, 1951.

Hsü Ti-hsin, who had studied at Futan University and was a graduate of the Shanghai College of Commerce, had also been an underground worker for the Party and had operated in and around Shanghai from 1933 until 1935. (It is also possible that at least three other members of the IPPE Committee may have worked in Shanghai as labor organizers before 1949. Han Hsi-ya, for example, was deputy chairman of the Shop Workers' Trade Union by 1951, while Ma Hsiao-ti and Shen Han were to appear as holders of responsible positions in the Shanghai trade union movement by 1955. However, this must remain speculative, as no details of their activities before 1949 are known, and it is not clear if they were Party members at the time.)

In addition to this group of Communists who had been trained in urban work, the leadership could also rely on the services of a number of prominent non-Communists. In his *Report* of March 5, 1949, Mao had instructed the Party to "develop" a group of non-Communist personages who had prestige and would be of use in the cities. In Shanghai at least this policy appears to have met with some success. A number of leading citizens, no doubt for a wide variety of motives, were willing to cooperate with the leadership.

Of special interest is the presence of a number of leading industrialists and businessmen on the IPPE Committee. The most important of these was Sheng P'i-hua, a native of Ningpo. Sheng had started his career as an apprentice but had risen steadily in the business world and eventually founded the Shangyüan Enterprise Company, which he was managing at this time. An outstanding patriot, he had been active in boycotting Japanese goods in the 1930's and had given time and money in support of anti-Japanese movements after 1937. Following the Sino-Japanese War, he became dissatisfied with the Nationalist regime and assisted Communist-instigated movements directed against the civil war, during which he permitted Communists to meet secretly on the premises of his firm. Since 1945 he had been director of the Shanghai branch of the China National Democratic Association.

Not all businessmen on the committee were "self-made" men; Jung I-jen, for example, was a second-generation millionaire.[61] A native of Wusih, he held important managerial positions in both the Shen Hsin Cotton Mills and the Fu Hsin Flour Company. Ching Shu-p'ing, Hu Chüeh-wen, and Sheng K'ang-nien were also men who possessed industrial and commercial experience and who knew Shanghai. Chao P'u-ch'u, who had been engaged in business in Shanghai since 1937,

[61] *New York Times,* January 2, 1966.

was one of China's most prominent lay Buddhists, and had been active in philanthropic and welfare work.

A number of committee members, both Communists and non-Communists, were "intellectuals." Chiang Yung, Ch'en Jen-ping, Shen Chih-yüan, and Shen Yin-mo were university or college professors, while Wu Hsüeh-chou was a distinguished scientist.

Chin Chung-hua and Hsia Yen had both worked at editing and writing, and Hsü Ti-hsin was a specialist in economic affairs.

The committee members were well placed in their relationships to the power structure of Shanghai, and represented all relevant sections of the Shanghai elite. At least thirty held government office at the municipal level. Two were deputy mayors, nine were directors, and three were deputy directors of municipal government bureaus, while three were chairmen and two were vice-chairman of committees of the municipal government. The secretary-general, two deputy secretaries-general, and eight members of the municipal People's Government Committee were members of the IPPE Committee also. Specialists in economic affairs and in inspection work were well represented by ten members of the municipal Economics and Finance Committee and five from the People's Supervision Committee. Some members held posts in the procuracy, trade unions, and the propaganda network.

Finally, Li Yü (secretary-general), Liu Hsiao (second secretary), Liu Ch'ang-sheng (third secretary), and P'an Han-nien (member of the standing committee) provided a close link with the municipal Party Committee. The IPPE Committee was, then, formidable in terms of power, status, and knowledge of the area. This was the cohesive and determined body that made possible the destruction of the status of the Shanghai bourgeoisie.

When the *wu-fan* campaign started, initial measures were taken to try to put pressure on the bourgeoisie through their own business organizations. The most important instrument of the campaign in this respect was the Shanghai Federation of Industry and Commerce, the preparatory committee of which had been established as early as August, 1949.[62] By 1952 it was obligatory for all heads of private business firms to be members.[63] This organization was responsible for communicating the leadership's wishes to the business community, and for supervising the business community's implementation of government policy. While the Executive and Supervisory Committee which

[62] *Shang-hai Chieh-fang I-nien*, p. 101.
[63] Barnett, *Communist China*, p. 144.

controlled it was composed largely of businessmen, many of these men also occupied positions of responsibility in the municipal government, and some Party members participated.

The federation played an extremely important part in the early stages of the *wu-fan* movement, which it began to help implement on January 12, when Sheng P'i-hua, its deputy director, addressed the business community on the need to wipe out the "poisons" of the old society and create a "new society of virtue." After noting that corruption was worse in Shanghai than in Peking, Sheng concentrated on the theme of the "two faces" of the bourgeoisie. He acknowledged the class's contribution to the campaign to resist America and aid Korea, but accused its members of merely looking after their own selfish interests and indulging in speculation. He reminded businessmen that the *san-fan* campaign had revealed the extent of collusion between corrupt cadres and unscrupulous capitalists.[64]

Four days later at an enlarged meeting of representatives of the Shanghai business world it was decided to set up a *wu-fan* committee for the federation; this, in turn, was to supervise inspection committees, offices, and branch committees on the basis of every occupation and *ch'ü.*[65] The businessmen were then divided into teams for small group discussion designed to rid them of their apprehensions and to foster the feeling that this campaign was the proper path for business development in accordance with the Common Program.

The federation's *wu-fan* committee itself was set up on January 17, 1952, and was closely controlled by the Shanghai IPPE Committee; its director was Sheng P'i-hua, and of his five deputies, three (Hu Chüeh-wen, Jung I-jen, and Wang Hsing-yao) were also members of the municipal IPPE Committee.[66] The committee instructed members of branch committees in each *ch'ü* to attack corrupt practices in every business, and also ordered their members to carry out "self-examination" and organize mutual inspections.[67]

The purpose of "self-examination" was, of course, to soften the business community by setting an example, and it was pursued with vigor by the leadership. Occasionally the offenses admitted were quite serious. For example, Hu Chüeh-wen, a leading figure in People's

[64] *CFJP,* January 13, 1952.
[65] *Ibid.,* January 16, 1952.
[66] *Ibid.,* January 18, 1952. This was actually a *sze-fan* (four anti) committee, but it changed its name a few days later.
[67] *Ibid.,* January 19, 1952.

Supervision, admitted that he had stolen "state economic secrets," and had improperly passed to his own firm information to the effect that the government intended to place large orders for machine tools. This had caused a rise in the prices of metal goods in Shanghai. Most of the "self-examinations" of businessmen, however, consisted of admitting less important sins. Thus Jung I-jen confessed that he had sold the Shanghai Municipal Cotton Cloth Company one thousand bales of yarn in December, 1949, and had failed to complete the order until the fall of 1951.[68]

The personal lead taken by these businessmen, who had been given the job of mobilizing their fellows, had only a limited effect. Although a certain number of others came forward to confess at that time, their confessions were considered inadequate in the Communists' eyes. The case of Yang Shu-fang was typical of many. This leading businessman, who was deputy director of the Electrical Equipment Industry Trade Association, made a self-examination of his own "profiteering ideology." However, while admitting his failings, he explained that his actions had been motivated by the desire to accumulate capital in order to expand production.[69]

Although it rapidly became apparent that most capitalists were not going to assist willingly in the leadership's bid to destroy their status, the federation was able to weaken the business community to some extent by means of its disciplinary powers. It could and did remove members from some of the positions through which they derived respect in the community. One example was the case of Chu P'ei-nung, a senior figure in the Min Feng and Hua Feng Paper Manufacturing Mills, who was accused of having committed serious tax evasion, and who had refused to take an active role in the campaign. In this instance the federation decided to terminate his membership on its Executive and Supervisory Committee, and he was also deprived of his deputy directorship in the Paper Industry Trade Association.[70]

The leadership, however, continued to encounter considerable resistance. While official claims of the "wild attack of the bourgeoisie" were somewhat exaggerated, frequent references to the fixing of "offensive and defensive alliances" should be taken more seriously. This charge was hammered home in a plethora of articles in the newspapers, and

[68] Hua, *San-fan Wu-fan,* p. 64.
[69] *Ibid.,* p. 65.
[70] *Ibid.*

had a central place in most major speeches. Rather than confess to real
or imagined transgressions, it is clear that many businessmen resorted
to "all sorts of tricks" to resist the leadership's attack.

At a meeting of the Shanghai People's Government Committee,
Sheng P'i-hua claimed that the federation had carried out initial work
and that seven thousand letters of denunciation and confession had
been received. He admitted, however, that many confessions "evaded
the difficult and took the easy [path]." He complained that many
unlawful businessmen were attempting either to flee or to resist. Some
continued to postpone confession and to "wait and see," while others
were guilty of intimidating their employees by the use of lockouts,
threats, and abuse. Han Hsi-ya, a trade unionist, noted that, in addition, some employers were using such methods as "leading the workers
astray," making false accusations, using beautiful women to ensnare
activists, and spreading rumors.[71] Han's claim that such shameful
conspiracies were always foiled because of the workers' firm class
standpoint could not be reconciled with the remarks just made by
Sheng, who had observed that these plots were "a serious obstacle" to
the movement's development.

Both men were commenting on a state of affairs which the leadership
was in the process of rectifying. On February 4, 1952, the municipal
government had published four regulations to deal with the problems.[72]
These decreed that managers, deputy managers, and senior officials in
private firms were not to leave their enterprises. Firms were forbidden
to go out of business, dismiss employees, withhold the supply of wages
or reduce them, withhold rations, reduce annual payments, or fix alliances with employees in state enterprises who had taken bribes. In
firms which had committed such offenses during the campaign, the
status quo ante was to be restored, and full restitution made to those
employees who had suffered. Furthermore, no one was to be penalized
for attending meetings called by the unions (presumably during working time). The factor of complicity in illicit dealings, which so complicated relationships in Shanghai's commercial world, and which was an
obstacle to the development of straightforward class struggle, was also
considered. Those employees who had been involved in unlawful acts
instigated by their employers were told that they would not be investigated themselves if they were prepared to denounce their employers.

[71] *CFJP*, February 6, 1952. The most commonly spread rumors at this time were (1)
the Americans would invade and Chiang Kai-shek would return, and (2) all classes were
to be purged in turn.

[72] *Ibid.*, February 4, 1952.

These were the leadership's initial attempts to deal directly with the bourgeoisie. The Communist Party also put great stress on the mobilization of the workers. In January and February an intensive campaign was mounted to induct the masses into active participation. While all enterprises, shops, and factories were affected by this process, the main target was the two hundred thousand shopworkers who formed just under 20 per cent of the city's employees; the Shop Workers' Trade Union was represented on the Shanghai IPPE Committee by Han Hsi-ya, its deputy chairman.

In order to weaken the relationship between employer and employed, the federation initiated a widespread denunciation movement. The first step in this direction was the convening of a meeting on January 21, 1952, which was attended by over one thousand shopworker cadres of the level of *ch'ü* "big team" chiefs and above who were themselves assigned the task of general mobilization. Ku Chün, a leading figure in tax collection work, addressed the meeting and stressed that shopworkers were to become absolutely certain of where their loyalties should lie. They were, he said, to gain a deep understanding of the nature of their own class and of the ways in which it differed from the bourgeoisie. Ku promised that the government would protect the workers should their employers attempt to intimidate them. Han Hsi-ya's speech attacked unlawful capitalists who coerced, led astray, or swindled union members, and called on all present to penetrate to the "basic levels," unite closely with the masses, and assuage their anxieties.[73]

The Shop Workers' Trade Union set up its own *wu-fan* committee with Han Hsi-ya as its director, and under its leadership *ch'ü* cadres began to establish branch committees and to hold a series of meetings for union members. Trade union cadres were ordered to "stand in the front line of the struggle," while young shopworkers were instructed to develop a "vanguard role" under the direction of its Youth League, and to mobilize older workers to take part in the campaign. Employees with some specialized knowledge of their firms, such as old shopworkers and accountants, were ordered to place their experience at the disposal of the government's tax collection personnel.[74]

Mass mobilization of the shopworkers was achieved by subjecting them to a series of daily meetings organized by the 2,000 basic organizations of the union in Shanghai. By February 7, 3,000 meetings had

[73] *Ibid.,* January 22, 1952.
[74] *Ibid.,* January 24, 1952.

taken place, attended by over 160,000 people. The union's *wu-fan* committee exercised strict control over the mobilization process at this stage. Thus, when a particularly important meeting of shopworkers' representatives was scheduled for February 7, 20 cadres were sent to *ch'ü* level to "assist" in the election of delegates, while *ch'ü* cadres themselves were sent to all basic organizations to help with this work. The insistence on close leadership even led Wan Ch'i-t'ing, deputy director of the *Wu-fan* Committee, to go to "direct the battle" in Laocha *ch'ü* in person.[75]

The meeting of February 7 was the largest and most crucial of the early period of the campaign, and was attended by thirty-six hundred union delegates. The emotional atmosphere was heightened by many dramaturgical techniques, such as employees marching in squads, bearing banners and beating kettle drums. In the case of the Laocha *ch'ü* delegation, a wooden cannon was displayed to demonstrate the employees' ferocity in "striking tigers."[76] The meeting was broadcast (a technique originating in Tientsin during the campaign to suppress counterrevolutionaries), and listeners sent letters or made telephone calls guaranteeing to help. Common forms of expressing personal commitment involved promises to transmit the meeting's "spirit" to shopworkers, offers to sign *wu-fan* "patriotic pacts," and the launching of a movement for "one denunciation per man."[77]

The leadership extended the movement organizationally by insisting that all "basic levels" of the union should set up their own branch committees and inspection centers. In a major speech Han Hsi-ya demanded that all shopworkers participate in the campaign, that there should be competitions in denouncing employers, and that unlawful capitalists be dealt with "trade by trade, firm by firm, level by level."[78] The process of creating the complex organizational structure of union *wu-fan* committees had taken only eighteen days.

Following the creation of suitable organizational forms, unceasing propaganda was directed at both employers and shopworkers. Violent psychological pressure played an important part at this stage of the campaign, which was designed to promote both denunciation and confession. The roles allocated to the activists involved were characterized by a high degree of specialization and were specifically localized; the targets were chosen with great care. It is useful here to consider the

[75] *Ibid.,* January 24, February 1, 7, 8, 1952.
[76] Hua, *San-fan Wu-fan,* p. 63.
[77] *CFJP,* February 8, 1952.
[78] Hua, *San-fan Wu-fan,* p. 64.

experiences of a "big team" of shopworkers employed in the metal industry of Laocha *ch'ü*. This is the most detailed case which has been found exemplifying the activities of the workers in the early period of the *wu-fan* campaign.[79]

The team's first problem was that of "choosing the tigers' den." It was necessary to find a group of capitalists who were particularly vulnerable, and whose cases would be of high "educational value." This team was located in the Manyinfang district, where metal shops were most numerous, and where the proprietors frequently took bribes, swindled, speculated, and made "excessive" profits. The team felt that "tigers" were most concentrated there and so focused on that area.

The next step was to "break through the mental block" caused by team members' fears—that they would be dismissed if they denounced their employers, that they would lose face with the employers to whom they were related, and that those of them who "did not have clean hands and feet" would "draw fire on themselves" by denouncing others. To overcome these difficulties, the team's work cadres, with the assistance of representatives from the *ch'ü* committee, used various methods of talking informally with those who were hesitant. Those who feared unemployment were told about the cases of others who had actively denounced their employers and who had been protected by the government. Those who feared that the capitalists would take revenge were reassured by the cadres, who told them of a case involving a proprietor in Hankow who was executed for harming his employees. Those who felt that denunciations would hurt feelings and would constitute a "loss of virtue" were regaled with stories of relatives denouncing each other. Reassurance was also given to those who had engaged in criminal activity by emphasizing that their past sins were the fault of the employers.

Thereafter the team moved on to the stage of "setting up Battle Headquarters in Manyinfang." Here, with a core of local trade union members, five departments were organized to receive material, and to be responsible for propaganda, liaison, planning, and broadcasting. This local command structure and the functional specialization of its members made it "possible to develop everyone's talents and expand work in an organized way."

Broadcasting was emphasized in the fourth stage, and it was then that the pressure was really applied to the capitalists. Those cadres responsible for broadcasting were praised for their clarity in listing the

[79] *CFJP,* February 10, 1952.

crimes of the accused. They gave examples of the passing off of old goods as new and bad goods as perfect, and of the sale of cheap goods at higher prices. Tax avoidance was revealed, and so were the methods by which the employers had led the cadres astray. During the broadcasts, a temporary "reception office" was set up to assist those making denunciations. Among the "many concrete problems" dealt with by this office were those which involved "enlightening those whose information on cases of unlawfulness was not clear," helping those who did not know how to denounce others, and (of the utmost importance) making provision to record the denunciations of illiterates.

In the fifth stage, which concentrated on the organization of an "effective propaganda battle," it was claimed that old (and presumably unsatisfactory) methods were avoided; thirteen blackboards were used to convey pointed messages, such as "you can fly over the sea but you cannot fly from the great fist of the people." Posters bearing the number of denunciation letters received were carried to all corners of the district, accompanied by a cadre ringing a hand bell. Well aware for whom the bell was tolling, unlawful business proprietors became concerned as the statistics of denunciations mounted steadily. One proprietor who had already confessed to his trade association ran to the "reception office" and confessed again. Others looked at their accounts, examined themselves, and went to the *ch'ü*'s tax bureau to confess.

The final stage was designed to ensure that those running the campaign had reached everyone concerned by "thoroughly visiting and getting rid of the blank spots." Small teams were set up to go from door to door, size up the situation in each shop, and begin to carry out propaganda and mobilization among employees in the shops which had not yet produced confessions. These teams heard the opinions of the shopworkers and asked if they had any difficulties. Most problems encountered were solved on the spot, but particularly complicated issues were handled with the assistance of the "reception office."

By these methods the businessmen of Manyinfang were exposed to the puritan ethics of the leadership, and the masses received experience of participating in mass activities. While it is virtually impossible to evaluate the effectiveness of such processes, some idea of the destruction of personal relationships in Manyinfang may be gauged by the fact that, by February 8, Laocha *ch'ü* had received eighteen thousand letters of denunciation as the result of this campaign.

Two very effective methods of communication used in the *wu-fan* campaign were the "broadcasting stations," mentioned above, and the newspaper reading teams. The "broadcasting stations" were established to communicate directly with people, orally, because of the low level of literacy found among the working class. These stations were merely loudspeaker systems set up at street corners, where they broadcast continually, often going through the night. The extent of penetration achieved by this method may be seen in the number operating in various *ch'ü*. Peichan had twenty-five, Laocha twenty-seven, Hungk'ou twenty-eight, Luwan twenty-six, Chiangwan thirty-nine, Hsinch'eng seventeen, Chapei twenty-seven, and Sungshan nineteen.[80] Great successes were claimed for this simple, inexpensive, and ubiquitous system. An article extolling the effectiveness of the thirty-seven stations of Huangp'u *ch'ü* claimed that their broadcasts had developed a "face to face" struggle with many unlawful businessmen who, because of "strong pressure," had become apprehensive and confessed. At the same time, exposure to this propaganda activity gave the shopworkers "education" and raised higher their "love of struggle."[81]

In explaining the principles for organizing the stations, the same article emphasized the division of labor which was so marked in this campaign. Generally, each station had two chiefs, one to look after policy and propaganda material, the other to lead and organize the "material collectors" and "liaison personnel." Five or six "reporters" handled the actual broadcasting, and three or four "editors" fitted material together and supplied the contents of propaganda. An additional two cadres were responsible for liaison with the *ch'ü* station.

The newspaper reading teams were designed, in part, to make the best use of newspapers by providing organizational units in which those who were literate read out the news to those who were not. These teams were set up by the trade unions of every *ch'ü* with the assistance of the propagandists, and were widely used during the *wu-fan* campaign. At first they were not always successful. An account of one team in Laocha *ch'ü* stressed that initially many people felt that reading newspapers was a chore, and was of little interest; people also resented the compulsory discussions which took place after reading sessions, in which their ignorance was revealed. A propagandist had to be sent to the team to clear up difficulties, and he blamed adverse reactions on the lack of "liveliness" in meetings. There were long discussions on why newspapers should be read, and the team members were taught that

[80] Hua, *San-fan Wu-fan*, p. 61.
[81] *CFJP*, February 10, 1952.

reading not only raised political consciousness but was also useful for solving problems related to concrete work. Eventually interest was reportedly kindled, and more and more people participated.[82]

Once such troubles were overcome, the importance of the newspaper reading teams became evident. An account of their activities was published in the form of a letter from the shopworkers of the Hsinch'eng branch of the union. This letter gave details of one of their "basic level" organization's experience with these teams. It was claimed that only five reading teams had been set up in this organization by the start of the *wu-fan* campaign. Through participation in the movement, however, the union members had their ideological consciousness raised, came to realize the importance of reading newspapers, and set up four more newspaper reading teams, bringing the total of those participating to ninety. Two of these teams held daily reading sessions, and the other seven met every other day. It was claimed that all were trying to find ways of increasing the amount of time spent on these activities. The paper read by teams was the *Chieh-fang Jih-pao* (Liberation Daily), "because we know it is the Party paper and the paper of the working class." Apart from serving as a forum for the discussion of policy as revealed in the newspapers, these teams were also used as units for organizing people to listen to broadcasts.[83]

Those who were members of such teams claimed that they obtained a wider picture of what was happening than those who were not, and it is evident that this was a significant step toward destroying the "isolation" of the workers from the elite. Consider the story of Chang Shih-chou, who wrote to the press of the benefits he had gained. He worked as an accountant in a firm owned by one of his relatives who, "from time to time, did small favors" for him. Although the proprietor was guilty of "criminal activities," Chang found himself "confused in class standpoint" because of his relationship, and held back from denouncing.

He began to read newspapers, however, and saw that the *wu-fan* movement was a vigorous struggle of a class nature; he read many accounts of children who denounced their fathers, brothers who denounced brothers, and wives who denounced husbands. As a result he began to question his own inaction and considered denouncing his relative, but he held back at the last moment because of "sentimen-

---

[82] *Ibid.*, April 5, 1952.
[83] *Ibid.*, March 30, 1952.

talism." Chang then joined a reading team and, he said, found enlightenment in many small group discussions. He felt that if he did not "rise up" he would be responsible for causing harm to the revolutionary task. Chang's resentment increased when he thought of how his capitalist relative was damaging his "working class standpoint," and he therefore denounced him. His success in winning his ideological struggle was, Chang claimed, "entirely due to reading newspapers."[84] The use of these teams, and the small group discussions which accompanied them, enabled individual problems to be handled in some depth, and there is no reason to doubt that such problems were often solved to the leadership's satisfaction.

All *ch'ü* carried out the work of organizing these teams. On March 30, it was reported that in Huangp'u *ch'ü* 1,706 were functioning for shopworkers alone, and there were 900 in Sungshan. In Hsinch'eng *ch'ü* 50 per cent of the shopworkers were members, and in Laocha one-third were reached in this way.[85]

Between January and March these techniques were applied to all sections of the community. It was claimed later that by February 20 the Shanghai Federation of Trade Unions had received 210,000 denunciations.[86] This figure may well inflate the number of people involved, as some people made denunciations more than once (one young shopworker of Laocha did so 80 times). Nevertheless, it reveals that the masses were being induced to show their activism by involving themselves in a process which demonstrated their acceptance of the regime's demand that they destroy old ties and acquire new loyalties and values very different from those to which they had previously subscribed. The main purpose of this stage of the campaign, apart from intimidating employers, was to transmit information to the masses, enlist their support, and acquire a considerable amount of information from them as to the "concrete situation" in the enterprises, factories, and shops in which they worked. The actual inspection of business enterprises was not carried out very intensively at this time; it was left largely to the properly designated officials, whose personnel was still limited, and there was little attempt to use the masses for the relatively skilled job of investigation. The main function of the masses was to make denunciations of a general nature. At times, as will be mentioned later, the

[84] *Ibid.*
[85] *Ibid.*
[86] *Ibid.*, May 21, 1952.

masses took it upon themselves to investigate their employers "in depth," but this was unsatisfactory, in view of their lack of training, and was frowned upon by the leadership.

Despite the vigorous measures taken by the leadership, the campaign did not reputedly result in speedy "victories" for them, partly because of the initial refusal of the bourgeoisie to be intimidated by the process of denunciation, and partly because of the existence of "rightist thought." The latter term referred to the tendency of many workers to ignore corrupt behavior, underestimate the skill of criminals, and show a lack of initiative and political awareness. While some businessmen were terrorized, a great many were not, and were presumably deriving some degree of hope from the fact that the masses did not respond as speedily or thoroughly as the leadership would have wished.

The patterns of action which the leadership was attempting to stimulate were being absorbed but slowly by the masses. However, from regulations which the leadership published the following month, it is clear that in some places where mass action had been successfully initiated, it was getting out of control. It appears that there was an excessive degree of "democracy" on some occasions, as workers took it upon themselves to initiate their own inspections, make their own arrests, and use a greater degree of brutality than the leadership deemed necessary.

Attempts to exert greater control began when the municipal IPPE Committee took steps to train really effective cadres for the campaign. From the middle of March each *ch'ü* held training classes and detached or transferred twelve thousand cadres and activists of "basic units," who were given instruction in class concepts and discipline. Some ten thousand of these cadres were formed into elite *"wu-fan* inspection brigades" and operated under the direction of the Shanghai IPPE Committee. About two thousand of these men were not, in fact, workers, but had been recruited from every organ in the city and, significantly, from army units. It was also stated that the brigades included cadres who had come from outside Shanghai to investigate *san-fan* material.[87]

In their training program, it was stressed that the *wu-fan* campaign was to be related to production. While the leadership claimed that this had always been a cardinal principle of the campaign, this was evidently not the case, and in earlier periods it had been noted that cadres had left their jobs in order to carry out mobilization activities.

[87] *Ibid.,* March 27, May 21, 1952.

These brigades were given a "trial run" between March 21 and March 24, when seventy-four of them were sent out to "test key points." The brigades were given ample time to study all the material which had been collected on a number of "seriously law-breaking" establishments, and inspection was furthered by "relying on workers, shop workers, and senior employees." This stage constituted a distinct shift of emphasis from the first months of the campaign, because now the leadership was actually "penetrating" factories, enterprises, and shops about which it already had gained some degree of knowledge from the denunciations of the earlier period. Moreover, the process was now more sophisticated, as emphasis was placed on securing the cooperation of senior employees, such as accountants and private secretaries, whose knowledge of the complex transgressions of their employers was obviously greater than that of the workers.

Direct action was forbidden by eight regulations which were announced on March 25; five of these were concerned solely with keeping the workers from carrying out their own unofficial inspections. No one was permitted to enter any factory, shop, or other enterprise, for the purpose of carrying out inspection work, without the express permission of the Shanghai (or *ch'ü*) IPPE Committee, without having prepared formal evidence, and without an armband of a *wu-fan* inspection brigade. The masses were to confine their activities to denunciations and were forbidden to take upon themselves the task of investigating capitalists unless authorized to do so by the IPPE committees. Similarly, the right to arrest and to deliver summonses was restricted to members of the public security apparatus and legal organs, who alone had the right to recover "plunder," block bank accounts, "take assets into custody," or confiscate property. The regulations stated that torture was not permitted; they also instructed all personnel to abide strictly by the orders of higher levels and to carry out conscientiously the "system of asking for instructions." These regulations revealed the partial inadequacy of the earlier instructions issued on February 4; it was now necessary to reiterate that capitalists were "not to resist, run away or avoid the main points of the question."[88]

In fact, it was largely because of bourgeois intransigeance that this extremely well-planned phase of the campaign was begun. On March 25, Ch'en I addressed a meeting of the municipal and *ch'ü* IPPE committees and announced the formal opening of the *wu-fan* campaign, an event which must have come as a considerable surprise to

[88] *Ibid.,* March 26, 1952.

those who had been involved in it for almost three months. One writer
has suggested that the reason for the leadership's action in prolonging
and intensifying the campaign at this stage was that industrialists and
businessmen had failed to surrender their capital, the acquisition of
which was certainly one of the major economic aims of the campaign.[89]
This is probably true; but it is also evident that the desired political
aims of the campaign were still not wholly satisfied.

Wang Yün-sheng, the chief editor of the *Ta Kung Pao* (Impartial
Daily), in an article of particular ferocity (entitled "Tear Down the
Defences of the Bourgeoisie of Shanghai"), revealed that the leadership still feared the potential of the Shanghai bourgeoisie. He warned
that the unlawful businessmen of the city were regarding the campaign
as a "whirlwind which quickly goes away," and stressed that although
the campaign had been basically completed everywhere else, in Shanghai it had just begun. Without victory in that city the campaign could
not be regarded as successful.[90] Hua Ming, a strongly anti-Communist
commentator, asserts that the belief was prevalent in Shanghai that
"the Communists are always having new movements, they change all
the time, and the *San-fan Wu-fan* will soon be over."[91] Many industrialists and businessmen appear to have been set on riding out this
particular storm.

Thus, new elite inspection brigades had to be created. The testing of
the seventy-four "key point" firms mentioned above was completed
with reasonable satisfaction by the end of March. In these firms many
businessmen had made "offensive and defensive alliances" with colleagues and relatives; some had "closed shop" and taken an attitude of
resistance. To overcome this, the inspection brigades not only mobilized workers and high level employees, but also put pressure on
capitalists' families in order to facilitate the destruction of relationships on which the businessmen's morale was based.[92] At the end of
March, following the "victory" of the seventy-four brigades involved
in "key point testing," one thousand inspection brigades were sent to
work.

The mobilization of the workers was also carried further at this time
by the creation of *"wu-fan* work brigades." These were set up by the
cadres of trade unions and mass organizations for the purpose of
encouraging the employees of private firms to air their grievances.

[89] Hua, *San-fan Wu-fan,* p. 82.
[90] *CFJP,* March 30, 1952.
[91] Hua, *San-fan Wu-fan,* p. 82.
[92] *CFJP,* March 27, 1952.

These brigades were closely controlled by means of a three-tier structure; thus, in the case of Yülin *ch'ü,* a "big brigade" was formed at *ch'ü* level, below which "medium brigades" were set up on the basis of occupational affiliations (in this case, metal, textiles, light industry, and building workers, shopworkers, and handicraft workers), beneath which "small brigades" functioned in individual firms.[93]

The work brigades were invariably small operational units, and in most cases had under twenty members, as in Ch'angning *ch'ü* where one hundred were set up with fewer than two thousand men.[94] Before "entering the struggle," the work brigades engaged in study and were given considerable guidance by trade union and Youth League cadres; the latter were particularly important, as many brigade members were young workers. The need to symbolize commitment was indicated by the extensive use of oath-taking ceremonies, where members wrote promises to obey the leadership, maintain discipline, be firm in standpoint, unite all the employees, and carry out the movement thoroughly.

By April 4, there were 30,000 employees in these brigades, and the number was increased to 50,000 by April 16. The brigades "penetrated" firms and organized the workers to "speak bitterness," the technique used effectively in the land reform program and now transposed to the urban environment. In a meeting of the employees of 78 metal shops in Peiszech'uan *ch'ü,* the brigade chief listed the crimes of the capitalists, after which brigade members directed discussions, led denunciations, and analyzed various problems in small group discussions. In this case 105 letters of denunciation resulted, while in the Yüan Cheng Steel Factory, "under the inspiration of the *wu-fan* work brigade" over 80 per cent of the employees denounced their employers.[95]

The work brigades also organized "confrontation meetings." At these, employers had to make reports on their unlawful actions, after which the brigades assisted the employees in carrying out "reasoned criticism" of their masters. Such activity was important because it went one stage further than the simple process of denunciation, which had often been done anonymously and had scarcely required a great deal of courage. On the employer's part, it contributed to his loss of respect by underlining the fact that he was answerable to his workers, and his consequent humiliation ensured that his future authority would

[93] *Ibid.,* April 8, May 21, 1952.
[94] *Ibid.,* April 8, 1952.
[95] *Ibid.,* April 8, 16, May 21, 1952.

be limited. In short, the working class was shown that it should "take the view of being the master."

By the middle of April it was apparent that the influence of the bourgeoisie was waning rapidly. It was claimed that in many cases great success had been achieved without much of a struggle, and that there had been a considerable number of "victories without fighting." This success was due in part to the use of the highly effective inspection brigades which, according to the leadership, frightened many unlawful capitalists.

Equally important, however, were the pressures which resulted from the loss of solidarity within the class itself. A consistent feature of the *wu-fan* campaign was its emphasis on reduced penalties for those who confessed or "became meritorious" by denouncing others. A number of employers were willing to do this by the middle of April, and the leadership was able to form with them what it termed a *"Wu-fan United Front."* The IPPE committees of every *ch'ü* worked on those who had confessed in the early stages of the campaign, and sent them to every district to talk about their "change of heart" and explain that their confession had resulted in lenient treatment of their past misdeeds. This process was formalized by the creation of "become meritorious small teams," consisting of repentant capitalists who visited their colleagues and urged them to confess.[96]

The leadership also set up "mutual help and criticism teams," another device for weakening the cohesion of the bourgeoisie. Where it was discovered that a number of employers were willing to confess, the *ch'ü* IPPE committees formed them into small teams in which they made reports on themselves and practised mutual criticism. Such a process led many businessmen to make very thorough reports of their misdeeds, and inevitably created disharmony within the group, because members strove to outdo each other in making suggestions concerning what their colleagues should admit.[97]

In the first half of April, attention was concentrated on small and medium-sized firms, which were for the most part guilty of relatively minor transgressions. By April 12, over 21,000 small and medium-sized firms had been handled. This figure rose to 41,154 by April 22; of these firms 27,906 were classified as "law-abiding," and 12,489 "basically law-abiding."[98] These classifications did not, however, imply that the

---

[96] *Ibid.*, April 16, 1952.
[97] *Ibid.*
[98] *Ibid.*, April 24, 1952.

leadership admitted that it had subjected a large number of firms to attacks for no valid reason. Because the regime's policy was to reduce punishment as a reward for confessions and "meritorious" activities, all but the handful of firms which gave the most bitter resistance could expect to receive more liberal treatment than would have been meted out on the basis of the initial accusations of criminal behavior.

Toward the end of April the number of small firms which had been handled rose to over seventy thousand, leaving only a few which remained obstinate and reputedly "completely isolated." By that time the leadership felt able to launch a major attack on large concerns; *ch'ü* IPPE committees called meetings of the unlawful capitalists from these firms and "ordered them to confess voluntarily," after which they were put into small teams where they were required to carry out self-examination and mutual criticism. By April 27, 74 per cent of the large firms scheduled for handling by that date had reported on their offenses, at a rate of one thousand a day. Because of the pressures exerted, in some areas it was unnecessary for the *ch'ü* IPPE committees to take any action at all. For example, in Hsühui *ch'ü* all the firms which the IPPE Committee had intended to inspect came forward and made voluntary confessions, apologizing for their sins.[99]

In the last ten days of April there was an intensified drive to break the resistance of the "big tigers," those capitalists who had consistently refused to cooperate. The senior employees of private firms were now sufficiently acquiescent to take a major part in exposing their bosses and, in some cases, relatives. The *ch'ü* committees held special meetings for them, at which policy was explained with great patience so as to give them "enlightening education." These meetings were designed not only to add to the list of enterprises guilty of actual breaches of the law, but also to obtain information on those measures taken by businessmen to cover up their crimes. At a meeting of senior employees of large firms in Hsinch'eng *ch'ü,* for example, the employees of the Cheng Fou Metal Plate Enterprise denounced not only their employer's unlawful acts, but also the "life and death" alliance which he had made with them.[100]

Inspection brigade members supervised meetings of the "mutual help and criticism teams," and at this stage the masses were encouraged to "assist their teams by urging capitalists to confess and by writing them letters of admonition." The "become meritorious small

---

[99] *Ibid.,* April 30, 1952.
[100] *Ibid.*

teams" also participated in the activities of the "mutual help and criticism team," urging the recalcitrant to confess. By the end of April, some sixteen hundred capitalists were "achieving merit" in this way. Such men were used within firms similar to their own, because "they were fully conversant with their own occupation's history and inside story, they knew the methods by which every firm carried out unlawful acts, and they had their finger on the pulse."[101]

Considerable attention was placed on the role that could be assigned to capitalists' families. The *ch'ü* IPPE committees organized meetings at which they were mobilized to urge their husbands and fathers to confess. This technique appears to have been highly effective; after such a meeting in Huangp'u *ch'ü* it was claimed that 90 per cent of the families present "proposed concrete plans" to help. Some of them wrote letters, others made telephone calls to the "mutual help and criticism teams," and others went home to exert pressure on their relatives. In some cases such exhortations took place in public, as when Wu Wen-fu, son of the proprietor of the Wu Fu Medical Instrument Enterprise in Hsinch'eng *ch'ü*, persuaded his father to confess thoroughly at a mobilization congress.[102]

For most "big tigers" pressure came from all sides. A case typical of many was that of the proprietor of the Ta Hua Copper Company. At a mutual help and criticism meeting he admitted obtaining 50,000,000 yuan by corruption. However, when he returned to his shop his employees, who were engaged in a meeting, called on him to confess. He then went home where he was admonished by his mother-in-law and daughter. In addition, he was visited at home by capitalists from the "become meritorious small teams," who tried to persuade him to confess. He became ill with worry, and after three days of anxiety, "feeling that there was no way out," confessed to unlawfully obtaining 2,300,000,000 yuan.[103] Even allowing for considerable exaggeration in the claims of the leadership, it is evident that such processes were extremely effective. The "isolation" of the unlawful capitalists was a reality.

On April 30, *Chieh-fang Jih-pao* was able to announce "basic victory in the *Wu-fan* campaign in Shanghai." A classification of firms which had been handled by May 5 revealed that of 77,616 small firms, 59,471 (76.6 per cent) were "law-abiding," 17,407 (22.7 per cent) were "basi-

---

[101] *Ibid.*, April 30, May 7, 1952.
[102] *Ibid.*, April 30, 1952.
[103] *Ibid.*

cally law-abiding," 736 (0.9 per cent) were "semi-law-abiding," and only 2 were "serious law-breakers." Of the 18,325 medium-sized firms which had been dealt with, 7,782 (42.5 per cent) were "law-abiding," 9,005 (49.1 per cent), were "basically law-abiding," 1,529 (8.3 per cent) were "semi-law-abiding," and 9 were "serious law-breakers." It was noted that some firms had received a lenient classification because they had confessed and "become meritorious."[104]

Although the campaign was not officially completed until late in June, by May the period of intensive, unremitting attack was generally over. It was claimed then that "the proprietors of the firms handled are grateful for the generosity of the government and the unselfish attitude of the workers, they actively participate in the *Wu-fan* and all manifest willingness to obey the leadership of the working class and state-operated industry."[105]

THE AFTERMATH OF THE WU-FAN CAMPAIGN

The industrialists and businessmen investigated in the campaign did not, for the most part, suffer imprisonment for their "crimes." P'eng Chen, in an "explanation of the draft regulations of the People's Republic of China for the punishment of corruption" which he made on April 28, claimed that in the whole country only 1 per cent of the business community fell into the category of "big robbing elements" who were "certainly no friends of ours." Such people were to be sentenced to imprisonment or labor reform. Even in these cases it was possible to be redeemed by confession, repentance, and "becoming meritorious."[106] On May 12, a "People's Tribunal" was set up in Shanghai to deal with such cases; eight of its seventeen members were from the Shanghai IPPE Committee.[107] Most "offenders" were penalized financially, however. Not only did they have to repay in full the sums they were supposed to have "stolen," but they were also fined heavily, and in some cases suffered the confiscation of their property.

Following this, the leadership implemented a series of different policies which combined to put industrialists and businessmen under extremely close and effective control. The psychological impact of the campaign appears to have been so great that little resistance could be offered. The dramatic destruction of the bourgeoisie's self-confidence was noted not only by Party leaders but also by leading representatives

---

[104] *Ibid.*, May 8, 1952.
[105] *Ibid.*
[106] *Jen-min Shou-ts'e* (People's Handbook) (Shanghai: Ta-kung Pao, 1952), pp. 52–55.
[107] *CFJP*, May 13, 1952.

of the class. Chang Nai-ch'i, a leading figure in the China National Democratic Construction Association, pointed out that it had been necessary to launch the campaign in order to make industrialists and businessmen "recognize their own smallness through the struggle of the masses," but he expressed concern about those who, because of this, had turned from being "egotists" into "self-debasing elements." Ch'en Shu-t'ung, another prominent "democrat," observed that there were a number of businessmen who feared that the leadership was no longer willing to tolerate the existence of the national bourgeoisie in China.[108] Ch'en also noted that some businessmen had adopted a "passive attitude" in business and shunned responsibility for factory production and management.[109]

The combination of economic hardship and psychological demoralization so weakened the bourgeoisie that the Party leadership was able to set up, or reinforce, a variety of economic, political, social, and ideological control mechanisms to prevent any resurgence of bourgeois power. The most general and far-reaching of these was the rapid extension of "state capitalism." The deterioration in the economic health of many firms brought about by the *wu-fan* campaign enabled the leadership to introduce the policy of "the state economy assisting the private economy," which meant that the state made loans to, and placed processing and purchasing orders with, private firms which found themselves in difficulties. However, assistance was neither unconditional nor universal. Only those firms which the leadership considered to be beneficial to the national economy and to the people were to be helped. Moreover, it was pointed out that "in aiding private enterprises, the state will guide them on the right track of operations in order to minimize blind production." Similarly, the state refused to help firms which were regarded as being of "an unsound nature"; instead, it would "educate" and "guide" them to change their trades.[110]

The capitalists of Shanghai were major "beneficiaries" of this system. In April state agencies and enterprises began to help firms in difficulties, and by June 10, 1952, over eighty-two hundred privately operated factories had received processing and purchasing orders, in comparison with three thousand in 1951. By this time the People's Bank had made loans to sixty-six hundred firms, an increase of 521.53 per cent over the corresponding period in the previous year.[111] Some

---

[108] NCNA, Peking, June 21, 1952, in *CB*, No. 199 (August 5, 1952).

[109] NCNA, Peking, August 15, 1952, in *SCMP*, No. 398 (August 20, 1952).

[110] *JMJP*, July 23, 1952, in *SCMP*, No. 397 (August 19, 1952).

[111] *Shanghai News*, August 28, 1952, in *SCMP*, No. 411 (September 9, 1952).

idea of the extent of economic control achieved by such measures may be seen by the fact that in June, 1952, government orders accounted for 54 per cent of the total output of private firms in the dyeing and weaving trades.[112] A further example of this process is provided by the case of the Chiangnan Paper Mill, where the state took over the job of marketing the firm's total production after the *wu-fan* campaign.[113]

Because many industrialists and businessmen were undercapitalized, isolated, and pessimistic about their future, they had no alternative but to accept such "assistance" and thus lost a considerable amount of independence. Acceptance did not necessarily mean financial loss; the leadership, in a number of editorials, emphasized that capitalists were to be allowed a good profit margin—especially those in efficient firms —and criticized the tendency of some state agencies to permit only a small profit.

While this may have "sugared the pill," it does not disguise the fact that the *wu-fan* campaign marked the beginning of the drive toward the full nationalization of private industry and commerce. Chou En-lai commented on the importance of the movement seven years later when he stated that it had "pushed private industry and commerce a great step forward towards state capitalism." Moreover, he asserted that because industrialists and businessmen had gone through stages which included the fulfillment of government contracts for processing, manu-facturing, and purchasing, they were able to accept their "socialist transformation" in 1956 without too much unwillingness.[114] The *wu-fan* campaign introduced a new era of economic construction based on a new relationship between the state-owned and privately owned sec-tors of the economy. In October, 1953, Li Wei-han, vice-chairman of the Financial and Economic Affairs Committee of the Government Administrative Council, observed that although private firms had ac-counted for 31 per cent of total production in 1952, there had been a "great improvement" in the share of the total which was produced by various forms of state capitalism other than jointly operated enter-prises.[115]

By the end of 1952 the "leading role" of the state sector of the economy was undeniable. Once state capitalism was fairly well estab-lished, the political and economic demise of the bourgeoisie was as-sured, as it was deprived of the strength derived from its place in the

[112] NCNA, Shanghai, August 13, 1952, in *SCMP,* No. 395 (August 15, 1952).
[113] *JMJP,* July 23, 1952, in *SCMP,* No. 397 (August 19, 1952).
[114] Chou, "A Great Decade," p. 56.
[115] NCNA, Peking, November 10, 1953, in *CB,* No. 267 (November 15, 1953).

"mixed-economy." Thus, a recent article written by "revolutionary rebels" in Shanghai has pointed out that the city's bourgeoisie was forced to accept "socialist transformation" in 1956 because it found itself confronted "by the powerful state-owned enterprises and the enormous superiority and absolute dominance of the daily increasing joint state-private enterprises."[116] The process by which this domination was achieved had been greatly accelerated in 1952.

Apart from the general extension of state capitalism which followed the campaign, other measures for controlling the bourgeoisie were introduced, or reinforced, at this time. One of the most important of these was the system of holding "labor-capital consultative conferences." This system had actually been introduced in 1950, but it was extended after the *wu-fan* campaign. Theoretically these conferences permitted the workers and employers to discuss questions of welfare and production to the mutual benefit of both sides. In actual fact, the conferences were an instrument through which the leadership could exercise control, as they provided a regularized channel through which the workers, led by the trade unions, could "persuade" the employers to follow policies which were in the state's interests. Both large and small firms were subject to such direction. In the case of the Ch'ang Fa Hsiung Porcelain Shop, the proprietor had previously sold only high quality goods and had not been willing to trade outside of Shanghai; this had raised costs and hindered the "urban-rural interflow of commodities." After the *wu-fan* campaign, however, his employees "untiringly educated him" at conferences and "persuaded him to change his business style." The case of the Yung Ta Dyeing and Weaving Mill, a relatively large Shanghai firm, also provides a good example of the influence employees could have on operational policy. There the conferences were used as a forum for the discussion and adoption of both the workers' "rationalization proposals" and the employers' schemes for the reform of production management. The degree of pressure which could be brought to bear on capitalists by means of these conferences is shown by the case of the proprietor of the Li Wen Radio Shop in Laocha *ch'ü*, who, having had his workers explain "policy" to him at such a conference, brought HK $7,000 from Hong Kong, "an asset which had not [previously] been entered in the books."[117]

Naturally the leadership's policy was not one of intimidation alone,

[116] "The Defender of Capitalist Economy," in *CB*, No. 836 (September 25, 1967), p. 35.
[117] *CFJP*, August 2, 1952, and *JMJP*, July 3, 1952; both in *SCMP*, No. 402 (August 26, 1952).

for the skills of the urban bourgeoisie were still required, and it was necessary to control not only industrialists and businessmen but also those workers who had become too "Leftist" during the campaign. The conferences were, therefore, used to effect a certain degree of reconciliation between employers and employees so that production would not suffer, and the task of fostering "economic unity" was given to the trade unions. The proprietor of the Yung Ta Mill mentioned above had been a major target in the *wu-fan* campaign, and he was regarded with hostility by some of the workers there, while the senior employees refused to talk to him or to eat at the same table. It is hardly surprising that this employer "became restless for fear of losing his political status and passed all responsibilities to the trade union." At the first conference held in this mill, the workers' representatives lectured him severely, with the result that no problems were solved. In order to implement the policy of "uniting with the capitalist so as to make a success of production," the trade union cadres called a meeting at which they persuaded the workers to moderate their views. Thereafter they were able to hold regular conferences in an "atmosphere of unity and equality."[118]

Trade union cadres occupied a very sensitive position in this system, and employers and managers were forced to rely heavily on them. The union committees became important mediators between management and labor. They collected the "opinions of the masses" on problems of production and welfare, on the basis of which they made proposals to the management. Similarly, suggestions from the management reached the workers only after they had been "filtered" through the union committees. Before meetings of the "labor-capital consultative conferences," the union cadres carried out extensive preparation so that it would be "easier to bring the opinions of the two parties closer."[119] Unions were naturally expected to look after the interests of their members, but it is evident that they were also expected to prevent them from making excessive demands which would harm economic production and intimidate the employers too much.

Industrialists and businessmen were placed under further control by the extension of "ideological reform." This had already been applied to bourgeois intellectuals, and after the *wu-fan* campaign was introduced to the business world, although in a somewhat milder form. Businessmen were instructed to "remold" themselves under the direction of

[118] *JMJP*, August 31, 1952, in *SCMP*, No. 402 (August 26, 1952).
[119] *Ibid.*

institutions which were effectively controlled by the elite. One of the most important of these was the China National Democratic Construction Association (CNDCA), the "Democratic party" to which many industrialists and businessmen belonged. At an important conference held by their association in Peking on July 2, 1952, Chang Nai-ch'i, one of its conveners, pointed out that because of the san-fan and wu-fan campaigns, many CNDCA members had "generally felt the need to review the past and to prepare themselves to greet the new and greater tasks" of economic construction which lay ahead. At the conference it was noted that the wu-fan campaign had given the bourgeoisie an education which was "incomparably profound." It was admitted that before the campaign many industrialists and businessmen had lacked adequate political understanding and had paid insufficient attention to study. The CNDCA felt that it was necessary to rectify this situation, and it called on all industrialists and businessmen to begin to study the Common Program, and to engage in criticism and self-criticism. By so doing they would bring into play their "progressive side," overcome their "passive and decadent side," and would then have a "glorious future."[120]

The demand that the bourgeoisie should carry out ideological reform was also made by the preparatory committee of the All-China Federation of Industry and Commerce. This organization was established after the wu-fan campaign to serve as a "transmission belt" which would facilitate the implementation of state policies among private enterprises. Within this organization Shanghai was well represented, as Hsü Ti-hsin and Sheng P'i-hua were vice-chairmen of the preparatory committee. On August 25, 1952, this committee called on all industrial and commercial associations in China to study the Common Program and to practise criticism and self-criticism. It was necessary for all capitalists to gain a clear understanding of the nature of the New Democracy and of the "significance of the people's democratic dictatorship." They were to understand the role of industrialists and businessmen in the New Democracy and develop an appreciation of the roles of the leadership of the working class and the leadership of the state economy. They were also to study the relationship between the general economic plans of the state and the development of private industry and commerce.

Industrial and commercial associations were to set up study units,

120 NCNA, Peking, July 12, 1952, in SCMP, No. 373 (July 13–14, 1952).

generally on the basis of the *ch'ü,* with special attention being paid to different trades. Apart from study classes, these units would hold lectures and forums, and "study guidance personnel" could be appointed by the associations to help with this work. The committee stressed the development of publicity work, including publications, "big character posters," and broadcasting relays. Local associations were required to report to the preparatory committee on study conditions from time to time.[121]

Thus, after the *wu-fan* campaign, the business community was "encouraged" to carry out extensive and intensive ideological reform based on study of those aspects of the Common Program which emphasized the leadership of the state-owned sector of the economy and the subjugation of "selfish" bourgeois interests to the general interest of the state and "the people." Only by so doing could the bourgeoisie be permitted to retain its place in the united front. One naturally suspects that in the case of many "bourgeois elements," the effects of ideological reform must have been only superficial. Nevertheless, when the other controls outlined above are taken into account, it seems quite probable that the bourgeoisie at least learned to behave in the manner which the leadership deemed appropriate.

The impact of the *wu-fan* campaign on the workers of Shanghai was of equal importance. William Kornhauser has observed that "People cannot be mobilized against the established order until they have first been divorced from prevailing codes and relations. Only then can they be made available for 'activist modes of intervention' in the political process."[122] In Shanghai such a trend took place in the first five months of 1952. The six hundred thousand employees in private firms were "reached" for the first time, and were subjected to an intensive campaign which attempted to reorient their values toward the society as a whole, and toward the bourgeoisie in particular. The campaign created new social and political patterns of behavior, and new loyalties. Boasts that the working class was united by this campaign contain a reasonable amount of truth, as a great deal of effort went into replacing pluralistic ties with what Kornhauser has termed "pseudo-community," a network of relationships and obligations created and controlled by the leadership. It would be dangerous to place too much emphasis on one campaign, but although it was merely one part of a

---

[121] *Ibid.,* August 25, 1952, in *SCMP,* No. 405 (August 29–30, 1952).
[122] William Kornhauser, *The Politics of Mass Society* (London: Routledge and Kegan Paul, 1960), p. 133.

much wider process of conscious destruction and renovation, it was of undoubted significance.

Being exposed for five or six months to the constantly reiterated message that dishonest dealings had no place in the public and business life of the new system, and the concomitant idea that the bourgeoisie was unworthy of respect, was a novel experience for the urban masses. By insisting that passive genuflections before the symbols of authority would not suffice, the leadership was able to create a fair degree of antipathy toward the industrial and commercial groups in the city. Demands that the workers denounce employers, either anonymously or publicly, were of the greatest importance, as was participation in the countless meetings which were held to criticize employers and to listen to their abject confessions. The individual was asked to identify with new heroes like Wang Chün, a young shopworker of Sungshan *ch'ü*, who had denounced eight people in the campaign to suppress counter-revolutionaries and who denounced his own nephew in the *wu-fan* campaign.[123] It is tempting to discount the effects of much of this activity, but in this particular campaign it is necessary to emphasize that they were probably quite deep because the leadership's message contained a reasonable amount of truth. The Shanghai bourgeoisie was guilty of corrupt practices which were harmful to society regardless of the form of government in control. It is perhaps going too far to accept the assertion that the "gangster and compradore mentality" was strong in 1952, but it must be remembered that even the Nationalists had eventually found Shanghai too corrupt and had launched a belated and unsuccessful attempt to cope with it under Chiang Ching-kuo in 1948. While the majority of Shanghai's private businessmen were not guilty of major crimes, the cumulative effects of their transgressions was great, and the leadership's claims could be viewed as credible by many.

Beyond the inculcation of new values lay the creation of a new "subelite" in Shanghai. To some degree the leadership's manpower shortage was reduced by the appearance of new cadres who were young, of urban background, and of a more genuine proletarian origin than their seniors. This was of great importance, in that the leadership was able to increase its legitimacy in the urban areas by providing urban workers with enhanced opportunities for advancement on condition that they actively support the policies of the regime. By the end of the *wu-fan* campaign there were sixty thousand workers in Shanghai who had been trained in the "*Wu-fan* work brigades," constituting 10 per

123 *CFJP*, February 3, 1952.

cent of the labor force in private firms.[124] Such activists, who "bubbled up" and received political education during the campaign, provided a reservoir from which the leadership could recruit cadres for urban work.

The major channel of advancement opened up at this time was through the trade unions. After the campaign the Party admitted that trade unions in private firms had often been inadequate; "because of the harm done by unlawful capitalists" union members had not always been "pure," and in some places the unions' authority had been usurped. In the campaign, however, the workers in many firms raised their "political consciousness" and held new elections for union officials, electing many activists to "basic level" committees. A number of "bad elements" were dismissed.[125]

In Luwan *ch'ü,* for example, the "basic level" trade union organizations underwent "organic readjustment" during the *wu-fan* campaign, and seventy cadres who had been "traitorous elements" were dismissed and replaced by activists.[126] A common pattern seems to have been that illustrated by the case of a rubber factory in Peiszech'uan *ch'ü.* Huang Wen-yüan, the deputy chief of the factory's union committee, was "in the pocket" of the proprietor. The employer had used the difficulties which ensued from a serious bombing raid as a pretext for laying off men; he had Huang draw up a list of the activists in the factory, whom he then fired. During the *wu-fan* campaign Huang helped the employer to bribe the senior office workers of the firm. Because of the development of the movement, however, there was a rise in "consciousness" among the employees, and Huang was reported to the higher levels of the union, which agreed to his dismissal. New elections were held; three members of the trade union committee were retained because of their "resolute standpoint," but others were dismissed. The factory engineer, who had denounced the employer, and a young workman who had "attacked and displayed heroism," were elected to the committee.[127]

It was noted that before the campaign many employers had been able to prevent the effective functioning of union organization. In the Hua Hsin Teaching Aids and Writing Materials Factory, for example, the employer had slandered the union's name and "dragged back the workers" by telling them, "You don't want to listen to the union, it is

---

[124] *Ibid.,* May 21, 1952.
[125] *Ibid.,* April 28, 1952.
[126] *Ibid.,* June 25, 1952, in *SCMP,* No. 368 (July 4–5, 1952).
[127] *CFJP,* April 28, 1952.

not reliable." During the campaign the union revenged itself by "laying bare the employer's plots" and thereby raised the workers' understanding of the nature of trade unions.[128]

The importance of family ties, which was mentioned earlier, had also hindered the effective functioning of trade union organizations in some areas. In the Yung Kang Draw-Silk Factory the chairman of the trade union committee had restricted union membership, giving preferential treatment to his relatives and those who were willing to give him presents. However, the higher level trade union organizations and the *ch'ü* IPPE Committee eliminated such "bad elements" while the campaign was in progress and persuaded the old workers to meet and be educated in trade union principles. New elections were held, and most of those elected were activists who had emerged from the *wu-fan* campaign.[129]

Apart from the reform of union organizations, there was also an expansion in union membership as more workers began to "take the attitude of being the masters." For example, the Shop Workers' Trade Union in Shanghai more than doubled its membership from 21,900 before the campaign to 44,029 after it; it was noted that some 14,000 shopworkers had played an "important role" in the movement.[130] Because of the elimination of corrupt elements and the recruitment of activists, it was claimed at the national level that relations between the leadership and the masses had become closer.[131]

This urban subelite was further strengthened by the growth of the Youth League. Detailed statistics on recruitment during the campaign have not been found, but by May, 1952, there were ninety thousand members in Shanghai.[132] It is reasonable to assume that this rise of thirty thousand, by comparison with the 1950 figure, was largely caused by the movement, in view of the fact that a substantial number of the activists were young.

A further means of advancement was offered by the propaganda network. By the end of the *wu-fan* campaign over sixteen thousand propagandists were operating in Shanghai (an increase of more than seven hundred compared with the figure for December, 1951). In August, 1952, the Shanghai Party Committee announced that it would expand the propaganda network in the second half of that year and

[128] *Ibid.*
[129] *Ibid.*, June 25, 1952.
[130] *Ibid.*, April 27, 1952, in *SCMP*, No. 329 (May 5–6, 1952).
[131] *KJJP*, July 1, 1952, in *SCMP*, No. 373 (July 13–14, 1952).
[132] *CFJP*, May 4, 1952.

would recruit fifty-four thousand new propagandists. Of these, forty thousand were to be recruited from among industrial workers and shopworkers.[133] Many of the new propagandists must, almost certainly, have been *wu-fan* activists; while the rank of propagandist was not a particularly exalted one, it did offer opportunities for demonstrating activism which could result in further promotion.

In some cases it was possible for activists to be admitted to the Party because of their work in the campaign. The rise in political awareness among the workers which took place during the *san-fan* and *wu-fan* campaigns caused the Party's East China Bureau to initiate a policy of "bold promotion," through which those workers who possessed the necessary qualification would be admitted to the Party.[134] This policy, however, appears to have applied more to *san-fan* activists than to those who rose in the *wu-fan*. This is, in fact, perfectly understandable, as the *san-fan* activists came from state-operated enterprises and therefore, one assumes, had undergone a longer period of "exposure" to the Party's policies than those in private firms. For the latter, promotion at this stage was generally through the trade unions and the Youth League.

While the leadership's position was strengthened by its ability and willingness to assist the workers' career mobility by inducting them into mass organizations, its influence was also increased by its "educational" policies. Claims that the increased political awareness of many workers resulted in increased demands for study, politics, and culture, if not actually demonstrating universal and voluntary action on the part of the working class, certainly do show that it had been brought under a fairly close degree of regimentation. Not all areas were subject to the penetration achieved in Huangp'u *ch'ü*, where 60 per cent of the shopworkers were in newspaper reading teams by the end of April, but this figure is indicative of the general trend.[135] The leadership made a determined effort after the campaign to regularize its lines of communication with the labor force, particularly with those workers who were employed in the private sector.

A large-scale "workers' political discussion forum" was opened on June 16 by the Propaganda Department of the Shanghai Party Committee in order to "consolidate and raise the standard of the activists and the basic level" cadres of the unions of privately-operated enter-

---

[133] *Ibid.,* August 12, 1952, in *SCMP,* No. 415 (September 14–15, 1952).

[134] *Ibid.,* September 7 and 18, 1952, in *SCMP,* No. 421 (September 23, 1952).

[135] *CFJP,* April 28, 1952.

prises." At this forum discussion took place on such themes as the new "labor-capital relationship after the *wu-fan* campaign," "class policy and education," "education on conditions and prospects," and "the Communist Party and the working class." By the end of June, it was claimed that 132,000 people had attended the forum.[136]

This process continued throughout the summer of 1952. In October, Liu Ch'ang-sheng was able to claim that the leadership had carried out "systematic education" among the 160,000 workers in privately operated factories, and was at that time developing education about communism and the Communist Party. He stated that political schools were being organized and that 220,000 workers were participating in professional and cultural studies.[137]

In addition to strengthening the leadership's control by disseminating the values of the elite, the provision of such "education" must also have given the urban workers yet another reason for being grateful to the Party. There seems little reason to doubt the claims of Chung Min, a committee member of the Shanghai Federation of Trade Unions, that in private industry the "Shanghai working class demarcated class lines in its ideology, strengthened discipline and organization, and the ranks were consolidated and enlarged."[138]

The *wu-fan* campaign was, then, of the utmost significance because it enabled the leadership to consolidate its power in urban China by extending its influence over both the bourgeoisie and the working class. The magnitude of the transformation which was brought about at this time was expressed succinctly by one newspaper in Shanghai, which declared that although "numerous mass movements have been staged in Shanghai before this, not one of them can approach the present one in scope, extensiveness, organization, discipline, influence and effect."[139]

Official interpretations of the campaign, made at the time and later, have been consistent in emphasizing its importance and the extent of the social, economic, and political benefits which the leadership derived

---

[136] *Ibid.*, June 28, 1952, in *SCMP*, No. 370 (July 9, 1952).

[137] Liu Ch'ang-sheng, *Shang-hai kung-jen nu-li ying-chieh wei-ta ti tsu-kuo chien-sheh shih-ch'i ti tao-lai* (Shanghai's Workers Strive to Usher in the Era of the Great Construction of the Motherland), in *Ch'ing-chu san-nien lai wei-ta ch'eng-chiu wei ying-chieh tsu-kuo ta kuei-mo chien-sheh wei-ta jen-wu erh chi-hsü fen-tou* (Celebrating the Great Achievements of the Past Three Years Which Have Resulted from Continually Struggling for the Task of Ushering in the Large-scale Construction of the Motherland) (Shanghai: Hua-tung Jen-min Ch'u-pan She, 1952), pp. 51–59.

[138] *CFJP*, May 11, 1952.

[139] *TKP*, Shanghai, June 9, 1952, in *SCMP*, No. 364 (June 27–28, 1952).

from it. The social issue involved was summed up by Ch'en Yün, a vice-premier of the People's Republic, when he addressed the preparatory committee of the All-China Federation of Industry and Commerce in June, 1952. He observed that the *wu-fan* campaign, together with the *san-fan,* had been a social reform movement aimed at changing old attitudes and habits. This in turn had economic effects because it created the necessary conditions for the economic construction of the state.[140] The economic impact of the campaign was stressed further in one Shanghai newspaper, which actually went so far as to state that it was a "necessary preparatory measure for carrying out full-scale economic construction projects in which private interests, as a component of the social economy of the new China, will play their part."[141]

A most interesting comment on the political role of the campaign was made in 1957, when Chang Chih-i, a leading figure in united front work, claimed that the *wu-fan* campaign had prevented the bourgeoisie from leaving the united front.[142]

This remark is worthy of note because it reflects the leadership's view that the bourgeoisie had "launched a wild attack" after the "liberation." This charge was made in numerous speeches and articles in 1952, and was reiterated by Chou En-lai in 1959 when he claimed that the campaign had "dealt a crushing blow to the offensive launched by the bourgeoisie." As recently as 1967, "revolutionary rebels" in Shanghai have claimed that the bourgeoisie of that city had spread the "five kinds of poisonous stuff" in order to "usurp the leadership of the state-owned economy," although, of course, such "frenzied attacks" had been repulsed.[143]

This charge did contain a kernel of truth. As has been demonstrated above, the bourgeoisie was an extremely powerful interest group within the New Democracy, and certain Party leaders had been prepared to compromise with it. Apart from the generally undesirable social effects of corruption, the dubious practices of the bourgeoisie, particularly bribery, did seriously weaken the role of the state. There is no reason to believe that corruption was deliberately practised with a view to hindering the expansion of Communist political influence, and for most industrialists and businessmen short-term financial goals were probably the main source of motivation. Nevertheless, the Party leadership

---

[140] NCNA, Peking, June 24, 1952, in *SCMP,* No. 365 (June 29–30, 1952).
[141] *Shanghai News,* August 28, 1952, in *SCMP,* No. 411 (September 9, 1952).
[142] *TKP,* Peking, March 21, 1957, in *SCMP,* No. 1522 (May 3, 1957).
[143] Chou, "A Great Decade," p. 49; "The Defender of Capitalist Economy," in *CB,* No. 836 (September 25, 1967), p. 33.

may well have been correct in regarding the campaign as a political battle which had to be won if the revolution were to continue. Hence the vituperative and repetitive allegation of the "wild attack."

In any event, the available evidence reveals that the Party leadership was successful in handling the problem of bourgeois corruption and was able to curtail severely the independence of the industrial and commercial groups after 1952.

The widespread demoralization of many businessmen has been well attested by the statements of both bourgeois and Party leaders, and it is clear that the effects of the *wu-fan* campaign were still being felt several years later. The Hundred Flowers campaign of 1957 provides several instances. For example, Hu Chüeh-wen, who had been a member of the Shanghai IPPE Committee, and who was deputy chairman of the Shanghai Federation of Industry and Commerce in 1957, complained that a major problem facing the Shanghai business world was that since the *wu-fan* campaign many people had persisted in the notion that all capitalists were bad. Other democratic leaders, the most notable of whom was Lo Lung-chi, also explained that many people were afraid of "blooming and contending" in 1957 because of their experiences in a number of the great campaigns of the consolidation period; the *wu-fan* movement was specifically mentioned.[144]

Although it is difficult to judge with precision the extent to which industrialists and businessmen were cured of their corrupt behavior after 1952, it appears that most of them were. Naturally, occasional cases of dubious dealings have appeared since the *wu-fan* campaign, and indeed even since 1956 when "socialist transformation" turned many of the proprietors and managers of China's privately operated firms into managerial personnel working under the leadership of the state. Such cases can be found in material which has appeared during the Great Proletarian Cultural Revolution. One source, for example, claims that Liu Shao-ch'i encouraged the promotion of "capitalist agents" when he visited Shanghai in April, 1957, and this resulted in the appointment of two capitalists who had been found guilty of corruption in the *wu-fan* campaign as deputy superintendents of the Shanghai Switches Factory. It is alleged that in the days of "socialist transformation" these men had ostensibly handed over their property but had secretly drawn out capital and practised embezzlement.[145]

[144] NCNA, Peking, May 22, 1957, in *SCMP*, No. 1550 (July 14, 1957).

[145] "Socialist Enterprises Can Never Be Allowed to be Dragged Astray onto the Road of Capitalism," *Hung Ch'i* (Red Flag), No. 13 (1967), in *SCMM*, No. 592 (September 11, 1967), p. 12.

Another source asserts that there was extensive speculation in Shanghai in 1962 because Liu's "agent" in the city had clamored for the opening of "free markets" there.[146] There is even a Chinese Nationalist article, based on "information from behind the enemy lines," which claims that there was widespread business malpractice in China in 1963.[147]

Other cases could be quoted, but, in this writer's opinion, they are significant only because of their rarity. Moreover, it is not always possible to know whether the "unlawful elements" involved are genuinely "bourgeois." A factory manager in Shanghai in the 1960's is just as likely to be a Party veteran or even a promoted worker as a "capitalist." Also, because of the enormous dislocations from which the Chinese economy suffered in the early 1960's, certain "unlawful practices" might well reflect nothing more than a slackening of controls in order to keep enterprises operating. What is evident, however, is that the Party leadership has not found it necessary to launch another great mass campaign against genuinely "bourgeois" corruption. One authority on the role of managers in Communist states (who actually studied capitalists in China before the Great Proletarian Cultural Revolution) has commented on the fact that corruption there was far less of a problem than in the Soviet Union.[148] He attributed this partly to the relative paucity of material incentives, such as bonuses, available to Chinese managers, which meant that they have not had the desire to carry out acts of doubtful legality in order to increase the performance of their enterprises. While this seems likely, it is also possible that China's capitalists still remember their painful experience in the *wu-fan* campaign. The curtailment of their independence in and after 1952 must also have made it much more difficult to escape detection and punishment for violations of the law.

The Great Proletarian Cultural Revolution is significant in this context because it reveals the relative lack of interest which the leadership shows in the bourgeoisie. One would imagine that a considerable number of bourgeois scapegoats would have been paraded during the movement in order to account for the decadent habits and ideas which have once more invaded the ranks of the Chinese Communist Party

---

[146] "The Defender of Capitalist Economy," in *CB*, No. 836 (September 25, 1967), p. 37.

[147] Wang Yao-t'ang, "Kung-fei ti hsin Wu-fan Yün-tung" (Communist Bandits' New "Wu-fan" Movement), *Fei-ch'ing Yen-chiu* (Research on Bandit China), VII, No. 1 (Taipei, January, 1964), 51–58.

[148] Barry M. Richman, "Capitalists and Managers in Communist China," *Harvard Business Review* (January–February, 1967), p. 62.

itself. This, however, is not the case. While a few capitalists have been held up as objects for condemnation, the majority of them (and there are still ninety thousand in Shanghai alone[149]) have not.

The essential point to note here is that the Great Proletarian Cultural Revolution has been directed mainly against Party members who have "taken the capitalist road." To a considerable extent the attack has been focused on the predilections of such people for pursuing a "bourgeois" strategy of economic development with all the "privilege" which that entails. Corruption in high places has been included in the charges laid against such men, and the Chinese (and Western) public has been regaled with the nefarious activities of a number of Party dignitaries who have engaged, or so it is alleged, in luxurious living. It seems quite feasible that many of these charges are true, for the secret "Work Bulletins of the People's Liberation Army" showed that the existence of privilege has been fairly widespread.[150]

Such corrupt behavior, however, has not been convincingly attributed to "the bourgeoisie"; indeed, many articles have not mentioned the class as such. What is under attack is "bourgeois ideology." To account for the appearance of this ideology in a situation where the role of the bourgeoisie has obviously been limited, it has been necessary to attribute "bourgeois" affiliations to these Party members under attack. Where possible this has been done by stressing kinship ties between those "taking the capitalist road" and genuine capitalists, landlords, and similar elements, or by emphasizing supposedly close friendships with such people.[151]

While these accusations appear to be largely spurious, they are significant because they reveal that the "Maoist" leadership has been unable to produce reasonably convincing "proof" of widespread opposition from the genuine capitalists within the country. Thus, an article in the authoritative theoretical journal *Hung Ch'i* (Red Flag) pointed out that many of the Party veterans who had been under attack recently had "degenerated precisely because they could not resist corruption by bourgeois ideology." The same article warned the new power holders who have arisen in the Great Proletarian Cultural Revolution to heighten their vigilance, for they will be "under the

---

[149] *New York Times*, January 2, 1966.

[150] See J. Chester Cheng, *The Politics of the Chinese Red Army: A Translation of the Bulletin of Activities of the People's Liberation Army* (Stanford, Calif.: The Hoover Institution, 1966).

[151] For example, Liu Shao-ch'i has been attacked because he has a "bourgeois" wife, and has allegedly been on very friendly terms with her "capitalist" brother as well as with other capitalists such as Sung Fei-ch'ing, the Tientsin industrialist mentioned in this study.

constant attack of the sugar-coated bullets of *bourgeois ideology.*"[152]

It seems then that the capitalists of China are no longer a real problem to the regime. They appear to work satisfactorily within the framework of the socialist economy, although no real analysis has yet been made of their motivations to do so. The *wu-fan* campaign marked the beginning of their political eclipse, and Richman's suggestion that they are left alone because they lack power is a convincing one.[153] The supreme irony would appear to be that although bourgeois corruption was eliminated successfully by the leadership, corruption within the Party was not. In one sense, the Great Proletarian Cultural Revolution is Mao's latest attempt to solve the basic problem: *Quis custodiet ipsos custodes?*

[152] "The Thought of Mao Tse-tung Illuminates the Road for Our Party's Victorious Advance," *Hung Ch'i,* No. 11 (1967), in *SCMM,* No. 587 (August 8, 1967), p. 5 (emphasis added).
[153] Richman, "Capitalists and Managers," p. 61.

ⅉⅉⅉⅉⅉⅉⅉⅉⅉⅉⅉⅉⅉⅉⅉⅉⅉⅉⅉⅉⅉⅉⅉⅉⅉ

JOYCE KALLGREN

Social Welfare and
China's Industrial Workers

. . . Communist states within the respective limits of their economic potential are, or try to be welfare states. Although the Communist world is primarily interested in rapid industrialization and a strong national defense—pursuits which require heavy investment yielding no (or no immediate) return to the customer—and although the level of economic development with which most Communist states were forced to start is relatively low, the ruling parties at least try to put a floor under the general living standard through social service schemes, free medical care and various other public services.[1]

This quotation from a recent article by Alfred G. Meyer entitled "The Comparative Study of Communist Political Systems" draws attention to an aspect of life in Communist societies "more readily associated with the democratic way of life than with the totalitarian."[2] Education, public health, and social welfare programs are popular internally and admired externally. If a Chinese version of the Alex Inkeles–Raymond Bauer study were available, it would probably indicate that among Chinese, as among Russians, the aspects of life generally viewed as "good" or "desirable" would be educational opportunities, medical care, and the pensions and awards available to workers.[3] Yet, of course, to the extent that these programs (themselves part of the modernization efforts of the Chinese) have been successful, that very success ironically poses troublesome problems for the Maoist leadership. Effective public health measures have heightened the popu-

[1] Alfred G. Meyer, "The Comparative Study of Communist Political Systems," *Slavic Review,* XXVI, No. 1 (March, 1967), 3.

[2] *Ibid.,* p. 6.

[3] Alex Inkeles and Raymond A. Bauer, *The Soviet Citizen* (Cambridge, Mass.: Harvard University Press, 1959), p. 242.

lation pressure. New educational opportunities have produced a generation of young people who search for opportunities not yet available and who (or so Mao seems to think) are dissatisfied with life in the countryside. Do similar problems result from the Chinese programs of social assistance?

This paper will analyze one aspect of social assistance, specifically the Labor Insurance Regulations (LIR) first inaugurated for China in 1951 and now reported to cover some twenty million people.[4] Examination of the Chinese counterpart—for the industrial work force—of the American "social security" system reveals that many of the anomalies implicit in industrialization and urbanization for developing societies are difficulties for the Chinese.

Governments of newly developing nations are committed to improving the welfare of their populations. But the facts of economic life, the scarcity of trained personnel, and the painful choices involved in the allocation of resources often restrict the kinds and amount of social assistance that can be provided. It is clear, from research such as that done under the United Nations' auspices over the past fifteen years,[5] that the effects of this resource scarcity are so grave that welfare programs often cannot go much further than providing an occasional "soup kitchen" for disaster relief. Communist China, however, at a very early date adopted several far-reaching programs of social welfare assistance, administered through its trade union organization and based upon firm and careful financial commitment.

Have the Chinese been able to avoid or cope with the financial stringencies that have confronted other nations? Have the social welfare programs broadened their coverage and benefits in the years since 1949? What have been the effects on the Chinese labor force of the protection and benefits accorded them by the labor insurance program? Have these programs heightened the revolutionary enthusiasm of the

[4] It is extraordinarily difficult to determine the total number eligible for services under the LIR program. First of all, the figures which the Chinese use refer only to those individuals covered and not to their dependents. Furthermore, the individuals now covered by various programs embodying very similar provisions to those of LIR are often not included in the figures cited by the Chinese. In 1965 when using the figure twenty million the Chinese indicate that this figure refers to productive workers as well as cadres, government employees, and so forth. Though the number eligible for various programs of social security has grown, it is still a minority. There have never been any figures of those covered under collective contract agreements.

[5] United Nations, Department of Economic and Social Affairs, *The Development of National Social Service Programmes* (New York: U.N. Publications, 1959), 70 pp.; U.N. Economic Commission for Asia and the Far East, *Problems of Social Development Planning with Reference to Asia and the Far East* (New York: U.N. Development Program Training Series No. 4, 1964), 71 pp.

workers and encouraged them to produce and sacrifice more as the costs of industrialization become apparent? Or have these programs contributed to the problems on which the Maoist critiques of the trade unions have focused since the start of the Great Proletarian Cultural Revolution, and do they help explain the subsequent suspension of the nationwide trade union organization and purge of its leadership? If, as some reports suggest, the industrial workers of China's major state enterprises have been reluctant to accept all the tenets of Mao and have even occasionally resorted to violence against the Red Guards, how can this be explained? Have the Chinese workers developed a stake in their society which makes them less responsive to the themes of Maoism, which stress selfless dedication to the long-range, ideologically determined goals, and what part does welfare play in determining the nature and importance of such a "stake"?

The analytical difficulties in answering these questions can be divided into two groups: those difficulties inherent in the reality of the social and economic policies of the regime, and those that result from individual workers' perceptions of welfare. Under certain circumstances, these two differing sets of considerations merge and reflect or reinforce each other. On one hand, the judgment about "stake" will vary with the individual, depending upon his economic and social position and his prospects for advancement. It is affected by the worker's perception of the past, to which the Chinese Communist Party (CCP) has given such emphasis, and by the extent to which the Party's image is meaningful to men and women in their twenties and thirties who have but a dim memory of conditions in the 1940's. Judgment is affected by the degree to which workers, collectively or singly, attribute present conditions to the leadership of the state, as well as by the workers' feelings about whether their interest might be jeopardized by the current activities of either the Party or the Maoists.

On the other hand, certain problems are inherent in the establishment and administration of welfare programs. Does labor insurance meet the real needs of China's workers, and what are the consequences of the fact that while some workers receive the additional protection of labor insurance, the peasants do not? During the Cultural Revolution the Maoists have accused their enemies of "economism," and the industrial workers and trade union cadres are certainly among those vulnerable to this charge. As one scholar, Dwight Perkins, has pointed out, the wages of China's industrial workers in real terms are now relatively high in comparison with peasants' real income, and are probably higher than the minimum level necessary to assure a continuous supply of new labor from the countryside.[6] The fact that some workers receive welfare benefits, while peasants do not, makes even more conspicuous the difference between the lot of the worker and of the peasant.

Apart from this issue of comparative well-being, there is the problem of adequacy. Measured against the need for medical care and income during old age, does the present system provide an adequate standard? Are the provisions administered fairly and without regard to any other standards except need? This paper considers first the degree to which the specific programs of the Chinese are geared to meet real needs and provide important services; and secondly the general effects of the program in a nation undergoing rapid industrialization.

LABOR INSURANCE REGULATIONS

There are difficulties implicit in any formal definition of what constitutes social welfare, but the Labor Insurance Regulations first announced by the Chinese in November, 1950, and made effective on February 26, 1951, fall within any reasonable set of criteria.[7] The Chinese Communist Party has always believed that it should have a welfare role, and the LIR represent a tangible effort by the Party to improve or at least ameliorate the conditions of some Chinese industrial workers.

---

[6] Dwight H. Perkins, *Market Control and Planning in Communist China* (Cambridge, Mass.: Harvard University Press, 1966), p. 146.

[7] There is an extensive terminology developed within the field of social welfare which is useful in an analysis of welfare problems. For the purpose of this paper, I will use the term "social security" as it was defined at the International Social Security Conference held in Vienna in March, 1953, under the auspices of the World Federation of Trade Unions. The definition is very broad, but approximates many of the goals that the Chinese have embraced. This definition was used by Mitsuoka Gen in his article, "Social Security in Communist China," published in the *China Research Monthly*, No. 161 (July 30, 1961), pp. 1–27, and translated in *JPRS*, No. 11802 (December 29, 1961). The author has since emerged as the leader of the Maoist faction (as of April, 1967) in the China Research Organization:

> True social security must be understood as basic social rights, guaranteeing by law all those who maintain livelihood by labor and their families and those who have become permanently incapacitated for labor temporarily or permanently. . . . The rights of social security must offer protection against the following accidents: sickness, confinement, incapacity for labor, old age, labor accidents, occupational diseases, total or partial unemployment and death.
>
> Social security must grant aid to all children so that their education and support can be secured. It must also provide workers with paid vacations, and family allowances.
>
> Social security must provide all people with cash benefits which guarantee the maintenance of a proper standard of living.

Although the commitment to improvement of working conditions and to providing labor insurance can be found in the Labor Law Outline of the Secretariat of the Chinese Labor Association of 1922, the opportunity to implement this commitment came only with the CCP's occupation and control of Manchuria. Between April 1, 1949, and the coming into force of the 1951 nationwide legislation, the LIR for the Northeast were effective for workers in several specified industries. "The program is to be practiced first on a trial basis in the following state enterprises: railways, mining, arsenal, military supplies, post office and tele-communications, electricity and textiles."[8] The benefits provided were medical care and modest income payments for disability (both work-connected as well as off the job), maternity care, and old age. The various levels of payments and the extent of free medical care were determined by the cause of the income interruption, the nature of the disability, the general work history of the individual, and his length of service in the given industry.

The experience of the CCP in Manchuria was only fifteen months old when announcement of the nationwide program was made, but the work summaries from the cities of Mukden and Harbin and other Manchurian areas provided valuable experience for the broader efforts of the Party and government after national "liberation."[9]

One basic dilemma inherent in the nationwide Chinese welfare effort represented by the LIR is clearly stated in the opening article of the 1951 regulations:

Article I. The present regulations are formulated in accordance with the *present economic conditions* for the purposes of protecting the health of workers and staff members and alleviating difficulties in their livelihood" (emphasis added).[10]

This problem of reconciling the present economic conditions of the state with the needs of specific programs and individuals is apparent in the initial provisions and has continued to shadow all subsequent welfare efforts.

[8] This is Article 1, Chapter 1, of the Wartime Provisional Labor Insurance Regulations for Public Enterprises in the Northeast (meaning Manchuria). The complete regulations are found in the book *Tung-pei Lao-pao Ching-yen Chieh-shao* (Introducing the Labor Insurance Experience in Manchuria) (Shanghai: Lao-tung Ch'u-pan-she, 1950), pp. 1–13.

[9] *Ibid.* General summary, pp. 91–117; Mukden, pp. 123–38; Harbin, pp. 139–47.

[10] For basic research on labor insurance regulations, the most complete collection is *Chung-yang Lao-tung Fa-ling Hui-pien* (Collection of Labor Laws and Regulations of the Central Government) (Peking, 1953) (hereafter cited as *LTFL*). For a brief collection of relevant documents, see the Foreign Languages Press collection, *Important Labor Laws and Regulations of the People's Republic of China* (Peking, 1961), p. 11 (hereafter cited as *FLP*).

Within two years (twenty-three months), the Chinese amended the 1951 legislation to provide more generous benefits. Since 1953, there has been discussion but no systematic review of the program. Various changes have been made in the 1953 legislation, but the effects are hard to document since the reporting of labor insurance implementation diminished markedly in 1956 and has been almost totally absent since 1958.

Two questions are central to an understanding of the LIR and their effect on the Chinese industrial work force. What benefits are provided by the LIR, and who is eligible to receive them? On the first question the provisions are relatively explicit. Any covered worker whose earning power is interrupted or terminated because of an accident (either work-connected or not), who becomes sick (whether or not the illness is due to working conditions), or who loses his working power because of old age, is guaranteed a percentage of his salary and, under certain conditions, free medical care. The specific benefits and the percentage of salary depend upon whether the injury or sickness *is* job-connected, as well as upon the work history of the individual and the length of his employment in the specific enterprise. The only risk excluded from coverage is unemployment (whether voluntary or nonvoluntary), on the premise that unemployment is a transitory phenomenon in China and hence should not be included in such basic legislation.

In addition to the income provisions, each worker is guaranteed certain services. The worker injured on the job is guaranteed free medical care until recovery or until permanent disability is determined. This care is provided without further consideration as to the length of his employment. The worker injured off the job or who becomes sick under non-job-connected circumstances is provided some free medical care but is required to pay for certain medicines and also for his food. The benefits vary in these non-job-connected injuries and illnesses, depending upon the present status of the worker (is he a labor hero?) and his prior occupation (is he a combat hero?). Dependents of workers are provided medical care at one-half cost and are eligible for a pension upon the death of the breadwinner. In addition, the legislation provides specific procedures for the development of collective welfare facilities, such as sanatoria, orphanages, and old people's homes, all necessary to implement the benefits provisions.

How did the individual qualify for these benefits? There were two steps: first, the specific enterprises were required to recognize and become part of the labor insurance system, and then the individuals within covered enterprises had to become subject to the legislative provisions.

The enterprises covered by the LIR were:

    a. State, joint state-private, private, or cooperative-owned factories and mines employing one hundred or more workers and staff members, and their ancillary units.

    b. Railway, water and air transport, post, and tele-communication enterprises and their ancillary units.

    c. Capital construction units of enterprises, mines, and transport enterprises.

    d. State-owned building companies.[11]

In the discussions and public study of the 1951 LIR provisions, the Party and government explained the basis for its decision about who was to be covered in the legislation. The basic criterion, it was pointed out, was aid to those enterprises wherein the majority of China's industrial workers were employed and those industrial fields central to the industrialization efforts of the CCP. Between the announcement and the effective date of enforcement of the 1951 regulations, banks were dropped from coverage on the ground that their employees did not face as difficult economic conditions as others. Cadres and soldiers who were being paid by the "fixed supply" system were not initially included, and the majority of state employees (for example, teachers) did not receive labor insurance benefits at this time.

It should be made clear at this point that enterprises not included in either the 1951 or 1953 legislation were not forbidden from developing their own programs of labor insurance. Various schemes for care of workers could be worked out between representatives of the enterprise and the relevant trade union cadres. The expectation of those writing about labor insurance, however, was that the standards of these provisions would be lower than the national legislation. Furthermore, the contract required the specific formal approval of the local labor department representative.

Even though an individual was an employee in an enterprise included within the legislative provisions of the LIR, he might still be excluded from its benefits. Benefits were in part determined by a variety of considerations which were political as well as economic in their origin. Those specifically excluded from labor insurance included certain former Kuomintang (KMT) officials (a category of relatively

[11] *Ibid.*

small proportions by the 1960's) and those who had been convicted of certain crimes and were working under surveillance in the factory. (The latter group also appeared to be relatively small in number.)

Much more significant considerations for each individual were the requirements about productivity and age which could limit an individual's benefits. Here the Chinese (as most other states) have used their welfare program to encourage or discourage specific types of conduct. Thus the policy has been to reward union membership by reducing benefits for non-union members. In general, a long work history produces higher disability benefits; achievement of special productive status (such as combat hero or labor hero) has definite advantages. In sum, one might say that the policy of the CCP, and hence of the state, has been to reward those who contributed more to the state, and to aid those who were hurt in the course of their productive labors.

How is the program administered, supervised, and implemented? Although the Chinese did receive advice from Russian colleagues, they never adopted *in toto* the Russian legislation in regard to either benefits or administrative procedures.[12] In the LIR, the Chinese called for trade union administration at all levels of the program, and for all the risks and benefits covered in the provisions. As in Manchuria, the trade unions were specifically charged with responsibility for conducting the work history studies which determined eligibility for both trade union membership and LIR coverage. In the early years of the People's Republic this was undoubtedly a more difficult task than is currently the case (today the new workers are frequently from villages, are youthful, and could not have the kinds of social histories and class backgrounds that would make their political beliefs suspect, as did some old foremen and workers who had worked in the pre-1949 days).

All enterprises now have either a labor insurance office, which is often part of the trade union office, or a specific individual responsible for advice on LIR matters. Newspaper accounts speak of the concern and enthusiasm of the Party secretary for the insurance system as well as his responsibility for overseeing the activities and needs of workers. However, interviews with refugees from mainland China suggest that the recommendations regarding specific benefits, coverage, and the like are generally made by trade union members specifically charged with this responsibility, or by the shop cadres. Certainly the forms provided for the administration of the LIR require trade union authorization

[12] Bernice Madison, *Social Welfare in the Soviet Union* (Stanford, Calif.: Stanford University Press, 1968), is the most complete study to date of the Soviet program.

(though the trade union official, at least at upper levels, may also be a Party member).[13]

The role of the government in this program seems to be relatively minor. But government approval is required for those cases involving negotiated contracts in enterprises excluded by size or activity from the compulsory provisions of the LIR. Here the problem of social welfare impinging upon the economic resources of the enterprise is extremely important. If disagreements occur about interpretation of provisions, the government must be consulted. Apart from this, though, the government is not directly involved, except in those cases where the government itself is administering the LIR provisions (as is apparent in the case of so-called "contract workers").[14]

The most frequent and basic barrier to labor insurance in a developing society is the fact that the cost of the program is generally seen as too great for the society. How have the Chinese met the financial costs of implementing their legislation?

The Chinese (like the Russians) point out that their efforts compare favorably to welfare endeavors in Western society because the worker does not have to contribute to the program. Payments for all income provisions of the LIR are made directly by the enterprise itself to the worker himself, or by the trade union (drawing upon a state bank account set up by the enterprise, to which the enterprise contributes).

The second chapter of the LIR legislation is entitled "Collection and Custody of Labor Insurance Funds," and it highlights the importance that the Chinese attribute to fiscal responsibility in this program.[15] Two alternative financing methods are used to pay for different types of benefits. The enterprise arranges for services such as medical care (that is, it contracts with a hospital for these services, provides the necessary identification for a worker and his dependents, and so on), and the enterprise pays the costs directly to the hospital. The trade union pays the benefits such as long-term disability; these payments are made by the union from the funds (legally, 3 per cent of the wage bill) which the enterprise must deposit monthly in a state bank.

Obviously, however, the costs of the LIR involve more than mone-

---

[13] *LTFL,* p. 328. This is a model application form for labor insurance payment.

[14] Informants in Hong Kong in the spring of 1967 spoke of workers who were paid by the Labor Department in the city. The department then contracted the workers to enterprises and always paid their labor insurance when they were not working and occasionally when they were employed.

[15] See *FLP,* p. 13.

tary payments for services and benefits. A large number of services are required to implement the LIR provisions. Consequently, the sum an enterprise allocates for the LIR is divided; one part is retained by the local trade union for such payments as it may expect to make, and another portion is forwarded to the provincial and nationwide trade union organizations to fund the construction of the union's collective welfare facilities, such as sanatoria and hospitals.

This brief discussion outlines the general provisions of labor insurance as it was enacted in 1951 and broadened in 1953. Since that time, there has been no publicly announced discussion and revision of the program. In 1956, a review of the program was undertaken, which apparently resulted in recommendations to broaden the provisions once again. The proposed general revisions have never been publicized, however. On the other hand, various changes apparently have occurred within the program from time to time; some of these changes are essentially administrative and others substantive in their effect.

With regard to the administrative changes, it appears that as difficulties emerged in the operation of the program, various modifications were developed to make the LIR consistent with other national social policies. For example, the original provisions provided for collection of a pension at the enterprise office. Obviously this precluded a retired worker from moving to the countryside, which has often been mentioned as an important goal of the state. Trade union offices have proliferated in China, and consequently there are now trade union offices in many of the *hsien* (county) towns adjacent to the rural areas, and these offices deliver pension checks.

Though the LIR are the model for protection, the government has developed other programs, patterned on the LIR but designed for different sectors of the economy. Thus, there are special provisions for leave and vacation, as well as labor insurance protection and medical care, for government employees.[16] There have been changes (according to both refugee informants and some newspapers) in the retirement ages for different professions. Since the information indicating these changes is so fragmentary in nature, and only partially corroborated by informant accounts, it is likely that welfare in China, as in so many other states, is subject to tremendous variation from place to place and time to time. Given the relative vagueness of various regulations, and

---

[16] See *FLP,* pp. 72–82; also see *JPRS,* No. 6908 (March 15, 1961), Regulations on Handling Demobilized National Servicemen, particularly Articles 6, 10, 11.

the fact that the union in each enterprise still is responsible for the implementation of its own program, there would appear in practice to be considerable autonomy in welfare administration in China.

Over time, there have been important shifts in the priorities assigned to various tasks by the Chinese Communists, and these affected welfare programs. In the years 1951–53, the press emphasized proper labor union work and the importance of trade union registration and labor insurance. After 1953, however, comments calling for close attention to labor insurance almost disappeared from the public view, except in 1956 when commercial enterprises were brought into the LIR program. From 1957 on, there was considerable discussion about cost experience with the program, particularly with medical care where there were reported to be inaccurate estimates of need and considerable overuse. During this period some of the leading economic journals discussed such problems as unreasonable welfare subsidies and high costs, and their effects on industrial development. *Kung-jen Jih-pao* (Workers' Daily) and *Jen-min Jih-pao* (People's Daily) often cited personal illustrations of misuse or overuse of medical facilities.[17]

In sum, though the Chinese established the main features of their welfare program in 1951, the daily operation of the program was affected by changes in the pattern of Chinese society and by important shifts in the regime's emphasis on various social goals. The individual charged with some portion of LIR work, whether it be accounting procedures or verification of need, found that his activities were either enhanced or hindered, depending upon which problems the regime perceived as most important at any particular time in China's dynamic society. There were unavoidable ongoing conflicts between societal goals and individual needs, and between enterprise aims and individual suffering, and such conflicts engendered tensions within the system.

NEED

Welfare programs are organized in response to needs, and to analyze any program one must ask: Is there a need for the program in general, and does the individual applicant need assistance? Welfare programs involve not only financial assistance, but frequently a service as well.

Theoretically, once policy makers have satisfied themselves that a need exists that is legitimately in the realm of state policy, a welfare

---

[17] For example, see *Chi-hua Ching-chi* (Planned Economy) XII (1957), 18; *Ts'ai-cheng* (Finance) (March, 1957), pp. 13–15; *Chung-kuo Kung-jen* (China's Workers), October 17, 1957, pp. 20–21; *JMJP*, April 13, 1957.

program may then be developed; and such a program may be administered in one of two ways: (a) on the general assumption that all persons in similar sets of circumstances will need the proffered assistance (this is often referred to as the "social insurance" approach); or (b) on the assumption that a specific need shall be demonstrated by each individual (the "public assistance" approach). In the former case, some financial loss is inevitable, in the sense that some individuals in the covered population will receive assistance even though they do not need it. Membership in the covered population is the primary determinant of eligibility, and need is simply assumed. Hence a Chinese worker seeking medical care merely presents a card showing his worker status; he does not have to demonstrate his financial incapacity to pay. Under the "public assistance" approach, however, the circumstances and procedures are somewhat different. One must have membership in the designated population covered by the program, but he must also demonstrate need in order to obtain assistance. When resources are extremely limited, a program may not be able even to meet all demonstrated needs; then additional requirements—usually political in nature and often understood though not prescribed—may be imposed. These two alternative approaches are combined in the Chinese program, which contains both "social insurance" and "public assistance."

The Chinese built their system primarily on social insurance principles. By tying benefits to worker status and length of employment in an enterprise, they moved toward developing a program of predictable benefits. But in actual practice, this reliance upon social insurance has been subject to considerable stress and modification in China. The Great Leap Forward, for example, as well as periodic demands that enterprises overfill production targets, created stresses which demanded modifications of the system in practice. In these circumstances the Chinese had to make difficult choices. Having very limited resources, they were apparently reluctant and hesitant to rely upon the general assumptions of a labor insurance program.

Both published accounts stressing the overuse of services and informant reports of the treatment of disabled workers and their dependents suggest that, in practice, when retirement or a pension is due, those administering the program inevitably raise questions of individual need.[18] Although on paper the regulations provide that the status of

---

[18] A labor insurance cadre from Canton gave examples of various coal miner families who, when hit by tragedy, would talk to the trade union cadre. He then looked into their specific need, found other jobs, and often provided only a lump sum payment, particularly when the recipient might be young.

the worker in his enterprise, his seniority, his wage level, and the circumstance of injury are what should determine his benefits, in actuality the enterprise or trade union officials are often unable to implement the regulations without modification. The industrial workers, as a special group in Chinese society, have received some relief from economic difficulties, but not all workers have been equally helped at all times. It should be noted that appeals for increased economic production always emphasize the poverty of the society as a justification for wage restraints; it is no wonder that in welfare programs individual need is often the controlling factor, despite the enabling legislation which prescribes benefits without regard to need.

In view of limited resources and the high general level of need in China, what were the original decisions about coverage and how were they made? In the extensive directives and guidelines that accompanied labor insurance promulgation,[19] the boundaries of the program were spelled out and explained. Basically, the productive tasks of the enterprise and its size determined initial eligibility. In setting these administrative limits, the Chinese attempted to take into account: (a) the needs of workers in particular industries; (b) their contribution to the industrial tasks facing China; and (c) the administrative ability of the society to undertake welfare programs along with other pressing tasks in the period 1949–52.

Less clearly stated, but obviously involved, was the fact that in the Party's eyes the workers occupied a central role, in Marxist terms as well as in achievement of modernization goals. The workers represented a visible portion of Chinese society, one that had been subject to great hardship and was in some respects most affected by the deterioration of the more traditional types of social welfare assistance.

Obviously, the industrial workers had real needs. The development of a welfare program could be a socially useful device to provide incentive and support for the labor discipline expected of the workers. This idea, of course, ignores the question of comparative need. China, like most societies, established priorities (putting industry and industrial workers high on the list). These priorities were then used as parameters applied to the population at large for determining who would receive help and who would be excluded. In regard to those who fell outside the groups covered, it was argued that no assistance was

---

[19] See *LTFL;* also see the following accounts: *T'ien-ching Daily,* June 13, 1953; *JMJP,* July 23, 1951; *KJJP,* February 28, 1951.

possible because of financial limitations,[20] and the individuals involved were counseled to seek help through contracts negotiated by their units or from the appropriate governmental unit, that is, the Civil Affairs Department or the Labor Department.

All individual workers covered by welfare programs in China are persons judged by the CCP to make a central contribution to Chinese modernization and industrialization. Party and government cadres, members of the People's Liberation Army, and factory workers in the larger enterprises all occupy important positions in regard to the major tasks of the society. In explaining the limitation of size, the regime argued that productivity played a central role in determining coverage of workers and of worker groups within the larger classification, and that productivity should be measured both quantitatively and qualitatively. The enterprise worker who is politically active as well as productive, the master worker with apprentices, the worker who is innovative as well as able to overfill his target all are entitled—in theory and in practice—to receive extra benefits, access to special sanatoria, and better food. Employees in dangerous or physically harmful occupations are also given special treatment, including food, to increase the chance of long and efficient productivity (given the unusual circumstances and extra demands of their tasks), and benefits such as early retirement to compensate for a reduction of life expectancy.

Thus, even though the CCP made its first decision about welfare (that is, the decision to institute labor insurance) with the primary emphasis upon meeting need, thereafter considerations more central to production and other goals of the nation received greater emphasis. Indeed, certain administrative procedures seem to treat need as irrelevant, or to assume a lack of need. A good example is provided by the eligibility of fathers and mothers for a pension upon the death of a son or daughter who is providing support. To be eligible, aged parents must have derived their support primarily from a worker-child. If they are supported by other sons and daughters who are engaged in agriculture, they forfeit the right to aid through labor insurance. If a husband and wife are both employed, the wife obtains labor insurance through her employment and finds it difficult to change her status to that of dependent through retirement or resignation.

---

[20] *KJJP*, January 27, February 4, 1953. Also see *Lao-tung Pao-hsien Kung-tso Ts'an-kao Tzu-liao* (Reference Materials on Labor Insurance Work) (Shanghai: Lao-tung Chu-pan-she, 1951), pp. 66–77.

A further, and significant, factor affecting the role of "need" in the Chinese labor insurance program must be noted. No guidelines as to the definition of "need" have ever been published. In neither the major legislation nor the detailed regulations that accompanied it was there a specific statement about what constitutes "need." In short, although there are provisions which depend for application upon the determination of need, there is no indication of how "need" is to be determined.

Many specific problems are involved. For example, for some time expensive drugs were, in the case of need, paid for by the enterprise. The responsibility for a decision about need fell on the trade union cadres involved in labor insurance work and the activists in a work section. But the guidelines for them to follow in making their determination (if in fact they exist) have never been included in the accounts of welfare programs.

Negative limitations have always been a part of the program. For example, with one exception, prior to 1958 a worker could never receive at retirement more than his wage prior to retirement. That exception was when a worker was specially asked to stay on, in which case he might receive a bonus for the additional period of work. In all other conditions, the reimbursement could not exceed his current wage level. Even if a worker's wages had been lowered because of reduced working capacity prior to retirement, that reduced level usually constituted the base against which his pension was computed.

All of these limitations, together with the low average wage levels and the percentage limitations in the original regulations which fixed pensions at a maximum of 85 per cent of wages, mean that the retiring workers have had a very modest floor for existence. The worker needs additional help from his family, or additional assistance from the trade union, or both, to live out his retirement years.

In fact, of course, this segment of the industrial work force (retired workers) is rather small by comparison with the total industrial population. The Chinese have never published nationwide figures on the number of recipients for a specific benefit, but their fragmentary reports convey the definite impression that retired workers who receive labor insurance constitute only a minor portion of the total number of persons aided by labor insurance. Given the age groups in Chinese society, the relatively small percentage of the population engaged in industry, and the even smaller number of individuals engaged in large enterprises (even after almost twenty years of development), this should be expected. As one informant commented, "Workers are generally very young . . . I myself have only seen one retiring worker."[21]

The other major group of recipients for labor insurance benefits are those receiving medical care and disability payments. The observations made above with regard to need also apply here, although to a lesser extent. A man who suffers a relatively brief interruption of earning power is better off than one who must face a prolonged period of idleness. In terms of social cost, the advantages to society of recovery and care are more apparent when he can be returned to productivity. In the extended care situation, the humanitarian aspect has more relevance, and consequently benefits are lower; the worker must draw upon the resources of family or friends or seek additional help from his trade union. In some cases, particularly where an industrial accident occurs, the state (or trade union or enterprise) aids the individual in more than simply financial terms. The enterprise is obliged to provide a man possessing "working power" with an alternative job, apparently at his old standard of pay. It is also obliged to aid the family through a variety of services (which will be discussed below) that redress to some extent the real loss of earning power involved either in permanent and total disability or in partial disability.

To this point, the discussion of "need" has involved considerations of eligibility, work history, and the various provisions of labor insurance. But an important aspect of the problem of China's industrial force falls outside the scope of benefits discussed above. Mention has been made of the worker whose benefits are insufficient to pay for such special costs as medical care, drugs, and the like. There is also the case of a worker whose wage is insufficient to maintain a large family or, perhaps, to meet the school fees required for his children. How does the system operate in these circumstances? Here, the usual questions about work history, eligibility, and so forth are involved, but they are complicated by the necessity to consider the problem of need. In practice, the Chinese tend to rely upon individual need individually determined.

How is the need determined and how needy must an individual family be to qualify for aid? The fact that the legislation lacks guidelines for determining who is needy has already been noted. Since affluence is certainly not a characteristic of China's work force, the

---

[21] This man worked in transportation. Probably the incidence of retiring workers differs depending on the importance and length of time the industry has been developed in China. I would expect that textiles in Shanghai might have a number of retiring workers.

determination of who shall be helped is difficult. Information on the operation of this aspect of "social security" in China is difficult to obtain and fragmentary. Apparently, though, the procedure for determining need is essentially rather simple. The worker makes application to the head of his basic level trade union organization or the labor insurance cadre for a specific sum, on either a short-term basis or in terms of continuing help. The matter may or may not be discussed at a meeting of the whole basic level trade union group. (In case of special expenses, that is, medical expenses of a family or school fees, where the amount may be comparatively nominal, the circumstances of the case and the amount tend to dictate the procedure.) At any rate, the income of the family is determined, and a judgment is made about its ability to undertake the specific expense. A sum requested may then be loaned, or given, or partially loaned and partially given.

Generally, for standard requests, the discussions and decision-making processes are rather simple. In other cases, particularly where comparatively long-term assistance may be involved or the cost may be large, home visits to obtain information may precede the discussions of the basic trade union group.

Frequently, a financial decision will be buttressed by the use of various rehabilitative services to prevent the recurrence of the cost, or to mitigate it where prevention is impossible. A job may be found for a mother; places may be made available in the enterprise nursery for young children. A loan or a grant may be made. In this program one sees similarities to the familiar programs of public assistance in Western society.

Chinese society, however, cannot afford to meet all the needs of the workers, nor to maintain wage scales generous enough to provide for the problem of large families. Wage scales, moreover, are generally based upon skills and productivity, not on need and seniority. The funds available to supplement the basic wages are limited to sums drawn from the enterprise welfare fund or from the trade union funds. In this situation, the need must be determined on a personal basis.

It should be noted that the Chinese are apparently involved here in a modest program of income supplement, that is, adding to the salary of a full-time worker when certain kinds of needs appear. In the determination of whether a grant should be made, the union appraises the political attitude of the worker, along with his individual need, since the request for assistance is beyond the guarantees of the basic legislation.

An individual worker and his family who receive this income supplement lose an additional increment of privacy under the demands of the system. In order to receive aid, he is subject to a "means test," that is, an appraisal of the resources available to him. This examination goes beyond income and savings and involves an intimate judgment about his possessions and attitudes. A trade union activist makes a home visit, consults with the neighbors, and investigates the tangible aspects of life, food, furniture, clothing, and the like, as well as political enthusiasm. Upon receipt of aid, according to all informants interviewed by the author, the family's actions would be subject to scrutiny and the possibility of criticism by the neighbors. The suggestion was that neighbors might exercise an unspoken veto over the individual recipient's actions. Neighbors' complaints might seem similar to the endemic American comments about welfare recipients who purchase cars or own television sets, but in China they involved more fundamental matters—such as the type of meals one ate and eating preferences —as a gauge of need.

Despite the personal aspects described above, the evidence is unclear about the program's actual provisions. It seems, though, that the trade union does develop some guidelines about actual costs of living for a worker and dependents. This standard, a rather minimal one, is then applied to the needs of an individual. One informant spoke of a monthly standard of nine yuan per individual; another spoke of twelve, and yet a third spoke of twelve for the ordinary individual but twenty-five for the worker. The differences may reflect variations in costs of basic items. Just as wage scales take account of regional differences in the prices of certain commodities, so too must the program of social assistance. The differences are incorporated into budgetary provisions.

The major source of information about this program of income supplement was interviews. Each individual seemed to know whether or not a program existed and how it operated. Furthermore, in the case of larger enterprises, the rules and general regulations as well as labor insurance provisions were common knowledge. Where the number of applicants might be substantial, or where the applications, though few in number, occurred with frequency, the procedures for handling the matter had become formalized and bureaucratized.

In China, the two methods of meeting workers' financial needs—social insurance and public assistance—modify each other. On one hand, procedures have become established for meeting some special needs, most probably including school fees and certain cases of long-term assistance where the causes are clear. These procedures have become bureaucratized, and they are predictable in their outcome. Thus, the program has some of the characteristics of social insurance in industrialized societies. On the other hand, other aspects of social welfare, handled either individually or collectively, involve the kind of judgments about "need" which characterize public assistance. The cost factor makes these judgments necessary, and equity introduces itself. "Need," even if judged as operative for a group, must enter the picture when a society of scarcity tries to implement social security. Though the Chinese Communists tried to move more quickly than most other developing states to foster welfare programs, Chinese society is simply not wealthy enough to pay the costs of a generous program of social insurance. In this situation, rather than change the provisions of the program, the administration has signaled (through the main channels of communication, such as the press) the importance of thrift to each decision.

The welfare program for the industrial worker of China involves another series of benefits, primarily nonmonetary in nature. These include such items as access to special facilities of various sorts, schools, vacation resorts, special foods, occasional grants of clothing, and a range of special services. For these types of benefits, and for the services that accompany them, the allocational principles are remote from the general assumptions of need. Services and grants beyond the basic items of food and shelter become subject to the political values of the society and the goals of the Party; they reflect the stress placed on productivity and the proper political consciousness.

Facilities such as nurseries and creches are designed to facilitate the employment of women and still maintain acceptable standards of labor discipline. In these cases, need is shared by all claimants, so the administrator must make his decision either on a graded standard of need among a group of needy individuals, or on the basis of alternate and important political values. The latter is what generally happens. Thus, the welfare program acquires a conservative quality; it is used to reinforce societal values which the regime considers central.

Services

The advantages of being an industrial employee in China involve more than the enjoyment of relatively good wages and labor insurance benefits. The factory worker has available to him various facilities and services which are a part of the enterprise for which he works. These services are developed especially for him and his dependents, and his payment for them, if any, is nominal. Such facilities and services are scarce in the countryside and in fact are unavailable to most urban dwellers not employed in the larger factories. The development of the service component of a welfare package is clearly an important part of the social change involved in urbanization and factory work.

Obviously social welfare goals cannot be achieved solely through the promulgation of directives. Operational requirements, such as personnel and facilities, have always been a limiting consideration. Since 1949, however, the Chinese have made a substantial increase in the facilities available to carry out their program of education, public health, and medical care. The official statistics in *Ten Great Years* indicate a rapid increase in schools, nurseries, kindergartens, hospitals, and clinics, all important in relation to governmental policy.[22]

The crucial factor of this development from the point of view of the worker is that their needs are specially provided for through the use of (a) trade union funds at the national and provincial levels to create hospitals and sanatoria for the special use of workers; and (b) enterprise funds for certain special service facilities associated with the enterprises themselves, notably nursing stations, occasional clinics, and workers' clubs. Although the regime hopes eventually to provide many of these services for all the people of China, proportionally more of the workers' needs are now met because the means to improve conditions were integrated into the original legislation for workers.

The emphasis on construction and development of welfare facilities, which was especially great in the immediate postliberation years, was altered when new tactics and priorities were adopted at the time of the Great Leap Forward in 1958. The essence of the Great Leap Forward was the attempt to achieve national development through labor mobilization and nonmaterial incentives. The growing discrepancy between urban and rural living necessitated a reduction of the emphasis upon amenities of daily life in the cities.

After the failures of the Great Leap Forward, the ensuing hardships of 1960–62 severely limited the resources available for welfare programs, at a time when the consequences of the Great Leap were placing

[22] *Ten Great Years,* comp. by the State Statistical Bureau (Peking: Foreign Languages Press, 1960), pp. 219–23.

in some jeopardy the standards achieved for medical care and labor protection. Taken altogether, the years 1958–62 were full of stress for Chinese urban dwellers.

A more positive result of this period, however, can be seen in two emerging characteristics of urban worker welfare programs: (a) the emphasis upon services designed to permit a more efficient use of time by the worker, primarily through help in his arrangements for daily living; and (b) various campaigns directed at specific problems that had emerged in the early years of the Great Leap Forward. The programs actually developed by the Party were designed to reduce, in the long run, the need for worker dependence upon social welfare. They demonstrated the ingenuity of the Party in mitigating strains of industrial life, within the framework of Party values, at minimal costs to the resources of the society.

Prior to considering these individual programs and mass campaigns, however, it is necessary to note that a substantial increase in facilities and personnel was essential to the operation of labor insurance even at minimum levels. The general shortage of facilities and personnel was not equally felt throughout China. For example, medical care requires special facilities, equipment, and personnel, all of which were more available in the urban and industrial centers of China; because of the regime's inability to develop comparable facilities and equipment in the countryside, the collectivization of medical practice and the supervision of young medical students and paramedical personnel between 1949 and 1958 favored the city dweller.

Yet the very successes and achievements of these early years raised a series of difficult administrative issues for the units responsible for allocation of medical care, as well as difficult problems for the recipients themselves. One thing that became clear as a result of the 1958 retrenchment of social welfare facilities was the necessity for planning. The Chinese, short of skilled personnel, found that economic waste occurred both because of excessively high standards of care and because of poor planning.[23] The inability to make efficient use of all hospitals, the difficulties of transportation, the inability to predict accurately needs for equipment and items of care all added to the basic costs of medical care. Consequently, the Party, of course, stressed the necessity for lower standards and for an emphasis on quantity rather

---

[23] The shortage of personnel skilled in statistics and planning has been noted by many economists. In welfare it produced the complaints of *KJJP*, February 25, 1958; *Kwang-hsi Jih-pao*, February 26, 1958; and Shanghai *Wen Hui Pao*, Shanghai, March 5, 1957.

than quality, especially during the Great Leap Forward. But such an emphasis immediately gave rise to complaints, which were especially strong when a service was attached to the enterprise itself. Criticisms such as "too few children in a nursery," "too few patients in a hospital," and "misuse of sanatoria facilities" reflected the basic problem of reconciling a low economic level and the unmet needs of the population, plus the enormous planning requirements demanded for efficient utilization.

The medical care and disability provisions of labor insurance programs were designed to aid those injured during their participation in factory life. They were accompanied by a program of labor protection, designed to make industrial working conditions safer and the worker aware of the extent to which accidents can be prevented. There has been a definite link between labor protection and insurance in China since 1949.[24]

Labor protection involves problems of financial cost and of time; consequently, it, like labor insurance, comes into direct conflict with other industrial needs. The contrasting pressures for improving protection and increasing production are felt by the worker, the enterprise, the trade union, and the relevant government units, all of whom participate in labor protection programs.

A program of labor protection requires not only protective equipment (that is, gloves, hard hats, safety belts) but also the introduction and enforcement of safety techniques in the normal procedures of factory life. As W. E. Moore noted: "The outstanding characteristic of factory work is the extent to which the timing and sequence of activities are regulated by machine."[25] To understand this statement is to take a significant step toward the achievement of protection.

The early focus of Chinese programs was on development of safety standards and equipment for plant operation, and on mass campaigns to alert the worker to his role in the program. Many special services were developed for those involved in hazardous work under dangerous conditions, such as, for example, coal miners and those working in high places. Such programs are essentially particularistic, in that they focus upon the special requirements of specific segments of the industrial work force.

The second aspect of the program, emphasized from 1960 on,

[24] The discussion from Manchuria made reference to the necessity for keeping both ideas together, but the major legislation was not passed until 1956. See *FLP*, pp. 32–72.

[25] W. E. Moore, "Industrialization and Social Change," in B. F. Hoselitz and W. E. Moore, *Industrialization and Society* (New York: UNESCO, 1963), p. 304.

stressed work protection in a more general sense: that is, the universal requirements for rest and recuperation. Both the cadres and the workers were sensitized to these requirements after the productive campaigns of the Great Leap Forward.[26] The enthusiasm of the Great Leap had resulted in increased factory accidents. Informant reports confirm what one might have expected: the combination of fatigue and poor equipment resulted in many personal injuries. One of the consequences of trying to solve problems on the spot, and of using substitutes when facing a shortage, was equipment failure and worker fatalities. Rising accident rates resulted in renewed emphasis in 1960–61 upon safety and the physical fitness of the workers as an important factor affecting production.

From another perspective, the labor protection problem involves a basic contradiction between industrial safety and productivity which is difficult to reconcile. An emphasis upon production is to be expected in any society attempting to industrialize, especially a nation as impatient as China for rapid change and achievement. In this context, the primary task of the enterprises and the trade unions is to encourage production. In the continual battle to achieve targets, the worker, the manager, and the trade union cadre discover that it may be impossible to observe safety requirements and procedures and still fulfill production targets. In Chinese society, there are no rewards for safety equal to those for production achievement. At the same time, the specific risk of accident in particular circumstances may seem small. Consequently, it is easy to understand the pressures and circumstances under which safety procedures may be suspended.

Informant reports suggest that industrial accidents are generally attributable to an individual taking a risk by short-cutting established procedures. When the goals of productivity and safety clash, the trade union cadre within an enterprise has no way to enforce the safety regulation even if he wished to. The cadre from the local Labor Department responsible for checking safety equipment is not able to prevent misuse or nonuse of safety equipment, nor can he always prevent extended work hours that result in a higher accident rate. All of these people share the interest in, and understand the importance of, production achievement—as well as safety standards. Finally, the industrial enterprise may also be faced with worker "fatalism" and the individual

[26] See *KJJP*, July 21, 1960, p. 1, August 12, 1960, p. 2, November 4, 1960, p. 1, November 11, 1960, p. 2.

worker's lack of understanding of labor protection and its consequences.

In the aftermath of the apparently mobile labor situation of 1958–59, the 1960 protection program emphasized the problem of inexperience and the necessity for providing intensive instruction to the newer workers who do not appreciate the necessity for care.[27] Here the employee, often from the countryside, or the casual worker drawn into the enterprise lacked the discipline and information necessary to implement effectively the labor protection regulations. The enterprise and trade union moved into the breach with an emphasis upon labor protection and its value. (Unfortunately, the medical care program was often least satisfactory for those most likely to suffer disabling accidents, since many of its provisions did not cover temporary or probationary employees.)

Another aspect of labor protection is rehabilitation. Here again, services as well as financial assistance are involved. If the skilled worker can be reintegrated into the enterprise, even with reduced working power, the ultimate cost of his injury to the enterprise will be less, and his experience can continue to be utilized. In addition there is a societal emphasis on productivity. The ultimate cost of the program is lessened if workers are given alternate jobs or light work, and their dependents hired where possible. To recognize the value of "rehabilitation" requires, as in the case of all other aspects of social welfare service, an ability to perceive long-range benefits, but the long-range view is often in conflict with the immediate productive goal.

Various criticisms of the rehabilitation program by workers indicates that some evasionary tactics have occurred. For example, an injured worker discovers that his job is gone, or the partially recovered worker is transferred to another enterprise. Moreover, the enterprise uses organizational categories for workers to limit promotions and regulate the availability of welfare.[28] It seems clear that from time to time the recurring themes of reducing costs and increasing productivity in the short run outweigh the welfare commitment of enterprise programs and affect the practical spirit of labor insurance service provisions.

Since 1958, the obligations of the trade unions in administering welfare assistance have broadened. At the same time, the economic

---

[27] This same comment is in a political report on the Harbin experience in 1949–50.
[28] *Yün-nan Jih-pao,* July 28, 1956; *CFJP,* Shanghai, January 29, 1956.

costs of the facilities and benefits have undergone re-evaluation. The new emphasis has been upon those services requiring minimal investment but closely related to the realities of daily life. Slogans praising thrift and frugality, injunctions against extravagance, and an emphasis upon the need to solve one's own problems—these moralistic prescriptions were utilized in the special welfare programs designed to improve the workers' dining halls and boarding houses. The object of these campaigns was to free the worker for more important tasks while still providing some tangible help in solving the real problems of poor meals, noisy accommodations, and "leaking roofs." Community teams repaired houses, after ascertaining the needs of workers and their families. Sewing groups repaired garments. Trade union and Party personnel worked with cooks.

These services, organized collectively, have represented attempts to solve real problems in the daily life of urban workers, particularly in periods where the pressure for high labor performance has been acute and has been reflected in extended work schedules. These services have actually highlighted to the worker the Party's concern and its attention to the individual's problems, but without involving the more tangible material incentives that represent a greater economic cost to the state. The provision of such services has also served to reduce tardiness, absences, and poor performance, and to promote labor discipline.

The services discussed above involve an interaction and perhaps a mutual reinforcement process between the worker and the regime's representative. In the various activities designed to meet real needs of the worker, the trade union representative and the Party man use the familiar techniques of social surveys, criticism sessions, and group discussion to pinpoint the difficulties of daily living. Once these problems are explicitly seen, methods that rely primarily upon organization and labor are used to mitigate or solve difficulties. The gain to the worker can be very real. The Party and the trade union cadre can reassert the advantages that accrue to those who participate in the productive process. The services themselves provide a transition from the family orientation of the countryside to the functionally organized urban life. The enterprise serves as the organizing unit and builds the web of relationships and advantages which insure individual performance and unit operation toward the expected goal.

In the evolution of the services, the trade union and the Party still must face the fact that incentives remain, at least for the present, an important factor. The attempt to develop a collective viewpoint must accompany the programs to reward achievement and acclimate the worker to the realities of planning, both for himself and for the nation. Promoting the idea that the necessity is for sacrifice today in order to achieve tomorrow is not simply a matter of communicating the message but also a problem of establishing habits of thrift and saving as permanent aspects of urban life. Consequently, this aim, too, is reflected in the welfare services. Although the worker may indeed require financial assistance currently, the purpose of a successful welfare program is not only to meet this current need, but also to provide him where possible with the institutions and techniques to effect the long-term solution of his own problems within the general theoretical framework provided by the Party.

An excellent example of such a program is the mutual saving program,[29] which was given considerable emphasis in 1961. If a worker is confronted with a special need, for example, school fees for his children, he has four options—his own resources, special assistance from the trade union, a loan from the enterprise, or keeping his children out of school. Some needs are unexpected or beyond the financial capabilities of the worker, but some are a result of mismanagement and lack of planning. The ability to postpone gratification is a function of maturity, but it also involves money management. The emphasis upon a mutual saving program had a number of important results. By strongly encouraging savings, it urged workers to accumulate some resources when state aid was limited or unavailable. Hopefully the long-run demands upon the state could then be reduced at the same time that workers learned about planning.

Although the program's operation varied, it generally had the following characteristics: the worker joined an enterprise or trade union mutual saving plan by agreeing to have a certain sum deducted from his salary. The sum might be one, three, or five yuan per month, which was then deposited in a bank account, frequently under the scrutiny of the trade union. The worker was able to borrow an amount based upon his contribution and pay it back over some period of time or withdraw amounts for his own use.

Informant accounts indicate some confusion about the program—who owned the money, and the difference between withdrawal and savings. Undoubtedly the savings served to help the industrial require-

---

[29] See, for example, three articles in *KJJP,* August 13, 1961, p. 1, discussing the program.

ments of the state. Probably for some workers the fund operated more as a loan than as a savings account. The program certainly relieved demands upon the enterprise and the trade union. Furthermore, here was a device to meet specific needs that emphasized habits useful for urban workers living in a money economy, where planning for the future was valued and future gratification or problem solving could, in theory at least, serve the purposes of both the individual and the state.

Social Welfare and the Worker

"There is an ample supply of alienated people in the new states; but industrial workers are not the most prominent among them both because the industrial sector remains small and because workers tend to be relatively secure and prosperous in relation to their country."[30] The available evidence suggests that this statement by Lloyd Fallers is applicable to contemporary China, where the industrial worker has the advantages of urban living, the *relative* stability of enterprise employment, a comparatively generous wage scale, and the additional benefits of labor insurance. The provisions of labor insurance, described in this paper, indicate the kinds of benefits provided to the worker. Though levels of worker satisfaction in contemporary China may depend first of all on wage levels, there can be no doubt that labor insurance is an important factor which can add to satisfaction.

This final section of the paper has two tasks. First, an attempt will be made to place in perspective the achievements and limitations which have characterized Chinese welfare efforts. Second, an attempt will be made to appraise the consequences of social welfare, and its administration, for the trade unions and the workers.

Social welfare programs (particularly those designed to assure minimum levels of income) are both an expression of the CCP's pattern of values and a functional device to meet real social needs; they not only reflect the utopian quality of Marxist thought but also symbolize the Party's acceptance of the welfare functions of the state. The modernization pattern of a state today is not likely to be a mere repetition of earlier centuries of Western experience. In the twentieth century, the industrial workers in newly developing countries, upon whom much of the success of industrialization depends, are not expected to endure the Dickensian conditions of the nineteenth century. However, welfare programs in many societies—whether short-term mass aid to cope with

[30] Lloyd Fallers, "Equality, Modernity, and Democracy in the New States," in *Old Societies and New States,* ed. Clifford Geertz (Glencoe, Ill.: The Free Press, 1963), p. 188.

disaster, or institutionalized programs of income maintenance—have a strong conservative quality. The programs are developed in or for times of social crisis, to meet urgent needs, when the alternative to their establishment may be social and political chaos; and in developing welfare programs a government is not only providing a mechanism to meet specific needs, it is also attempting to reinforce the values of the society which it supports.

In an industrialized society, the conservative quality of such programs is quite clear. In the United States the 1935 "social security" bill is an example, just as were Bismarck's nineteenth-century medical programs for Germany. What about developing societies such as China? In the newer states undergoing modernization and industrialization, this conservative quality is not so clear, since the programs frequently result from the success of a revolutionary movement and hence have both a radical and a conservative quality, depending upon one's reference point.

Welfare programs can help to establish or support new social patterns that a modern government wishes to encourage. In non-Western societies, including China, welfare programs for the urban worker reinforce bonds which undermine the fusion of economic functions with the family, and hence, of course, they reinforce new patterns of urban living and new relationships between individuals and enterprises.

As leaders of a developing society, the Chinese Communists have had considerable success in coming to grips with the needs and difficulties of economic life for the enterprise worker. Following the decision to implement a program of welfare legislation, the fact that the Chinese established a broad-scale coverage of risk and provided programs offering considerable services and benefits, rather than minimal programs, emphasized the utopian aspects of Marxism, but also gave evidence of a grasp of the economic realities of the workers' difficulties. The important limitations of the programs have reflected two factors: (a) that China has not been able to escape the dilemma of cost in terms of resource allocation; and (b) that Marxism, while providing ideological impetus for welfare programs, also acts as a limiting factor in terms of the program's economic aid. Each of these two issues will now be considered in further detail.

Economic reality did not deter the decision to undertake welfare, but it did and does compromise the program at a number of points. The regulations clearly indicate that those individuals centrally involved in the industrial process receive priority treatment and fare best under most welfare programs. The more remote the contribution to industrialization—whether because of skill or age—the lower the benefits. Rationally, this is probably an understandable and acceptable emphasis, even if personally harsh in some of its consequences. Less acceptable, however, is the insistence that political attitudes be taken into account in allocating benefits. Even in those cases where a worker's productive contribution is clear, the further condition of political activism enters the picture, and only after this condition is met is "need" again considered.

As Martin Wolins noted in his account of the functions of welfare,[31] the state views the program as a mechanism for reinforcing the values of the society. In the Chinese case, the program does reinforce the value of productivity to the industrial effort, but it also supports the concept of political activism. To some extent all welfare programs, anywhere, have a political component in their eligibility provisions, whether stated or unstated—the most obvious of which in the West might be citizenship or state residence requirements. These are, of course, predictable, and the guidelines for fulfillment are clear. In the Chinese case, however, the intrusion of political activism as a criterion provides an opportunity for the most capricious of judgments with respect to eligibility, and at a minimum largely removes the predictability and hence reduces the security provided by the program. This uncertainty does not permeate all of the programs, by any means, but it apparently is involved in an important way in the social assistance program, where need is likely to be most clear.

Another manifestation of the intrusion of both cost considerations and political factors can be seen in the service apsects of the program. For example, Party members apparently have an advantage in terms of admission to special medical facilities, sanatoria, and the like. Although this limits the egalitarian aspects of Chinese society, the consequences may be minimal for the efficient operation of welfare, provided that the selected Party members need the service.

When the welfare programs are diverted from their intended users, or where facilities are taken over by other organizational units or agencies, the intended contribution of the service or facilities is ob-

[31] Martin Wolins, "The Societal Function of Social Welfare," *New Perspectives*, I (April, 1967), 1–18. Wolins argues: "Social welfare is a device for maintaining or strengthening the existing social structure of an industrial society," p. 2.

viously reduced. In the absence of hard data on the extent to which a diversion of facilities has occurred in China, it is impossible to be precise about the size of this problem, but newspaper comments and continual criticism from refugee informants suggest that this phenomenon is not infrequent.[32] (Obviously, informant reports on this question may have a significant bias.)

Given the twin goals of easing economic difficulties and encouraging productivity, there is an additional area in which the Chinese welfare experience has seemed to be counterproductive. The development of labor insurance and labor protection has resulted, not unexpectedly, in a broad range of new administrative problems and needs, such as the determination of disability and benefits, and the provision of wages. The Russians attempt to solve this problem by having government administrators provide the expertise, but the Chinese do not.

Rehabilitation and pension disability would obviously benefit from the development of detailed standards and the use of the skilled knowledge that the government, drawing upon the medical profession, could offer. But the Chinese, who have relied primarily on trade unions and enterprises to administer key welfare programs, have not tried this approach. While the governmental units at the city and provincial level are involved more directly than the legislation itself suggests, there is no evidence that the welfare system takes maximum advantage of the expertise available within governmental ministries. For example, while the disability classifications are derived from the experience of the People's Liberation Army, the actual determination of disability appears to be primarily a function of enterprise committees that have a doctor serving as a member. This reluctance to centralize responsibility may reflect indecision within the whole of the Chinese economy, where the issue of centralization versus decentralization has yet to be completely resolved.

There are a variety of problems, similar to the issue just mentioned, which could probably be more equitably resolved on a centralized basis. A simple example is the whole question of work-connected disability. In China, the system has not reached the complexity of workmen's compensation cases in the United States, but there are significant problems that are meaningful for the individuals involved, if occasionally humorous in their description. Is a worker who falls

---

[32] Informants commented on the temporary use of facilities by the army and Party. There have been letters in the newspapers on this issue.

asleep bicycling home after participating in a marathon production drive, and consequently suffers a severe injury, hurt on the job?[33] Such cases are amenable to decision, but the determination of equity on a broader basis than seems to be the case in China would permit the system to operate in a fashion more faithful to its goal of meeting needs.

Another aspect of the problem of cost involves the very crucial problem of forced social change. In developing societies, welfare programs—and this is certainly true of those in China—serve to reinforce the separation of the economic functions from the family. But society is not really able or prepared to shoulder the welfare tasks formerly met by the family, and, indeed, the leaders wish to lessen the reliance of ordinary people on state programs. Thus, the Chinese wish to encourage women to enter into productive labor, but they also want to minimize the costs necessary to permit such a program. In this situation, the prospective woman worker will often seek to enlist aged grandparents to solve the problem of child care; even this alternative may not be attractive to the state, since it increases the urban population and reinforces old family and generational ties. Even though the state does wish to emphasize its contribution to the welfare and wellbeing of its citizens, for example the aged, it does not wish to undertake general responsibility for financial support of the aged, because such a task is beyond the means of the state budget.

In non-Marxist settings, there is more willingness to use traditional social assistance at the same time that the modernization process is developing. In China, the strong reluctance of the state to permit the continuance of old values or traditions seen as harmful to the building of a socialist state complicates the process of social change, raises the costs of industrialization, and places the welfare process under some restraints.

The majority of examples cited up to this point have dealt with various aspects of development as the LIR have slowly taken on the formalized character of a welfare program in an industrialized society. Various additional problems result from the relative inflexibility of the general welfare orientation. For example, a most difficult issue, particularly since 1957, has resulted from the emphasis upon labor immobility in the LIR provisions. The Chinese constructed their welfare program to encourage and reward labor immobility. Obviously, when they wished to transfer an individual, his benefits and seniority were trans-

---

[33] An informant cited the bicycle example and said the man was considered covered.

ferred with him. However, in cases where the Chinese wish to encourage workers to return to the countryside for a lifetime rather than for a year or so, the costs to the individual are considerable. Thus, the worker who is transferred to a hardship post is asked to volunteer for a future in which he has to forego values that have been described as the essence of the CCP's contribution to his life.

What has happened, of course, is that national policy, and the general assumptions underlying it, have altered since the early years, and the LIR system has not been revised to meet the changes. Welfare lags behind the growth and change of the society. This is a relatively common characteristic in many societies, and often results in a considerable dissatisfaction on the part of both the welfare recipients and the state.

In sum, the basic thrust of China's welfare program would profit from a review of both the operative principles upon which it is based and the institutional arrangements that support it. In the absence of such a review, the system has developed *ad hoc* operating procedures, some of which seem to be of doubtful value, either for modernization or for the welfare goals. For example, the development of a hierarchy of classifications for workers—such as temporary, apprentice, part-time, contract—with differing benefits, designed to limit enterprise and welfare costs, may not always serve the industrial functions of the state, and cannot help but discredit the integrity of welfare programs.

Finally, it is necessary to consider the tasks of the trade union cadre or activist as he participates in the many facets of social welfare. The decision to rely on the trade unions, to the comparative exclusion of other possible social organizations, in administering welfare programs was understandable, in the light of domestic considerations in 1949. The Chinese Communists wanted to develop a strong trade union organization to mobilize worker support and insure labor discipline. This task required the development of files and information about the workers in industrial enterprises. Worker participation in the labor unions, however, needed either a relatively high degree of coerciveness or some positive benefit, particularly at a time when the wage levels were quite low. Since the administration of a labor insurance system required much the same information, the welfare task could be subsumed in the task of organizing the trade unions. Labor union membership would gain some increment of support by virtue of the positive benefits accruing to those who were members.

Since 1949 trade union membership has become almost universal and relatively routinized. The tasks of the trade union cadres in relation to labor insurance, however, have remained and indeed grown as the program and its benefits have developed and multiplied in a developing society.

If one reviews the social welfare tasks of the trade union cadres, it is clear that they involve providing help to individual Chinese workers. Since both the Chinese and Soviets have specifically eschewed a "helping profession," in the individual sense in which Western societies think of social workers, the functions of "help" are to be found in other institutions, specifically the trade unions and neighborhood associations. In China the emphasis has been upon group work, and there are abundant injunctions to cadres about learning from the workers, helping where possible, or explaining the necessity of less desirable actions (from the individual's point of view). The concepts of leadership demanded of the Party, and to a lesser extent of the trade union cadres, require the most intimate and continued contact with the workers. What is the effect of such a close relationship and of intervening in such personal problems?

In light of the welfare tasks set by the CCP, the services involved, and the demands for participation placed upon both trade union cadres and workers, it may well be that a kind of conservatism and perhaps a sense of separateness have developed among industrial workers and union cadres in China. The extent and degree of either of these qualities is very difficult to judge. First of all, it is clear that trade union cadres have always had an important role in directing and insuring worker productivity, and in heightening worker political consciousness and education. In many situations, these goals clearly run counter to and have dominated the values and operation of welfare programs. In the urban setting, the CCP has tried, despite severe economic restraints, to make the enterprise a total unit providing for as many of the individual worker's needs as possible. The role of the trade union worker or the worker-activist has been to stress the obligations of the worker to the industrial goals of the nation, to emphasize the political and economic sacrifices that are entailed in this effort. What has not been sufficiently emphasized in the study of contemporary China is the fact that there has also been a consistent welfare component to CCP programs. Certainly the trade unions of China have been expected to transmit the various messages of the Party—but they have also been responsible for administering an important and valuable aspect of enterprise employment. Given the emphasis upon productivity, with its implied admiration of skill, the absorption in tasks which characterizes many of China's workers, and the sense in which the wages and welfare of the worker give him a modest "stake" in society, has not this constellation of factors produced a group somewhat conservative in relation to the messianic implications of Maoist theory expounded in the Great Proletarian Cultural Revolution?

Appendix

MICHEL OKSENBERG

Sources and Methodological Problems in the Study of Contemporary China

Diversity in sources marks research on contemporary China. In broadest terms, primary sources fall into one of five categories: (1) the mainland press[1]—books, journals, and newspapers—and monitored radio broadcasts; (2) interviews with and publications of former residents of the Chinese People's Republic (CPR);[2] (3) accounts by people who have visited the mainland;[3] (4) Chinese fiction, particularly novels and short stories; and (5) secret Chinese documents and other data obtained *covertly* and released by non-CPR agencies. In addition to these five primary sources, various governments and private institutions publish summaries of the mainland press and compile statistics, chronologies, bibliographies, and biographical directories on China.[4] Moreover, several competent analysts survey the primary

---

[1] For bibliographies of Chinese periodicals available in the West, see in particular G. Raymond Nunn (comp.), *Chinese Periodicals, International Holdings, 1949–1960* (Ann Arbor, Mich.: Association for Asian Studies, 1961), 3 vols.; U.S. Library of Congress, *Chinese Scientific and Technical Serial Publications in the Collections of the Library of Congress* (Washington, D.C.: Government Printing Office, 1961); Union Research Institute, *Catalogue of Mainland Chinese Magazines and Newspapers* (Hong Kong: Union Press, 1962).

[2] For example, Eric Chou, *A Man Must Choose* (New York: Knopf, 1962); Chow Ching-wen, *Ten Years of Storm* (New York: Holt, Rinehart, and Winston, 1960); Robert Loh, *Escape from Red China* (New York: Coward-McCann, 1962); Mu Fu-sheng, *The Wilting of the 100 Flowers* (New York: Praeger, 1962); and Teng Chi-ping, *The Thought Revolution* (New York: Coward-McCann, 1966).

[3] See note 27, p. 172.

[4] For a guide to United States governmental sources, see John M. H. Lindbeck, "Research Materials on Communist China: United States Government Sources," *Journal of Asian Studies*, XVIII (1958–59), 357–63.

sources and chronicle developments on the mainland in a journalistic fashion. The publications of the better analysts, in fact, have achieved the status of "primary source material."[5] Finally, secondary sources include the ever increasing number of scholarly books and journal articles.[6]

Naturally, this classification scheme is not easily applied. Many specific sources do not fit easily into one category. Moreover, the boundary between primary and secondary sources is hazy. The difficulties encountered in categorizing specific items, however, are linked to important methodological problems. For instance, are the biographies of model workers and the histories of model production units classified as "mainland press" or "fiction"? The question is intertwined with the more general problem that fact and fiction form less of a dichotomy than a continuum in China, so that one is never sure where a particular news item should be placed on that continuum. To cite another question, do we classify those non-CPR statistical compilations based partially on overt and partially on covert sources as "primary" or "secondary" materials? The question is relevant to the more general problem of how to evaluate data when we are unable to ascertain how the data were acquired. The attempt to categorize specific sources of information is, in short, a worthwhile exercise; it forces us to confront important methodological problems.

This paper, however, addresses itself to questions on a different level, questions arising from the very diversity in the sources of information. First, how is one's perspective affected by the sources one employs? Second, what are some of the principal strengths and weaknesses of each source? What skills should be developed to exploit each source effectively? And third, what are the implications for research and analysis of the discontinuities in the sources?

The underlying theme is that thorough research on China, no matter what the inquiry, requires the use of all types of sources—the mainland press, interviews, fiction, visitor's accounts, and the secret documents. Analysis must weave information derived from many sources into a coherent pattern; in essence, documentation involves the search

---

[5] Among these are *Chinese News Analysis, Current Scene, Tsu Kuo,* and *Far Eastern Economic Review.*

[6] A comprehensive bibliography is Peter Berton and Eugene Wu, *Contemporary China: A Research Guide* Stanford, Calif.: The Hoover Institution, 1967); also important is the annual Association for Asian Studies compilation, "Bibliography of Asian Studies," a special issue of the *Journal of Asian Studies.*

for convergence among a variety of sources. Confidence in the analysis rests upon the extent to which the available sources point in the same direction.

The following pages develop this theme by first showing that the problems we raise are genuine. Next, we compare quantitative data on local leaders—the data derived from different sources—to indicate that, in fact, the sources produce somewhat different impressions of the subject studied. Then we assess the principal sources of information, their possible limitations and biases. This leads us to consider the implications of the continual change in sources through time, as first one source, then another, is more heavily drawn upon. In our conclusion, we restate our basic theme and argue that it has more general applicability. Although this paper deals exclusively with research on China, we believe that it sensitizes us to the methodological problems which pertain to the study of any society; the problems are merely more acute in the Chinese case.

THE PROBLEM SPECIFIED

The fundamental problem, so noticeable in the case of China but existent everywhere, stems from the limited perspective provided by any source of information. No matter what his inquiry, the social scientist must constantly ask how his perspectives have been shaped and his data skewed by the sources he employs. He must ask the same question about the books he reads. For example, the underlying perceptions and judgments are noticeably different in three of the more important, broadly conceived books on China, Edgar Snow's *The Other Side of the River: Red China Today,* Franz Schurmann's *Ideology and Organization in Communist China,* and A. Doak Barnett's *Cadres, Bureaucracy, and Political Power in Communist China.*[7] In extremely oversimplified terms, Snow paints a vast China in the throes of industrialization; Schurmann sees China through Mao's eyes, a society seething in its contradictions; Barnett leaves the impression of China as an extraordinarily complex bureaucratic apparatus. Naturally their books reflect the authors' divergent educations and values,

[7] Edgar Snow, *The Other Side of the River* (New York: Random House, 1961); Franz Schurmann, *Ideology and Organization in Communist China* (Berkeley and Los Angeles: University of California Press, 1966); A. Doak Barnett (with a contribution by Ezra Vogel), *Cadres, Bureaucracy, and Political Power in Communist China* (New York: Columbia University Press, 1967).

as well as the distinctive purposes the books were intended to serve. But our interest here prompts another observation. Each author relied primarily on different sources: Snow on an extensive visit to China, Schurmann on the press, and Barnett on interviews with former cadres of the CPR. China from the windows of a train is in the throes of industrialization. In the pages of *People's Daily,* China is the dialectic at work. And from the lips of former cadres, China is a huge bureaucracy. These authors, it would appear, were inescapably the captives of the perspectives provided by their sources. It seems important to ascertain what perspectives are commanded by each source.

This is only part of the problem, however. Charting the development of a country requires data comparable through time. Lacking comparability, one cannot be sure whether perceived development represents real phenomena or merely reflects changes in the data. Yet, the study of China must be undertaken in the face of strong discontinuities in the sources. Compare, for example, the available sources for the mid-1950's with those for the mid-1960's. To study developments in 1954–57, researchers are able to turn to an informative national press, local newspapers, ministerial journals,[8] legal compendia,[9] reports issued by the Chinese statistical bureau,[10] published proceedings of national congresses,[11] and the accounts of travelers who were just beginning to visit the mainland in those years. In 1954–57, the systematic interviewing of recent émigrés from the mainland by Western-trained social scientists had not yet developed; there were few émigrés and pitifully few scholars around to interview them.[12] A favorite source for measuring "public opinion" on the mainland was letters from mainland residents to relatives living abroad.[13] The community of professional

[8] For example, *Ts'ai-cheng* (Finance) published by the Ministry of Finance, *Chung-kuo Chin-jung* (Chinese Money and Finance) published by the People's Bank, *Chung-kuo Nung-pao* (Chinese Agriculture) published by the Ministry of Agriculture, and *Chung-kuo Shui-li* (Chinese Water Conservancy) published by the Ministry of Water Conservancy.

[9] Some principal compendia are: *Collected Laws and Regulations of the CPR,* Vol. 1–13 (1954–63); *Collected Financial Laws and Regulations of the Central Government;* and *Collected Banking Laws and Regulations.* For a bibliography on Chinese law in translation, see Lin Fu-shun (ed.), *Chinese Law Past and Present: A Bibliography* (New York: East Asian Institute of Columbia University, 1966).

[10] Especially published in *T'ung-chi Kung-tso* (Statistical Work).

[11] See especially *Proceedings of the National People's Congress,* available for several sessions.

[12] An exception was A. Doak Barnett. See his *Communist China: The Early Years, 1949–1955* (New York: Praeger, 1965).

[13] See, for example, Richard Walker, "Hunger in China: Letters from the Communes," *New Leader* (June 15, 1959), supplement.

"China watchers" was assembling in Hong Kong, and the chronicles of the China scene were just beginning to appear.[14]

In comparison, the sources for 1963–65 are considerably different. The national press for this period was less informative, more propagandistic. Banned for export, local newspapers and ministerial journals for those years were only occasionally available,[15] and legal compendia, published proceedings from national congresses, and any kind of firm statistics were extremely rare.[16] New sources of information developed, however. Secret mainland documents, obtained surreptitiously, were released by the United States government and the Republic of China (Taiwan).[17] Typescripts of provincial radio broadcasts became more widely available. Social scientists recorded their interviews with former residents of the mainland, and the interview protocols were filed at several universities.[18] As China became increasingly accessible to non-American tourists and journalists, a flood of "China travelogs" appeared on the book market, many of which contained interesting information. The Hong Kong community of "China watchers" had jelled, and their myriad analyses were readily available. Authorities on Taiwan began to make their analyses available. The pattern of available sources, it is clear, had changed considerably within a decade.

Unique sources of information, moreover, exist for each of the periods into which students of China like to subdivide the history of the CPR. Perhaps most significantly, these sources provide a strong temptation to generalize beyond what is legitimately supported by the data. Impressions of developments throughout China during a particular period repeatedly have been influenced by suddenly available sources that in fact apply to more limited topics or sectors of society.

The period of rehabilitation and consolidation, 1949–55, is distinguished by its coverage in the memoirs of Westerners who lived in

---

[14] *China News Analysis* first was published in 1953, the *Union Research Service* in 1955, *Contemporary China* in 1956, and *Current Scene* in 1959. The *Far Eastern Economic Review* also improved the quality of its reporting of China in the late 1950's.

[15] Provincial papers have gradually changed their format, making them less valuable than in the 1950's. There is less local news, more reprinting of news items appearing in the national press.

[16] For a discussion of statistical problems, see Li Choh-ming, *The Statistical System of Communist China* (Berkeley and Los Angeles: University of California Press, 1962); John Emerson, *Nonagricultural Employment in Mainland China, 1949–58* (Washington, D.C.: Bureau of the Census, 1965), pp. 11–25; Leo Orleans, "Trouble with Statistics," *Problems of Communism,* XIV, No. 1 (January–February, 1965), 39–47.

[17] A collection of these documents is at the Hoover Institution.

[18] Scholars at Harvard, Columbia, Michigan, and California (Berkeley) in particular hold such protocols.

China during those years.[19] Typically, these people wrote of their arrest and imprisonment. During the same time, Chinese immigrants to Hong Kong described the violence of land reform in Kwangtung, and United States soldiers captured by the Chinese during the Korean War described the psychological stress of the prison camps. The sources added up to a China totalitarian and harsh.

The first Five Year Plan, 1953–57, saw the maturation of China's statistical system and the availability of journals and provincial newspapers. Perhaps to a greater extent than for any other period, the Chinese Communists themselves supplied the information relied upon for the study of their country. Partly as a result, for these years there emerges an image of a unified, dynamic, pragmatic leadership guiding an orderly, politically progressive, economically developing China. To students of China, the 1953–57 period has become the regime's halcyon days.

The Hundred Flowers campaign of 1957 produced outspoken criticism of the regime, voiced particularly by the intelligentsia and students. Here was fresh information that bore upon a crucial unknown —public opinion and discontent in China. Published in *ta-tze-pao* (wall posters) and newspapers, the comments were widely distributed and continue to be studied in the West. Partly on the basis of these data, the literature is prone to say that by 1957 the government had alienated some of its initial supporters.

The Great Leap Forward of 1958–60 witnessed a reduction in the flow of hard information from the mainland. Local newspapers, ministerial journals, and firm statistics became unavailable. Students of China became more vulnerable to rumor and gossip. Speculation centered on why Ch'en Yün's speech to the Central Committee's Third Plenum remained unpublished, why the Politburo and Secretariat added personnel in 1958, why Mao resigned as head of state in early 1959, and why P'eng Teh-huai was removed as Minister of Defense in September of that year. (Disclosures during the Cultural Revolution underlined the importance of these questions, key to an understanding of Chinese politics since 1957.) Partly because of the change in source availability, the literature on the Great Leap presents a somewhat different image of policy formulation than the literature on the 1953–57 period. The secondary literature on the mid-1950's has been

[19] Allyn and Adele Rickett, *Prisoners of Liberation* (New York: Cameron Associates, 1957); Harriet C. Mills, "Thought Reform: Ideological Remolding in China," *Atlantic Monthly* (December, 1959); A. Bonnichon, "Cell 23–Shanghai," *The Month* (January, 1955), pp. 1–32; Harold Rigney, *Four Years in a Red Hell* (Chicago: Regnery, 1956).

heavily influenced by economists, who use the available statistics to weave a narrative of policy heavily influenced by economic determinants.[20] The literature on the Great Leap has been greatly influenced by political commentators, who trade on speculation to tell a tale of policy affected by power struggle.[21]

Noted sources for the 1959–64 period of "readjustment, consolidation, filling out, and raising standards" are the secret army bulletin, the 1961 *Kung-tso T'ung-hsün,* and the secret documents from a county in Fukien, the 1963 Lien-chiang documents.[22] These materials provide an inside view of the procedures in the Chinese army and county organization, as well as the problems faced by the regime following the collapse of the Great Leap. The 1962 exodus of emigrants from the mainland, including a number of former cadres, also provided new sources of information. The sudden availability of these sources enabled students of China, who had been deeply impressed by the role of organization during the Great Leap, to emphasize the bureaucratic nature of the Chinese government and to apply organizational theory in their analyses.[23]

---

[20] For example, Li Choh-ming, *Economic Development of Communist China* (Berkeley: University of California Press, 1959); Kenneth Walker, *Planning in Chinese Agriculture* (London: Cass and Company, 1965); T. J. Hughes and D. E. T. Luard, *The Economic Development of Communist China, 1949–60* (New York: Oxford University Press, 1961); and Alexander Eckstein, *Communist China's Economic Growth and Foreign Trade* (New York: McGraw-Hill, 1966), pp. 1–86.

[21] For example, Harold Hinton, "Intra-Party Politics and Economic Policy in Communist China," *World Politics,* XVI, No. 4 (July, 1960), 509–24; Roderick MacFarquhar, "Communist China's Intra-Party Dispute," *Pacific Affairs,* XXXI, No. 4 (December, 1958), 323–35; Robert Bowie and John Fairbank, *Communist China, 1955–1959: Policy Documents with Analysis* (Cambridge, Mass.: Harvard Center for International Studies and East Asian Research Center, 1962), introduction; David Charles, "The Dismissal of Marshal P'eng Teh-huai," *China Quarterly,* No. 8 (October–December, 1961), pp. 63–76; Schurmann, *Ideology and Organization in Communist China,* chaps. i and ii. Two exceptions are Alexander Eckstein, "The Strategy of Economic Development in Communist China," *American Economic Review,* No. 2 (May, 1962), pp. 508–17, and Peter Schran, "Economic Planning in Asia: Communist China," *Asian Survey* (December, 1962), pp. 29–42.

[22] See J. Chester Cheng, *The Politics of the Chinese Red Army: A Translation of the Bulletin of Activities of the People's Liberation Army* (Stanford, Calif.: The Hoover Institution, 1966); and S. C. Chen and Charles P. Ridley, *The Rural People's Communes in Lien-chiang* (Stanford, Calif.: The Hoover Institution, in press 1968).

[23] For example, Ezra Vogel, "From Revolutionary to Semi-Bureaucrat: The 'Regularisation' of Cadres," *China Quarterly,* No. 29 (January–March, 1967), pp. 35–60; G. William Skinner, "Compliance and Leadership in Rural Communist China" (paper read to the annual meeting of the American Political Science Association, September 8–11, 1965); Schurmann, *Ideology and Organization in Communist China,* and H. Franz Schurmann, "Politics and Economics in Russia and China," in Donald W. Treadgold (ed.), *Soviet and Chinese Communism: Similarities and Differences* (Seattle: University of Washington Press, 1967), pp. 297–326.

Finally, during the 1962–67 socialist education campaign and Cultural Revolution, disclosures in the Red Guard publications and charges leveled against the victims of the purge provided another view of the political process. Although these materials have not yet been sifted with care, it appears that they will produce a new image of politics that in part will involve this: policy in China is the product of an intricate combination of Mao's whims, factional disputes, and bureaucratic infighting.[24]

The discussion above perhaps caricatures and certainly oversimplifies the emerging literature on China. Much of the writing on China maintains a balanced perspective. Moreover, the research on the various phases in the CPR's history is based upon more than a few unique sources. The many different sources available to us indicate that the 1949–54 period was generally one of harsh rule, the 1954–57 period was one of pragmatic rule, the 1957–65 period was marked by intense internal political debate, and so on. Thus, to state the argument more precisely, while the unique sources generally create valid impressions, they also tend to make us lose sight of subtleties and crosscurrents.

In addition to shaping an image of a period of history, each of these sources generated research on specific topics. The availability of informants who had been imprisoned in China led to research on thought reform.[25] The outburst during the Hundred Flowers increased the interest in the fate of intellectuals on the mainland.[26] The release of the *Kung-tso T'ung-hsün* spurred research on military affairs.[27] If precedent is a guide, the materials obtained during the Cultural Revolution will provide the necessary incentive for further study of policy formulation. Here, the problem is to establish the validity of the study for other time periods. To what extent, after all, are the studies on thought reform, based upon sources of 1949–54, applicable to other periods?

[24] See Philip Bridgham, "Mao's 'Cultural Revolution': Origin and Development," *China Quarterly,* No. 29 (January–March, 1967), pp. 1–35; Cheng Chu-yuan, "Power Struggle in Red China," *Asian Survey* VI, No. 9 (September, 1966), 469–84.

[25] See Edgar H. Schein *et al., Coercive Persuasion* (New York: Norton, 1961), and Robert Lifton, *Thought Reform and the Psychology of Totalism: A Study of "Brainwashing" in China* (New York: Norton, 1961).

[26] See Roderick MacFarquhar, *The Hundred Flowers Campaign and the Chinese Intellectuals* (London: Atlantic Books, 1960); Dennis Doolin, *Communist China: The Politics of Student Opposition* (Stanford, Calif.: The Hoover Institution, 1964); Merle Goldman, *Literary Dissent in Communist China* (Cambridge: Harvard University Press, 1967); Chalmers Johnson, *Communist Policies Toward the Intellectual Class* (Hong Kong: Union Research Institute, 1959).

[27] See especially articles in *China Quarterly,* No. 18; and Ralph Powell, *Politico-Military Relationships in Communist China* (Washington, D.C.: U.S. Department of State, 1963).

How long should the images produced by the *Kung-tso T'ung-hsün* characterize aspects of military affairs? The questions point to a real danger in the development of contemporary Chinese studies. In perhaps an excessive fascination with the more glamorous "one shot" sources, researchers seem to be exploiting first one source, then another, in a noncumulative way.

Clearly, the continual changes in sources of information only partially explain the discontinuities in perspectives and research efforts. The changes in the financial resources available to different people and institutions in the China field, the rise of a younger generation of China specialists—many of whom have never been to the mainland—and the retirement of others, political events (such as the Sino-Soviet dispute, the war in Vietnam, and the Chinese detonation of the bomb), as well as intellectual developments apart from contemporary Chinese studies, have inevitably caused scholars in the field to strike out in new directions. The increasing discontent of those in the field of comparative politics with the totalitarian model, and the growing comparative literature on the politics of industrializing societies, for example, have had their impact on students of China. As a result, there is somewhat less interest today in how the rulers mobilize the people, but more interest in how the masses manipulate their rulers and how the alternatives available to the rulers have been shaped and narrowed by societal constraints. This does not necessarily mean that China is less of a mobilization system today than it was ten years ago; rather, different aspects of the political system have attracted attention. Similarly, America's increased interest in problems of guerrilla war, coupled with the Sino-Soviet dispute, the accessibility of fresh information on CCP history, and the seminal work by Chalmers Johnson on the Yenan epoch, has prompted a re-evaluation of the Chinese Communists. No longer considered captives of Soviet influence, they now tend to be viewed as captives of their own guerrilla past. Such discontinuities and reappraisals are not to be decried. On the contrary, they are the hallmark of intellectual creativity and growth. Rigorous adherence to the same perspective and dogged reliance upon the same sources would be sure signs of dogmatism and stagnation.

Our argument is therefore a more limited one. Scholars must be the masters of their data, not vice versa. As we have attempted to show above, students of China face a continually shifting pattern of sources. This demands an awareness of how perspectives shift and data change simply because the sources have altered. In turn, this requires a sensitivity to the perspectives and biases embodied in each source. Since the Chinese do not provide us with information comparable through time, moreover, trends can be studied only by independent construction of series of comparable data. These seem to be some of the methodological problems posed by the diversity and changes of sources of information on post-1949 China.

A COMPARISON OF SOURCES: A CASE STUDY

This section compares data on local leaders[28] derived from four sources: interviews, the mainland press, fiction, and travelogs.[29] We aggregate and compare data drawn from these four sources on the educational level, Party and Youth League affiliations, and geographic origins of local officeholders, and discover that each source yields a somewhat different impression of the background of local leaders. In comparison, the press pictures a slightly better educated local elite, in which members of the Chinese Communist Party (CCP) monopolize positions of power. From the interviews comes the impression of a less educated local elite, in which non-CCP members have limited access to positions of power. Chinese fiction, when compared to the other sources, devotes more attention to officials who serve in their native place and to poorly educated officials who triumphed over adversity. Finally, data derived from the travelogs are noteworthy primarily for their comparability to the interview data.

While these subtle differences among the sources are important, in most general terms all sources point in the same direction. Local leaders received surprisingly little formal education. Their average age increased from 1955–57 to 1962–65. With a few important exceptions, they served in their native place. Finally, local officials, except on the lowest levels, were predominantly Party or Communist Youth League (CYL) members. It is satisfying to know that the four sources converge on these matters. But beyond these broad generalizations, the four sources suggest slightly different conclusions.

Before reporting the findings, I must add a strong word of caution. These data in no sense represent a random sample of the total commu-

---

[28] Any attempt to identify "local leaders" encounters considerable conceptual and definitional problems. At what level does government cease to be "local"? Who are "leaders"? For purposes of this paper, "local leaders" are defined as those with power and influence up to and including the county (*hsien*). This definition and the problems it presents are discussed at greater length in my paper, "Local Leaders in Rural China, 1962–65: Individual Attributes and Bureaucratic Positions" (see pp. 155–215).

[29] See notes 24, 25, 26, 27, and 28, pp. 171–73, above.

nity of local leaders. As a result, when I state that the average formal education of local officials varies from the 6.4 years reported in the press to the 4.2 years reported in fiction, *I certainly do not imply* that in fact the average educational level of local officials is in the range of 4.2 to 6.4 years of formal schooling. Rather than yielding precise information on local leaders, these data only allow a comparison of the images of local leaders projected by different sources. To repeat, the figures below, although suggestive, do not necessarily provide accurate information on local leaders.

EDUCATION

Educational data were provided for 172 of the 353 local leaders studied. The press reported a strikingly higher average educational level than did the other three sources. The press reported an average of 6.4 years, travelogs 4.8 years, interviews 4.5 years, and fiction 4.2 years (see Table 47).[30]

TABLE 47

EDUCATION OF LOCAL LEADERS, BY SOURCE, 1962–65

Source of Information	Total Number	Number, Educational Data Available	Percentage of Total	Average Number Years, Formal Schooling
Interviews	125	119	95%	4.5
Press	84	18	21%	6.4
Fiction	63	9	15%	4.2
Travelogs	81	26	32%	4.8
Total	353	172		4.8

What is the reason for the discrepancies among the sources? One possibility might be that they are reporting on different types of local leaders. For example, interviews yielded biographies of fifty-one leaders on the subvillage level, while the press, travelogs, and fiction together yielded a total of two such biographies. Since subvillage leaders tend to be less well educated than those above them, perhaps the interview data have a downward bias. When subvillage leaders are eliminated, however, the pattern remains much the same, with the

---

[30] For complete rigor, the data derived from the following tables should be tested for their statistical significance. However, such tests would grace the data with greater precision than they deserve. To apply such tests would create an illusion of rigor, while all we intend to do is employ quantitative data to raise suggestive hypotheses.

educational level from the interviews only slightly elevated (Table 48). Thus, the low level reported in the interviews does not appear to result from the inclusion of greater numbers of team leaders.

Another possible source of downward bias in the interview data is a tendency of the informants, claiming a relatively high six to nine years of formal education themselves, to underestimate the educational attainment of those below them. Or perhaps local leaders in Kwangtung, the native province of the informants, are less well educated than local leaders in other Chinese provinces, which would also account for the

TABLE 48

Education of Local Leaders above the Team Level,
by Source, 1962–65

Source	YEARS IN SCHOOL			
	0–2	3–6	7–12	N
Interviews	28%	46%	26%	68
Press	18%	25%	57%	16
Fiction	44%	22%	33%	9
Travelogs	31%	46%	23%	26

downward bias in the interviews. These possibilities seem unlikely however, since the travelogs, lacking these biases, yielded comparable educational levels.

Another likely source of bias is that the press tended to report the educational level of the better educated local leaders, and to omit information about the less well educated. In describing local leaders, the press reported their educational level less often than other characteristics. It disclosed the educational level for eighteen of eighty-four local leaders for whom partial data were obtained. In comparison, the press gave the age for fifty-eight, Party affiliation for forty-one, and place of origin for forty-four of the eighty-four. Finding the lower educational attainments less congenial, the press may have neglected reporting them.

An additional source of upward bias in the press might be its emphasis on model cadres. It well might be that model cadres are better educated than the more typical cadres described in the interviews.

PARTY AFFILIATION

All sources point to the domination of local politics by members of the CCP or CYL. For the years 1962–65, however, the sources differed in their images of the degree of domination (see Table 49). The press and fiction conveyed the impression that all local leaders were members either of the CCP or the CYL. If the leader described was not affiliated with these organizations, his lack of affiliation went unreported. In fact, the press and fictional accounts did not explicitly describe one single official as non-Party (*fei-tang*) or non-CYL, while these sources described sixty-two officials as *tang-yüan* (Party member) or *t'uan-yüan* (league member). In the interviews, on the other hand, 29 per cent of the leaders described were neither CCP nor CYL members. Again, the data from the travelogs yielded similar results; 21

TABLE 49

PARTY AFFILIATION, BY SOURCE, 1962–65

Source	Total Number	Number for Whom Data on Party Affiliation Available	Percentage of Those Reported CCP or CYL Members	Percentage of Those Reported Non-Party
Interviews	125	119	71%	29%
Press	84	41	100%	0%
Fiction	63	21	100%	0%
Travelogs	81	52	79%	21%

per cent of the local leaders described in these sources were neither CCP nor CYL members.

These results cannot be solely attributed to the fact that the sources focus upon local leaders serving on different levels. If we compare the sources just on their reporting of village level leaders—the only level for which we have a sufficient number of cases to make comparison worth while—the same conclusion emerges (Table 50).

It is difficult to evaluate the bias of each source here. One reasonable hypothesis is that the Party-controlled press tended to exaggerate the role of Party members in the society. Moreover, the data suggest that, *in comparison to the press,* the interview data were less likely to overestimate Party membership. The interviews clearly indicate that the informants, none of whom claimed CCP or CYL membership, either were not well informed about Party and CYL organization on the brigade level or chose not to be completely candid for fear of CCP reprisals. In any case, eleven of the sixteen informants claimed not to know how many CCP or CYL members were in their brigade; three of the sixteen were unable to identify all the CCP members in their

TABLE 50

PARTY AFFILIATION OF VILLAGE LEVEL OFFICIALS
BY SOURCE, 1962–65

Source	Percentage of Those Reported CCP or CYL Members	Percentage of Those Reported Unaffiliated	N
Interviews	76%	24%	50
Press	100%	0%	14
Fiction	100%	0%	10
Travelogs	81%	19%	16

team.[31] Some informants, in short, may have erroneously described a few brigade and team leaders as not being CCP or CYL members.

The few available surveys of Party and CYL affiliation of local leaders[32] gave lower percentages of membership than do the data in Tables 49 and 50, suggesting that all our sources had an upward bias. Moreover, each source may have had an upward bias for a different reason. Under certain policy guidelines, such as those that may have prevailed in 1962–65, the Party-controlled press may have been told to dwell upon the merits of local leaders with CCP or CYL membership. Visitors touring rural areas perhaps tended to come into more frequent contact with CCP and CYL members. Many informants, impressed by the power of the CCP, possibly were prone to exaggerate the dominance of Party members. Our conclusion here must be a limited one. In their reporting of individual biographies, the press and fiction portrayed a higher percentage of local leaders as Party and CYL members than did the interviews and travelogs. All sources, however, may have had an upward bias.

NATIVE–OUTSIDER

Next, we compare the images of the ties local leaders had to the areas they served. Did the sources differ in their portrayal of "natives"

[31] See Production Team interviews, Responses to Question No. 31; Production Brigade interviews, Responses to Question No. 21. Confirming these responses, Informant H stated: "So far as non-Party members in the Production Brigade are concerned, most people in the brigade know little about Party branch affairs. In fact, most people only know who the Party secretary was; others on the branch committee might be known as Party members, but their posts would be unknown to most." Informant H, Interview 4 (November 5, 1965), p. 3. (These protocols are available upon request.)

[32] See Chalmers Johnson, "Lin Piao's Army and Its Role in Chinese Society," Part 2, *Current Scene*, IV, No. 14 (July 15, 1966), 7; John M. H. Lindbeck, "Transformations in the Chinese Communist Party," in Treadgold (ed.), *Soviet and Chinese Communism*, p. 86; Barnett (with Vogel), *Cadres, Bureaucracy, and Political Power*, pp. 153–54.

and "outsiders"? We have already discussed the significance of this question and the complex analytical problems it poses (see pp. 192–94). Because of the complexity, to classify local leaders into native and outsider categories and then to aggregate and compare the data from the different sources would oversimplify matters. Two examples make this clear. *Chinese Youth* gave the biography of a thirty-two-year-old county level cadre who had served in a remote area of Kweichow Province for eleven years; he had been dispatched to this county as part of the invading People's Liberation Army (PLA) forces.[33] One of the main themes of the article was to show that the cadre had become a part of the local society. So loved was the cadre, the article states, that the natives tried to arrange a marriage for him with a local girl. The offer was refused by the cadre, who insisted that "revolutionary activity comes first." Later, the story recounts that the cadre seized the first opportunity to visit his native Anhwei to marry a girl from his home town. This incident indicates that in spite of the main theme of the story, this local official still longed for his old home place. In another example, peasant informant Li, coming from a lineage long established in his village, classified his forty-five-year-old brigade chairman and Party branch secretary Ch'en as an outsider. Informant Li also disclosed that the Ch'en family had moved to his village in 1947, prior to Communist rule, that leader Ch'en had several kin in the village, and that the Ch'en family had moved its household registry to the village. This evidence suggests that leader Ch'en probably considered himself a native of the village by the mid-1960's, although less of a native than Li.

In view of these analytical problems, it may be best to evaluate the sources here on a qualitative basis. Each source did give a somewhat different impression of the proportion of outsiders and natives among local leaders and the degree of public receptivity to outsiders. The press dwelt upon youths who had volunteered to serve in non-native areas; these youths became schoolteachers, accountants, technicians, propaganda workers, and lower level civil servants. The press also devoted considerable attention to higher level cadres assigned to lower level, non-native posts. Though these youths and cadres were outsiders, they generally were received, according to the press, as though they were natives. The press conveyed an image of outsiders warmly welcomed and integrated into local communities. At the same time, the

[33] *Chinese Youth*, No. 17 (1967), pp. 4–11.

press described the native officials, by and large, as people devoted to the nation's welfare. Deviant behavior of native local leaders was less a matter of loyalty to the native community than a matter of personal corruption or promotion of the interests of one's immediate family. In short, only rarely did the press describe a gap between an outside leader and the native population, or picture a native as the articulator of his local community's interest.

Fiction emphasized almost exclusively local leaders of native origin. Fictional accounts did portray "outsiders," but only those serving on a temporary basis, in the role of cadres sent down (*hsia-fang kan-pu*), cadres "squatting at a point" (*tun-t'ien*), cadres in work teams (*kung-tso tui*), and so on. It may well be that in the effort to extol self-reliance, the writers chose to highlight virtuous native officials.

The travelogs upon occasion recorded whether the local leader was born in the area he served, but tended not to explore the native-outsider issue as a problem in human relations. In the travelogs, the matter was not a salient issue.

The interviews with people from Kwangtung, however, placed the issue in different perspective. Informants were quick to note whether a leader was a native or an outsider. They suggested that the outsider did not easily become a part of local society, and that resentment against outsiders was strong and persistent. Moreover, in comparison to the other sources, the interviews tended to portray native leaders as more loyal to their home area and more willing to defend the interests of their community. Here, the interview data may reflect their geographic bias: Kwangtung informants, resentful of northerners who had somewhat different customs and spoke a different tongue, may have been more sensitive to native-outsider relations. At the same time, the other sources may simply have underplayed the ill feelings which locals harbor against leaders sent from the outside.

In short, when judged in a qualitative way, the sources differed in their reporting of native and outside local leaders.

AGE

In this instance, the similarity among the sources, not their differences, deserves comment. The convergence, moreover, increases confidence in the conclusions reached. As Table 51 shows, the sources yielded similar average ages of local leaders, both for 1955–57 and 1962–65. They all indicated that the average age of local leaders

TABLE 51

AVERAGE AGE OF LOCAL LEADERS,
BY SOURCE, 1962–65

Source	1955–57	1962–65	Change
Interviews	31	35	+4
Press	29	37	+8
Fiction	31	35	+4
Travelogs	34	38	+4
Total	31	36	+5

increased in the last ten years, underlining a trend of an aging elite which has been observed throughout the political system.[34]

A comparison of the sources according to their distribution of local leaders among age groups (see Table 52) points to only two small differences. When compared to the other sources in 1962–65, fiction described a higher percentage of local leaders in the "below twenty-five" age bracket. Fiction, in short, focused upon the role of youth. In the same years, visitors seem to have met very few rural leaders in this age bracket; only 7 per cent of local leaders described in the travelogs

TABLE 52

AGE DISTRIBUTION OF LOCAL LEADERS 1955–57 AND 1962–65, BY SOURCE

Source	Year	AGE				N
		Over 45	35–44	25–34	below 25	
Interviews	1955–57	3%	28%	44%	25%	32
	1962–65	10%	36%	41%	13%	108
Press	1955–57	0%	21%	36%	43%	14
	1962–65	32%	25%	21%	22%	44
Fiction	1955–57	19%	15%	15%	50%	26
	1962–65	26%	20%	13%	40%	15
Travelogs	1955–57	19%	26%	22%	33%	27
	1962–65	33%	25%	35%	7%	52
Total	1955–57	11%	23%	29%	37%	99
	1962–65	24%	27%	35%	16%	219

[34] See Donald Klein, "The 'Next Generation' of Chinese Communist Leaders," *China Quarterly,* No. 12 (October–December, 1962), p. 60; Frederick Teiwes, *Provincial Party Personnel in Mainland China, 1956–1966* (New York: East Asian Institute, Columbia University, 1967), p. 7; also my "Paths to Leadership in Communist China," *Current Scene,* III, No. 24 (August 1, 1965), p. 2.

were under twenty-five. But the convergence among the sources is more striking than the divergence. As Table 52 indicates, each source reported a noticeable drop in the proportion of leaders under twenty-five years of age, and a noticeable increase in the proportion over forty-five years of age.

SUMMARY

Quantitative comparisons show that interviews, the press, fiction, and travelogs presented somewhat different images of local leaders, an important aspect of the Chinese governmental system. Greatest divergence among the sources occurred in their reporting of the formal education and Party affiliations of local leaders. There was greater convergence on the age and native-outsider dimensions, although the sources appeared to differ qualitatively in their treatments of the native-outsider aspect of local elite. One is tempted to generalize beyond this study: the sources probably differ in their treatment of other aspects of the governmental system also. To identify and compensate for the bias of any single source, convergence must be sought among several sources.

Evaluation of Sources

Bias in reporting of specific aspects of the political system is only part of the broader problem; namely, each source has its own set of strengths and limitations. The discussion below explores some important limitations of the major types of sources on China, and concludes that research drawing upon a wide range of sources is required to escape the limitations imposed by any one source.

The Press

Four broad methodological problems are confronted in the use of the mainland press: its ideological and cultural world view, its deliberate distortion, its discontinuity in coverage, and its unintentional inaccuracy. The first two, while difficult to handle, at least raise identifiable problems. The press employs Marxist-Leninist categories, as well as many Chinese historical and literary allusions. The press, in short, views the world through Chinese, Marxist-Leninist eyes. At the same time, it deliberately distorts developments both in China and abroad. Playing a heavy hortatory role, moreover, it tells more about how things *ought* and *ought not* be done than how things actually *are* done. Pekingology is the art of compensating for deliberate distortions and of conveying the Chinese system and views to audiences who think in different categories. Remaining sensitive to Chinese cultural and linguistic peculiarities, reading between the lines, decoding esoteric communications, and making proper allowance for discrepencies between verbal statements and actual behavior are some of the techniques that can be acquired to overcome deliberate distortions and Chinese distinctiveness.[35]

Discontinuity in coverage presents other interpretive and methodological problems. China's newspapers and journals, as with journalism everywhere, tend to emphasize the issues that are particularly important to their publishers and fail to place these issues in perspective. The heavy emphasis upon the government's momentary concerns makes it difficult to chart trends. When a particular issue is no longer mentioned, has it merely lost its salience, or has it ceased to exist? Press treatment of the involvement of veterans in village politics provides an excellent example of the interpretive problem.

In the mid-1950's, articles and legal enactments continually appeared on the problems of integrating the demobilized PLA soldier into village political life. These statements stressed that the PLA veterans were a valuable source of township, village, and subvillage officials, and articles on cooperatives frequently headlined the news that ex-servicemen in fact had become village officials in large numbers.[36] In the mid-1960's, fewer such headlines appeared. For example, the index to *Jen-min Jih-pao* (People's Daily) for 1963 cited only three articles on the role ex-servicemen played in village life,[37] and the United States Consulate General translation series contained very few articles on the

---

[35] For other discussions of Pekingology and the use of the press, see Schurmann, *Ideology and Organization in Communist China*, pp. 13–16, 62–68; Donald Zagoria, *The Sino-Soviet Conflict, 1956–1961* (Princeton, N.J.: Princeton University Press, 1962), pp. 24–35; Alan J. P. Liu, *The Press and Journals in Communist China* (Cambridge, Mass.: MIT Center for International Studies, 1966), pp. 72–95, 111–18; for a brilliant series of studies based upon sensitivity to the nuances of the Chinese language, see T. A. Hsia, *Metaphor, Myth, Ritual and the People's Commune, A Terminological Study of the Hsia-fang Movement*, and *The Commune in Retreat as Evidenced in Terminology and Semantics* (Berkeley: Center for Chinese Studies, mimeograph, 1961–64).

For a discussion of Kremlinology, one of the intellectual antecedents of Pekingology, see: the symposium in *Survey*, No. 50 (January, 1964), pp. 154–94; Wolfgang Leonhard, *The Kremlin Since Stalin* (New York: Praeger, 1962), chap. i; Myron Rush, *The Rise of Khrushchev* (Washington, D.C.: Public Affairs Press, 1958).

[36] For example, see HHYP, No. 67 (May, 1955), pp. 70, 71; No. 69 (July, 1955), pp. 60, 61; No. 70 (August, 1955), p. 259; No. 73 (November, 1955), pp. 52, 53; No. 78 (February 21, 1956), p. 16; No. 84 (May 21, 1956), pp. 23, 25; No. 92 (September 21, 1956), p. 24.

[37] *1963 Jen-min Jih-pao So-yin* (Index to *People's Daily*), ed. by the Library of *People's Daily* (Peking: People's Daily Press, 1965), p. 314.

subject for 1965 and 1966. In both the 1950's and 1960's, articles did appear describing the role of the demobilized soldier in county level politics,[38] the need to give preferential treatment to the families of PLA martyrs and active servicemen, and the participation of active servicemen in village affairs. What seems to have drastically decreased were the descriptions of ex-PLA soldiers returning to their native villages, where they immediately assumed active leadership roles. Three possible reasons, not mutually exclusive, may explain the change. First, it may be that the problem became less acute: fewer and younger soldiers probably were mustered out of the service annually in 1962–65 than in the mid-1950's, when the size of the PLA was being reduced from approximately five million men to two and one-half million men.[39]

But could a second reason be that, unlike the 1950's, in the 1960's most veterans were absorbed by government, industry, and the huge state farms in Sinkiang, Heilungkiang, and elsewhere? If so, the change in press coverage hinted at an important shift both in the recruitment patterns of village leadership and in the power of the PLA to place its soldiers in attractive positions. Or could a third explanation be that the whole process of demobilization had become routinized by 1962–65 and was no longer worthy of press attention? A more likely hypothesis, this also would have been a significant development. It must be remembered that in traditional China and particularly during the late Ch'ing dynasty and the Republican period, army veterans frequently turned to banditry and organized outlaw bands.[40] If ex-servicemen were peacefully and automatically reintegrated into local society, it means the People's Republic was dealing effectively with a major problem of the old society. However, the press does not enable us to determine which of the above three hypotheses most accurately explains the shift in press coverage of the demobilized soldier.

Other discontinuities pose problems to those using the press, and

[38] For some examples during the 1950's, see *Hsin Hu-nan Pao,* February 16, 19, May 11, June 4, August 22, 1957; *Che-chiang Jih-pao,* February 12, May 22, August 8, December 2, 1957.

For a discussion of this during the 1960's, see Johnson, "Lin Piao's Army," p. 6. Johnson erroneously implies, however, that the infusion of ex-servicemen into government posts dates only to the early 1960's.

[39] John Gittings, *The Role of the Chinese Army* (New York: Oxford University Press, 1967), p. 305. Gittings does not provide figures for the 1960's, but he estimated demobilization figures for the 1950's.

[40] See Frederic Wakeman, *Strangers at the Gate* (Berkeley and Los Angeles: University of California Press, 1966), chap. v; Chow Yung-teh, *Social Mobility* (New York: Atherton Press, 1966), pp. 158–65; Ralph W. Powell, *The Rise of Chinese Military Power, 1895–1912* (Princeton, N.J.: Princeton University Press, 1955), pp. 22, 341.

particularly to those using content analysis.[41] Both the antirightist campaign of 1957 and the Cultural Revolution in 1966 brought sweeping changes to China's publishing industry. The *People's Daily,* among others, experienced considerable change in its editorial staff during both purges. During 1957–58 and 1966–67, some newspapers and journals became more prominent, while others became less important or ceased publication. For example, for a time during the Cultural Revolution, *Chieh-fang Chün-pao* (PLA Daily) emerged as the authentic voice of the group around Mao, with the *People's Daily* following its lead. As a result, a content analysis of the Maoist line would have to use the *People's Daily* for one time span and the *PLA Daily* for another time span. In an earlier section we discussed the problems arising from discontinuities in the availability of sources. Now, we suggest that even if a particular source is available through time, the characteristics of the source—its concerns, its political functions, its structure, and the access its reporters have to hard information—may have altered. These changes must be understood before the source can be well employed.

The fourth problem in using the press is its unintentional inaccuracy. Journalists can be no better than the accuracy of the information they obtain, and China's weak statistical network seriously affects the quality of data available to the press.[42] As one example of the problem, as of 1959 neither the regime nor its press had accurate data on the number, geographic distribution, and employment of ex-servicemen. One would think that the Ministry of Defense and the Ministry of Internal Affairs would be able to tabulate the number of soldiers released annually and to record their initial employment. But such expectations are dispelled by an article in a journal discussing data problems. The article observed: "How many veterans are there in a county or special district or even the nation? This is not known for many places."[43] If these data are inadequate, what is the reliability of data on other aspects of the political system, such as CCP membership, where the presumption of accuracy is lower?

The vastness of China, when coupled with the low educational level

[41] See Paul Wong, *Content Analysis of Documentary and Biographic Materials: Methodology* (Berkeley: Survey Research Center, University of California, mimeograph, 1967).

[42] See note 16, above.

[43] Kuo T'ai-yen, "Lüeh-t'an chia-ch'iang min-cheng-pu-men tzu-liao kung-tso ti chung-yao-hsing" (A Brief Discussion of the Importance of Work on Research Materials in the Offices of Internal Affairs), *Nei-wu-pu t'ung-hsün* (Bulletin of the Ministry of Internal Affairs), No. 6 (June, 1959), p. 43.

of local leaders, hinders the development of a comprehensive statistical network. In addition, local officials have learned, to some extent, to control the upward flow of information.[44] Failure to use sophisticated survey techniques to surmount these difficulties adds to the inaccuracies of government and press reports. There is little evidence to indicate that the Chinese are employing proper sampling techniques in their surveys, or have experimented with improved survey designs.

It appears that when the government senses a particular problem or desires particular information, Mao and his associates use the same procedures now as they did ten years ago.[45] They dispatch investigators to several localities, or telephone local officials (usually the harried secretary—*mi-shu*—or accountant—*k'uai-chi*) to gather the needed data. For a rural survey, only the crudest attempt seems to be made to secure a cross section of different kinds of local communities. Typically, data are gathered from both backward and advanced villages in the plains, hilly regions, and mountain areas. Apparently, rural surveys in China attempt to gather data on a topic to fill the following matrix:

	Mountains	Hills	Plains
Advanced Area			
Backward Area			

But the mere dispatching of a survey team or the telephoning of a local official do not guarantee that the higher level officials secure accurate information. Survey designs do not appear to have built-in checks to insure accuracy. Nor is any attempt made to weight the matrix in order to obtain a more representative sample. Often the figures will be added and averaged with no apparent concern for the problem of securing a representative sample. Newspaper reports based upon such crude survey techniques are bound to contain errors.

Finally, another source of unintentional press error results from the CPR's penchant for secrecy. Errors are not always due to deliberate distortion; sometimes the press reporters are simply denied access to vital information.[46] Unfortunately, no sure test exists to determine

---

[44] For examples, see Production Team interviews, Question No. 20; *SCMP*, No. 3370 (January 5, 1965), pp. 30–34, and No. 3383 (June 22, 1965), pp. 20–21; and Lien-chiang Documents.

[45] Compare, for example, the surveys found in the 1963–64 Lien-chiang Documents with the surveys of the mid-1950's appearing in *T'ung-chi Kung-tso*.

[46] For a discussion, see MacFarquhar, *Hundred Flowers*, pp. 61–63, 68–69.

which are the "sanitized" articles rooted in classified data and which are based upon more limited information.

The problems of interpreting the Chinese press that arise from its unintentional inaccuracy can be summarized in this way. To employ in an impressionistic manner qualitative data that are rooted in hard fact is acceptable. To employ in an impressionistic manner qualitative data that are themselves based upon questionable or infirm data, on the other hand, is perilous practice, for in such a case, where is the firm base for all these impressions?

To summarize, to rely excessively upon the Chinese press is to be a captive of the rulers one is studying. One is prey to their deliberate distortions as well as victim of their ignorance. Although skills can be acquired to overcome some of the difficulties in interpreting the mainland press, a great deal remains hidden. On the other hand, research on China would be impossible without the press. Newspapers, particularly on the provincial and county levels, and journals published by the ministries are especially valuable for their frank discussions of specific policy issues. They enable the student to chart broad trends. The press also provides the vocabulary used in interviews. Thus, the press is extremely useful, but because of its inherent weaknesses, conclusions derived from it merit documentation from other sources.

INTERVIEWS OF FORMER CPR RESIDENTS

Survey research and in-depth interviews of former CPR residents are invaluable for the study of Chinese society and politics.[47] Information unavailable in the press can be obtained from knowledgeable informants; they bring the Communist jargon to life. Only through in-depth interviewing of former cadres, for example, have we learned about the tasks actually performed by various local officials, the development of the Chinese bureaucracy, and the legal processes.[48] Inter-

---

[47] For discussion of interviewing, see Barnett (with Vogel), *Cadres, Bureaucracy, and Political Power*, pp. x–xix; H. Franz Schurmann, "Research on Chinese Society through Displaced Persons" (informal agenda paper for the subcommittee on Chinese Society, March 5, 1962); Richard H. Solomon, "Refugee Interviewing in Hong Kong" (unpublished MS); Robert Marsh, "On Interviewing Chinese Displaced Persons" (paper prepared for Conference on Research on Chinese Society, Vancouver, B.C., May, 1962); Jerome Alan Cohen, "Depth Interviewing as an Aid to Legal Research on China" (paper prepared for conference on Chinese Communist Law: Tools for Research, Bermuda, May, 1967).

[48] For studies which profit from their heavy reliance upon interviews, see Ezra F. Vogel, "Voluntarism and Social Control," and Jerome Alan Cohen, "The Criminal Process in China," both in Treadgold (ed.), *Soviet and Chinese Communism*, pp. 168–84 and 107–43; Barnett (with Vogel), *Cadres, Bureaucracy, and Political Power;* and Stanley Lubman, "Mao and Mediation: Politics and Dispute Resolution in Communist China," *California Law Review*, LV, No. 5 (November, 1967), 1284–1359.

views and surveys provide the best ways to explore such subjects as the Chinese political culture and attitudinal change under Communist rule.[49] But a study of Chinese politics cannot depend solely upon interviews with former residents of the CPR. Informants are no better than the questions asked of them, and to ask the important questions requires considerable knowledge. Much of this knowledge has to be derived from the press.

Moreover, the suggestive data presented on local leaders raised the possibility that information derived from interviews contains biases that are hard to define and eliminate. We found, it will be recalled, that non-CCP informants appear to have been imprecise in reporting Party membership figures, and well-educated informants may have underestimated the formal schooling of the less educated officials. Undoubtedly some other biases went undetected.

Other factors detract from the value of informants. Their dim memories of the 1950's mean they cannot be fully relied upon for information about that period. Informants obviously remember with greatest clarity the situation at the time of their departure. To judge from my interviews and the experience of others, the time dimension is one of the hardest to obtain from informants. Only the unusually perceptive informant displays sensitivity to the process of change. Impressions derived from the informants, therefore, tend to be more static than dynamic.

In addition, one has the handicap of dealing with an unrepresentative sample. The ages, geographic origins, socioeconomic backgrounds, and former mainland occupations of the informants are not representative of the total population. Kwangtung peasants and fishermen, Shanghai, Canton, and Peking intellectuals, Cantonese and Fukienese with overseas Chinese connections, a scattering of lower level officials, and people who have run afoul of the law constitute a large portion of the informant pool. Former provincial, special district, and county cadres, as well as former residents of the Northeast, Northwest, and Southwest, are very few in number. In addition, their very act of leaving signifies that the former residents thought that, in some way, their life would be better outside of China. Émigré informants rarely enjoyed considerable career success on the mainland and still remained

---

[49] Richard H. Solomon, *The Chinese Revolution and the Politics of Dependency* (Ann Arbor, Mich.: Center for Chinese Studies, 1966); Paul Hiniker, *Chinese Attitudinal Reactions to Forced Compliance: A Cross-Cultural Experiment in the Theory of Cognitive Dissonance* (Cambridge, Mass.: Center for International Studies, M.I.T., mimeograph, 1965).

committed to the regime. The image of China obtained from informants, in short, is more applicable to the coastal regions than to the inland, more applicable to the 1960's than to the 1950's, more applicable to those who, in some sense, are disaffected or disappointed with the CPR than to those who remain committed and are successful in the system.

Admittedly, many of these difficulties can be overcome. Carefully designed interview procedures reflecting sensitivity to Chinese culture and language can minimize many sources of error. Judicious handling of the interview data, especially through careful writing of interpretations, further reduces the margin of error. At the same time, the bias and error inherent in interview data mean that, when possible, interview data should be interpreted in light of information from other sources.

TRAVELOGS

The limitations of this source are not easily summarized, for visitors differ in their perceptiveness, interests, length of stay, and prior acquaintance with China.[50] Obviously, the visitor is better equipped if he knows Chinese, is acquainted with pre-1949 China, is able to visit a locality for long periods of time, and tours with a focused inquiry in mind. Few visitors have all these attributes; at the same time, most travelogs have some passages of redeeming value. For example, in the comparison of reporting of local leaders, the travelogs were useful. Several writers provided important information. Jan Myrdal's *Report from a Chinese Village* was rich in the biographical data it contained. Indeed, the book revealed the age, income, kinship, and Party affiliation of almost every village official. Rewi Alley was eager to report the native place of his local officials, while the eighty-one-year-old Anna Louise Strong was quick to note the age of the younger officials. For our comparison, the chief value of the travelogs was that their limited data provided a convenient comparison with the interviews. The similar data yielded by the travelogs suggested that the Kwangtung origins of the informants did not distort the data unduly.

While the travelogs proved useful for our purposes, they suffer from two major handicaps. First, the number of visitors knowledgeable enough to ask penetrating questions is small. Second, the Chinese have erected barriers to prevent in-depth coverage. Only a handful of ex-

[50] For other discussions of the problems faced by sojourners and tourists, see Hobbs, *I Saw Red China:* Lindquist, *China in Crisis,* pp. 97–105; Herbert Passin, *China's Cultural Diplomacy* (New York: Praeger, 1962), pp. 116–31.

perts in any particular field have personally investigated and then written about Chinese activities in the area of their expertise.[51] A few others, particularly students and teachers, were located at the right place during the right time (Peking University during the Hundred Flowers campaign, Shanghai during the Cultural Revolution), and have written about their experiences.[52] Such reports by competent observers are invaluable, but are all too few. Obstacles to good reporting are in part the result of Chinese restrictions on travel. Tours of particular units are usually quite brief: see a commune in half a day, inspect a school in two hours, and so on. The data recorded on such hasty visits are obviously subject to inaccuracy.[53] The visitor also learns that, although in theory any question is permissible, according to custom certain questions are considered crude, ill mannered, and embarrassing. Thus, while the reports of visitors to the mainland have their use, their limitations prevent them from serving as the most useful source of information. The travelogs can be used, however, for the corroborative material they often contain.

FICTION

In our comparison of the sources, it became clear that, at least in their description of local leaders, novels and short stories were what they claimed to be: fiction. The data derived from fiction differed from the other sources on all aspects studied. Fiction presents, in sum, an idealized version of reality.

Yet, fiction can be quite enlightening.[54] Short stories and novels

---

[51] Examples of such reports include S. D. Richardson, *Forestry in Communist China* (Baltimore: Johns Hopkins University Press, 1965); W. R. Geddes, *Peasant Life in Communist China* (Ithaca, N.Y.: Cornell Society for Applied Anthropology, 1963); Barry M. Richman, "Capitalists and Managers in Communist China," *Harvard Business Review* (January–February, 1967), pp. 57–78; Geoffrey Oldham, "Science in China: A Tourist's Impressions," *Science*, CXLVII, No. 3659 (February 14, 1965), 706–14.

[52] Rene Goldman, "The Rectification Campaign at Peking University: May–June, 1957," *China Quarterly* (October–December, 1962), pp. 138–53; Neale Hunter, "Three Cadres of Shanghai," "Port in a Storm," and "The Cultural Arm," in *Far Eastern Economic Review*, No. 231 (June 1, 1967), pp. 491–95; No. 234 (June 22, 1967), pp. 663–67; No. 236 (July 6, 1967), pp. 22–24.

[53] For example, K. S. Karol reported that Nanking's October Commune had 10,546 members, grouped into 1,857 families; Oldham, visiting China at almost the same time, reported that the same commune's 10,554 members were grouped into 2,420 families. (Karol, *China*, p. 444; Geoffrey Oldham, "Visits to Chinese Communes," letter to Institute of Current World Affairs [CHGO-45, January 18, 1965], p. 2). The discrepancies are not encouraging to anthropologists wanting data on the average number of people in rural households.

[54] For studies based on fiction, see A. S. Chen, "The Ideal Local Party Secretary and the 'Model' Man," *China Quarterly*, No. 17 (January–March, 1964), pp. 229–40; Richard

frequently portray interesting examples of fundamental aspects of Chinese politics, such as generational conflict, bureaucratism, and the career choices confronted by youth. These examples present the "flavor" of politics.

Perhaps more important, the stories occasionally describe informal group activities and provide intimate glimpses of individual thought ("Li San thought to himself . . ."). Neither the press nor the travelogs penetrate these dimensions of society. In this way, fiction is a useful supplement to refugee interviews, which also shed light upon informal processes and private thoughts. Convergence between fictional accounts and interview data increases confidence in the validity of the observations.[55]

DOCUMENTS OBTAINED COVERTLY

In recent years, the United States and the Republic of China on Taiwan (ROC) have begun to release surreptitiously obtained, classified CPR documents, including secret directives, descriptions of mainland conditions, and reports of local surveys. The documents, apparently authentic, are extremely revealing and have added immeasurably to our understanding of Chinese politics in the 1960's.

The problem of interpretation centers on the criteria for the release of these documents. Doubtless, not all captured documents have been released to the academic community. This raises the question of how decisions are made to release particular documents. One hopes the value of the document is taken into account: the more valuable the document, the more likely its release. Protection of the supplier of the document is no doubt a factor; if release carries little risk of "blowing a cover," a given document supposedly will be more readily released. But is there any attempt to release selectively documents that, say, either would do the most damage to the image of the CPR or would support the official United States or ROC interpretations of mainland politics? Would the ROC, for example, release statistical reports that show substantial economic progress? The mere posing of the question indicates that data acquired from these sources must be handled with

---

H. Solomon, "Educational Themes in China's Changing Culture," *China Quarterly,* No. 22 (April–June, 1965), pp. 154–70; and several articles in Cyril Birch (ed.), *Chinese Communist Literature* (New York: Praeger, 1963), esp. pp. 158–225.

[55] For an important study which combines these two sources, see Ezra Vogel, "From Friendship to Comradeship: The Change in Personal Relations in Communist China," *China Quarterly,* No. 21 (January–March, 1965), pp. 46–60.

the same caution that one uses in handling data obtained from the mainland itself.

DATA COMPILATIONS

A number of biographical directories, chronologies, statistical compilations, and translation series are prepared by private and public institutions around the world.[56] These sources, which fall on the border between primary and secondary sources, are invaluable research aids, but have their own methodological problems.

Some of the chronologies, biographical directories, and statistical series are more reliable than others. Only through considerable research experience does the student of China acquire the ability to judge the reliability and thoroughness of these research aids. This is particularly true of the biographical directories; none of the major ones cite references, which makes it difficult to trace questionable information to its original source.

Moreover, here too the researcher must be sensitive to discontinuities in coverage. A change in personnel at the United States Consulate in Hong Kong, where several economic series are prepared, may affect, say, the estimates of grain production. A reported drop in production could reflect, in part, the different analytical techniques of the new official, rather than a real drop in production. In addition, some institutions improve their compilations, while others deteriorate in quality. The well-equipped researcher in the China field knows which chronologies best cover specific time spans, and which biographical directories are best for specific kinds of information.

The publicly available translation series also raise methodological problems. To the best of our knowledge, no one has studied carefully the criteria for selection of material to be translated and released. Most series—the BBC-monitored radio broadcasts, the press translations of the United States Consulate in Hong Kong, the intragovernmental United States Joint Publications Research Service, to mention the major ones—are government sponsored. They are intended primarily to serve the policy needs of government. That is, they are to assist policy makers in their assessment of China's goals, strategies, and capabilities in world affairs. The translation series therefore appear to pay closest attention to items directly relevant to China's foreign policy. They seemingly pay somewhat less attention to Chinese domestic developments that have no obvious foreign policy implications.

[56] See Berton and Wu, *Contemporary China.*

In addition, since analysis of contemporary China is based both on the press translations and on the monitored radio broadcasts, there is a need to know whether these two sources differ in their interpretations and coverage of the news. As long as social scientists rely heavily upon the translation services—a glance at the footnotes in the *China Quarterly* indicates the extent of this reliance—they must be sensitive to possible biases introduced by the selection process.

SUMMARY AND CONCLUSION

Research on China draws upon many sources, each with its distinctive attributes. As the use of first one source, then another, becomes easier or more fashionable, interpretations of China are thereby affected. An examination of the secondary literature suggests that the characterization of each period since 1949 reflects the sources available for the study of that period. Moreover, evaluations of the various sources suggest that each has its limitations and inherent biases. For example, four general sources—the mainland press, interviews with émigrés, fiction, and travelogs—present somewhat different images of local leaders. The student of China, desiring to master his subject must be aware of how his perspective has been shaped by the data he employs.

Three further conclusions emerge. First, the China field does not face a scarcity of sources. The real problem is to cope with the diversity. Second, in order to penetrate beyond the limits of any single source, research must be based upon several different sources. Conclusions are most sound when supported by convergent data from several sources. Third, no methodological panacea can solve the research problems we have been discussing. The problem can be handled only with intelligence, imagination, and total familiarity with the sources. Increased use of computers, quantitative content analysis, and other advanced research techniques cannot eliminate the problems; the danger is that they may camouflage them.

The implications of this paper extend beyond contemporary Chinese studies to cross national comparative research.[57] Obviously, the same

[57] The better comparativists are aware of the problem. See Richard L. Merritt and Stein Rokkan (ed.), *Comparing Nations* (New Haven, Conn.: Yale University Press 1966), esp. pp. 3–80, 131–68, 217–238; Sidney Verba, "The Uses of Survey Research in the Study of Comparative Politics: Issues and Strategies," in Stein Rokkan, Sidney Verba, Jean Viet, and Elina Almasy, *Comparative Survey Analysis* (The Hague: Mouton, 1968); and Sidney Verba, "Some Dilemmas in Comparative Research," *World Politics*, XX, No. 1 (October, 1967).

methodological problems exist in the study of any society. These stem from the diversity of sources, each with their different perspectives and limitations, and the discontinuities in the availability of particular sources. As the Chinese case makes so abundantly clear, sensitivity to these problems is required before sound research can be undertaken on any nation. How does one design social surveys and in-depth interviews in the particular culture? Which particular journalists in which newspaper are most relevant to one's inquiry? Which statistical series are most reliable? What are the inherent biases of the sources one employs? What combination of sources should be employed to increase the reliability of the analysis? And so on. Considerable familiarity with a country is required before these questions can be adequately answered.

Index

The following abbreviations are used throughout the index:

CCP	Chinese Communist Party
CKCN	*Chung-kuo Ch'ing-nien* (Chinese Youth)
CPR	People's Republic of China
CYL	Communist Youth League
GPCR	Great Proletarian Cultural Revolution
IPPE	Increase Production and Practice Economy (Shanghai Committee)
KMT	Kuomintang
LIR	Labor Insurance Regulations
MPC	Municipal People's Council (Wuhan)
PLA	People's Liberation Army
UPM	Unified Purchasing and Marketing

CONTRIBUTORS

A. DOAK BARNETT. Born in China. Member of the Department of Political Science and the East Asian Institute, Columbia University. Field research in Asia during 1947–55 and 1964–65. Author of *Communist China and Asia: Challenge to American Policy* (1960); *Communist China in Perspective* (1962); *China on the Eve of the Communist Takeover* (1963); *Communist China, The Early Years: 1949–1955* (1964); *China After Mao* (1967); and *Cadres, Bureaucracy, and Political Power in Communist China* (with a contribution by Ezra Vogel) (1967).

THOMAS P. BERNSTEIN. Born in Germany. Member of the Department of Government, Indiana University. Field research in Hong Kong during 1964.

R. J. BIRRELL. Born in Australia. Member of the Department of Sociology, Indiana University.

JOHN GARDNER. Born in England. Member of the Department of Government, University of Manchester. Field research in Hong Kong and Japan during 1963–64, and in Hong Kong from March through May, 1968.

ROY HOFHEINZ, JR. Born in the United States. Member of the Department of Government, Harvard University. Field research in Taiwan during 1963–65, and in Japan during 1964–65.

JOYCE K. KALLGREN. Born in the United States. Member of the Department of Political Science, University of California at Davis. Vice-chairman of the Center for Chinese Studies, University of California at Berkeley. Field research in Hong Kong during 1967.

YING-MAO KAU. Born in China. Member of the Department of Political Science, Brown University. Field research in Hong Kong and Japan during 1965–66.

ILPYONG J. KIM. Born in Korea. Member of the Department of Political Science, Indiana University. Field research in Hong Kong and Taiwan during part of 1964–65.

MICHEL OKSENBERG. Born in Belgium. Member of the East Asian Institute, Columbia University. Field research in Hong Kong during 1964–65.

MARK SELDEN. Born in the United States. Member of the Department of History, Washington University. Field research in Taiwan and Japan during 1964–66.

RICHARD H. SOLOMON. Born in the United States. Member of the Department of Political Science and research associate of the Center for Chinese Studies, University of Michigan. Field research in Taiwan and Hong Kong during 1964–65.

JAMES R. TOWNSEND. Born in the United States. Member of the Department of Political Science and the East Asian Program, University of Washington. Field research in Hong Kong during 1962–63 and 1966–67. Author of *Political Participation in Communist China* (1967), and *The Revolutionization of Chinese Youth: A Study of* Chung-kuo Ch'ing-nien (1967).